Penguin Reference Books

The Penguin Dictionary of English and European History, 1485–1789

E. N. Williams was born in Leicester, educated at Pembroke College, Cambridge, and served in the Royal Artillery during the war. He has taught history and English in three grammar schools, and was head of the history department at Dulwich College from 1957 to 1977. He is also the author of *The Eighteenth-Century Constitution*, the very successful *Life in Georgian England*, the Pelican *Documentary History of England*, vol. 2 and *The Ancien Régime in Europe* (Penguin).

D1019153

The Penguin Dictionary of

English and European History, 1485–1789

E. N. Williams

Penguin Books

Penguin Books Ltd, Harmondsworth, Middlesex, England
Penguin Books, 40 West 23rd Street, New York, New York 10010, U.S.A.
Penguin Books Australia Ltd, Ringwood, Victoria, Australia
Penguin Books Canada Ltd, 2801 John Street, Markham, Ontario, Canada L3R 1B4
Penguin Books (N.Z.) Ltd, 182–190 Wairau Road, Auckland 10, New Zealand

First published 1980
Published simultaneously by Allen Lane
Reprinted 1982, 1984

Made and printed in Great Britain by
Richard Clay (The Chaucer Press) Ltd, Bungay, Suffolk
Set in Monotype Times

TO BETTY AND ROY

A dictionary of this length has to be selective, and for the sake of students and others interested in this period I have thought it wiser to provide substantial articles on the important personalities and topics, instead of fragments on everybody and everything. For the same reason, the articles follow the mainstream of political history without diverging too far into economic history, cultural history and so on. On the other hand, much more detailed information is provided than might at first appear. This is made readily available by the numerous cross-references (indicated by words in SMALL CAPITAL LETTERS) and by the comprehensive Index where, for example, under the heading of each of the major Powers of the period, the following subjects are treated: Army, Church, Economy, Education, Foreign Policy, Government, Society. By referring back to the text, the reader can thus pick up the threads of the subjects that interest him, and the cross-references will lead him on to associated articles to amplify the information.

Finally, it gives me great pleasure to record my gratitude to my erstwhile mathematical colleague, Raymond Payne, who has very kindly read through the typescript and saved me from many errors. Fortunately, he has a sharp eye and never minces his words, and I have benefited greatly from his candid criticisms.

Dulwich   ENW

admin	administration, administrative
Archbp	Archbishop
Archbpric	Archbishopric
b	born
Bn	Baron
Bp	Bishop
Bpric	Bishopric
c	*circa*
C	century
Cab	Cabinet
Capt	Captain
Card	Cardinal
Cath	Catholic
Ch	Church
C-in-C	Commander-in-Chief
Co	Company
d	died
D	Duke
dept	department
Dss	Duchess
E	east, eastern
ed	educated
El	Elector
eld	elder, eldest
Emp	Emperor, Empire
Empss	Empress
Gen	General
Gov	Government, Governor
H of C	House of Commons
H of L	House of Lords
HQ	Headquarters
HR Emp	Holy Roman Emperor, Holy Roman Empire
Hug	Huguenot
i/c	in command
K	King
Kdom	Kingdom

Ld	Lord
Lieut	Lieutenant
m	married
Maj	Major
Med	Mediterranean
Mlle	Mademoiselle
MP	Member of Parliament
N	north, northern
nr	near
Parl	Parliament, Parliamentary
PM	Prime Minister
Pp	Pope
Pr	Prince
Pres	President
Prof	Professor
Prot	Protestant
prov	province, provincial
Prss	Princess
Q	Queen
R	River
RC	Roman Catholic
S	south, southern
Sch	School
Sec	Secretary
Tr	Treaty
Univ	University
Vt	Viscount
W	west, western

During this period two Calendars were in use. The Julian or Old Style (OS) Calendar was in general use until 1582, when Pp Gregory XIII introduced the Gregorian or New Style (NS) Calendar. The OS was 10 days behind the NS until C18, when it was 11 days behind. Since different States adopted the NS at different dates (some not before C20) both Calendars were in use from 1582 onwards. Great Britain, for example, did not adopt the NS until 1752, and Russia not until after the Revolution. Dates given in this Dictionary are in the Style in use in the country concerned. International events involving States using different Calendars are given in both Styles: eg the battle of Blenheim took place on 2/13 Aug 1704. In all cases the year is taken to begin on 1 Jan.

Abbot, George (29 Oct 1562–4 Aug 1633) Moderately Puritan Archbp of Canterbury (4 Mar 1611) under JAMES I and CHARLES I of England.

b at Guildford, Surrey; son of a textile worker; ed at Guildford Grammar Sch and Balliol, Oxford.

Abbot was a moderate Puritan, a Calvinist in theology and way of life, hostile to Rome, and to the ARMINIAN (ie semi-Roman) party in the Ch of England; but fully supporting the full discipline of the Ch of England, with the K at its head, if disapproving of the royal favourites and their influence at Court and on policy. He opposed the pro-Spanish policy of the Howard faction. He opposed the divorce of the Countess of Essex (1613), so that she could marry the K's new favourite, Robert CARR; and, incurring the latter's hostility, he was active in introducing the last favourite, BUCKINGHAM, to Court in 1615. Unfortunately, doubts were cast on Abbot's fitness for office in 1621, for while hunting a buck he accidentally killed a gamekeeper. However, his career was saved by the casting vote of the K. Under Charles I he opposed the Spanish-marriage project, as well as the trend towards Arminianism and the growth of arbitrary power. When he refused to license the publication of a sermon advocating non-resistance to the K's order for a forced loan (1627), he was suspended from office for a year while his work was taken over by a commission headed by LAUD.

Absolutism The form of Gov (also known as New Monarchy, or Renaissance Monarchy, in its early stages) which was emerging in most European states during C16, C17 and C18. In these states the monarch's power was theoretically unlimited except by divine or natural law, or by his own laws. Absolutism replaced the early-modern CORPORATIVE STATE (*Ständestaat*), which had replaced the medieval feudal State. In the corporative states the K's power was limited by the legislative and judicial rights of vassals, churches, semi-independent provs, municipal corporations etc, especially when all of these were represented in Estates (or Diets, Parliaments, Cortes etc). Moreover, the K's orders depended for their execution on the co-operation of troops and administrators provided by these representative institutions. In addition, these rulers suffered from external restrictions on their power placed by the HR Emp, or the Pp. Absolute rulers, on the other hand, succeeded in raising a standing army and bureaucracy directly under their own command, paid for out of taxes which did not require the approval of the Estates, and carrying out policies which did not require their assent either, or the agreement of any external authority. Under absolute monarchs the institutions of the previous era were either suppressed or allowed to continue as empty ceremonies. Absolutism was justified by such political theorists as Bodin, Bossuet and Hobbes; and exemplified by such rulers as LOUIS XIV of France and FREDERICK WILLIAM, the Great El, of Brandenburg-Prussia. *See also* ENLIGHTENED ABSOLUTISTS.

Alba (Alva), Fernando Àlvarez de Toledo, 3rd D de (29 Oct 1507–11 Dec 1582) Spanish general and leading minister of PHILIP II of Spain whose unsuccessful attempt to terrorize the Netherlands into submission helped to consolidate the REVOLT; and who later conquered Portugal for Spain.

Making himself master of the most up-to-date methods of warfare, he rose rapidly in the armies of the Emp CHARLES V and Philip II. Proud, domineering and able, he became one of Philip II's 2 chief ministers in the period up to his downfall in 1573. As a Grandee and head of a large family and CLIENTAGE network of wealthy landowners, admirals and generals, he was the leader of a powerful faction at Court which shared power with a rival faction headed by the Pr of Eboli. In June 1565 he represented Philip at Bayonne in the conversations with CATHERINE DE MEDICI which led to the 2nd of the FRENCH WARS OF RELIGION. He was hard and brutal, convinced that the only way to deal with rebellion was to terrorize the people by cutting off the heads of a sufficient number of leaders, after paying little attention to the fairness of their trials. For this reason, when the Revolt of the Netherlands was in its early stages, he was appointed Gov. In Apr 1567 he left Spain for Milan where he picked up 9,000 men and marched them over the Mont Cénis pass, through Franche Comté and Lorraine, to reach Brussels in Aug 1567. While WILLIAM I (the Silent) and his brother, Pr LOUIS OF NASSAU, went into exile to organize armed resistance, Alba set up the apparatus of centralized absolutism and religious persecution. His agents trampled on the long-entrenched constitutional privileges of nobles, provs and cities. During his rule, 12,302 Netherlanders appeared before his 7-man kangaroo court – the 'Council of Blood' – and 1,105 were executed or banished. With a view to terrorizing the S into quiescence so that he could march N to deal with Louis of Nassau's invasion of Groningen – he beat the Spanish at Heiligerlee there on 23 May 1568 – he beheaded 18 noblemen at Brussels on 1 June 1568, a few more the next day, and then on 5 June he cut off the heads of the 2 chief loyalist magnates, Egmont and Hoorn, in the Great Market Square before a large crowd. Paying scant attention to the protests of the States-Gen, he attempted, not very successfully, to enforce 3 new taxes: the 100th Penny, the 20th Penny and the 10th Penny. In 1572, while he concentrated his forces in the S to face the invasion threatened by the French gov now under COLIGNY, and repulse the attack of Louis of Nassau on Mons, Hainault, the Sea Beggars – the rebel fleet – took the Brill in Zeeland on 1 Apr 1572, then Flushing, and soon established a grip over the 2 chief provs of the N – Holland and Zeeland. When the Massacre of St Bartholomew eliminated the French threat and allowed him to march N, he found it impossible to make any progress against these provs sheltering behind waters dominated by the Sea Beggars, while he lacked both money and ships.

His rule had succeeded in turning a traditionalist movement of constitutional resistance by the high nobility into a patriotic war against Spain, complicated by a mass striving after religious toleration, political freedom and social reform, and aided by foreign powers. His failure provided the opportunity for the Eboli faction at Madrid. They favoured conciliation in the Netherlands and war on England, while Alba had consistently dissuaded Philip from invading England during the rebellion of the Northern Earls there (Nov–Dec 1569) and while the Ridolfi Plot of 1571 was being hatched. In 1573 he was recalled from the Netherlands at his own request, and then coldly dismissed by a K who had no use, as the saying went, for a squeezed orange.

He had to wait 7 years for his recall, this time to command the forces conquering Portugal. He made a swift success of it. He crossed the border near Badajoz, Estremadura, on 27 June 1580, and Lisbon fell on 25 Aug 1580.

Albuquerque, Afonso de (between 1445 and 1462–15 Dec 1515) 2nd Viceroy of Portuguese India (1509–15) and leading emp builder. He made many naval expeditions to the E African coast, the Red Sea, and the W coast of India (1503 onwards) until he was appointed Gov of India, superseding Francisco de Almeída, who arrested him on his first arrival (1508), but released him later. During his term of office he pursued an imaginative but clear-sighted policy of laying the foundations of the Portuguese sea-borne Emp in the Indian Ocean and SE Asia. He aimed to give Portugal the monopoly of the spice trade, orientating it round the Cape, instead of through the Red Sea, and eliminating such rivals as the small Moslem powers of the Indian Ocean, the Mameluk Emp of Egypt and Syria, the NW Indian state of Gujarat, Java in SE Asia, and Spanish encroachment from the Far E. He ended the indiscriminate attacks on Arab traders, and the unnecessary involvement of Portugal in local Asian politics – both of which had characterized the era begun by Vasco da GAMA. Instead he concentrated on creating a network of safe sea-routes for Portuguese merchants, policed by naval squadrons operating from strongly-held naval bases scattered over a wide area.

Starting with the naval superiority provided by Almeída's defeat of the Egyptian fleet off Diu in the Gujarat (1509), he seized Goa on the W Indian coast (1510), and made it the Portuguese HQ. He captured Malacca on the Malay Peninsula (1511), and made contact with China. In 1513 he besieged Aden at the mouth of the Red Sea, though without success. He nevertheless explored the Red Sea, somewhat to the alarm of Egypt, as this was the first European incursion into this area. During the same year he helped to arrange the installation of a friendly ruler at Calicut, who allowed the Portuguese to build a fortress there. In 1515 he captured Ormuz at the mouth of the Persian Gulf. In the meantime, he worked hard to reform the imperial admin, and started a campaign against corruption. Eventually rivals at Court secured his dismissal, and he d at sea off Goa on his way home.

Alexander VI (Rodrigo Borgia) (prob 1 Jan 1431–18 Aug 1503) Pp (1492), father of Lucrezia and Cesare BORGIA, and extreme case of a worldly prelate.

b at Valencia, Spain, ed in law at Bologna, Italy, he worked at the papal HQ where his uncle Alonso, as Pp Calixtus III (1455–8), was very good to him in the matter of Ch preferment. More or less buying his way to the papal throne – his siring of at least 4 bastards seeming to present no obstacle – he spent his time as Pp steering a zig-zag course between the powers attempting to dominate Italy in the HABSBURG–VALOIS WARS; jockeying for position among the warring petty Prs of the peninsula; evading attempts, eg by SAVONAROLA, to reform the Ch; dividing the colonial world between Spain and Portugal in a series of Bulls leading up to the Tr of TORDESILLAS (1494); making complaisant decisions in favour of his patrons FERDINAND II and ISABELLA I of Spain, giving them control of the Spanish INQUISITION and Ch preferment; but paying most

15

attention to the problem of carving out suitable inheritances for his bastard children. He was highly gifted in statecraft and a patron of Renaissance art, but his values were not those of a statesman, let alone a spiritual leader. He organized the Emp, Spain, Venice and Milan into the Holy League of Venice on 31 Mar 1495 to drive CHARLES VIII of France out of Italy. He then invited LOUIS XII, the next French K, into Italy, granting him a divorce and giving d'AMBOISE, his chief minister, a Card's hat; all in return for Louis' help in finding a bride for Cesare, and in providing a diplomatic and military back-up to Alexander's conquest of the Romagna. He also found a series of husbands for Lucrezia. In fact, all was going very well when he d suddenly at Rome; with the subsequent election of a deadly rival as Pp JULIUS II the Borgia bubble burst.

Alexis (Aleksei Mikhailovich) (10 Mar 1629–29 Jan 1676) Tsar of Russia (13 July 1645), from whose reign Soviet historians date modern Russian history, principally because of the formation then of the all-Russian market by commercial capitalists, though his reign is notable in other ways also. At home the Law Code of 1649 was passed, the centralizing autocracy was strengthened on the basis of the serving nobility and serfdom, the Ch schism was caused by NIKON, strong W cultural influences were felt, and Stenka Razin's peasant revolt was suppressed; while abroad the frontiers were consolidated and Russia gained the Ukraine, though not a foothold on the Baltic coast.

b at Moscow, son of Tsar MICHAEL and his 2nd wife, Eudoxia Streshneva; ed in reading, writing and Orthodox ritual, but also to a certain extent in W ways by his tutor, *boyar* B. I. Morozov; m 1st (1648) Maria Miloslavskaia (d 1669, having had 13 children, including Tsars Theodore III and Ivan V, and Regent Sofia); 2nd (1671) Natalia Naryshkina (for love), a young Westernized member of favourite Artamon Matveev's household (d 1694, leaving her son, PETER I). Tall, robust and bright, with simple daily habits, deep religious convictions, and a taste for W music and drama, he was gentle and benevolent – traditionally known as the 'quietest tsar' – but also now and then capable of terrible anger and ruthless action reminiscent of IVAN IV ('The Terrible'), the details of whose reign fascinated him.

At home: (a) Morozov, his tutor, ran the gov (1645–9), making many enemies with his cuts in gov salaries, his new salt tax, his state monopoly of tobacco (condemned by the Ch), his replacement of office-holders in the central depts (*prikazy*) with his own clique, and his lack of attention to the interests of the service nobility (*dvoryane*) and the townsmen. His immense wealth excited envy, too, with his 30,000 serfs scattered over 300 different establishments. Disturbances in the provs (1646–7) and then a violent rebellion in Moscow (June 1648) forced the Tsar to exile his tutor in order to save his life. To satisfy grievances, he called a *zemskii sobor* (parliament) (Sept 1648–Jan 1649) which produced (b) the 1649 Code of Law (*ulozhenie*), much of which stayed in force untill C20. Its 800 and more clauses generally backed the *dvoryane* and townsmen at the expense of the *boyars*, the peasants and the clergy. It completed serfdom, among other ways, by abolishing the time limit after which fugitive slaves could not be recaptured. Bad harvests, plague and oppression by landlords and the state produced further popular disturbances, eg at Pskov (Feb 1650), Novgorod (Mar 1650), and Moscow (July 1662), the last partly caused by the debasement of the coinage with copper. (c) The schism, which gave birth to the dissenting Old Believers who survived into C20, resulted from the opposition of traditionalist and patriotic Russians to the programme (1652–66) of Patriarch Nikon, supported by Alexis, to reform the Russian Ch in conformity with the Greek. Nikon was Alexis' chief minister (1652–8) till even the mild Tsar eventually had his fill of his overbearing manner and his attempts to place the Ch above the state; when Nikon resigned in 1658 in order to pressurize the Tsar, he found himself out of office for ever. (d) Stenka (Stepan) Razin's revolt (1670–71) was a far more grandiose affair than the riots earlier in the reign. Known to Soviet historians as the 2nd Peasant War, it was similar to the 1st – Bolotnikov's (1606–8) during the TIME OF TROUBLES. Razin, a Don Cossack freebooter who raided round the Caspian Sea and the Lower Volga, switched to politics in 1670 and advanced on Moscow with a horde of runaway serfs, peasants, colonial tribesmen, religious dissidents, bandits and other malcontents, to the number at times of 200,000. His proclamations breathed fire against property owners and state functionaries, and looked to a benevolent Tsar for land and justice. Organizing such a motley movement was no easy task, and Razin was heavily defeated by gov troops nr Simbirsk on the Volga on 1–4 Oct 1670. He fell back on the Don, but the Cossacks captured him (14 Apr 1671) and handed him over to the authorities. He was executed in Red Square, Moscow, on 6 June 1671, dying a barbarous death (he was torn limb from limb), but living for ever in Russian folklore. (e) The gov continued the trends of Michael's reign, steadily tightening its grip over the community, becoming more absolute and more centralized, and depending more on regimentation by its bureaucracy and army of *dvoryane* and less on the *boyars* and on elected institutions. The *zemskii sobor* declined into an occasional accompaniment to gov, meeting only in 1645, 1648–9, 1650 and 1651–3. The *boyars*' *duma* weakened in prestige also, its work as the tsar's chief council being taken over in the 2nd half of the reign by the *Prikaz* of Secret Affairs. A *Prikaz* of Accounts was formed to reform the finances, and attempts were made to bring some order into the medieval confusion of the *prikazy*. In the provs the admin of the towns was reformed (1649–52), but the prov governors (*voevody*) still tyrannized over their subjects – the elected sheriffs (*gubnie starosty*) did not provide the check they were supposed to – and still enriched themselves at public expense – even though the *kormlenie* (feeding) system of paying them was supposed to have ended (*see* IVAN IV). (f) The economy made significant strides, with the development of the national market – especially in grain – with Moscow at its centre; with the diversification of Russian manufactures; and with the expansion of foreign trade through the only port, Archangel. A native bourgeoisie was slow in growing, and what capitalism existed was dominated by foreign merchants and by the Tsar himself, though the gov gave some encouragement to Russian merchants with the regularization of internal customs (1653 and 1667) and the New Commercial Regulations of 1667, which kept foreigners out of retail trade, and put high tariffs on foreign goods. Prosperity grew steadily, and economic growth was not something invented by PETER I. (g) Westernization did not wait for Peter's reign either, for it was already present to inspire him in his father's day. Both Alexis and his 2nd wife were much influenced by W scholarship, literature and art – once the Ch had pronounced them not sinful – and so were the leading courtiers: Boris Morozov, Afanasy Ordin-Nashchokin and Artamon Matveev. W knowledge and manners penetrated Russian life along many channels: with the foreign experts who reformed the army; with the growing Foreign Quarter (*Nemetskaia Sloboda*) built just outside Moscow after the fire of 1652, where foreign merchants, professionals and technicians lived; with foreign trade, especially with England and Holland; with the conflict in Poland-Lithuania; with the diplomatic involvement in European affairs; with the annexation of the Ukraine and especially Kiev; and with Nikon's reforms of the Ch on Greek lines.

Abroad: Alexis was involved in the 13 Years War (1654–67) with Poland and Sweden: (a) 1654–6 with Poland, (b) 1656–8 with Sweden, and (c) 1658–67 with Poland. (a) The 1654–6 Polish War was a further push W, into the Ukraine, and NW into Lithuania towards the Baltic, this time in alliance with Bogdan Khmelnitski (Bohdan Chmielnicki), Hetman (leader) of the Dnieper Cossacks in what Soviet historians regard as the Ukrainian war of liberation against JOHN II CASIMIR of Poland. On 1 Oct 1653 the *zemskii sobor* (the last of these assemblies) voted to incorporate the Ukraine into Russia and at Khmelnitski's request Alexis' representatives met him on the square at Pereyaslavl (Perejaslaw), Ukraine (8/18 Jan 1654), and concluded an oral agreement, subsequently put into writing (Mar 1654) whereby Russia accepted the sovereignty of the Cossacks, while allowing them to keep their self-gov, social system and laws. The 1st result was a joint attack on Poland in which Russia took Smolensk (Oct 1654) and advanced deep into Poland and Lithuania until the outbreak of the Northern War (1655–60) – in which CHARLES X GUSTAV of Sweden also attacked Poland – forced Russia to change her policy. In Moscow there was always disagreement between those who favoured attacking the Ukraine and those who favoured concentrating on the Baltic, and this time the latter won. Russia made peace with Poland and helped her fight Sweden, by the Tr of Vilno (24 Oct/3 Nov 1656), which gave her much of White and Little Russia. (b) The 1656–8 Swedish War consisted of Alexis' campaigns to win a foothold on the Baltic – he especially attacked Riga, Livonia – till he acknowledged his failure to do so in a 3-year armistice (Dec 1658), confirmed by the Tr of Kardis (21 June 1661). (c) The 1658–67 Polish War, in which the Ukrainian Cossacks, in an effort to create an autonomous State for themselves, switched alliances between Russia, Poland, Sweden, and Turkey, exhausted both Russia and Poland. The war also devastated the Cossack lands – it is a period known in Ukrainian tradition as 'the Ruin' – but marked the emergence of Russia as a stronger military power than Poland – a big change since the Time of Troubles. Eventually, fear of a joint Cossack–Tatar–Turkish attack prompted Russia and Poland to make peace (Tr of Andrussovo, 30 Jan/9 Feb 1667), whereby Russia gave up much of her Vilno acquisitions, but kept Smolensk and the E bank of the Dnieper as well as Kiev on the W. Henceforth Russia and Poland had to concern themselves jointly with defence against Turkey.

Allen, William (1532–16 Oct 1594) Card (1587), English Cath exile under ELIZABETH I, who founded the seminary at Douai and led the movement for training English priests for missionary work, and possible martyrdom, in England.

b at Rossall, Lancs; ed at home and at Oriel, Oxford (1547). A firm Cath, he prospered in Oxford, the academic HQ of the Cath revival under MARY I; but after Elizabeth's Prot Ch settlement he went into exile at Louvain Univ (1561). Ordained at Malines (Mechlin), Netherlands, in 1567, he founded a seminary at Douai, Netherlands, in 1568 for the education of exiled English youths, and for the preparation of priests for missionary work in the homeland. He transferred it to Rheims, France, in 1578, after quarrelling with the Spanish authorities. He went to Rome and helped to found the English College and place it under the control of the JESUITS (1579). The 1st Douai priests landed in England in 1574, and the 1st Jesuits, led by PARSONS and CAMPION, in 1580. In the 1580s he moved into political activity, plotting with MARY, Q OF SCOTS in England and the Guises in France; and becoming especially involved in PHILIP II's plans for the invasion of England. It was at Spain's request that Pp Sixtus V made him a Card; and he was destined for high office in England had the ARMADA succeeded. Before it sailed, he angered Englishmen with his pamphlet 'An Admonition to the Nobility and People of England and Ireland, concerning the Present Wars, made for the execution of His Holiness' Sentence' (1587), calling upon English Caths to support the Spanish invasion. And here was his great mistake, and perhaps the mistake into which he led Philip II: he believed that all English Caths were ready to rise in support of Spain. He was a sincere Cath, but an inept politician, out of touch with Cath opinion in England. When the defeat of the Armada ruined his political hopes, he concentrated once more on the academic side of the English Cath movement, helping in Rome to revise the Vulgate and bring out the so-called 'Douai Bible' in England. He did not succeed in winning England for the COUNTER-REFORMATION, but his missionaries, especially the Jesuits, fortified the faith of a hard core of English Caths, stopped the rot whereby Caths went to Anglican services but kept mental reservations, and saved English Catholicism from extinction – thus preventing possible reconciliation between England and Rome.

Amboise, Georges d' (1460–25 May 1510) Card (1498) and chief minister to LOUIS XII of France.

A typical political prelate of the period, he was made Bp of Montauban (1484), Archbp of Narbonne (1493), Archbp of Rouen (1493). Under CHARLES VIII he backed Orléans, the future Louis XII – suffering 2 years' imprisonment for his pains – and, when Orléans became K, Amboise became his chief minister, rising to a position in Ch and State similar to that of WOLSEY in England: accumulating benefices for himself and his family, controlling foreign policy, supporting the Italian invasions with the aim of becoming Pp, and organizing the reforms in the central admin which marked Louis' reign.

American Independence, War of (1776–83) in which the 13 American colonies of Great Britain under GEORGE III rebelled against increasing economic and constitutional centralization, and with French and other help defeated the British gov and established the independent USA.

The causes evolved from cool clashes of economic interest at the start into proud struggles over constitutional principle. As far as (a) economic matters were concerned, the American colonies were controlled (1650 onwards) for the benefit of the mother country by the old navigation system, which not only forced the colonists to trade in a long list of goods only via Great Britain and in

British or colonial ships, but also limited colonial manufacture of certain goods if they rivalled British products. In fact, the system benefited the colonists as well as Great Britain, witness their growing population, prosperity, and self-confidence – all factors contributing to the rebellion and its success. Until the reign of George III, the colonists accepted the system because it was only loosely enforced, and because they needed British military protection. The SEVEN YEARS WAR (1756–63) put an end to this truce. Firstly, the colonists felt that they no longer needed British protection against the French, the Spanish and the Indians. Secondly, the slack admin of the old system ended in 1763 when Great Britain, in common with other European powers (eg the ENLIGHTENED ABSOLUTISTS) tightened up imperial control in the interests of efficiency, security and, above all, revenue, which was short in the post-war depression. In resisting the new imperialism, the colonists elevated the quarrel into (b) a constitutional struggle. They advanced the argument that the British Parl had no right to tax the Americans as they were not represented in it, ie they denied the sovereignty of the British Parl over America. This was a constitutional theory no one in Great Britain, apart from a few eccentrics, could accept, not even such men as ROCKINGHAM and PITT, who otherwise advocated lenient treatment of the colonists. In America, however, it was widely accepted among educated colonists, steeped as they were in the self-help attitudes of pioneering frontiersmen and in the individualism of the Puritan congregations. For them, the ideas of Locke and the Country philosophy of the British oppositions were still live issues. They lived in provs where constitutional struggles were endemic; where representative assemblies based on comparatively wide electorates were accustomed to resisting the absolutist pretensions of governors sent out from Great Britain. Moreover, with 5,000 km of ocean between them, mutual misunderstanding was unavoidable, so that the stridency of the American protests surprised the British, and seemed out of proportion to the provocation.

The run-up to the war took the form of 3 increasingly severe crises caused by restrictive legislation in Great Britain provoking resistance in America, followed by concessions in Britain. The provokers were GRENVILLE, Townshend and NORTH.

(a) The Grenville admin (1763–5) naturally took the view that 13 separate colonies were not competent to regulate their commerce on an imperial scale, nor could they defend their frontiers against France, Spain and the Indians. Moreover, they felt that the colonists should begin to pay their fair share of the expenses involved in these 2 imperial responsibilities. In consequence, Britain issued the Proclamation of 7 Oct 1763, defining the boundaries of the 13 colonies as well as those of Canada and E and W Florida, and limiting migration westwards to enable Britain to garrison the Indian areas and control relations with the Indians so as to avoid a recurrence of the great Indian uprising under Pontiac (1763). At the same time Grenville tightened up the enforcement of the old navigation system, and in 1764 alone doubled the list of enumerated goods which the colonists were obliged to export via Britain. He passed the Revenue Act – or Sugar Act – (1764) which halved the sixpenny duty on foreign sugar, but enforced its collection with unprecedented vigour, using the navy to seek out smugglers. He passed the Stamp Act (1765) which laid a tax on legal transactions, playing cards, newspapers etc, after giving the Americans a year in which to suggest an alternative way of raising revenue. The American resistance to the Stamp Act made it impossible to enforce. Colonial legislatures passed resolutions against it (eg the Virginia Resolves of May 1765); and some colonies sent delegates to the so-called Stamp Act Congress in New York which began to co-ordinate resistance (Oct 1765). Americans also began to refuse to implement the Quartering Act (1765), whereby colonies were supposed to provide billets and upkeep for British troops passing through them. In Britain the new Gov – the Rockingham admin (1765-6) – repealed the Stamp Act (1766), but passed the Declaratory Act (1766) which declared that Parl had full sovereignty over the colonies.

(b) Charles Townshend, the Chancellor of the Exchequer in the Pitt admin (1766-8), introduced in his Revenue Act (1767) duties on the import into the colonies of glass, red and white lead, painters' colours, paper and tea. He was seeking a source of revenue to pay British officials in America so as to make them independent of the colonial assemblies which had paid them thus far. Moreover, he thought he had answered the colonists' objections to the Stamp Act, for these would theoretically be external duties for regulating commerce, not internal duties for raising revenue. These duties, as well as other measures taken at the same time to make the collection of customs revenue more efficient, intensified the opposition in America, where mob violence and resistance by the authorities made the collection of revenue almost impossible. The Massachusetts Assembly sent a Circular Letter to the other colonies (Feb 1768) calling for joint resistance to taxation of any kind without representation, a position which entailed independence, since sending MPs to London was not in their minds. Shortly after, the colonists began to make non-importation agreements with one another. In Britain, the GRAFTON admin (1768-70) created a new office of Sec of State for the American Colonies, and the holder of it, the Earl of Hillsborough, prepared to coerce the colonists, landing troops under Gen Gage in Boston, Massachusetts, on 1 Oct 1768.

(c) The North admin (1770-82) tried to lower the temperature by repealing the Townshend duties (Mar 1770) while retaining the tax on tea in order to assert the principle that Britain could tax the colonies. In America, violent incidents showed that the opposition was rising: eg the Boston Massacre on 5 Mar 1770 (when troops guarding the custom-house fired on a crowd, killing 5); the burning of the *Gaspée* on 10 June 1772 (when Rhode Islanders set fire to a revenue cutter); and the formation by the radicals of Boston of the Committee of Correspondence on 2 Nov 1772 (the beginnings of a revolutionary organization). It was North's Tea Act (May 1773) which produced the next big wave of violence. This Act was designed to help the finances of the E India Co by allowing it to unload its surplus tea in America, without paying the 12 pence duty to England, though still collecting the 3 pence duty in America. American radicals regarded this cheap tea as British bait to seduce colonists into breaking the boycott and paying the hated duty. The result was the Boston Tea Party (16 Dec 1773), when Bostonians dressed as Indians threw 3 ship-loads of tea into the harbour. The British Gov could not ignore this act of defiance, and passed a series of Coercive Acts (the Intolerable Acts in American eyes). The Boston Port Act (1774) closed Boston to shipping until the city paid compensation. The Massachusetts Government Act (1774) gave the Gov more dictatorial powers. The Administration of

Justice Act (1774) allowed cases to be tried in Britain or another colony if a fair trial for a British official could not be expected in Massachusetts. The Quartering Act (1774) enforced the billeting of troops. At the same time, the British Gov angered the Americans by the enlightened Quebec Act (1774), which fixed the border of Canada so as to give it the vast area between the Ohio, the Great Lakes and the Mississippi (thus shutting out the Americans from the fur trade and westward migration), and set up a form of Gov which gave Caths full rights and the executive strong powers (thus causing the Americans to fear for their religious and political liberties). Representatives from all colonies except Georgia met in the 1st Continental Congress at Philadelphia (5 Sept 1774) to co-ordinate anti-British measures and to formulate American constitutional rights. Though the moderates on both sides made several attempts at conciliation, the authoritarians in the Gov (especially the K) and the radicals in the colonies steadily carried the 2 sides towards war. Both sides adopted positions from which retreat was impossible; and there was a gap between the two which no amount of goodwill could bridge: the Americans refused to acknowledge what Britain insisted upon, namely, the mother country's powers of taxation and rights of legislation. George III had the support of his Cab, the majority of Parl, and most of the nation – except the Radicals – in his determination to make the Americans submit. It was only a question of a tiny minority of radicals, it was thought. It was doubtful, however, if George could ever have defeated the colonists; and certain that, if he did, they would soon rebel again rather than bow the knee to British sovereignty.

The war: (a) 1775–7. Fighting began in Massachusetts when British troops on their way to capture a colonial arms store at Concord got into a skirmish at Lexington (19 Apr 1775). The 2nd Continental Congress, which met on 10 May 1775, made war preparations, appointing George Washington C-in-C of a Continental army. The British, hemmed in at Boston, beat an American attempt to hold positions overlooking them at Bunker Hill (17 June 1775), though with very heavy losses. Great Britain pronounced the colonists rebels on 23 Aug 1775, while the Americans invaded Canada from the Hudson valley, taking Montreal on 13 Nov 1775. On 9 Jan 1776 Tom Paine published his pamphlet *Common Sense* blaming George III for everything (as did the British opposition) and urging the colonists to form an independent republic. This had a deep influence on American public opinion, and on 4 July 1776 the American Declaration of Independence was signed. Meanwhile, the British had to evacuate Boston in Mar 1776 and refit at Halifax, Nova Scotia, awaiting reinforcements. In Canada, the Americans were repulsed at Quebec and had to abandon their invasion (June 1776). The British under Gen Howe and his brother, Admiral Ld Howe, landed on Long Island, New York, beat Washington at Brooklyn (Aug 1776), and steadily forced him up the Hudson, then S across New Jersey and beyond the R Delaware, though without succeeding in bringing him to battle. During that winter American defeatism was rife and the militia was melting away till Washington restored morale by suddenly recrossing the Delaware and beating the British forces at Trenton, NJ, on 26 Dec 1776. In London, Ld George Germain – the Sec of State for the American colonies, who was in charge of the land operations – formed a plan to bisect the American colonies and then eliminate each half separately. The Hudson was to be the dividing line, and this was to be taken in a co-ordinated pair of campaigns – southwards from Canada, and northwards from New York. Gen Burgoyne made slow progress in his descent from Canada, and so Howe in New York decided to fill in the time by capturing Philadelphia. This change of plan was approved by Germain and known to Burgoyne, but dilatoriness in communications led to misunderstandings among the commanders, and then to disaster. Howe left New York for Philadelphia, defeated Washington at Brandywine Creek, and took Philadelphia (25 Sept 1777), by which time it was too late to get back to help Burgoyne who in the meantime had reached Saratoga, where he had no alternative but to surrender to Gen Gates on 17 Oct 1777. This was a turning-point in the war. It stiffened American morale, and brought in France and Spain on the anti-British side. Moreover, the British allowed Washington to rest undisturbed at Valley Forge, where he employed the terrible winter in refitting his men and fortifying their fighting spirit.

(b) 1778–82 saw a chastened Britain begin to realize that, even if the Americans could be defeated in battle (and this was questionable), the British could not permanently hold down a whole continent of patriots. In these years Britain gave up trying to conquer New England and Pennsylvania, and instead – keeping New York as a base – concentrated on conquering the S colonies (where there was a higher proportion of loyalists), at the same time using the navy to make sporadic raids on the American coast and shipping, and mounting a big attack on the French W Indies. France signed an alliance with the Americans on 6 Feb 1778, and a French fleet arrived off the American coast, with the result that, burdened with the extra responsibilities of winning command of the sea in the Caribbean and defending Great Britain itself, the British navy could no longer adequately reinforce and supply the troops in America, especially as the menace of American privateers increased annually. In America, the British abandoned Philadelphia (June 1778) and invaded Georgia (Oct 1778), taking Savannah on 29 Dec 1778. Spain declared war on Britain on 16 June 1779, and the summer of 1779 saw an attempted Franco-Spanish invasion of Britain, as well as threats to Gibraltar and Minorca. In the W Indies (1778–82) the French captured Dominica, St Vincent, Grenada, Tobago, St Kitts, Nevis and Montserrat, while Britain took only St Lucia (Dec 1778). In America, the British campaigned in S Carolina, taking Charleston on 12 May 1780. In Europe, Britain declared war on Holland (20 Dec 1780) for resisting the British claim to search neutral vessels; while the formation of the Armed Neutrality (1780) – an alliance of Russia, Sweden and Denmark to oppose the British right-of-search claim – added to the pressure on the British navy. In the Med, Gibraltar held out, but the British garrison on Minorca surrendered to a Franco-Spanish expedition on 4 Feb 1782. In the American S, the victorious British advanced into N Carolina and then into Virginia, where they dug themselves in at Yorktown, hoping to make it a base which could be supplied from the sea. Unfortunately, the French navy was in command at that point, and the British had to surrender to the French-American armies (19 Oct 1781), a disaster which ended the military operations in America. On the other hand, the British defeated the French at Les Saintes, W Indies, on 12 Apr 1782, a victory which gave them back the command of the Caribbean and the Atlantic; while Gibraltar – continually under siege – was finally saved from a serious attack in Sept 1782. Nevertheless, the news of Yorktown led to the fall of North (Mar 1782) and the conclusion of peace.

By the Tr of Versailles (Sept 1783) (a) In America, Great Britain recognized the independence of the colonies (the USA) and ceded to them the land between the Ohio, the Mississippi and the Great Lakes which had been Canadian by the Quebec Act of 1774. (b) In the W Indies, Great Britain and France restored each other's islands, and in addition Britain ceded Tobago to France. (c) In Africa, Britain restored Senegal and Goree to France. (d) To Spain, Britain ceded Minorca and Florida, while Spain recognized the British right to the Bahamas and to logwood cutting in Honduras.

Anabaptists Part of the radical wing of the REFORMATION (the other main part being the SPIRITUALISTS), consisting of preachers and congregations in the tradition of medieval mysticism and millenarianism who believed that LUTHER and ZWINGLI had stopped halfway towards reform by compromising with existing governments and churches. They were given this name by their enemies, though they were not a united or a uniform movement, but a group of separate (if sometimes mutually influenced) religious movements in different places and at different times all over Europe, with many differences between them, though also with certain broad common characteristics: ie (a) They usually belonged to the underprivileged layers of society, being poor miners, or depressed craftsmen, or dispossessed peasants (though not the labouring poor), and their programmes contained a mixture of social and religious aspirations. (b) They based their doctrines on the Scriptures, but also on the 'continuous revelation' which God's chosen people received by being 'filled with the Spirit', hearing voices, seeing visions etc. (c) They practised adult baptism. (d) They believed that the Elect were surrounded by the forces of Antichrist, in the form of existing churches, governments and other institutions, with whom co-operation (in the form of holding public office, performing military service, taking oaths etc) was sinful; and that the saintly should form their own communities, separate from the rest of mankind, sharing goods in common, and working to destroy the established order and usher in the Kingdom of Christ on Earth. Their chief centres were Saxony (where Thomas Müntzer was important); Zürich, among the radical followers of Zwingli; Augsburg and the upper Danube (where the ex-Zwingli-ite Balthasar Hubmaier was influential); Austria, Moravia, Tyrol (where the leader, Hubmaier, was burned at the stake in Vienna in 1528, and was followed by the Tyrolean Jakob Huter who, by the time he was executed at Innsbruck in 1536, had established the Moravian Brethren as an indestructible puritan movement based on communal agriculture); Poland–Lithuania, where baptism by immersion was a variant; Italy, where the anti-Trinitarian views which influenced Servetus were stressed; the lower Rhine and the Netherlands, to which the message was brought via Strassburg by ex-Zwingli-ites from Zürich; where the fanatical violence and sexual heterodoxy of the Siege of Münster gave Anabaptism a filthy name for all time to come (even though atypical) and where Menno Simons (1496–1561) organized those who survived the Münster bloodbath into a pacific and quietist community which was the origin of modern Baptism.

Anna (Ivanovna) (28 Jan 1693–17 Oct 1740) Empss of Russia (1730), who was placed on the throne by a faction of *boyars* and *dvoryane* in an unsuccessful attempt to turn the autocracy into a limited monarchy. During her reign Russia was ruled by Germans under her favourite, Biron; and this period was marked (1) at home by the decrease in the control exercised by the Crown over the provs and the nobility, and by the increase in the power of the nobility over the serfs; while (2) abroad Russia won control over Poland in the WAR OF THE POLISH SUCCESSION (1733–5/8), but gained only Azov in the expensive Russo-Turkish War (1735–9).

b at Moscow, 2nd daughter of Ivan V (half-brother of PETER I, and joint Tsar with him, 1682–96) and his wife, Praskovia Saltykova; m (1710) Frederick William, D of Courland, who, however, soon d (1711). She lived in straitened widowhood in Mitau, Courland (now Jelgava, USSR), till she was made Empss of Russia by the Supreme Privy Council, who thought she would obey their orders. In the *Conditions* which she signed in Jan 1730 she handed over power to the Supreme Privy Council, ie to the Golitsin, Dolgoruky and other *boyar* families; but with the support of the chief opponents of oligarchy – namely the top 4 ranks of the *dvoryanstvo* (service nobility) as well as the rank-and-file and prov *dvoryane* – she tore up the *Conditions* (Feb 1730), abolished the Supreme Privy Council (Mar 1730), revived the Senate, but soon superseded it in policy-making with a 3-man Cab. Supreme power, in fact, was placed in the hands of her coarse and grasping lover, Count Ernst Johann Biron (or Bühren), and his German followers from Courland and Livonia, to such a degree that this period in Russian history is known as the *Bironovshchina*. Other leading foreigners were Count A. I. Osterman and Count B. C. Münnich – controlling foreign and military affairs, respectively – with whom Biron was frequently at loggerheads. While the Biron régime cruelly oppressed the Russian people – using the Secret Chancery (security police) to institute a reign of terror – the tall and fat Empss – who had no education and little interest in gov – devoted herself to hunting and shooting and to practical jokes, as well as to crude and extravagant Court orgies in which her dwarfs, giants, jesters and other freaks played a prominent part.

At home, the decline in the effectiveness of the centralized autocracy, which had become evident since the death of Peter I, continued apace. (a) Peter's attempts to create systematized central control over prov and local gov were abandoned, and Russia relapsed into its traditional federal structure in which prov power was exercised by practically autonomous *voevody* (governors) who oppressed the public at will. (b) Moreover, the Empss made important concessions to the *dvoryane*. In 1730 she repealed Peter I's Entail Law of 1714, which had required landowners to bequeath all their estates to one heir, so as to leave the rest available for service. She made the nobles responsible for collecting the soul-tax from their serfs, thus intensifying serfdom (1731). She established a Noble Cadet Corps at St Petersburg (1731) in which the sons of nobles could receive their training without serving in the ranks. From 1736, state service was reduced from life to 25 years (though this concession was soon suspended on account of the Russo-Turkish War); service was to begin when nobles were aged 20 instead of 15; and one male per family was excused service so that he could supervise the estates. (c) At the same time, the status of the serfs declined in proportion. They could be moved about from one region to another without warning (1732). Fugitive serfs could be punished by lords at their discretion (1736). Serfs were deprived of the right to own land or carry on business in their own name (1737). (d) Business prospered in this period, perhaps because of Crown weakness. More and more Crown monopolies in manufacturing and commerce were created and farmed out to enterprising individuals.

Abroad, Russia took a more active part in European affairs under Osterman, whose policy was based on an alliance with Austria to support their common aims in Poland and Turkey. Russia participated successfully in the War of the Polish Succession (1733–5/8), ousting the French from Poland, and establishing the Russian candidate – Augustus III – as K. Towards Turkey, Russia continued her centuries-old hostility. The 2 states were deadly rivals in many areas – Persia, Poland, the Crimea and the Black Sea – as well as worshipping different gods; while Russian military success in Poland encouraged the war parties in both capitals. The Russo-Turkish War (1735–9) was the result, with Austria joining Russia in the Austro-Turkish War (1737–9). Russia won some early victories, but could not sustain a long war, especially as Austria fought so badly and made a separate peace – Tr of Belgrade, Sept 1739. In the Russo-Turkish Tr of Belgrade (Sept 1739) Russia managed to gain only Azov with its fortress dismantled, a meagre profit from such an exhausting outlay. It is not surprising that the oppressive *Bironovshchina* did not long outlast the Empss. She d in St Petersburg, where she had moved the Court.

Anne (6 Feb 1665–1 Aug 1714) Q of Great Britain and Ireland (18 Mar 1702), the last of the Stuart dynasty, in whose reign the UNION WITH SCOTLAND was achieved, the War of the Spanish Succession was fought, party warfare between WHIGS and TORIES was fierce, and the Crown lost power to the leading political 'managers'.

b at St James's Palace, London; 2nd daughter of James, D of York (future K JAMES II) and his 1st wife, Anne Hyde; ed as an Anglican; m (28 July 1683) Pr George of Denmark (d 1708), 2nd son of K Frederick III of Denmark, a dull but pleasant soldier, fat but faithful, by whom she had 18 pregnancies (1683–1700) 5 of them live births, none of them surviving childhood. During the REVOLUTION OF 1688 she left London with the Bp on 25 Nov 1688 to join the Midlands rebels at Nottingham, a betrayal of her father about which she felt guilty for the rest of her life. Sweet-voiced, but dull, blinkered, pious and prejudiced and, in later life, corpulent and weak in health, she lacked the industry, interest and intellect to gov the country in the way WILLIAM III had done. Her likes and dislikes swayed her political judgement. Her affection for succeeding Bedchamber women – 1st Sarah, Dss of Marlborough, then Mrs Masham – placed her too much in their power; and more than one able Whig found his career hindered by her hatred of his irreligion or immorality. Britain was gov on her behalf by a trio of non-party 'managers': MARLBOROUGH (Capt-Gen, 1702–11), GODOLPHIN (Ld Treasurer, 1702–10) and HARLEY (Speaker, 1702–4; Sec of State, 1704–8; Chancellor of the Exchequer, 1710; Ld Treasurer, 1711–14). 1702–4 saw the triumvirate in alliance with the Tory Earl of NOTTINGHAM (Sec of State) waging the War of the Spanish Succession (1702–13/14) against France (see LOUIS XIV). The fighting went well, but the Gov was distracted in the Tory H of C of the 1st Parl (Oct 1702–Mar 1705) from its main job of voting war finance by 2 groups of Tory extremists: (a) Nottingham and his High Ch faction tried 3 times to pass the Dissenter-persecuting Occasional Conformity

Bill (1702, '03, '04), the 3rd time 'tacking' it to the Land Tax Bill in an effort to ensure its passing; (b) the Country Tories – back-bench squires – abetted by Henry St John (later BOLINGBROKE) obstructed the war effort by their objections to war finance, high taxation and the 'money'd' interest. To counter this sabotage, Harley brought into the Gov moderate Tories (St John became Sec-at-War, Apr 1704) and moderate Whigs (Newcastle became Ld Privy Seal, Apr 1705), while he himself replaced Nottingham as Sec of State (May 1704).

1704–8 saw the triumvirate in the evenly balanced Whig–Tory 2nd Parl (Oct 1705–Apr 1708) leaning more and more for support on the pro-war Whigs for voting men and materials for the front, and for passing the Act of Union with Scotland (6 Mar 1707). Harley disagreed with Marlborough and Godolphin when they decided to bring Whigs into the Gov, while they for their part suspected he was plotting to overthrow them by cultivating his cousin, Mrs Masham, who by this time had a great hold on the Q. He was suddenly dismissed in Feb 1708, and Whigs replaced Tories in the Gov.

1708–10 saw a Whig H of C in the 3rd Parl (Nov 1708–Sept 1710), and a Gov consisting of Marlborough and Godolphin and the Court Whigs known as the Junto. In the peace negotiations of 1709 they loyally backed their intransigent allies, the United Provinces and the Emp LEOPOLD I, and pitched their terms so high (eg insisting that Louis XIV should help them drive his grandson, PHILIP V, out of Spain – 'No peace without Spain') that France preferred to go on fighting. They were accused then and later of continuing the war because it was so profitable to them. War-weariness was seizing the nation, however, and buoying up Harley, who was rallying the Tories once more on a programme of peace, as well as the usual Country demands. Anne herself became convinced that a change was necessary by the pro-Tory excitement which exploded over the trial of Henry Sacheverell. This high-flying Tory parson had celebrated the 21st anniversary of 1688 by casting aspersions on the Revolution; and the Gov made the mistake of prosecuting him and so turning him into a hero and martyr. Anne dismissed her ministers one by one during 1710–11, beginning with Godolphin on 7 Aug 1710 and ending with Marlborough on 31 Dec 1711. In between, she appointed Harley, St John and the Tories, while a general election returned a Tory H of C.

1710–14 saw Harley as Earl of Oxford and in effect prime minister, with St John (Vt Bolingbroke) as his deputy, and backed by a Tory majority in the 4th Parl (Nov 1710–July 1713) and a bigger Tory majority in the 5th (Feb–July 1714). This Gov overcame a serious financial crisis, and restored credit by dispelling City prejudice against Tories. It passed the Occasional Conformity Act (1711) to prevent Dissenters from qualifying for public office simply by taking Anglican communion occasionally. It passed the Schism Act (1714) to cut off Dissent (and therefore much Whiggism) at its source by closing down Dissenting schools. Its chief task was to negotiate the very advantageous Tr of Utrecht (1713). Britain in effect gave up fighting in 1711, and Marlborough's successor, the D of Ormonde, was given 'restraining orders' on 10 May 1712, the French being informed of this behind the allies' backs. Oxford's peace preliminaries were passed by Parl, but only after Anne had swamped the Whig H of L with 12 new Tory peers (1711). By 1714, however, the Gov was tottering. Firstly, Oxford and Bolingbroke were at daggers drawn, with Bolingbroke determined to oust his moderate chief at the head of the high-flying Tories. Secondly, the Tories were split over some key questions: the persecution of Dissenters, the peace terms, and the succession to the throne. There were Jacobite Tories, Hanover Tories and Tories who were undecided; while the Whigs were united in favour of GEORGE I. Thirdly, and partly as a result, Oxford was ill, depressed, debauched and falling down on his job. On 27 July 1714 the Q dismissed him, and she d 5 days later at Kensington Palace. In that short time Bolingbroke panicked and the Tories hesitated. At the meeting of the Privy Council on 30 July 1714, the pro-Hanover minority seized the initiative and recommended the Q to appoint the Whig D of Shrewsbury to succeed Oxford as Ld Treasurer. She agreed, and her ministers – including the Tories – then proceeded to make all the necessary arrangements for the Hanoverian succession as she lay dying.

Armada, the Spanish The great military and naval expedition which PHILIP II of Spain sent to invade England in the summer of 1588, though without success.

Anglo-Spanish antagonism gradually built up during the 1580s. As far as Spain was concerned, England was, firstly, a heretic country, ruled by an illegitimate Q, ELIZABETH I, who had no right to the throne. Secondly, she had become a menace to Spanish communications with the Netherlands through the Channel, and to Spanish commerce across the Atlantic. And, thirdly, she was the friend of Spain's enemies: the N provs in the REVOLT OF THE NETHERLANDS, and the Huguenots in the FRENCH WARS OF RELIGION. The idea of reconquering the N Netherlands and establishing a Spanish monopoly over the Indies after first conquering England and replacing Elizabeth I by Philip II was raised as early as Aug 1583 by the Marquis of Santa Cruz; and plans for it were gradually worked out, modified and remodified, as Anglo-Spanish relations deteriorated. Events in the Netherlands and France led to active English intervention in both theatres. In the Netherlands, the assassination of WILLIAM I (the Silent) on 10 July 1584 and the conquest of Antwerp by FARNESE on 17 Aug 1585 caused Elizabeth to sign the Tr of Nonsuch on 10/20 Aug 1585 whereby 6,000 men under the Earl of LEICESTER went to the aid of the Dutch in Dec 1585. In France, the death of the D of Anjou (Alençon) on 10 June 1584, leaving the Hug, HENRY of Navarre, heir to the throne, caused the revival of the Cath League, which now allied with Spain in the Tr of Joinville (Dec 1584), causing K HENRY III of France to ally with them both by the Tr of Nemours (July 1585) – all leading to the War of the Three Henries (1585–9), in which Elizabeth gave financial support to the Hugs. Diplomatic relations between England and Spain ended when Elizabeth expelled the Spanish ambassador in Jan 1584 for involvement in the Throckmorton Plot; and war was brought nearer by DRAKE's piratical activities in the Spanish W Indies (1585–6).

The preparations for the Armada now went ahead, with the D of Medina Sidonia in charge of fitting out, and Farnese and Santa Cruz in charge of strategy. The final plan was the result of inadequate dovetailing by Philip II of 2 separate schemes: that of Santa Cruz for a naval descent on England from Spain, and that of Farnese for an invasion from the Netherlands. According to it, Farnese was to withdraw his army from fighting the Dutch, assemble it at Dunkirk and Nieuwpoort, where the Armada would pick it up, land it near Margate, Kent, and guard its supply-lines while Farnese conquered England. At the same time, stepped-up

Spanish intervention in the French Wars of Religion would prevent France from aiding England. Preparations, however, were slow, but the execution of MARY, Q OF SCOTS on 18 Feb 1587, leaving Philip with a strong claim as heir, called for speed. Farnese was ready in 1587, but Santa Cruz favoured delay until he had overwhelming superiority; but in any case Drake's raid on Cádiz in Apr 1587 (he eliminated 24 Armada ships, and captured supply-ships carrying barrel-staves) prevented departure that year. Further difficulties were caused by the death of Santa Cruz on 9 Feb 1588 and his replacement by the very reluctant Medina Sidonia, who was diffident about switching from admin to active service.

The campaign began in May 1588 when 130 ships carrying 22,000 sailors and soldiers, as well as 2,431 pieces of artillery, set sail from Lisbon. On 9/19 June they were scattered by a storm off Corunna, causing a month's delay for re-assembly and repairs. On 19/29 July they appeared off the Lizard and then made their way in tight crescent-shaped formation along the Channel towards Calais. They were fitted with short-range guns suitable for damaging enemy ships with a view to grappling and boarding. On the other hand, the small English ships evaded contact and attacked with long-range artillery which was, in fact, too light to do great damage. The Armada, with orders not to engage the enemy till after the rendezvous with Farnese, maintained superb order and discipline during the 9-day battle, in which they were continually attacked from the stern by Drake and his ships which, warping out of Plymouth after the Armada had passed, had the advantage of lying to windward throughout the engagement. Medina Sidonia anchored off Calais on 27 July/6 Aug, and for the 1st time learned about a serious defect in Philip's planning. The rendezvous with Farnese was impossible because Dunkirk was not deep enough to take the Armada, and Farnese had only canal boats with which to ferry his men out under the eyes of the Dutch navy. During the night of 28–9 July/7–8 Aug the English scattered the Armada by sending in 8 fireships, and on 29 July/8 Aug, while Farnese was obediently embarking his men at Dunkirk and Nieuwpoort, the 150-strong English fleet pounded the Spanish as they drifted off Gravelines, sinking only 4, but wreaking heavy damage among the rest. A strong SW wind now drove the Armada into the N Sea; and it made its way back home via the N of Scotland. Medina Sidonia reached Santander on the N coast of Spain, semi-delirious from his privations, on 23 Oct 1588. About a third of the shipping failed to return; but the most serious loss was in manpower. The defeat of the Armada did not immediately change the naval balance of power, but it dealt a severe blow to Spanish self-confidence, and marked the start of Spain's slow decline. It also raised the morale of Prots all over Europe to a degree which cannot be calculated.

Arminians The inaccurate name given by their PURITAN opponents to the High Churchmen of early C17 England, of whom Lancelot Andrewes and William LAUD were leading examples. The name was borrowed from Holland, where the followers of Jacobus Arminius (1560–1609) formed a moderate faction in the Ch, denying predestination and irresistible grace, and affirming human free will to co-operate with God or not. The English Arminians revived elements of doctrine and worship which had been typical of the early Ch, but which had been swept out by the Calvinists in C16. They stressed the importance of ceremonial, vest-ments and Ch decoration, and preferred ornate and learned sermons to the extempore efforts of the Puritans. In their view, men were free to resist divine grace or fall from it having accepted it; in fact, they practically held the Cath view that men could deserve grace by their actions and state of mind. Characteristically, also, they believed that discipline and uniformity, enforced by the Bps, were an essential element of the Ch. They also supported the authority of the Crown which, in the person of CHARLES I, strongly reciprocated. He promoted Laud and his like in preference to the Puritans; and soon this minority was able to impose its views on the Ch and universities, provoking resentments which were an important cause of the CIVIL WAR.

Augsburg Confession, The (1530) The statement of Lutheran beliefs presented to the German Diet of Augsburg, which the Emp CHARLES V had called with the aim of achieving German unity by reconciling the Prots. At that time the West was threatened by a Turkish invasion under SULAIMĀN II, The Magnificent. The chief author of the creed (originally called the Articles of Schwabach) was MELANCHTHON, though it had been sent to LUTHER for his approval before it was presented to the Diet on 25 June 1530. As was to be expected, Melanchthon went out of his way to be conciliatory in his phraseology, and 21 of the 28 Articles showed no disagreement with the Roman Caths; but the Roman delegation, led by Lorenzo Campeggio and under orders from Pp CLEMENT VII, were intransigent, as their reply – the *Confutatio* of Aug 1530 – showed. The Diet ended in Nov 1530 with a Recess confirming the Edict of Worms (1521); but the Prots had already withdrawn, bequeathing in the Confession what many have regarded as a watered-down version of their position.

Augsburg, Peace of (25 Sept 1555) The Tr which ended the German religious wars of the REFORMATION period. It was the product of the Diet of Augsburg (Feb–Sept 1555) at which the Emp was represented not by CHARLES V, who was abdicating, but by his brother, FERDINAND I. It marks the defeat of the Emp's attempts to unite Germany politically and religiously (failures which were repeated in the THIRTY YEARS WAR of 1618–48 and in the Trs of Westphalia of 1648) and thus represents an important stage in the evolution of Germany into a collection of petty states instead of a united absolute monarchy. Among its chief terms were: (a) The religion of each state – RC or Lutheran, but no other – was to be settled by the Pr (a principle known later as *cujus regio, ejus religio*); and dissenters were to be free to emigrate. (b) In free cities and Imperial cities where there were RCs and Lutherans, both were to be tolerated. (c) Lutheran knights and towns within RC ecclesiastical states were to continue to worship freely. (d) All ecclesiastical land secularized by Lutherans before the Tr of Passau of 1552 was to remain Lutheran, but in future the Ecclesiastical Reservation was to apply: ie any ecclesiastical prelate turning Lutheran was not allowed to take his office, lands and revenues with him. This last was Ferdinand's version of the proceedings, but the Lutherans did not accept this clause.

Austrian Succession, War of the (1740–48) A complex series of campaigns, the chief ones being (1) between FREDERICK II of Prussia and MARIA THERESA of Austria for the possession of Silesia; (2) between LOUIS XV of France and Maria Theresa of Austria over the break-up of the Habsburg monarchy; (3) between

PHILIP V of Spain and Maria Theresa of Austria over who should control Italy; (4) between GEORGE II of Great Britain on one side and France and Spain on the other for the naval supremacy in the Med and the Atlantic, as well as the control of India, and of America (where it was called K George's War). Britain took the leading part – with diplomacy, subsidies, military and naval support – in persuading as many Continental states as possible to make peace with one another so as to become free to attack France. Moreover, as far as the hostilities between Britain and Spain were concerned, the war had begun in 1739 as the War of Jenkins' Ear. At the end of the war, the Tr of Aix-la-Chapelle (the result of general exhaustion) was not definitive. The issues continued to be contended for, diplomatically in the DIPLOMATIC REVOLUTION, and militarily in the SEVEN YEARS WAR – though there was no ambiguity about one result, and that was the emergence of Prussia as a great power. The war can be divided into 5 main periods.

1740–42. On the sudden death of the Emp CHARLES VI on 20 Oct 1740, leaving his inexperienced daughter, Maria Theresa, as his heiress (according to the Pragmatic Sanction), Frederick II, the new K of Prussia, invaded Silesia (Dec 1740) and defeated Austria at Mollwitz (Apr 1741). At the same time, Charles Albert, El of Bavaria, also claimed the inheritance, and a Franco-Bavarian army invaded Austria (Aug 1741), and then Bohemia, taking Prague on 26 Nov 1741. In this crisis, Maria Theresa as Q of Hungary appealed for Magyar help, guaranteeing all their privileges (Diet of Pressburg, Sept 1741). She also made a truce with Frederick II (Tr of Klein-Schnellendorf, Nov 1741), followed by a peace (Tr of Berlin, July 1742), allowing him to keep Silesia, and thus ending the 1st Silesian War. Her purpose was to free herself to concentrate on the Franco-Bavarian invasion, which succeeded in getting Charles Albert elected as H R Emp Charles VII on 24 Jan 1742 – the 1st non-Habsburg for over 300 years. At the same time (winter 1741–2), in the Med, Philip V of Spain used the Franco-Spanish navy to reinforce his position in Naples, where his son was K Charles III; after which he attacked Austrian positions in central and N Italy. Meanwhile, Great Britain under CARTERET subsidized Austria, organized the so-called Pragmatic Army in the Netherlands (made up of contingents from Britain, Holland, Austria, Hanover and Hesse), and, reinforcing the Med fleet, helped Maria Theresa by severely restricting Franco-Spanish activity in Italy.

1742–4. Thus strengthened, Austria threw the Franco-Bavarian armies out of Bohemia, and conquered Bavaria (1742–3); while the Pragmatic Army under the command of George II himself marched up the Rhine and defeated the French at Dettingen (16/27 June 1743), nr Frankfurt-on-Main. In negotiations at Hanau, Carteret tried to persuade Bavaria to make peace with Austria; and then he induced Charles Emmanuel of Savoy-Sardinia to join Austria and Britain (Tr of Worms, 2/13 Sept 1743). Maria Theresa was thus now in a position to cross the Rhine into France. This apparent diplomatic and military victory for Carteret only led, however, to the Franco-Spanish alliance (Tr of Fontainebleau, Oct 1743), a renewal of the Family Compact. A Franco-Spanish army then invaded Charles Emmanuel's prov of Piedmont and joined up with the Spanish army from Naples. France also invaded the Netherlands (May 1744). Moreover, Frederick II now felt that Austria was growing too strong, and he renewed the war.

1744–5. Frederick II opened the 2nd Silesian War by invading Bohemia in Aug 1744, forcing Maria Theresa to withdraw her army from the Rhine. Her position improved, though, with the death of Charles Albert of Bavaria (the Emp Charles VII) on 20 Jan 1745. His son, Maximilian Joseph, signed the Tr of Füssen with Austria (Apr 1745) whereby he recognized her in possession of the Austrian monarchy while she returned Bavaria to him. On the other hand, France beat Britain at Fontenoy, Netherlands (30 Apr/11 May 1745) and over-ran the whole prov. Moreover, though Frederick II had had to retreat from Bohemia into Silesia, he nevertheless beat the pursuing Austrian army at Hohen-friedberg, Silesia, on 4 June 1745. He then invaded Saxony – which had joined Austria in Jan 1745 – and beat their army at Kesseldorf on 15 Dec 1745, and took Dresden. Meanwhile, Britain had to withdraw her troops in order to deal with the French-backed Jacobite invasion – the 'FORTYFIVE' (June 1745–Sept 1746). Frederick II then felt secure enough to end the 2nd Silesian War and signed the Tr of Dresden with Austria on 25 Dec 1745, Maria Theresa under British pressure once more having to accept the loss of Silesia. In Canada, Great Britain took Cape Breton Isle and its fortress of Louisbourg, which commanded the St Lawrence estuary (1745).

1746–8. In Italy, France and Spain co-operated as badly together as Austria and Savoy-Sardinia, and each was in intermittent touch with the enemy. The Franco-Spanish army overran Parma and Lombardy (1745), but then withdrew into France (1746); while an Austro-Savoyard-Sardinian invasion of Provence, aided by the British fleet, retreated (1747) without having reached its target, Toulon. Little further action occurred in this theatre. Further N, the French followed up their success in the Netherlands by invading Holland, causing a constitutional revolution which brought William IV to full power as Stadholder, Capt-Gen, and Admiral-Gen (1747). This, however, did not prevent the French from taking the important fortress of Bergen-op-Zoom (Sept 1747). In India, the French captured the British town of Madras (Sept 1746). On the Atlantic coast, however, the British navy had two great successes over French fleets setting out to reinforce their colonies: off Cape Finisterre, Spain, in May 1747, and off Belle Ile, France, in Oct 1747: actions in which Britain captured many valuable prizes. In N Europe the Empss ELIZABETH of Russia at last entered the war. She had hitherto delayed because of palace revolutions at the start, then because of the war with Sweden (1741–3) (caused by Sweden's attack on Russia, instigated by France), and then because of Russia's slowness in appreciating that Frederick II's expansionism constituted a threat to the stability of N Europe. She signed a Tr of alliance with Austria (22 May/2 June 1746), but the Russian army moved across Germany to the Rhine so slowly that it saw no action before the peace was signed.

The Tr of Aix-la-Chapelle (7/18 Oct 1748) brought about a wholesale res-toration of conquered territory, except that (a) Prussia kept Silesia, (b) Philip V's son, Don Philip, gained Parma, Piacenza and Guastalla from Austria, (c) Charles Emmanuel of Savoy-Sardinia made small gains in Lombardy, and (d) the Prag-matic Sanction in Austria and the Hanoverian Succession in Britain received general recognition.

Bacon, Francis (22 Jan 1561–9 Apr 1626) Knight (1603), Baron Verulam (1618), Vt St Albans (1621); Solicitor General (1607), Attorney General (1613), Privy

Councillor (1616), Ld Keeper of the Great Seal (1617), Ld Chancellor (Jan 1618–May 1621); statesman under ELIZABETH I and JAMES I of England, and also essayist, and philosopher of science of European renown.

b at York House, Strand, London, 8th son of Sir Nicholas Bacon, Ld Keeper of the Great Seal, and his 2nd wife, Ann, the Puritan blue-stocking daughter of Sir Anthony Cooke; ed Trinity, Cambridge (1573–6), where, still a boy, he decided that the prevailing study of Aristotle was 'barren of the production of works for the life of man'; then (1576–9) in France with Sir Amias Paulet, the English ambassador, where he observed the FRENCH WARS OF RELIGION. On the early death of his father (1579) he had to return and begin a career in law. He m (1606) Alice Barnham, daughter of a City of London alderman (no children). He was called to the Bar in 1582, but in spite of his brilliant and original mind, immense industry, insatiable ambition and family connections, he found the path to high office strewn with obstacles. His faulty judgement of men, his cold arrogance and self-interest, perhaps his homosexual tastes, aroused distrust and hostility in others.

Under Q Elizabeth I he became MP for Melcombe Regis, Dorset (1584), Taunton (1586), Liverpool (1589), but he received little help from Burghley, for the latter regarded him as a rival to his own son, Robert Cecil (SALISBURY). Thus in the 1590s he joined the ESSEX following, but his opposition to a taxation motion in 1593 did not endear him to the Q, and it was COKE, not he, who became Attorney General in 1594 and m Burghley's granddaughter, the wealthy widow, Lady Elizabeth Hatton, in 1598. After warning Essex against opposing the Q, Bacon left the faction and reaped popular execration for his part in the conviction of Essex (Feb 1601) after his abortive rebellion. Henceforth Bacon was a convinced supporter of strong monarchy.

Under James I he rose in the K's service, though less swiftly than he would have liked, having still to compete with Coke till the latter began to oppose the Crown in defence of the Common Law. With BUCKINGHAM's help Bacon became the leading law officer of the K, strong in the defence of the royal prerogative, prominent in the execution of RALEGH (1618), and taking the lead with Buckingham in the Star Chamber prosecution for embezzlement of the Ld Treasurer, the Earl of Suffolk – the leader of the Howard faction, which now fell from power (1618).

The 3rd Parl of James I, while investigating monopolies, found evidence that Bacon had accepted bribes, and the H of C impeached him before the H of L on 3 May 1621. 23 charges were made, and Bacon made a full confession, claiming, however, that his judgements in Chancery had not thereby been affected. He was found guilty, and among other punishments he was committed to the Tower of London (in practice only for the night of 31 May 1621), and fined £40,000 (but this was remitted by the K). His political career was ruined, even though he later received a general pardon (1624). He retired to his estate at Gorhambury, St Albans, Herts, where he made strenuous efforts to restore his reputation and fortune – eg, by applying unsuccessfully for the post of Provost of Eton – and concentrated on his literary and philosophical work.

Law and politics had occupied only part of his mind, and he had established a separate reputation as a writer. His *Essays* – 10 in the 1st edition (1597), 38 in the 2nd (1612), and 58 in the 3rd (1625) – have become part of the proverbial wisdom of English-speaking people, with their aphoristic compactness and vivid physical imagery: 'Money is like muck, not good except it be spread'. His *Advancement of Learning* (1605), *Novum Organum* (1620) and *New Atlantis* (1627) embody his ambitious programme for scientific research in the service of mankind, which, if not original, had a profound effect on the formation of the Royal Society (1662) and the European scientific revolution of C17 and C18. 'I have taken all knowledge as my province,' he said, meaning knowledge derived from experimentation and the observation of nature, and excluding metaphysics. 'We cannot command nature except by obeying her,' he believed, and his purpose was 'the relief of man's estate'. He himself was a thinker rather than a practical scientist, and he failed to appreciate some of the best experimental work of his day. On the other hand, he himself experimented a great deal in his last years, and met his death at Highgate through catching a chill while stuffing a fowl with snow to see whether this would be as effective as salt in preserving the meat.

Balance of Power The situation that arises in a given states-system (eg Italy in C16, or Europe from C16 onwards, or the world today) where there is a rough equilibrium between the members, and no one state dominates the rest. When one power grows too strong (eg CHARLES V in C16, or LOUIS XIV in C17) the others join together in opposition to restore the balance. The endless shifting of alliances to preserve the balance of power became a regular aim of foreign policy from C16 onwards. It replaced the medieval notion of the international scene as an unchanging hierarchy of states under the leadership of the HREmp; and it formed the presuppositions of peace Trs such as those of Westphalia (1648) and Utrecht (1713).

Bancroft, Richard (Sept 1544–2 Nov 1610) Archbp of Canterbury (1604) under K JAMES I of England, and who continued WHITGIFT's policy of repressing Puritanism.

b at Farnworth, Lancs; ed at Christ's, Cambridge; chaplain to Sir Christopher Hatton, then Whitgift (1592), and the latter's chief detective in the police action against the Presbyterians in the 1580s and '90s. His writings and sermons were sarcastic and provocative, and stressed the danger of Presbyterian separatism to the social and political order. As far as the Caths were concerned, he joined with Robert Cecil (the future Ld SALISBURY) in trying to separate the bulk from the pro-Spanish, Jesuit-led minority, by offering an end to persecution in return for political loyalty. In June 1591 he was consecrated Bp of London, and acted as Archbp in Whitgift's old age before being elevated himself. He played an important role in the conciliatory Hampton Court Conference (Jan 1604), but provoked Puritan ire by his hostile attitude thereafter. The Canons of 1604, produced by Convocation and licensed by the K in Sept 1604, enforced subscription by the clergy to all the *39 Articles* and to everything in the Prayer Book. As a result, about 90 clergy lost their livings, and in addition the common lawyers attacked the ecclesiastical courts, and the H of C protested at this attempt to legislate outside Parl. At the same time, Bancroft made strenuous efforts to put a stop to the alienation of lands which had so weakened the Ch of England since the reign of HENRY VIII; and in 1610 he put a programme before the Lords to ensure that the Ch received its full dues in tithes and other fees, and proposed raising a fund out of taxation to repurchase all the impropriated benefices – ie those in lay hands, about 40% of the total – an attack on property-rights established since the DISSOLUTION OF THE MONASTERIES which aroused the enmity of the Parl gentry. Altogether Bancroft added fuel to at least 3 quarrels which were dividing England in the years leading up to the CIVIL WAR: the misunderstanding between Crown and Parl, the mutual suspicion of the Puritans and the hierarchy, and the anticlerical sentiments of the laity.

Bethlen Gábor (1580–15 Nov 1629) Pr of Transylvania (1613), K of Hungary (1620), Calvinist Hungarian protégé of Turkey who from time to time co-operated with the anti-Habsburg allies in the THIRTY YEARS WAR by raiding Hungary, Moravia and Austria from the E.

b of Hungarian nobility; m (1626) Catherine, sister of the Elector GEORGE WILLIAM of Brandenburg. As a young man he supported Istvàn Bocksay, the Turkish-backed Pr of Transylvania in his war against Emp RUDOLF II (1590–1606), as well as his successor, Gabriel Báthory, whom he later overthrew, becoming Pr himself with the support of Sultan Ahmed I. Emp MATTHIAS recognized him as Pr of Transylvania in May 1615. A dark-skinned adventurer and a convinced Prot, he was an ambitious and talented war-leader who hoped to win a Kdom for himself in the shifting military scene in E Europe (where the power of Turkey, the Austrian Monarchy, Poland and Moscow overlapped) by co-operating with the alliance of the Hague who were attacking Austria from the W.

(1) In alliance with the Bohemian rebels (1619) he invaded Hungary, took Pozsony (Pressburg) on 15 Sept 1619, besieged Vienna (Oct–Nov 1619), and then made a separate peace with the Emp FERDINAND II on 4 Feb 1620. (2) Invading Hungary, where the Prot Estates elected him K, he besieged Vienna, took part in the battle of the White Mountain (Nov 1620), besieged Poszony unsuccessfully in Aug 1621, and then signed the Tr of Mikulov (Nikolsburg), Moravia, with the Emp on 31 Dec 1621, renouncing Hungary, but gaining parts of Slovakia. (3) In Aug 1623, with Tatar and Turkish help, he plundered Hungary, without being of much help to his W allies, and then signed the separate Tr of Vienna with the Emp on 8 May 1624, confirming Mikulov. (4) He took part in the Dutch-organized joint attack on Vienna of 1626. MANSFELD joined him and they both faced WALLENSTEIN together on 30 Sept 1626, but without giving battle. In general, his incursions brought no great advantage to the anti-Habsburg cause because of the formidable difficulties in co-ordinating all-European military action, and because of the propensity of Bethlen Gábor and his horsemen to be content with brief raids after booty.

Blake, Robert (Aug 1599–7 Aug 1657) English admiral who fought for Parl in the CIVIL WAR on land and sea, helped to professionalize the navy, and won victories against Holland and Spain that turned England into a leading naval power.

b at Bridgwater, Somerset; son of Humphrey Blake, a prosperous merchant; ed at Bridgwater Grammar School and Wadham, Oxford (1615–25). During the Civil War he achieved prominence through his military exploits in the SW. A tough and thick-set Puritan, fearless and enterprising, he successfully defended Lyme, Dorset, from the Royalists till ESSEX relieved the town (June 1644); and captured Taunton, Somerset (July 1644) and then successfully defended it against great odds until May 1645. Appointed by Parl to be 1 of 3 Generals at Sea (Feb 1649) in command of the navy, he put to sea in Apr 1649 to destroy the Royalist navy under Pr Rupert. He chased him from Kinsale, Ireland, to Lisbon, Portugal (where Blake captured several Portuguese ships, May 1650), and then into the Med, where Blake destroyed most of the Royalist ships at Cartagena, Spain, in Nov 1650. The following year he cleared the Royalists out of their refuge in the Scillies (May–June), and took Jersey, Channel Islands (Oct 1651). In concert with CROMWELL and the other Puritan leaders he was on the Council of State (Dec 1651–Mar 1652), a member of Barebones Parl (4 July–12 Dec 1653), and was closely associated with the programme which first created the professional navy in England, as well as its aggressive use: the ship-building programme of sizeable and heavily armed vessels (1649–51), the development of the new line-of-battle tactics, the preparation of the *Fighting Instructions*, *Articles of War*, and so on. In the 1st Dutch War (1652–4) he was involved in 4 battles. He beat Tromp off Dover (19 May 1652); drew at least with de Ruyter and de Witt at the Kentish Knock (28–9 Sept 1652); lost to Tromp off Dungeness (29–30 Nov 1652); and defeated him in the 3-day running battle from Portland to Calais (18–20 Feb 1653).

In pursuance of his active colonizing policy, Cromwell sent Blake to the Med (Sept 1654), where he demonstrated the presence of the English fleet in several ports, and destroyed a Barbary pirate squadron at Porto Farina, Tunis, on 4 Apr 1655. He then probed round the coast of Spain, for the 1st time blockading it all through the winter (1656–7). One of his lieutenants captured much of the R Plate treasure fleet (Sept 1656); while he on 20/30 Apr 1657 sank another treasure fleet and silenced the shore batteries at Santa Cruz Bay, Tenerife, Canaries, without himself losing a single ship. The treasure unfortunately had already been taken ashore. During the journey back to England he caught what his doctors called 'scorbutic fever' and d at sea an hour from Plymouth. He had made English sea-power formidable for years to come.

Bolingbroke, Henry St John, 1st Vt (16 Sept 1678–12 Dec 1751) Tory leader under Q ANNE – deputy to HARLEY – who fled abroad to join the Old Pretender on the accession of K GEORGE I, but who later was allowed to return to England, where he organized the opposition to WALPOLE, and formulated the Tory theory of non-party Gov under a 'Patriot K'.

b at Lydiard Tregoze, Wilts, son of the Restoration rake, Sir Henry St John, Bart, and his wife, Mary Rich, daughter of the 3rd Earl of Warwick (she d just after his birth); ed possibly at a Dissenting academy; then on the Grand Tour (1698–1700); m 1st (1700) Frances Winchcombe, a Berkshire beauty and heiress whom he treated so shamefully that even his contemporaries were shocked (d Nov 1718); m 2nd (1719) Marie-Claire de Marcilly, Marquise de Villette, a widow with 3 daughters (d 18 Mar 1750). There were no children by either marriage.

Handsome and charming, with a sharp mind and insatiable appetites, Henry was a witty conversationalist and brilliant orator who divided his time between literature and scholarship, wine and women, politics and admin. His friends were notorious libertines, but he was also intimate with celebrated poets and philosophers; and the driving passion of his life was political ambition. Unfortunately, he lacked the common touch, was always short of money, and lacked long-term views; he was highly-strung and over-sensitive to criticism, as well as being unreliable and likely to act rashly on the spur of the moment. He knew that others thought him hypocritical, but he was incapable of seeming sincere. What deeply felt views he had were the prejudices of the Tory squires, but he was always ready to adapt his ideas to circumstances.

1701–10 were years of co-operation with Harley. He was MP for the family borough of Wootton Bassett, Wilts, 1701–8, but out of Parl 1708–10 because his father insisted on being a candidate for the seat and Bolingbroke did not succeed in finding another. At first (1701–4) he became prominent among the back-bench, high-flying Tories, supporting their Country attacks on WILLIAM III's Whig ministry, and backing High-Ch projects such as the 3 Occasional Conformity Bills. He became such a nuisance to the Gov of MARLBOROUGH, GODOLPHIN and Harley – who simply wanted Parl to vote supplies for the War of the Spanish Succession (1702–13/14) – that he was made Sec-at-War to tone him down (Apr 1704). A hero-worshipper of Marlborough and Harley, he now moderated his political conduct and worked hard at his job of supplying men and materials for the war, and piloting the necessary finance bills through the H of C. He resigned with Harley in Feb 1708, when Marlborough and Godolphin decided to take the Whigs into the Gov. During 1708–10 he lived on his estates and picked up the country squires' war-weariness and hatred of the high land-tax.

1710–15 saw him as Sec of State in Harley's Gov (for the N, 1710–13, for the S, 1713–14); MP for Berks (1710–12); and Vt Bolingbroke (June or July 1712). They also saw his breach with Harley, and the ruin of the Tories. Thrusting, head-strong, and resentful at being a Vt and not an Earl, he thirsted for political power, and tried to outpace his chief in Parl, in the Cab, and at Court. In Parl, he lost patience with Harley's chosen role as 'manager' for the Q, employing moderates of both parties as well as independents. Bolingbroke envisaged taking office at the head of a united Tory party; and while Harley's grip on affairs loosened through ill-health, family bereavement and drink, Bolingbroke did all he could to appeal to the prejudices of the back-bench Tory pressure-group, the October Club: their hatred of the war on the Continent, their suspicion of foreigners, especially the Dutch, their dislike of the land-tax, and their intolerance of Dissenters. He led the campaign for the Schism Act (1714), designed to conquer Dissent by closing down its academies. Unfortunately for him, he lacked the ability to lead men; and in any case the Tories were split on what, with the Q's declining health, became the most important issue of the day: the succession. With a strong force of Hanover Tories on one side, a body of convinced Jacobites on the other, and many undecided in between, a united Tory party was impossible; and that was quite apart from NOTTINGHAM and his group, who split on another issue and voted with the Whigs against making peace until Spain had been conquered. In the Cab he had violent clashes with Harley, eg over the unsuccessful expedition to take Quebec (1711), which he sponsored in order to please the 'blue-water' Tories; and over the peace negotiations with France, which Harley kept firmly under his own control, while Bolingbroke as Sec of State exceeded his instructions and tried to take the negotiations into his own hands, giving the French the false impression that the English Gov was pro-Jacobite. At Court Lady Masham, now his ally, replaced the Dss of Marlborough as the chief influence on the Q, and, though Anne could not trust such an irreligious, immoral and dishonest rake as Bolingbroke, she was worn down in the end, and dismissed Harley in July 1714. This was only 5 days before she d, however, and her rapidly declining health caught Bolingbroke without any firm plans for the succession. He went to pieces while the Whig lords confidently organized the Hanoverian succession. He attended the coronation of K George I (Oct 1714), resting his hopes on a Tory victory in the 1715 elections. When this did not materialize, and the Whig ministry asked him to surrender his papers, he panicked and made the fatal error of fleeing the country (27 Mar 1715).

1715–51 saw him sometimes in exile, but mainly in England, tirelessly but in vain producing the ideas with which he hoped to recreate the ruined Tory party, and then use it to overthrow Walpole and the Whigs, and bring himself to supreme power once more. In France he became the Sec of State of the Old Pretender (1715), but was dismissed (Mar 1716), and made the scapegoat for the failure of the incompetently run Jacobite rebellion of 1715 (the 'FIFTEEN'). An Act of Attainder was passed against him in England (1715), and for the rest of his life the Whigs were able to taint both him and the Tories as Jacobites and keep them out of power. In France he studied history, philosophy and religion, made contact with the Enlightenment, became a Deist, and eventually persuaded George I (partly by bribing his mistress, the Dss of Kendal) to pardon him (May 1723). Later, an Act of Parl restored his estates to him (May 1725); but Walpole would never allow him to recover either his title or his seat in the H of L, and thus he never succeeded in becoming anything more than a non-playing captain of the opposition. His home at Dawley, Middlesex, became the meeting-place of opposition intellectuals and politicians (eg Swift, Pope, Gay, Arbuthnot and Pulteney) and he contributed nearly 100 articles to the chief opposition weekly, the *Craftsman*, which ran from Dec 1726 to Apr 1736. In these and other more extended writings – such as the *Idea of a Patriot King*, 1738 – he tried to create an up-to-date Tory philosophy (*see* TORIES). Unfortunately, he was up against the political skill of Walpole on the one hand, and the inability of the various opposition groups to unite for long at a time, on the other. No positive party capable of taking (or even wanting) office could be made out of Jacobites, Tories, Country Whigs and Whig Outs, though negative successes were sometimes possible, eg when forcing Walpole to withdraw his excise scheme in Apr 1733. Worst of all, he was dogged by his own reputation and his own rashness, eg supplying the French ambassador with inside information on English politics and even accepting money from him to run the opposition campaign. It only required a few hints from Walpole to ruin him even in the eyes of the opposition; and after the failure of the Tories in the election of 1734, a mixture of despair and a desire to save his own skin drove him to further exile in France (1735–44). He returned again after his father's belated death in Apr 1742 had improved his financial position. He lived in the family house at Battersea, nr London, where he d of cancer of the cheek-bone.

Bonner, Edmund (*c* 1500–5 Sept 1569) Bp of London (1539–49, 1553–9), conservative career-Bp under the Tudors who gained notoriety for his support of Q Mary I's persecution of the Prots.

ed Pembroke, Oxford, Chaplain to WOLSEY (1529) after which he rose in the royal service, like GARDINER performing important diplomatic and legal tasks for K HENRY VIII, especially in connection with the divorce from CATHERINE OF ARAGON. Made Bp of Hereford in 1538, then of London in 1539, he accepted the Henrician REFORMATION but, with Gardiner, was conservative when it came to moves in the direction of Protestantism. Thus under K EDWARD VI he was deprived of his see and imprisoned after a commission had elicited doubts about the Royal Supremacy as exercised by an infant K. Under Q MARY I he was released and restored (Aug 1553) and took a leading part in the Marian reaction. His diocese contained most of the heretics, and he earned an evil reputation among Londoners for his coarse and bullying participation in the burnings. On the accession of Q ELIZABETH I he was deprived once more (1559) for refusing to take the oath laid down in the Act of Supremacy.

Borgia, Cesare (1475–12 Mar 1507) Son of Pp ALEXANDER VI, who unsuccessfully tried to conquer a state for himself, and was admired by MACHIAVELLI.

2nd son of the Pp and his Roman mistress, he was made Archbp of Valencia in 1492, Card in 1493; but when his elder half-brother, the D of Gandia, was murdered in June 1497, possibly with Cesare's help, the latter decided to pursue a worldly career. He abandoned his cardinalate, and was released from his holy orders on the grounds of illegitimacy in Aug 1498. In the mutually advantageous arrangement between Alexander VI and K LOUIS XII of France whereby the Pp annulled the K's 1st marriage and the K backed the Borgia military campaigns in the Romagna, Cesare was created D de Valentinois, travelled to France with a Card's hat for the French chief minister, Georges d'AMBOISE, and m Charlotte d'Albret, sister of the K of Navarre in 1499. He returned to Italy in Louis' army of invasion at the start of the 2nd HABSBURG–VALOIS WAR. In the Romagna Cesare fought 3 campaigns against the semi-independent lordships (1499–1502) with a view to carving out a new principality for himself in central Italy. An unpleasant character, though with certain charismatic qualities, he took Imola in Nov 1499, Forli in Dec 1499, Rimini and Pesaro in Oct 1500 and Faenza in Apr 1501. He seems to have organized the murder – at the 2nd attempt – of the 2nd husband of his sister Lucrezia (Aug 1500); and got himself created D of Romagna by his father (May 1501). Subsequently, he took Urbino in 1502, but was then held up by the Conspiracy of La Magione – a town near Lake Trasimene where some of his captains plotted a rebellion against him in Oct 1502. Cesare patched up a reconciliation with them, and then, to use the words of Machiavelli who was there, he 'gently whistled' them to a meeting in Sinigaglia on 31 Dec 1502 and treacherously had them murdered. This was another act of cruel opportunism which earned him the admiration of Machiavelli, who saw in him 'a new power in Italy' who was unlike 'other petty princes'. With the sudden death of his father, however, on 18 Aug 1503, when Cesare was ill and unable to control events, the Cards elected the short-lived Pius III, and then the enemy of his family, Pp JULIUS II (1 Nov 1503). His position in the Romagna now crumbled, and the petty lords one by one retook their cities. He was placed under papal arrest from Nov 1503 to Apr 1504, and then transported by K FERDINAND II to Spain for 2 years' imprisonment. Escaping in Oct 1506, he took service with his brother-in-law, the K of Navarre, and was killed at the siege of Viana, a rebel citadel.

Boris Godunov (c 1551–13 Apr 1605) Tsar of Russia (Feb 1598), under whom the TIME OF TROUBLES began.

Son of a minor noble family of russified Tatars, though reputedly illiterate, he rose high in the admin of IVAN IV till he m (c 1570) Maria, daughter of G. L. Maliuta Skuratov-Belsky (favourite of Ivan IV and head of the *oprichniky*), while his sister Irina m the future Tsar THEODORE I, son of Ivan IV (1580), to mark which occasion Boris was raised to the rank of *boyar*. Appointed 1 of 4 guardians of the feeble Theodore, Boris managed by dint of remarkable political cunning to push aside his rivals and become sole ruler of Russia by 1587. As Regent he was sufficiently ruthless, by torture, imprisonment, murder and exile, to thin out the ranks of rival *boyar* families, eg the Romanovs, whose head, Theodore Nikitich Romanov, was forced to take the tonsure under the name of Filaret, while his son, the future Tsar MICHAEL, was made to live away from Moscow. Moreover, the faction surrounding Dmitri – Ivan IV's other surviving son – was exiled to Uglich; and there on 15 May 1591 Dmitri mysteriously had his throat cut. Whether it was an accident during an epileptic fit, or whether Boris had him murdered – as many believed – is a problem that has never been solved. On Theodore's death without heirs, Boris was able with strong Ch help to organize a compliant *zemskii sobor* (a kind of estates general) which, meeting on 7 Feb 1598, acclaimed him Tsar, though he felt it wise to delay his coronation till 1 Sept 1598. Thenceforth he pursued wise policies, backed by paranoiac terror, reminiscent of Ivan IV's as far as the *boyars* were concerned, but more benevolent to the *dvoryane* (serving nobility) and the Moscow masses.

Abroad, his reign was mainly peaceful, and he signed commercial trs with England and the HANSEATIC LEAGUE. (a) In the W he was at peace with Poland, but in his war against Sweden (1590–95) he regained territories which Ivan IV had lost in 1583; but he failed to reach the Baltic. (b) In the E, using the merchant family of Stroganov, he established firmer control over the Tatars of W Siberia; while (c) in the S the frontier against the Crimean Tatars was advanced, the arm of Moscow reaching as far as the Caucasus.

At home (a) the Russian Ch gained in world prestige, thanks to Boris's diplomatic guile with Jeremiah, the Patriarch of Constantinople, when the Russian Metropolitan was raised to the rank of Patriarch (1589), and thus equal to the other leaders in the Orthodox world: of Constantinople, Alexandria, Antioch and Jerusalem. The 1st Patriarch was Boris's henchman, Job. (b) In education Boris favoured western influences, and sent 18 young men to study abroad, but clerical prejudice prevented him from founding a Univ. (c) The peasants moved nearer to serfdom with Boris's law of 1597 ordering peasants who had fled since 1592 to return to their masters. He was here concerned to protect the *dvoryane*, and prevent the *boyars* from enticing away their precious labour force, but the effect was to tie the peasants more firmly to the soil. Economic catastrophe, moreover, exacerbated the oppressions of the Gov. The years 1601–3 brought harvest failures, famine and disease on a gigantic scale. Frost was recorded in Aug 1601. The people ate the bark from the trees and practised cannibalism, while 100,000 are said to have perished in Moscow alone. This popular distress, coming on top of the absolutist savageries of the reign of Ivan IV (1547–84) and adding to the many other causes of disquiet under Boris Godunov – such as the resentments of rival *boyar* families, the resistance of colonial tribesmen to

Russian centralization, the ambitions of foreign powers, and the disputed succession to the throne – inaugurated the Time of Troubles by giving birth to the powerful rumour (1601 onwards) that Pr Dmitri was still alive and that someone else had been killed at Uglich. (d) False Dmitri I, backed by the recognition of K SIGISMUND III of Poland, and the support of some Polish magnates and JESUITS, as well as many COSSACKS, invaded Russia in Oct 1604, and immediately benefited from the multifarious discontents with Boris, whose reign was on the point of collapse. The nearer False Dmitri I approached Moscow, the bigger grew his army till on 13 Apr 1605 Boris Godunov suddenly d – how, we do not know. Rival *boyars* took over in Moscow, murdered Boris's wife and son Theodore II (10 June 1605), and recognized the pretender, who entered Moscow on 20 June 1605. Boris Godunov became the subject of a drama by Alexander Pushkin (1831), on which Modest Mussorgsky based an opera (1874).

Bucer, Martin (11 Nov 1491–28 Feb 1551) Moderate German Prot reformer.

Influenced by the HUMANISM of ERASMUS and the arguments of LUTHER, he left the Dominicans in 1521, became chaplain to the Prot knight, Franz von SICKINGEN, and pastor of Landstuhl, Palatinate, in 1522, where he m the ex-nun, Elizabeth Silbereisen. In 1523 he became minister at Strassburg, preaching in the cathedral. The REFORMATION in this city, of the type advocated by ZWINGLI, was put through in 1525 by Wolfgang Capito and the chief magistrate, Johann Sturm; but they were so tolerant to refugee ANABAPTISTS that their movement was in danger of being swamped by radicalism. Bucer established himself as the leader, from 1527 onwards, of a Ch in Strassburg and other S German states which rejected Anabaptists, stressed predestination, remained theoretically independent of the state, supported the role of the inferior magistrates and Estates in opposition to centralized absolutism, used simplified forms of Ch service, and employed the 4-fold ministry of pastors, elders, doctors and deacons. In all these fields, Bucer greatly influenced John CALVIN, who stayed in Strassburg, 1538–41. Bucer's religious position was somewhere between those of Luther and Zwingli; and making use of the distinction between essentials and inessentials (about the second of which Bucer proposed that men should agree to differ) he also played a leading conciliatory role in all the conferences of the 1520s, '30s and '40s designed to bring together Lutherans and R Cs, and then Lutherans and Zwinglians. He was particularly skilled in the formulation of disputed issues in vague phraseology and in assembling package deals. He failed, however, to get Luther and Zwingli to compromise over the Eucharist at the Marburg Colloquy of 1529; and he refused to sign the AUGSBURG CONFESSION of 1530, but drew up the more radical *Confessio Tetrapolitana* instead, on behalf of the cities of Strassburg, Constance, Lindau and Memmingen. In 1536 he brought the S Germans into the Lutheran movement by the Wittenberg Concord, which he negotiated with MELANCHTHON. When his position at Strassburg became unsafe owing to the victory of CHARLES V over the Prots at Mühlberg (Apr 1547), he moved to England on the invitation of CRANMER, and was appointed Regius Professor of Divinity at Cambridge (Dec 1549). He d there, and was buried at St Mary's; but under Q MARY I his body was exhumed and burnt at the stake on Market Hill.

Buckingham, George Villiers, 1st D of (28 Aug 1592–23 Aug 1628) Master of the Horse (1616), Knight of the Garter (1616), Earl of Buckingham (1617), Master of the Wardrobe (1617), Marquess of Buckingham (1618), Ld High Admiral (1619), D of Buckingham (1623), favourite of K JAMES VI AND I of Scotland and England, and became his chief minister, as well as that of K CHARLES I. Until his assassination he was an important cause of the alienation between K and Parl which led to the CIVIL WAR.

b at Brooksby, Leics, younger son of Sir Charles Villiers by his 2nd wife; ed at Billesdon, Leics, then in France.

Under James I he attracted attention as a tall, handsome and athletic youth, powerfully built and yet graceful. He first met the K in Aug 1614 at Apethorpe, Northants, and soon eclipsed Robert CARR in the K's affections. 'I never yet saw any fond husband,' wrote a contemporary, 'make so much or so great dalliance over his beautiful spouse as I have seen King James over his favourites, especially Buckingham.' 'No one dances better, no man runs or jumps better,' wrote another. 'Indeed he jumped higher than ever Englishman did in so short a time, from a private gentleman to a dukedom.' By 1618 he dominated the Court, forcing the resignation of the Howard faction, who had governed hitherto, and who had in vain produced their own handsome young man. In 1620 he m Lady Catherine Manners, only daughter of the Earl of Rutland, a brilliant match. He became very rich, not only accumulating estates and sinecures, bribes and gifts, pictures and manuscripts, but also building up a vast CLIENTAGE network of office-holders and monopolists, headed by his family and friends whom he enriched with posts and remunerative marriages. Worst of all, the doting monarch, who could not keep his hands off him even in public, allowed him to dominate policy-making, and thus, firstly to alienate powerful groups in Parl and the country, and then to sacrifice valuable ministers such as BACON and CRANFIELD in a vain attempt to appease them. The 3rd Parl of James I (Jan 1621–Jan 1622) turned their guns on the outworks of Buckingham's empire, impeaching Sir Giles Mompesson and Sir Francis Mitchell for monopoly offences. They then impeached Ld Chancellor Bacon for accepting bribes, and Buckingham sacrificed him to save his own skin. Parl also criticized Buckingham's Spanishmarriage policy, and thus started the wrangle over whether they had the right to discuss foreign affairs, which led to the voting of the Protestation (Dec 1621), a document which the K tore out of the H of C Journals with his own hands. Buckingham then accompanied Pr Charles on the abortive marriage journey to Madrid (1623), the failure of which led to a complete reversal of policy: war against Spain, and a French marriage – to Henrietta Maria (May 1625). The 4th Parl (Feb 1624–Mar 1625) did not attack Buckingham. With no strong views of his own, he had spread his patronage across a wide spectrum of political and religious opinion. In any case, Parl supported his anti-Spanish policy; and he allowed them to impeach Ld Treasurer Cranfield, his former protégé and ally, who opposed the war, and aimed at ending the Court prodigality, of which Buckingham was the prime cause and chief profiteer. Even the pacific K allowed the war preparations to proceed, so completely enslaved was he in his senility. 'And so God bless you, my sweet child and wife,' James wrote to him in one of his last letters (Dec 1624), 'and grant that ye may ever be a comfort to your dear dad and husband.' But Buckingham had also established an ascendancy over

Pr Charles, and on the old K's death (27 Mar 1625) he nimbly crossed the hazardous divide to become the chief minister in the new reign.

Under Charles I the relations between K and Parl deteriorated once more as the basic problems were raised as to whether Parl could make the K follow policies and appoint ministers they approved of, and if so how it could be done. The 1st Parl (June–Aug 1625) opposed the K's religious policy: his support of Arminian clergy and his relaxation of the penal laws against Caths. They also began to attack Buckingham's foreign policy and the incompetence with which it was carried out. Buckingham had signed Trs with Denmark and Holland for English participation under Mansfeld in the Danish War phase of the THIRTY YEARS WAR. He had also negotiated the marriage Tr with France, lent RICHELIEU 8 ships with which to attack the Hug stronghold at La Rochelle, but failed to get active French intervention in the Thirty Years War. He threw together an armada to attack Cádiz. In their suspicious frame of mind, Parl authorized tunnage and poundage (customs) for 1 year only instead of the duration of the K's life, and voted inadequate taxation for the war, thus increasing the ineffectiveness of Buckingham's measures and providing further grounds for attacks on him as the minister responsible. Three-quarters of Mansfeld's 12,000 pressed men perished aboard ship without even going ashore in the Netherlands, let alone engaging the enemy (1625); while the 15,000-man enterprise against Cádiz (Oct–Nov 1625) was a complete failure, thanks to hopelessly bad training and equipment. The 2nd Parl (Feb–June 1626) was deprived of opposition leaders such as COKE and Wentworth (later STRAFFORD), for the Court had had the bright idea of making them sheriffs. Unfortunately, new and more radical leaders took charge. ELIOT launched eloquent attacks on Buckingham, and when he began impeachment proceedings against the chief minister, Charles dissolved the Parl. Buckingham now reversed his French policy and declared war in order to aid the Hugs (1627). France and Spain were the 2 chief protagonists for European domination at that time, and England was at war with both of them. Buckingham led a motley force of 6,000 men to liberate La Rochelle. He landed on the Isle of Rhé, just off the city, on 10/20 July 1627, and left it on 8/18 Nov 1627, having achieved nothing except the loss of half his men. 'Since England was England,' said Denzil Holles, 'it received not so dishonourable a blow.' The 3rd Parl (Mar 1628–Mar 1629) passed the Petition of Right, and Charles was constrained to give it the royal assent on 7 June 1628. Parl continued to attack Buckingham – the 'grievance of grievances', as Coke called him. They sent the K a Remonstrance (17 June 1628) explaining how they feared for their religion, their Gov, and their success in war if Buckingham remained in office, but Charles clung to his minister and prorogued Parl (26 June 1628). Buckingham went to Portsmouth to organize another sea-going expedition where he was stabbed to death in his house by John Felton, a Suffolk gentleman who had taken part in both the Cádiz and the Rhé disasters and formed a very poor opinion of Buckingham, on both public and private grounds. At Westminster Abbey where the funeral was held the body had to have military protection to save it from the cheering crowds.

Burghley, Sir William Cecil, 1st Bn (13 Sept 1520–4 Aug 1598) Principal Sec (1558), Ld Treasurer (1572) and chief minister to Q ELIZABETH I of England.

He was a great statesman who collaborated closely with the Q, at home, in following conservative religious, constitutional, economic and social policies aimed at uniting a nation hitherto divided by the REFORMATION and disturbed by economic development; and abroad, in exploiting the political rivalry between France and Spain and the religious warfare between Caths and Prots so as to preserve England as long as possible from foreign attack and then defeat it when it came, and in reply lay the foundations of the British colonial empire and world trading system.

b at Bourne, Lincs, heir to a minor Welsh gentry family which had supported K HENRY VII at Bosworth and subsequently prospered in the service of HENRY VIII and EDWARD VI and profited from the DISSOLUTION OF THE MONAS-TERIES; ed at Grantham and Stamford Grammar Schools, St John's, Cambridge (1535–41), where he was deeply influenced by the prevailing HUMANISM and Protestantism, and then at Gray's Inn, London; m 1st (1541) Mary Cheke, sister of his tutor and daughter of a Cambridge inn-keeper (she d in 1543); 2nd (1545) the scholarly Puritan Mildred Cooke, daughter of the Gov of Pr Edward. He became an MP from 1543 onwards; and as a bureaucrat rather than a politician survived the violent changes of regime which marked the reigns of Edward VI and MARY I.

His admin talents were too good to miss. Enjoying the realities of power rather than the outward trappings, and possessing a sharp mind, capacious memory, stamina, patience, prudence, judgement and tact, he was the ideal servant of a monarch who wanted the last word. Q Elizabeth I appointed him Sec at the start of her reign (he had been Surveyor of her estates since 1550), and he served her till he d, becoming Master of the Court of Wards and Liveries (1561) – a post of great importance for the royal income, but also of great profit for the Cecil family – Baron Burghley (1571) and Ld Treasurer (1572). Skilfully self-effacing while guiding the course of events, he nimbly evaded the hazards presented by a headstrong and demanding Q and by the mutually hostile Court factions, who resented his rise from obscurity – whether they were leaders of the old nobility, such as the 4th D of NORFOLK, or personal favourites of the Q, such as Robert Dudley, Earl of LEICESTER, and Robert Devereux, 2nd Earl of ESSEX. Only the broad features of his policies can be sketched in here, for his political career is impossible to disentangle from the general history of Elizabeth's reign.

At home, he sought order, stability and the widest possible consensus. He was valuable to the Q for his management of Parl, earlier in the Commons, later in the Lords; and he put much effort into propagating the Gov's point of view in a series of pamphlets. He helped to produce the broad compromises of the religious settlement, and was later moderate in his attitude towards Puritans and Caths. Pious and ascetic himself, he was a Puritan in the sense that he favoured reform in the Ch, a better endowed, educated, and more assiduous clergy; but he opposed the Presbyterian and other opponents of the Prayer Book and episcopal Ch Gov as threats to the social and political order. Similarly, he had no time for Caths who dabbled in treason, and was ruthless in his destruction of the D of Norfolk and MARY, Q OF SCOTS. In economic and social affairs, he is no longer regarded as the master-mind behind a coherent policy designed to bring England into the modern world; but rather as an old-fashioned healer applying *ad hoc* remedies to the multiple symptoms of capitalist growth in agriculture, industry and trade. His aim was to preserve tradition and stability, while making England as self-sufficient as possible, especially in armaments.

Abroad, he was very mindful of the threat posed to English independence by the Cath powers of France and Spain; but, unlike some of his more Puritan colleagues, such as Leicester and WALSINGHAM, he did not see foreign policy purely as an anti-Cath crusade. On the contrary, he was prepared to take every advantage of the political rivalries of the Cath powers, and co-operate with one or the other as the situation allowed. He quickly appreciated the need to support the Prots in Scotland against Mary, Q of Scots and her foreign allies, whether French or Spanish; and he organized the armed intervention of 1560 and nego-tiated the Tr of Edinburgh (July 1560), one of his greatest achievements. At this stage he maintained England's traditional friendship with Spain, based on fear of France and desire to trade with the Spanish Netherlands; but when the FRENCH WARS OF RELIGION began to cripple France and the REVOLT OF THE NETHER-LANDS brought a Spanish army to the Netherlands, his main preoccupation was to keep the Spanish troops out of the Channel ports of France and the Nether-lands – the area which now replaced Scotland as the base for a possible invasion of England. It was Burghley's initiative in Dec 1568 which brought about the seizure in the English Channel ports of the Spanish treasure on its way to pay the Spanish army, a risky adventure which weakened Spain, but which also led to a mutual trading embargo lasting until Jan 1573. He favoured giving all possible support to the Prots of France and the Netherlands short of war, but when war actually came (Aug 1585) he ran it. It developed into a long-drawn-out series of engagements which included Leicester's expedition to the Netherlands, the defeat of the Spanish ARMADA, the attempt by Essex to aid K HENRY IV of France, the transatlantic plundering expeditions of DRAKE and HAWKINS, and the campaigns in Ireland.

Burghley clung to office until his death. The man who had survived the joint attempt of Norfolk and Leicester to unseat him in 1568, who had defeated the REVOLT OF THE NORTHERN EARLS in 1569, and all the plots surrounding Mary, Q of Scots, outlived his old rivals and founded 2 dynasties: that of Thomas, later Earl of Exeter, to whom he left Burghley House, Stamford, and the bulk of his property; and that of Robert, later Earl of SALISBURY, to whom he left his mansion of Theobalds, Herts, and the bulk of his political power.

Bute, John Stuart, 3rd Earl of (25 May 1713–10 Mar 1792) Politically inadequate favourite of K GEORGE III and his chief minister (1760–63) who helped to break up the Old Corps of WHIGS, and ended the SEVEN YEARS WAR (1756–63). Though forced to resign by public execration, whipped up by political Outs, he continued to advise the K 'behind the curtain' for several years afterwards.

eld son of the 2nd Earl of Bute (d 28 Jan 1723) and his wife, Lady Anne Campbell, daughter of the 1st D of Argyll; ed at Eton and Leiden Univ, Holland, and in the household of the D of Argyll; m (1731) Mary, daughter of the Hon Edward Montagu, who inherited her father's enormous coal-mining fortune.

Under GEORGE II, Bute sat in the H of L (1737–41) as one of the 16 Scottish representative peers; moved into the Leicester House group which had formed around Frederick, Pr of Wales (1747 onwards), after, it is said, making a fourth at cards with him during a shower at Egham races. After Frederick's death (1751), Bute became the chief adviser to his widow, Prss Augusta, and then tutor, and eventually second father, to the future K George III, who usually called him 'my dearest friend'. Bute's tuition produced the unworkable paradox of a K endowed with the philosophy of a back-bencher. From Bute, George imbibed the typical Country and Tory precepts of the mid C18 opposition, as formulated, above all, by BOLINGBROKE. In foreign affairs, Bute was isolationist, opposing Continental entanglements for the defence of Hanover, and favouring peace, or at most maritime and colonial warfare: the 'blue-water' policy. In domestic affairs, he believed that the Old Corps of Whigs – led 1st by WALPOLE, then by PELHAM and NEWCASTLE – had corruptly used patronage to organize a party and with it impose their wishes on George II in an unconstitutional way. Bute fostered in the impressionable young George the ideal of becoming a Patriot King (to use Bolingbroke's phrase) who would reclaim the rightful powers of the Crown from the Whig magnates, form a Gov of the best men irrespective of party, reduce Gov expenditure – especially by cutting back on places, pensions and all other means of corruption – and generally initiate a reign of virtue.

Under GEORGE III (Oct 1760 onwards) Bute and the K embarked on this programme, beginning by winding up the Seven Years War and dismissing the Newcastle–Pitt admin (1756–61) which ran it. It was made clear that Bute as Groom of the Stole (Nov 1760) was the sole channel of communication with the K, a political revolution which angered the politicians, since Bute was simply a courtier – not even a member of either House of Parl, and without experience of either politics or admin. Shy, scholarly and radiating aristocratic *hauteur*, he was naïve in the rough and tumble of politics, and untrained in the daily drudgery of Gov, and, what is more, Scottish into the bargain. He became Sec of State (N) on 25 Mar 1761, but PITT the Elder, who had been running the victorious war, resigned on 5 Oct 1761 when Bute and the K refused to extend the war to Spain. Bute continued the war, benefiting from Pitt's planning, not only to capture Martinique (Jan 1762) and other French sugar islands in the W Indies, but also to declare war on Spain itself on 2 Jan 1762, capturing Havana and Manila (Aug and Oct 1762). As far as the Continental war was concerned, however, Bute decided against renewing the subsidy to Prussia and further reinforcing the Army of Observation (Apr 1762), policy changes which led to the resignation of Newcastle (May 1762). Bute became 1st Ld of the Treasury in his place and carried through his main task: negotiating the Preliminaries of the Tr of Paris (signed 3 Nov 1762), and getting them approved by Parl (9 Dec), in the latter enterprise stooping to use the very methods of corruption he had sworn to root out. Henry FOX, continuing as Paymaster-Gen, was promoted Leader of the H of C, and he replaced all Old Whig placemen, great and small, if they opposed the Preliminaries. This 'Massacre of the Pelhamite Innocents' – as Horace Walpole called it – marks the break-up of the Old Corps, a grouping which had dominated English politics for 40 years. The deafening outcry of the stricken against the Gov's strongarm methods, against the peace, and against the Cider Tax it introduced in Mar 1763 – an excise which revived all the fears, and the arguments, of 1733 – focused on Bute himself. He was traduced as an upstart

Scot, a royal favourite, a lover of the Q Mother, and a reviver of royal despotism. He was attacked by mobs, hanged in effigy and execrated in print – especially in the *North Briton* (June 1762 onwards), a brilliantly outspoken weekly, edited by John WILKES and Charles Churchill, and sponsored by Earl Temple. On the verge of nervous collapse, Bute resigned (Apr 1763) to the distress of the K, who continued to consult him regularly for the next 2 years. By 1766, however, his hold over the K had gone, though the legend that he was one of the 'King's Friends', secretly giving unconstitutional advice 'behind the curtain', lived on into Whig historiography. Out of politics, Bute travelled, and indulged his deep interest in botany, and patronized other scholarly and literary activities. He played an important part, eg in the development of the royal gardens at Kew, a special interest of Prss Augusta.

Cabot, John (Giovanni Caboto, *c* 1450–?1499) Italian navigator who explored the NE coast of N America for K HENRY VII of England.

b probably in Genoa, he became a Levant spice merchant, and a naturalized Venetian (1476). Planning to find an Atlantic route to the Far E he went to England in the early 1490s, having failed to find support elsewhere, and was commissioned by Henry VII on 5 Mar 1496 to find new lands. Cabot and the merchants of Bristol were to provide the capital, and then enjoy the monopoly of the new trade. He seems to have made his 1st journey that year, and on 2 May 1497 he set out on his 2nd trip, in the *Matthew* (50 tons) with about 20 men. He sighted land on 24 June 1497, explored the coastline of what was probably Nova Scotia, and was back in Bristol by 6 Aug 1497, convinced that he had found Asia. On 10 Aug 1497 he had an interview with Henry VII, who gave him £10 and a pension of £20, and he became a celebrated public figure at Court. He set off for his 3rd voyage in May 1498 with 5 ships and *c* 200 men, and it is conjectured that he sailed down the coast of N America as far as Chesapeake Bay, and possibly did not return. The last record marks the drawing of his annuity in 1499, but the drawer could have been his wife.

Cabot, Sebastian (*c* 1470–?1557) Navigator and cartographer under the Tudors, who explored the NE coast of America and sponsored the Russian voyage of Willoughby and Chancellor.

b in Venice (or possibly Bristol), son of John CABOT who came to England in the early 1490s. Although he was a gifted teller of travellers' tales, there is no evidence that he was on any of his father's voyages. He led a Bristol expedition of 2 ships in 1508 or '09 in search of the NW passage to the E; for he had realized that America was not Asia, but was separate from it. From his accounts it appears that he probably discovered Hudson's Strait and part of Hudson's Bay, where his men made him turn back because of the ice. After exploring the coastline probably as far S as Delaware Bay, he returned to England. The reign of K HENRY VIII was unpropitious for geographical exploration, and Cabot spent 1512–48 in the service of Spain where in 1518 he was appointed Pilot Major to K Charles I, later Emp CHARLES V. He was in command of an expedition from Seville (1526–32) which explored the Rio de la Plata for a passage to the E. It was as a map-maker and navigator of European renown that he was brought back to England in 1548, where the Gov under both SEYMOUR and DUDLEY was once more favourable to overseas exploration. He was the 1st Gov of the Merchant Adventurers of England (1551), and was behind the Willoughby and Chancellor expedition in search of the N E passage to the E (1553); and when the subsequent Muscovy Co was founded (1555) he was the 1st Gov.

Cabral, Pedro Álvares (1467/8–?1520) Portuguese discoverer of Brazil.

Son of a minor noble family, he became a member of the Court of K Manoel I (1495–1521), who gave him command of a 13-ship trading expedition to India which left Lisbon on 9 Mar 1500, following up the 1st Indian voyage of Vasco da GAMA. Sailing somewhat W of the normal route to the Cape (whether by accident or design is not clear), he sighted the coast of Brazil on 22 Apr 1500. Spending 10 days there, he claimed it for Portugal as Terra da Vera Cruz (Land of the True Cross), though he was possibly anticipated in Brazil by the Castilian expedition of Vicente Yáñez Pinzón of 1499–1500. Continuing to India, he lost 4 ships and all hands (including DIAS) in a storm off the Cape of Good Hope, and reached Calicut on the Malabar Coast via Mozambique, E Africa. Though opposed there and in other Indian ports by rival Moslem merchants, he arrived back in Lisbon on 23 Apr 1501 with 6 ships loaded with sufficient spices and other merchandise to more than pay for the whole enterprise.

Calvin, Jean (10 July 1509–27 May 1564) French leader of the REFORMATION in Geneva.

Son of a successful lawyer of humble birth; ed at the Univ of Paris (1523, theology), Orléans and Bourges (1528 and 1529, law) and then at the humanistic Collège de France, Paris (1531, Greek). By now a scholar of HUMANISM who admired ERASMUS, he published his 1st book, a commentary in Latin on the Stoic Seneca's *De Clementia*. At some point between 1528 and 1533 (according to his own account) he experienced 'a sudden conversion' to the reformed doctrines; and henceforth this retiring intellectual, with his powerful mind and austere moral intensity, never doubted that he was God's chosen instrument in the regeneration of the world. He had to flee Paris to escape the attentions of the persecuting Univ (1533) and live (1533–6) in other parts of France, as well as in Switzerland and Italy. His great work *The Institutes of the Christian Religion* was first published during this period (1536). This lucid exposition of Christian doctrine as found in the Scriptures went through several revisions and enlargements until the final edition of 1559. In July 1536, by sheer accident, he went to Geneva which was to be the scene of his life's work. He had been en route for Strasbourg, but the HABSBURG–VALOIS; WAR (1536–8) forced him to make a detour through Geneva, where the Prot leader, Guillaume Farel (former associate of LEFÈVRE D'ÉTAPLES at Meaux) persuaded the very reluctant Calvin to stay and help. (Farel was a fiery preacher, but a poor organizer.)

The Reformation in Geneva took place in association with the armed struggle of the city to achieve its independence from the neighbouring Dukes of Savoy, and their relatives, the Bps of Geneva. Not yet part of Switzerland (until 1815), Geneva allied with the Swiss cantons of Berne and Fribourg against the House of Savoy, and in the year of their success in this the city adopted religious reform (May 1536). Within Geneva itself, however, there was a struggle between, on the one hand, a patrician group (called the 'Libertines'), who favoured mild reform on the lines pioneered by their political allies in Berne, putting the magistrates securely in charge of the clergy, and, on the other, Farel and Calvin, who demanded radical changes and ministerial control. When the Libertines got the ascendancy, Farel and Calvin fled to Strassburg (1538), where Calvin spent 3 very happy years ministering to a congregation of French exiles; learning much from BUCER about doctrine, liturgy and church organization; attaining European status for his part in the Cath–Prot conferences at Hagenau (1540), Worms and Regensburg (1541); translating his *Institutes* into French; and marrying (July 1540) Idelette de Bure, a widowed convert from the ANABAPTISTS (d 1549). Meanwhile Geneva, divided and chaotic, invited him back, and after a long hesitation he returned (Sept 1541) to devote his life to a long, bitter, but ultimately successful struggle to impose his version of liturgy and church organization, theological doctrine and moral behaviour, upon the loose-living Genevans and their Erastian-inclined magistrates.

Calvin, who was immensely learned and heartlessly logical, derived his view of Christianity from the Bible, being much influenced at the same time by St Augustine and LUTHER. In his view, totally corrupt man confronts an omnipotent and omniscient God, remote and inscrutable, who before the universe began predestined some (the elect) for eternal salvation and the rest (the reprobate) for everlasting damnation; and who saves his chosen few by the operation of divine grace (through his incarnation in Christ) which is irresistible and cannot be earned by man's merits, and which brings to the believer faith, repentance, and the inner conviction of salvation. The outward means used by God to bring about and support this regeneration is the organized Ch with its discipline, its preaching, and its sacraments. Calvin disagreed with the RCs, and Luther and ZWINGLI, in his interpretation of the crucial phrase, 'This is my body', in the Eucharist. For him, Christ was spiritually partaken during the bodily ceremony. As for Ch order, his *Ecclesiastical Ordinances* (1541) laid down a Bible-derived form of Gov (the model for PRESBYTERIANS the world over) based on 4 orders of men: pastors, elders, doctors and deacons. The Consistory (of pastors and elders) maintained strict supervision over Ch life, as well as over public and private morality, using excommunication, whipping, even the stake as punishments. Since the elders were city councillors, they provided the link between Ch and state. In so far as they were subject to popular appointment they introduced an important element of democracy into Ch Gov; and on the outcome of the power-struggle between pastors and elders within the Consistory depended whether the Ch became Erastian or the state became theocratic. Calvin's Geneva was oligarchic and, eventually, theocratic. It became the ideal for Calvinists everywhere; and with its Academy (founded 1559) it developed into the powerhouse of world missionary activity as well as the refuge for the persecuted.

As Calvinism spread throughout the world it demonstrated over and over its immense powers of survival, with its clear body of doctrine, its high moral standards, and its tightly-knit, strictly-disciplined congregations of believers who were totally convinced that they were the chosen agents of God, and who with their popularly elected leaders were independent of existing churches and states, and able to fight off all attacks, whether from the Caths on their right or the sects on their left. Although Calvin said that rulers must be obeyed, he also said enough on the right of people (using their representative institutions) to resist an ungodly Pr, for his followers to become the ideological backbone of a variety of political revolutions, especially when fortified by the political theories of resistance worked out by Calvin's successor at Geneva, Theodore Beza, and by Philippe du Plessis-Mornay.

Campion, Edmund (25 Jan 1540–1 Dec 1581) English Cath exile under Q ELIZABETH I of England, who landed with the 1st underground Jesuit mission, was caught, and executed for treason.

He was ordained in the Ch of England (1568), but because of Cath convictions abandoned a highly promising academic career and went to Dublin, then to the English College at Douai (1571), where he joined the Cath Ch, then to Rome (1573) in order to join the JESUITS for whom he worked in Prague. He was picked to join the 9-man Jesuit secret mission to England under Robert PARSONS, and landed at Dover in June 1580. They had been prepared in their training for danger and possible martyrdom. Constantly in flight from the alerted authorities, he moved frequently from house to house, preaching, saying Mass, hearing confessions, and inspiring renewed faith in the Ch and deep affection to himself by his selfless devotion and moving oratory, and fortifying the doubters with his *Decem Rationes* (10 reasons why the Cath Ch was the true Ch), which Parsons had printed on his underground press. Though he scrupulously avoided political activity – 'we travelled only for souls', he said subsequently on the scaffold, 'we touched neither state nor policy' – he was nevertheless working for a Ch whose leaders promised that the assassination of the Q would be 'a glorious work' and not a sin. Moreover, Pp Gregory XIII chose this period to launch an invasion of Ireland in support of the Fitzgerald rebellion. It was for these reasons that, when this apolitical saint was captured in hiding at Lyford, Berks, he was lodged in the Tower, charged with treason – adhering to the Q's enemies – and tortured on the rack. Tried on 14 Nov 1581, he was hanged, drawn and quartered at Tyburn.

Carlos, Don (8 July 1545–24 July 1568) Eld son of K PHILIP II of Spain, whose insane behaviour led his father to arrest him, and then be suspected of causing his mysterious death.

Inheriting the blood of Joanna (the Mad), who was the grandmother of both his parents, he grew into a pitiful creature, loathed by all. With his outsize head and frail body, his constant stammer and frequent illnesses, he soon seemed physically unfit to inherit the vast responsibilities of the Spanish monarchy; but it was his strange behaviour that convinced Philip that he must be barred from the succession. He was an irascible paranoiac, and a sadistic *voyeur*. Neither the ministers, the clergy nor the citizens of Madrid were exempt from his insults, nor were their daughters immune from his perverted advances. In his anxiety to escape from the clutches of his disapproving father, he concocted unrealistic and treasonable plans of fleeing to the Netherlands or to Naples and Sicily. In 1565 and '66 he contacted Egmont, and then Montigny, the representatives of the Netherlands at Madrid at the start of the REVOLT. He asked ministers to let him have money and troops. The K was kept fully informed, and finally resolved to perform his painful political duty for the preservation of the monarchy. On the night of 18 Jan 1568, Philip, the Pr of Eboli and a small guard entered Don

Carlos's bedroom in the Alcázar in Madrid and placed him under arrest there. Six months later he d, but the cause of death has never been satisfactorily established, whether illness, suicide or murder.

Carlstadt, Andreas Rudolf Bodenstein of (c 1480–24 Dec 1541) Religious radical during the German REFORMATION.

b Karlstadt, Franconia; ed Univs of Erfurt and Cologne; in 1505 began to teach at the Univ of Wittenberg. He became a supporter of LUTHER, and debated grace and free will with Johannes Eck at the Leipzig Disputation of 1519. While Luther was in hiding in the Wartburg, Carlstadt grew more radical, possibly under the influence of Müntzer and other radical preachers from Zwickau. Moving towards the position of the SPIRITUALISTS or the ANABAPTISTS, he stressed the passivity of the soul to divine inspiration, as opposed to the use of faith or scholarship. He m Anna von Mochau, aged 16, administered communion in both kinds, gave up vestments, then shoes, and got such a hold on the town council and people of Wittenberg that Luther risked emerging from his hiding place for a time in 1522 in order to preach them back into line. Henceforth Carlstadt wrote and preached radical Protestantism in various parts of Germany. Though he did not stress social revolution, he was with Müntzer during the PEASANTS' WAR, but managed to escape the bloodbath of Frankenhausen (15 May 1525), Luther giving him shelter for a time. He later became Professor of Old Testament Theology at the Univ of Basle (1534), and d there (plague).

Carr, Robert (c 1590–July 1645) Vt Rochester (1611), Earl of Somerset (1613), favourite of K JAMES VI AND I of Scotland and England, till his fall because of a scandal.

He first attracted the royal notice in 1607 at a tilt, when he fell from his horse and broke his leg. James visited his bedside and soon became his slave, for he was flaxen-haired, handsome and full of life, if shallow and uncultured. Henceforth Carr rose rapidly, from being knighted in 1607 to being appointed Ld Chamberlain in July 1614. He became not merely the K's intimate friend, but also his gen sec (particularly after SALISBURY's death, 1612), through whom all business with the K had to pass. He thus grew very rich, from both the bribes of suitors and the gifts of the doting monarch. He also fell in love with Frances Howard, daughter of the Earl of Suffolk, who had been m as a child to the Earl of Essex. In order to please him, James packed a commission of bps and judges who gave her a divorce (1613) in a travesty of legality which seriously damaged the K's reputation in the eyes of respectable men. But worse was to follow. The lovers married on 26 Dec 1613, and Carr ceased to behave as the K's agent, becoming instead the arrogant leader of the Howard faction. He made many enemies, and unfortunately Lady Frances presented them with plenty of ammunition. In 1615 it came out – through the confession of the Lieut of the Tower – that it was she who had organized the poisoning of Sir Thomas Overbury in the Tower in Sept 1613. Overbury, who was in prison for offending the K, was an old friend of Carr, and a fierce enemy of the Howards, and he had incurred the hostility of Lady Frances by trying to dissuade Carr from marrying her. These revelations ruined Carr's credit with the K, who in any case had already met and taken a fancy to BUCKINGHAM. The pair were tried before the H of L in May 1616, found guilty and sentenced to death; but the K pardoned them and kept them in the Tower till 1622. Probably no other escapade of James did as much damage to the reputation of the Court as this.

Carteret, John, 2nd Bn, then Earl Granville (22 Apr 1690–2 Jan 1763) Diplomat and Sec of State under GEORGE I and GEORGE II, and for a time (1742–4) chief minister of the latter.

Eld surviving son of George, 1st Bn Carteret; ed at Westminster Sch and Christ Ch, Oxford; m 1st (1710) Frances, daughter of Sir Robert Worsley (d 1743); m 2nd (1744) Lady Sophia Fermor, daughter of the 1st Earl of Pontefract and 30 years his junior (d 1745). An arrogant and idle *bon vivant* of enormous intellectual power and broad culture, he was one of the greatest classical scholars of his day, with fluency in French and German, and a detailed grasp of the politics of the H R Emp which endeared him to the 1st 2 Hanoverian Ks. Under Q ANNE, he had supported the Hanoverian succession, and then attached himself to the Sunderland faction. On his 1st appointment as ambassador to Stockholm (1719) he successfully negotiated the end of the GREAT NORTHERN WAR (1700–21) on behalf of the Sec of State, STANHOPE, and achieved the freedom of the Baltic for British ships. As a protégé of Stanhope, he was appointed Sec of State (S) in Mar 1721, on the break-up of the Stanhope–Sunderland admin; but the new PM, WALPOLE, soon had him removed (Apr 1724) and sent to Dublin out of harm's way as Ld Lieut of Ireland (Oct 1724). Carteret was a rival that Walpole felt he had to push aside, with his forward foreign policy that went right against Walpole's grain, with his credit with the K, with his aloof attitude towards the details of patronage and Parl management, and with his independent-minded refusal to take orders.

Back in England (1730), he continued for the rest of his life to be grit in the Walpole–Pelham political machine, denouncing, along with Pulteney, the Gov's isolationist foreign policy, until Walpole was forced out of office in Feb 1742. In the reconstructed ministry – an uneasy alliance of remnants of Walpole's Old Corps and Carteret's friends, the New Whigs – Carteret was appointed Sec of State (N) on 12 Feb 1742 to run the WAR OF THE AUSTRIAN SUCCESSION (1740–48). Travelling abroad with the K, he indulged himself extravagantly in foreign affairs, his favourite pastime being 'knocking the heads of the kings of Europe together, and jumbling something out of it that may be of service to this country'. He busied himself in the expensive business of forming elaborate Continental alliances around Austria against France, which, however wise as foreign policy, brought his downfall at home. In the opposition, PITT the Elder roused the Country back-bench prejudices against a policy which pursued the European interests of Hanover to the neglect of England's trade and colonies, and which in any case was being incompetently carried out, both diplomatically and militarily (*see* War of the Austrian Succession, 1742–4, page 31). In the Cab, PELHAM and NEWCASTLE determined to get rid of a high-handed colleague who did not tell them what he was doing, who followed extravagant policies abroad which they had the impossible task of 'selling' to the H of C, and who monopolized the ear of the K. Carteret believed he was impregnable: 'Give any man the Crown on his side,' he said, 'and he can defy everything.' He was mistaken, however, for a PM also needed the backing of the H of C, and Carteret never took the slightest trouble to form a party. On 23 Nov 1744 the Pelham brothers (possibly aided by Walpole) persuaded the K to dismiss him; but the Old Corps' troubles were not over. The K still consulted Carteret (who had become Earl Granville on the death of his mother, 18 Oct 1744) 'behind the curtain', and even planned his return to full power. The Pelhams therefore forced the K to face political reality by resigning in a body (10–11 Feb 1746) and proving to the K that Carteret was incapable of forming an admin that could command a majority in Parl. The Pelhams were recalled to office, and Carteret retired – not unwillingly – to his books and his burgundy. By 1751, when Pelham carried out a minor reshuffle, Carteret was sufficiently innocuous politically to be recalled to office. He was made Ld Pres of the Council in June 1751, a post he retained in a succession of admins: the Newcastle (1754–6), the Devonshire–Pitt (1756–7), the Newcastle–Pitt (1757–62), and the Bute (1762–3); in the last of which he officially signed the Tr of Paris on his death-bed, quoting an appropriate passage from the *Iliad* as he did so.

Cartier, Jacques (end of 1491–1 Jan 1557) French explorer of the R St Lawrence, on whose discoveries was based the French claim to Canada.

b at St Malo, Brittany, he was sent by K FRANCIS I to look for gold and find a NW passage through America to the Far E. On his 1st voyage he left St Malo with 2 ships in Apr 1534, and explored the coast of Newfoundland and Labrador, landed on Gaspée (proclaiming it French), and returned to St Malo in Sept 1534. On his 2nd voyage he took 3 ships (May 1535), and explored the St Lawrence as far as the sites of Quebec and Montreal (proving it to be a river and not a strait) and reached St Malo again in July 1536. His 3rd voyage with 5 vessels (May–Oct 1542) was an unsuccessful attempt to colonize the St Lawrence valley.

Cartwright, Thomas (c 1535–27 Dec 1603) Leading thinker and publicist of Presbyterianism under Q ELIZABETH I of England.

b in Herts of a yeoman family; ed at Clare Hall and St John's College, Cambridge; under the Cath Q MARY I he left the Univ to study law, but returned under Elizabeth I, becoming a Fellow of St John's, and then of Trinity. Appointed Lady Margaret Prof of Divinity in 1569, he gave a course of lectures advocating the abolition of Bps and the reform of the Ch of England on Presbyterian lines. The Vice-Chancellor of the Univ, John WHITGIFT, deprived him of his post for this seditious talk (1570), and he paid a visit to Geneva, returning to Cambridge in 1572, only to be deprived of his Fellowship of Trinity. As one of the most effective Presbyterian publicists he had to flee abroad in 1573 to escape the attentions of Whitgift's Commission for Ecclesiastical Causes which had issued orders for his arrest. He moved about the Continent from one Calvinist centre to another, publishing among other works the English translation of Walter Travers' Latin advocacy of Presbyterianism: the *Full and Plain Declaration of Ecclesiastical Discipline* (1574). With help from BURGHLEY and LEICESTER he was allowed back into England in 1586 to become Master of the hospital which Leicester had founded in Warwick, a post which he held until his death, and which he doubled with a good deal of literary and organizational work for the Presbyterian movement. He was examined by the Ecclesiastical Commission in Oct 1590, but refused to take the *ex officio* oath. He was locked up in the Fleet Prison from Nov 1590 to May 1592, appearing again before the Commission in May 1591 and the Star Chamber in June 1591. He was not convicted of any crime, and on his release he went to Guernsey until 1598, after which he returned to Warwick where he d.

Catherine I (1684–6 May 1727) 2nd wife of PETER I of Russia and Empss (Jan 1725) after his death.

b in Lithuania, daughter of a peasant, she became Peter's mistress, wife and carousing companion after spending some time as the property of Pr A. D. Menshikov. Since Peter did not name his successor, Menshikov (his *arriviste* favourite) seized power with a faction of guards officers, and placed Catherine on the throne – buying the acquiescence of the *boyars* by accepting the creation of a new central institution, the 6-man Supreme Privy Council. Coarse and corpulent, licentious and illiterate, Catherine left the Gov to Menshikov, undoing Peter's work by inaugurating a period of declining autocracy and crumbling central-ization. Menshikov tried to feather his own nest by persuading her to nominate as her successor the 11-year-old grandson of Peter I (the future Emp PETER II), and to agree to the boy's betrothal to his own daughter, Maria. In foreign affairs, which were managed by Vice-Chancellor A. I. Osterman, Russia played a peaceful role, signing a Tr with Austria (Aug 1726), an alliance which became the basis of Russian foreign policy for several decades.

Catherine II (The Great) (21 Apr/2 May 1729–7/18 Nov 1796) Empss of Russia (1762), under whom (1) at home the organs of prov and local Gov spread out from St Petersburg and Moscow to the rest of Russia, and over into the conquered provs; the nobility and the bureaucracy gained privileges at the expense of the State and the peasants; the Pugachev rebellion was bloodily suppressed; the Ch was further reduced in power and wealth; Physiocratic policies helped to promote economic growth comparable to that in Western Europe; the Enlightenment shaped the outlook of the educated classes; while (2) abroad Russia won im-portant victories over Turkey, conquered and colonized the Black Sea coast, and profited from the 3 partitions of Poland.

b at Stettin, Pomerania, as Pss Sophie Auguste Fredericka; daughter of Pr Christian August of Anhalt-Zerbst, Governor of Stettin, and his wife, Johanna Elizabeth of Holstein-Gottorp; ed as a child as a Lutheran, but as a grown-up self-ed in the European Enlightenment through the medium of French; brought to Russia by Empss ELIZABETH to be the bride of the future Emp PETER III, whom she m at St Petersburg in Aug 1745, after being received into the Orthodox Ch as Catherine Alekseyevna (1744).

Gifted with great personal charm, a warm heart, a ruthless will, a powerful intellect, and bottomless political guile, she received the title 'the Great' in her own day. She enjoyed a long succession of lovers for, as Pushkin later put it, 'many were called, and many chosen'. At least 21 have been identified, including Gregory Orlov, Gregory Potemkin and Platon Zubov – but they were not allowed undue political influence. She ruled as well as reigned, after successfully surviving the suspicions of Empss Elizabeth and the hostility of her own husband. Shortly after Peter's accession she overthrew him with the help of the Orlovs and their supporters in the guards, and then probably organized his assassination.

Being politically nimble, she avoided the usual fate of becoming the prisoner of the faction who had helped her. Her wide reading and personal contacts filled her head with the beliefs (or at least the phraseology) of the Western European Enlightenment, and she has been interpreted as an example of an ENLIGHTENED ABSOLUTIST, a phrase which is more appropriate to her aspirations than to her achievements. To be sure, she reformed the admin system, plundered the Ch, liberalized the economy, emancipated the nobility, and helped it to absorb Western culture; but at the same time she increased the degradation of the peasants, serfs and colonial tribesmen, drowned the Pugachev rebellion in blood, persecuted the Enlightened Radishchev, opposed the French Revolution, and pursued a foreign policy of traditional Russian expansionism. These discrepancies are not easy to explain. Was she a tyrant for whom the Enlightenment was merely cynical window-dressing or was she an idealist who became frustrated by the realities of harsh political life?

At home, as far as (a) Gov is concerned she began to give to Russia the blessing of a uniform legal-administrative system, manned by bureaucrats under the central supervision of the Senate. Hitherto this had been limited to the environs of Moscow and St Petersburg, and the rest of Russia had suffered under the primitive form of prov and local Gov which simply placed the public at the mercy of all-powerful governors (*voevody*) who ruled with the army, independent of central control. (i) A Legislative Commission was called (July 1767–Dec 1768) representing all social groups except private serfs but dominated in practice by the nobility, to recodify the law after the long interval since the Law Code of 1649 in the reign of ALEXIS. As a guide to its work she issued her *Instruction* (which she spent 2 years in writing), based on the ideas of Montesquieu and Beccaria. This commission was in many ways politically inept, and it was dissolved before any laws were passed, but it did have certain advantages for Catherine. It allowed important interests to express their hopes and grievances: the nobles, the townsmen, the peasants, the Cossacks, the Baltic provs etc. It painted for Catherine a vivid picture of what reforms were urgent and what could wait. Above all, perhaps, its meetings and the publication of the *Instruction* introduced educated Russians to the ideas of Western Europe and helped to spread political consciousness, to sow seeds whose fruit would ripen in the following century and a half. (ii) The Law on the Administration of the Provinces (7 Nov 1775) decentralized and elaborated the admin structure inherited from PETER I, ie about 18 Govs (*guberniia*) each divided into provs (*provintsiia*), each of which was divided into districts (*uezda*). By the end of Catherine's reign, there were 50 Govs and about 360 districts, while the provs had been eliminated. Secondly, the powers of the central Colleges were transferred to the head of each Gov, the *gubernator*; and at Gov and district level these powers were split up among separate boards for finance, justice and welfare. Thirdly, the judicial system was reorganized to separate criminal from civil justice, and to provide 3 distinct hierarchies of courts for the nobility, the town-dwellers and the peasants. And, fourthly, the various boards at each level were to be manned by personnel, some locally elected and some centrally appointed. This system gradually expanded into the empty spaces, and provided Russia with its admin structure down to Soviet times. Despite the expansion, however, the bureaucracy still remained comparatively thin on the ground. In proportion to population it was only about a third the size employed by Western European states. (iii) The Charter of the Cities (21 Apr 1785) divided townspeople into hierarchies of six different guilds, based on wealth. These were to elect the municipal council, which was to choose a 6-man committee to run urban affairs. Unfortunately, the bourgeoisie was a frail growth in Russia, and most towns remained subject to the bureaucrats. (iv) The central Gov did not change greatly in Catherine's time, except that, unlike her immediate predecessors, she was a fully-employed working ruler like Peter I. The Senate expanded its activities as the highest decision-making body in the day-by-day running of judicial and financial affairs and home affairs generally. It gained in authority, thanks to the work of A. A. Viazemskii and to the confidence Catherine placed in him as Prokuror-Gen, 1764–93. In 1768 a 9-man advisory State Council was formed to mediate between the Empss and the Senate. The Colleges, for their part, became less collegial as their Pres behaved more and more like ministers, and less important as much of their work was pushed out to the new *gubernii*. (v) The Russification of the conquered areas went ahead also from the 1780s onwards. The Ukraine, the Baltic provs, Finland, Siberia and ultimately Poland and Lithuania were all cut up into Govs and districts, while their inhabitants were turned into serfs and serving nobles.

(b) The social order of lord and serf consolidated itself generally and became impervious to Gov control. (i) The Charter of the Nobility (21 Apr 1785) was only one of several measures which raised the status of the nobles and relaxed the power of the autocracy over them – a continuing trend since the death of Peter I. This charter guaranteed the rights which the nobility had already acquired, and added some new ones. It gave them as individuals the same legal safeguards against arbitrary power as were enjoyed by the citizens of Western European countries. It allowed them as a group to form corporations in their Govs and districts, meeting in assemblies every 3 years; though these assemblies had nothing like the powers of Western European Estates, nor could the nobility meet in a national assembly. But if the nobility did not acquire the power to resist the Crown as a class, they did so as individual civil servants. By an edict of 1767 and other concessions, Catherine allowed automatic promotion based on seniority to become the rule, instead of taking into account hard work and ability. The personnel became sharply divided into 2 categories: the *dvoryane* – a title thenceforth held only by the top ranks, ie landowners, officers and hereditary *dvoryane* – and the *chinovniki* – the bottom ranks, the career bureaucrats in the humbler clerical jobs. The career open to the talents envisaged by Peter the Great's Table of Ranks ceased to exist (in so far as it ever did) and the Crown lost control of its bureaucracy. Broadly speaking, Russia became divided into 2 areas: one where the *dvoryane* tyrannized over their serfs, and the other where the *chinovniki* ruled the destinies of the peasants belonging to the State and the Ch. The Crown's activity became limited essentially to foreign policy and raising revenue. It was far less capable of improving the lot of the humblest citizens than the more limited monarchies of the West. (ii) The serfs in these circumstances were bound to suffer. As an Enlightened ruler, Catherine may well have favoured emancipation on humanitarian and economic grounds, but she was incapable of carrying out reforms which the *dvoryane* would not execute. The only improvement she achieved was to forbid the use of the hammer at serf auctions (1792). Otherwise, she allowed lords to sentence serfs to hard labour with the Admiralty (1765);

forbade serfs to complain against their lords on pain of knouting and penal servitude for life (1767); and added to their number by enserfing many Ch peasants (1764 onwards) and the peasants of conquered provs (1780s onwards). Catherine's policies first raised hopes then caused deep suffering and savage discontent. (iii) The Pugachev rebellion (1773–4) was the biggest of the numerous riots and rebellions of the persecuted groups whose position deteriorated in Catherine's reign. Emelian Pugachev, a Don Cossack and ex-member of the Russian army turned outlaw, 1st raised the Yaik Cossacks to revolt in 1773. With his angry and skilfully composed manifestos – in which he claimed to be the Emp Peter III – he soon rallied 20,000–30,000 partisans of diverse discontented peoples: serfs, peasants, factory workers, Cossacks and frontier tribesmen. He offered the old religion, land and freedom. He took Kazan (except for the Kremlin) on 12 July 1774, and posed a serious threat to Moscow and St Petersburg until troops released from the Russo-Turkish War suppressed him. Captured on 15 Sept 1774, he was taken to Moscow in an iron cage and in Jan 1775 was broken on the wheel, beheaded, dismembered and burnt. Similar savagery was meted out to the other rebels, the Yaik Cossacks being reorganized and renamed the Ural Cossacks. This insurrection is known to Soviet historians as the 4th Peasant War; like its predecessors, it achieved nothing, except that the fear it inspired was an important cause of the prov and local Gov reforms that began in 1775, and of the continuing alliance between the autocracy and the nobility.

(c) The Ch was further plundered and subordinated. In 1764 Catherine confirmed the decrees of Peter III nationalizing all land belonging to Chs and monasteries and bringing it under a new Gov dept, the College of Economy. The monks and clergy were paid salaries by the State, becoming something like *chinovniki*. The million or so Ch peasants became State peasants and thus available to Catherine as serfs, to be given away as presents. About half the monasteries were dissolved. In the 1790s the boundaries of the Bprics were redrawn to match the boundaries of the civil admin so as to make it easier for the Govs to control the Ch. In contrast with Western European experience during the REFORMATION, the Russian Ch seems to have accepted this rape without a murmur.

(d) The economy continued to flourish as it had in mid C18, and Catherine followed the liberal policies favoured by the Physiocrats. She confirmed Peter III's decree abolishing many State monopolies and allowing free public participation in the trade of most goods. Industry was also opened up by the decree of Oct 1762, allowing all the estates to start manufactures, except in the 2 capitals, and by the decree of Mar 1775, which allowed all ranks except serfs to participate in all industries – though vodka-distilling remained a noble monopoly. Catherine's policies stimulated both trade and industry, but concentrated them in the villages rather than the towns, and put them in the hands of nobles and peasants rather than townsmen. This last small group suffered a serious blow when Peter III repealed Peter I's law allowing merchants to buy serfs (Feb 1762). Without this source of labour they could no longer compete with the other classes, as their complaints to the Legislative Commission showed. Only 4.1 % of Russians were urban at that time, compared with 20.5 % of the French and 32 % of the British. Agricultural output also expanded, not because of improved farming methods – which in the more advanced areas had reached only the level of the 3-field system – but because of the enlargement of the cultivated area, especially after the colonization of the Ukraine and the steppe lands down to the Black Sea. All sectors of the economy were stimulated by the expanding machinery of Gov, and by the rise in population, which from 14 million at the death of Peter I grew to 36 million at the death of Catherine (including 7 million gained in the conquered territories).

(e) The Westernization of the Court and the top nobility in manners, morals and culture intensified during Catherine's reign, and its effects spread out into the prov towns and cities. She appointed I. I. Betskoi – who had lived in the West – as Pres of the Academy of Arts and director of the St Petersburg Military Academy. Under his influence, educational provision for the privileged expanded with the setting up of the Moscow Orphanage (1763), the St Petersburg Orphanage (1772), the Smolny Convent at St Petersburg for nobles' daughters (1764) and a second girls' school for commoners (1765). A general system of elementary and high schools in the capitals of each Gov and district was inaugurated when the Statute of Popular Schools was issued in Aug 1786: this scheme was worked out by Catherine's other educational collaborator, Fedor Yankovich de Mirievo. By this time, private tutors and academies also proliferated for the rich, and the chief products of Western European culture were readily available in Russian translation. At the same time, the soldiers' schools and the Ch schools continued their more humble forms of instruction. By the end of Catherine's reign, the high nobility at least were fully a part of the European Enlightenment, and were already beginning to feel its seditious effects. Alexander Radishchev, whose *Journey from St Petersburg to Moscow* (1790) exhibited deep disquiet over serfdom, autocracy and bureaucracy (and got him sent to Siberia), was only the most notorious of a generation infected, as Catherine complained, by the 'French madness'. Not surprisingly, the erstwhile Enlightened Empss was one of the severest critics of the French Revolution.

Abroad, Catherine's reign brought Russia to a new peak of European power and influence, thanks to the size of her armed forces, the skill of her commanders, and the bravery and endurance of her troops.

(a) Poland continued to suffer from Russia's interference, though Catherine was able to pretend that in preventing any reform of the Polish system of Gov (anarchy modified by civil wars) she was defending constitutional liberties against absolutism, and that in stimulating dissident religious groups (such as the Orthodox Christians and the Uniates) she was supporting religious freedom against RC intolerance, propaganda which fooled many of her admirers among the Enlightened. In 1763 she invaded the Duchy of Courland – a Polish fief with ice-free ports – turned it into a subject prov, and later annexed it (1795). On the death of K Augustus III of Poland in Oct 1763, a Diet dominated by the powerful pro-Russian Czartoryski family elected as the new K one of their family: Count Stanislas Poniatowski, a former lover of the Empress (1764). Soon, however, he began to show sufficient independence of mind to try to turn Poland into an effective hereditary monarchy and reduce the nobles' powers. As a result, Catherine intervened once more and forced him to sign the Polish-Russian Tr of Feb 1768, whereby Russia guaranteed the Polish constitution 'for all time to come'. A separate agreement protected the freedom of the dissident religious groups. Finally, with a change to a more unambiguously aggressive policy, Catherine annexed large tracts of Polish territory. Announcing that she was liberating Russian subjects and .euniting them with the fatherland, she participated in the 3 notorious partitions of Poland: the 1st (1772) with Austria and Prussia, the 2nd (1793) with Prussia, and the 3rd (1794/5) with Austria, and joined by Prussia in Oct 1795. One of the largest States in Europe had disappeared from the map.

(b) Turkey continued to be Russia's main enemy as Russia pressed W into Poland and S towards the Black Sea. It was an ancient hostility in which power politics, commercial rivalry and religious differences all played their part; while in St Petersburg dreams of expelling the heathen Turks from Europe and setting up a Russian ruler in Constantinople seemed to accord with Enlightened philosophy. Spurred on by Catherine's success in Poland, angered by Russian border raids, and encouraged by France, Turkey launched (i) the 1st Russo-Turkish War (1768–74) at a moment when Russia was unprepared. The fighting showed that the Turkish armed forces were in a state of ripe decay and that Russia could handle military and naval operations at vast distances from the capital. Catherine's armies conquered Moldavia, Wallachia and the Crimea. A Russian fleet sailed round through the English Channel, across the Med, and into the Aegean, there annihilating most of the Turkish fleet off Scio and Chesme, Asia Minor, in June 1770. By the peace Tr signed at Kutchuk-Kainardzhi, Bulgaria (July 1774), Russia made important gains. She was confirmed in her possession of Azov, and gained the Black Sea littoral between the Bug and the Dnieper, as well as part of Kuban and Terek. The Crimean Tatars became independent of Turkey and ripe for subversion by Russia. Russian merchantmen could sail the Black Sea and pass through the Straits. Moreover, Russia received vaguely worded rights to protect the Christians in the Ottoman Emp – rights which could form the basis of later interference. Turkey kept Moldavia, Wallachia and the Greek islands. (ii) The Crimea – after being subjected to several years of Russian subversion – was peacefully annexed by Catherine in Apr 1783. (iii) The 2nd Russo-Turkish War (Aug 1787–Dec 1791/Jan 1792) resulted from Russian aggression – aided (1788–91) by Austria, who performed disastrously. The Russian generals – especially Pr Gregory Potemkin and Field-Marshal Alexander Suvorov – showed high accomplishments, capturing Ochakov (Dec 1788) and other Black Sea territories. On the other hand, Catherine's hope of taking Constantinople was disappointed, and by the Tr of Jassy (Dec 1791/Jan 1792) she had to rest content with the annexation of Ochakov and the coast between the Bug and the Dniester, as well as the recognition by Turkey of Russia's possession of the Crimea.

(c) Sweden managed to end the Russian tutelage it had suffered since the GREAT NORTHERN WAR (1700–21). In Aug 1772 K Gustav III set up an absolute monarchy and thus ended Catherine's attempt to cripple Sweden by defending aristocratic constitutionalism. Taking advantage of the 2nd Russo-Turkish War, Sweden made war on Russia (June 1788–Aug 1790), though without success. The Tr of Verelä (Aug 1790) restored the pre-war situation. Sweden had failed to regain any of her lost territories, but Russia had also failed to turn Sweden into another Poland. Nevertheless, when Catherine d of a stroke at St Petersburg, she had extended the Russian Emp by about 200,000 square miles, and added some 7 million new subjects.

Catherine of Aragon (1485–7 Jan 1536) 1st Q consort of K HENRY VIII of England, and mother of Q MARY I. It was in order to divorce Catherine that Henry began the English REFORMATION.

Daughter of K FERDINAND of Aragon and Q ISABELLA of Castile; m Arthur, Pr of Wales (Nov 1501), then his brother Henry (June 1509), in accordance with the Anglo-Spanish alliance. For the 2nd marriage a dispensation was obtained from Pp JULIUS II (Dec 1503) dispensing them from the impediment of affinity; and the marriage was solemnized at Greenwich, 2 months after Henry succeeded to the throne. By 1525 they had ceased to live together. Henry had grown tired of her (she was 7 years his senior) and, moreover, she had failed to provide a male heir. (Apart from her daughter Mary, who later became Q, Catherine produced 5 children, who were stillborn, or who d soon after birth.) This barrenness convinced Henry that his marriage to his deceased brother's widow did not have the divine blessing. Moreover, Catherine was the aunt of the Emp CHARLES V, whose unco-operative attitude in foreign affairs at this juncture rendered Henry willing to seek vengeance through Catherine. And, finally, he fell in love with Anne Boleyn. This mixture of motives led Henry to set in train the divorce proceedings in 1527. Pp CLEMENT VII used delaying tactics, never providing the K with just the unequivocal pronouncement he required – for Henry's case was weak in canon law, while Clement could not afford to alienate Charles V. A Legatine Court under Cards WOLSEY and Campeggio opened at Blackfriars on 18 June 1529 before which both Henry and Catherine appeared; but it failed to reach a decision before the (Roman) law vacation began on 31 July 1529. Catherine, a well-educated and high-principled student of HUMANISM, throughout behaved in a dignified, almost heroic manner. The K spent a further year sending envoys to Rome, and at CRANMER'S suggestion asking Oxford and Cambridge, as well as the French and Italian univs, for their opinion (which in 8 cases was favourable); but by Aug 1530 he had decided on a completely new line of attack. Instead of going cap in hand to Rome, where the Pp now proposed to try the divorce, Henry put forward a revolutionary new view of the position of England in the world and of the monarchy in England. Briefly, he asserted that no Englishman could be cited before a foreign court, and that, to use a phrase that one of his agents used to a papal nuncio, 'the K is absolute emperor and pope in his kingdom' (Sept 1530). Accordingly, when Anne Boleyn became pregnant by the K (in Dec 1532, probably) the machinery for a purely English solution to the divorce problem was swiftly set in motion, as Thomas CROMWELL became the chief minister of the Crown. The Act in Restraint of Appeals was passed in Mar 1533 prohibiting appeals to Rome from the Archbps' courts in testamentary and matrimonial cases; and a special court at Dunstable under Cranmer (recently consecrated Archbp of Canterbury) opened on 10 May 1533 to try the case. Catherine refused to appear, either in person or by proxy; and on 23 May Cranmer declared her marriage with Henry null and void, by which time the K had already secretly m Anne (25 Jan 1533). A year later at Rome, 7 years after the divorce proceedings had begun, and after reviewing the whole case 4 times, the Consistory pronounced Catherine's marriage to Henry to be valid (Mar 1534). This was too late to have any practical effect in England, or to mitigate the humiliations Catherine had to endure as she was separated from her daughter (later Mary I), and forced to live in meaner and meaner material circumstances. She d at Kimbolton, probably of cancer. Her steadfast behaviour assured her the affections of the English people, but only the contempt of her husband and K, who is said to have celebrated her death by appearing at a banquet at Greenwich dressed in yellow from head to foot.

Catherine de Medici (13 Apr 1519–5 Jan 1589) Q consort of K HENRY II of France, mother of K FRANCIS II, CHARLES IX and HENRY III, and of François, D of Alençon. She was Regent for them or a dominant influence on them during the FRENCH WARS OF RELIGION, in which she unsuccessfully tried to prevent the power and prestige of the Crown from sinking under the weight of its many difficulties, the chief of which were the rival noble CLIENTAGE networks, religious antagonisms, prov separatism and foreign interference.

b at Florence, daughter of Lorenzo dei Medici, D of Urbino, and Madeleine de la Tour d'Auvergne; m (Oct 1533) the future Henry II (5 sons and 5 daughters). On Henry's death on 10 July 1559, her eldest son, Francis II, became K till his death on 5 Dec 1560, when her 2nd son succeeded as Charles IX, aged 10. The Guise faction which had dominated Francis was ousted, and Catherine, co-operating with Antoine de Bourbon, the 1st Pr of the Blood and leading rival of the Guises, got herself recognized as Regent by the Estates-Gen of Orléans in Dec 1560, Bourbon being appointed Lieut-Gen of the Kdom. She was faced with the same problems that plagued all the would-be absolutist rulers of France before the Revolution, but in addition she was hamstrung by the disadvantages of being a woman, a foreigner and a Regent.

Athletic in a heavily built way, she was a *bon vivant* who helped to spread Renaissance aesthetic taste in France, as well as Italian *haute cuisine* and Machiavellian political methods. Fearless in the defence of her children's interests, tireless in her incessant manoeuvrings among the factions, she was never afraid of hard work, but usually had her eye on short-term political gains rather than on long-term statesmanship. Being a tepid R C amidst the fierce conflicts between the Catholicism of the COUNTER-REFORMATION and the Protestantism of CALVIN, she enjoyed the advantages of pursuing a *Politique* policy, but also the disadvantage of never really appreciating the depth of feeling behind the Wars of Religion, never being able to understand why the 2 sides could not indulge in the kind of horse-trading she was so fertile in proposing as the way to peace. For some kind of compromise was all she could offer. She could never allow one side to defeat the other, for the victor could then turn on her. And in any case, the great nobles involved could never be eliminated. They owned such vast estates and commanded such extensive clientage retinues that the gov of France was impossible without their co-operation. Catherine began by sponsoring R C–Prot discussions at the Colloquy of Poissy (Sept–Oct 1561); but, discovering that C16 theologians were not adept at arranging package-deals, she made concessions to the Hugs in the January Edict (1562) and in the Tr of Amboise which brought an end to the 1st War of Religion (Apr 1562–19 Mar 1563). She then unwittingly caused the 2nd War (Sept 1567–Mar 1568) by meeting her daughter, Q Elizabeth of Spain, and the D of ALBA at Bayonne in June 1565, an innocent family gathering which convinced the Hugs that they were about to be suppressed by Spanish troops. During this and the 3rd War (Aug 1568–Aug 1570), Catherine continued to aim at compromise, angering the Guises, who left the Court, and giving COLIGNY, the new Hug leader, the opportunity (1570–72) of using his magnetic personality on the receptive Charles IX to persuade him to back his ambitious scheme for uniting the French factions in the marriage of Catherine's daughter, Margaret, with Antoine de Bourbon's heir, the future K HENRY IV, and in a patriotic war against Spain – helping WILLIAM I of Orange in the REVOLT OF THE NETHERLANDS. Catherine's political calculations and maternal instincts turned her against Coligny. She was aware of the risks France would run in fighting a Spain now apparently so strong after her victory over the Turks at Lepanto (Oct 1571); and at the same time she was outraged by the thought of her son taking advice other than her own. Urged on by her 3rd son, the future Henry III, and the Guises, she descended from her elevated position above the factions, and ordered Coligny's assassination, the bungling of which led to the Massacre of St Bartholomew (23/4 Aug 1572). This fatal deviation from neutrality put her at the mercy of the Guises, and her influence was never so strong again. Her role, and that of the Crown, shrivelled into one of pathetic manoeuvring between the noble factions which really governed France. Abroad, she somewhat irrelevantly got her son Henry elected as K of Poland (May 1573), and then successfully preserved the French Crown for his return on the death of Charles IX on 30 May 1574. She continued to dominate him and his policy, conceding liberties to the Hugs, and then withdrawing them as the power-balance fluctuated. And it was her flexible negotiations with the various chieftains that were mainly responsible for the long peace of 1577–84 – as far as the Crown was concerned, a peace of impotence. Her period of power was over, however, and in 1588 Henry III became his own man by dismissing the ministers she had told him to appoint. By the time of her death of pneumonia at Blois she was unimportant. According to a contemporary, Pierre de L'Estoile, her demise 'made no more stir than the death of a goat'.

Catholic Reformation The pre-Lutheran reform movement in the Cath Ch, as distinct from the more aggressive COUNTER-REFORMATION, which it broadened into. The result of the same historical circumstances that made the REFORMATION possible (ie the corruption of the Ch, the rise of an educated laity demanding higher standards from the clergy, the conciliar movement, anti-clericalism, Erastianism, HUMANISM and mysticism), the Catholic Reformation expressed itself in various ways, in various countries. In Spain, Card XIMÉNEZ DE CISNEROS tightened up clerical discipline, reformed the religious orders, and encouraged scholarship at school and univ level. In the Netherlands, the C14 Brethren of the Common Life (lay and clerical) produced the *Devotio moderna*, which stressed the inwardness of Christianity and its expression in practical life, eg in secondary education, a field in which they were very influential. One of their products was ERASMUS, a powerful expression of the Catholic Reformation. In Italy, the 5th Lateran Council (1512–17) proposed reforms to Pps JULIUS II and LEO X, which they did not enforce, however. Moreover, the Oratory of Divine Love (a brotherhood of higher clerics and laymen) was founded near Rome in 1517 – though its origins were elsewhere – to foster asceticism and good works in everyday life. Among its members were Gian Matteo Giberti (1495–1543), who later reformed his bpric of Verona; Gaetano (Cajetan) da Thiene (1480–1547), one of the founders of the Theatines (1524), an order of priests working in the world but living in monastic austerity; Gian Pietro Caraffa, the other founder, who later became Pp PAUL IV; Jacopo Sadoleto (1477–1547), reformer of his bpric in Carpentras, France; and Gasparo Contarini (1483–1542) who was made a Card (1535) by Pp PAUL III. Kindred spirits at this stage were Giovanni Morone (1509–80), later Bp of Modena and leading papal negotiator at the COUNCIL OF TRENT, and Reginald Pole. Pp Paul III, who made Sadoleto and Caraffa Cards in 1536, included such reformers in his commission of 9 (1536) which had the task of investigating abuses in the Ch, and suggesting reforms. Their report (1537) – the *Consilium de emendenda ecclesia* (Advice on the Reform of the Church) – by its assumption everything would be well with the Ch once the abuses had been looked into – showed the inadequate appreciation by this generation of the full Prot revulsion from Rome. By this time, the Reformation of LUTHER had already swept past, and the Counter-Reformation – the stern and persecuting counter-attack on the Prots – was a different matter altogether from the methods of these reasonable Humanists.

Charles I (19 Nov 1600–30 Jan 1649) K of Great Britain and Ireland (27 Mar 1625), who inherited an aggressive generation of Parl nobility and gentry, but who was largely himself to blame for appointing men in Ch and state, and pursuing policies in foreign affairs, religion and taxation, which either jeopardized English religion, liberties or property, or broke the law, or both. Consequently, when the chance came in 1641, Parl was practically unanimous in enacting severe limitations on the royal power. The more radical M Ps and citizens, however – so devious was the K on the surface – sought further concessions in order to safeguard these; and the CIVIL WAR was the result – so intransigent was he at bottom. Charles then lost the war, and conducted the peace negotiations with such a lack of political skill that even more radical men were able to seize power and execute him. He was a genuine connoisseur of the arts, and left a collection of buildings, paintings and sculptures unequalled in the history of the English crown.

b at Dunfermline, Fifeshire, Scotland, 2nd son of K JAMES VI AND I of Scotland and England, and Q Anne of Denmark; ed at Court, though that coarse, immoral, and intellectual environment could hardly have suited this shy, delicate, artistic and conscientious boy, who was mentally slow, disliked public appearances, could not get rid of his stammer or his Scots accent, and soon learned to retreat behind a façade of dissimulation. It says much for the gifts of BUCKING-HAM, his father's chief minister and favourite, that he was able to overcome the young Pr's initial reserve and establish as much dominion over Charles's mind as he had over James's body. In the last few years of the old K's life, Charles and Buckingham effectively ruled Britain, and it was their idea to make the abortive marriage journey to Madrid in 1623 and then to switch suddenly to a French alliance, as a result of which Charles m K HENRY IV's daughter, Henrietta Maria, and soon after became K. He became a devoted husband to her, and father to her children: CHARLES II, JAMES II and 5 others.

His reign divides into 5 periods: 1625–9 under the 1st 3 Parls, when the rule of Buckingham led to a break-down in the relations between K and Parl; 1629–40, the 11 years' Personal Rule, a period of authoritarian gov without Parl by LAUD and STRAFFORD, at first successful, but brought to an end when Scotland was provoked into a war; 1640–42, when the Long Parl united long enough under

PYM to destroy Strafford and Laud, and force the K to accept serious limitations on his power; but then split over Ch reform and the extent of the Crown's future subordination to Parl. Out of these fragments formed the Royalists and the Parliamentarians, and the Civil War ensued; 1642–6, the 1st Civil War, which Parl won, being better placed for a long struggle, especially with the Scots alliance and the creation of the New Model Army under an outstanding leader, Oliver CROMWELL; 1646–9, when the Army quarrelled with Parl, and divided into 2 factions, moderate and radical; while the K negotiated simultaneously with Parl, the Army and the Scots, making promises, but intending never to make concessions. After the Army won the 2nd Civil War – a series of local, but not necessarily Royalist, risings against Parl and the Army, aided by a Scottish invasion – it seized control of affairs, occupied London, purged Parl, tried the K, and executed him.

(1) 1625–9: The 1st 3 Parls (June–Aug 1625, Feb–June 1626 and Mar 1628–Mar 1629) saw the breach widen between K and Parl. Unlike his father, Charles did not indulge in provocative theoretical expositions of the royal power. His messages to Parl were short and sharp; but in practice he defended his prerogatives with vigour, and he felt his responsibilities deeply, especially as head of the Ch. Disputes arose over several issues: (a) Buckingham's disastrous foreign policy, involving the failure of Mansfeld's intervention in the THIRTY YEARS WAR (1625), the abortive attack on Cádiz (1625), the disgraceful Isle of Rhé expedition, all leading to billeting, martial law and other grievances; (b) Charles's promotion of Arminian clergy and relaxation of the laws against Caths; (c) Parl's grant of Tunnage and Poundage for one year only instead of for the duration of the K's life, and its subsequent refusal of further supplies (one cause of the foreign disasters); leading to (d) the collection of a Forced Loan, the dismissal of Chief Justice Sir Randolph Crew for refusing to affirm its legality; followed by (e) the arbitrary imprisonment of 76 gentlemen who refused to pay, and the King's Bench ruling (5 Knights' Case, or Darnel's Case, 1626) that their arrest was lawful; (f) attempts by MPs to impeach Buckingham, whom the K saved by dismissing Parl; (g) the passing of the Petition of Right (signed by the K in June 1628) which forbade arbitrary imprisonment, non-Parl taxation, billeting and martial law; (h) the assassination of Buckingham on 23 Aug 1628, and (i) the violent session of the H of C, fomented by ELIOT, in which the tearful Speaker was held down in his chair while 3 Resolutions were passed condemning non-Parl taxation and innovations in religion.

(2) 1629–40: The 11 years' Personal Rule saw Charles attempting the perhaps not impossible task of turning England into an absolute monarchy. (a) In foreign affairs, war was impossible without Parl grants, and so peace was signed with France (Tr of Suze, Apr 1629) and Spain (Tr of Madrid, Nov 1630), while English aggressiveness in taking advantage of the Thirty Years War was diverted into the expansion of trade and transatlantic colonial settlement. (b) In the Ch, Laud and his minority of Arminian clergy were given extravagant promotion and allowed to impose their ritualism on the majority by tyrannical means, causing offence not only to PURITANS but also to conservatives who resented the growing habit of socially inferior clergy dictating to the laity. (c) In social policy, the bad harvests of 1630 and 1631 necessitated extra efforts to protect the weak from the strong, and this period saw unusual activity by the Privy Council

and Star Chamber, as well as by Strafford in the N and in Ireland, to enable the state to encroach paternalistically on the self-gov communities of county and borough in order to enforce the Poor Laws, the Enclosure Acts and wage assessments under the Statute of Artificers of 1563. (d) The revenue was expanded by a series of devices which up to 1637 appeared to ensure the success of this experiment in non-Parl gov. With the judges' approval, Tunnage and Poundage continued to be collected, though not granted by Parl; and increased income was extracted by virtue of the K's position as feudal over-lord, as well as from monopolies. In addition, dubious dormant rights of the Crown were exploited: eg fines were levied for encroachments – perhaps a C old – on the royal forests or on common land; likewise, men with £40 a year and above who had not become knights at the coronation were all fined. Similarly, Ship Money, which the K could levy on coastal areas for defensive purposes, was expanded. It was imposed on the coast in 1634, and then extended to the inland counties in 1635 and after, though it was by no means certain that there existed a national emergency. The test case of John HAMPDEN (1637) favoured the Crown, but by the smallest possible majority of the judges; and this, together with the K's use of the navy on the Spanish and Cath side in the Thirty Years War, caused a tax-payers' strike and a fall in receipts from 1637 onwards. (e) Scotland, however, finally ruined Charles's schemes by bringing war. With their policy of resuming alienated Ch and Crown land (Act of Revocation, 1625), capped by the sudden proclamation of an Anglican-type liturgy for Kirk (1637), Charles and Laud achieved the difficult feat of uniting the nobility and clergy against them. The Scots rebelled, their national pride and their religious beliefs outraged. They drew up the National Covenant (Feb 1638) pledging themselves to oppose these innovations by all means within their power. Charles abandoned the new Prayer Book, but the Scots raised an army under Alexander Leslie and began to attack episcopacy. The K assembled his vassals at York and the bloodless border manoeuvring of the 1st Bishops' War took place, the penniless K soon yielding by the Tr of Berwick on 18 June 1639. He now recalled Strafford from Dublin (Sept 1639) who advised calling Parl; but under the leadership of Pym the Short Parl (13 Apr–5 May 1640) refused supplies before redress of grievances, and was dissolved. Strafford still advised war, using his army from Ireland, but the Scots started the 2nd Bishops' War by invading Northumberland and Durham, and again the K was forced to give in. By the Tr of Ripon (Oct 1640) the Scots were to hold their positions and receive £850 a day until the religious disputes had been settled. Charles had no option but to call another Parl.

(3) 1640–42: The work of the Long Parl (3 Nov 1640 onwards) in this period divides into 2 phases: before and after the recess in the autumn of 1641. In the 1st phase Pym's management achieved a united Parl which (a) released and compensated Prynne, Burton, Bastwick, Lilburne, and other victims of Star Chamber and High Commission persecution; (b) impeached, attainted and executed Strafford, imprisoned Laud (executing him on 10 Jan 1645), while the other ministers fled abroad; and (c) clipped the Crown's powers with the following statutes: (i) Triennial Act (Feb 1641), guaranteeing a 50-day session of Parl at least every 3 years; (ii) Act against the dissolution of the Long Parl without its own consent (May 1641); (iii) Tunnage and Poundage Act (June 1641), settling the dispute over impositions in Parl's favour and voting customs

to the K for 2 months only; (iv) Act for the abolition of Star Chamber (July 1641); (v) Act for the abolition of High Commission (July 1641); (vi) Act abolishing Ship Money (Aug 1641); (vii) Act defining the boundaries of the royal forest (Aug 1641); (viii) Act against vexatious proceedings touching the Order of Knighthood (Aug 1641). These reforms, which ruled out absolutism for the future, represent the real, permanent revolution of this period, for they were eventually incorporated into the Restoration settlement of 1660.

In the 2nd phase (beginning Oct 1641, after a 6-week recess) Pym could no longer postpone the emergence of the 2 underlying sides which eventually fought one another as Roundheads and Cavaliers. The chief issues were the reform of the Ch and the further limitation of the executive power. While there was practically universal criticism of the Arminians, Parl was divided when it came to constructing something to take their place: ie between the extremists, or Root and Branch party, who favoured Presbyterianism and a fully revised Prayer Book, and the moderate, or limited episcopacy party, who simply wished to reduce the powers and pretensions of bps and make a few alterations in the Prayer Book. As for the executive, Pym demanded a Parl veto on the K's ministers, and Parl control of the armed forces which had to be raised to suppress the Irish rebellion of Oct 1641. 'By God, not for an hour,' said Charles. When Pym put the issue to the vote in the Grand Remonstrance in Nov 1641, he achieved a majority of only 11. In the increasingly frenzied atmosphere of mutual suspicion, in which each side expected violence from the other, with the K and Q negotiating for help from City financiers and Cath powers, and Pym keeping in touch with radical aldermen and preachers in the City, and publishing the Grand Remonstrance in order to widen the basis of support, it was Charles who struck first. On 4 Jan 1642 with 400 soldiers he invaded Parl to arrest 5 MPs, but 'the birds had flown', as he put it. They had already gone by water to the safety of the City where, in the nick of time, the radicals had won control of the Common Council in the elections of Dec 1641. The K and the royal family left London on 10 Jan 1642, and both sides prepared for war.

(4) 1642–6: The K lost the 1st Civil War, in spite of having the loyalty of most of the nobility and gentry and their lower-class dependants; and his conduct of it demonstrated his weaknesses just as clearly as his role in the Parl struggle: his inability to think quickly, act decisively, inspire trust, give effective leadership, or follow a consistent course. He appointed a Council of War, but gave it little scope and failed to carry out its decisions. His supporters raised local armies in the N and W under effective noble commanders who nevertheless disagreed among themselves, while the K failed to provide any overall co-ordination. Having left London – with its psychological, administrative and financial advantages the greatest asset either side could have – he failed to take it in 1642, blocked by the drawn battle of Edgehill, nr Warwick (23 Oct 1642), and the confrontation at Turnham Green (13 Nov 1642), W of London, his nearest approach to the capital. He set up his HQ at Oxford, and seems to have planned for 1643 a co-ordinated 3-fold attack on London – from the N, the W and from Oxford – but, if so, it did not materialize as the N and W royalists were reluctant to leave their areas. In Sept 1643, Charles signed a truce with the Irish rebels and released troops for service in England; but Parl acquired the far more valuable asset of the Scots, with whom the Solemn League and Covenant was signed in

London in Sept 1643, including an ambiguous promise to set up Presbyterianism in England. It was now too late for the dilatory K to win the war, for a long struggle gave the advantage to Parl, in the form of time to collect revenue and to train troops. The chief event of 1644 was the decisive victory of Parl and the Scots over the Royalists at Marston Moor, nr York (2 July 1644), where Oliver Cromwell's cavalry swung the issue; and the K's fate was sealed the following year when Parl advanced beyond the concept of local levies to the creation of a national army – the New Model – and expelled their half-hearted commanders – Self-Denying Ordinance (Mar 1645). Under FAIRFAX and Cromwell the New Model beat the K at Naseby, nr Market Harborough, Leics, on 14 June 1645, Cromwell's cavalry again winning the day. In 1646 the Royalist remnants were mopped up; the K left Oxford in disguise on 27 Apr 1646, and gave himself up to the Scots near Newark on 5 May 1646.

(5) 1646–9: In these fluid post-war years Charles condemned himself to death by his readiness to negotiate specious concessions with the various power groups which came in turn into prominence, while at the same time barely concealing his basic determination to remain steadfast in the defence of the monarchy and the Ch as he had inherited them. As a Machiavellian he was not a success, hamstrung as he was by a willingness to die for what he saw as his duty. The sticking points, as far as he was concerned, were the Crown's powers over the army and over the Ch; and control of the Ch, he once said, 'I hold to be of equal consequence to that of the militia; for people are governed by pulpits more than by the sword, in times of peace.' His Civil War opponents now split into 3 broad groups: the Scots, Parl and the Army – while Parl divided into a majority, the 'Presbyterians' and a minority, the 'Independents', at the same time as the Army split between the generals, the Grandees, and the junior officers and men, represented by the Agitators, their elected agents. Moreover, the 'Independents' were themselves an alliance of 2 groups – the radicals and the middle group – who eventually split apart. Thus the K was faced with 6 main interest groups, strung across the whole spectrum from conservative to radical in accordance with the amount of change they wanted in the existing political, religious and social system: the Scots, the 'Presbyterians', the middle group, the radicals, the Grandees and the Agitators. The Scots were only interested in setting up their form of theocratic Presbyterianism in England. The 'Presbyterians', consisting of Presbyterian MPs, but also Independents and others, favoured an alliance with the Scots to negotiate peace with the K, in order to head off further radical change, political, religious or social. Led by Denzil Holles, they reflected the fear of the Army which now gripped the landed classes because of the high taxation it required, the distress its billeting caused, and the 'levelling' nature of its programme. They determined to disband it. The middle group (Pym's old party) at first worked in alliance with the radicals to form the 'Independents', consisting of Independents, sectaries and others, led by Oliver St John and Sir Henry Vane. They wished to keep the Army in being, fearing the loss of everything they had fought for – especially religious toleration – if they disarmed themselves before the K had been brought to heel. The Grandees, led by Cromwell and IRETON, with increasing difficulty bridged the gap between Parl and the Army, who moved further apart as the Army increasingly thought of itself as an interest in its own right, more representative of the people than Parl. At the same time, the Grandees had

to adopt increasingly more radical policies so as not to lose the support of the rank and file. The Agitators – the elected representatives of the officers and men of the regiments – pushed the Grandees from behind with their programme, much influenced by Lilburne and the LEVELLERS, for a democratic republican settlement involving radical social and religious reforms. For his part, the K sat passively by, waiting for bids from these various groups, discussion of which he would string out as long as possible, hoping ultimately to profit from their discords, but doing little in a positive way to form his own party. The Scots left England (1647) handing the K over to Parl, which moved him to Holmby (or Holdenby) House, Northants, in Feb 1647. At the same time, the 'Presbyterian' majority in Parl ordered the Army to disband or serve in Ireland, though offering only 6 weeks' arrears of pay instead of the 18 weeks owed to the infantry and the 43 weeks owed to the cavalry. The 'Independents' supported the Army; and the split in Parl was further widened when the K told them (May 1647) that he was prepared to accept a Presbyterian Ch settlement for 3 years and also allow Parl to control the militia for 10. Meanwhile, the Army grew restive, and when Cornet Joyce took possession of the K and brought him to Newmarket (June 1647) the Grandees did not repudiate the coup – possibly they had even planned it. A Council of the Army was formed, consisting of Grandees and Agitators, and in its name Cromwell offered the K a moderate scheme for a settlement known as the *Heads of the Proposals* (Aug 1647). This split the Army, however, and the Agitators produced their own settlement, the *Agreement of the People* (Oct 1647), which the Grandees discussed with them at Putney (Oct–Nov 1647), but found too radical to accept. Cromwell ordered the Agitators back to their regiments and put down a mutiny by force (Nov 1647), while the K turned down the *Heads of the Proposals* and tried a new tack. He escaped from the Army to Carisbrook Castle, Isle of Wight (Nov 1647) and made a deal with the Scots (the 'Engagement', Dec 1647), whereby he agreed to accept Presbyterianism for 3 years and to suppress the sectaries: an alliance which led to the 2nd Civil War. This consisted of a series of regional risings, in Wales (Mar 1648), Kent (May 1648) and Essex (June 1648), followed by the mutiny of about half the fleet (May 1648) and the invasion of England by the Scots 'Engagers'. It was not only Royalists that were involved, for these risings were also the protest of the moderates in the county communities against the oppressions of the Army and its centralizing structure of gov, worse than 'Thorough' under Laud and Strafford. One by one the rebellions were put down, and at Preston, Lancs (Aug 1648) Cromwell defeated the invading Scots. By now the patience of the Army was exhausted, and at a prayer meeting at Windsor on 22 Apr 1648 it decided that it was time to call 'Charles Stuart, that man of blood, to an account for blood that he had shed'. The 2nd Civil War also broke up the 'Independent' alliance in Parl, the radicals backing the Army, the middle group joining the 'Presbyterians' for further negotiations with the K, known as the Newport Treaty, beginning in Sept 1648. The K was happy to oblige, but these discussions sealed his fate. At Army HQ, Ireton made the decisive moves, while Cromwell hesitated long in the N, ostensibly finishing off the 2nd Civil War. When the Newport discussions seemed to be succeeding, Ireton made the critical decision to use the Army against Parl, keeping the Agitators quiet with a committee to revise the *Agreement of the People* (Nov 1648). On 30 Nov 1648 the Army took possession of the K and advanced on the capital. On 6 Dec 1648, Pride's Purge took place, with Col Thomas Pride and his men preventing any MPs from sitting with the exception of about 60 of the radical wing of the 'Independents', henceforth known as the Rump. Cromwell arrived in London that evening and reluctantly approved this action as the only way to keep the Army united and in being. A revolutionary minority of the Rump now took charge of events. Receiving no co-operation from the H of L, the H of C appointed a High Court of about 150 members to try the K. In the public hearings in Westminster Hall (20–27 Jan 1649) Charles refused to plead before this illegal tribunal, claiming to stand for the liberties of the people of England. 'For, if power without law may make laws,' he said, '. . . I do not know what subject . . . can be sure of his life, or anything that he calls his own.' He was beheaded outside the Banqueting Hall of Whitehall on 30 Jan 1649, moving all observers with the depth of his convictions and the courage with which he faced his end.

Charles II (29 May 1630–6 Feb 1685) K of Great Britain and Ireland who achieved the Restoration and consolidation of the monarchy after the CIVIL WARS.

b at St James's Palace, London, eld surviving son of K CHARLES I and his Q consort, Henrietta Maria; ed until 1642 by the Bp of Chichester and the Earl of Newcastle, and then in the hard school of the Civil War, which doubtless fostered his self-confidence, his cynicism, his realistic judgement of men, and his skill in handling them. From 1645 he was a refugee in Jersey, France and the Netherlands until he landed in Scotland (June 1650) to head a Presbyterian rising against England, leaving his father's supporters – the followers of Montrose – in the lurch. The Scots were defeated by Oliver CROMWELL at Dunbar (3 Sept 1650), and then, invading England, at Worcester (3 Sept 1651), after which Charles fled abroad again, having hidden for 6 weeks in the oak tree at Boscobel and other refuges. During the vacuum created by the death of Cromwell (3 Sept 1658), Charles's chief minister, CLARENDON, negotiated the Restoration with MONCK, the commander of one of the republican armies, on the basis of Charles's Declaration of Breda (Apr 1660) in which the K promised an amnesty, liberty of conscience, a land settlement and arrears of pay for the army – the details to be worked out by a Parl.

Charles landed at Dover on 25 May 1660 amid popular rejoicing. Though he was too lazy and pleasure-loving to make the Crown permanently absolute over a wary upper class, he had the political skill to avoid becoming the prisoner of either the factions at Court or the parties in Parl, and even ruled without Parl for the last 4 years of his reign. Tall, dark and athletic, he was energetic in his search for pleasure, and his Court soon radiated a licentiousness which contrasted strongly with the Puritan period just over. He had many mistresses, notable among them being Lucy Walter, Barbara Palmer (Lady Castlemaine, Dss of Cleveland), Nell Gwynn and Louise de Kérouaille (Dss of Portsmouth); and though he acknowledged 14 bastards, of whom MONMOUTH was the chief, he fathered no legitimate children. There were 5 main phases in his reign.

Rule of Clarendon (1660–67): (a) The Restoration settlement was made by the Convention Parl (Apr–Dec 1660) and the Cavalier Parl (May 1661–Jan 1679). It confirmed the legislation of 1641 (which made the growth of absolutism very difficult, perhaps impossible). It pardoned all those involved in the Civil War (except the regicides, of whom 11 were executed). It restored Ch and Crown lands, and the lands of Royalists which had been confiscated – but not lands which had been sold to pay Cromwellian taxation. It granted a revenue of £1.2 million a year to the Crown, which was inadequate in view of the K's extravagance. It restored the Anglican Ch, and by a series of statutes known as the 'CLARENDON CODE' persecuted dissenters. Charles himself favoured toleration, but his 1st Declaration of Indulgence (Dec 1662) was blocked by Parl. (b) His foreign policy generally strengthened France (England's long-term enemy), and consisted of (i) the sale of Dunkirk to France for financial reasons (Oct 1662); (ii) the alliance with Portugal (June/July 1661), whereby Charles m Catherine Bragança (May 1662) and received Bombay and Tangier, and trading concessions in the Portuguese empire, while England aided Portugal in their revolt against Spain, thus weakening Spain in France's interests; and (iii) the 2nd Anglo-Dutch War (Feb/Mar 1665–July 1667) – the result of English commercial and colonial aggression, and not of Clarendon's wishes. England won the battle off Lowestoft, Suffolk (3 June 1665), lost the Four Days' battle in the Thames (1–4 June 1666), and suffered the humiliation of seeing the Dutch sail up the R Medway and set fire to the English fleet at anchor in Chatham, Kent (13 June 1667). By the Tr of Breda (July 1667) with Holland and France, England kept New Amsterdam, which she renamed New York. To the strains caused by the war were added the Great Plague, the last bubonic epidemic in England (at its height in Sept 1665), and the Fire of London (Sept 1666) which destroyed 89 parish churches and 13,200 houses. Charles dismissed Clarendon in Aug 1667, sacrificing him to popular discontent, and giving a younger generation of politicians their chance.

The Cabal (1667–73): was not a united cabinet, but a motley group of ministers whose initials happened to make up that word: Sir Thomas Clifford, the Earl of Arlington, the 2nd D of Buckingham, Ld Ashley (later SHAFTESBURY) and the Earl of Lauderdale. During this period the K's actions aroused those deep suspicions which shortly became the basis of the support for Shaftesbury's Whig Party. (a) He gave his real confidence to Clifford and Arlington, Cath sympathizers. (b) He joined Sweden and Holland in the Triple Alliance against France (Jan 1668); but (c) signed the Secret Tr of Dover with France (May/June 1670) whereby LOUIS XIV gave him a subsidy and he promised to declare himself a Cath, to restore the Cath Ch in England, and to declare war on Holland. (d) He treacherously launched the 3rd Anglo-Dutch War (Mar 1672–Feb 1674) in support of France – expensive, unsuccessful and unpopular. (e) He issued the 2nd Declaration of Indulgence (Mar 1672), suspending the penal laws against Cath and Prot Dissenters; but Parl by this time was no longer so royalist. It forced him to withdraw the Declaration (Mar 1673) – as only Parl could suspend the laws – and sign the Test Act (Mar 1673), which drove all Caths from public office. The Cabal disintegrated. The D of York (future K JAMES II) resigned as Ld High Admiral (June 1673), and Clifford resigned as Ld Treasurer (June 1673), dying, perhaps by his own hand, on 18 Aug 1673. Shaftesbury was dismissed in Nov 1673, and the rest followed shortly after.

The rule of DANBY (1673–9): at first calmed the deep fears of French absolutism and Roman Catholicism which had been aroused by rumours of the K's pro-French foreign policy and by the revelation that the D of York – the heir to the throne – was a Cath. Danby reassured Parl and the business world with his deliberate support of Anglicanism (eg by enforcing the Penal Laws), with his hostility to France (eg by his sponsoring of the marriage of the D of York's daughter, Mary, to William, Pr of Orange (future WILLIAM III) in Nov 1677, and with his financial skill. Moreover, he made sure of majorities in both Houses of Parl by creating the Court (later called the Tory) Party, using methods of Parl management which became general in C18. Pragmatic and statesmanlike, he narrowed the gap between the pro-French, pro-Cath K and his anti-French, anti-Cath people; but he could not survive the upheaval caused by the POPISH PLOT and Ralph Montagu's revelation to Parl in Dec 1678 of Danby's nego-tiations with France in search of a subsidy for the K. (Montagu was ex-ambassa-dor to France, and the enemy of Danby, who had not promoted his career.) The Cavalier Parl grew increasingly hostile. It passed the Parl Test Act (Nov 1678) excluding all Caths except the D of York from both Houses. It began impeach-ment proceedings against Danby (Dec 1678). The K dissolved it (Jan 1679), and exiled York to Brussels (Mar 1679); but the new Parl – the 1st Exclusion Parl (Mar–July 1679) – had a 2–1 opposition majority after an election fought on party lines. It forced Danby to resign (Mar 1679) and continued the impeachment proceedings. The K gave him a royal pardon (Mar 1679). The H of C ruled that this was illegal. The H of L imprisoned him in the Tower (Apr 1679) where he remained for 5 years.

The Exclusion Crisis (1679–81): was dominated at first by SHAFTESBURY (under whom it is described). He transformed the arts of electioneering and Parl management, but the K was victorious in the end, thanks partly to his easy-going ability to sit tight and ride out the storm, and partly to financial help from Louis XIV. The 1st Exclusion Parl passed the Habeas Corpus Amendment Act (May 1679), which increased the rights of the subject and decreased the powers of the State in political trials; but when the H of C passed the 1st Exclusion Bill, the K ordered a dissolution. In the 2nd Exclusion Parl (Oct 1679–Jan 1681), which did not meet until Oct 1680, the 2nd Exclusion Bill was defeated in the H of L thanks to HALIFAX, who split the Exclusion forces. Charles himself was present at the debates, standing with his back to the fire. He dissolved Parl, and ordered the 3rd Exclusion Parl (Mar 1681) to meet in Oxford to avoid the City mob. The Court occupied Christ Church, Merton and Corpus; the Whigs stayed at Balliol; and as soon as the H of C began to debate Exclusion, Charles ordered the dis-solution. He could afford to do so, having just agreed with France (Mar 1681) to receive about £400,000 over the next 3 years in return for England's good be-haviour in European affairs.

Absolute rule (1681–5): marked Charles's last years, aided by his ministers, Rochester, SUNDERLAND, GODOLPHIN and Halifax, and characterized by Whig ruin and Tory triumph. Shaftesbury had over-exploited Exclusion and the Plot, and a sated public swung back behind the K. Shaftesbury fled into exile and death, while his lieutenants soon became implicated (perhaps innocently) in the Rye House Plot (1683), a wild, radical scheme to assassinate the K and his brother at Newmarket, Suffolk. William Ld Russell and Algernon Sidney were executed, the Earl of Essex cut his own throat, and the others involved fled abroad. At the same time, the K conducted a fierce campaign to destroy the basis of Whig strength in the boroughs. London and 50 other boroughs either surrendered their charters voluntarily or were forced to do so under so-called *quo warranto* proceedings. They then received them back 'regulated' – a process which eliminated Dissenters (in accordance with the Corporation Act, 1661) and ensured Tory domination. Meanwhile, thanks to French subsidies, the up-turn in trade, and the financial reforms of Danby and Rochester, Charles had no intention of calling a Parl, though after Mar 1684 he was acting illegally according to the Triennial Act. And even if he had called one, he was quite safe from a Whig majority. He d at Whitehall from a stroke.

Charles II (6 Nov 1661–1 Nov 1700) K of Spain (17 Sept 1665), an invalid under whose rule the decline of SPAIN accelerated. Having no children and being expected to die at any moment, he created a succession problem which galvanized European diplomacy and led, on his death, to the War of the Spanish Succession (1702–13/14).

Son of K PHILIP IV and his 2nd Q consort, Maria Anna, sister of Emp LEOPOLD I; m 1st (Nov 1679) Marie Louise, daughter of Philip, D of Orléans (brother of K LOUIS XIV of France) (she d Feb 1689); m 2nd (May 1690) Maria Anna (Mariana) of Neuburg, sister-in-law of Leopold I (d 1740).

1665–75, during the Regency of the Q Mother, power was in the hands, 1st, of her German Jesuit confessor, Father Johann Eberhard Nithard (1665–9), and then of her favourite, Fernando de Valenzuela (1669–75); while the K's vain and incompetent bastard half-brother, Don John of Austria – whom Nithard had expelled from Court – tried unsuccessfully to seize power in a military coup backed by Aragon (1669). In this sorry period the favourites enriched themselves while the Crown went bankrupt, the grip of Madrid over the provs slackened, the bureaucrats circulated paper from one Council to another and made what profit they could on the money they had invested in buying their jobs; real power became disseminated among the prov Grandees and other strong men. The ministers of the Q Mother harassed trade by manipulating the currency, and they could only cower before the aggressions of K Louis XIV of France. They signed a Tr of Commerce with Great Britain (May 1667) inviting British intervention in the Spanish economy. They conceded independence to Portugal (Feb 1668) ending a war which had begun with the REVOLUTION OF PORTUGAL (1640). They had to endure the French invasion of the Spanish Netherlands in the War of Devolution, 1667–8 (*see* LOUIS XIV), and lost Lille and 11 other fortresses on the border in the Tr of Aix-la-Chapelle (May 1668).

1675–1700 saw no essential change in the gov of Spain as Charles came of age. Currency manipulation and economic depression reached their worst in 1680 when the Crown defaulted once more; while the prov nobility continued to defy the authority of Madrid with increasing insolence.

Charles was the grotesque end-product of generations of Habsburg inbreeding. Small and weak, and subject to many physical disorders, he was incapable of masticating because he had the 'Habsburg jaw' to such a degree that his upper and lower teeth did not meet. At the same time, he was too lazy to do a proper day's work as a ruler; and he jeopardized Spain's future by not producing an heir. (He had been rendered impotent by witchcraft, it was believed.) At the start, Don John carried out a successful coup from Aragon (1676), throwing out Valenzuela, and putting the Q Mother in a convent in Tours. He had no staying power, however, and Charles ruled henceforth through a succession of chief ministers, only one of whom – the Conde de Oropesa, who ruled 1685–91 – made serious efforts to make the machinery of gov function and to modernize the economy. Abroad, Spain suffered the aggressions which France perpetrated in the Franco-Dutch War, 1672–9. The Spanish Netherlands, Franche Comté and Catalonia were invaded, and by the Tr of Nijmegen (Sept 1678) Spain had to cede Franche Comté as well as exchange some fortresses with France so as to strengthen the border with the Spanish Netherlands. In the next period (1679–84), Charles could do nothing to stop Louis' annexation of Spanish property in the Netherlands (eg Luxemburg, June 1684) through his *Réunions*. In fact, he had to recognize them in a 20-year truce (1684). In the War of the League of Augsburg, 1689–97, French armies once more marched over the Spanish Netherlands and invaded Catalonia, taking Barcelona (1697), once the British fleet was not there to protect it. However, by the Trs of Rijswijk (1697), Louis returned all his conquests to Spain. He was moderating his behaviour owing to the decline in Charles's health. He hoped soon to acquire much of the Spanish empire through diplomacy, not war. When Charles's attacks of fever, giddiness, rashes and discharges became punctuated by grave illnesses, it was decided that the time had come for him to make his will. The 2 chief claimants were Louis XIV and Leopold I, whose mothers and wives were respectively daughters and grand-daughters of K Philip IV, Louis being linked to the eld girl in each case. Leopold decided to aim at the whole inheritance even if it meant war. Louis, on the other hand, was realistic enough to know that for either Austria or France to inherit the whole would upset the BALANCE OF POWER to such a degree that Britain, the United Provinces and the rest of Europe would not stomach it. He therefore agreed with WILLIAM III in the 1st Partition Tr (Oct 1698) to share out the inheritance (Spain, the American colonies, the Spanish Netherlands, Sardinia, Milan, some Tuscan ports, Naples and Sicily) between France, Austria, and a 3rd claimant, Joseph Ferdinand, the 7-year-old Electoral Pr of Bavaria. grandson of Leopold and his 1st (Spanish) wife. In Madrid, Charles manfully refused to break up his dominions and left everything in his will to Joseph Ferdinand. Unfortunately, the latter soon d (Feb 1699) and opened up the whole question again. While the French and Austrian embassies competed for influence round Charles's sick-bed, Louis and William signed the 2nd Partition Tr (June 1699), dividing up the inheritance differently. In Madrid the dying K patriotically insisted on the unity of his possessions, while the pro-French faction triumphed. Just before he d, Charles made another will (Oct 1700), making Louis' grandson, Philip of Anjou, his sole heir. When Louis accepted it, the War of the Spanish Succession, 1702–13/14, could hardly be avoided.

Charles III (20 Jan 1716–14 Dec 1788) D of Parma (1732), K of Naples and Sicily (the Two Sicilies, 1734), and K of Spain (Aug 1759), who was an EN-LIGHTENED ABSOLUTIST in both his Kdoms. In Spain and the colonies he reformed the central, prov and local admin in ways which gave the State more power to impinge on all aspects of life. He increased the revenue, expanded the army, subordinated the Ch, modernized higher education, stimulated the economy and formed the Spanish nation out of what had been a collection of peoples with prov loyalties. On the other hand, he left behind certain funda-mental problems which he failed to tackle. Abroad, he raised Spain once more to the rank of a great power, and intervened in the SEVEN YEARS WAR (1756–63) and the WAR OF AMERICAN INDEPENDENCE (1776–83), in the latter regaining Minorca and Florida.

Eld son of K PHILIP V and his 2nd Q consort, Isabella Farnese; ed broadly under the direction of the Conde de San Estabán; m (May 1738, by proxy) Maria Amalia, daughter of Augustus III, K of Poland and El of Saxony (d 1760). A short, thin, long-nosed and round-shouldered man, he behaved in a simple, informal – even rustic – manner. He endured a long widowerhood in complete chastity; and he preferred frugal habits, country sports and a regular routine of work to the ostentations of Court life; though he was ever mindful of his supreme responsibilities as K, and always ready to assert his absolute power. He chose his ministers with sound judgement, and he was as reluctant to change them as he was his timetable or his clothes.

His reign passed through 2 stages: 1759–66: Rapid reform under Esquilache; 1766–88: Steady reform under Aranda, Floridablanca and Campomanes.

1759–66. Reaching Madrid from Naples in Dec 1759, Charles retained many of FERDINAND VI's ministers, but brought his own right-hand man with him: the Marchese di Squillaci. He appointed him Sec of the Treasury (1759), then, in addition, Sec of War (1763). The new chief minister soon became hated in Spain, but he paid no attention, except that his name changed to the Spanish form of Marqués de Esquilache. (a) In foreign affairs, the new K abandoned the suicidal neutral policy of his predecessor, and joined in the Seven Years War. He wished to tilt the balance against Great Britain, which, under the leadership of the imperialistic PITT the Elder, was a dangerous menace to the economy of the Spanish Emp. He signed a Tr of alliance with France (3rd Family Compact, Aug 1761), and Britain declared war on Spain on 2 Jan 1762. Spain lost Havana, Cuba, in Aug 1762, and Manila, Philippines, in Oct 1762, both to Britain; but took Sacramento, a colony which Portugal had established across the R Plate from Buenos Aires. By the Tr of Paris (Feb 1763) – to which Spain adhered in Aug 1763 – Spain ceded Florida to Britain, allowed Britain to cut logwood in Honduras, and renounced her claims to share the fishing in Canada. She also returned Sacramento to Portugal; but regained Havana and Manila from Britain; and gained Louisiana from France. (b) In home affairs (i) Esquilache set up a committee – the *Junta del Catastro* – to reform the revenue collection, using a single tax based on wealth; but the bitter opposition of the nobility and other privileged groups blocked any basic reform in practice. (ii) He alienated the nobility also by another change. He reorganized the Council of Castile, and recruited *manteístas* (career lawyers and bureaucrats from the minor nobility) in place of *colegiales* (children of titled nobility and grandees who had been to the exclusive schools which channelled them into the top positions). (iii) He antagonized the Five Major Gilds of Madrid – the richest bankers and merchants in the country – by trying to control their prices. (iv) He angered the clergy by further measures of *regalismo* (ie the policy of increasing the power of the Crown over the Ch, and decreasing that of the Pp). He increased clerical taxation, reduced the powers of the Ch courts, banned the publication of papal bulls and briefs without royal permission and decreed that newly-acquired Ch property would in future pay the same taxes as lay property. (v) He harassed the lower classes of Madrid and other cities by measures to improve city life with street lighting, water supply, refuse collection, vagabond hunting and crime prevention. His decree of Mar 1766 forbidding the wearing of the traditional long cloak and broad-brimmed hat – on the ground that they made it difficult to identify criminals – caused the riots which flared up into the so-called Mutiny of Esquilache. The people were already suffering from very high food prices, brought on by the droughts of 1760–66 and the free trade in grain which Esquilache had decreed in 1765. On Palm Sunday 1766, a mob sacked the minister's house and demanded his death. Madrid suffered two days of rioting and pillage until the K dismissed Esquilache and got him out of the country, withdrew the dress regulations and fixed lower food prices. The contagion spread to other cities as well, and it is still not clear whether the riots were spontaneous or organized by noble and clerical opponents of change. In any case, from then on Charles chose ministers who were more circumspect towards the interests they antagonized, and who moderated the pace of reform accordingly.

1766–88 was a period dominated by 3 Enlightened reformers: the Conde de Aranda, an Aragonese aristocrat influenced by the *philosophes*, who was President of the Council of Castile, 1766–73, then ambassador to France; and 2 Cath *manteístas*: Conde Pedro Rodríguez Campomanes, a *fiscal* of the Council of Castile, 1762–83, then President of the Council of Castile, 1783–91; and José Monino y Redondo, Conde de Floridablanca, a *fiscal* of the Council of Castile, 1766–76, and Sec of State and Sec of Ecclesiastical Affairs, 1776–92.

(a) In foreign affairs Spain continued to follow a mainly anti-British policy in alliance with France. (i) The Falkland Islands crisis (1770–71) arose from the longstanding Spanish claim to these British-ruled islands off the W coast of S America. Charles sent a Spanish force to occupy them in June 1770; but war was avoided thanks to the refusal of LOUIS XV of France to back Spain in this affair, and to the pacific attitude of the British gov under NORTH. Spain withdrew on North's unwritten promise (Jan 1771) that Britain would later surrender the islands. (ii) The War of American Independence (1776–83) gave Spain another opportunity to attack Britain. At first she joined France in supplying the rebels secretly; then she offered mediation, which Britain refused; then she declared war on Britain (June 1779). The Franco-Spanish attempt to invade England (July–Sept 1779) was a failure; and Spain concentrated on Gibraltar and Minorca. Gibraltar fought off several attacks, notably the assault of Sept 1782; but a Spanish invasion of Minorca (July 1781) eventually forced the British garrison to surrender (Feb 1782). The Tr of Versailles (Sept 1783) was the most favourable settlement Spain had signed for 200 years. She regained Minorca and Florida from Britain, though she once more confirmed the British right to cut logwood in Honduras. She also regained Sacramento by the Tr of San Ildefonso with Portugal (Mar 1778). (iii) The colonial Emp claimed much of the K's attention. In this era of triumph Spanish ministers were well aware of the unwisdom of supporting rebels against their lawful rulers, and fully conscious that, once independent, the USA could be just as dangerous to the Spanish empire as Britain had been. They set about improving the admin of the colonies, increasing central control by sending out *intendentes*, improving imperial defences, ending Cádiz's monopoly of colonial trade by opening up the emp to 9 other Spanish ports (1765), and in 1778 establishing more or less free trade between Spain and the colonies. The last decades of Charles's reign saw a great economic revival in the Spanish emp and an increase in gov revenues, though it is not certain how far this was due to gov intervention and how far to natural economic growth. Whatever the case, the K's attempts at Enlightened imperial reform had their dangers. They disturbed the position of the privileged groups, and stirred the hopes of the unprivileged; in both cases feeding a desire for colonial self-gov.

(b) At home Charles and his ministers fought a steady battle for reform against the entrenched beneficiaries of traditional privilege: the Ch, the univs and schools, the *municipios* (municipalities), the *señoríos* (lordships over towns and villages owned by nobles, monasteries, bps and Military Orders), the Mesta (a vast sheep-raising combine controlling large tracts of grazing land) and the gilds. Imaginative plans were produced, but only modest reforms achieved. Nevertheless, the plans were inherited by C19 Liberals. (i) The Gov continued to improve in efficiency. At the centre, the Council of Castile became once more the chief organ, with its *fiscals* and presidents acting as ministers. The K took decisions with each minister separately until 1787, when the *Junta de Estado* was formed – a Council of State to co-ordinate the policies of the different departments. In the bureaucracy, merit and experience counted more and more in appointments and promotions, while wealth and birth alone were less valued as qualifications. As the civil service became more elaborate, specialization of function increased, with the *intendentes* limiting themselves to military and revenue matters, and the *corregidors* concentrating on law and order. Elaborate regulations on civil-service structure, salaries and duties etc, were published in the 1770s; and 1783 saw a further bout of rationalization whereby the *corregidors* were to bring the *municipios* further under bureaucratic control, especially in matters concerning justice, finance and conscription for the army. These reforms, however, applied only to royal land, and the privately-owned towns of nobles, bps, monasteries and Military Orders went their independent way. The army improved in size, quality and self-consciousness, and by the end of Charles's reign it formed a separate power in the land, ready to intervene in politics. In local gov, little was done to remove the noble oligarchs from power, though the problem was continually under discussion. All that Charles achieved was to bring them under pressure from above and below: from above, by the *corregidors* and *intendentes*; from below, by the semi-democratic institutions brought in by Campomanes in 1766, immediately after the Mutiny. In each commune, the rate-payers elected 4 *diputados del común* and a *síndico personero* to sit on the town council and vote on matters of food supply. From 1768 onwards the big cities were divided into sections, in each of which the rate-payers elected an *alcalde de cuartel* to put down crime; and into sub-sections which each elected an *alcalde de barrio* to supervise law and order, hygiene, weights and measures, pauperism etc. They proved frail democratic plants, however. (ii) The Ch continued to receive the attentions of the K, who strongly favoured *regalismo*. Ch courts were weakened in relation to State courts. Asylum was restricted to 1 or 2 churches in each town. Higher ecclesiastical taxation was enforced. The INQUISITION – independent until then of both Pp and K – was brought under State supervision. It became less barbarous in its punishments, but continued to function as the terror of the Enlightenment. Moreover, the JESUITS were blamed, rightly or wrongly, for causing the Mutiny of Esquilache, and in Apr 1767 were expelled from Spain and the colonies, and deported to Rome. On 21 July 1773, under strong pressure from Floridablanca,

Pp Clement XIV abolished the Order altogether. At the same time the Jansenist reformers, Enlightened Caths who favoured a reduction in the power of the Pp, were given their head. Under their influence the Ch was made to cut down all the worldly indulgences which accompanied its festivals. The Age of Reason also insisted that for hygienic reasons corpses should be buried outside the churches, and that meat could be eaten on Sundays. Another aspect of the same Enlightened campaign was the foundation, with State encouragement, of learned societies to further science, the arts and economic progress: eg the Basque *Amigos del Pais* (Friends of the Country) of 1765, and the Madrid Royal Economic Society of 1775. These and many other societies all over Spain gave prizes, published journals, founded lectureships, opened schools and generally campaigned for the liberalization of the economy from its traditional restraints.

(iii) The economy has already been mentioned in connection with the liberalization and growth of imperial trade. In Spain itself, Charles's reign saw great improvements in commerce and industry, but not in agriculture. The Treasury and the improved civil service generally saw its task not simply as raising revenue, but as stimulating economic activity. One sign of improvement since the C17 DECLINE OF SPAIN was population growth. Between 1700 and the census of 1786, the population rose from about 7 million to 10.4 million. Communications also vastly improved, and under Floridablanca's impulse Madrid was connected with the capitals of the peripheral provs of Catalonia, Valencia, Andalusia, Galicia and the Basque provs by a network of trunk roads. Industry developed greatly in these provs; eg Barcelona was importing British spinning-jennies in the 1780s, and installed its 1st steam-engine in 1790. Castile, on the other hand, remained backward, and industry stagnated at the small workshop stage. Similarly, agriculture remained for the most part locked in traditional practices. Some improvements occurred, of course. In 1786 the Mesta lost its right of *posesión* (its perpetual grazing rights at fixed rents over vast tracts of Spain); while in 1788 landlords were given permission to enclose and plough up the pastures. Moreover, some landlords acted as miniature Enlightened absolutists on their estates. By the time Charles caught a severe chill and d in Madrid, however, he had failed to touch Spain's basic agricultural problem: the masses of under-employed landless labourers on the one hand and, on the other, the vast stretches of uncultivated land kept off the market artificially by perpetual owners through *mortmain* in the Ch, entail among the nobility, and all the rights of the *municipios*.

Charles V (24 Feb 1500–21 Sept 1558) D of Burgundy (1506–55), K (Charles I) of Spain (1516–56), Holy Roman Emp (1519), who, in spite of a lifetime's perseverance, was unable to solve the manifold problems of his many domains – far too extensive for one man to rule – and abdicated, retiring to a monastery.

b at Ghent, Netherlands, 1st son of PHILIP THE HANDSOME, D of Burgundy and Joanna (The Mad), later Q of Castile; m Isabella of Portugal (1526); crowned Emp by Pp CLEMENT VII at Bologna, Italy (1530); retired to a house by the Monastery of San Gerónimo de Yuste in Estremadura, Spain (1557); d of fever. Without great mental or physical qualities, but dominated by a zealous sense of obligation towards the RC Ch and his vast political responsibilities (he identified the interests of the two), Charles was overwhelmed by the multiplicity of his tasks and retired from public life, haunted by a feeling of all-round failure. For clarity's sake, each of his separate responsibilities will be treated in turn, as indeed he had to treat them himself, whether as D of Burgundy, K of Spain, ArchD of Austria, or HREmp; his all-European entanglements are treated under the HABSBURG–VALOIS WARS.

Burgundy (ie the Netherlands), the source of much of his revenue, which he visited 10 times, and where he spent a total of 28 years of his life, was ruled 1st by his aunt Margaret of Austria (Regent 1509–30), then by his sister Mary of Hungary (Regent 1531–55). Their policy was to introduce central judicial and financial institutions without provoking revolt; and no serious inroads were made on the independence of the 17 provs, no reforms were made in the Ch, and only Burgundians were employed in the admin (3 precautions later neglected, to his cost, by K PHILIP II, Charles's eld son and successor). The Regents did all they could to moderate the extent to which the wealth created by Burgundian commerce and industry was taxed by Charles V and squandered in his wide-ranging international wars, of little concern to Netherlanders, though the provs appreciated that being a cog in his machine gave them protection from France, their permanent enemy. However, exploited beyond endurance, the people of Ghent revolted (1539). They were savagely suppressed, however, and Charles in person ordered the abolition of Ghent's ancient constitutional privileges (1540). Another change in Burgundy's position resulted from the Augsburg Compromise (1548). Hitherto the N provs had been fiefs of the Emp. Now they were joined with the rest into the Burgundian Circle, independent of it.

In Spain Charles was K of Aragon and co-ruler of Castile with his mother. In all he paid 7 visits to Spain and spent 18 years there, ultimately establishing himself as a strong monarch capable of exploiting Spanish resources in men and treasure in his interests as HREmp, but at first finding himself confronted with serious trouble. On the death of FERDINAND II (1516) the centres of resistance to absolutism broke out in revolt, partly as a result of hostility to Charles as a foreigner who spoke no Spanish, and who angered the Castilian Grandees by appointing one Burgundian, Guillaume de Croy, to be Archbp of Toledo, and another, Adrian of Utrecht (later Pp) to be Regent (among other tactless moves). In the Crown of Aragon, the towns of Valencia formed a revolutionary union (the *Germanía*) in Dec 1519, while in Castile a league of towns called the *Comuneros* broke out in revolt (June 1520), aided at first by the Grandees and clergy. Both revolts grew so radical, however, that the gov was able to split the opposition and use the now frightened Grandees to put down the towns (which were led by the minor nobility). The forces of the *Comuneros* were defeated at Villalar (nr Toro on the R Duero, Apr 1521); the *Germanía* was gradually suppressed in the summer of 1522. The alliance of the Crown with the Grandees at the expense of townsmen and peasants continued for the rest of the reign, as Charles enforced the authority of the royal agents, the *corregidores*; as he more tactfully associated the Grandees with the high offices of State (not merely in Spain, but in Germany, Italy and the Netherlands as well), left untouched their privilege of paying no taxes, saw that they had more than their fair share of ecclesiastical patronage; as he gave his full support to the INQUISITION and the RC Ch; as he exploited to the full the military virtues of the Spanish upper classes in his widespread warfare in all parts of Europe; as he backed CORTES and PIZZARO and the other *conquistadores* of Mexico, Peru, Venezuela and the Indies; as he enacted the New Laws of the Indies (1542) taking the colonies out of the hands of these private-enterprising robber-barons and incorporating them in the general admin structure of Spain – with a view, partly, to enforcing the ideas of Las Casas in favour of protecting the blacks from excessive white exploitation. Under the Councils (of Castile, of Aragon, of the Indies, of the Inquisition) Spain became the most absolute, the most efficiently governed by the most sophisticated institutions, and the most profitable part of all his possessions. Unfortunately, Charles made a big contribution not only to Spain's Golden Century, but also to her later DECLINE. Firstly, the success of the COUNTER-REFORMATION locked the Spanish mind in archaic attitudes in a world where the prizes which history was awarding were going to free thought, capitalistic enterprise and advanced technology. Secondly, Charles squandered Spanish wealth on non-Spanish projects, causing a steady haemorrhage which was hidden from view during his reign by the dazzling inflow of silver from America. Unfortunately, this input did no economic good to Spain, but flowed out again to pay for imports which the Spanish ought to have produced themselves, to finance Charles's European wars, to pay the debts he owed to German and Italian bankers. His policy ensured that, one day, not only the Crown but the nation as a whole would go bankrupt.

Spanish foreign policy continued to lay most stress on hostility to France (in the Habsburg–Valois Wars) and to Turkey, which was thrusting by land at Vienna (*see* FERDINAND I) and by sea in the Med area (*see* SULAIMĀN II), endangering not only Charles's possessions in Italy (Naples, Sicily, Milan, Sardinia), but also the Spanish mainland itself, with its persecuted Moslem minorities. In spite of a continuing struggle and serious losses in both areas, a rough equilibrium was maintained, for both Spain and Austria were too far away from Constantinople to be in serious danger.

The Habsburg family provs (future Austrian Monarchy) were handed over by Charles to his younger brother FERDINAND I (1521, 1522), who also deputized for him as H R Emp during his frequent absences from Germany.

To the Holy Roman Emp (Germany) Charles made 9 visits, spending about 8 years of his life there – insufficient time to supervise a field in which his problems were the thorniest and his failures the most humiliating. In Germany, he not only inherited his grandfather MAXIMILIAN I's problem of the clash between imperial power and princely independence (complicated by the need to defend imperial interests from Franco-Turkish threats in the Balkans, in Italy and on the W front); but also found them raised to a higher degree of complexity and intensity by the REFORMATION, led by Martin LUTHER, which sanctified princely ambitions, attracted foreign aid, and gave ideological comfort to socio-economic unrest among the knights and peasants. Although determined to preserve the religious and political unity of his Emp, Charles was unable or unwilling to pursue either of the two possible courses open to him – suppression or conciliation – through to a conclusion. Instead, he dithered between the two, chary of harsh measures, on the one hand, when he required the Prs' support against the Turks and the French, and prevented, on the other, from instituting Ch reform and making overtures towards the Prots because of the hostility of the Pps, who were his political rivals in Italy and Europe in general, and who opposed the convening of a Gen Council in case it should turn the Ch into a limited – instead of an absolute – monarchy. And the Cath Prs were a further complication: for they were for him as Caths, but against him as Prs. On top of that, he spent roughly 30 of his 38 years as Emp out of Germany, dealing with the internal and external problems of his other states. Charles was elected K of the Romans (ie Emp designate) partly because he could spend more on bribes (850,000 florins) than his rival, FRANCIS I of France. After his coronation at Aachen (Oct 1520) he attended the Diet of Worms (Jan–May 1521), where the confrontation with Luther, and the Ban of Empire published against him (26 May 1521) were only part of the agenda. During his subsequent absence (until 1530) Protestantism took firm root; the 1st Diet of Speier issued a tolerant edict (1526) allowing each Pr or city to decide upon the religious question pending the calling of a Gen Council; while the 2nd Diet of Speier cancelled this (1529) and demanded the enforcement of the Edict of Worms. Against this, 6 Lutheran Prs and 14 reformed cities signed the Protest (Apr 1529) which gave the Prots their name. Returning to Germany, Charles called the Augsburg Diet (June 1530) to reconcile the two sides in the face of the Turkish danger. The conciliatory AUGSBURG CONFESSION of the Prots, however, did nothing to soften the papal position, and the final decree of the Diet (Nov 1530) threatened force against innovators in religion and confiscators of Ch property. As a result, the leading Prot Prs and cities met at Schmalkalden (Thuringia) and signed a Compact (Feb 1531) setting up a military organization to defend Protestantism, which during Charles's second long absence (1532–41) gained further adherents in Germany, and made contact with Francis I of France and HENRY VIII of England. On his return, Charles made another attempt to reconcile Caths and Prots at the Diet of Regensburg (Apr–July 1541); but he was alone in wanting a settlement, for neither side was by this time prepared to budge from their entrenched positions. Reluctantly, he decided on force. The Tr of Crépy-en-Laonnois (Sept 1544) released him for the time being from the Habsburg–Valois Wars. The opening of the COUNCIL OF TRENT (Dec 1545) relieved him of the religious problem. He was free to tackle the political one, ie the insubordination of Prs and cities. Making an alliance with a Prot, MAURICE of Saxony, he defeated the Schmalkaldic League at the battle of Mühlberg in Saxony (Apr 1547), making prisoners of the leaders John Frederick, El of Saxony, and Philip, Landgrave of Hesse. Entering Wittenberg and seeing Luther's tomb, he seemed to be at the height of his power, but it was an illusion. For the military victory made no difference to his religious problem. The capture of a few Prs availed little against the by now well-organized network of Prot congregations. And when the delegates at Trent effectively sabotaged the Gen Council by moving to Bologna (Mar 1547) and thus put the ecclesiastical question back into Charles's court, his attempt at the Diet of Augsburg (Sept 1547–May 1548) to impose his idea of a compromise – the so-called Interim – had no success at all. Neither had Mühlberg solved the political problem, for Charles's authoritarian behaviour aroused the fears of all the Prs (including Caths), and even caused a rift with his brother Ferdinand. Maurice of Saxony now rebelled, and along with other Prot leaders made an alliance with K HENRY II of France (Tr of Chambord, Jan 1552), ceding him the imperial bprics of Metz, Toul and Verdun in Lorraine in return for financial aid. The ensuing war, in which the revolt of the Prot Prs (1552–5) merged into the last Habsburg–Valois War (1552–9), found Charles prematurely old and utterly unprepared. He lost both combats. In Germany, Maurice forced him to flee for safety from Innsbruck, Austria, down to Villach in Carinthia (May 1552), and then to sign the Tr of Passau with Ferdinand (Aug 1552), on to whose shoulders he was now beginning to unload all his German problems. This Tr gave Lutherans equal treatment with Caths, and promised that Germany would be gov by the Diet, as in the past – a confession of failure which Charles had to confirm by his signature of the Tr at Munich (15 Aug 1552). In Lorraine, Henry II occupied Metz, Toul and Verdun, and Charles's attempt to retake Metz failed completely. Having left the Emp to his brother Ferdinand, he now handed over Burgundy and Spain to his son PHILIP II (Oct 1555, Jan 1556). Leaving his heirs to negotiate the German PEACE at AUGSBURG (25 Sept 1555) and the Habsburg–Valois peace at Cateau-Cambrésis (3 Apr 1559), he himself retired to Yuste to await death.

Charles VI (1 Oct 1685–20 Oct 1740) Head of the Austrian Monarchy (17 Apr 1711), H R Emp (12 Oct 1711), the last male in the Habsburg line, he ruled over a federation of provs at last rescued from the menace of Turkey, and thenceforth able to revive under the influence of COUNTER-REFORMATION piety and baroque culture. At home, he was preoccupied with the problem of how to guarantee the integrity of Austria after his death without a male heir. He wanted all his dominions to descend to his daughter, MARIA THERESA; but he unwisely tried to achieve this by securing international signatures to an agreement to this effect – the Pragmatic Sanction – instead of providing the monarchy with a firm structure of centralized absolutism. Abroad, he entertained ambitions against Spain, France and Turkey, which were beyond Austria's strength, and he left her in a vulnerable international position.

2nd son of Emp LEOPOLD I and his 3rd wife, Eleonora Magdalena of Pfalz-Neuburg; ed by JESUITS, and deeply influenced by his experiences in Spain (1705–13) as the self-styled 'K Charles III'; m (1708) Elizabeth Christina of Brunswick-Wolfenbüttel (d 1750), a Lutheran converted to the R C Ch. Unsmiling, haughty and distant, Charles took readily to the piety and ponderous Court ceremonial he found in Spain. He went there during the War of the Spanish Succession (1702–13/14, *see* LOUIS XIV) as the candidate of Austria, Britain, Holland and their allies, in competition with Louis XIV's candidate, PHILIP V. The British fleet disembarked him in Catalonia (Aug 1705) where he headed the prov rebellion against Castile (which supported Philip V), staying there until 1711, when the death of his brother, Emp JOSEPH I, on 17 Apr 1711, forced him to return to Vienna. Here he ended the Hungarian war of liberation (1703–11) by the conciliatory Tr of Szatmár (Apr 1711). The War of the Spanish Succession was ended by the Trs of Utrecht, Rastatt and Baden (1713/14). By this settlement Austria received Milan, Naples, Sardinia and the Spanish Netherlands (Belgium). Nevertheless, Charles never abandoned hope of gaining Spain as well; and he imported into Austria his *camerilla* of Spanish advisers, as well as Spanish extravagance, with a Court of 2,000 employed persons and 30,000 parasitic place-seekers. Spanish mysticism also enslaved him: he trusted in God, but did not keep his powder dry. His favourite diversions were the opera, horsemanship in the Spanish Riding School and hunting.

At home, his reign brought little progress in the direction of unifying his dominions. (a) The gov was too fragmented at the centre, and too swayed by Court factions, for him to exercise firm overall control. He lacked the intellectual power, force of character, industry and decisiveness to dominate the Privy Conference and use it to co-ordinate the work of the various organs, ie the Treasury, the Supreme War Council and below them the separate prov boards: the Austrian, Bohemian and Hungarian Chancelleries, the Netherlandic Council and the Spanish Council (for the Italian provs). While team-work was lacking in Vienna, the Diets in the provs kept such a grip on the traditional liberties of raising revenue and recruiting troops that Charles never had resources adequate to his foreign ambitions. By the same token, the gov lacked the machinery to stimulate economic progress, and thus raise the taxable capacity of the inhabitants. (b) The economy languished in the presence of a number of unfavourable circumstances. The Austrian monarchy lay in the back-waters of S E Europe, lacking sea communications with world trade. Commerce and industry were hampered by prov tariff barriers, as well as the lack of navigable rivers and passable roads. They were also kept backward by the archaic powers of the gilds, and the shortage of manpower. The enserfment of the peasants and the racial variations in the towns hindered social mobility. The anti-capitalistic teachings of the Counter-Reformation strangled enterprise. As a result, Charles raised half the revenues enjoyed by GEORGE II of Great Britain, with $2\frac{1}{2}$ times the population; and out of his 25 million subjects he could produce only 100,000 soldiers compared with FREDERICK WILLIAM I of Prussia's 80,000 from $2\frac{1}{2}$ million subjects. Spurred on by Charles – whose experiences in Barcelona had given him a taste for commerce – the gov took mercantilist measures to encourage business. S Hungary and other areas devastated by the wars against Turkey were repaired and re-settled. Royal factories making porcelain, glass and textiles were set up. The Ostend Co to trade with the E Indies was chartered in 1722. Banks were opened, and roads built. Trieste and Fiume were developed as ports, and a highway (the *Karolinenstrasse*) was constructed to connect them with Austria and Hungary. It was all in vain. Capitalism would not flourish in a society where the State fostered the Counter-Reformation, shored up racial and social rigidities, and did little to break the antique powers of the gilds and the prov separatism of the Diets. (c) Culturally Austria succumbed to the Counter-Reformation at the time when more-developed states were experiencing the Scientific Revolution. Religious exaltation gripped the faithful who had just rolled back the Turks, suppressed or exiled the Prots, and victimized the Jews; and they fortified themselves against further heresy by putting Austria in a state of intellectual quarantine. Aided by the monarchy, the Ch kept science and reason at bay through its control of the univs, the schools, the pulpits and the press; and it turned men's minds towards other-worldly concerns through the enchantments of baroque architecture and ceremonial. Moreover, the same architects who built sumptuous churches and monasteries to the glory of God – J. B. Fischer von Erlach, Johann Lukas von Hildebrand and Jacob Prandtauer – also raised palaces to heighten the prestige of the monarchy. Led by the Court, Vienna flourished. No longer a fortress on the edge of Christian civilization, the city became a centre of fashion, renowned for its music, theatre and the other arts.

Abroad, Charles had fingers in more pies than was good for Austria. He put his trust in military and diplomatic adventures in scattered parts of Europe, instead of building sound institutions at home. He had conflicts, not only with Turkey, Spain and France, but also at times with Britain and Holland, his usual allies. (a) The Austro-Turkish War (1716–18) was Charles's response to Ottoman attacks on Venetian posts in the Morea (1715). Pr Eugen defeated the main Turkish army at Peterwardein (1716) and captured Belgrade (1717). By the Tr of Passarowitz (July 1718), Austria gained the Bánát of Temesvár (ie the rest of Hungary), the N part of Serbia including Belgrade, and parts of Bosnia and Wallachia. (b) The Austro-Spanish War (1717–20) flared up because Austria and Spain had not made peace at Utrecht (1713). Philip V of Spain had ambitions in Italy: ie he wanted principalities for the 2 sons of his Q, Isabella Farnese. Charles, for his part, refused to abandon hope of gaining the whole of the Spanish inheritance. Spain invaded Sardinia and Sicily (*see* PHILIP V) and Austria joined the peace-keeping Triple Alliance of Great Britain, France and Holland, making it the Quadruple Alliance (1718). This group dictated the peace settlement of Jan 1720. Spain returned Sardinia and Sicily; Austria recognized Philip V's kingship of Spain, and promised the succession to Parma-Piacenza and Tuscany to Isabella Farnese's sons. Austria also received Sicily from Savoy, handing over Sardinia in return. (c) Austrian diplomacy (1720–32) was complicated by 2 projects to which Charles gave high priority, and for which he was prepared to make sacrifices: ie the Ostend Co (chartered in Dec 1722 to trade in the E Indies where Great Britain and Holland were paramount) and the Pragmatic Sanction (an agreement which guaranteed that the provs of the Austrian monarchy would descend 'indivisibly and inseparably' to Charles's heirs in perpetuity). The Pragmatic Sanction began as a Habsburg family agreement, and was later endorsed by the Prs of the H R Emp, and then by the great powers. Charles revealed it first to his ministers in Apr 1713. In 1716 his only son d, and he named Maria Theresa, his eld daughter (b 13 May 1717), as his heiress. He spent 1720–24 persuading the Habsburg provs to sign, and for the rest of the decade the Prs of the Emp, most of whom finally agreed at the Diet of Regensburg (Feb 1732). The great powers signed one by one: Spain in 1725, Russia in 1726, Britain in 1731, France in 1735. In return for each signature Charles made concessions which weakened the Crown in favour of the provs, and Austria in favour of the powers. Austria and Spain caused a minor diplomatic revolution by forming an alliance (1st Tr of Vienna, Apr 1725) by which Charles hoped that the Ostend Co – which was making no headway in the E against British and Dutch hostility – could benefit from trade in the Spanish colonies. This created the counter-alliance of Great Britain, France, and their allies in the Tr of Hanover (1725). War seemed imminent, but Austria was not prepared to go so far in Spanish interests. Britain and France negotiated the 2nd Tr of Vienna (1731) whereby Austria allowed Spanish troops into Parma-Piacenza and Tuscany, and closed down the Ostend Co, while Britain recognized the Pragmatic Sanction. (d) The WAR OF THE POLISH SUCCESSION (1733–5/8) saw Charles involved in profitless warfare, beyond his resources. In accordance with the Austro-Russian Tr of alliance (Aug 1726), Charles supported the Empss ANNA in her war to place the Russian candidate on the Polish throne, and not the French. Moreover, this candidate – the El Frederick Augustus of Saxony – earned Charles's support by recognizing the Pragmatic Sanction. In the event, Charles was not able to campaign in Poland for he was simultaneously attacked in W Germany and Italy by France, Spain and Savoy, while receiving no help from his ally, Britain (*see* WALPOLE). By the Tr of Vienna (Nov 1738), the Austro-Russian candidate became K of Poland as Augustus III; but in return the French candidate – Stanislas Leszczyński – was given Lorraine and Bar, whose D – Francis Stephen, Charles's son-in-law – took Tuscany in compensation. In addition, Austria ceded Naples and Sicily to Don Carlos (the eld son of Isabella Farnese, and future K CHARLES III) and Tortona and Novara to Savoy, receiving in return the dubious advantage of France's signature to the Pragmatic Sanction. (e) The Austro-Turkish War (1737–9) was the disastrous contribution which Charles made to the Russo-Turkish War of 1735–9, Charles being dragged in because of his alliance with Russia. Unfortunately for Austria, the Ottoman Emp was going through a period of revitalization in which a French adventurer – Bonneval Pasha – carried out important military reforms. The Austrian army took the fortress of Niš and then lost it again (summer 1737), as a result of which Gen Doxat was beheaded and his C-in-C, Field-Marshal Seckendorf, placed under arrest. The new C-in-C, Field-Marshal Oliver Wallis, lost the battle of Grocka (Kroszcka), nr Belgrade (July 1739), and then had to fall back on Belgrade – a defeat for which he was gaoled for the rest of Charles's reign. By the Tr of Belgrade (Sept 1739) Austria had to make a hurried and humiliating peace behind Russia's back. All Pr Eugen's gains of the 1716–18 war were surrendered except the Bánát of Temesvár. Austria was thus in a weak position when Charles d. In the E, her ally, Russia, was becoming a rival in the Balkans; in the W, enemies were gathering to break up the monarchy as soon as his daughter, Maria Theresa, should succeed.

Charles VIII (30 June 1470–8 Apr 1498) K of France (1483), who gave her the advantages of increased centralized absolutism and the disadvantages of the HABSBURG–VALOIS WARS, which he started by invading Italy.

Son of K Louis XI and Charlotte of Savoy; feeble in body and intellect, and only 12 on succeeding, he was dominated (1483–92) by his elder sister, Anne, and her husband, Pierre de Bourbon, Ld of Beaujeu. On the death of the absolutist Louis XI, discontented aristocrats (including the future K LOUIS XII) rose against the Crown, helped by the as yet independent Duchy of Brittany, and such foreign powers as the Netherlands and England. Authoritarian Anne established order in France, defeated Brittany at Saint-Aubin-du-Cormier (July 1488), and m Charles to Anne of Brittany in Dec 1491.

At home, his reign was marked by internal peace and consolidation, comparative economic well-being, and gov reform. Steadily the foundations of the *Ancien Régime* continued to be laid: ie the superimposing of the institutions of a centralized, bureaucratic, absolute State onto a Medieval France consisting essentially of a loose federation of semi-autonomous provs, governed by the personal relationships of feudalism, and characterized by over-mighty subjects, an independent-minded Ch, regional variations and prov separatism. The chief ingredients of the new monarchy were a royal Council not dominated by the high nobility, a hierarchy of royal courts of justice to supervise the feudal and urban tribunals, a royal standing army in place of feudal levies, a taxation system to supplement the income from the royal domain and free from interference by the Estates-Gen. Though Charles was not keen on the drudgery of gov, his reign continued the tradition of his father and saw significant developments in all these fields.

It is a pity that his foreign policy was not equally realistic. In 1492 he was swayed by favourites such as Étienne de Vesc to overthrow the Beaujeu group and strike out on his own, and in particular to invade Italy. Charles had a questionable and remote claim to the Kdom of Naples, but his head was also seething with archaic notions of chivalry and vague and romantic ambitions to crusade against the Infidel, conquer Jerusalem, and be crowned Emp in Constantinople. As far as Italy was concerned, the invitation of Ludovico SFORZA, ruler of Milan, turned the scale. Charles safeguarded his rear by buying off K HENRY VII of England with cash (Tr of Étaples, Nov 1492), by ceding Roussillon and Cerdagne (near the Pyrenees) to K FERDINAND II of Aragon (Tr of Barcelona, Jan 1493), and by giving up Artois and the Franche Comté to MAXIMILIAN of the Netherlands (Tr of Senlis, May 1493). Thus, giving up the hard-won gains of his predecessors, and sacrificing the real and near interests of France to the foolish pursuit of will-o'-the-wisps in distant parts, Charles entered Italy through Piedmont (Aug 1494), and marched S through Pisa, Florence and Rome to enter Naples without a battle (Feb 1495). The Holy League of Venice (the Pp, Emp, Spain, Milan and Venice) was soon formed against him (Mar 1495), and Charles retreated, fighting the 15-minute-long, indecisive battle of Fornovo (6 July 1495) with the League, but managing to escape with his army intact home to France. Meanwhile, the absurdity of French ambitions in Italy was revealed as K Ferrantino of Naples re-established his control with the help which Ferdinand sent from Sicily. Moreover, Charles's aggressiveness led to the union against him of his chief enemies, the Emp Maximilian and Ferdinand and ISABELLA of Spain, an alliance cemented by the double marriage of their children: PHILIP the Handsome to Joanna the Mad, and Margaret to Don Juan (Oct 1496). These lessons were lost on Charles, however, for he was preparing a further Italian adventure when he d after an accident at Amboise in which he struck his head on a low doorway. He left no children.

Charles IX (27 June 1550–30 May 1574) K of France (1560) during the FRENCH WARS OF RELIGION.

2nd son of K HENRY II and CATHERINE DE MEDICI, he was only 10 when he succeeded his brother, FRANCIS II; and his mother ruled as Regent until he was proclaimed of age on 17 Aug 1563. He m (Nov 1570) Archdss Elizabeth of Austria, daughter of Emp Maximilian II, but left no children except for the D d'Angoulême, by his mistress, Marie Touchet. Sad, sickly and vacillating, he was dominated by his mother, whose policies contributed to the outbreak of the Wars of Religion in Mar 1562. Alternately in the grip of the Guises and the Bourbons, he had little effect on events except during the brief period of Hug ascendancy at Court, 1570–72, when the Hug leader COLIGNY, acting as a 2nd father, advocated unity at home in a patriotic war against Spain by sending troops to help the Dutch in the REVOLT OF THE NETHERLANDS. Coligny almost extracted Charles from the maternal influence, but not quite, for, by histrionically playing on his emotions and appealing to *raison d'état*, she eventually persuaded him to back the momentous decisions which led to the murder of

Coligny and the Massacre of St Bartholomew (23/4 Aug 1572). Depressed by remorse, he d at Vincennes of tuberculosis.

Charles X Gustav (8 Nov 1622–13 Feb 1660) K of Sweden (1654), who launched the War of the North (1655–60) against Poland and Denmark.

Eld son of John Casimir, Count Palatine of Zweibrücken and his wife, Catherine, sister of K GUSTAV II ADOLF, who were refugees in Sweden from the THIRTY YEARS WAR; ed carefully as a soldier, including touring abroad (1638–40) and service with the Swedish army in Germany (1642–5). He and his cousin, Q CHRISTINA, formed an adolescent romantic attachment which he would have liked to transmute into marriage and political power. She, with her subsequent distaste for marriage, instead had him appointed C-in-C of the Army (1648); and then used the crisis of 1650 to coerce the nobility into recognizing him as her heir (Oct 1650). He was crowned the day she abdicated, and shortly after he m (Oct 1654) Hedvig Eleonora of Holstein-Gottorp (d 1715), by whom he had 1 son, the future K CHARLES XI.

At home, he inherited a critical situation (*see* OXENSTIERNA) in which the long-term constitutional struggle between the Crown and the nobility was exacerbated by the urgent need to make the aristocracy disgorge some of its wealth in order to save the Crown from bankruptcy and to pacify the lower Estates in the Diet (*riksdag*) – burghers, clergy and peasants – who were growing mutinous at their high taxation. Decisive, ruthless and energetic, Charles adopted the policy long demanded by the commoner Estates: the *reduktion* (resumption) of Crown lands which had been donated to the nobility by profligate monarchs or sold to them by others for ready cash. In the Diet of 1655 he used the support of the 3 lower Estates – a traditional alliance in Swedish history – to force through a law to make the nobles give up 25% of the lands granted to them since Nov 1632, the date of Christina's accession. In practice the Commission appointed to carry this out achieved little, since the War of the North immediately began to monopolize the gov's attention.

Abroad, he started the War of the North by attacking the Poland of JOHN II CASIMIR though, impenetrable and unpredictable as he was, it is impossible to say exactly why. The chief factor was probably the apparently imminent collapse of Poland under the onslaught of the Cossack Rebellion (1648–57) and the Russian War (1654–6). Charles considered it urgent to occupy Poland before Russia did, as ALEXIS's westward advance threatened the Swedish emp in the E Baltic. Additional motives were the Cath John II Casimir's persistence in claiming to be K of Sweden; and Charles's desire to unite his restive people by deflecting their feelings against a foreign enemy. Whatever the case, Europe was soon electrified by his swift and daring 2-pronged attack: in the W through Pomerania to take W Poland and race high up the Vistula valley; in the E from Riga to penetrate deep into Lithuania. In the W he took Warsaw (29 Aug/8 Sept 1655) and Cracow (9/19 Oct 1655); allied with FREDERICK WILLIAM, the Great Elector of Brandenburg (Tr of Königsberg, Jan 1656); and forced John II Casimir to flee. In the E, Alexis stopped fighting Poland in order to attack Sweden (1656–8) in an unsuccessful attack on the port of Riga. In both there were numerous Polish magnates ready to swear homage to Charles as K. In 1656–7 John II Casimir managed to head a patriotic and Cath revival against

Sweden. He retook Warsaw (June 1656), but lost it again to Charles and the Great Elector after the 3-day battle of Warsaw, 18–20/28–30 July 1656. At this stage, however, Charles was abruptly forced to abandon his Polish exploits, for at home Denmark had declared war on Sweden (June 1657), encouraged by Holland and supported by Austria, while the Great Elector changed sides, joining Poland in the Tr of Wehlau in Sept 1657. Full of surprises as ever, Charles did not hasten back to Sweden, but invaded Denmark from the S, overrunning Jutland, and from there – in the exceptional winter of 1657–8, when the seas froze – hopped from island to island across the Little Belt and the Great Belt to attack undefended Zealand and Copenhagen. Denmark was forced to make peace (Tr of Roskilde, Feb 1658), ceding to Sweden Skåne, Halland and Blekinge (provs which completed Sweden's control of the Swedish peninsula N of the Sound) as well as the Island of Bornholm and the Norwegian territories Trondhjem and Bohuslän. Other clauses in the Tr led to protracted negotiations and Danish resistance until Charles decided that the only guarantee of Swedish security was complete Swedish control of Denmark, and thus of both sides of the Sound. He suddenly attacked Denmark (Aug 1658), but Copenhagen saved the day with a heroic defence (Feb 1659) led by K Frederick III and a patriotic citizenry, and helped by the Dutch fleet, and by Brandenburg and Poland. Charles d suddenly at Göteborg, where he had called a Diet to raise war taxes. His son was only 4, so a Regency took power and brought an end to the war in 3 Trs. In the Tr of Oliva (Apr/May 1660) with Poland, Brandenburg and the Emp, John II Casimir renounced his claim to the Swedish throne, Sweden gave up her recent conquests in Poland, and the Great Elector was recognized as the sovereign of E Prussia. By the Tr of Copenhagen with Denmark (May/June 1660) Denmark recovered some of her losses of Roskilde (Trondhjem and Bornholm) and Sweden gave up trying to close the Sound to foreign warships. The Tr of Kardis with Russia (June 1661) recognized that, so far, Sweden had been able to prevent Russia from seizing a foothold on the Baltic coast. This settlement marks the limit of Swedish expansion, when she had twice as much territory as she has today.

Charles XI (24 Nov 1655–5 Apr 1697) K of Sweden (1660), who overthrew the high nobility, turned Sweden into a bureaucratic absolutism, reformed the admin and the armed forces, and in foreign policy enabled Sweden to survive as a 2nd-rate power, independent of foreign subsidies.

Only son of K CHARLES X GUSTAV and his Q consort, Hedvig Eleonora of Holstein-Gottorp; ed under the Q Mother and Regents arranged by his father, with an outdoor rather than an academic bias; m (1680) Ulrika Eleonora, pious sister of K Christian V of Denmark (d 1693). His reign falls into 2 parts: 1660–72, The Regency, before he came of age, when a self-interested oligarchy of the high nobility plundered the Crown lands and led Sweden into an ignominious satellite position abroad; and 1672–97, The Personal Rule, when Charles allied with the minor nobility and the 3 commoner Estates (clergy, burghers and peasants) to give the Crown absolute power, supported by an efficient bureaucracy, and adopting a foreign posture of neutral independence, all paid for by a policy of vigorous *reduktion*: ie the resumption of Crown lands which had been alienated to the high nobility.

The Regency had been chosen by Charles X to continue his reform policy, including the *reduktion*, but a group of titled nobles led by the young K's uncle, Count Magnus de la Gardie, persuaded the *riksdag* (Diet) to set aside the will, and thus allow the lax and incompetent de la Gardie and his group to monopolize the Regency. Abroad, they brought an end to the War of the North (*see* CHARLES x) with the Trs of Oliva, Copenhagen and Kardis (1660–61) with Poland, Brandenburg, the HREmp, Denmark and Russia. After that they pursued a policy of oscillation between LOUIS XIV of France and his enemies, in the expectation of receiving subsidies to maintain the army and navy, though in the hope of never actually having to use them. At home, the *reduktion* was abandoned – to the great profit of the high nobility – and foreign subsidies filled the gap in the royal coffers. Though trade improved and certain progress was made – eg the foundation of the Univ of Lund, 1668 – sooner or later this dependence upon foreign powers for money was bound to lead the Regents into policies against Sweden's interests. In Apr 1668 Sweden joined the anti-French Triple Alliance with Great Britain and Holland. In Apr 1672 she allied with Louis XIV, who was about to launch the Franco-Dutch War, 1672–9. De la Gardie intended not to fight but to remain a neutral mediator, but France forced him to earn his keep by invading Brandenburg, where he was defeated at Fehrbellin (18/28 June 1675) by FREDERICK WILLIAM, the Great Elector. And while Sweden was being driven out of her strongpoints in Swedish Pomerania, Denmark seized the opportunity to overrun Holstein-Gottorp, and to launch the Scanian War (1675–9) on the Swedish peninsula itself. The incompetence and improvidence of the Regency was clear for all to see.

The Personal Rule of Charles began in theory when he came of age in Dec 1672, but not in practice until 1674, when he took charge in the crisis of the war. (a) Foreign affairs, dominated by the Scanian War, enabled him to assume dictatorial powers. By dint of total dedication and reckless bravery, rather than military genius, he defeated the invading Danes at Lund (3 Dec 1676) and by 1678 had cleared them out of Scania, a victory recognized in the Swedish–Danish Tr of Lund (Sept 1679). In N Germany, Charles was rescued by the long arm of Louis XIV, who forced Brandenburg to give most of Pomerania back to him by the Tr of St Germain-en-Laye (June 1679). Thenceforth, Charles followed a neutral foreign policy, taking no part in the War of the League of Augsburg, 1689–97, and generally maintaining a tentative peace with Denmark while nevertheless backing the D of Holstein-Gottorp, whose lands in the S of Denmark could give him a back entrance into Denmark if necessary. He was able to maintain his independent stance in Europe thanks to his governmental changes at home. (b) Domestic affairs were dominated by the consolidation of the absolute powers he had assumed as a war measure; and this involved stripping the high nobility of their wealth and power. He himself contrasted strongly with the Regents and their extravagant, Versailles-type style of life. Pious and narrow-minded, short-tempered and painfully shy, he was conscientious and abstemious. In alliance with the lower nobility, and with clergy, burghers and peasants, he overturned the constitution by constitutional means in a series of measures passed by the *riksdag*, 1680–93. (i) He revived the *reduktion*, introduced but not properly enforced by his father. He extended it, moreover, beyond the 25 % limit set by his father and, by means of the Great Commission, made the high nobility disgorge the royal properties they had taken over during the Regency. By the end of his reign the Crown held 30% of all land instead of the 1% it had held at the start; and the income from it freed him from great-power bullying abroad, and financed his wide-ranging reforms at home. (ii) The *råd* (Council) – the magnates' institution and the traditional defender of constitutional rights against absolutism – lost power during the Scanian War, as emergency measures had to be taken, and as Charles was able to play upon the rivalries between the magnates and the other social groups. The *riksdag* of 1680 declared that the K was not bound by the decisions of the *råd*. In 1682 its full name was changed from Council of State to K's Council. In 1693 the *riksdag* declared the K to be 'by God, Nature, and the crown's high, hereditary right . . . an absolute sovereign king'. (iii) The army was placed on a new footing: the *indelningsverket* or allotment system. It was a conscript, citizen army, paid by being given farms, or revenues from farms, on the lands which had returned to the K in the *reduktion*. It became the best trained and equipped force ever to leave Sweden, as its clockwork mobilization and early victories under K CHARLES XII later proved. (iv) The bureaucracy was much improved by a highly industrious K. The Table of Ranks (1680) made promotion depend upon service and merit rather than birth; and, though the civil service was still dominated by the nobility, it became progressively more open to commoners. Regularly paid and closely supervised, it became the well-oiled machine which governed Sweden during the 15-year absence of K Charles XII, and then ensured the preponderance of the *riksdag* in the so-called Age of Liberty after his death. There is no telling what glories it might have achieved under Charles had he lived. Unfortunately, he was only 41 when he d at Stockholm of cancer of the stomach.

Charles XII (17 June 1682–30 Nov 1718) K of Sweden (1697), a young and ascetic military hero who maintained the absolute rule set up by his father, K CHARLES XI, and led Sweden in the GREAT NORTHERN WAR, 1700–21, spending his whole reign – until his death in action – defending her against a coalition of Denmark, Saxony-Poland and Russia, later joined by Brandenburg and Hanover.

Eld son of K Charles XI and his Q consort, Ulrika Eleonora of Denmark; thoroughly ed, by good tutors in preparation for the kingship, in science, mathematics, philosophy, theology and the Arts, as well as political and military studies, in which his father gave him a practical grounding by taking him with him on official business; he loved music, architecture and the theatre, and was fluent in Latin and German as well as Swedish; he remained a bachelor, saying he was 'married to the army'. A 5-man Regency, trained by Charles XI, had been left to govern during the boy-king's minority, but in Nov 1697 the high nobility – the leaders of the constitutional resistance to absolutism – offered the K full powers, thinking a 15-year-old K would be easier to dominate than would the Regents. The obsequious commoner Estates concurred, and so the *riksdag* (Diet) declared Charles of age. The young K, however, continued the absolutism of his father. Tall, slim and fair, he impressed his subjects with his powerful will and his steady devotion to the religious and political duties he had learned from his father. He practised self-control, toughening himself physically and morally by self-denial and hard exercise. He was chaste, abstemious and brave, even rash; and he led his men in person into battle to arouse a like spirit of self-sacrifice in them. There was a tragic inevitability in the uneven struggle which Sweden faced in his reign, and in the total dedication with which he steeled himself to his impossible task. C17 Sweden had exploited favourable circumstances to conquer a Baltic emp which she was, in the long run, incapable of defending – in view of her small population and resources – against a coalition of her victims, especially when led by a new great conqueror, PETER I of Russia. Charles's enemies seized the opportunity of a minority gov to exact their revenge by launching the Great Northern War; and in it Charles's life was totally absorbed, from his invasion of Denmark (1700), through his victory over Russia at Narva (1700), his conquest of Poland and pacification of Saxony (1700–6), his invasion of Russia (1707–9) and his defeat at Poltava (1709), his long exile in Turkey (1709–14) to his homecoming and subsequent death in action at Fredriksheld, Norway, from a bullet which might have been fired by one of his own men. On his death, the civil service, which had governed Sweden during his absence, carried out the measures (1719) which established Parl Gov and inaugurated the Age of Liberty. At the same time the new Gov made peace with all Sweden's enemies, ceding Bremen and Verden to Hanover, yielding Stettin and most of Pomerania to Brandenburg, giving up her exemption from the Danish Sound dues and also her special support of Holstein-Gottorp, and transferring her Baltic provs – Livonia, Estonia, Ingria and part of Karelia – to Russia. Swedish absolutism was over – if only temporarily; but Sweden as a great imperial power was finished for ever.

Christian IV (12 Apr 1577–28 Feb 1648) K of Denmark-Norway (1588), whose ambitions for the domination of the Baltic and N Germany during the 1st half of C17 aroused the suspicions of Holland and other interested powers, provoked the resistance of the Danish nobility, and were eventually frustrated by the military superiority of K GUSTAV II ADOLF of Sweden.

Son of K Frederick II of Denmark, and his wife, Sophia of Mecklenburg; ed as a Lutheran; m 1st (1597) Anna Katerina of Brandenburg (d 1612); m 2nd (1615) Kirstine Munk (d 1629). (His sister, Anne, m K JAMES VI of Scotland.) He was elected K while still a minor and came under a Regency provided by the Council (*rigsråd*) till 1596, when he assumed what few powers the crown of Denmark enjoyed. A bluff, red-faced, hard-drinking hedonist, who could command the fleet in battle as well as plan new cities, he achieved a place in the affections of the Danish nation. Throughout his reign he was hamstrung by the short-sighted opposition of the nobility in their Council, which left him short of resources, and cramped economic progress with their subjection of the burghers and their practical enserfment of the peasants.

At home, he created a navy, but not an army. He encouraged investment in industry and mining, built new towns, improved the defences, extended the ports, and beautified Copenhagen. He founded Glückstadt in 1626 to out-trade Hamburg; but he was no more successful in this venture than he was in his ambitions for his E and W Indies Companies.

Abroad, he was able to play the great power, thanks to the income he received from the Sound Dues which shipping had to pay to pass through the narrows between Denmark and the Scandinavian peninsula, both coasts of which were his. His foreign policy was characterized by his rivalry with Gustav II Adolf of Sweden for supremacy in the Baltic, and by his brief intervention in the THIRTY YEARS WAR in the hopes of securing some cities of the HANSEATIC LEAGUE, such as Hamburg, Lübeck and Bremen, as well as a secularized bpric or two in NW Germany – Osnabrück and Halberstadt, for example – to add to Bremen and Verden which his family already controlled. He failed in both areas, for the nobility refused to provide backing for adventures which they regarded as more in the interests of the royal family than of the Danish State, especially his incursions into Germany which he pursued as D of Holstein, and thus as a member of the HREmp. (a) In the 1st Swedish War (or Kalmar War, 1611–13), he captured Älvsborg, but failed to conquer Sweden. The Tr of Knäred (Jan 1613) thus registered short-term victory but long-term defeat. Gustav Adolf had to repurchase Älvsborg with a large ransom; but Denmark failed to re-create the Union of Kalmar (which K GUSTAV I VASA had broken up in 1523) and still had to allow Sweden exemption from the Sound Dues. Moreover, Christian's aggressiveness threw Holland and the Hanse cities onto the Swedish side. (b) In the Thirty Years War, Christian made a brief and unsuccessful intervention in the so-called Danish War (1624–9), when, as the chief military arm of the anti-Habsburg alliance organized by Holland and RICHELIEU in the Tr of the Hague (Dec 1625), he was defeated by the army of the Cath League under Tilly at Lutter in Lower Saxony on 27 Aug 1626. He was forced to withdraw from Germany and witness the ravaging of Jutland by Tilly and WALLENSTEIN; and, though he made a brief alliance with Gustav Adolf to force Wallenstein to abandon the siege of Stralsund (Aug 1628), he withdrew from the Thirty Years War in the Tr of Lübeck (May 1629), signed with the Emp FERDINAND II. He relinquished his territorial ambitions in Germany, where his rival Gustav Adolf now took his place as the Prot leader. (c) His 2nd Swedish War (1643–5) may have begun with a surprise attack by Sweden, but it had been provoked by Christian's anti-Swedish diplomatic moves, his raising of the Sound Dues 8 times between 1629 and 1639, his attempts to limit Sweden's exemption from them, and his blockade of Hamburg in 1643. Denmark was decisively defeated, and by the Tr of Brömsebro (Aug 1645) had to recognize Sweden's complete exemption from the Sound Dues, give her the E Baltic islands of Ösel and Gotland, as well as the Norwegian provs of Jämtland and Härjedalen, and leave her in occupation of Bremen and Verden. Moreover, Sweden was to occupy Halland for 30 years (permanently, in fact), a geographical revolution which gave her the N side of the Sound – a stretch of international water which could no longer be regarded as a Danish river, as Christian had claimed. Humiliation thus marked his declining years, when, abroad, Sweden took Denmark's place as the chief power in the N and, at home, his indebtedness offered further opportunities to the nobles on the Council to reduce the powers of the Crown.

Christina (8 Dec 1626–19 Apr 1689) Q of Sweden (1632–54), who abdicated and became a Cath.

Daughter of K GUSTAV II ADOLF and his Q consort, Maria Eleonora of Brandenburg; ed, after being separated from the bad influence of her neurotic mother (1636), by Bp Johannes Matthiae, according to her father's will, like a man. Until she came of age on 8 Dec 1644, Sweden was ruled by a Regency under

Axel OXENSTIERNA who admitted her to Council meetings from the age of 14, and with whom she increasingly disagreed in her 'teens. She had 'naught of a child except age', said a contemporary, and 'naught of a woman except sex'. Stocky, masculine, early-rising, headstrong, vain and highly intelligent, she had a romantic attachment to her cousin, the future K CHARLES X GUSTAV, but by the mid 1640s she had ended it. She had determined not to m, but nevertheless to secure the recognition of Charles Gustav as her successor. Oxenstierna and the nobility opposed both these decisions, but she eventually forced them into compliance during the economic and social crisis of 1650, which was partly created by her extravagant gifts and sales of royal land to the nobility (see OXENSTIERNA). In the Diet (riksråd) of 1650 she backed the non-noble Estates – burghers, clergy and peasants – and scared the nobles into making a bargain with her. By Oct 1650, all Estates had recognized Charles Gustav as her heir, and she henceforth abandoned the radicals and reassured the nobles again. She also differed from Oxenstierna in foreign policy, being willing to make concessions in order to bring an end to the THIRTY YEARS WAR in the Tr of Westphalia (Oct 1648). As well as being a keen horsewoman, Christina was a gifted linguist and devotee of scholarship, philosophy, music and the visual arts. Her restless researches led her into secret contact with the JESUITS and by 1652 she was probably a convinced Cath, possibly swayed in this direction partly by her conversations with René Descartes, who spent some unhappy months in Stockholm (1649–50) and d there. Since conversion to Rome was a criminal offence in Sweden, her religious views were undoubtedly a powerful motive impelling her towards the very rare act of voluntary abdication. Others were the desperate financial position of the Crown, and the social unrest which came in the wake of the 1650 crisis, when civil war was in the air. She first announced her desire to abandon the throne to the Diet in Aug 1651, but she was talked out of it, and did not hand over to her cousin until 6 June 1654. In Brussels she was secretly received into the Cath Ch (Dec 1654); at Innsbruck she ceremonially embraced the faith in public (Nov 1655); and she entered Rome incognito (Dec 1655) and settled there. Though short of money, she became a leading participant in Rome's social and cultural life, and also intervened frequently in Vatican politics and international diplomacy – hardly the pious type of Cath the Pp had expected. She employed Scarlatti for her choir and Corelli for her orchestra. Bernini was her friend. In the Franco-Spanish war that dominated the 1650s she at first backed Spain, but soon swung to the French side. She visited France (1656 and 1657–8) to negotiate a foolhardy secret scheme with MAZARIN (Tr of Compiègne, Sept 1656) whereby France would conquer Spanish-held Naples and make her Q, then she would leave it to France in her will. Nothing came of it, however, for her Court Equerry, the Marquis of Monaldesco, let the secret out, a crime for which she had him executed at Fontainebleau in 1657. Back in Rome, she lived (and d) in the Palazzo Riario, meddling in papal elections, promoting the opera, trying to get up a crusade against Turkey, and accumulating an important assembly of pictures, books, manuscripts, medals etc.

Civil War, the English (1642–6) Between the armies of K CHARLES I and Parl, in which Parl defeated the K, but was then itself overthrown by Oliver CROMWELL and the Army, who executed the K and declared a republic. (For the course of the Civil War, *see* CHARLES I and CROMWELL.) Here follows an explanation of the immediate causes, the deeper causes and the causes of the victory of Parl.

The immediate causes began with the growth of hostility to the K compounded of 4 main elements: constitutionalist resistance to absolutism; separatist opposition in county and borough to centralization (practised by STRAFFORD, and others); Puritan and anti-clerical hatred of the Arminian measures of LAUD; nationalist shame and aggressiveness at the disastrous pro-Cath foreign policy of BUCKINGHAM. This hostility found expression in the 1st 9 months of the Long Parl which the K was forced to call on 3 Nov 1640 because he was bankrupt, having lost the Bishops' Wars against the Scots, on whom he had been trying to impose Arminian Anglicanism. By Aug 1641 a series of statutes, passed by a united Parl and signed by a defeated K, deprived him of the men and the powers which had aroused the opposition; this legislative revolution could have been the end of the matter except for 2 chief questions over which the K put his foot down and Parl divided into what later became the Royalists and Roundheads: (a) what kind of Ch was to replace that of Laud? and (b) what further concessions should be demanded from the K in order to safeguard those already gained? Charles by this time had aroused complete mistrust, and PYM and his party, appealing to nascent urban radicalism outside Parl, demanded control of the Army, and a negative voice in the choice of ministers. Fearing this – and determined throughout to defend to the death the monarchy he had inherited, by whatever means, however impolitic – Charles initiated the use of force in trying to arrest 5 MPs and 1 Lord (Jan 1642) who escaped to the protection of the City of London where opponents of the K had just won the elections. The Civil War began soon after.

Deeper causes. The events just outlined would not have occurred, and could not have resulted in such deep divisions in English society without developments which had evolved over the whole Tudor and Stuart period. In *Gov*, the Crown had failed to build a standing army and bureaucracy, and Parl had grown into a regular and essential partner in raising revenue and changing the law. In *the economy*, the growth of capitalism in agriculture, commerce and industry, along with the increase in population, the PRICE REVOLUTION, and the geographical discoveries, was transforming medieval life in all its aspects. In *society*, big transfers of wealth had occurred, strengthening the gentry and the professional classes, weakening the feudal aristocracy, diversifying the social structure, increasing social mobility and replacing service bonds with commercial relationships. In *ideas*, the revolutionary stimulus of the Renaissance and REFORMATION, the growth of science and reason, and the spread of lay education were filling men with new aspirations and values, Puritanism in England being an especially important element in the rise of an independent-minded and self-confident revolutionary group.

The victory of Parl can be ascribed to the following causes. (a) Charles and his generals – Pr Rupert, Hopton, Newcastle etc – were inferior in powers of organization and fighting ability to Pym, FAIRFAX and Cromwell. (b) Parl controlled the rich and populous S and E, including London and the chief ports, and also enjoyed the support of WARWICK and the navy. This gave them the material and psychological advantage of possessing the centre of admin and communications, a convenience which promoted a unified command and produced taxation, credit, prestige, manpower, war materials – all decisive in the long run, once the K, by not capturing London, had wasted the short-term advantages he had in the gifts of cash and plate and the superior fighting qualities of the aristocracy – who soon quarrelled among themselves. (c) Parl drew strength from the religious fervour and the superior numbers of the Puritans, especially in the cavalry, and especially when the war party gained control with the New Model Army and the Self-Denying Ordinance. (d) Parl was aided at a crucial point by the Presbyterian Scots, whereas the K suffered loss from his dependence on the Irish.

Clarendon, Edward Hyde, 1st Earl of (18 Feb 1609–9 Dec 1674) Moderate opponent of K CHARLES I of England who changed sides to become a leading Royalist in exile, who organized the settlement at the Restoration, and who was K CHARLES II's Ld Chancellor and chief minister until his dismissal and exile.

Eld son of Henry Hyde, a lawyer turned country gentleman; ed at home by the vicar, then Magdalen, Oxford, and the Middle Temple, practising as a lawyer; m 1st for love (winter 1631/2) Anne, daughter of Sir George Ayliffe (d 6 months later of smallpox); and 2nd (1634) Frances, daughter of Sir Thomas Aylesbury, Master of the Mint, forming a connection which brought him legal posts in the admin; elected MP for Wootton Bassett, Wilts, in the Short Parl (Apr–May 1640), and for Saltash, Cornwall, in the Long Parl (Nov 1640 onwards). In the 1st phase of the Long Parl (1640–41) he played a leading part in passing the revolutionary legislation which reduced the arbitrary powers of the Crown and championed the Common Law. In the 2nd phase (Oct 1641 onwards), when Parl split into what later became the 2 sides in the CIVIL WAR, he voted against the Root and Branch party in favour of limited episcopacy, and opposed PYM's Grand Remonstrance (Nov 1641), as well as his demand for Parl control of the army and Parl veto on ministers, and his appeal to public opinion outside Parl. Clarendon now became a royal adviser (Oct 1641), but was unable to persuade the K of the necessity of seeking a compromise with Parl. Clarendon was never fully accepted as a royalist, and the K did not consult him over his attempted arrest of the 5 members (4 Jan 1642). On the outbreak of the Civil War, Clarendon joined the K at York in May 1642, and thenceforth tried to be a moderating influence on the Royalist side. From Feb 1645 onwards, he was at the head of the council appointed to advise the Pr of Wales (who became K Charles II on his father's execution on 30 Jan 1649). He shared the Pr's exile – mainly in Brussels – vainly trying to educate him in his own image; and eventually, through the Declaration of Breda in concert with MONCK (Apr 1660), secured the bloodless overthrow of the Cromwellians and the restoration of the monarchy.

Becoming Ld Chancellor (June 1660) and Earl of Clarendon (Apr 1661), he was the chief minister in CHARLES II's 1st ministry (1660–67). This Gov was dominated by the older generation of the K's advisers, to whom Charles at first had to show deference and gratitude, but who soon demonstrated that they were out of touch with the 1660s, clashing with Parl, with the pleasure-loving Court, and with the new generation of ambitious politicians eager to take their place. Clarendon was high-principled and incorruptible, but rigid, aloof and censorious. He failed to foster a following among either the ex-Royalists or the ex-Parliamentarians, and did not appreciate the importance of Parl management; so that, when his diverse enemies united to overthrow him, the K was glad to see the back of his elderly and arthritic headmaster. His Gov was responsible for the Restoration financial settlement, which left the Gov short of money. His lack of Parl control allowed the persecuting so-called 'CLARENDON CODE' to be passed (1661–5), whereas he favoured a comprehensive Ch with limited episcopacy. His foreign policy led to the K's m with the Portuguese prss Catherine of Bragança (May 1662), though her barrenness was not his fault. He was also responsible for the sale of Dunkirk to France (Oct 1662). The 2nd Dutch War (Feb 1665–July 1667) did not have his approval, but he was blamed for its mismanagement, especially for the Dutch attack on the Medway (June 1667). He did not cause the Plague (1665–6) or the Fire of London (1666) or the intense cold of the winter of 1666/7, when the Thames froze over, but he was the necessary scapegoat. Moreover, his daughter Anne had m the future JAMES II, the K's brother (Sept 1660); and his overmighty pre-eminence as the father and grandfather of the future royal family was more ammunition for his enemies, among whom was the beautiful but irascible reigning royal mistress, Lady Castlemaine. Thus the disasters and the criticisms accumulated, but Clarendon failed to read the signs, or listen to the advice from Charles and James that his day was over. In the end the K had to dismiss him (Aug 1667); and he fled abroad in Nov 1667 to avoid impeachment. There, before he d, he completed the great literary works which are such important sources for the period: his *History of the Rebellion* and his *Life*, published 1702–4 and 1759, respectively.

'Clarendon Code' The inaccurate name given to a series of statutes passed by the Cavalier Parl of K CHARLES II of England to persecute Dissenters – inaccurate because CLARENDON, like the K, was in favour of a more tolerant policy. The Presbyterians, who were numerous in the Convention Parl, could probably have secured 'comprehension' – a Ch settlement which embraced all respectable Dissenters in one body; but, asking too much, they were out-manoeuvred into delaying a decision. The Cavalier Parl was dominated by Anglicans who had been convinced by the CIVIL WAR that Dissenters were social revolutionaries, a prejudice confirmed by the abortive London rebellion of the FIFTH MONARCHY MEN (Jan 1661) in the immediate expectation of Christ's reign upon earth. Out of revenge and fear, the Anglicans passed the 4 Acts which created the 2 separate worlds of Anglicanism and Nonconformity, so important in later English history: (1) *The Corporation Act* (Dec 1661) in effect limited municipal office to Royalist Anglicans. (2) *The Act of Uniformity* (May 1662) re-enforced the Prayer Book of Q ELIZABETH I, with no concessions to Dissenters, and led to the uncompensated ejection from their livings of 1,760 ministers and 150 dons and schoolmasters. (3) *The Conventicle Act* (May 1664) penalized anyone who attended a Dissenting congregation, or preached at one, or let any building be used for one. (4) *The Five Mile Act* (Oct 1665) drove ejected clergy away from towns and the places where they had ministered, and forbade them to teach or take in boarders.

This 'Code' resulted in a period of harsh persecution for all forms of Dissent, but Nonconformity nevertheless took firm root, especially in the 2-year interval between the expiration of the 1st Conventicle Act and the passing of the 2nd (1667–70), and in the 1-year intermission provided by Charles's 2nd Declaration of Indulgence (Mar 1672).

Clement VII (Giulio de' Medici) (26 May 1478–25 Sept 1534) Pp (1523), who concentrated on Italian and European power-politics and opposed Ch reform, and who was unable to prevent the domination of Italy by Spain, the spread of the movement of Martin LUTHER in Germany, or the divorce of K HENRY VIII of England and the subsequent breach with Rome.

Illegitimate son of Giuliano (brother of Lorenzo the Magnificent) and cousin of Pp LEO X, who made him Archbp of Florence and Card (1513). Industrious and conscientious, but vacillating and procrastinating, he did what he could for the Ch so long as it was not inconsistent with his 1st 2 priorities: the advancement of the Medici family and the strengthening of the Papal States. In the 5th HABSBURG–VALOIS WAR of 1521–6 he fought on the Habsburg side against K FRANCIS I of France; but changed sides after the latter's defeat at Pavia on 24 Feb 1525, and joined the League of Cognac (May 1526) and reaped his reward with the Sack of Rome (May 1527) by the Emp's army, during which he was locked up in the Castel Sant'Angelo. He became the Emp CHARLES V's prisoner, and in consequence he lost control of Florence where the Medici were ejected by the restored Republic (May 1527); and he was also unable to grant Henry VIII his divorce from CATHERINE OF ARAGON, who was the Emp's aunt, or prevent the separation of the English Ch from Rome. He threatened to excommunicate Henry in 1533, but this gesture came too late to be of any help to English R Cs loyal to Rome. His concern with the effect of international politics on Italy, coupled with his ignorance of the real situation inside Germany, also prevented him from any co-operation with Charles V in dealing with Luther. Fearful of adding to the Emp's power and terrified of the mere idea of a Council to reform the Ch, he instructed his legates to the various religious conferences (eg Campeggio at Augsburg, June–Sept 1530) to block all concessions to the German Prots. Moreover, his encouragement of French anti-Habsburg moves in Italy kept Charles V so tied up with international war and diplomacy that he had no time or strength to deal with the Lutherans himself by force until it was too late. Switching back to an alliance with Charles in the Tr of Barcelona of June 1529, Clement crowned him as K of Italy in Bologna on 22 Feb 1530, and as H R Emp 2 days later. For his part, Charles overthrew the Republic in Florence and restored the bastard Alessandro de' Medici as hereditary D (1531), a revolution confirmed by the Florentines in Apr 1532. Charles and Clement met again at Bologna from Dec 1532–Feb 1533 and concluded a Tr in Feb 1533 which was wide-ranging but practically meaningless in view of Clement's objection to a Ch Council and his renewed friendship with France, clinched when he travelled to Marseilles to meet Francis I, and to marry his cousin twice removed, CATHERINE DE MEDICI, to the future K HENRY II of France (Oct 1533). On Clement's death, the Medici were firmly in control of Florence, but Italy was at the mercy of the great powers, and large areas of the Ch had turned Prot.

Clientage ('Bastard feudalism') The system prevalent in CORPORATIVE STATES whereby great nobles – 'overmighty subjects' – acquired followings, and therefore power-bases, independent of the monarch, similar to feudal retinues of earlier times and political parties of later. Clientage networks were hierarchical, and stretched across the social strata; and the followers were bound to their leaders by several of the following ties: feudal vassalage, prov sentiment, religious creed, patronage, blood relationship, marriage, cash, blackmail or terrorism. Typical examples were the barons involved in 'livery and maintenance' under K HENRY VII of England, or the participants in the WARS OF THE ROSES, the FRENCH WARS OF RELIGION, the English CIVIL WAR, the FRONDES in France, or the REVOLT OF CATALONIA against Castile. One of the crucial tasks performed by rulers in states where ABSOLUTISM was emerging was to eliminate clientage by making the Crown the most attractive force in the country and giving it the first call on the people's loyalty.

Coke, Sir Edward (1 Feb 1552–3 Sept 1634) Judge under Q ELIZABETH I, K JAMES I and K CHARLES I of England, Attorney Gen (1594), Knight (1603), Chief Justice of the Common Pleas (1606), Chief Justice of the K's Bench (1613–16). His writings contributed massively to the process of moulding the traditional Common Law to fit later conditions, the chief being his *Reports* (1600–15, 1650–59) and his *Institutes* (1628–44). As a judge he defended the Common Law, as interpreted by Parl, against the ecclesiastical and other prerogative courts; and as an M P he led the Parl attack on the 1st 2 Stuarts.

b at Mileham, Norfolk (gentry); ed Norwich Grammar, Trinity, Cambridge, and the Inner Temple; called to the Bar 1578; m 1st (1582) Bridget Paston (d 1598); m 2nd (1598) Lady Elizabeth Hatton, a beautiful and wealthy widow 26 years his junior, with whom he soon quarrelled. She was the granddaughter of BURGHLEY, and it was under the latter's patronage that Coke became Solicitor Gen in May 1592, Speaker of the H of C in Feb 1593 and Attorney Gen in Apr 1594, defeating in the last instance his rival BACON, who was the nominee of Burghley's rival, ESSEX.

As a judge whose knowledge of the law was without equal he was domineering, bad-tempered and brutal in his prosecution of such defendants as Essex (1601), RALEGH (1603) and the men behind the GUNPOWDER PLOT (1606). As Chief Justice of the Common Pleas he stoutly defended the Common-Law courts against the encroachments of such prerogative courts as High Commission, Requests, the Council of the N and the Council of the Marches and Wales. James trembled with anger at being told that the law was superior to the K and, as a punishment and a warning, he promoted Coke to the less remunerative office of Chief Justice of the King's Bench. Coke did not come to heel, however, but persisted in proclaiming the superiority of the Common Law as interpreted by Parl over the royal prerogative. He denied the K's claim to legislate by proclamation (1610). In *Peacham's Case* (1615) he opposed the desire of the K to consult the judges individually before hearing the case. In the *Commendams Case* (1616) he refused to delay the hearing so that the K could speak to the judges. James reached the end of his patience and dismissed him in Nov 1616. Henceforth, Coke's platform was the H of C, and under his leadership the twin attacks on the Crown by Parl and the Common-Law courts fused into one aggressive campaign. Coke's zeal in defence of the law was inflamed by personal animosities. Although he reluctantly agreed (1617) to marry his beautiful daughter Frances to BUCKINGHAM's mentally deficient brother (giving her a very generous portion and settlement), he failed to get the Treasurership or any other office, except membership of the Privy Council. In James's 3rd Parl (Jan 1621–Jan 1622), he was prominent in the impeachment of the monopolists,

Mompesson and Mitchell, and of his old rival, Chancellor Bacon, for bribery. He also led the attack on Buckingham's Spanish-marriage policy, a controversy which raised basic questions about Parl's right to discuss foreign policy and about the status of Parl's privileges: were they dependent upon the K's 'grace and permission' or were they their 'ancient and undoubted birthright'? The latter view was recorded in the Protestation which the whole House voted on 18 Dec 1621, and which the K tore out of the Journals on 30 Dec 1621. Coke and others were arrested on 27 Dec and kept in the Tower for 8 months. In the 4th Parl (Feb 1624–Mar 1625), he supported the war against Spain (to which Buckingham had swung round on the failure of the Spanish marriage trip) and backed the impeachment of another rival, Ld Treasurer CRANFIELD (May 1624). In Charles's 1st Parl (June–Aug 1625), he stood out as an opponent of the Crown in a Parl which voted customs (Tunnage and Poundage) for one year instead of for the K's life, imprisoned the Arminian, Dr Montagu, and attacked Buckingham's conduct of foreign affairs. He was excluded from the 2nd Parl (Feb–June 1626), for, along with other opposition leaders, he had been made Sheriff – though typically he appeared at Westminster with a wealth of precedents for Sheriffs being made MPs. In the 3rd Parl (Mar 1628–Mar 1629), he suggested the idea of preparing the Petition of Right – hitherto a method used for private grievances only – and it received the royal assent on 7 June 1628. He did not sit in the 1629 Session of this Parl, but went into retirement; and while he lay on his death-bed at Stoke Poges, Bucks, the K's officers were searching his house and seizing his papers. 'We shall never see his like again,' wrote his widow, 'praises be to God!'

Colbert, Jean-Baptiste (29 Aug 1619–6 Sept 1683) One of the chief ministers of LOUIS XIV of France, concerned mainly with financial and economic policy.

Son of Nicolas Colbert, merchant and office-holder, and his wife, Marie Pussort; ed in commerce and banking; rose in the service of the chief minister, MAZARIN, and was recommended by him on his death-bed to Louis XIV, who found him just what he wanted: an able and industrious policy-maker and administrator who could dominate France but remain the K's servant and never become an over-mighty subject. Cold, gloomy and austere, with a passion for figures and a head for detail, but also an awareness of the broad view and the long term, he began his rise to power by organizing the downfall, trial and imprisonment of his chief, Nicolas Fouquet, the Superintendent of Finances, whose wealth and power were an affront to the K's new policy of himself ruling without a chief minister. Colbert became the leading member of the Council of Finances (1661), Superintendent of Royal Buildings, Arts and Manufactures (1664), Controller-Gen of Finances (1665) and Sec of State for the Navy (1668), among other offices. He helped the K to extend the absolute power of the monarchy into all aspects of French life. He was chiefly responsible for the consolidation of the new bureaucratic machinery under the Intendants, for the improved policing of Paris, and for the new law codes, but his main concerns were (a) the royal finances, (b) agriculture, (c) commerce, (d) industry and (e) the arts.

The royal finances were greatly improved by tighter admin efficiency at the centre and in the provs; by careful budgeting based on a thorough survey of resources; by the punishment of peculation and waste; by the close scrutiny of false titles to nobility and other fraudulent methods of tax evasion; by the sale of honours and offices; by the repudiation of some Crown debts and the conversion of others to lower interest rates; by the resumption of alienated parts of the royal domain and the more profitable exploitation of all the K's property, especially the forests; by manipulating the currency; by uniting all the various farmed taxes into one General Farm (1680) and exacting better terms from the tax-farmers. These reforms enabled Colbert to increase the royal revenues while decreasing the burden on the peasants; but his grandiose plans for the rational reform of French revenues – eg for levying taxes in accordance with wealth, and assessing wealth by a land survey – were never fully implemented. The Crown's expenditure always exceeded its income, thanks to the chief curses of the *Ancien Régime*: the unlimited power of the monarch to indulge in extravagant policies on the one hand, and the taxation privileges of the clergy, the nobility and the office-holders on the other.

Agriculture tended to be left to its own devices as, in the thinking of the time, it did not add directly to the nation's stock of capital. Moreover, being dependent upon nature for its ups and downs, it was less susceptible than commerce and industry to Gov control, even that of Louis XIV. Colbert steered a middle course between conflicting interests. He needed low food prices for his urban workers, but he needed a prosperous peasantry to pay his taxes.

Commerce received much more of Colbert's attention, for only a favourable balance of trade, he reasoned, could enrich the nation, thus increasing its taxable capacity, and adding to the royal income. Using the new Council of Commerce set up in 1664 he applied in a thorough-going fashion the usual mercantilist policies favoured in his day. He encouraged the export of home-manufactured goods, and discouraged the import of foreign. He discouraged the export of raw materials used in industry and encouraged their import. He forbade skilled craftsmen to emigrate, and persuaded Dutch weavers, German miners and Italian silk and glass experts to settle in France by offering special privileges. He built a navy and a merchant fleet; he improved roads, bridges, canals, rivers and harbours; he tried to eliminate the internal customs duties which cluttered French trade at all points, though without much success, as there were too many powerful fingers in that pie. He created overseas trading companies, assisting them with capital and monopolies, though they showed little staying power, and failed to attract investment from the French bourgeoisie, for the latter preferred to buy gov *rentes* or offices rather than risk their savings in the West Indies Co (1664–74), the Northern Co (1669–84), the Levant Co (1670–90) or the E Indies Co (1664) – the only one to survive Louis' reign. He encouraged the colonization of Canada (New France). He tried to loosen the grip which the United Provinces had on the French economy and on world commerce: he imposed the prohibitive tariff of 1667, and he supported the Franco-Dutch war of 1672–9 (*see* LOUIS XIV).

Industry – the ultimate source of a favourable trade balance and therefore of the K's income – had a special place in Colbert's thinking: not the small crafts serving local French markets, but large-scale industry exporting to the world. He helped such firms with capital, expertise, monopolies, high tariffs, buildings, raw materials and even the royal name, as in the many *manufactures royales*. His Intendants and Inspectors of Manufactures imposed uniform standards of length, breadth, weight and quality of finish; and, though they eventually became a drag on private enterprise, they established the world reputation of the French as producers of the finest luxury goods: silks, lace, glassware, clocks, carpets, tapestries, jewellery and clothes.

The arts, crafts and sciences came under Colbert's scrutiny, to make sure they were used to the greater glory of the Sun King. Through its role as the chief builder of palaces, and as the top audience for opera, in fact through its influence as the main market for artistic products of all kinds, and through its control of the Academies which trained all the artists, the monarchy imposed a uniform style on all French output (for it was copied by the nobility and bourgeoisie) which impressed Europe just as forcibly as Louis' victories in war. In 1663 Colbert founded the Little Academy of Inscriptions and Medals to supervise the wording on medals, coins and monuments, and brought the private Academy of Painting and Sculpture under State control. Later foundations were the Academy of Science (1666), the French Academy in Rome (1666), the *Académie Française* (brought under the State in 1671), the Academy of Architecture (1671) and the Academy of Music (1672).

More than any other minister, Colbert was responsible for providing the resources which enabled Louis XIV to establish absolutism in France, and France to become the chief power in Europe. Colbert also enriched himself and his family. His brother, Colbert de Croissy, became Foreign Sec. His nephew, Nicolas Desmaretz, became Controller-Gen of Finances. His 1st son, the Marquis de Seignelay, became Minister of the Marine; his 2nd became Archbp of Rouen. 3 of his daughters m dukes. On the other hand, his impact on France fell short of his plans, and the gains he made for her were jettisoned in the K's insatiable lust for glory. When he d in Paris, he had for some time been eclipsed in the K's councils by Louvois, his war-monger rival.

Colet, John (?1467–16 Sept 1519) Dean of St Paul's (1505), English exponent of HUMANISM and RC reformer.

Son of Sir Henry Colet (of the Mercers' Co and twice Ld Mayor of London) and Christian Knyvet (member of a well-known Norfolk gentry family); ed London, Oxford, France and Italy. He then began his famous course of lectures at Oxford on the Epistles to the *Romans* and to the *Corinthians* (among others), which were innovatory in at least 2 ways: they were a return to the Scriptures anticipatory of the whole drift of Protestantism, and they approached the texts as a Humanist might treat a Roman or a Greek author. Colet attacked the abuses in the Ch, criticizing the worldliness of the clergy and the mechanical image-worship of the laity; he believed that the only way back to holiness was through the study of the Bible, whose truths were now being fully revealed by the New Learning. As Dean of St Paul's (1505–19) he preached many sermons with this message; and as a practical step forward he founded St Paul's School (1510) with the fortune his father left on his death. He placed the school under lay governors: the Mercers' Co. His advanced views once brought him before the Ch courts for heresy (his accuser being the Bp of London), but Archbp William WARHAM dismissed the case; and, together with MORE, ERASMUS and others, he did much to shape the mentality of the generation of educated Englishmen who supported the REFORMATION of K HENRY VIII.

Coligny, Gaspard de Châtillon, Comte de (16 Feb 1519–24 Aug 1572) Leader of the Hugs during the FRENCH WARS OF RELIGION till he was assassinated in the Massacre of St Bartholomew.

Son of Gaspard de Coligny and Louise de Montmorency (sister of the future Constable, Anne de MONTMORENCY) he rose in the French Court and military forces under the patronage of his uncle, who was a leading minister to FRANCIS I, HENRY II and CHARLES IX. He served in the Italian campaign of 1544, became Col-Gen of the Infantry (1547) and Admiral of France (1552). During the last HABSBURG–VALOIS WAR, when he was Gov of Picardy, he unsuccessfully defended St Quentin from a Spanish attack in Aug 1557, and was held prisoner at Sluys, Netherlands, until the Tr of Cateau-Cambrésis (Apr 1559) released him. During this period he was converted to Calvinism after an intense study of the Bible; and he and his 2 brothers became an important addition to the Hug cause during the Wars of Religion which now broke out. Unlike many noble converts who hoped to manipulate the Hug cause for their own political ends, Coligny was a sincere believer, an ingenuous and uncomplicated idealist, whose aim was to eliminate the forces of anti-Christ in France, or at least secure freedom of worship for the Hugs. His personal magnetism, his patent honesty and his hostility to plans for overthrowing the monarchy or overturning the social order conferred respectability on the Hug cause, and attracted support from otherwise suspicious members of the upper classes. He played a central role, along with Louis, Pr de CONDÉ, and Theodore Beza, in the unsuccessful attempts to secure a religious compromise (1560–62), and then reluctantly followed Condé into action when hostilities could no longer be avoided. After the latter's defeat and death, Coligny was elected C-in-C of the Hug forces at a conference at Cognac in Mar 1569; and, though he was beaten at Montcontour, Brittany, in Oct 1569, his exceptional powers of leadership saved the Hug cause from extinction. Under his inspiration, the civil service had been penetrated by Hug supporters (alternatively, a Hug admin structure parallel with the official one had been set up). The result was that Coligny was able to command support from whole regions of France, especially in the W and S, and thus survive defeat in the field to achieve the favourable Tr of St Germain (Aug 1570). Coligny now became dominant at Court, ousting the Guise network, and securing a personal hold on the fatherless young K Charles IX, who called him *Mon Père*. In the years 1570–72 Coligny devoted himself to a high-minded, but unrealistic scheme to unite the French in a joint attack on Spain in the Netherlands, in alliance with WILLIAM I of Orange and ELIZABETH I of England; but the Q mother, CATHE-RINE DE MEDICI, both jealous of Coligny's influence over the K and appreci-ative in her practical way of the strength of the Spanish army, decided that the safety of France required Coligny's removal. He was shot but not killed by the Guise faction on 22 Aug 1572; and then, as the chief victim of the Massacre of St Bartholomew, he was wounded in his bed by François, D de GUISE, and thrown out of the window on to the street. The mob hanged him on a gibbet.

Columbus, Christopher (Cristóbal Colón) (c 1451–20 May 1506) Discoverer of America.

Son of Domenico Colombo, an Italian weaver, and Suzanna Fontanarossa;

m (c 1478) Filipa Moniz Perestrello, a noble lady by whom he had his son Diego. He had another son, Fernando, b out of wedlock to Beatriz Enríquez.

A navigator from boyhood, he arrived in Portugal when he swam ashore from his ship which had caught fire. His mind full of a mixture of scientific reasoning and wild fantasy, he accepted the opinion of the day that the world was round, and planned a voyage to Asia by sailing W. When this idea was turned down by K John II in 1484, he migrated to Spain where FERDINAND II and ISABELLA, after long consideration (1486–92), decided to support him, promising him the Governorship of the lands he discovered, a proportion of the profits and so on. He made 4 voyages, discovering America, but failing to reach Asia, though he believed he was very near.

On his 1st voyage he sailed from Palos, Huelva, on 3 Aug 1492 with the *Santa María*, the *Pinta* and the *Nina*; observed land on 12 Oct 1492, disembarked on one of the Bahama Islands (later named San Salvador), discovered Cuba and Hispaniola (Haiti); and arrived back at Palos on 15 Mar 1493, having lost the *Santa María*, and leaving 39 men behind on Hispaniola with supplies for a year.

His 2nd voyage, unlike the 1st which aimed at Asia, really began European voyages of discovery aiming at colonizing the New World, with the double object of exploiting the people economically and converting them to Christianity. He left Cádiz on 25 Sept 1493 with 17 vessels and between 1,000 and 1,500 men, and discovered Guadalupe, Puerto Rico and other islands. On reaching Hispaniola, he found that the party he had left there had been massacred by the native population. Nevertheless, he founded Isabella on the island, the 1st European city in the New World; from this base he explored the coast of Cuba, certain it was the mainland, and discovered Jamaica in May 1494. Then, leaving his brothers Bartolomé and Diego in command, he returned home, reaching Cádiz on 11 June 1496, where he had some difficulty in re-establishing his position with Ferdinand and Isabella whose confidence in him had been undermined by rivals.

On his 3rd voyage he left Sanlúcar at the mouth of the R Guadalquivir on 30 May 1498 with 6 ships and 200 men excluding sailors. He discovered Trinidad (July 1498) and the mainland of S America (Aug 1498), which he thought was another island. Intrigues by rivals in Spain and rebellions by colonists on Hispaniola led Ferdinand and Isabella to appoint Francisco de Bobadilla as Gov over his head in May 1499, thus bringing the New World directly under the Spanish Crown. Columbus and his brothers resisted him when he arrived, but they were arrested in Sept 1500, and Columbus landed in Spain once more, this time in chains. With some difficulty he managed to regain royal favour, though he never regained his former political position in the New World.

On his 4th voyage he sailed with 4 ships from Cádiz on 9 May 1502, and explored the coast of Honduras, Nicaragua and Panama. He was plagued by mutinies and shipwrecked on Jamaica in June 1503; and on his return landed at San Lúcar in Nov 1504. He spent the rest of his life taking legal action and sending petitions to the Crown in unsuccessful attempts to regain the vast honours, power and wealth he had been promised on his 1st voyage. He d, still convinced that it had been Asiatic lands he had explored.

Condé, Henry II de Bourbon, 3rd Pr de (1 Sept 1588–26 Dec 1646) 1st Pr of the

Blood under K HENRY IV and LOUIS XIII of France, who led the magnates in rebellions until c 1620, after which he fought for the Crown.

Posthumous son of Henry I de Bourbon, 2nd Pr de Condé, and Charlotte de la Trémoïlle; ed as an RC, though his family had been Hug leaders during the FRENCH WARS OF RELIGION; m (1609) Charlotte Marguerite de Montmorency, who proved so attractive to Henry IV that the young couple fled to Brussels for the rest of the reign. Returning in July 1610, after Henry's assassination, Condé led the Prs of the Blood and magnates in their factional struggles at Court, interspersed with rebellions in the provs, with the purpose of extracting the maximum number of places, pensions and other perquisites, from a Crown weakened by the minority of Louis XIII and the Regency of MARIE DE MEDICI. He revolted in 1614, forcing the Gov to call the Estates-Gen of that year, and again from Aug 1615 to May 1616, involving the Hug nobility, but not the towns, but gaining concessions at the Tr of Loudun in May 1616, including the leadership of the Council for a month. When the favourite, Concini, strengthened the Gov, Condé was imprisoned at Vincennes (Sept 1616–Oct 1619) but, on his release by LUYNES, he henceforth supported the K, whose heir he was – after the K's brother, Gaston, D d'ORLÉANS – until the very late birth of the future LOUIS XIV on 5 Sept 1638. Condé helped to suppress the various rebellions of magnates and Hugs (1619–29), and then took part in the campaigns of the THIRTY YEARS WAR. His son, Louis, became the Great Condé.

Condé, Louis I de Bourbon, 1st Pr de (7 May 1530–13 Mar 1569) Pr of the Blood and Hug general in the early stages of the FRENCH WARS OF RELIGION.

Youngest son of Charles, D de Vendôme and Françoise d'Alençon; and thus the brother of Antoine de Bourbon, K of Navarre; m 1st (1551) Élénore de Roye (d 1564), who is said to have converted him to Calvinism during an illness in 1558; m 2nd (1565) Mlle de Longueville. As heirs to much of the property in central France of Charles III, D de Bourbon, his family headed one of the most powerful clientage networks in France. He fought in the armies of K HENRY II in the 9th HABSBURG–VALOIS WAR (1552–9), seeing action at the siege of Metz (Nov 1552–Jan 1553), the battle of St Quentin, Picardy (10 Aug 1557), and the capture of Calais from the English (7 Jan 1558). When the accession of K FRANCIS II in July 1559 brought the rival house of Guise to power, Condé made himself military protector of the Hugs. They for their part needed support in high places, and he hoped to use their religious ardour and disciplined organization to lever himself into office. A loose-living hunchback and unprincipled power-seeker, he did not take up arms in the Wars of Religion for idealistic reasons, unlike his ally COLIGNY. He was motivated by the belief that his eld brother, as senior Pr of the Blood, should be in power during the royal minority in place of the Guise family. He was behind the Conspiracy of Amboise (Mar 1560) to capture the K, but on its failure he was arrested at Orléans on 31 Oct 1560, and sentenced to death. His life was saved, however, by the early demise of the K on 5 Dec 1560: for the Q Mother, as Regent for K CHARLES IX, needed the Bourbon connection as a counterweight to that of the Guises. Condé was made Gov of Picardy, and was at the centre of the ultimately abortive attempts to achieve an RC–Prot compromise in the Colloquy of Poissy (1561) and the January Edict (1561); but when François, D de GUISE, massacred the Hugs at

Vassy (Mar 1562), and then took Paris, Condé joined Coligny at Meaux, and then took Orléans (Apr 1562), unaccountably failing to get hold of the K and the Q Mother, who now joined the Guises in Paris. In the 1st War of Religion (Apr 1562–Mar 1563), Condé in desperation ceded Le Havre to England in return for military and financial aid (Tr of Richmond, Sept 1562); but when he marched on Paris he was defeated and captured at the battle of Dreux on the W edge of the Ile de France (Dec 1562). After the Pacification of Amboise in Mar 1563, he supported the Q Mother until her pro-Spanish policy and his resentment at his inadequate advancement led to the 2nd War (Sept 1567–Mar 1568), which opened with the Conspiracy of Meaux, the unsuccessful attempt by Condé and Coligny to get possession of the K. Condé once more marched on Paris, only to be defeated at St Denis (Nov 1567), after which he signed the Tr of Longjumeau (Mar 1568). In the 3rd War, which soon broke out in Aug 1568, Condé was defeated at Jarnac, Poitou, by the future K HENRY III (15 Mar 1569). He was shot in the head and killed.

Córdoba, Gonzalo Fernández de (El Gran Capitán) (?1453–1 Dec 1515) Spanish gen and military innovator.

2nd son of the Grandee Pedro Fernández de Córdoba (Gov of Andalusia) and Elvira de Herrera; ed at Court, he took part in the war to establish ISABELLA on the throne of Castile (1474–6), but established his reputation as a gifted soldier in the conquest of Granada (1482–92), where he developed techniques which made the Spanish infantry (hitherto unknown) unbeatable for the next century. Militarily, he developed the Swiss square, making the cavalry subordinate to the infantry, adding pikes and arquebuses, and making the units more mobile, able to fend off cavalry and then counter-attack. The Great Capt now achieved European fame in the HABSBURG–VALOIS WARS in Italy. Fighting with the Holy League of Venice against K CHARLES VIII of France, he drove the French out of Naples (1495). When war broke out between Spain and K LOUIS XII of France over the border between their two halves of Naples, he defeated the French at Cerignalo (28 Apr 1503) and on the R Garigliano (27 Dec 1503), thus ensuring the Spanish domination of S Italy.

Corporative State (Ständestaat) The name given to States at the stage of social and political development midway between feudalism and ABSOLUTISM, in which the power of the monarch was limited by institutions formed by groups of individuals for their mutual help. To put it another way, they were States in which tasks later performed by the organs of absolute monarchies (or modern States) were then shared by these other institutions. Typical institutions at work in corporative states were Estates (assembling as a Parliament, or a Diet, *Reichstag, Cortes, Zemskii Sobor, États-Généraux*), municipalities, provinces, universities, gilds, monasteries and CLIENTAGE networks. Poland under K SIGISMUND III and JOHN II CASIMIR was an extreme example of the corporative state. Holland and England were moderate examples, while Russia was a state where corporative institutions were a very weak growth.

Cortés, Hernán (c 1485–2 Dec 1547) Spanish conqueror of Mexico.

Son of a minor-noble family; ed in law (against his will) at Salamanca, whence he ran away to Hispaniola (1504). He fought in the expedition under Diego Velázquez which conquered Cuba (1511–13); and was later sent by Velázquez to explore and trade with the mainland of Central America. He sailed on 19 Feb 1519 with 600 volunteers in 11 ships, and armed with weapons unknown to the Indians – 16 horses and about the same number of cannons and muskets. He first landed at Tabasco, then at a point further along the coast, where he destroyed his ships (so that there could be no turning back) and founded Vera Cruz, whose citizens (ie his men) elected him Capt-Gen, thus enabling him to renounce Velázquez and come directly under the Spanish crown with a certain air of legality. Before making for Tenochtitlán (Mexico City), the capital of the 5-million-strong Aztec Emp which stretched from the Atlantic to the Pacific, he explored the surrounding area, displaying high powers of leadership in the way he exploited the Spanish thirst for heroic action, appreciated the political situation and the religious aspirations of the Indians, and treated them with less cruelty than was normal at that time. With the help of the people of the mountain town of Tlaxcala (hostile to the Aztecs) he penetrated peacefully into Tenochtitlán (a city of up to 500,000 inhabitants in the middle of Lake Tezcuco and approached by 3 causeways) where the Emp Montezuma mistook him for Quetzalcoatl, a god whose incarnation was at that time expected (Nov 1519). He imprisoned Montezuma, intending to rule and Christianize the Aztecs peacefully through him. However, Velázquez sent a force under Pánfilo de Narváez to replace him, and the peaceful period was over. Leaving part of his army in Tenochtitlán, Cortés marched against Narváez and overcame him, incorporating much of his expedition into his own army. On returning, he found that the oppressive rule of the party he had left behind had caused the Aztecs to rise against Spanish rule, and renounce and kill Montezuma. Cortés was forced to abandon the city (June 1520); having beaten his pursuers at Otumba (July 1520) he took refuge with the Tlaxcaláns while he refitted for a counter-attack. He besieged Tenochtitlán for 3 months (May–Aug 1521) before re-entering the now semi-derelict city and re-establishing control over the whole Emp. CHARLES V appointed him Gov and Capt-Gen of New Spain (Mexico) (Oct 1522). Using vast quantities of Indian labour, Cortés swiftly rebuilt the ruined city (1522–3) in the Spanish style as Mexico City, the capital of New Spain, and soon more populous than any city in metropolitan Spain. While he spent the 1520s organizing the Gov and economy of Mexico, exploring the Pacific Coast, and looking for a route to the Far E, his enemies at home persuaded the Court to supersede him. In general, Charles V's Gov was opposed to the way the *conquistadores* were carving out for themselves large, semi-feudal estates (*encomiéndas*) worked by Indian slaves; and was anxious to replace these private-enterprise heroes with bureaucrats and businessmen. Cortés spent 1528–30 in Spain pleading his cause. He succeeded in getting himself created Marqués del Valle de Oaxaca (the site of his 23,000-strong *encomiénda*) and Capt-Gen – but not Viceroy or Gov. Back in Mexico (1530) he led further expeditions and explored Lower California (1533–5) returning to Spain (1539), where he took a modest part in Charles V's unsuccessful attack on Algiers (Oct 1541) – but otherwise was kept at arm's length by the Court.

Cossacks The wandering peoples of the steppes on the S fringes of Russia and Poland-Lithuania on the lower reaches of the Volga, the Don, the Donetz and the Dnieper. Consisting mainly of fugitive peasants and outlaws from Russia, Poland, Lithuania and Turkey, as well as Tatars, they lived by hunting and fishing, keeping cattle and bees, and by plundering their neighbours, whether Turks, Tatars, Russians or Poles. Conforming to none of the more usual social systems, they settled in fortified towns and organized themselves on semi-military lines, mainly to defend themselves against raiding Tatar bands and their Turkish overlords, but sometimes to mount rebellions against Russia or Poland, as during the TIME OF TROUBLES (1598–1613) and during their revolts against the Poland of SIGISMUND III, WLADYSLAW IV and JOHN II CASIMIR in 1625, 1630, 1637–8, 1649–51, 1654–67. Russia and Poland in their turn pushed S as they gradually colonized the steppes and brought many Cossacks under their control, who became known as 'registered Cossacks'. The Dnieper Cossacks of the Ukraine became especially difficult as religious differences exacerbated their political and social hostility to Poland, the former being Orthodox, the latter Cath. These Cossacks hoped to form an independent state, and in C17 played off Russia, Turkey and Poland – and even Sweden and Austria – against one another in a series of wars which accelerated the decline of Poland, but resulted only in the eventual incorporation of the Cossacks in the Russian and Polish States.

Counter-Reformation, The (to be distinguished from the CATHOLIC REFORMATION) The name given to the complex movement whereby the Cath Ch reformed itself, defined its doctrine, tightened its discipline and otherwise prepared itself (and sympathetic secular rulers) for the task of winning back the regions which had been lost to Protestantism during the REFORMATION. The point at which the swing from the reasonable reforms of the Cath Reformation to the severe persecution of the Counter-Reformation took place can be seen in the life of Pp PAUL IV, who began as a reformer but went over to the offensive in the 1540s before being elected (1555). The Counter-Reformation took many forms.

The COUNCIL OF TRENT (1545–63) was one important aspect. This achieved a clear definition of doctrine and ritual, and ordered the reform of abuses at all levels; and as a result of the skilful management of its sessions the Pps emerged with greatly increased power over the Ch (a development similar to the growth of ABSOLUTISM in many States).

The Papacy was also much improved by a series of reforming Pps: PAUL III (1534–49), Julius III (1550–55), Paul IV (1555–9), Pius IV (1559–66), Pius V (1566–72), Gregory XIII (1572–85) and Sixtus V (1585–90).

New religious orders were founded to lead the Cath offensive, notably the JESUITS, founded by Ignatius LOYOLA in 1534, which not only invigorated Cath Europe, but also won back Prot areas such as Poland, Austria and Bavaria, and made converts all over America, Africa and Asia.

Other institutions which made a powerful contribution were the INQUISITION and the INDEX.

Certain lay rulers were prominent in support of the Counter-Reformation, forming what might be called its political wing: PHILIP II of Spain, MARY I of England, the Guises and the Cath League during the FRENCH WARS OF RELIGION, SIGISMUND III of Poland, the Emp FERDINAND II and MAXIMILIAN I of Bavaria.

Cranfield, Lionel (1575–6 Aug 1645) Bn Cranfield (1621), Earl of Middlesex (1622), successful merchant and financier who became a reforming Ld Treasurer under K JAMES I of England until he was impeached.

Younger son of Thomas Cranfield, merchant; ed at Mercers' and St Paul's; apprenticed for 7 years in 1590 to Richard Sheppard, general importer and exporter; admitted to membership of the Mercers' Co and founded his own business (1597); m 1st (1599) Elizabeth Sheppard, daughter of his old master (d 1617); m 2nd (1619) Anne Brett, cousin of BUCKINGHAM's mother (d 1664); made member of the Merchant Adventurers by Sept 1602; moved out of trade into financial speculation and made a fortune. With a shrewd head for business he was ruthless and thrusting, but patient enough to bide his time before making a killing. With the aid of his 1st patron, Henry Howard, Earl of Northampton, Ld Privy Seal, he entered the royal service in July 1613 as Surveyor-Gen of the Customs. His financial skill brought him rapid promotion, aided later by his 2nd patron, Buckingham. He became Master of the Court of Requests (1616), Master of the Great Wardrobe (1618), Master of the Court of Wards and Liveries (1619), Chief Commissioner for the Navy (1619), leading Treasurer Commissioner (early 1619), Privy Councillor (1620) and Ld Treasurer (1621). Moreover, he was MP in the 2nd (Addled) Parl (Apr–June 1614), and in the 3rd Parl (Jan 1621–Jan 1622). All through these years until his fall he slaved away at his 2 principal tasks: increasing his fortune, which was easy, and reforming the royal revenues, which proved impossible. On the expenditure side, James I was incorrigible; on the income side, improvement could only be partial and temporary since the Court, the Household and the Gov depts – from Buckingham down to the humblest clerk – all took their slice of it. In consequence, all the reforms he made – reducing pensions, cutting out fraud, stopping perquisites, enforcing payment of debts to the Crown, raising Crown rents, restricting encroachments on the royal forests, extracting better terms from customs-farmers – added to the number of his enemies. By 1624 it was clear that his patron, Buckingham, was now his chief enemy on 2 counts: as head of a vast network of patronage which blocked reform, and as instigator of the financially ruinous war against Spain on the failure of the marriage trip to Madrid. It became a battle to the death at Court, as one or the other had to go; and, as the K refused to dismiss Cranfield, Buckingham arranged his destruction in Parl. On charges of bribery, extortion and others, he was impeached before the H of L (May 1624), fined £50,000, imprisoned briefly in the Tower, and stripped of all his offices. He spent the rest of his life in the political wilderness.

Cranmer, Thomas (2 July 1489–21 Mar 1556) Archbp of Canterbury (1533–53) leader of the English REFORMATION under Ks HENRY VIII and EDWARD VI, and Prot martyr under Q MARY I.

Ed at Cambridge, he became a Fellow of Jesus and pursued an academic career, taking part in the discussions at the White Horse Tavern of the distinguished group of Lutheran sympathizers, until he was unwillingly dragged into high politics when through GARDINER he suggested to Henry VIII the idea of getting the theological support of the univs of Europe for the divorce from Q CATHERINE OF ARAGON, since the legal approval of the courts was proving so hard to obtain. As Chaplain to Anne Boleyn's father, the Earl of Wiltshire, he travelled to consult the Italian univs, and also undertook other diplomatic work for Henry (1529–33); but, being a retiring academic rather than a typical civil-service cleric, he reluctantly obeyed the K's orders to become the Archbp of Canterbury on WARHAM's death. He m twice (1515 and 1532); he also gradually adopted religious opinions which went beyond those of the K in the direction of Protestantism. His fundamental belief, however, was in the importance of absolute monarchy, and he was prepared to accord almost total obedience to the divinely appointed K of England. This led him to arrange Henry's divorces and marriages in the search for an heir, and to organize under Thomas CROMWELL the Henrician Reformation. In the 1530s and 1540s he led the Prot party in Henry's council, sponsored the Great Bible (1539), composed the English Litany (1545), opposed the Act of 6 Articles (1539), which forced him to keep his wife in seclusion, survived the attempts of NORFOLK, Gardiner and other conservatives to destroy him (thanks to the peculiarly warm trust and affection that K Henry had for him), and was included, unlike the conservatives, in the Council of Regency which Henry left in his will to advise K Edward VI. Under the new K he led SEYMOUR in the direction of Continental Protestantism; and was chiefly responsible for the 1st Prayer Book in English, which from June 1549 became the only legal form of worship by the 1st Act of Uniformity. This was skilfully worded by Cranmer so as to embrace the widest range of supporters between the extremists of the Prot and RC sides. Under DUDLEY Cranmer dissociated himself from the extreme attack on the Ch (including the spoliation of its material wealth), but revised his Prayer Book in a Prot direction to satisfy the criticisms made by BUCER and other Continental Protestants whom he respected. These alterations were incorporated in the 2nd Prayer Book which became legal from Nov 1552 by the 2nd Act of Uniformity. Cranmer was also responsible for the compilation of the *42 Articles*, which received the royal assent in June 1553, and later became the basis of the Elizabethan *39 Articles* (1563). Unfortunately for himself, Cranmer's deference to divine-right monarchy led him to sign K Edward VI's will designating Lady Jane Grey as his successor; for on the failure of that enterprise and the succession of Mary I he was found guilty of treason on 13 Nov 1553 and imprisoned in the Tower. Like LATIMER and RIDLEY, he had to defend his doctrinal position before a delegation at Oxford appointed by Convocation (Mar 1554), and his opinions were found to be heretical. In Sept 1555 his trial opened at St Mary's Ch in Oxford before a commission appointed by Rome. He was condemned as a heretic, handed over to the secular power, and publicly degraded in a humiliating ceremony – also at St Mary's – on 14 Feb 1556. Under great pressure to recant, and seriously perplexed by the now agonizingly paradoxical consequences of his belief in the divine right of rulers, when the ruler was an RC, Cranmer submitted and made four partial and two complete recantations. However, at the ceremony at St Mary's at which he was to have made this public – thus acting as valuable propaganda for the régime – he solemnly withdrew his recantations and d a heroic death at the stake the same day (21 Mar 1556). Thrusting the hand that had signed the recantations into the flames and holding it there until the end, he made an unforgettable impression on all present, quite the opposite of what Mary had intended.

Cromwell, Oliver (25 Apr 1599–3 Sept 1658) Outstanding Puritan general of the

Parl Army in the English CIVIL WAR, who defeated and executed K CHARLES I, and set up an army-controlled republic, to which he unsuccessfully tried to give constitutional form and permanence.

2nd son of Robert Cromwell and Elizabeth Steward, both members of yeoman families which had gained land and gentry status under the Tudors, profiting from the DISSOLUTION OF THE MONASTERIES. Oliver was the great-grandson of Richard Williams, a nephew of Thomas CROMWELL, whose name he adopted; ed at Sidney Sussex, Cambridge (1616–17), a Puritan college, leaving after only a year because of his father's death; m (1620) Elizabeth (d 1672), daughter of Sir James Bourchier, a City merchant; became a farmer nr Huntingdon, then at St Ives (1630), then, on receiving a legacy, at Ely, Cambs (1636). At about this time he seems to have undergone conversion to Calvinism, after passing through a phase of deep, neurotic melancholia. His subsequent life divides into 4 main phases: (1) 1640–46, when, beginning as a backbench MP, he emerged as the most successful commander in the Parl army, defeating the Royalists, and creating in the New Model Army a power-base which made him the strongest man in England. (2) 1646–9, the period of negotiations between the K on the one hand and, on the other, the leading power-groups which had emerged in the Civil War: the Scots, the 'Presbyterians', the 'Independents' (the 2 main factions in Parl) and the Grandees and the Agitators (the 2 main parties in the Army). Cromwell 1st backed the 'Independents', then headed the Grandees, purging Parl of the 'Presbyterians', suppressing the Agitators in the Army, winning the 2nd Civil War, putting the K on trial, and executing him. (3) 1649–53, when Cromwell and the purged Parl – the Rump – set up the Puritan republic, conquered Ireland and Scotland, fought the Dutch, until Cromwell forcibly ended the Rump's life when it failed to produce the social and political reforms the Army wanted and tried to perpetuate its own power, instead of co-operating with Cromwell in giving his military dictatorship a Parl basis in a new constitution. (4) 1653–8, when Cromwell ruled as Protector, conducting an aggressive, imperialistic foreign policy and trying in vain to devise a form of Gov which would be based on popular consent, and which would nevertheless desire only the reforms he approved of.

1640–46: Cromwell was MP in Charles I's 3rd Parl (Mar 1628–Mar 1629), and MP in the Short Parl (Apr–May 1640) and the Long Parl (Nov 1640 onwards), a leading backbencher, opponent of STRAFFORD and LAUD, and supporter of PYM and HAMPDEN. He was an eloquent, vigorous, even violent, defender of the little man against oppression, of the rights of the commons against enclosing landlords, of religious INDEPENDENTS against either Anglican or Presbyterian persecution, of toleration against an imposed uniformity – though not toleration for Caths or Anglicans. What particular religious sect he favoured is not clear. As he once said, 'I can tell you, sir, what I would not have, though I cannot, what I would.' But in addition to being a Puritan idealist, he was also a social and political traditionalist, and an earthy pragmatist. In consequence, he opposed the LEVELLERS and other radicals who at first looked to him for leadership; and he was capable of the most ruthless political realism, hesitating for weeks while seeking God's will in the turn of events – 'waiting on providences' – but acting relentlessly once he was sure that it was God's work he was doing – the beheading of the K being the most striking example. Oscillating between opportunism and principle, he also swung between melancholy and excitement, between hypochondria and incapacitating illness on the one hand, and horse-play and wild laughter on the other. When the Civil War came, he secured Cambridge for Parl (Aug 1642), mustered a troop, then a regiment, of cavalry (the future Ironsides) and played an increasingly successful part in bringing E England under Parl control, fighting at Edgehill, nr Warwick (23 Oct 1642), Winceby, Lincs (11 Oct 1643), becoming Lieut-Gen and Commander, under MANCHESTER, of the army of the Eastern Association, and commanding the left wing in the great victory at Marston Moor, nr York, on 2 July 1644. Though without military experience, Cromwell adapted himself resiliently to his new tasks, profiting from the C17 military revolution of MAURICE of Nassau and GUSTAV II ADOLF, and relying on the conviction that soldiers, however humble, who fight for a cause they have faith in, are superior to mere professionals or aristocrats. 'Truly,' he said, 'I think he that prays best will fight best.' In addition to higher morale, his men enjoyed better training, higher pay, superior equipment, greater numbers and sterner discipline than the Royalists. Moreover, Cromwell favoured an all-out effort to beat the K as well as religious toleration; and this put him on the side of the 'Independents' in Parl, and against the 'Presbyterians' to which his dilatory C-in-C, Manchester, belonged. The latter sought a negotiated peace with the K, and feared the radical social consequences of allowing sects to exist outside a State-controlled Presbyterian Ch. Cromwell criticized him strongly in Parl, and with great political skill successfully campaigned in Parl for the New Model Army (Feb 1645) and the Self-Denying Ordinance (Apr 1645). The New Model – with FAIRFAX as C-in-C, and Cromwell i/c of the cavalry – was a national army under a unified command, replacing the separate Association armies, and benefiting from the energetic leadership which Fairfax and Cromwell supplied. The Self-Denying Ordinance prevented members of either House holding military or civil posts, and it thus eliminated from the Army ESSEX, Manchester and other insufficiently bellicose, 'Presbyterian' and aristocratic commanders. An exception was eventually made of Cromwell, and he retained both his seat and his command. Along with Fairfax, he beat the K decisively at Naseby, Northants (14 June 1645), and Langport, Somerset (10 July 1645), ending the war with the surrender of the K's HQ at Oxford (20 June 1646).

1646–9: In the complex post-war jockeying between the K and the main factions (the Scots, the 'Presbyterians' and 'Independents' in Parl, the Grandees and Agitators in the Army) Cromwell sometimes controlled events, sometimes allowed himself to be swept along by them. As an 'Independent' MP (1646–7) he worked in Parl to prevent the 'Presbyterian' majority from disbanding the Army and setting up a Presbyterian Ch; but as the Army and Parl drifted further and further apart he threw in his lot with the former (June 1647), 2 days after Cornet Joyce had taken possession of the K on the Army's behalf. In the Army he led the Grandees, and kept the Agitators in line by a judicious mixture of empty concessions, debating skill and brute force. On the one hand, he and the Grandees offered the K the moderate settlement called the *Heads of the Proposals*, constructed by Henry IRETON (under whom it is summarized) and published on 1 Aug 1647, but rejected by the K. On the other hand, he formed the Gen Council of the Army, consisting of the generals and 2 officers and 2 men from each regiment, and with it he argued against the Agitators' proposed settlement – the Leveller-influenced *Agreement of the People* – in the Putney Debates (Oct–Nov 1647), eventually ordering the Agitators back to their regiments, and putting down a mutiny by force (Nov 1647). Unity was now required to fight the 2nd Civil War, which the K had brought about with the aid of the Scots Presbyterians and the forces of prov separatism in England. Cromwell marched N to beat the invading Scots at Preston, Lancs (17–19 Aug 1648), and then unaccountably lingered there while Ireton took the historic decision to use the Army, whose patience was exhausted, against the Parl majority, which still wanted further negotiations with the K. Cromwell returned to London to find the Army in possession of the K, occupying London, and in the process of carrying out Pride's Purge: ie dispersing all the MPs except about 60 of the radical wing of the 'Independents' (Dec 1648), henceforth known as the Rump. Cromwell said 'that he had not been acquainted with the design, yet since it was done he was glad of it'. The Army had already voted to try the K – 'that man of blood' – for the blood he had shed; but Cromwell hesitated until the end of Dec 1648 before he became convinced that Charles would have to die. Confident at last that 'the providence of God hath cast this upon us', he acted swiftly. The K was tried by a special court (20–27 Jan 1649) and beheaded on 30 Jan.

1649–53: The Rump ruled during this period, acting through the Council of State which it nominated in Feb 1649, with Cromwell as its first chairman. The monarchy and the H of L were formally abolished on 17 and 19 Mar 1649, and on 19 May 1649 an Ordinance declared England 'a Commonwealth or Free-State'. Though it represented the last tenuous link with legality, the Rump had ceased to represent anything but an eccentric minority of public opinion. Its violent measures had been pushed through by a revolutionary minority, but, once that was done, the Rump became anxious to recover constitutional respectability, and soon encouraged the return to Parl of the moderates, who in their turn ensured that this was as far as revolutionary change would go. Henceforth, the cautiously conservative measures of the Rump aroused the opposition of all those radical idealists who had hoped for a thorough-going reform of Ch and State. The law was not reformed, the franchise was not extended, tithes and gentry-presentation to livings were still preserved, and another Leveller outbreak was suppressed in London (Mar 1649) and in the Army (May 1649). Cromwell himself was out of London during much of this period reconquering Ireland and Scotland. In Ireland (Aug 1649–May 1650) he broke the back of Irish resistance which had been active since 1641, and achieved lasting notoriety at Drogheda on 11 Sept 1649 when it refused to surrender. He slaughtered the garrison and all the priests he could catch in order to encourage other towns to surrender – and thus save lives by shortening the war. On 11 Oct, Wexford received similar treatment. After Cromwell's departure the mopping up was completed, and English Prots were settled on land confiscated from Irish Caths, while Ireland was united with England (1653–60), sending MPs to the English Parl. In Scotland, where K CHARLES II had landed in June 1650, Cromwell was victorious at Dunbar (3 Sept 1650); and then, luring the Scots S into England, he defeated them at Worcester on the same day a year later. Scotland was united with England (1653–60). It sent MPs to Westminster, and its admin was considerably modernized. For the Scots campaign Cromwell had been promoted C-in-C, as Fairfax refused to invade Scotland. In foreign affairs, the Rump tried a Dutch alliance (1651) based on common Protestantism, then a Dutch War (1652–4), resulting from commercial rivalry. This war, in which MONCK was afloat as Gen-at-Sea, and in which BLAKE several times defeated the Dutch, was stimulated by the Navigation Ordinances of 1650 and 1651, measures designed to develop colonial trade as a British imperial monopoly. Cromwell's attitude to the Dutch War is not completely clear, though he brought it to an end as soon as he achieved supreme power as Protector. This new régime came about when Cromwell eventually lost patience with the Rump's persistent refusal to dissolve itself and make way for a form of Gov more deeply entrenched in popular consent. On 20 Apr 1653 he brought musketeers into the House and dispersed what was left of the Long Parl. He remained as sole ruler, by virtue of his position as C-in-C of the Army.

1653–8: Until the end of his life, Cromwell's insoluble problem continued unchanged: how to find a form of Gov which reconciled popular consent with God's providence, how to elect a Parl which would not immediately try to overthrow all he stood for – the philosophy, unfortunately, of a small minority. And Cromwell honestly sought a Parl régime. He was embarrassed by naked military power; and his policies in any case needed great revenues which only Parl consent could satisfactorily produce.

Barebone's Parl (4 July–12 Dec 1653), named derisively later after one of its humbler members, was an assembly of 140 members selected by the gens from nominees of the Independent congregations, men 'fearing God and of approved fidelity and honesty'. It was an attempt by Cromwell to give practical form to the ideals of Major-Gen Thomas Harrison, a leading FIFTH MONARCHY man. Unfortunately, Cromwell neglected the matter of Parl management, and the more radical 'saints' took the bit between their teeth with socially disruptive plans for legal and ecclesiastical reforms, until one morning the conservative minority assembled especially early and voted their own dissolution.

The *Instrument of Gov* (16 Dec 1653), a written constitution devised by Gen LAMBERT and the Council of Officers, was the basis of Gov for the rest of Cromwell's life; and by it England was to be ruled by a Ld Protector, a Council of State and a triennial Parl sitting for at least 5 months at a time. This was hardly the form of Gov for which men had fought the Stuarts, for, built into it, and beyond discussion, was a standing army, revenues to maintain it and wide powers for the Protector to issue Ordinances and control appointments. Parl was to be chosen by owners of £200 worth of property, and many 'rotten' boroughs were suppressed, their seats being redistributed to the counties: an electoral system which produced Parls of very independent country gentry, with whose views Cromwell no longer had patience. The idealist period of Cromwell's life could be said to be over with the suppression of the Levellers, and the disappointing performance of Barebone's Parl. Henceforth, Cromwell was the conservative guardian of law and order, and the existing social structure. (a) The 1st Protectorate Parl (Sept 1654–Jan 1655) insisted on trying to amend the Instrument so as to bring the executive under Parl control; Cromwell dissolved it as soon as he legally could. A different form of Gov was tried soon after as a result of Col John Penruddock's easily suppressed Royalist rising in Wilts in Mar 1655: (b) Major-Generals: In Aug 1655 the country was divided into 11 districts, each under a major-gen and about 500 men, with the task of stimulating the normal magistrates to increase their vigilance against Royalists and un-Puritan behaviour. It was an invasion by the executive of the self-governing rights of county and borough more offensive than anything the Stuarts had attempted, and it effectively inoculated England against military rule for centuries to come. But, like the Stuarts, Cromwell was forced to call another Parl to provide revenues for his foreign policy and, unlike them, to provide a legal basis for his power. (c) The 2nd Protectorate Parl (Sept 1656–Feb 1658) was made more amenable by the Major-Gens' influence over the elections, and by the exclusion of about 100 MPs of a radical persuasion. This friendly body abolished the Major-Gens (Jan 1657), and then produced an amended constitution, called the *Humble Petition and Advice*, whereby the Protector could name his successor and choose his Council. A second chamber was also provided (the Other House), and an outline of an established Independent Ch with toleration for sects. They also wanted Cromwell to become K but, after some hesitation and probably under Army pressure, he refused, and this clause was amended before he accepted the *Petition* on 25 May 1657. And here is further evidence of Cromwell's inadequacy as a Parl manager. In accordance with the *Petition*, the 100 excluded radicals were allowed to sit, while about 30 of Cromwell's chief supporters were promoted to the Other House, leaving the majority in the hands of the Republicans. When they began attacking the Other House and taking up the grievances of the soldiers, Cromwell lost his temper and dissolved them, saying: 'If this be the end of your sitting and this be your carriage, I think it high time that an end be put to your sitting. And I do dissolve this Parliament. And let God be Judge between you and me.' In Church affairs the impact of the Protectorate was as hesitant and muffled as each of the previous revolutionary régimes: strong on destruction, weak on creation. The Long Parl had appointed the Westminster Assembly to advise it on Ch policy – 121 clergy, 10 Lords, 20 MPs, with Scots advisers, beginning their deliberations in July 1643. Disputes between theocratic and Erastian Presbyterians, Independents and sectaries, as well as between the Assembly and Parl, both then and later, made progress difficult, though stage plays were forbidden by Parl (Sept 1642), Sunday observance strictly enforced (Apr 1644), and Christmas abolished (Dec 1644). The Assembly published its Directory of Worship (Jan 1645) to replace the Prayer Book; and laid down a form of Presbyterian Ch organization (Aug 1645), though the Parl Ordinance enforcing it was not passed till Jan 1648, by which time there was so much opposition to it from Independents and sectaries that it did not spread very far outside London. In Oct 1646 Archbps and Bps were abolished and their lands sold, Deans and Chapters following in 1649; but throughout the succession of different régimes, tithes and lay patronage – important property rights – were left untouched. Cromwell himself believed in a form of State Ch with toleration, and under his Protectorate an Ordinance of Mar 1654 set up a central committee of Triers to vet clerical candidates, while a further Ordinance of Aug 1654 established county commissions of Ejectors to eliminate 'scandalous, ignorant, and insufficient ministers and schoolmasters'. Both these Commissions represented a very broad spectrum of the many variations of Puritan opinion extant at that time. In general, except under the Major-Gens, the interference of the State in Ch matters was muted and, in the ecclesiastical free-for-all resulting from the destruction of the Ch of England, a rich variety of sects flourished, with Anglicans and Caths being the main sufferers. The foreign policy of Cromwell under the Protectorate raised England's diplomatic and military position high above the level to which it had fallen under JAMES I and Charles I, and set her on a new aggressive course based on sea-power, commerce, colonization, sugar and the slave trade. Cromwell ended the Dutch War which he had inherited from the Rump, by the favourable Tr of Westminster (Apr 1654), and made commercial Trs with Sweden (Apr 1654), Denmark (July 1654) allowing English merchants access to the Baltic trade, and with Portugal (July 1654), opening her emp to English trade. He sent Blake to the Med (1654–5) to safeguard English merchants from the Barbary pirates of Algiers and Tunis; and with the spread of Protestantism in mind as much as the increase in trade he adopted a pro-French, anti-Spanish policy. With his Western Design he gave the backing of the State to schemes pioneered by private adventurers such as Sir Walter RALEGH, and the Providence Island Co of Pym's day – schemes involving colonization in the W Indies so as to invade Spain's American monopoly, and capture her silver and trade. He made a commercial Tr with the France of MAZARIN (1655), one consequence of which was the ending of French persecution of the Vaudois Prots in Savoy. He dispatched a naval expedition to conquer Hispaniola in the W Indies, but it turned out a disgraceful failure, and Jamaica was captured instead (May 1655) – a disappointment at the time, but an acquisition of crucial importance in the later build-up of the British Emp. Pursuing the war with Spain, he made a joint attack with France on the Spanish Netherlands, winning the Battle of the Dunes, E of Dunkirk (13/23 June 1658), and keeping Dunkirk as an English Continental foothold, though without great significance for the future.

Just before Cromwell d of pneumonia on the anniversary of Dunbar and Worcester, he named his son Richard as his successor, but in fact his republic had only 20 months of very disturbed existence left, thanks to the activities of 2 of his generals, Lambert and Monck. But if Cromwell's régime was transitory, the effects of his career were permanent. He had led England through a decisive period in which she rejected both absolute monarchy and democracy. With a fine appreciation of both principle and expediency, Cromwell had called on the aid of the lower classes just sufficiently to defeat the K, and had leaned on the Royalists just enough to defeat the masses. Above all, perhaps, Englishmen had gone through the experience of operating, or at least discussing, every possible type of political institution. In so doing, they made errors, but learned a great deal. Henceforth the property-owning nobility, gentry and middle classes entered upon a wonderful period of unrestrained development: of self-Gov in Parl, county and borough, of religious toleration and intellectual freedom, of social mobility, free enterprise and imperialistic aggression.

Cromwell, Thomas (c 1485–28 July 1540) Chief minister (1533–40) to K HENRY VIII of England during the REFORMATION. His rule represents one of the most creative periods in the history of English gov, but was cut short by his execution for treason.

Son of Walter Cromwell, a brewer, blacksmith and fuller who was related to the Notts gentry, he seems to have spent much of his life until 1512 abroad as a soldier and banker in Italy, and as a merchant in Antwerp. He m a gentlewoman, Elizabeth Wykys (*c* 1512), who d in 1528–9. After practising as a lawyer in London, he became WOLSEY's general man of business by the early 1520s; and at the latter's downfall he somehow managed to remain faithful to him while simultaneously attracting the K's favourable notice. He was elected MP in the Parl of 1523 and in the Reformation Parl, speaking on the anti-clerical side. In early 1530 he entered the royal service; by Nov 1530 he was a member of the Council; and in Nov 1531 he was a member of the inner ring. Cromwell was a new man who was unencumbered by the feudal and RC traditionalism which blinkered the K's other – noble – ministers. His experience of Continental business and diplomacy, and his reading of such Italian political theorists as Marsiglio of Padua, had given him not only a clearsighted view of what was to be the main European development of the next few centuries (ie the triumph of the sovereign, parl, bureaucratic State over all possible enemies), but also the pragmatism to assist at its birth-pangs. And he acquired in addition a leaning towards the views of Martin LUTHER. Very quickly he accumulated offices until he was the K's chief minister: Master of the K's Jewels (1532), Clerk of the Hanaper (1532), Chancellor of the Exchequer (1533), Principal Sec (1534), Master of the Rolls (1534), Vicegerent in Spirituals and Vicar Gen (1535) and Ld Privy Seal (1536). Working through his numerous offices he was in day-to-day control of the momentous programme of constitutional, ecclesiastical, social and economic change which marked the 1530s: ie the breach with Rome, the divorce from Q CATHERINE OF ARAGON, the DISSOLUTION OF THE MONASTERIES, the entrenchment of Crown-in-Parl as the sovereign authority in England, the establishment of the omnicompetence of statutes, the admin revolution (in the Council, in the Council of the North, in the development of the Exchequer and the establishment of 5 new revenue courts, in the royal Household), the incorporation of Wales into the English system of gov, and the start of the Tudor Poor Law. To all these tasks and others, Cromwell brought the tireless zeal and creative imagination of a managerial genius; but, though historians agree that he was the driving force which impelled the machinery of gov during that unprecedented decade of purposeful activity, they disagree over how far he originated the revolutionary policies.

It is equally difficult to disentangle Cromwell's contribution to Henry's foreign policy, though he appears to have been more worried than the K that England's isolation after the breach with Rome would encourage a joint attack by a reconciled Emp CHARLES V and K FRANCIS I. His policy consisted of repairing England's defences, and seeking an alliance with Charles V or, failing that, with the Emp's chief enemies, the Lutheran Prs of Germany. During the crisis of 1538–9 when meetings between Charles V and Francis I led to fears of invasion in England, Cromwell led Henry so far along the road to an alliance with the Lutheran Prs that, when it turned out to be an *impasse*, he fell from power. The K had at least 3 objections to Cromwell's diplomatic moves: (a) he had no liking for Anne of Cleves, a crucial part of the bargain; (b) he refused to turn Lutheran, while the Germans would entertain no political alliance unless Henry adopted the AUGSBURG CONFESSION in England; and (c) he shrank from active involvement in the wars between the Lutheran Prs and the Emp. Moreover, this matrimonial, religious and diplomatic blunder strengthened Cromwell's enemies at home, the 3rd D of NORFOLK and Bp GARDINER and their followers.

They accused Cromwell of making England Prot, having recently got through Parl the very conservative Act of Six Articles; and they now brought Norfolk's nubile niece, Catherine Howard, to Court to take the K's mind off Anne of Cleves. The manner in which the Norfolk faction talked a perhaps over-suggestible Henry into throwing his greatest minister to the wolves is wrapped in mystery. As late as 18 Apr 1540, Cromwell was created Earl of Essex, and then Ld Great Chamberlain of the Household the following day; yet on 10 June 1540 he was arrested at a Council meeting at Westminster by the Capt of the Guard and taken by water to the Tower. Denied a proper trial, he was convicted of treason and heresy in an Act of Attainder (29 June 1540) and beheaded at Tyburn.

Danby, Sir Thomas Osborne, Vt Latimer, Earl of (20 Feb 1632–26 July 1712) Later Marquis of Carmarthen (1689) and D of Leeds (1694) Chief minister under K CHARLES II and K WILLIAM III of Great Britain, helped to found the TORIES by his skill at Parl management on behalf of the Court, sponsored the marriage of William and Mary, and played a key part in the REVOLUTION OF 1688.

Son of Sir Edward Osborne, Bart, a Royalist in the Civil War, and his 2nd wife, Anne Midelton; ed at home; m (1653) Bridget, daughter of Royalist leader, Montague Bertie, 2nd Earl of Lindsey; rose in Yorks politics under the patronage of the 2nd D of Buckingham, becoming Sheriff (1661) and MP for York (1665). Attaching himself to Buckingham, he helped to bring down CLARENDON; and under the Cabal became joint Treasurer of the Navy (1668), then sole Treasurer (1671) and member of the Privy Council (1673). On the break-up of the Cabal he became Ld Treasurer (June 1673) and chief minister (1673–9) (*see* CHARLES II).

Pale and proud, vigorous and determined, he soon established himself in the K's eyes by restoring the royal finances, and creating a Court party (later called the Tories), using patronage and all the other subtle devices of Parl management. At the same time he calmed the public fears caused by the K's pro-French, pro-Cath attitude with his vigorous support of the Anglican Ch and his negotiation of the marriage of the K's niece (future Q Mary II) and the Prot Dutch Pr of Orange (future K William III) in Nov 1677. His arrogant indifference to criticism, however, and his confident pulling of political strings, were insufficient to withstand the POPISH PLOT and the Exclusion crisis which swept him from office. He was impeached in Parl on 23 Dec 1678. The K pardoned him in Mar 1679, but the H of C declared this tactic illegal, and he resigned on 26 Mar 1679. The H of L lodged him in the Tower of London in Apr 1679, where he remained without trial until Feb 1684. For the rest of the reign he retired to private life; and likewise refused to support the Cath and absolutist policies of K JAMES II. He was one of the famous seven conspirators who signed the Invitation to William of Orange, and during the Revolution of 1688 he raised the N of England behind the invading Pr. In the debates on the settlement he was a leading proponent of the joint rule of William and Mary which was eventually incorporated into the Bill of Rights (Dec 1689). He was appointed Ld Pres of the Council (Feb 1689) in the mixed ministry which opened the new reign, emerging by early 1690 as the chief minister. His main task was to engineer majorities in a Parl riddled with factions, in order to vote the legislation necessary to fight the War of the League of Augsburg (1689–97); and he achieved this with his old managerial finesse until 1694. During that year the Parl situation forced the K to shed Tories and take in the Whig Junto, a reshuffle which toppled Danby from his dominating position. Then on 29 Feb 1695 came the final opportunity for the legions of his enemies: he was impeached for receiving a bribe from the E India Co. The charge was not pursued, but his day was over.

Dias, Bartolomeu (c 1450–29 May 1500) Portuguese discoverer of the Cape of Good Hope.

His early life is unknown, but he was probably much concerned with the voyages of exploration to the W African coast sponsored by K John II. In command of one of these, he set off in Aug 1487 with 3 ships and passed Latitude 21°50′ S – the furthest point S hitherto reached. Continuing S he passed the Cape without seeing it; on turning N he reached the coast on 3 Feb 1488 at Mossel Bay (22°23′ E), the 1st expedition to round the Cape. He then explored the E coast as far as the Great Fish River – as far as his men would let him – confirming that he had discovered the sea-route to India. On the return journey he landed at the Cape (possibly calling it the Cape of Storms), and reached Lisbon in Dec 1488. He was not chosen to organize the Portuguese expedition to India, only sailing with Vasco da GAMA as far as the Cape Verde Islands in July 1497. He was also a member of CABRAL's Indian expedition which discovered Brazil on 22 Apr 1500 and then lost 4 ships and all hands rounding the Cape. Dias was one of them.

Diggers, The A group of 20–50 landless peasants who occupied and cultivated the commons at St George's Hill, Walton-on-Thames, Surrey (Apr 1649–Mar 1650). Their leader was Gerrard Winstanley (c 1609–1660+), son of a Wigan, Lancs, clothier, an unemployed apprentice in London, whose book *The Law of Freedom* (1652) blamed most human afflictions on the institution of private property. 'True freedom lies where a man receives his nourishment and preservation,' he said, 'and that is in the use of the earth.' He advocated a utopia without class distinctions, property or money, in which land was exploited communally. Like Continental ANABAPTISTS and others, he believed in the inner light; unlike CALVIN, he declared that all men could be saved. Though they were also known as the 'True Levellers', the Diggers belonged to a social stratum below that of the LEVELLERS, whose appeal was to yeomen and artisans, and who opposed communism. The Gov – the Rump – took alarm and sent the C-in-C, FAIRFAX, to intervene; but he regarded the Diggers as harmless cranks, and it was the local landowners and peasants who eventually broke up the movement.

Diplomatic Revolution, The (1749–56) Also called reversal of alliances.

The period between the end of the WAR OF AUSTRIAN SUCCESSION (1740–48) and the start of the SEVEN YEARS WAR (1756–63). When it was complete, the chief pairs of enemies were still the same, but their allies had exchanged places: that is in E Europe Prussia still fought Austria, while in W Europe Great Britain still fought France, but Britain was allied to Prussia instead of Austria, and France was allied to Austria instead of Prussia. The rise of Prussia and

Russia on the one hand, and the colonial rivalry between Britain and France on the other, had changed the balance of power with the result that the traditional enmity between the H R Emp and France ceased to be the chief polarity in Europe. In Austria, Kaunitz realized as early as Mar 1749 that Prussia, not France, was the chief enemy, and MARIA THERESA's Gov began to negotiate with France on these lines. At the same time, Britain had made it only too clear in the War of the Austrian Succession that she was interested in Austria only as an enemy of France, and that Austria could expect no help from Britain in trying to recover Silesia from Prussia. The French K did not respond to Austrian advances, however, till events in N Europe made him change his mind. Britain signed the Convention of St Petersburg with the Empss ELIZABETH of Russia on 30 Sept 1755: a traditional agreement whereby Russia would keep an army on the Prussian border (paid for by Britain) to defend Hanover if it were attacked. Thinking, wrongly, that this signified an Anglo-Russian–Austrian threat to Prussia, FREDERICK II signed the Tr of Westminster with Britain (Jan 1756), whereby both powers promised not to wage war in Germany. When the news reached Paris of this independent action of their satellite, the French Gov were so angry that they began to respond to Austrian overtures (which had been under active negotiation since Aug 1755). In May 1756 France and Austria signed the 1st Tr of Versailles, a defensive alliance. Meanwhile, Elizabeth of Russia was also offended by the Anglo-Prussian rapprochement, for she regarded the Anglo-Russian Convention of St Petersburg not as a defensive precaution, but as an essential element in her plan to dismember Prussia. She now bent her diplomatic efforts to negotiating an offensive alliance with Austria and France, but LOUIS XV (with a colonial war against Britain already in being) refused to encourage a European war as well. In his turn, Frederick II suspected that a vast coalition of the great powers was preparing to attack him, and so, typically, he struck first. He invaded Saxony on 29 Aug 1756, and by so doing provoked the imagined alliance into being, France signing the 2nd Tr of Versailles with Austria on 1 May 1757: an offensive alliance. The Diplomatic Revolution was complete, and the Seven Years War under way.

Drake, Sir Francis (c 1543–27/28 Jan 1596) The most dashing of the English seamen under Q ELIZABETH I, the 1st Englishman to sail round the world, and Vice-Admiral against the Spanish ARMADA, whose daring piratical exploits against the Spaniards stimulated Protestantism and patriotism among the English, and whetted their appetites for sea-going commerce.

Son of Edmund Drake, a Prot yeoman who became a lay preacher to the sailors and dockers of Chatham. Drake learned seamanship as an apprentice on a coasting vessel in the Thames estuary, and in 1566 accompanied John Lovell on a voyage to the W Indies with slaves from the Guinea coast of Africa. He m 1st (1569) Mary Newman (d 1583); m 2nd (1585) Elizabeth, daughter of Sir George Sydenham. He was a member of his cousin, John HAWKINS's, 3rd slaving expedition (1567–69), during which, commanding the *Judith*, he abandoned Hawkins when the Spanish had trapped him at San Juan de Ulúa (Vera Cruz, Mexico) in Sept 1568: a mysterious flight which has never been cleared up.

Drake was an outstanding leader and original tactician as well as a fierce patriot and fanatical Prot, and henceforth he achieved European fame with his audacious invasions of Atlantic and Pacific waters, which the Spanish and Portuguese regarded as their monopoly.

(1) The 1st W Indies Voyage (1571–2) when he led a profitable reconnaissance and raiding expedition against Spanish ports.

(2) The Nombre de Dios Expedition (1572–3) during which he ambushed a Spanish mule-train transporting silver from Peru across Panamá to the shipping point of Nombre de Dios; he saw the Pacific for the 1st time (11 Feb 1573); and arrived back in Plymouth (Aug 1573) with a handsome profit.

(3) The Circumnavigation (Dec 1577–Sept 1580) which, like so many Elizabethan undertakings, was at one and the same time a joint-stock business venture and a branch of the Q's foreign policy. It took up a scheme which had been originally worked out by Sir Richard GRENVILLE. Drake set out on 13 Dec 1577 with the 100-ton *Pelican* and 4 other vessels, and about 160 men. His flagship was later renamed the *Golden Hind* after the crest of Sir Christopher Hatton, who held a big piece of the stock. He sailed down the coast of Africa, then crossed to Brazil, putting into Port St Julian in present-day Argentina, where he abandoned 2 ships and refitted the rest. The 3 ships made a swift 16-day passage through the Straits of Magellan (Aug–Sept 1578), only to be separated by storms in the Pacific. The *Marigold* disappeared, the *Elizabeth* returned to England while Drake was driven S of Tierra del Fuego, enabling him to establish the fact that S America did not continue as a great continent as far as the Pole. He now sailed N up the Pacific coast of S America, raiding Spanish ports and ships and capturing much silver and other booty, including the cargo of the treasure-ship *Cacafuego*, which carried one-third of a year's output of silver. After refitting somewhere on the coast of what is now California (which he claimed for the Q under the name of New Albion) he set out across the Pacific (July 1579) to the Moluccas (where he loaded up with cloves) then Java, and so back to England round the Cape of Good Hope, reaching Plymouth on 26 Sept 1580. He had not only played havoc with the security of the whole Spanish colonial empire, but he had also made a profit of 4,700% on the original investment. The Q showed her appreciation of both exploits by knighting him aboard his ship at Deptford on 4 Apr 1581. Her profit had been about £160,000 – 6 months' income.

(4) The 2nd W Indies Voyage (Sept 1585–July 1586) when, with 29 ships, including 2 of the Q's, he sacked Spanish settlements at Santo Domingo, Hispaniola (Haiti), Cartagena on the mainland and St Augustine, Florida. He failed to intercept the silver fleet, but brought home RALEGH's colonists from Roanoke (in present-day N Carolina).

(5) The Cádiz Raid (Apr–June 1587) – better known as 'the singeing of his Catholic Majesty's beard' – was perhaps Drake's most important contribution to the war against Spain. With great daring he sailed into Cádiz harbour, destroyed over 20 ships, and so upset the provisioning of the Armada that its sailing was delayed till 1588, giving England a year to prepare her defences. Before returning home, Drake captured the silver ship, the *San Felipe*, in the Azores.

(6) The Spanish Armada (1588) saw him as 2nd i/c to Ld Charles Howard of Effingham. He played a leading part in the action, especially in the attack off

119

Gravelines on 29 July 1588; though the story about him finishing his game of bowls before joining battle dates from a century later, and does not sound like Drake.

(7) The Portugal Expedition (Apr–June 1589), an ambitious reply to the Armada under the joint command of Drake (navy) and Sir John Norris (army), was a complete disaster, owing to inadequate victualling, ambiguous orders which were not in any case obeyed and arguments between the 2 commanders. Drake was court-martialled and in disgrace for 5 years.

(8) The last West Indies Voyage (Aug 1595–Jan 1596) under the joint command of Drake and Hawkins was another failure, instead of being a repetition of the triumph of 1585–6 which it was meant to be. Divided counsel again hampered operations, and the Spanish defences had been much improved. Hawkins d off Puerto Rico on 12 Nov 1595, and 10 weeks later Drake caught dysentery and d off Porto Bello, Panama.

Dudley, Edmund (*c* 1462–17 July 1510) Law and finance minister of K HENRY VII of England whose oppression of the rich led to his execution by K HENRY VIII.

Son of John Dudley, a Sussex gentleman; ed in the law at Gray's Inn; m 1st Anne Wyndesore; m 2nd Elizabeth Grey, by whom his eld son was John DUDLEY, later D of Northumberland. He became a member of Henry VII's Council in 1485; Speaker of the H of C (1504) and Pres of the Council. He is chiefly known, along with EMPSON, for his work as a member of a committee of the Council known as the Council Learned in the Law (beginning Sept 1504) which used legal and semi-legal pressures to collect the K's debts, and otherwise extract fines from the nobility and wealthy citizenry for breaches of the law (eg smuggling). By making the revenue-collecting machinery efficient to the point of oppressiveness, he increased the royal income during Henry VII's last years, made a fortune himself and caused deep resentment among the nobility which erupted on the K's death. One of the new K's methods of placating the baronage was to allow the destruction of Empson and Dudley. Dudley was found guilty of constructive treason before a special tribunal in Guildhall in July 1509 and executed a year later. During his imprisonment he wrote a political allegory called the *Tree of Commonwealth,* which advocated strong monarchy, but criticized corruption in Ch and State.

Dudley, John (1502–22 Aug 1553) Viscount Lisle (1542), Earl of Warwick (1547), D of Northumberland (1551). Tudor soldier, sailor and statesman, who became the chief minister of K EDWARD VI of England, made rapid changes in the direction of Protestantism, and was executed under Q MARY I for his role in the unsuccessful attempt to make Lady Jane Grey Q of England.

Son of Edmund DUDLEY and Elizabeth Grey, he was freed from the penalties of his father's attainder in 1512, and rose in the service of K HENRY VIII as a soldier, sailor and politician; m Jane, daughter of Sir Edward Guildford. He was appointed Ld High Admiral in 1543, invaded Scotland with SEYMOUR in May 1544, led the attack on Boulogne in Sept 1544, commanded the Channel fleet against the French invasion attempts of June and Aug 1545; and with Seymour headed the Protestant opposition to the faction of the 3rd D of NORFOLK, in the K's Council. During the death throes of the old K he aided Seymour in the overthrow of the whole Norfolk faction just before Henry's death, and backed his *coup d'état* just after it. During Seymour's Protectorate under the boy K Edward VI, Dudley added to his military reputation by being chiefly responsible for the English victory over the Scots at Pinkie (Midlothian) on 10 Sept 1547, and for the suppression of social unrest in England, defeating Ket's rebellion at Dussindale, nr Norwich, in Aug 1549. Less scrupulous and more realistic than Seymour, Dudley organized his overthrow and execution in stages between 1549 and 1552, and replaced him as the chief minister of Edward VI, though without the title of Ld Protector. He became Ld Admiral again in 1549, Great Master of the Household in 1550, Earl Marshal of England on 20 Apr 1551 and D of Northumberland on 11 Oct 1550. A skilled political manipulator, authoritarian and ruthless, he was motivated in the policies he now pursued by nothing more than an appetite for wealth and a pleasure in power – though what was good for Northumberland was not necessarily bad for England.

In foreign affairs, he reversed traditional policy in the light of the decline of the Emp CHARLES V and the rise of the French K HENRY II in the last of the HABSBURG–VALOIS WARS (1551–9). England became subservient to France (with her army, navy and fortresses depleted through lack of funds, and with the French dominant in Scotland, she had little choice) and unfriendly to Charles V (who was the cousin of MARY, the rightful heiress to the throne). Towards the social crisis he adopted the opposite view from that of Seymour, supporting property against poverty, repealing the laws against enclosure, repressing rural unrest and dropping agrarian reform. Although some further debasement took place, Dudley more than Seymour realized the importance of a sound coinage, and he promoted a recoinage, as well as a general overhaul of Gov finance and admin (under William Cecil, later Ld BURGHLEY) from which the reign of Q ELIZABETH I drew the benefit. Moreover, trade and industry flourished during his short reign. He founded the joint-stock company which sent Willoughby and Chancellor in search of the NE passage; and he built the dockyard at Chatham, another project which fructified under Elizabeth I.

In religious affairs, he supported a policy of headlong moves in the direction of Protestantism, not because he was a Calvinist or a Zwinglian, but probably because this policy enabled him and his supporters to secularize land belonging to the Bps – monastic and chantry properties having been already confiscated under Henry VIII and Seymour. Conservative Bps were deprived and replaced by Prots who were forced to hand over large amounts of land. Meanwhile, Parl ordered images to be removed from churches (1550), and CRANMER's 2nd Prayer Book (1552), from which all remnants of Catholicism still left in the 1549 version had been removed, was enforced by the 2nd Act of Uniformity, which also authorized the Prot Ordinal, prepared in 1550 to change RC priests into Ch of England ministers. And the creation of the Protestant Ch was completed by Cranmer's formulation of the Christian faith in his *42 Articles*, which received the royal assent on 12 June 1553, and later formed the basis of the Elizabethan *39 Articles*.

The succession question was a vital problem for Dudley, for his power would end with the fragile life of Edward VI if the legitimate laws of succession operated, and Mary Tudor became Q. To avoid this disaster, Dudley browbeat the K (though the initiative may well have come from Edward himself) to sign a document on 21 June 1553 excluding Mary and her sister Elizabeth from the succession on grounds of their illegitimacy. In their place, Lady Jane Grey was pronounced to be the monarch next in succession – and she had recently married Dudley's 4th son, Guildford Dudley, on 21 May 1553. Accordingly, he kept Edward's death (6 July 1553) secret for 3 days while he made his preparations, and proclaimed Jane Q on 10 July 1553. One vital thread in the plot was missing, however: he had failed to secure Mary herself, who got away to E Anglia, the heartland of the Norfolks. As Dudley went after her, his followers in London began to panic, while in the provs the people instinctively supported the rightful Tudor heiress. Having no troops capable of dealing with this situation, thanks to the gov's penury, Dudley gave up at Cambridge on 20 July 1553, and was executed at the Tower of London, shortly after Mary had established herself.

Edward VI (12 Oct 1537–6 July 1553) K of England (28 Jan 1547), a boy K whose reign was dominated by two magnates in succession and notable for the Protestantization of the Ch.

3rd child of K HENRY VIII and Q Jane Seymour; ed in Christian HUMANISM by Sir John Cheke, Richard Cox, Sir Anthony Cooke and Roger Ascham, to become an adept at Latin, Greek and French, a very studious Prot, haughty, priggish, and old for his years, independent-minded and keen on theology; betrothed to the future MARY, Q OF SCOTS (Tr of Greenwich, July 1543) and then to Elizabeth, daughter of K HENRY II of France (Tr of Angers, July 1551). Living less than 16 years, he was overshadowed in Gov by his uncle, Edward SEYMOUR, D of Somerset, and then by John DUDLEY, D of Northumberland, who had been the 2 chief members of the Council of Regency appointed by Henry VIII just before his death. The former defeated the Scots at Pinkie (Sept 1547) and united them in hatred against England, made moderate moves, aided by CRANMER, in the direction of Protestantism, and stimulated unrest among the poor and resentment among the rich by his adoption of policies worked out by the 'Commonwealth Men'. The latter followed a policy of subservience to France, support for enclosing landlords, encouragement of trade and full Protestantization of the Ch of England. From Aug 1551 onwards, Edward sat on the Council, and the intense pressures to which he became subject played havoc with his feeble health. As Mary, the heiress to the throne, was R C, neither Northumberland nor Protestantism would be safe in the event of the K's early demise, and so Edward signed an order in June 1553 excluding the future MARY I and ELIZABETH I from the succession in favour of Northumberland's daughter-in-law, Lady Jane Grey. In the event, the coup failed and the Tudor dynasty continued. The Tudor system of Gov survived also, after a reign which had witnessed a minor on the throne, a revival of the struggle between over-mighty subjects, a REFORMATION carried too far and too fast, deep economic and social disquiet, and profitless foreign adventures. Its survival was a testimonial to the soundness of the foundations laid by HENRY VII and Henry VIII.

Eliot, Sir John (20 Apr 1592–27 Nov 1632) A fiery orator who radicalized the Parl attack on BUCKINGHAM and K CHARLES I of England, who imprisoned him in the Tower until he d.

Only child of Richard Eliot, a landowning gentleman; ed at Blundell's, Tiverton, and Exeter, Oxford, as well as at the Inns of Court and on a Continental tour, where he met Buckingham, his future patron; m (1609) the heiress Radigund Gedy (d 1628). Under James I he was M P in the 2nd Parl (Addled) (Apr–June 1614) and, becoming a client of Buckingham, who was favourite and by 1618 chief minister, he was knighted in 1618 and made Vice-Admiral of Devon in 1622. In the 4th Parl (Feb 1624–Mar 1625) he emerged as a leading orator, supporting Buckingham by favouring the war against Spain and attacking CRANFIELD, but at the same time opposing non-Parl taxation and defending freedom of speech in Parl.

Under Charles I he broke with Buckingham because of his incompetent handling of foreign affairs, especially in the disastrous attack on Cádiz (1625), the victims of which he saw dying in the streets of Plymouth, Devon. He attacked the mismanagement in the 2nd Parl, and took the lead in impeaching Buckingham. Charles imprisoned him for 8 days in the Tower for sedition, and saved Buckingham by dissolving Parl. During the interval between Parls he was arrested again (1627–8) as one of the 76 who refused to pay the Forced Loan. In the 3rd Parl he spoke eloquently against arbitrary taxation and Arminianism, and took a leading part in the Petition of Right debates. As leader of the new generation of politicians, he voiced the extremist views and backed the violent tactics which broke the united front of Lords and Commons and led to the 11 years without Parl. It was Eliot who drew up the 3 Resolutions condemning anyone who introduced popery or Arminianism, or advised or paid non-Parl taxation. The K had ordered the H of C to adjourn, but Eliot's supporters held the Speaker, Sir John Finch, weeping in his chair until the Resolutions were passed (2 Mar 1629). Next day Eliot and 8 others were imprisoned in the Tower, and Eliot (along with Denzil Holles and Benjamin Valentine) was tried before the King's Bench (Jan–Feb 1630). He was fined £2,000 and imprisoned for as long as he refused to acknowledge his guilt and give security for good behaviour. As he refused, he d in the Tower of consumption, and the K refused to allow his family to have his body for burial in Cornwall.

Elizabeth I (7 Sept 1533–24 Mar 1603) Q of England (Nov 1558) whose statesmanship united a people deeply divided socially and ideologically, and saved it from foreign conquest. At home, she devised a *politique* religious settlement which embraced the widest possible consensus, and then defended it from Cath and Prot extremists. She enjoyed the adulation of a nation at that time unusually creative in literature, music and the visual arts. She held the reins of a restive society which was profoundly stimulated by overseas trade and exploration as well as by agrarian and industrial innovation; and for the time being she successfully headed off the political discontents of thrusting social groups by skilful management of Parl, and soothed economic wounds with policies of social welfare. She succeeded in establishing the authority of the Crown with a Gov which represented all the powerful interests, and passed a sound inheritance on to her heir, though not without its problems, due in part to her very success. Abroad, where the independence of England was gravely threatened by the Cath powers of France and Spain, she manoeuvred in the twilight zone between diplomacy and war with outstanding skill; stretching narrow resources to the limit, she struck with success wherever danger loomed: in Scotland, the Netherlands, France, Spain or Ireland, across the Atlantic, or in the English Channel.

Daughter of K HENRY VIII and his 2nd Q Consort, Anne Boleyn; ed in HUMANISM by John Cheke, William Grindall and Roger Ascham, she was familiar with Greek and Latin literature, and good at French, Italian, Spanish and music. When she was 2 years and 8 months old, her father divorced and beheaded her mother, making Elizabeth illegitimate, until the Succession Act of 1544 and Henry's will of Dec 1546 declared her to be in line for the throne after EDWARD VI and MARY I. Under K Edward VI, Henry's widow, Catherine Parr, who had become a 2nd mother to Edward, m Thomas, Ld Seymour of Sudeley, brother of the Protector, Edward SEYMOUR; but he tried to seduce Elizabeth – who was then aged 15 – and was executed. Under Mary I, she was regarded with suspicion as the Prot heiress, and spent 2 months in the Tower after Wyatt's rebellion. Nothing was proved against her, and in the latter part of the reign she lived at Hatfield Palace enjoying the protection of K PHILIP II of Spain (Mary's husband), who preferred her as heiress to MARY, Q OF SCOTS who, though Cath, was pro-French. On the death of Mary I Elizabeth succeeded without trouble and was crowned at Westminster Abbey on 15 Jan 1559.

Tall, red-haired and gaudy, she was every inch a Q, tough, dominating and unfathomable. She could be abrasive and soothing by turns and, though at times swept off course by anger or affection, she was normally guided by an unflinching devotion to her interest and duty. She was utterly cold to the religious and other idealistic enthusiasms of her day, and could concentrate her efforts single-mindedly on the preservation of the unity and independence of England and her own security within it. She picked a small, efficient Council, representative of the chief interests in the politics of her day, where differences could be hammered out in the light instead of festering unseen. The Council plied her with information and advice, and pushed her this way and that; but she took the decisions herself, sometimes after long delays, interpretable either as masterly patience or weak procrastination. Her reign divides into 2 main eras. 1558–88 was a period marked by (a) the religious settlement; the attacks on it by (b) the Puritans and (c) the Caths; complicated by the problem of (d) Elizabeth's marriage; which in its turn involved (e) foreign policy, where 3 phases are notable: (i) 1558–68 when fear of France predominated, (ii) 1568–85 which brought peace with France and a growing quarrel with Spain, and (iii) 1585–8, bringing war with Spain, culminating in the ARMADA. 1588–1603 was a period marked by (a) continuous warfare against Spain (i) in the Netherlands, (ii) in France, (iii) in the Spanish emp itself and (iv) in Ireland; and (b) domestic problems heralding the break-up of the Elizabethan political system.

1558–88

(a) The religious settlement was the most urgent task facing the new Q. Circumstances at home and abroad required her to be a Prot and a Cath at one and the same time, and thus to delay a decision; but Parl pushed her into precipitate action. On the one hand, she needed to avoid provoking the Cath powers of France and Spain then ending the long HABSBURG–VALOIS WARS at the Tr of Cateau-Cambrésis (Apr 1559), and thus free for a joint attack on England. She also had to consider the Cath consciences of all her bps, and most of her clergy and people. On the other hand, in Cath eyes she was illegitimate and not the rightful Q; moreover, the Pp, not the Q, was the head of the Ch – 2 views she could not accept. In addition, some of the best minds in the English Ch had spent Mary's reign in Calvinist churches on the Continent. They now returned, full of determination to remodel the Ch on authentic Prot lines. And ready to collaborate with them was a knot of Puritan MPs, whose leverage over the Q derived from the fact that any settlement had to be by Act of Parl because of the precedents set in the previous 3 reigns. In consequence, Elizabeth was denied the luxury of procrastination and was forced into a settlement more Prot than she wanted, enshrined in the Act of Supremacy (Apr 1559), which in effect reversed Mary's reconciliation with Rome and declared the Q in Parl to be the 'supreme governor' of the Ch; and in the Act of Uniformity (May 1559), which enforced the more Prot 1552 Prayer Book of Edward VI, modified in a Cath direction as far as the Communion service and clerical vestments were concerned. This compromise between Q and Parl, and Cath and Prot, was accepted by most of the clergy and laity; however, on the one hand, it was disliked by the Q, and rejected by all the bps but one as too Prot (they were replaced by Prots); on the other, it was regarded by the militant Prots just back from exile as but the first tiny step on a long Puritan road. Not surprisingly, it soon came under attack from PURITANS and Caths.

(b) The Puritans took a radical view of the REFORMATION. To the moderate members of the Ch of England, the Reformation was simply a matter of removing the abuses that had crept into the Ch while it was under Rome; to the Puritans it was a question of creating a new Ch from the very foundations, in which not only clerical corruption would be eliminated, but also many Cath elements, such as vestments, ornaments, holy days, kneeling at the altar, using the sign of the cross in baptism and the ring in marriage, on the grounds that they had no warrant in the Bible. Such opinions were passionately expressed by a vigorous minority of clergy in Convocation, and nobility and gentry in Parl, and sympathetically viewed by people in high places: Archbps such as PARKER and GRINDAL, Privy Councillors such as LEICESTER and WALSINGHAM. The *first wave* of Puritan activity in the 1560s focused mainly on clerical vestments and other aspects of ritual (the Vestiarian Controversy). The Q refused their demands, whether in Convocation or Parl, and ordered Parker and the bps to exercise discipline. By the late 1560s the moderate Puritans had been battered into obedience, leaving a hard core of intransigents moving to more extreme positions. In the *second wave* (1570s onwards), the Puritans naturally began to question the authority of those – whether in the State or the Ch – who were blocking their progress. In the state, MPs such as Thomas Norton, Walter Strickland and Peter WENTWORTH advanced views of the privileges of Parl which conflicted with the prerogatives of the Crown. In the Ch, the Puritans, led by Thomas CARTWRIGHT, Professor of Divinity at Cambridge, demanded the abolition of bps and the erection of the full Presbyterian form of Ch Gov. In many parishes from 1564 onwards, the unofficial rudiments of this were being constructed (or so it seemed to Elizabeth) by the 'prophesyings', or informal spiritual and intellectual exercises of clergy and laity to raise their religious level. She ordered Archbp Grindal to suppress them, and then suspended him when he refused. In the 1580s the so-called 'classical' movement spread over a large part of the SE and centre of England: an underground, 'shadow' Presbyterian Ch within the Ch of England, with synods and provincial and national assemblies. More extreme still were the Brownists and the Barrowists who demanded independent congregations and no national Ch. All forms of Puritanism contained a fatal flaw in Elizabeth's eyes: the element of social and political insubordination; and at last she found in WHITGIFT a like-minded Archbp who was prepared to hammer them in the Inquisition-like Court of High Commission, while she resolutely rejected all their bills in Parl. Between them they purged the Ch clean by the end of the reign; but left outside it a discontented and determined minority of clergy and laymen to plague the 1st 2 Stuarts – as well as an unreformed Ch to be shot at.

(c) The Catholics declined in morale and numbers from 1558–68. They were not persecuted in England, and were not helped from abroad, it being PHILIP II of Spain's view then that a Cath victory in England would only strengthen France. A Cath revival gathered way from 1568 onwards with the imprisonment of Mary, Q of Scots in England (1568–87); the REVOLT OF THE NORTHERN EARLS (1569); the papal bull excommunicating and deposing the Q (Feb 1570); the 3 plots aimed at destroying Elizabeth and replacing her with Mary, Q of Scots, led by Ridolfi (1571–2), Throckmorton (1582) and Babington (1586); the arrival (1574 onwards) of priests trained in William ALLEN's seminary at Douai, Netherlands; the landing (1580) of the 1st Jesuit mission under CAMPION and PARSONS; the 'Enterprise of England' (1572 onwards) bringing Spanish attacks on Ireland; the quarrel with Spain, becoming open war from 1585, and reaching its climax with the Armada in 1588. Pressed by her ministers and Parl, the Q sharpened the anti-Cath laws – on political rather than religious grounds. In 1571 an Act made it treason to introduce papal bulls and other instruments from Rome. In 1581 an Act made it treason to withdraw subjects from their obedience to the Q or their membership of the Ch of England, and raised the fine for non-attendance at Ch from 12d a week to £20 a month. In 1585 an Act ordered Jesuits and seminary priests to leave the country within 40 days, after which priests could be charged with treason. In 1593 an Act ordered all Caths to remain within 5 miles of home. By this time, however, the persecution was easing off. By the use of fines, prison, exile, torture and the execution of about 120 clergy and 60 laymen, Elizabeth had eliminated Caths as a danger to the State. Only the Jesuits and their handful of followers looked to Spain for a lead. The secular priests and their congregations were English patriots, as they demonstrated during the crisis of the Armada.

(d) Elizabeth's marriage and the succession question were vital political problems to which there seemed to be no solution. Marriage to an English noble would have raised up an over-mighty subject and reduced the Q to the level of a faction-leader. Marriage to a Continental Pr would have repeated the mistake of Q Mary I and made England the satellite of a foreign power. Thus statesmanship – and possibly her own wishes, and even physique – required her to remain the 'virgin Q'. On the other hand, her death without an heir – except for Mary, Q of Scots – threatened danger to the Ch of England and other aspects of English life – as her subjects saw so vividly when she almost d of smallpox in Oct 1562. Like the Ch, the Q's marriage became a constitutional issue between Crown and Parl (1566, 1576 and 1593). To Elizabeth, it was one of those 'matters of state' which Parl had no business to debate. At the same time, she used the marriage question constantly as a weapon of foreign policy.

(e) Foreign policy was a matter of defending the security of England and the Q against the dangers posed by the traditional enemy, France, and the traditional ally, Spain. This would have been a serious danger indeed if these 2 could have united in their Catholicism; but usually their material rivalry enabled the Q to play one off against the other, irrespective of the religious issue. (i) 1558–68: Fear of France was the principal theme, for the dominant noble faction there, under François, D de GUISE, aimed at a French–Scots–English emp through his niece, Mary, Q of Scots, who was married to the *dauphin* – the future K FRANCIS II – and was the Cath claimant to the throne of England. Elizabeth boldly attacked this plan in 2 wars. First, she invaded Scotland in support of the Prot nobles, and by the Tr of Edinburgh (July 1560) the French agreed to leave the country. Second, under the Tr of Hampton Court (Sept 1562), she fought for the Hugs against the Guises in the 1st of the FRENCH WARS OF RELIGION, though without success, for by the Tr of Troyes (Apr 1564) she had to accept the permanent loss of Calais, which had been lost to France under Mary I. It was because the overthrow of Elizabeth would strengthen France that Philip II restrained papal or other attacks on her during the 1st decade of the reign, in spite of her Prot Ch settlement. (ii) 1568–85: Uneasy peace with France and growing quarrel with Spain evolved through a change in France's situation. The Wars of Religion left France no longer formidable; and in this period Spain and England therefore no longer needed one another's alliance. In fact, they could afford to drift into enmity, and were encouraged to do so by 3 sets of events. First were the imprisonment in England of Mary, Q of Scots, the REVOLT OF THE NETHERLANDS, the plots against Elizabeth and the efforts of the COUNTER-REFORMATION, backed by the Pp and Spain, to make a counter-attack in Ireland and England. Second came the invasions by DRAKE, HAWKINS and others of the Spanish Atlantic empire in order to block the flow of silver, especially Drake's Nombre de Dios raid (1572–3) and his circumnavigation of the world (1577–80). Third was the growing semi-official aid given by Elizabeth to the Dutch in their Revolt against Spain. In this new situation, there were times when Elizabeth made an alliance with France, partly to keep her from joining Spain, partly to have some say in French attempts to take over the Revolt of the Netherlands. The 1st occasion was from 1570–72 when COLIGNY was in power in France, and there was talk of a French attack on Spain in the Netherlands, helped by England. The Q sent Walsingham over to negotiate a marriage between herself and Henry, D of Anjou, the French K's younger brother, and to sign the Anglo-French Tr of Blois (Apr 1572). Anjou envisaged a princely role for himself in the liberated Netherlands, and Elizabeth was anxious to prevent French dominance there; and she worked for French friendship until the Massacre of St Bartholomew (23–4 Aug 1572) brought an end to the whole episode. The 2nd occasion was during the period 1578–84, when marriage proposals were dangled before the D of Alençon, the French K's youngest brother, who was similarly hoping to carve out a kingdom for himself in the Netherlands. His sudden death in June 1584 ended this episode. Elizabeth's main preoccupation as far as the Netherlands and France were concerned was to keep the Dutch and French ports out of the hands of any power strong enough to use them as bases for an invasion of England. She would have preferred Spain to remain in possession of the Netherlands, though without an army, of course. She feared that the victory of WILLIAM of Orange would only lead to the military presence there of France. She certainly had no intention of supporting the Dutch in a Prot crusade, as Walsingham and other members of the Council wanted. In any case, she objected in principle to supporting rebels against legitimate authority. Hitherto she had sanctioned only indirect aid to the rebels. She took possession of the Spanish treasure sheltering in English ports on its way to the Netherlands in Dec 1568. She allowed the Sea Beggars to use English ports, and then expelled them with momentous results (proclamation of Mar 1572). She allowed volunteers to go and fight; but when the death of Alençon (now called Anjou) was followed by the assassination of William of Orange (10 July 1584) and a series of Spanish victories under FAR-NESE, Elizabeth had to opt for open war. 1585–8: (iii) The War with Spain came with the Tr of Nonsuch (Aug 1585), the expedition of LEICESTER to the Nether-lands (1585–7), and the presence of English troops there for the rest of the reign. Other blows at Spanish treasure and pride were Drake's piratical West Indies expedition of 1585–6 and his attack on Cádiz, where part of the Armada was assembling (1587). Meanwhile, the international scene, and the position of England in it, had greatly changed from the point of view of Philip II. From 1580 onwards N Europe took 1st place in his calculations, as he broke off the war with Turkey, conquered the maritime Kdom of Portugal, and prepared to deal once and for all with the Prot rebels of France, Holland and England. He was no longer restrained from attacking Elizabeth by the fear that her defeat would strengthen the French. France had long been prostrated by the Wars of Religion. With the death of Alençon, the Hug Henry of Navarre was heir to the French throne, and Henry, D of GUISE, far from being a rival of Spain, was by the Tr of Joinville (Dec 1584) her satellite. In other words, the preconditions for the preparation and dispatch of the Armada were there; by destroying this when it sailed, Elizabeth not only saved England, but contributed incalculably to the independence of France and Holland, and to the survival of Protestantism.

1588–1603

(a) Continuous warfare against Spain on a wide front and on an exhausting scale characterized the remaining years of the Q's life. (i) In the Netherlands a small expeditionary force served with MAURICE of Nassau until the end of the reign, though paid for by the Dutch from 1598 onwards. (ii) In France HENRY IV was helped financially, and small armies were sent to Dieppe, Normandy, in 1598, to St Malo and Brest, Brittany, from 1591–5, and to Rouen, Normandy, 1591–3 – until France made the separate Tr of Vervins with Spain (May 1598), after which Elizabeth rightly began to feel that a new situation had arisen, with France the danger once more. (iii) With Spain there was unremitting warfare. Every year between 100 and 200 private-enterprise piratical expeditions set out from England, bringing in between £150,000 and £300,000 per annum in prizes. At the same time, official attempts were made to ruin Spain by a silver blockade: eg the disastrous Portugal Expedition of Drake and Norris (Apr–June 1589); the unsuccessful attempt to waylay the silver fleet which culminated in GRENVILLE's heroic defeat on his *Revenge* (Sept 1591) – a triumph for Spain's new policy of convoying the fleet; the last calamitous W Indies expedition of Drake and Hawkins (Aug 1595–Jan 1596); the Cádiz Expedition of ESSEX and Howard of Effingham (June–Aug 1596), which defeated the Spanish fleet and held Cádiz for a fortnight; the Islands Voyage under Essex (July–Oct 1597) – an unsuccessful attempt to destroy the new Spanish armada and capture the silver fleet, the last of its kind. Meanwhile, Spain assembled 2 armadas with a view to invading England from Ireland, both of which were dispersed by bad weather in Oct 1596 and Oct 1597. (iv) In Ireland, where Elizabeth continued the uphill task of bringing order out of chaos by alternately crushing and employing one or other of the various tribal chieftains (eg in the rebellion of Shane O'Neill in Ulster, 1559–66, and the conspiracy of Sir James Fitzmaurice Fitzgerald in Munster, 1569–72), the problem intensified as papal and Spanish involvement injected ideological fervour into the war by bringing the Irish under the influence of the COUNTER-REFORMATION. It took Elizabeth from 1579 to 1583 to subjugate the Fitzgeralds with their Roman money and Spanish troops. She then confiscated 200,000 acres of land for redistribution among English 'undertakers', and Ireland gave no trouble during the Armada crisis. From 1593, however, the Irish lead was assumed by Hugh O'Neill, Earl of Tyrone, claiming to be the K of Ulster. From 1586 onwards he had active Spanish help, eg the Armadas of 1596 and 1597, and the force which captured Kinsale harbour on the S coast in Nov 1601. Elizabeth had to make a very serious effort, at crippling expense. The expedition of Essex was a failure (Apr–Sept 1597); but in Charles Blount, Ld Mountjoy, she found a general equal to the task. He drove the Spanish out of Kinsale in Dec 1601, and completely subjugated the island, receiving the surrender of Tyrone just after the Q's death in Mar 1603.

(b) Domestic problems, which had always been present, assumed critical dimensions in the last years of the reign, when the Q's skill at soothing away pain declined, though there were flashes of the old magic at times. The great tidal wave of economic, social, religious, intellectual and political change which had swept over England during the Tudor period now washed up powerful groups of malcontents in all classes, who either feared the pace of change, or kicked against the obstructions lying in the way. The immense financial strain of the long war against Spain, and the 5 consecutive bad harvests from 1594 onwards, heightened tension everywhere, and the State increasingly had to intervene. Most of its measures were conservative – aiming to hold back economic and social change – and paternalistic – providing relief for the victims of progress. Acts were passed against enclosures; attempts were made to control prices and fix wages. The Parl of 1597 provided that rogues and vagabonds should be sent back to their parishes for punishment and forced labour (Act for the Punishment of Rogues, Vagabonds, and Sturdy Beggars, 1598). The famous Poor Law Act of 1598 (usually known by the year 1601, when it was modified) inaugurated a system of relief based on parish rates which lasted until 1834. Not that these measures were very effective in practice. Lacking revenue, armed forces and a bureaucracy, and not having the right to change the law or levy taxes without consent of Parl, the Crown was too weak to take adequate measures. Moreover, in a period when practice was making Parl more efficient, and M Ps were growing wealthy, confident and aggressive, the Q lost the leaders in Ch and State who by their regular contact with Puritans and other extremists had knitted all groups together in one political system. Archbp Grindal d in 1583, Leicester in 1588, Walsingham in 1590, Burghley in 1598. In the Ch, Archbp Whitgift attacked discontent with terror, not reasonable reform. In the State, the Q lost her old skill at balancing the factions; and the new generation of Privy Councillors failed to give an adequate lead in Parl. The bitter Court rivalries of Essex, Robert Cecil, RALEGH and Francis BACON and the desperate rebellion of Essex and his retinue in Feb 1601 show what rifts were forming in the Elizabethan political world. Though in the Parl of 1593 neither James Morrice, who tried to initiate Puritan measures against the Ch, nor Peter Wentworth, who made a last attempt to stir up the succession question, found any following – the heat was out of the issues for the moment – yet the Parls of 1597 and 1601 were extremely restive over taxation. The H of C heard some strong speeches, especially against monopolies – the device by which the Q paid her ministers, who then had to recoup by soaking the public. Some MPs were even spoiling for a constitutional fight, but with her timely retreat and her 'golden speech', Elizabeth won them round and showed that the régime was in no danger so long as she lived. 'Though God hath raised me high,' she said to a deputation of 140 MPs on 30 Nov 1601, 'yet this I count the glory of my crown, that I have reigned with your loves . . . Though you have had and may have many mightier and wiser princes sitting on this seat, yet you never had nor shall have any that will love you better . . . And I pray you, Mr Comptroller, Mr Secretary, and you of my council, that before the gentlemen depart into their counties you bring them all to kiss my hand.' Sixteen months later at Richmond Palace she d in her sleep in the early hours of the morning, and the much-feared succession went peacefully ahead, thanks to the prior planning of Robert Cecil and K JAMES VI of Scotland. It is possible to argue that she papered over many long-term problems with short-term tactical victories – and thus made life difficult for the Stuarts – but she preserved the unity, the independence and the peculiarity of England, and there can be no doubting her greatness.

Elizabeth (Petrovna) (7 Dec 1709–25 Dec 1761) Empss of Russia (1741) under whom Russia experienced a period of steady and efficient Gov, when the Court and the top nobility became more westernized, business flourished under Enlightened economic policies, and Russia played a leading part in European politics, successfully checking Prussia in the SEVEN YEARS WAR.

Daughter of Emp PETER I and his 2nd wife, Empss CATHERINE I; ed in French, German and dancing, but little else; remained in tactful obscurity during ANNA's reign (1730–40), then took power in a palace coup when the guards of the Preobrazhenskii Regiment helped her to overthrow the baby-Emp Ivan VI and his German entourage. Ivan VI (the son of Anna Leopoldovna, the daughter of Empss Anna's sister, Catherine) had been named Emp by his great-aunt Empss Anna, with her favourite, Biron, as Regent. Biron had neglected to cultivate the guards, or any other section of the Russian nobility, or even many of his fellow Germans; and he had been overthrown and sent to Siberia by Anna Leopoldovna and some guards in 1740. Anna Leopoldovna then ruled as Regent for her son until Nov 1741 when Elizabeth and her faction of guardsmen (supported by the top-rank *dvoryane* as well as the rank and file, and aided by the French and Swedish ambassadors) overthrew and exiled them. This coup was accompanied by the usual torturings, judicial murders, deportations and confiscations of property, Ivan VI himself being imprisoned for life until he was eventually murdered under Empss CATHERINE II (5 July 1764).

Elizabeth was a most attractive, vivacious and warm-hearted woman, who gave herself up without shame to pleasure and extravagance, enjoying food, clothes, religious observations and parties, as well as a succession of good-looking guards officers, mostly of lowly origin. She did not marry, but finally became deeply attached to Alexis Razumovsky, an illiterate Ukrainian Cossack with a wonderful voice. It was not easy for her ministers to obtain an interview with her to discuss State business and, though she intervened in politics much more than Anna, she left the main burden of Gov to others.

At home, the main thrust of Gov activity anticipated the work of Catherine II, though the latter blackened Elizabeth's reign in order to exaggerate her own originality. (a) In Gov the Cab was replaced by the Privy Chancery (1741) as the arena where high policy was thrashed out; and this in turn was replaced by the 10-man Conference (1756); but such institutions gained or lost importance according to whether the current favourite or ministers used them or not. Things were different with the Senate, which she revived (1741) along with its Gen Prokuror (Pr Nikita Trubetskoi). This institution handled not policy but the daily detail of justice and admin. Its steady work was crucial to the gradual co-ordination of prov Gov by St Petersburg, to the formation of a systematized form of rule. At the same time the Secret Chancery (security police) continued its sinister work in brutally repressing any sign of dissidence. (b) The economy continued to flourish under Enlightened Gov policies which relaxed the control of the State in order to encourage private enterprise. Internal customs duties were replaced by high import and export duties at the ports (1753–7). A decree of 1753 set up the State Bank of the Nobility to provide low-interest capital. On the other hand, economic growth could never soar without an enterprising middle class, and this did not develop in the absence of public confidence. The State continued to hand out monopolies and other privileges in order to interest the nobility in trade and industry; but private people were reluctant to take risks when all successful businesses found their profits tapped by a permanently indebted State or a corrupt admin machine. (c) The nobility added to their privileges, their chief aims being to reduce their service to the State and increase their power over their serfs. In the long years of peace (1743–57) the *dvoryane* could spend more time tending their estates; but, though they were powerful as a class (witness their role in palace coups), as individuals they and their property were still at the mercy of a capricious and arbitrary State without the rule of law. On the other hand, by decrees of 1746 and 1748 the *dvoryane* achieved the monopoly of serf-ownership (except for the Crown and the Ch). Moreover, they increased their arbitrary power over the economic and social life of their serfs to such a degree that peasant flight and rebellion became a constant preoccupation of the Gov. (d) The Westernization of Russia continued apace. French language and culture became the fashion among the top nobility, but Russian life was affected also by all the scientific and technological advances of the W European Enlightenment. Thanks to the Empss's favourite, Ivan Shuvalov, the Univ of Moscow (Russia's first) and 2 secondary schools were founded by a decree of 1755. Shuvalov was also concerned with the foundation of the Academy of Arts (1757); and the historian, Vasily Tatishchev, wrote much of his *Russian History* in this period, though it was not published until 1768–74. St Petersburg continued to grow during Elizabeth's reign, the great Paris-born architect, Bartolomeo Francesco Rastrelli, being responsible for the Hermitage, the Smolny Convent and other rococo palaces, where the minuet and the quadrille were all the rage.

Likewise the army, navy and diplomatic service kept pace with the W, enabling Russia to play the part of a great power in European affairs.

Abroad, Russian policy was mainly in the capable hands of Count A. P. Bestuzhev-Ryumin from his appointment as Vice-Chancellor in 1741, until he was ousted by rivals in 1758. (a) The Russo-Swedish War (1741–3) which he inherited arose from Sweden's desire to take advantage of the palace coup which overthrew Biron to win back some of the provs lost in the GREAT NORTHERN WAR. The Count attacked Sweden with great vigour, and by the Tr of Abo (Aug 1743) Russia annexed another slice of Finland (the prov of Kymmenegard) and still kept Swedish internal affairs under her tutelage. (b) The WAR OF AUSTRIAN SUCCESSION (1740–48) found Russia neutral owing to the tug-of-war between Bestuzhev-Ryumin (who favoured an alliance with Austria against France and Prussia) and rivals at Court who favoured an alliance with Prussia. Eventually, the Count's view – that the rise of Prussia upset the balance of Europe to the peril of Russia – prevailed, and his diplomacy played a leading part in bringing about (c) the DIPLOMATIC REVOLUTION (1749–56) (though this was not his intention) and (d) the SEVEN YEARS WAR (which led to his disgrace). It was the death of the Empss at St Petersburg in the crisis of the war that rescued FREDERICK II from imminent defeat; for her successor, PETER III, was an ardent admirer of the Prussian K, and immediately stopped the war against him.

Empson, Sir Richard (d 17 Aug 1510) Lawyer and finance minister to K HENRY VII of England whose oppression of the rich led to his execution by K HENRY VIII.

Ed in law at the Middle Temple; worked for Ks Edward IV and Richard III and then Henry VII; MP in 1491, Speaker of the H of C (Oct 1491), Chancellor of the Duchy of Lancaster (1504) and knighted in Feb 1504, he became notorious with Edmund DUDLEY for his extortions as a member of the Council Learned in the Law, was arrested at the very start of the reign of K Henry VIII, condemned for constructive treason at Northampton Assizes (Oct 1509), attainted by Parl (Jan 1510) and executed in London.

Enlightened Absolutists The name applied to rulers of the second half of C18 who continued the build-up of ABSOLUTISM, fortified by the theories of the Enlightenment. Their motives were primarily practical – ie they needed to strengthen the power of their central Govs in order to suppress anarchic tendencies at home, and provide security against dangers from abroad – but they could not but be influenced by the current teachings of the *philosophes*. (Neither could their opponents, the guardians of tradition.)

The Enlightenment was not a coherent body of thought, but was broadly the collection of ideas which were in vogue among thinking men in the second half of C18. Deriving ultimately from classical times and the Renaissance, these ideas were developed in C17 Holland and Britain: eg by René Descartes with his rationalistic approach and habit of systematic doubt; by John Locke who based his philosophy and political theory on observation; and by Isaac Newton, who demonstrated the powers of observation and experiment with his laws of motion and gravitation. In C18, these ideas were further developed in France, and publicized all over Europe in French, the international language of the time, in such works as Montesquieu's *De l'Esprit des Lois* (1748), Condillac's *Essai sur l'Origine des Connaissances Humaines* (1746), the *Encyclopédie* of Diderot and d'Alembert (1751 onwards), Voltaire's *Dictionnaire Philosophique* (1764) and Rousseau's *Contrat Social* and *Émile* (1762). Although the *philosophes* did not form a school of thought, they subscribed together to a number of broad propositions. They had been taught by the Renaissance and REFORMATION to adopt the ideas of the classical writers, free from any bondage to medieval dogma. These had shown that the basis of knowledge was reason and observation, not reliance on authorities; and the first result of this new approach, in the late C17, was the Scientific Revolution in the physical sciences. The thinkers of the Enlightenment believed that human behaviour also followed laws which could be discovered by reason and observation, and which could be applied to morality, Gov, the economy and the social order. The Enlightened Absolutists believed that these laws had been discovered, and that it was their duty to apply them strictly. (It would have been pointless to do otherwise, they thought, just as in geometry, for example, it would be pointless not to follow Euclid strictly.) Whereas in the disturbed C17 political theorists had been concerned to find arguments to justify the exercise of power, or resistance to it, in the more settled C18 the Enlightenment accepted the state and focused its attention on ways of using political power to better human life. Moreover, life in the century after the THIRTY YEARS WAR (1616–48) became more secularized, with men paying less attention to their eternal salvation than to their earthly happiness. In addition, men took an optimistic view of the possibilities of improving life on earth, if Govs applied the laws of human nature like engineers applying the laws of physics. Finally, in political theory, they believed that power is a trust from the community. This was a doctrine which, of course, encouraged radical resistance to absolutism; but it could also justify despotism – in fact, a despotism far more ruthless than was ever envisaged by earlier thinkers who defended monarchy with arguments from divine right or long-established tradition. An Enlightened Absolutist regarded the State as a sacred entity. It was superior to himself in importance, and there was no limit to what he would do in its interests. He thought of himself as 'the first servant of the State'; and there is no tyrant so oppressive as the ruler who is ready to jeopardize himself and his eternal salvation – sacrifice anything, in fact – for this earthly master.

In Gov the Enlightened Absolutist aimed at centralizing his State by eliminating the constitutional privileges enjoyed by provs through their Diets, Estates, Cortes etc, the chief privileges being in the collection of revenue, the raising of armed forces and the dispensing of justice. Some rulers tried to erase the very boundaries of the old provs by creating new sets of provs and districts based on rational principles. Similarly, where there was a national Diet or other representative body with powers of consent to taxation or changes in the law, monarchs battled hard to eliminate this limitation on their absolutism. They tried to replace traditional central, prov and local officials – especially those who had bought their offices – with bureaucrats who were trained, appointed, promoted and dismissed in accordance with the latest political and economic theories. These new civil servants had to follow, not their individual whims, as in the past, but uniform procedures laid down by the K; and in multilingual empires such as the Austrian monarchy they all used the dominant language. In other words, the Enlightened Absolutists were building the admin machinery of the modern State, whose wheels could go on turning without the detailed personal intervention of the ruler. (a) In taxation they tried to eliminate the immunities enjoyed by the nobles or clergy or municipal élites; and, after counting the population, and surveying the land, they hoped to base taxation on ability to pay. (b) The army was as far as possible withdrawn from the control of prov feudal lords or professional military entrepreneurs, and entrusted to a department of State, which alone had the resources – admin, technical or financial – adequate for C18 warfare. (c) Judicial reform was another important aspect of the Enlightened ruler's work. It usually involved the compilation of codes of criminal and civil law, uniform throughout the provs and based on humane and rational principles. Torture and capital punishment were usually frowned on by Enlightened Absolutists. At the same time, they tried to set up a network of district and prov courts of appeal, manned by trained jurists and following uniform procedures, to supervise the judgments of the old manor, Ch and town tribunals. In this unifying work, the new courts came under the watchful eye of the supreme court in the capital city; and one of the chief tasks of the new system was to iron out the legal privileges enjoyed by social groups or districts, and create what was for them the ideal situation: the equality of all citizens before the law.

The economy of the country occupied the attention of the Enlightened Absolutists because of its intimate connection with the revenue, and its possible effect on public order. In a depression, the masses refused to pay taxes and rioted in the streets. (a) In agriculture – the chief branch of the economy (being the sole source of wealth, according to the Physiocrats) – Govs invested great efforts to drain marshes, clear wastes, settle immigrants, teach new methods, develop better crops and improve cattle and sheep. Serfdom was regarded as an uneconomic and inhumane method of production, and in central and E Europe, where it was common, rulers did all they could to abolish, or at least regularize or reduce, compulsory labour services (*Robot, corvée*). In general, they succeeded on their royal domains, but not on noble or Ch lands. The rulers aimed at a free, prosperous and mobile peasantry, paying less money to their lords and priests, and more to the State. They were to form a buoyant market for manufactured goods, and, if need be, have the right to leave the manor in order to participate in urban industries. (b) In industry – following the Physiocrats – the Enlightened Absolutists used the powers of the State to eliminate all the artificial obstructions to the natural working of the economy, whether in the form of serfdom, gild monopolies, prov privileges, urban immunities or mercantilist state regulations. At the same time, in a more positive way, they encouraged enterprise by lending capital, guaranteeing markets, easing access to raw materials, establishing uniform weights, measures and currency, and imposing protective tariffs – sometimes even setting up royal factories for porcelain, glass or fine cloth. Where entrepreneurs were missing, bureaucrats filled the gap. (c) Commerce, similarly, was liberated and encouraged. Internal customs barriers round cities or between provs were reduced; roads, rivers, canals, ports and posts were improved; merchant ships were built, and commercial treaties negotiated.

Cultural life came equally under their scrutiny, the 2 chief objects being to reduce the powers of the Ch and to modernize the system of education. (a) The Churches had to retreat before the regalism of the absolutists. Externally, the power of the Pp was reduced: taxes to Rome were cut; papal Bulls needed royal permission before promulgation; agents from Rome lost their powers of visiting monasteries. Internally, the training and work of the clergy were taken over by the State, which regarded priests more as agents for education, health and welfare than as the means of eternal salvation. Monasteries – particularly purely contemplative houses – were dissolved, and their wealth confiscated. The censorship of the press was taken from the Ch, and administered by the State, sometimes in favour of Enlightened writers. Toleration was extended to economically useful minority groups, whether Prots, Orthodox Christians or Jews. In many states, the JESUITS were expelled and the INQUISITION tamed; and, with these guardians of tradition swept aside, the State could reshape the education system. (b) Education was expanded and improved at univ, secondary and elementary level. Practical subjects and modern methods combined to train civil servants, technicians and manual labourers, who were all programmed with upright behaviour and conscientious toil on behalf of the economy and the state.

The social order was modified, whether deliberately, or simply as a by-product of other measures. In general, Enlightened Absolutists preferred a situation where all Estates, classes, races, religions and provs were equal in their subjection to the monarchy; but in practice they had to encourage different groups as necessity required. The nobles had to be protected as leaders of the army; the burghers encouraged as the source of enterprise; the peasants supported as the beasts of burden of the economy and the backbone of the army. (*See also* CATHERINE II, CHARLES III, FREDERICK II, JOSEPH II.)

Erasmus, Desiderius (?26 Oct 1466–9–12 July 1536) Leading exponent of Christian HUMANISM, critic of the Ch, but opponent of the REFORMATION.

Illegitimate son of Roger Gerard, priest, and Margaret, daughter of a physician of Severnbergen; ed at Gouda, St Lebwin's at Deventer where his teachers were members of the Brethren of the Common Life who introduced him to the *Devotio Moderna* as well as to Italian Humanism, then at 's Hertogenbosch (or Bois-le-Duc), and finally at the Augustinian monastery at Steyn, nr Gouda, where his teachers unwittingly turned him against monks for the rest of his life. Ordained priest in 1492, he became secretary to the Bp of Cambrai until, with the Bp's help, he went to learn theology at the Collège Montaigu in Paris, earning his keep by private coaching. One of his pupils, Ld Mountjoy, invited him to England in 1499, where his contact with COLET transformed his life.

He soon established a European reputation. Moving about frequently from one intellectual capital to another, giving lectures to students, having discussions with other advanced intellectuals, writing vast quantities of letters to rulers and eminent men in all countries, publishing highly successful popular satires, and preparing editions of the Scriptures and the Fathers which he cleansed of all the accretions of scholasticism with the help of the linguistic apparatus provided by Humanist scholarship, he reached a peak of fame and influence never achieved, perhaps, by any other scholar before or since. He spent the years 1500–6 mainly in France and the Netherlands, moving to England in 1506, where he became friendly with MORE and WARHAM. Then he toured Italy, taking his DD degree at Turin in 1506, and witnessing the, to him, disgusting spectacle of Pp JULIUS II's martial entry into Bologna, which he had just reconquered. Erasmus also visited Venice, Padua, Florence, Siena and Rome. From 1509–14 he was mainly in England, in close contact with Colet, More, Grocyn, LATIMER, Warham and FISHER, and teaching principally at Cambridge, where he was Prof of Divinity and of Greek. His chief works were *Adagia* (1500), a collection of classical quotations with a commentary; *Enchiridion militis christiani*, or *Manual of a Christian Soldier* (1501); *Encomium moriae*, or *In Praise of Folly* (1511), sarcasm at the expense of corrupt and worldly Ch leaders and secular rulers; *Julius Exclusus* (1513), an attack on Pp Julius II and other Pps; his edition of the Greek New Testament (1516) and of St Jerome (1519), followed by other Fathers; *Colloquia* (1519), followed by amended editions till 1524, dialogues on contemporary affairs, including some sharp criticism of Ch abuses; and *De libero arbitrio* (1523), affirming free will against LUTHER's doctrine of divine determinism. Motivated by the piety of the *Devotio Moderna* and the scholarship of the Renaissance, Erasmus saw true Christianity not as the regular routine of Ch observances or as salvation by some miraculous means, but as the imitation of Christ in daily life in the pursuit of truths revealed to men by sound scholarship. His writings combined biting sarcasm with common sense, humour, sincerity and the best Renaissance scholarship, together with the ability to make an impact on the ordinary reader. Typical of the pre-Lutheran CATHOLIC REFORMATION, he attacked the paganism of the extreme Italian Humanists; and he criticized the abuses in the Ch, which he assumed could be cured by a few minor adjustments, not a revolution. During Luther's revolt he advocated the reconciliation of the Prots while refusing to join them. He believed in moderation and the middle way. The dogmatic extremes of both the REFORMATION and the COUNTER-REFORMATION were not his style, and he and his like became increasingly isolated, until all his writings were placed on the INDEX in 1559.

Essex, Robert Devereux, 2nd Earl of (10 Nov 1566 or 1567–25 Feb 1601) Over-ambitious but politically inept favourite of the ageing Q ELIZABETH I of England, who was executed as an over-mighty subject after trying to seize power at the head of his clientage connection.

Eld son of Walter Devereux, 1st Earl of Essex, and his wife Lettice Knollys, whose mother was Mary, sister of Q Anne Boleyn, he was the Q's cousin; and when on the death of his father his mother secretly m the Earl of LEICESTER (1577 or 1578), he also became the stepson of her favourite; ed as a ward of the Crown in the household of BURGHLEY and at Trinity, Cambridge (1579–81). He accompanied Leicester on his expedition to the Netherlands (1585–6), and showed daring at the battle of Zutphen (22 Sept/2 Oct 1586). Back in England, he made rapid progress at Court and in the affections of the Q, till it was said that 'he cometh not to his own lodging till the birds sing in the morning'. She made him Master of the Horse (1587) and Knight of the Garter (1588), and gave him the lucrative farm of the duties on sweet wines. On Leicester's death on 4 Sept 1588, Essex inherited his clientage network. He was brave, handsome and gallant, an ideal courtier and natural favourite; but unfortunately he aimed at the highest office in the State, though he was unskilled in political manoeuvre and incapable of administrative drudgery. He was a truculent boy, outwitted by veteran statesmen of the calibre of Burghley and his son, Robert Cecil, future Earl of SALIS-BURY. Unable to get his own way, Essex used to quarrel petulantly with the Q. He failed to appreciate that lovers' quarrels and fits of pique were entirely inappropriate techniques for bending the will of the most hard-headed monarch in Europe. Against the Q's orders he accompanied DRAKE and Norris on their unsuccessful Portugal Expedition (Apr–June 1589); but she forgave him eventually, as she did his marriage to Frances, daughter of WALSINGHAM and widow of Sir Philip Sidney (1590). As a result of pleading for 3 hours on his knees, he was given command of the expedition sent to Normandy (1591–3) to help K HENRY IV of France against Spain; but he angered Elizabeth in various ways, not least by creating too many knights on the field of battle, thus cheapening the honour. As well as performing heroic feats on distant battlefields he tried to amass a political following at Court, though he naturally found it difficult to combine these two activities. In 1593 he became a member of the Council. In the election of 1593 he acquired a number of borough seats for his followers. He employed Francis BACON as his political adviser and Anthony Bacon as his expert on foreign intelligence. He led a pack of discontented aristocrats headed by the Earls of Southampton, Rutland, Sussex and Bedford. In general, he was the leader of all those who chafed at the long monopoly of power and patronage held by Burghley, and who were determined that it should not be inherited by his son. He represented the young against the old, the nobles against the men of business, the soldiers against the civilians, the Outs against the Ins; and he also sheltered under his wing Puritan preachers at one end of the religious spectrum, and Cath conspirators at the other, who were involved in the Gunpowder and other plots in the next reign. Essex and the Cecils became deadly rivals for the favours of the Q, and especially for vacant offices for their followers. The Cecils steadily gained, as when the Cecil nominee, Edward COKE, became Attorney Gen. Part of the trouble was that Essex's weakness for military heroics on distant shores gave plenty of opportunity to the Cecils to steal marches on him during his absences from Court; and any glamour that he gained as the darling of the younger sons of the nobility and of the public in general was usually outweighed by the advances that the Cecils made on the back-stairs. He was in joint command with Howard of Effingham of the Cádiz Expedition (June–Aug 1596) in which he captured Cádiz on 22 June 1596 and set fire to it. But he also disobeyed orders, quarrelled with Howard, and brought back few spoils. Moreover, in his absence, Robert Cecil had been appointed Principal Sec (July 1596); and it was not till Mar 1597 that he was reconciled with the Q, made Master of the Ordnance, and given joint command with RALEGH of the Islands Voyage (July–Oct 1597) – a botched attempt to destroy the new Spanish Armada and capture the silver fleet. While Essex was in the Azores quarrelling with Ralegh and departing from instructions, Robert Cecil became Chancellor of the Duchy of Lancaster and Howard of Effingham became Earl of Nottingham (1597). In Mar 1599, after assiduous canvassing, Essex became Ld Lieutenant of Ireland and was sent (Apr–Sept 1599) with an unusually large army to suppress Tyrone's rebellion. While he was away, Robert Cecil was given the lucrative post of Master of the Court of Wards; meanwhile Essex disobeyed orders, signed a truce with Tyrone, and left his post without permission in order to explain himself to the Q. Back in England, he was tried (June 1600), forbidden to exercise his offices, and confined to his home, Essex House, for 3 months. Moreover, the Q refused to renew his farm of the sweet-wine duties. At last, crazed with frustrated ambition and desperate with debt, he and about 300 followers decided to overthrow the Gov by force. Taking to their horses on 8 Feb 1601, they rode through the City shouting slogans, but it was soon over as there was no response from the citizens. On 19 Feb 1601 he was tried before his old rival, Coke, with his old ally, Francis Bacon, giving evidence against him; a week later he was beheaded on Tower Hill.

Essex, Robert Devereux, 3rd Earl of (Jan 1591–14 Sept 1646) C-in-C of the Parl forces in the English CIVIL WAR, who, being a 'Presbyterian' and thus an opponent of a vigorous prosecution of the war against the K, was removed by the war party.

Son of the 2nd Earl of ESSEX and Frances Walsingham; m 1st (1606) Frances Howard, daughter of the Earl of Suffolk, from whom K JAMES I arranged his divorce (1613) so that she could marry the favourite, Robert CARR, a scandalous proceeding which did not endear Essex to the Stuart Court; m 2nd (1631) Elizabeth, daughter of Sir William Paulet – also an unhappy union. In 1620 he served with Sir Horace Vere's volunteers in the *Palatinate War* period of the THIRTY YEARS WAR; was vice-admiral on BUCKINGHAM's mismanaged expedition to Cádiz (Oct–Nov 1625); and was one of those who refused the Forced Loan of 1626. K CHARLES I appointed him 2 i/c in the 1st Bishops' War (1639); in 1640 he favoured the execution of STRAFFORD; and in 1641 he was one of the more respectable members of the opposition whom the K as a concession made a member of the Privy Council. When the Civil War broke out, Essex was appointed C-in-C of the Parl armies (July 1642), though he never achieved any unified control over them. A solemn Puritan of delicate health, who went to war with his coffin and winding sheet at the ready, he was a reluctant and incompetent military leader, but a rich and powerful aristocrat and conscientious public servant whose support PYM and Parl required at this early stage. At Edgehill, nr Warwick (23 Oct 1642), and Turnham Green, nr London (13 Nov 1642), he was lucky that the K did not make a really determined attack on London, as it might have succeeded. He took Reading, Berks (Apr 1643), and relieved Gloucester (Aug–Sept 1643), and then fought the inconclusive 1st battle of Newbury, Berks (20 Sept 1643). In 1644 he moved SW, relieving Lyme, Dorset, then Plymouth, Devon, but advancing so far from his base that he became trapped in a hostile Cornwall. At Lostwithiel on 2 Sept 1644 his 6,000 infantry surrendered, and he had to escape by water. Along with MANCHESTER, he was subjected to strong criticism by Oliver CROMWELL and the win-the-war party. Essex was a leading 'Presbyterian', favouring the Scots alliance and a negotiated peace, and apprehensive of the radicalism which the war had brought to the surface. 'Our posterity will say,' he remarked, 'that to deliver them from the yoke of the king we have subjected them to that of the common people.' The formation of the New Model Army (Feb 1645) ended his military career, and he resigned the day before the passing of the Self-Denying Ordinance (3 Apr 1645), which forbade members of either House to hold military or civil posts.

Fairfax, Sir Thomas (17 Jan 1612–12 Nov 1671) 3rd Bn Fairfax of Cameron

(1648) in the Scots peerage, C-in-C of the New Model Army who defeated K CHARLES I in the English CIVIL WAR.

Eld son of Ferdinando, 2nd Bn Fairfax, a leading Yorks opposition MP at the head of a large clientage connection, who was made C-in-C of the Parl forces in Yorks (Sept 1642) on the outbreak of the Civil War; ed at St John's, Cambridge (1626); fought in the Netherlands under Sir Horace Vere (1629–31), whose daughter, Anne – a very keen Presbyterian – he m (1637) (she d 1665). He raised a troop of dragoons for service in the Bishops' Wars (1639–40), and at the start of the Civil War he was made commander of the Yorks cavalry. In 1643 he took Leeds and Wakefield and retained Parl control of Hull, joining MAN-CHESTER and CROMWELL in Lincs to defeat the Royalists at Winceby (11 Oct 1643). On 24 Jan 1644 he relieved Nantwich, Cheshire (which was besieged by troops from Ireland), then took Selby and besieged York, commanding the right wing at the decisive victory of Marston Moor (2 July 1644). Though gentle in manner, diffident, gloomy and reserved, and suffering from frequent attacks of the stone and rheumatism, he was an attacking Gen, heroically brave and very popular with his men, becoming Capt-Gen of the New Model Army (Feb 1645) when the Self-Denying Ordinance (3 Apr 1645) eliminated the 3rd Earl of ESSEX and the 2nd Earl of Manchester, who had till then fought reluctantly against the K. Fairfax created and trained the New Model Army, with Cromwell i/c the cavalry, and Philip Skippon the infantry. He defeated the Royalists at Naseby, Northants (14 June 1645) and at Langport, Somerset (10 July 1645), subsequently extending Parl control over the SW, taking Bristol (11 Sept 1645), Exeter (Apr 1646) and Oxford (20 June 1646). During the post-war negotiations (1646–9) he could have been the most powerful man in England, but he allowed the political initiative to be snatched from him by IRETON and Cromwell, being incapable of giving a lead either for or against them. He typified the inertia of those PURITANS who wanted a 'Godly Reformation' on the one hand, but no change in the political or social system on the other. He supported the soldiers against Parl in their grievances over pay, pensions and disbandment; but, un-willing to use the Army to interfere in politics, he hoped for a compromise between Parl and the K; nevertheless retaining his command so as to keep it out of the hands of more radical men – INDEPENDENTS or LEVELLERS. Completely at sea in politics, he drifted with events, being forced to accept Cornet Joyce's seizure of the K (June 1647), reluctantly occupying London (Aug 1647), playing a vigorous part in suppressing the Agitators (the Army radicals), putting down Kent and Essex in the 2nd Civil War (May–June 1648), but helplessly carried along in the wake of Pride's Purge (Dec 1648) and the trial and execution of the K (Jan 1649). He was appointed a member of the special court which tried the K, but did not attend. When his name was called, his formidable wife, sitting masked in the spectators' gallery, shouted: 'He has more wit than to be here.' He opposed the setting up of the republic, yet became a member of its Council of State (Feb 1649). He remained C-in-C of the Army, but refused to invade Scotland when it became necessary. He gave way to Cromwell, and retired to his estate at Nun-appleton, Yorks (1650) to enjoy his hunting and verse-writing. He did not emerge into public life again until the anarchy of 1659 which followed Cromwell's death. He backed MONCK's moves to bring about the restoration of the monarchy, and made a vital contribution to his success by taking York (1 Jan 1660) and rallying

Yorks to his cause. MP for Yorks in the Convention Parl (Apr–Dec 1660), he voted for the return of CHARLES II, but against the exhumation and execution of Cromwell's corpse.

Farnese, Alessandro (27 Aug 1545–2/3 Dec 1592) D of Parma (1586), Gov of the Netherlands on behalf of K PHILIP II of Spain, and his greatest gen during the REVOLT.

Son of Ottavio Farnese, D of Parma (grandson of Pp PAUL III), and Margaret of Austria (natural daughter of the Emp CHARLES V); ed at the Spanish court along with Don JOHN OF AUSTRIA; he lived in Brussels, 1556–9, then Spain, 1559–65; m (1565) the Infanta Maria of Portugal in Brussels (d 1577); then settled in Parma. Here he served in the Italian forces of Don John, and was present at the victory of Lepanto over the Turkish fleet on 7 Oct 1571. In 1577 he once more joined Don John – now Gov of the Netherlands – and helped him win the battle of Gembloux, Brabant, on 31 Jan 1578. On Don John's death on 1 Oct 1578, Farnese succeeded him, and soon transformed the whole situation in the Netherlands. An impressive figure, and a great patron of the arts, he was Philip II's most successful gen and most statesmanlike minister; and the policy he adopted saved the S Netherlands for Spain, and might have regained the N as well had Philip followed his advice. He began by winning over the Walloon nobles in the deep S to sign the Tr of Arras in May 1579; and from that base he reconquered the towns of the middle (Flemish) S, including Antwerp on 17 Aug 1585 after a record 14-month siege. He then proceeded to establish bridgeheads across the Rhine, Maas and other rivers, behind which the N provs were sheltering, and by 1588 he was about to begin the reconquest of Holland and Zeeland when he was ordered by Philip II to mass his troops at Dunkirk and Nieuwpoort on the Flemish coast, preparatory to embarking them on the Spanish ARMADA in order to invade England. He had taken Sluys in Flanders in Aug 1587, and this enabled him to ferry his troops to the coast along the inland waterways, a necessary manoeuvre as the Dutch controlled the sea. There was, unfortunately, a serious gap in Philip's planning which nullified all these moves. Neither Nieuwport nor Dunkirk was deep enough a port to take the ships of the Armada, which consequently had to remain off-shore; while Farnese had nothing better than canal-barges with which to ferry his men out under the guns of the Dutch navy. The invasion of England had to be abandoned; as he resumed his land operations against the Dutch, Farnese was blamed for the failure; but he was in any case disliked by his Spanish commanders who resented having to serve under an Italian. Before long, Philip again mistook his priorities, and ordered Farnese to march his army into France to snatch victory from K HENRY IV in the FRENCH WARS OF RELIGION and to support Philip's visionary scheme for incorporating France into the Spanish Emp. Always frankly outspoken, Farnese did not endear himself to his sovereign when he sharply criticized this neglect of the Netherlands – but neither did he succeed in changing Philip's mind. Three times Farnese was ordered into France: 1st, to relieve Paris in Sept 1590; 2nd, to relieve Rouen, Normandy, in Apr 1592; while on the 3rd expedition he d at the Abbey of St Vaast, nr Arras. Unknown to him, his devious and ungrateful master had already dismissed him and appointed another commander, the Count of Fuentes, in his place.

Ferdinand I (10 Mar 1503–25 July 1564) ArchD of Austria (1521), K of Bohemia (1526), K of Hungary (1527), K of the Romans (1531), H R Emp (Feb 1558), who was important in 2 main fields. (1) In the Austrian Monarchy (as it later became) he united Austria, Bohemia and Hungary under one ruler, gave them the beginnings of centralized Gov, defended them against Turkey, first contained the Prot movement and then counter-attacked it; but also eventually divided his lands among his 3 sons. (2) In the H R Emp (Germany) he served as loyal deputy to CHARLES V until he became Emp himself, generally adopting a less doctrinaire position than his predecessor.

2nd son of PHILIP I (The Handsome), D of Burgundy, and Joanna (The Mad) of Castile – and thus the brother of the Emp Charles V; m (1521) Anne Jagiello, sister of Lewis II, K of Bohemia and Hungary, thus confirming their earlier marriage by proxy under the Tr negotiated in 1516 by Ferdinand's grandfather, the Emp MAXIMILIAN I.

In the Austrian Monarchy (ie the Habsburg family provs) Ferdinand became ruler as Charles V handed over responsibility to him. By the partition of Worms (Apr 1521) he received the Gov of Upper and Lower Austria, Styria, Carniola and Carinthia; and by the secret Trs of Brussels (Jan and Feb 1522) he was made Regent of Tyrol, Vorarlberg, the upper-Rhine lands and Würtemberg. On the death of Lewis II, at the battle of Mohács (29 Aug 1526), Ferdinand claimed both Kdoms. In Bohemia, the Estates elected him K in Oct 1526 without much opposition, in view of the constitutional and financial concessions he made; but in Hungary the nobility were divided. A Turkish-backed majority elected John I Zápolyai, Pr of Transylvania, as K on 10 Nov 1526, while only a minority elected Ferdinand as K on 17 Dec 1526. This split involved Ferdinand in decades of warfare with John Zápolyai and Turkey, in which the latter besieged Vienna (Sept–Oct 1529), invaded Carinthia and Styria (1532), and threatened Vienna again (Sept 1532). Numerous truces were signed and broken. By the Tr of Grosswardein (Feb 1538), Ferdinand recognized John Zápolyai as ruler of Hungary and was in turn recognized as his heir. On the death of John Zápolyai, however, on 21 July 1540, the Turks occupied all Hungary except a narrow W strip which was all that Ferdinand could hold (1541–3). In later truces of Sept 1545 and June 1547 Ferdinand was recognized as ruler of his strip of W Hungary in return for an annual tribute to Turkey of 30,000 Hungarian ducats. Further warfare followed, but the Tr of Constantinople of June 1562 changed little; and Austria had to put up with this limited success till late in C17. Nevertheless, Ferdinand's reign marks an important stage in the creation of the Austrian Monarchy. He effected the union with Bohemia and Hungary which lasted until 1918. He turned Bohemia from an elective into an hereditary monarchy (1547). He sketched out the beginnings of an all-Austrian central admin by setting up the *Geheimer Rat* (Privy Council) in 1527, the *Hofkammer* (Treasury) in 1527 and the *Hofkriegsrat* (Supreme War Council) in 1556, though the Estates of the Kdoms and provs resisted every inroad on their privileges. And his conflicts with the Estates were exacerbated by religious differences, for the various branches of Protestantism spread rapidly all through his reign, affecting all classes and races, Lutheranism especially affecting the German-speaking nobility and townsmen, Calvinism propagated in Latin deeply affecting Hungary, and Anabaptism recruiting strongly among the masses of Moravia and Tyrol. Ferdinand was forced to be permissive at first, for he needed the financial and military support of the various Estates in his struggles with Turkey. In his bridge-building attempts between the confessions he unsuccessfully tried to persuade the COUNCIL OF TRENT to countenance clerical marriage and communion in both kinds. In the 1550s, however, and especially after the TREATY OF AUGSBURG of 1555, he began an RC counter-offensive, aided by the JESUITS under the leadership of Peter Canisius. This Austrian wing of the COUNTER-REFORMATION, however, did not begin to be really effective till after the THIRTY YEARS WAR (1618–48). Moreover, Ferdinand's action on his death in splitting up the Austrian Monarchy once more among his sons seems to contradict the whole of his life's work. The 1st son, Maximilian, inherited Upper and Lower Austria, Bohemia and Hungary; the 2nd, Ferdinand, received Tyrol, Vorarlberg and the upper-Rhine area (Württemberg having been lost in a humiliating war with the German Prs backed by France: Tr of Kaaden, June 1534); and Charles, the 3rd son, took Carinthia, Carniola, Styria and the lands on the Adriatic. The explanation is that Ferdinand expected Maximilian to turn Prot, and feared that his younger brothers would quarrel with him for the inheritance.

In the Empire Ferdinand was President of the *Reichsregiment*, or Regency Council, ie CHARLES V's deputy, till he became Emp himself. In both capacities he was more flexible and pragmatic than his brother in his approach to the chief German problems: ie at home, the struggle with the separatist Prs, now intensified by the REFORMATION, and, abroad, the war and diplomacy required to defend Imperial interests against the threats from Turkey, France, the Papacy and so on. Ferdinand remained a loyal supporter of his brother until they quarrelled over the succession in the late 1540s. Charles decided that to split the Habsburg possessions would be dangerous, and wanted Ferdinand to make way for Charles's son, the future PHILIP II, who was to inherit everything. Ferdinand refused, and eventually a family compromise was arrived at in Mar 1551 whereby Ferdinand would succeed, to be followed by Philip, and then by his own son, Maximilian: a plan never put into operation, as Philip abandoned his claims on his marriage to Q MARY I of England, and as Charles eventually did in fact divide his dominions. In these years, Ferdinand failed to support Charles in his last attempts to subdue the Prot Prs and their ally, France. In any case, Ferdinand favoured compromise, realizing that with the division of the Habsburg family into the Austrian and Spanish branches, the Emp would be shorn of the wealth of the Indies and the Netherlands, and would thus be incapable of defeating his enemies. Thus it was Ferdinand, and not Charles, who negotiated the Tr of Augsburg (Sept 1555) which brought about a compromise peace between German RCs and Prots, and which lasted until the Thirty Years War.

Ferdinand II (9 July 1578–15 Feb 1637) ArchD of Styria (1590), K of Bohemia (1617), K of Hungary (1618), HR Emp (Aug 1619), whose policies of centralized absolutism and enforcement of the COUNTER-REFORMATION had some early success in the Austrian provs, but not in Hungary, Bohemia and the Emp, where he helped to precipitate the THIRTY YEARS WAR. He was successful in this until 1629, but the threat he posed to the German Prs, the German Prots, and his international rivals, France and Sweden, produced counter-alliances which frustrated his designs in the Emp, though not in Austria and Bohemia, where he suppressed the Prots and tamed the Estates.

Eld son of ArchD Charles of Styria and Maria of Bavaria; ed at the College at Ingolstadt, Bavaria (1590–95), along with his cousin the future El MAXIMILIAN I of Bavaria, where he swallowed whole the Jesuit precepts favouring the propagation of Cath dogma by authoritarian means; m 1st (1600) Maria Anna, sister of Maximilian (d 1616); m 2nd (1622) Eleonora Gonzaga, sister of Vincenzo II of Mantua. Ginger-haired, apple-cheeked and pot-bellied, he talked and ate too much, and heard Mass twice a day. Genial and ascetic by turns, he managed to be privately amiable and kind-hearted while pursuing his joint aims of absolutism and orthodoxy with unflinching ruthlessness, if insufficient realism. He is notable for his enforcement of Counter-Reformation absolutism in Inner Austria and his involvement in the Thirty Years War.

In Inner Austria, where he took over the Gov of Styria, Carinthia, Carniola and Gorizia in 1595, he at once attacked the Estates and town councils which shared power with the ArchD, and where at that time the nobles, burghers and peasants were predominantly Prot. Preachers were exiled, churches destroyed, books burnt; and in general Ferdinand set such an example of Habsburg ardour and drive that the family chose him to succeed Emps RUDOLF II and MATTHIAS – his childless cousins – instead of their childless younger brothers. This agreement, signed by Matthias in Graz (June and July 1617) and known as the Oñate Tr after the Spanish ambassador who negotiated it, provided that Ferdinand should be elected K of Bohemia and HR Emp, while K PHILIP III of Spain gave up his claim, receiving in return a promise of Habsburg fiefs in Alsace and Tyrol and imperial fiefs in Italy.

The Thirty Years War broke out when Ferdinand, having been elected K of Bohemia on 17 June 1617, was deposed on 26 Aug 1619 by Prot noble rebels who objected to his attempts to limit their religious and constitutional privileges. During the Bohemian War (1618–20) he employed the army of Maximilian I of Bavaria to defeat the Bohemian rebels at the White Mountain (8 Nov 1620), drive out the new K Frederick V, the El Palatine, and reduce the Austrian Prot rebels who had risen in sympathy under the Calvinist noble, Georg Erasmus von Tschernembl. After this success, he spent the next decade turning Bohemia, except Silesia, into a Cath, authoritarian, economically declining colony of Austria. During the Palatinate War (1621–3) Bavarian armies conquered the Upper Palatinate, and Bavarian and Spanish armies between them overran the Rhenish Palatinate. Ferdinand illegally transferred the Palatinate and the title of Elector from Frederick V to Maximilian I (Jan 1621). During the Danish War (1624–9) Ferdinand resented his dependence on the Bavarian army under Tilly, and raised an imperial army under WALLENSTEIN (Apr 1625), and the 2 generals brought him to the peak of his reign. Denmark was knocked out of the war, Wallenstein conquered much of the N German coast, and began to build a fleet. During the year of the Emperor's Pride and Fall (1629–30) Ferdinand issued the Edict of Restitution (Mar 1629), ordering the return to the Ch of all lands taken over by Prots since 2 Aug 1552. The German Prs, Prot and Cath alike, now opposed Ferdinand as a threat to German liberty, and at the Regensburg Electors' Meeting (June–Aug 1630) they forced him to dismiss Wallenstein.

The Swedish War (1630–35) marked the turn of the tide against Ferdinand, when Sweden, financed by France, intervened against him, and forced Brandenburg and Saxony to do likewise. Tilly was defeated at Breitenfeld, Saxony, on 17 Sept 1631, and Ferdinand was compelled to resort to Wallenstein once more. He skilfully drew the Swedes away from Prague and Vienna, but was himself defeated at Lützen, Saxony, on 16 Nov 1632. Wallenstein now appeared to Ferdinand as an over-mighty subject of doubtful loyalty, and the Emp dismissed him again, and had him murdered (25 Feb 1634). Ferdinand's army, now under the command of his son, the future Emp FERDINAND III, joined a recently arrived Spanish army under Ferdinand, the Card-Infant; and together they defeated the Swedish and Prot army of the League of Heilbronn at Nördlingen, Swabia, on 5/6 Sept 1634. The German period of the War now ended as Ferdinand in effect abandoned his more extreme Cath and absolutist ambitions, and the majority of the German Prs signed the Tr of Prague (May 1635). During the Franco-Habsburg War (1635–48), Ferdinand had to rely more and more on his son, as he grew prematurely senile and often incapacitated by asthma.

Ferdinand II (10 Mar 1452–23 Jan 1516) K of Aragon (1479), K (Ferdinand V) of Castile (1474); whose marriage to ISABELLA I, Q of Castile (1469) united the 2 Kdoms later known as Spain, the 2 sovereigns being called the 'Catholic Kings', the title given them by Pp ALEXANDER VI (1494). Ferdinand supported the voyages of COLUMBUS; and gained Navarra and Granada, thus uniting the whole Spanish peninsula except for Portugal. He ruled with the most advanced forms of centralized absolutism to be found in Europe, both in Ch and State. At home, he attacked Jews and Arabs; abroad, he entwined his enemy, France, in a network of alliances and made territorial gains from her in Italy and the Pyrenees.

Son of John II, K of Aragon, and his 2nd wife, Juana Enríquez, daughter of the Grand Admiral of Castile; m 1st Isabella, and 2nd (1506) Germaine de Foix, niece of K LOUIS XII of France.

The constitutional basis of the union of the 2 Kdoms, which was a loose confederation where each State retained its own separate identity, was simply the marriage contract of Ferdinand and Isabella. However, on the death of K Henry IV of Castile (Isabella's half-brother) in 1474, Ferdinand claimed the throne for himself; but he gave way when Isabella and her Castilian supporters insisted on her rights, and agreed to rule jointly. But before this could happen, a rival claimant had to be defeated. This was Prss Juana, the late K's daughter, who was backed by the K of Portugal and another group of Castilian nobles. The supporters of Isabella claimed that Juana was not the daughter of K Henry IV (known as *El Impotente*) but of a Portuguese noble called Beltram de la Cueva (hence her nickname, Juana *La Beltraneja*). After Isabella's party defeated Juana's party at the battle of Toro (1476) and brought an end to the civil war (1479), they began to rule jointly in both Kdoms (1481). On Isabella's death (1504) the two Kdoms almost separated again as their daughter Joanna (the Mad) and her husband PHILIP The Handsome, D of Burgundy, claimed the throne of Castile, backed by the Grandees. Ferdinand contested this and, on Philip's early death (25 Sept 1506), he managed to get himself recognized as Regent of Castile for his insane daughter. To these 2 Kdoms he now added a third, Navarra, for

Gaston de Foix, close claimant to the throne of Navarra, was the brother of Ferdinand's 2nd wife, Germaine de Foix. On Gaston's unexpected death at the battle of Ravenna (11 Apr 1512) Ferdinand talked K HENRY VIII of England into invading Aquitaine while he conquered Spanish Navarra (1512) and annexed it to Castile (1515), without, however, changing its form of Gov. Earlier, he had carried out the conquest of Granada, the last remaining Arab Kdom (1482–92). With the fall of the city of Granada (Jan 1492), the conquered territory was annexed to the crown of Castile. Ferdinand and Isabella now ruled the whole Spanish peninsula except Portugal, and the 800-year-old dynamism of the *Reconquista* was ready to spill over into colonial conquest: for 7 months later Columbus set sail (Aug 1492) to discover the New World.

At home, the institutions of Gov were transformed under Ferdinand and Isabella to give Spain the most up-to-date admin in Europe: the basis of her greatness under CHARLES V and PHILIP II. These reforms were all planned to replace the anarchy of late-medieval times with centralized ABSOLUTISM whose main features (in each of the separate Kdoms, not in Spain as a whole) were designed to increase the central power of the monarchs and their bureaucrats and soldiers at the expense of all rivals: the Ch, the nobility, the towns and the provs, the brigands and the bandits. (a) In each State, the monarch was represented by a Viceroy. (b) The central Councils (of Castile, of Aragon) were reorganized and staffed by middle-class lawyers (*letrados*) instead of over-mighty Grandees, and turned into bureaucratic executors of royal orders instead of makers of high policy. New councils similar to them were added: of the *Hermandad* (1476–98), of Finance (1480), of the INQUISITION (1483), of the Military Orders (1489). (c) The *Cortes* (Parl) of Castile, which was dominated by the towns, was called only infrequently; while the various *cortes* of Aragon still preserved their considerable ancient privileges. In Castile, the *Cortes* was used mainly to pass anti-Grandee legislation, of which 2 examples follow. (d) The *Cortes* of Toledo (1480) authorized the resumption by the Crown of vast amounts of royal property which had been alienated to the nobility in previous reigns. (The towns preferred this solution to the alternative: an increase in taxation.) (e) The *Cortes* of Madrigal (1476) authorized the reorganization of the *Hermandad* (already mentioned). This medieval, voluntary, peace-keeping association of cities was now centralized under the Crown with a central Council, which collected taxes and raised militia, using them to put down all infringements of the public peace, especially the lawlessness of the nobility. So successful was it in creating prov law and order within 20 years that its powers were drastically reduced in 1498. (f) Further centralization resulted from the appointment of a royal *corregidor* to each municipal council. The cities were no longer democratically run, but had become dominated by oligarchies of local nobles; and the job of the *corregidor* was to see that the municipal finances, common lands, justice and police etc, were admin in the royal and general interest. (g) A further big transfer of power, patronage and wealth from the nobility to the Crown was brought about when, by arrangement with the Pp, Ferdinand took over the Grandmasterships of the Military Orders of Calatrava (1487), Alcántara (1494) and Santiago (1499) – medieval knightly associations which had accumulated a vast acreage of land plundered by them from the Arabs during the Reconquest. (h) The papacy also made its contribution to royal absolutism by granting the Crown such power over the Ch that a Reformation on the lines of that of K Henry VIII of England would have been pointless. A Bull of 1482 gave the Crown the right to appoint all prelates – a right which it used to fill the bprics with loyal and religious servants, instead of unruly Grandees. A Bull of 1494 gave the Crown the right to reform the religious orders, which Cardinal XIMÉNEZ used with great effect. A Bull of 1482 granted the Crown three-quarters of the income derived from the *Cruzada* – an indulgence (which all Spanish laymen were expected to buy) created to finance the conquest of Granada – a tax which was still collected even when the crusade was over. A Bull of 1478 established the Spanish Inquisition, a council under royal control. At first designed to inquire into the orthodoxy of the *conversos* (ie Jews converted to Christianity; also called *Marranos*, meaning 'swine'), it soon became a powerful instrument of royal absolutism in all cultural fields, creating religious uniformity at the cost of eliminating all the elements making for intellectual and economic progress. An anti-Jewish campaign was set on foot by Isabella (who was extremely pious), leading to their piecemeal expulsion from various bprics and then (Mar 1492) their wholesale expulsion from the whole Kdom. About 150,000 out of 200,000 Jews fled from Castile alone, depriving the country of an invaluable élite of merchants, financiers, doctors and intellectuals; and, what is more, handing them over as a valuable present to future enemies of Spain, notably Holland. In Castile, moreover, the forced conversion of Arabs to Christianity carried out by Ximénez – in conflict with their Tr of surrender which had guaranteed freedom of worship – led to an Arab revolt (1499–1502) after the defeat of which, Moslems who refused conversion were expelled from Granada (1502). Those who were baptized (called *Moriscos*) were feared and despised by the Old Christians of pure Spanish blood, and permanently threatened with the attentions of the Inquisition. (i) The Catholic Ks also took measures to encourage sheep-rearing and textile-manufacturing, to stimulate trade with the colonies (through the *Casa de Contratacion* established at Seville, 1503) and generally develop the economy of Spain so as to boost the royal revenues. Castile developed well (having the monopoly of the Americas was one reason) while the economy of the Crown of Aragon (flourishing in the Middle Ages) continued to decline. (j) A final contribution to royal power was the creation of a standing army, whose state of training under CORDOBA turned it into the greatest body of infantry in Europe.

In foreign policy Ferdinand was ruthlessly realistic, and he profited from the gullibility of his contemporaries (K HENRY VII of England excepted) in a manner much admired by MACHIAVELLI. Under his influence Spain pursued Aragonese rather than Castilian interests, and (the first ruler outside Italy to establish a regular diplomatic service) he spent most of his reign contesting with France in war and diplomacy, with a view to making territorial gains in Italy and in the Pyrenees. He also safeguarded his position in the Spanish peninsula itself by marriage alliances with Portugal. He surrounded France with a network of alliances: eg with England (by the marriage of his daughter CATHERINE OF ARAGON to K Henry VIII, 1509); and with the Emp and Burgundy (by the marriage of his daughter Joanna with the Emp MAXIMILIAN I's son Philip, 1496; and by that of his son Juan to the Emp's daughter Margaret, 1496). A master of guile, he duped his allies (eg Henry VIII) into fighting his wars for him while he reaped the benefits; and out of the Italian wars of Ks CHARLES VIII and LOUIS XII of France he gained Cerdagne and Roussillon in the Pyrenees (Tr of Barcelona, Jan 1493), Naples (battle of Garigliano, 27 Dec 1503, and Tr of Blois, Oct 1505) and Navarra (1512). He also gave lukewarm support to the crusade of Ximénez in N Africa (1505–11), in which Mers-el-Kebir (1505), Peñón de la Gómera (1508), Oran, Bugia, Tripoli, Algiers (1509–11) and other towns were conquered. When he d, Ferdinand had set Spain on the route to great splendour, but also to ultimate decay, for the unexpected deaths of so many of his offspring (and theirs) left Spain to be inherited by Joanna, and then her son, who became not only Charles I of Spain, but also, fatally for Spain, CHARLES V of the H R Emp.

Ferdinand III (13 July 1608–2 Apr 1657) K of Hungary (1626), K of Bohemia (1627), K of Rome (1636), H R Emp (Feb 1637), who succeeded in the middle of the THIRTY YEARS WAR, and who, more flexible than his father, FERDINAND II, recognized the necessity of making the compromises with the German Prots, the German Prs, Sweden and France, which were enshrined in the Tr of Westphalia (Oct 1648). These sacrifices enabled him to strengthen the Habsburg and Cath grip on Austria, Bohemia and the small strip of Hungary not occupied by the Turks.

Eld son of the future Emp Ferdinand II and Maria Anna of Bavaria; ed at home; m 1st (1631) Maria Anna of Spain (d 1646); m 2nd (1648) Maria Leopoldina of Tyrol (d 1649); m 3rd (1651) Eleonora Gonzaga of Mantua (d 1686). A vigorous ruler and a skilful gen, as monarchs go, he was sad, shy and taciturn, though fluent in 7 languages. He was too artistic and scholarly to be the heroic crusader for Ch and Emp that his father had been. His chief priority was the Austrian Monarchy; and to secure this he was more prepared than his father to sacrifice parts of the Emp, or the interests of the Ch, or the safety of Spain. He played a positive part in the imperial council from the age of 19, and helped to organize the dismissal and murder of WALLENSTEIN, the C-in-C of the imperial army. He took over the command himself in Apr 1634, advised by the professional, if inebriate, Count Matthias Gallas. Ferdinand forthwith marched his army to join that of his Spanish brother-in-law, Ferdinand, the Card-Infant, and the 2 together defeated the Swedes and the German Prots at Nördlingen, Swabia, on 5/6 Sept 1634, changing the whole character of the War. The majority of the German Prs now accepted the Tr of Prague (May 1635), and the last period of the War – the Franco-Habsburg War (1635–48) – was a European power-struggle rather than an internal German civil or religious war. On the death of his father on 15 Feb 1637, Ferdinand took over full control, and found himself steadily pressed back to Vienna from his distant outposts. While his main ally, Spain, was in clear decline, the Emp was constantly attacked from the W by the French and Swedes through the Black Forest and Bavaria, and from the N by Swedish thrusts through Bohemia, at one point in alliance with Transylvania striking from the E. The Swedes defeated him at Wittstock, Brandenburg (4 Oct 1636), at the 2nd Breitenfeld, Saxony (2 Nov 1642) and at Jankov (Jankau), Bohemia (24 Mar 1645). The French and Swedes took Breisach on the Rhine (17 Dec 1638) and successfully advanced down the Danube into Bavaria. The French destroyed the Spanish army at Rocroi, Ardennes (19 May 1643). Meanwhile, at the peace conferences in Westphalia – at Münster with the French, and at Osnabrück with the Swedish – Ferdinand's diplomats were realistically prepared to sacrifice the high religious and imperial ideals of his father, in order to secure peace, and the Austrian Monarchy. In 1648, when he and MAXIMILIAN I of Bavaria were beaten at Zusmarshausen, Bavaria (17 May 1648), when his joint thrust with Spain at Paris was thrown back at Lens, Artois (20 Aug 1648), and when the Swedes were besieging Prague (July–Oct 1648) and capturing the suburbs, he decided that the game was up, and signed the Tr of Westphalia on 24 Oct 1648. Though in addition to the sacrifices Ferdinand had to make there the Swedes and French tried to end the monopoly of the H R Emp by the Habsburgs, the Emp managed to persuade the Electors to choose his son Ferdinand as K of the Romans (May 1653), thus guaranteeing his succession. This son d of smallpox, however (9 July 1654); and during his lifetime Ferdinand did not succeed in making the same arrangement for his 2nd son, LEOPOLD, thanks to the counter-diplomacy of MAZARIN. Nevertheless, soon after he d the Electors unanimously elected Leopold as Emp on 18 July 1658.

Ferdinand VI (23 Sept 1713–10 Aug 1759) K of Spain (1746) under whose able and reforming ministers Spain prospered at home, and abroad abandoned her ambitions in Italy in order to concentrate on the security of the colonial empire by peaceful neutrality between France and Great Britain – a pacifism taken to suicidal extremes.

2nd son of K PHILIP V and his 1st Q consort, Maria Luisa of Savoy; m (1729) Barbara of Braganza, daughter of K John V of Portugal (d 1758, no issue). A gloomy and retiring person who spent his last 4 years in a state of acute depression, he supported art and scholarship, and favoured peace and reform; and, though mediocre himself, appointed very capable ministers.

1746–54 saw Gov confided to Ensenada and Carvajal. Ferdinand inherited Zenón de Somodevilla, Marqués de la Ensenada, from his father's reign. As Sec of State, of the Treasury, of War, and of the Navy and the Indies, Ensenada continued his programme of admin reform and the build-up of centralized ABSOLUTISM. The routine-ridden and noble-controlled Councils were bypassed by the Sec of State – a career bureaucrat from the minor nobility – and the central Gov increased its impact on the provs, eg by creating (1749) a number of *intendentes* to supervise the *corregidors* in their districts; and by basing the appointment and promotion of civil servants as far as possible on merit rather than on birth or purchasing power. Ensenada used his greater State leverage to rebuild the navy, expand the army, build trunk roads, reorganize the post-office, improve tax-collection (eg by abolishing tax-farming) and stimulate the economy; though this creative thinker left far more schemes on paper than he was ever able to implement. Foreign affairs were in the care of Don José de Carvajal y Lancaster who, after helping to bring the WAR OF THE AUSTRIAN SUCCESSION (1640–48) to an end by the Tr of Aix-la-Chapelle (*see* PHILIP V), turned Spain's back on ambitions in Italy to contest British economic aggression in the colonies – and to contest it by negotiation, not war. He preferred a neutral position between France and Britain to a French alliance, for he was convinced that Spain and France – even when united in the Family Compact – were not strong enough to defeat Britain. Consequently, he signed the Anglo-Spanish Commercial Tr (Sept/Oct 1750) whereby Britain abandoned the *asiento* in return for £100,000 compensation to be paid to the South Sea Co, while the other Anglo-Spanish disputes were skated over. In the same spirit, he signed the Tr of Aranjuez (June 1752) with Britain, neutralizing Spanish possessions in Italy; and negotiated a concordat with Pp Benedict XIV (Jan 1753) which ended a long quarrel, but which furthered Spanish *regalismo* (ie it increased the power of the Crown over the Spanish Ch at the Pp's expense). Carvajal was generally pro-British, while Ensenada was pro-French; and on the former's death (8 Mar 1754) the latter entered into secret negotiations with France which led to his sudden dismissal by the K (July 1754).

1754–9: Ricardo Wall headed the Gov – the K himself was practically insane. A member of an exiled Irish family, and born in France, Wall took the K's pacific policy to extremes. He maintained a strictly neutral posture during the DIPLOMATIC REVOLUTION (1749–56) and the SEVEN YEARS WAR (1756–63), thus allowing Britain to upset the transatlantic balance of power by defeating France in Canada. When he d Ferdinand left the Spanish colonies more vulnerable to British imperialism than ever.

'Fifteen', The (Sept 1715–Apr 1716) An unsuccessful attempt by James Edward Stuart – the Old Pretender – to overthrow GEORGE I, and restore the Stuart dynasty. The Hanoverian succession in 1714 had ruined the careers of TORIES and Jacobites, and James Edward in exile was advised that their anger would make him K, even though he remained a Cath. In this he was mistaken, and when the Gov got wind of the plot, they received full support in Parl for taking the necessary precautions of raising troops, arresting suspects and seizing Cath horses and arms. Moreover, after LOUIS XIV's death on 1 Sept 1715, the rebels received no French help. In England there were stirrings in the SW and the N. In the SW, the D of Ormonde appeared off the coast of Devon in Oct 1715, but returned to France after finding no support. In the N there was a certain amount of marching and counter-marching till the rebels surrendered at Preston, Lancs (13 Nov 1715). In Scotland, the Earl of Mar – Sec of State under ANNE, but dismissed by George I – raised the Pretender's standard at Braemar (Sept 1715) and took over most of the country except Edinburgh. The royal forces under the D of Argyll fought Mar at Sheriffmuir on the edge of the Highlands (13 Nov 1715). It was an indecisive battle, but after it the rebels' cause was hopeless, even though the Pretender himself landed at Peterhead, Aberdeen, in Dec 1715. The Earl of Cadogan with reinforcements from England drove the rebels N into the Highlands and in Feb 1716 the Pretender sailed back to France, taking Mar with him.

Fifth Monarchy Men, The A radical religious movement, active in the 1650s in England, and broadly representing aspirations and grievances of the same social groups as the LEVELLERS, but aiming at the rule of the 'saints' rather than a democracy. According to their calculations, based mainly on *Daniel* and *Revelations*, there had been 4 monarchies in the ancient world – Babylon, Persia, Macedon and Rome – the 4th still continuing as the Papacy, or the Great Beast, or AntiChrist. Its days were numbered, however, for the time was ripe for the 2nd Coming, which would bring to pass the 5th Monarchy, or the reign of Christ; and it was the duty of men to 'overturn' existing institutions – 'carnal

Gov' – and prepare the way. An important convert was Maj-Gen Thomas Harrison (1606–60), a butcher's son whose victories in battle gave him the intoxicating conviction that he was doing God's work; and it was partly in deference to him that Oliver CROMWELL put the ideas of the 5th Monarchy Men to the test in Barebone's Parl (July–Dec 1653), an unsuccessful attempt to inaugurate the rule of the 'people of God'. The enthusiastic, lower-class MPs – though a minority – took the bit between their teeth with a programme of political, legal, social and economic legislation so extreme as to threaten property and the social order: eg the abolition of Chancery, the simplification of the law into a code 'within the bigness of a pocket-book', the abolition of a State Ch and the elimination of tithes and lay patronage. Cromwell and LAMBERT dispersed them by trickery and force, and this was the last of Cromwell's attempts to bring about a 'Godly reformation' with the help of radicals. Harrison and the 5th Monarchy movement broke with the Protector, identifying him as the 'Old Dragon' and the 'Man of Sin'. Harrison was twice imprisoned by Cromwell and then executed by CHARLES II as one of the regicides (13 Oct 1660). The movement survived him, but the last serious expression of it was the attempted rising in the City of London in Jan 1661 by Thomas Venner, a cooper, and his congregation. It was soon suppressed by MONCK, and its leader executed.

Fisher, John (c 1469–22 June 1535) Bp of Rochester (1504–35), Card (1535), leading opponent of K HENRY VIII'S REFORMATION in England and RC martyr.

Son of a merchant, ed Cambridge, where he became a don, and Chancellor (1504–35); was appointed chaplain and then confessor to Lady Margaret Beaufort, the mother of K HENRY VII. A saintly, scholarly, reforming humanist, he became a fierce defender of the privileges and doctrines of the Ch, and he earned a European reputation with his writings against LUTHER. From the start in 1527 he opposed the K's divorce from CATHERINE OF ARAGON, writing, according to his own account, at least 7 books and preaching many sermons against it, as well as guiding Catherine through the intricacies of the Canon Law and preparing her defence, and leading the opposition in Convocation to the motion that Henry was not legally married to her (Apr 1532). He also led the opposition in the H of L to the legislation against the Ch in the early sessions of the Reformation Parl (1529–31), fulminating ever more boldly against the Henrician Reformation, even taking the treasonable step of sending a secret appeal to the Emp CHARLES V to use force against Henry, and ultimately being the only prelate to resist to the very end. He became implicated in the affair of Elizabeth Barton, the 'Nun of Kent', who was hanged for prophesying against the K's marriage to Anne Boleyn, and was named with her associates in the Act of Attainder passed in Mar 1534 for misprision of treason, and fined £300. In Apr 1534, in spite of several attempts to persuade him, he steadfastly refused to take the oath required by the Succession Act – in particular, he opposed the Royal Supremacy and the divorce – and while he was imprisoned in the Tower the new Treasons Act enabled this offence to be construed as treason. Henry was further enraged when Pp PAUL III made Fisher a Card; Fisher was tried on 17 June 1535 by a special court at Westminster and beheaded at Tower Hill. He was canonized in 1935.

'Fortyfive', The (June 1745–Sept 1746) The last Jacobite rebellion, in which Charles Edward Stuart – Bonnie Pr Charlie, or the Young Pretender – failed to overthrow K GEORGE II and restore the Stuart dynasty. In the middle of the WAR OF THE AUSTRIAN SUCCESSION the Pr left Nantes in France on 22 June 1745 with 7 followers, and arms and ammunition in 2 ships (one of which had to return after an encounter with the British) and landed on Eriskay Island, in the Hebrides, W Scotland, on 23 July 1745. He reached the mainland 2 days later, where his personal charm and the glamour of his cause attracted promising support among the Highland clans. He took Edinburgh (Sept 1745) and defeated the British at nearby Preston Pans (21 Sept 1745); and with 5,000 men at his back was ready to invade England. Taking the W route through Carlisle, Preston, Manchester and Macclesfield, he reached Derby on 4 Dec 1745. The heart went out of the enterprise, however, with the absence of either any Jacobite rising in England or hoped-for French invasion, and he turned N again with the intention of concentrating on Scotland. Here he was comparatively successful until his exhausted army was defeated by the D of Cumberland at Culloden, nr Inverness, on 16 Apr 1746. Cumberland proceeded to earn his nickname 'Butcher' by terrorizing the Highlands, and Charles Edward escaped to France on 20 Sept 1746.

Fox, Henry (28 Sept 1705–1 July 1774) 1st Bn Holland (1763), rapacious political manipulator under GEORGE II and GEORGE III, who made a fortune out of his office as Paymaster-Gen (June 1757–May 1765) and provided an over-indulgent upbringing for his son, Charles James Fox.

Younger son of Sir Stephen Fox (who had grown rich as steward to K CHARLES II in exile and after) and his 2nd wife, Christian Hopes; ed at Eton (1715–20) and Christ Ch, Oxford (1721–4) and on the Grand Tour; m (1744) Lady Caroline Lennox, eld daughter of the 2nd D of Richmond, in a clandestine, though very happy, marriage (she d 1774). Beginning as a supporter of WALPOLE, he became MP (1735–41) and received the post of Surveyor-Gen of the Works in 1737. A formidable debater, who was highly industrious in any task leading to his own advancement, he and his contemporary, PITT the Elder, emerged as the 2 greatest H of C politicians during the ministries of Walpole (1721–42), PELHAM (1742–54) and NEWCASTLE (1754–6). No PM was comfortable without one or both in his Gov.

Under the Pelham admin Fox became a Ld of the Treasury (1743–6), then Sec-at-War (1746), in which capacity he gravitated towards the faction led by George II's brother, the D of Cumberland, who was Capt-Gen (ie C-in-C).

Under the Newcastle admin he faced disappointment. On Pelham's death (6 Mar 1754) he expected to be made PM, but his cynical lack of idealism and his naked self-interest alienated the backbenchers, while his connection with Cumberland antagonized the Leicester House faction (the household of the future George III and his mother). Moreover, he had recently quarrelled with Ld Hardwicke – a leading member of the Old Corps of WHIGS – who had just passed the Marriage Act (1753) designed to prevent the clandestine kind of marriage Fox himself had made. In any case, Pelham's brother, Newcastle – the leader of the Old Corps – took office himself as 1st Ld of the Treasury, and offered the post of Sec of State to Fox, though without the H of C leadership, ie control of patronage. Fox refused, and moved into vigorous opposition along with Pitt until he got his way, becoming Sec of State (S) and leader of the H of C – though without full control of appointments – in Nov 1755. Unfamiliar with the international scene and incompetent at foreign affairs, Fox was unhappy holding office during the critical years of the DIPLOMATIC REVOLUTION and the first disasters of the SEVEN YEARS WAR as well as facing the tirades of Pitt. He resigned in Oct 1756, and Newcastle soon after.

The Devonshire–Pitt admin (1756–7) was forced on the K after Fox had been given the task of forming a Gov and had failed, mainly because of Pitt's refusal to serve with him. George II was most unhappy, and was soon persuaded by Fox and Cumberland to dismiss them (Apr 1757).

The Newcastle–Pitt admin (1757–61), which successfully ran the Seven Years War, included Fox as Paymaster-Gen (1757). Fox thus chose the rich pickings of politics, while Pitt made his mark on history by winning the war. Through Fox's department flowed the vast public funds which paid the troops and provided their victuals and kit; and Fox not only pocketed the commission paid by the bankers and merchants involved, but also invested the tax-payers' money on his own account during the long period between receiving and disbursing it.

The Bute admin (1762–3) – the 1st of the new K, George III – ended the long ascendancy of the Old Corps of Whigs, and brought the Leicester House faction into power. Thanks to Cumberland, Fox obtained from the K 2 sinecures for the lives of himself and his 2 sons: the Writership of the Tallies and Counter-Tallies, and the Clerkship of the Pells in Ireland – worth about £2,500 a year on average. But Fox soon forsook his old leader to help the K's friends. He remained Paymaster, but gained a seat in the Cabinet and the leadership of the H of C (1762). His task was to get the preliminaries of the peace Tr of Paris through Parl, which he did with complete success, for war-weariness had gripped the country. When it was safely passed (Dec 1762) with unprecedented thoroughness, he removed from office all who had opposed it. This 'Massacre of the Pelhamite Innocents' – as Horace Walpole called it – broke up the emp of patronage which had sustained the Old Corps in office since Robert Walpole's day.

The Grenville admin (1763–5) ousted Fox as soon as it could. He received the reward he had been promised for his services to K and Tr, being made Bn Holland in Apr 1763, but Grenville in a momentarily strong position forced the K to remove him from his post as Paymaster (1765). Fox retired to enjoy private life on the fortune he had made, and provide an excessively permissive and expensive upbringing for his brilliant and precocious son. It took many years of detailed investigation to separate his private funds from those of the Gov, and when he d 8 years of accounting still remained to be done before his affairs as Paymaster were finally settled.

Francis I (12 Sept 1494–31 Mar 1547) K of France (1515) who, flamboyant, authoritarian and pleasure-loving, continued the foreign policy of his 2 predecessors in the HABSBURG–VALOIS WARS; while his reign at home was characterized by (1) the growth of ABSOLUTISM, (2) the spread of HUMANISM and (3) the spread of Protestantism and its subsequent persecution.

Son of Charles of Valois-Orléans, Count of Angoulême and Louise of Savoy; m 1st (1514) Claude, daughter of K LOUIS XII, and heiress to the Duchy of

Brittany (d 1524); m 2nd (1530) Eleonore, sister of the Emp CHARLES V, in accordance with the Trs of Madrid (Jan 1526) and Cambrai (Aug 1529).

The build-up of centralized absolutism which marked the reigns of CHARLES VIII and Louis XII was intensified under Francis. He was the 1st French K to be called *Your Majesty*, for example, a title hitherto reserved for the Emp. At the centre, the *Conseil du Roi* began to specialize its activities, allotting some days to finance, others to justice etc; while decisions of high policy were taken by a small inner ring, sometimes called the *Conseil des Affaires*; and more and more work (outside the Council) was taken on by the royal Secs (the Secs of State in embryo). In finance, much was done by Chancellor Antoine Duprat to raise the vast revenues required by Francis's extravagant foreign policy and personal life. The *taille* (a direct tax) was increased, and so were the voluntary *aides* demanded from the clergy. The creation of new offices for sale, the sale of titles of nobility, of offices, of the right to nominate successors to offices were all exploited in a more systematic way. He also raised many loans, among which the experiment of 1522 was important for the future. On this occasion the interest (*rente*) was backed by the revenues of the City of Paris corporation. In 1522-3 Duprat carried out a wholesale reform of the tax-collecting and accounting system, placing financial admin under the close supervision of 2 central officials, the *Trésorier de l'Épargne* and the *Receveur des Parties Casuelles*. In the judicial sphere, Francis made active use of a court called the *Grand Conseil*, an offshoot of the royal Council created in 1497, but only in this reign emerging as the chief agent of royal centralization and co-ordination in the field of civil and criminal justice. On the other hand, he had a running battle with the PARLEMENT of Paris, which objected to royal policy in many fields (eg the sale of offices, the 'evocation' of cases from the Parlement to the royal Council, the financial exactions of the Crown, the Concordat of Bologna, ecclesiastical preferment, the toleration of heresy) and it was not until after his return from captivity in Madrid (1526) that he managed to make it submit. He also reorganized the jurisdiction of the prov Parlements and the royal courts immediately below them (the *bailliages* and the *sénéchaussées*), and steadily ensured that their personnel behaved more like centrally appointed bureaucrats than locally elected magnates. The codification of customary law also continued; and the Ordinance of Villers-Cotterêts (Aug 1539) ordered that all legal documents had henceforth to be in the French language and asserted that the royal courts were superior to those of the Ch – a decree symbolizing the extension of the power of the Crown in two areas, the nobility and the provs on the one hand, and the Ch on the other. As regards the former, Francis absorbed into the monarchy the last of the great semi-independent fiefs: the lands of the D of Bourbon (a state within a state) from 1523 onwards in practice; those of Alençon by escheat in 1525; those of Albret by the marriage of the K's sister, Marguerite d'Angoulême to Henry II d'Albret, K of Navarre (1527); those of Burgundy when Charles V abandoned his claim to the Duchy in 1529; those of Brittany by the decree of 1532 that the duchy was henceforth indissolubly linked with the Crown of France; though the penetration of royal power into the internal affairs of these and other fiefs was a long and painful process, not complete by 1789. As regards the Ch, the Concordat of Bologna (1516) gave Francis in theory what the French Crown already had in practice since the Pragmatic Sanction of Bourges (1438): ie the patronage of about

600 of the chief benefices. What the Parlement of Paris objected to (and they registered the Concordat only under duress as late as Mar 1518) was the restoration of the legality of judicial appeals to Rome, which were believed to undermine the Gallican liberties. The Parlement also opposed the K over the Prot problem.

The spread of Italian Humanism was encouraged by the royal family in various ways. The Habsburg–Valois Wars brought Franco-Italian contact; Francis employed Cellini, Primaticcio, Leonardo and others on such royal châteaux as Fontainebleau, Blois and Chambord; and, influenced by Guillaume Budé, the leading classical scholar, he founded in 1530 what later became the Collège de France where humanist teaching was given, free from the medievalism of the Univ of Paris; and his sister and other courtiers patronized LEFÈVRE D'ÉTAPLES and other members of the Meaux circle which, while remaining true Caths, nevertheless, with their application of humanist scholarship to the Scriptures and their strong dash of German mysticism, prepared the French mind for the reception of Protestantism.

The persecution of Protestantism did not begin at once. In the 1520s, the reform movement spread by the native humanists was reinforced by Prot influences from Germany and Switzerland, and groups of so-called Lutherans began to form among the lower clergy and educated laity in many parts of France. The Univ of Paris formally condemned Lutheranism (Apr 1521) and the Parlement of Paris began to charge humanists with heresy; but Francis, as a humanist (perhaps persuaded by his sister), as an ally of the German Prot Prs, but above all as an absolutist, did all he could to block the persecuting measures of these two opponents of absolutism. If the Prots were to be suppressed (his policy went) then only the K could do it. And he turned hostile in the 1530s as the radical Protestantism of the image-breaking type took hold and threatened public order – the last straw being the so-called Affair of the Placards (Oct 1534) when broadsides insulting to the Mass appeared on the walls of Paris and other cities – even the K's bedchamber-door at Amboise not being spared. Henceforth Francis, the Parlement and the Univ co-operated in a campaign of severe persecution, during which the Card de Tournon played a leading role; the Univ published lists of forbidden books; a score of villages were destroyed and 3,000 Waldensians massacred in a military campaign in Provence in 1545; and 14 were executed at Meaux in 1546.

Francis II (19 Jan 1544–5 Dec 1560) K of France (1559).

Eld son of K HENRY II and Q CATHERINE DE MEDICI; m MARY, Q OF SCOTS (1558). Poor in health and pliable in character, he was only 15 when he succeeded to the throne on the accidental death of his father, and was dominated by his wife's uncles: François, D de GUISE, and his brother Charles, Card of Lorraine, whose aggressively anti-Prot policy contributed to the outbreak of the FRENCH WARS OF RELIGION.

Frederick I (11 July 1657–25 Feb 1713) El Frederick III of Brandenburg (1688), K of Prussia (1701), who in a less dynamic way continued the build-up of the Brandenburg-Prussia of FREDERICK WILLIAM, the Great Elector, as a European power, his main achievement being the acquisition of the royal title and the conspicuous expenditure that went with it.

3rd son of the Great Elector and his 1st wife, Louisa Henrietta of Orange; ed by Eberhard von Danckelmann; m 1st (1679) Elizabeth Henrietta of Hesse-Kassel (d 1683); m 2nd (1684) Sophie Charlotte of Hanover (d 1705); m 3rd (1708) Sophie Louise of Mecklenburg (d 1735). Deeply religious, but physically and mentally unimpressive, Frederick set his heart early on the title of K, but did not manage to get the Emp LEOPOLD I's consent until the latter needed Frederick's alliance in the War of the Spanish Succession (1702–13/14). In the Crown Tr of Nov 1700 Frederick promised 8,000 soldiers and diplomatic support. In return he was allowed to crown himself 'K in Prussia' at Königsberg (Jan 1701) – that city not being in the HR Emp. To support his new dignity, Frederick built new châteaux and filled them with works of art and Versailles-type ceremonial. Other 'prestige' outlays were the Univ of Halle (1694), the Academy of Arts (1696) and the Academy of Sciences (1701), the last under the leadership of Gottfried Wilhelm Leibniz. This whole programme was largely inspired by his attractive, able, cultured and pious 2nd wife, Sophie Charlotte. Frederick concentrated on ostentation and, unlike Prussian rulers immediately before and after, he left the daily toil of Gov to chief ministers: 1st (1688–97) his tutor, von Danckelmann, an energetic career bureaucrat who followed the sound policies of the Great Elector; and 2nd (1697–1711) Count Kolbe von Wartenberg, a flattering courtier, who encouraged Frederick in his extravagances, lined his own pockets, and left the actual work of Gov to his Sec of State.

At home, the population rose, aided by the influx of Hugs who found refuge there. The economy continued to evolve; the royal income doubled. The outlines of central, prov and local bureaucracy sketched out by the Great Elector were steadily filled in. The standing army increased from 30,000 to 50,000. The Supreme Court of Appeal was established in Berlin (1702), from which there was no longer any appeal to the HR Emp. Education was fostered; Pietism spread; the Enlightenment started its course; while Brandenburg-Prussia rightly enjoyed a reputation for religious toleration.

Abroad, Frederick followed the last lead of his father and committed himself fully to the European coalition that fought LOUIS XIV in the War of the League of Augsburg (1689–97) and the War of the Spanish Succession. The troops he lent to WILLIAM III to defend the lower Rhine allowed the latter to leave the United Provinces and carry out the REVOLUTION OF 1688 in Britain; while the troops he provided for Leopold (14,000 rising to 50,000) played a distinguished part in the major campaigns, especially under MARLBOROUGH and Pr Eugen in the Netherlands. Brandenburg-Prussia was a client State which depended on the subsidies which richer States paid for the use of its troops, but which consequently had to follow a foreign policy dictated by them. It has been argued that Frederick would have been wiser had he kept out of the wars in the W and played an active part in the GREAT NORTHERN WAR (1700–25) in the E. Instead, in this area he dithered between Sweden on one side and Poland and Denmark on the other, achieving nothing by his attempts at mediation, and standing helplessly by as foreign armies devastated N Germany.

Frederick II (The Great) (24 Jan 1712–17 Aug 1786) K of Prussia (1740), a cool and ruthless Machiavellian who raised Prussia to great-power status by conquering Silesia in the WAR OF THE AUSTRIAN SUCCESSION (1740–48); successfully

defended her against a coalition of great powers in the SEVEN YEARS WAR
(1756–63); acquired W Prussia in the 1st Partition of Poland (1772); and led the
German Prs against the expansionist designs of the Emp JOSEPH II. A leading
ENLIGHTENED ABSOLUTIST, and highly gifted, for a K, in literature and the
arts as well as in statesmanship and warfare, he devoted his life as 'the first
servant of the State' to the tasks of expanding the army and the revenue, and
raising the economic, cultural and judicial level of his subjects, while maintaining
them in social and political leading-reins. Before he d there were many signs that
the rigidities of the gov system and social order were preventing the fulfilment of
his altruistic aims.

3rd and eld surviving son of K FREDERICK WILLIAM I and his Q consort,
Sophia Dorothea, daughter of K GEORGE I of Great Britain; ed, according to
the brutal and spartan precepts of his semi-deranged father, in religious and
military affairs to the exclusion of 'effeminate' arts subjects; then (1730 onwards)
in posts in the Prussian admin; later self-ed at his own household at Rheinsberg
(1736 onwards) in philosophy, history, poetry, music, mathematics and science,
often reading and taking notes till far into the night, and already making a start
on his own writings by corresponding with Voltaire; m (1733) Elizabeth Christine,
daughter of D Ferdinand Albert II of Brunswick-Bevern (d 1797, no issue).
Small, delicate and sensitive, with great dark-blue eyes and a gentle, captivating
voice, he was encyclopaedic in conversation, tireless in industry, swift in his
thinking, iron in his determination and unshakeable in his fortitude. He rarely
saw his wife, but formed deep attachments with a series of male friends. He spent
hours at his desk, and his published *Works* and *Political Correspondence* run into
scores of large volumes. He also composed symphonies, over 100 sonatas, and
concertos for the flute – he was himself a competent flautist. He suffered from
gout, indigestion, constipation, migraine, cramp and insomnia. He aged early
and became bent and stiff with rheumatism. Like his father, he was probably
a sufferer from that rare metabolic disorder, porphyria. Father and son were at
daggers drawn, and it was probably in resistance to his father's philistinism that
Frederick developed his powers of dissimulation and endurance. On his part,
K Frederick William hated never knowing 'what goes on in this little head'.
Frederick once tried to escape from Prussia, in the summer of 1730. The plot
failed and the K locked him up in the fortress of Küstrin. His friend and ac-
complice, Hans Hermann von Katte, was beheaded immediately in front of his
window while Frederick was forced to watch by Grenadiers holding his head.
The old K's cruelty was foiled, however, for Frederick fainted away. After this
crisis, he went through a form of reconciliation with his father. He pretended
to co-operate and took a post in the admin to learn his trade. His pragmatic
attitude contrasted strongly with his father's piety. 'It is better that the sovereign
should break his word,' he once said, 'than that the people should perish.' Once
he became K, this irreligious and cynical misanthrope worked himself into a
premature old age in the service of his country.

In his foreign policy Frederick shocked Europe within 7 months of his accession by invading Silesia (Dec 1740) and precipitating the War of the Austrian
Succession (1740–48). Thanks to the superb army and bureaucracy he had
inherited, and to his own nimble diplomacy and swift campaigns (he combined
the 2 roles of Head of State and C-in-C) he conquered and kept the rich and

populous prov, and by the Tr of Aix-la-Chapelle (Oct 1748) secured inter-national recognition for his conquest. Thereafter, he sought only peace, but Austrian desire for revenge kept him permanently on the alert. His diplomacy was a leading feature of the DIPLOMATIC REVOLUTION (1749–56), in which Prussia allied with Great Britain, and Prussia's erstwhile ally, France, joined up with her old enemy, Austria. Frederick was convinced that a big anti-Prussian coalition was being negotiated, and he decided to strike first. 'Negotiations with-out arms,' he thought, 'produce as little impression as musical scores without instruments.' He invaded Saxony (Aug 1756) and began the Seven Years War (1756–63), bringing the feared coalition into existence, consisting of France, Austria, Russia, Sweden and Saxony. His ally was GEORGE II of Great Britain, who paid him an annual subsidy and relieved French pressure on him by main-taining the Army of Observation in W Germany, raiding French coastal stations, and fully engaging French forces in the colonies. Frederick spent every cam-paigning season on the move, desperately parrying blows from his numerous enemies, contemplating suicide, but somehow finding the will to endure. With the advantage of uniting in himself both political and military command he was able to launch vigorous attacks on enemies who were more accustomed to the defensive manoeuvring typical of the period. 'If you must go to war,' he once wrote, 'fall on your enemy like thunder and lightning.' His aim was to destroy armies, not conquer ground; and he made up for the modest size of his armies by the perfection of their drill, the intensity of their fire-power, and his own mental dexterity at the height of the battle. Disaster seemed inevitable, however, when George II d and PITT resigned. GEORGE III reduced British aid; but in the end Frederick was rescued by the death of the Empss ELIZABETH of Russia (25 Dec 1761/5 Jan 1762). Her successor, PETER III, was an ardent admirer of Frederick, and he immediately made peace with Prussia (Apr/May 1762), returning all Russian conquests. By the Tr of Hubertusburg (Feb 1763), which ended the Seven Years War in E Europe, Prussia kept Silesia. After that it was more essential than ever for Frederick to keep the peace through skilful diplomacy. He allied with CATHERINE II of Russia (Mar/Apr 1764); supported the election of her candidate, Count Stanislas Poniatowski, as K of Poland (Aug/Sept 1764); reluctantly acquiesced in the Russian subjection of Poland; and made the best of a bad job by taking part in the 1st Partition of Poland (July/Aug 1772) along with Russia and Austria. By this shameless act of piracy Prussia gained W Prussia, which contained 600,000 inhabitants. It included the valley of the R Vistula, and joined up the isolated prov of E Prussia with the main body of the State. His principal problem after this was to contain the aggressive designs of Austria. The 1st crisis came in the War of the Bavarian Succession (1778–9). When the El Maximilian Joseph d (30 Dec 1777) without issue, Austria claimed one-third of Bavaria and occupied it. Frederick took the lead in defending the German Prs against this aggression and thus preserving the *status quo*. He invaded Bohemia (July 1778), but neither side was anxious to join battle. In any case, the troops on both sides spent most of their time seeking food – hence this war was called the Potato War. By the Tr of Teschen (May 1779) Austria had to abandon her pretensions, taking only the face-saving little triangle of land known as the Inn Quarter. Frederick continued to lead German resistance to Austrian ambition when the restless JOSEPH II became head of the Austrian monarchy (Nov 1780). When in 1784 the latter announced his plan for annexing Bavaria in exchange for the Austrian Netherlands (Belgium), Frederick organized the League of Princes (*Fürstenbund*), beginning with the alliance of Prussia, Hanover and Saxony (July 1785). Against the determination of these 17 States, Austria had to back down once more. Frederick's methods in E and central Europe have been roundly condemned by later historians. He has been accused of lowering the moral tone of international relations and splitting, and therefore weakening, Germany, as well as endangering her by encouraging the Wward advance of Russia – charges which are either unjust or anachronistic.

At home, as far as the gov is concerned, he made few changes in the bureaucratic absolutism bequeathed him by his father. Prussia continued to be ruled *aus dem Kabinett*, the K sitting at his desk at Potsdam every day and, helped by 5 secs, receiving written information or requests, and issuing written orders. Uncluttered by family life, undistracted by Court intrigues, he dispatched all business quickly, postponing nothing and expecting instant obedience. He raised the army from 83,000 to 200,000, the revenue from 7 million to 19 million thaler, and the State treasure from 8 million to 51 million thaler. The population doubled to 5 million. The 500,000 thaler adverse balance of trade became a 3 million favourable balance. The economy thus prospered, thanks to the efforts, not of an enterprising bourgeoisie (all its talent was attracted into the army and bureaucracy), but of the mercantilist State machine. In Prussia the State had more or less the monopoly of capital, enterprise and purchasing power; and in an era when all other Enlightened States were moving in the Physiocratic direction of free trade, Frederick's civil servants founded overseas trading companies; organized a marine insurance company; dredged rivers and linked them by canals; managed mines, quarries and forests; set up a State bank to ease credit; started new industries by granting monopolies, finding experts and lending capital; taught scientific farming to the peasants; stabilized food prices by setting up grain depots; drained swamps, cleared wastes and settled immigrants (300,000 of them during the reign, domiciled in 900 new villages). Culturally, Frederick's reign produced the great change from Pietism to the Enlightenment, but this switch made little practical difference to the educated classes, since both philosophies preached the virtues of conscientious endeavour on behalf of the public. In 1763 Frederick promulgated a detailed scheme of elementary education, designed to produce a generation of obedient citizens, each with a useful trade. At the same time, the middle classes thronged the private schools to secure jobs in the Ch and the middle ranks of the army and bureaucracy. This piece of private enterprise, however, resulted in over-production, and Prussian towns filled with Enlightened graduates, either unemployed or following humble careers, and deeply hostile to the privileges of the nobility (though not questioning the omnicompetence of the State). These were the readers who sustained the German literary revival of this period: the *Sturm und Drang* movement, the new generation of stars led by Lessing, Herder, Goethe, Schiller and Kant. For his part, Frederick had no sympathy for early German Romanticism. Calling German a 'semi-barbarous tongue', and speaking it 'like a coachman', he wrote in French and looked for intellectual stimulus to Voltaire and the French *philosophes*. Similarly, he built in the rococo style: the Berlin Opera House (1742), the Château of Sans Souci and the *Neues Palais* at Potsdam

(1747 and 1769); and when he revived the Berlin Academy of Sciences (1740) it was Pierre Louis Moreau Maupertuis, the French mathematician, who became President. The social order which Frederick inherited maintained the strict separation between Junkers, peasants and burghers. With military discipline in mind, Frederick reserved all the top posts in the State (but not in the Ch) to the nobility. The same consideration prevented any improvement in the condition of the peasants. In fact, their position deteriorated with the wider spread of *Gutsherrschaft*: ie large-scale commercial agriculture run by feudal lords, using their serfs as forced labour. For their part, the burghers became further subservient to the State machine, and remained locked up in their towns to facilitate the collection of the excise.

Weaknesses in the Prussian State and society which were apparent in Frederick's lifetime became dangerous when he was replaced by successors who lacked his genius. The rigid social order served the interests of the army, but hampered economic growth. The bureaucrats may have been steeped in economic theory, but the people lacked the vertical and horizontal social mobility that advanced economies require. The Gov also began to ossify as the bureaucracy sank into a routine which could just as easily resist orders as carry them out. Sometimes departments fed the K with false information; sometimes they were incapable of quick action because overloaded. The channels of communication silted up with slowly moving paper, and Frederick found it expeditious to bypass the benumbed Gen Directory and deal with prov War and Domains Chambers directly, or even create new departments separate from it, such as the Ministry of Mines and the Ministry of Forests. Against the Gen Directory's wishes he created the *Régie* (1766) to collect customs and excise duties. It was run by a French tax-farmer, de Launay, employing 200 Frenchmen, and it took the Prussian bureaucrats 20 years to eliminate (1786) this foreign invasion. During Frederick's reign there was a general resurgence of the Junkers. His predecessors had created Prussian absolutism by eliminating their powers of resistance in the provs, and incorporating them into the centralized State. Under Frederick – and encouraged by him – the nobles monopolized the commanding positions in that State – in the army, the bureaucracy and the judiciary (where the prov *Regierungen* were bureaucratized by Samuel Cocceji (1746 onwards), continuing his judicial reforms initiated under K Frederick William I). By the end of Frederick's reign, the Junkers were ready to turn his dictatorship into a limited monarchy, not through parl institutions as elsewhere, but through their control of the State machine. The Army became intoxicated with its own success, opposed reform, and failed to keep up with the times. It lagged behind the army of K LOUIS XVI of France, eg, in both training and equipment, and eventually fell at Jena before the armies of the French Revolution (1806). The economy failed to take off. Enterprise withered under the dead weight of State regulations, gild controls, the Kanton system of recruitment, the sharp separation of town and country, the absence of social mobility and the lack of a buoyant home market. The political education of the Prussian people, moreover, did not fit them for progress, whether they were degraded serfs or subservient burghers. The Prussian monarchy with its all-providing paternalism took the sting out of the bourgeoisie. It made them concentrate on the task of creeping rank by rank up the lower levels of the public service, and brainwashed them into admiring the system which oppressed them. It paid the price in the C19, however, for Frederick left behind a middle class lacking both political wisdom and business enterprise; while his successors on the throne proved incapable of correcting these faults.

Frederick III (The Wise) (17 Jan 1463–5 May 1525) El of Saxony (1486), protector of LUTHER, though without becoming a Lutheran or meeting him.

Son of Ernest, El of Saxony, and Elizabeth, daughter of Albert, D of Bavaria; ed in HUMANISM, he patronized the painters Dürer and Cranach at his court in Wittenberg, founded the Univ there in 1502 and assembled a large collection of relics – over 5,000 in 1509, including 33 fragments of the Cross. A leading member of the Imperial-reform party under the Emp MAXIMILIAN I, he was considered in 1519 as a suitable candidate for the Emp instead of the rivals CHARLES V and FRANCIS I, but he refused. He appointed Luther Prof of Theology in 1512 and MELANCHTHON Prof of Greek in 1518; and achieved fame by protecting Luther when he was under papal and imperial condemnation, eg by having him taken to the Wartburg from 1521–2.

Frederick Henry (29 Jan 1584–14 Mar 1647) Pr of Orange, who led the United Provinces in its Golden Age and during the renewed 80 Years War with Spain (part of the THIRTY YEARS WAR).

Youngest son of WILLIAM I (the Silent) and his 4th wife, Louise de Coligny; ed at the Univ of Leiden, in the army under his brother MAURICE, and in France with his mother; m (1625) the plump and beautiful Amalia von Solms, maid of honour to Elizabeth, wife of Frederick V of the Palatinate, at that time exiled in the Netherlands. On the death of Maurice on 23 Apr 1625 Frederick Henry succeeded as Stadholder (Gov) of Holland and 4 other provs, and as Capt-Gen and Admiral-Gen of the United Provinces, in which capacities he led the fighting against Spain in the renewed 80 Years War, 1621–48 (a continuation of the REVOLT OF THE NETHERLANDS).

1621–9: he fended off Spanish attacks on the N Netherlands while Admiral Piet Heyn captured all but 3 of the Spanish silver fleet off Matanzas, Cuba, in Sept 1628.

1629–39: he took the offensive against the S Netherlands, capturing Wesel on the German border (19 Aug 1629), Bois-le-Duc ('s Hertogenbosch), Brabant (14 Sept 1629), Maastricht (23 Aug 1632) and Breda (10 Oct 1637), and conquering a strip of N Flanders, Brabant and Limburg, which eventually became part of the United Provinces as the 'Lands of the Generality'. At the same time, in the Channel, Admiral Martin Harpertzoon Tromp defeated the vast Spanish fleet of Don Antonio de Oquendo in the Battle of the Downs (21 Oct 1639). As this Armada was on its way to reinforce the S Netherlands, its destruction was a material as well as a moral blow in favour of Frederick Henry. This run of successes turned him into a popular hero, and during this period he occupied an almost monarchical position in the Dutch federation. As commander of the armed forces in time of war, he naturally enjoyed great power; but he added to it by his astute political management of the States-Gen, which in the Act of Survivance (1631) made his offices hereditary, and in 1637 gave him the title of 'Highness'. He and Amalia annoyed the Regents – the urban patrician oligarchs who normally governed the Netherlands – by maintaining a princely court at the

Hague, promoting the nobility, and following a foreign policy the Regents disapproved of. Frederick Henry tried to reunite the N and S Netherlands. As he invaded the S, he tried to stimulate a popular rebellion against Spain, but without success. Nor did the year-long negotiations between the 2 States-Generals produce union. The Cath S did not trust the Calvinist-dominated N to tolerate their religion. Moreover, the Regents of Amsterdam and Holland also opposed reunion, for this would have reopened the R Scheldt and revived the trade of their economic rival, Antwerp.

1640–47: saw a deterioration in Frederick Henry's position. He suffered from gout and jaundice, and became feeble-minded and hen-pecked. His military successes came to an end, but he would not break the alliance with France and make peace, as the Regents wanted. He also annoyed these Calvinist republicans by marrying his son, the future WILLIAM II, to Mary, daughter of K CHARLES I of England (1641), and supporting the Cavaliers instead of the Roundheads. A further move towards monarchy was the marriage of his daughter, Louise Henriette, to the El FREDERICK WILLIAM I (the Great Elector) in 1646. He disapproved strongly of the peace negotiations between the United Provinces and Spain at Münster, but d before peace was signed there in Jan 1648.

Frederick William (The Great Elector) (16 Feb 1620–9 May 1688) El of Brandenburg (1640), a masterful ruler, tall and powerfully built, with piercing blue eyes, who founded Brandenburg-Prussia as a European power, by imposing unity on scattered, independent provs, and by playing an energetic part in European war and diplomacy. As means to this end, he created a standing army, crushed the Estates and constructed an all-Prussian bureaucracy centred on Berlin.

Son of the El GEORGE WILLIAM and his wife, Elizabeth Charlotte, sister of Frederick V, the El Palatine; ed (1634–7) in Holland (Univ of Leiden and household of Pr FREDERICK HENRY), learning the latest in science and technology, politics and warfare, and developing the austere piety and moral force of the dedicated Calvinist; m 1st (1646) Louisa Henrietta, daughter of Frederick Henry (d 1667); m 2nd (1668) Dorothea of Holstein-Glücksburg (d 1689). Frederick William inherited 3 main groups of scattered territories: Brandenburg in the centre, E Prussia stretching E to the R Niemen, Cleves-Mark far away W on the R Rhine. These provs had many disadvantages: they had no all-Prussian loyalties (Frederick William was their only possession in common) and no natural frontiers; and they were poor, thinly populated and unproductive. They were also wide open to foreign conquest, as the THIRTY YEARS WAR proved; for Frederick William's father had been unable to prevent his lands being the battleground for the rival armies of Sweden and the Emp. Moreover, in each prov, the El was merely a constitutional ruler, and the Estates in each – dominated by the Junkers (nobles) – passed laws, authorized taxation, collected and spent it, raised armed forces and dictated their use. In addition, the Junker-dominated Government (*Regierung*) in each prov kept the El at arm's length as the final court of appeal for the prov and its day-to-day ruling committee. Frederick William's achievement was to give Brandenburg-Prussia, not merely external security, but also a positive international role, by creating a standing army, destroying the powers of the Estates, and replacing them with a centralized absolutism based on his new bureaucracy and sentiments of patriotism. In the international field he had the advantage of ruling at a time when Poland was in decline, when Sweden was over-extended, when the Emp, threatened by Turkey and France, had to retreat before the German Prs, when Russia was still too weak to impinge on W affairs, and when France was glad to use Brandenburg-Prussia as a counter-weight to the Emp, so long as Sweden's interests were safe-guarded.

1640–48, the last years of the Thirty Years War, saw him skilfully extricate himself from the fighting and clear his lands of foreign troops. He did it by not acknowledging any obligations to the Emp under the Tr of Prague which his father had signed (May 1635), while making a separate peace with Sweden, Tr of Stockholm (July 1641). In the Tr of Westphalia (Oct 1648) which ended the Thirty Years War he had to be content with the E half of Pomerania and the Bpric of Kammin, leaving the W and better half – with Stettin and the mouth of the R Oder – to Sweden. In compensation, however, he gained the Bprics of Halberstadt and Minden, along with the succession to the Archbpric of Magde-burg, which he achieved in 1666. Moreover, he successfully championed the Calvinists in the negotiations at Westphalia, and secured for them the same rights as the Lutherans enjoyed, an achievement for which he was acknowledged as the leader of the German Prots.

At home, he applied the lessons that these experiences taught him: the crucial importance of building a standing army so as to avoid going cap in hand to allies. An army in its turn depended on increasing the royal revenues and extri-cating them from the control of the Junkers. Here the breakthrough came in Brandenburg, where he had a series of confrontations with the Estates (1649–53), who refused to vote taxes for the use of other provs. At last in the so-called Recess of 1653 he reached a compromise which seemed like a victory for the Junkers. It not only enlarged and guaranteed their economic and social privi-leges, including the opportunity to turn more peasants into serfs, it also confirmed their political role, guaranteeing that the El would always consult the Estates over policy and appointments. In return, the Junkers voted Frederick William a sum of 530,000 thaler, payable over the next 6 years. With this money the El founded an army which he was eventually able to use to collect more taxes without waiting for the Estates' consent. He believed that the 'general welfare' and 'extreme necessity' were more important than the privileges of the nobility; and thus armed he was in a position to pursue a successful foreign policy and turn Brandenburg-Prussia into a centralized absolutism.

In foreign policy his chief aims were (a) to gain the full sovereignty of E Prussia, instead of holding it as a fief from the K of Poland (JOHN II CASIMIR at that time); and (b) to acquire W Pomerania from Sweden. He achieved the former in the War of the North (1655–60), but failed to achieve the latter, though he raised Brandenburg-Prussia to the rank of a European power by his sinuous diplomacy and ruthless use of force, all in the interests of an implacable egoism. (a) In the War of the North in E Europe, when CHARLES X GUSTAV of Sweden invaded Poland, he fought at first for Sweden, seeing important action in the 3-day battle outside Warsaw (18–20/28–30 July 1656), and being recognized by Sweden as sovereign of E Prussia (Tr of Labiau, Nov 1656). He then changed sides, and was recognized by Poland as sovereign of E Prussia in the Tr of Wehlau (Sept 1657), and also in the Tr of Oliva which ended the war (23 Apr/

3 May 1660). (b) In LOUIS XIV's wars in W Europe, Frederick William showed the same ability to earn foreign subsidies and raise Brandenburg-Prussia's price by timely changes of side. Between 1660 and 1688 he drew funds from most of the European powers in turn, without having to do a great deal of fighting. His normal posture, insofar as he had one, was in alliance with Holland, England and the Emp, but the need for French money and anger at his own side for not helping him sufficiently would put him at times on the French side. In the Dutch War (1672-9) he supported Holland (1672-3), then France (1673-4), then Holland again (1674-9). During this last period, Louis XIV persuaded Sweden to attack him from the rear by invading Brandenburg (Dec 1674), but Frederick William defeated Sweden at Fehrbellin, Brandenburg (18/28 June 1675). It was only a skirmish, but to defeat Sweden was an enormous moral fillip, and Frederick William went on to take Stettin (Dec 1677) and other strong points, and clear the Swedes out of W Pomerania. At the end of the war, however, Louis XIV forced him to return all his conquests to Sweden (Tr of St Germain, June 1679). The next period, 1679-85, saw Frederick William in French pay, but the Revocation of the Edict of Nantes on 18 Oct 1685, and the persecution of the French Prots, injected a religious element into international politics which Frederick William could not ignore – especially in view of the economic advantages which the French Prots would bring to Brandenburg-Prussia. He replied in the Edict of Potsdam (Nov 1685) offering the Hugs shelter in Brandenburg-Prussia. And at the same time he came to terms with Holland and the Emp and the other powers that were forming the League of Augsburg, though without actually breaking with France by the time of his death.

At home, meanwhile, he was increasing his revenues by reforming their admin and stimulating the economy, all in order to expand his standing army. His revenues (apart from foreign subsidies) came from 2 sources: the royal domains and taxation. The domains, which produced income from rents paid by tenant farmers and from the profits of direct exploitation by the Crown of its own corn, cattle, timber, coal etc, were extensive in comparison with those of most European monarchs. He greatly improved their yield by more efficient management. He used 3 tiers of functionaries: bailiffs at the local level, Domains Chambers at the prov level, all supervised in Berlin by the central Chamber (the *Hofkammer*) set up just after his death. As for taxation, he continued the traditional *Contribution* in the country (a land tax paid by the peasants), but in the towns he gradually enforced the Excise, a sales-tax which enabled him to tap rising output. He also improved the yield from taxes by creating a 3-stage hierarchy of new bureaucrats: Excise Commissars (*Steuerräte*) in the towns and *Contribution* Commissars (*Landräte*) in the country, supervised by Prov War Commissars, under the Gen War Commissars in Berlin. He did not attempt to eliminate the traditional functionaries of the provs and towns working for the Estates and the municipalities, but during the next century his 2 new pyramids of bureaucrats gradually took over all their work leaving them to decay as empty shells. With these civil servants – over whose selection, training, discipline and promotion Frederick William and his successors took exceptional care – the Great El extended his sway over all his provs, collected his revenues and raised, trained and supplied his army. He also used the same men to stimulate economic growth by such measures as canal building, land drainage, the settlement of empty areas, the welcoming of skilled immigrants such as the French Prots, the dispatching of colonizing ventures to Africa and America, and the founding of State-aided manufacturing companies, all of which were intended to swell his subjects' wealth and add to their taxable capacity. To man the middle and lower ranks of the Gov machine, Frederick William employed burghers, but in the top positions – as *Landräte*, as Prov and Gen War Commissars, as Prov and Central Domains personnel, above all as army officers, he gradually persuaded the Junkers to work for him, to drop their traditional hostility and follow profitable careers in the royal service. In the post-Thirty Years War depression, the Junkers were glad of the money. This bureaucratic framework, moreover, was steadily extended from the central Brandenburg area to E Prussia and Cleves-Mark. In E Prussia the Estates and the great city of Königsberg put up a hard struggle in defence of their prov rights (1660s and 1670s), but Frederick William broke them in the end by occupying the prov with his army and eliminating the recalcitrant leaders by imprisonment and hanging. In Cleves-Mark on the Rhine and the Ruhr, with sophisticated inhabitants and a social structure on W lines, there was determined resistance to outside interference. For example, Frederick William made 9 separate attempts to introduce the Excise, all failures. He managed to make them give up their right to conduct foreign policy and exclude his troops, but the Estates retained the right to assemble whenever they wanted and to vote their own taxation. These problems notwithstanding, the progress made by the Great El in founding Brandenburg-Prussia as a centralized, absolute State amounted to a veritable revolution from above. It was a State whose chief job was tax-collecting and troop-training; and by the end of his reign he had trebled his revenues and raised an army of 30,000 men. It was a State where the nobles co-operated with the Crown because they were left free to exploit the peasants; but it was also a State which could begin to take care of itself in the dangerous world of international relations.

Frederick William I (15 Aug 1688–31 May 1740) K of Prussia (1713), who consolidated the centralized and absolute monarchy created by FREDERICK WILLIAM (the Great Elector) and K FREDERICK I. Known as the Sergeant-King, he doubled the size of the army, militarized the bureaucracy and society in general, stimulated economic development and doubled his revenue. Under his rule, Prussia ceased to be a client state living off foreign subsidies, and managed to afford her own independent foreign policy, which was one of peace, except that Frederick William joined Russia at the end of the GREAT NORTHERN WAR (1700–21) against Sweden, and gained Stettin and part of Swedish Pomerania. In general, Frederick William created the means by which his son, FREDERICK II (the Great), turned Prussia into a great power.

Son of K Frederick I and his 2nd Q consort, Sophie Charlotte; ed as a Calvinist by refugee Hug tutors, who disturbed his peace of mind with their awesome teaching on predestination; further ed (age 15 onwards) by sitting regularly at his father's Privy Council meetings, and by serving under MARLBOROUGH and Pr Eugen in the War of the Spanish Succession against LOUIS XIV of France; m (1706) Sophia Dorothea, daughter of K GEORGE I of Great Britain (d 28 June 1757). A coarse, fat brute, who loved his food and drink, and whose social life rarely rose above an evening's beer-drinking and pipe-smoking in the company of a few army cronies, he behaved towards his family and his subjects like an enraged sergeant-major. He was prudish and parsimonious, and prone to sudden bouts of uncontrollable temper when generals or bureaucrats might get a black eye from his fist or a broken head from his stick. His eldest son, Frederick II, tried to leave home and flee the country. Religious anxieties tortured him, as well as gout, boils, migraine, colic, melancholia and other plagues. He may have been a victim of the hereditary metabolic disorder known as porphyria. His devotion to duty was neurotic in its intensity. Regarding the success or failure of Prussia as God's judgement upon himself, he devoted himself to her interests in lifelong drudgery and attention to detail. Moreover, at the age of 23 he became converted to Pietism, the form of Lutheranism preached at the Univ of Halle, which taught that the proof of a Christian's rebirth lay in his striving to bring about God's Kdom on earth: ie in his attempts to improve society (not, as in Calvinism, to improve only himself). It cannot be doubted that Frederick William's idio-syncrasies – his belief in punctuality, regularity, obedience, frugality and con-scientious application to work – must have been a powerful influence in the formation of the Prussian national character, and hence in that of Germany generally. He made sure – through the Ch, through the univs and schools, through appointments and promotions in the army and the bureaucracy – that his attitudes were indelibly stamped on more than one generation of his subjects.

The Gov of Prussia was his personal daily task. He ruled *aus dem Kabinett*: ie he did not consult ministers or ask their advice – he received their information or requests on paper in his office, and then issued orders by means of marginal comments or letters. As soon as he mounted the throne he pruned away his father's extravagances and initiated a cheese-paring campaign in every walk of life except the army. Unlike other States, Prussia soon enjoyed a State treasure, not a national debt. The army rose from 39,000 to over 80,000 by the time of his death, when it ranked 3rd or 4th strongest in Europe, while Prussia was only tenth in size and thirteenth in population. A new Table of Ranks (1713) set the tone: a Field-Marshal ranked higher than a Lord Chamberlain, and at all levels the military were superior to the civil. The K wrote the full Infantry Regulations of 1714 himself; and he collected from all over Europe his own special battalion of Grenadiers, all gigantic in size. Conscription was universal: the Junkers becoming the officers, the burghers the NCOs and the peasants the rank and file. The Kanton System (inaugurated 1733) maximized the recruitment of men and minimized the damage to agriculture, by calling up serfs as soldiers to serve under their lords as officers. After initial training, both officers and men spent most of the year at home on their estates, except for summer manoeuvres. Foreign recruits – and they amounted to about a third of the army – were billeted in towns where they were given leave to take jobs in industry. Commanders sent up annual reports (*Conduitenlisten*) on the professional and private conduct of their officers. The admin – whose main task was raising men and money for the army – continued to expand. The Berlin *Hofkammer* – which supervised the Domains Chambers in the provs and the bailiffs in the localities – was reorganized on collegial lines as the Gen Finance Directory (1713). This raised the income from the royal domains. The other half of the K's income – taxation – was still handled by the Berlin Gen War Commissariat, which controlled the prov War Commissariats, which in turn supervised the local commissioners: ie the *Steuer-*

räte in the towns and the *Landräte* in the countryside. These 2 bureaucratic pyramids were fused together at all levels by Frederick William's Instruction of Dec 1722. By this means he hoped to eliminate the friction that had arisen between them. At Berlin, the fusion produced the *General-Ober-Finanz-Kriegs-und-Domainen-Direktorium* – usually known as the Gen Directory – which supervised the unified boards at prov and local level. Each office in this hierarchy had its written *Règlement* explaining what to do in minute detail. Individual initiative was superfluous as any problem not catered for in the regulations had to be passed upwards for solution. The judiciary was centralized by Samuel Cocceji (Supreme Minister of Justice, 1738 onwards), who had 3 main aims: to impose a Supreme Court at Berlin over the *Regierungen* (traditional prov supreme courts under Junker control); to develop uniform procedures in all provs; and to compile an all-Prussian body of law. Though his centralizing schemes were opposed by the Junkers every inch of the way, Cocceji achieved the first 2 aims. The 3rd had to wait for the reign of Frederick II.

The economy prospered, and Frederick William raised his annual revenue from 3,655,000 thaler in 1714 to 7,000,000 in 1740. Whether this success was due to, or in spite of, State planning is debatable; but industry and commerce occupied much of the Gov's attention. In such a militarized and bureaucratized society private initiative was absent. Entrepreneurial drive had to be provided by the State; and so did technical expertise, capital and markets. Civil servants created the woollen industry and gave the lead in coal and metal mining. They tried to establish luxury industries in silk and porcelain, clocks and watches, such as all ENLIGHTENED ABSOLUTISTS loved to own. In agriculture, technical progress was possible on the royal domain where bureaucrats reigned supreme. On the Junkers' estates where *Gutsherrschaft* was the general practice (ie where the feudal lord acted as a large-scale agrarian entrepreneur, using his serfs as forced labour) technical progress was minimal. The serfs bore the brunt of the whole Prussian system: working for the lord, paying taxes to the State, and fighting for the K. Well aware of this, Frederick William followed a policy of peasant *Konservation*: ie keeping the total amount of peasant land steady by preventing the Junkers from absorbing peasant holdings without replacement.

The social order hardened in its 3-fold divisions of Junkers, peasants and burghers. Social mobility between classes, and between town and country, was minimal. At first, when the aggressive absolutism of the Prussian monarchy seemed to pose a threat to Junker independence and prov rights, the nobles opposed the Crown, and Frederick William encouraged the bourgeoisie as their rivals. Halfway through his reign, though, he changed his policy. He began to value the Junkers for their qualities as commanders and admin leaders. In turn, the Junkers warmed to the monarchy and began to appreciate its financial rewards. Nobles, who till then had used their prov Estates and *Regierungen* to resist the army and bureaucracy, began to send their sons to serve the K of Prussia as soldiers and civil servants. The K, in his turn, guaranteed their social superiority and economic dominance.

The culture of Prussia did not escape being profoundly affected by Frederick William's reign. As far as the Ch was concerned, the K followed a policy of religious toleration in order to attract foreign refugees to fill the empty lands of E Prussia. When the Archbp of Salzburg drove out the Prots from his diocese, the K invited them to Prussia (Feb 1732) and settled about 20,000 on new farms. He naturally tried to centralize and unify Ch life. The prov Consistories were made subordinate to Berlin, while visitations became more frequent and more penetrating. He failed in one of his aims – to unite the Calvinists and the Lutherans – but he made sure that all the clergy preached the necessity of submission to earthly authority. In education he ordered universal schooling at the elementary level (1717); and made the Univ of Halle into a centre of Pietism. The public servants also studied Cameralism – a combination of law, economics and admin – and Frederick William set up 2 chairs in this, one at Halle and one at Frankfurt-on-the-Oder.

In foreign affairs the Sergeant-King was totally unwarlike, partly because of his conviction that 'God forbids unjust wars', and partly because of his reluctance to risk his precious army. His only aggressive act was to join PETER the Great (Apr 1715) in the last stages of the Great Northern War against Sweden. Peter handed over Stettin to Prussia, and Prussia helped her allies conquer Stralsund (12/23 Dec 1715) and Wismar (4/15 Apr 1716). By the Tr of Stockholm (Jan/Feb 1720) Sweden ceded Stettin at the mouth of the R Oder, and the S part of Swedish Pomerania, as well as the islands of Usedom and Wollin. For the rest of his reign Frederick William was at peace, and for most of it in alliance with the Emp CHARLES VI, whose help he needed to win a further prize on which he had set his heart. This was the Duchy of Berg in W Germany, where the ducal family was about to become extinct. One exception to this pro-Austrian stance was the minor diplomatic revolution caused by the alliance of the erstwhile hostile Spain and Austria by the 1st Tr of Vienna (Apr 1725). Frederick William joined Britain, France and their allies in the Tr of Hanover (Aug/Sept 1725), but not for long. He soon renewed his alliance with the Emp by the Tr of Wusterhausen (Oct 1726) and strengthened it by the Tr of Berlin (Dec 1728), by both of which Charles VI promised him the succession to Berg. In fact, Charles VI did nothing to back Prussia's claim, and it was a profoundly disillusioned Frederick William who eventually recognized this betrayal and signed a secret alliance with France (Apr 1739) whereby Louis XV promised to back his Berg claim. Thus, when Frederick William d, hostility to Austria was strong in Prussia, and it made its contribution to the success of Frederick II's sudden invasion of Silesia. Frederick William may have been clumsy and ingenuous in his foreign policy – to the extent of being hoodwinked by the Emp – but he did achieve one important success. Thanks to his financial policies, Prussia had ceased to be a client state and was ready to become a great power.

French Wars of Religion, The (Mar 1562–Apr 1598) A series of petty and inconclusive civil wars between great noble connections fighting for the control of the Crown, and supported on the one side by the Prots (Hugs), aided from time to time by England, Holland and German Prots; on the other, by the Cath League, supported by Spain, Savoy and Rome.

The causes included (a) the structural weaknesses of the monarchy, whose steady build-up of centralized absolutism under CHARLES VIII, LOUIS XII, FRANCIS I and HENRY II constantly aroused the resistance of the nobility and the separatism of the provs, and whose internal weaknesses, due to bankruptcy (1557), the sale of offices, and the incompleteness of the new bureaucratic framework, left the throne vulnerable to counter-attack whenever it was not occupied by a powerful and hard-working monarch. (b) The personal weaknesses of the monarchs became evident when the unexpected death of K Henry II on 10 July 1559 left power in the hands of his foreign widow, CATHERINE DE MEDICI, and her 4 inadequate sons: FRANCIS II, CHARLES IX, HENRY III and François, D of Alençon. (c) The ambitions of 3 extensive clientage networks fuelled the wars: headed respectively by the Bourbons (strong in the S and in Picardy), the Guises (with big estates in the E) and the Montmorencies (powerful in the N and centre) – families which were aiming to fill the power-vacuum at the centre, or even take the throne itself or, at the very least, stop the Crown's encroachments on their independence. (d) The economic depression in France, which was partly due to the switch of capital and labour away from profitable enterprise into the wasteful HABSBURG–VALOIS WARS (a diversion made possible by the lack of parl control of taxation) aggravated the discontents of all ranks, especially those of the lesser nobility, many of whom, after the Tr of Cateau-Cambrésis (Apr 1559), had only civil war to fall back on as a means of earning their livelihood in the traditional manner. (e) The growth of the Calvinist Ch in spite of the fierce persecution of Francis I and Henry II; its pyramidical structure of neighbourhood consistories, local colloquies, prov synods and national synod (the 1st of which took place in Paris in May 1559); its semi-democratic sources of authority based on elections at every stage; its independence of existing Gov or ecclesiastical institutions; its invigorating contact with missionaries sent by CALVIN and Beza from Geneva; its spread among the peripheral provs of Normandy, Brittany, Guyenne, Languedoc, Provence and Dauphiné – as well as in cities such as Orléans and Lyons – where royal authority was at its most tenuous; its converts among the nobility and gentry, the lower clergy and friars, and the educated urban classes of lawyers and bureaucrats, teachers and doctors, merchants and manufacturers; above all, its acceptance – thanks to Beza – of the military protection of the Bourbon connection: an alliance which donated to the Bourbons a moral cohesion and force never before enjoyed by an over-mighty subject. (f) Foreign interference in the form of diplomatic, military, naval and financial meddling in French affairs by Spain, England, Holland, the German Prots and the Pp prolonged the wars when the combatants were otherwise exhausted.

In the run-up to the wars after the death of Henry II, the new K, Francis II, aged 15, was dominated by the uncles of his wife, MARY, Q OF SCOTS: François, D de GUISE, and his brother, Charles, Card of Lorraine, who now ousted the previous chief minister, Anne, D de MONTMORENCY, Constable of France, from power and began a campaign of severe Hug persecution. Opposing the Guises was Louis de Bourbon, Pr de CONDÉ, who believed that his elder brother, Antoine de Bourbon, K of Navarre, as chief Pr of the Blood, should be in power. He strengthened himself by becoming military protector of the Hugs. After the failure of the badly planned Hug Conspiracy of Amboise (Mar 1560) to capture the K and destroy the Guises, Condé was arrested and sentenced to death by the Guises on 31 Oct 1560; but he was rescued from this fate by the death of the K on 5 Dec 1560, a contingency which put power into the hands of the Q Mother as Regent for K Charles IX, aged 10. She aimed at a policy of reconciliation by bringing to Court Antoine de Bourbon and Montmorency as counter-weights to the Guises; and by attempting a religious compromise at the unsuccessful RC-Prot Colloquy of Poissy (Sept–Oct 1561), after which the Guises, as well as Montmorency and his ally, the Maréchal de St-André, left the Court. The Q Mother now issued the January Edict (Jan 1562) – the work of Beza and COLIGNY – which allowed the Hugs to worship freely outside towns, and in private houses in them, and also to hold synods. The outraged D de Guise raised the temperature of the dispute by massacring a Hug congregation at Vassy in Champagne (1 Mar 1562), killing over 70 and wounding over 100; after which he entered Paris with his army (15 Mar 1562), forcing the Q Mother and the K to join him there. In retaliation, Condé occupied Orléans (Apr 1562), henceforth the Hug HQ; and, morally supported by Beza's manifesto, theologically justifying armed rebellion, Hug congregations rose in arms all over France, taking power in cities such as Lyons, Tours, Blois, Rouen and others.

In the 1st War (Apr 1562–Mar 1563), Condé negotiated the Tr of Richmond (Sept 1562) whereby England promised him troops and a loan of 140,000 crowns in return for Le Havre, which was to be exchanged for Calais at the end of the war. Nevertheless, Guise beat the Hugs at Dreux (a W bastion of the Ile de France) on 19 Dec 1562, a battle in which Montmorency was captured by the Prots and Condé by the RCs. Antoine de Bourbon was killed at Rouen and Guise at Orléans. This elimination of the leaders enabled the Q Mother to negotiate the Pacification of Amboise (Mar 1563), which allowed Hug nobles to worship freely, but limited commoner worship to 1 town in each judicial district (*baillage* or *sénéchaussée*), but not Paris. Both sides then co-operated in driving the English out of Le Havre (July 1562) and making ELIZABETH I abandon her claim to Calais by the Tr of Troyes (Apr 1564). Meanwhile, Catherine de Medici's meeting with her daughter, Q Elizabeth of Spain, accompanied by the D of ALBA at Bayonne (June–July 1565), followed by Alba's march from Milan to the Netherlands (June–Aug 1567), convinced Condé and his ally, Coligny, that a Franco-Spanish plot was afoot to eliminate the Prots in France and the Netherlands. These fears led to renewed civil war.

The 2nd War (Sept 1567–Mar 1568), which began with the Conspiracy of Meaux, a botched attempt by Condé and Coligny to capture the K, followed by a general rising of the Hugs, was marked by the intervention of Spain on the RC side, and of the Elector Palatine's son, John Casimir, on the Prot. Condé marched on Paris, but was beaten at St Denis (10 Nov 1567), a battle in which Montmorency was fatally wounded. The Tr of Longjumeau (Mar 1568), which re-established the position laid down by the Pacification of Amboise, calmed the fears of neither side, and fighting soon broke out again.

The 3rd War (Aug 1568–Aug 1570) was the bloodiest of the series. The D of Anjou (future K Henry III) beat the Hugs at Jarnac in Poitou (13 Mar 1569) – where Condé was killed – and at Montcontour in Brittany (3 Oct 1569). In spite of these serious setbacks, Coligny, who was now in sole command of the Hugs, managed by brilliant manoeuvring to re-establish Prot strength in the S, and force a war-weary Gov to concede the Tr of St Germain (Aug 1570), which restored the old position and introduced the new feature of allowing the Prots to garrison 4 *places de sûreté*: Cognac, La Charité, Montauban and La Rochelle. The Hugs now became dominant at Court as the Guises decamped, and Coligny managed to establish an ascendancy over the young K with his unusual personality and his grandiose plan for uniting France in a patriotic war against Spain in the Netherlands in conjunction with WILLIAM I of Orange and his brother, LOUIS OF NASSAU, not to mention Q Elizabeth of England. The Guise faction grew desperate as the new policy took shape; as the *Politique* party emerged under François de Montmorency, son of the Constable, who favoured mutual toleration between Caths and Prots; as the Tr of Blois was signed with England (Apr 1572); as Nassau captured Mons in an attack from France (23 May 1572); as Coligny prepared to give general aid to the Dutch in their REVOLT; above all, as the guests arrived in Paris for a ceremony which would extinguish Guise hopes for ever: the marriage of Catherine de Medici's daughter, Margaret of Valois, with Antoine de Bourbon's heir, K Henry of Navarre (future HENRY IV) in Aug 1572. The Massacre of St Bartholomew (23–4 Aug 1572) was the result: a tragic descent by the Q Mother from her position above the factions in her desperation at seeing the K slip out of her control. She decided to solve all her problems by assassinating Coligny, but this scheme was bungled when the Guises shot him but failed to kill him (22 Aug 1572). As religious tension rose in Paris, she determined on the panic measure of eliminating all the Hug leaders, so conveniently assembled in the capital; after 2 hours of persuasion she got the K to agree, using the argument that the Hugs were about to strike first. A handful of Hugs were selected for murder, beginning with Coligny, who was stabbed in his bed at 2 a.m. and then thrown out of the window. Unfortunately, the Parisians were the most fanatical R Cs in France, and it was not long before these organized killings exploded into a spontaneous massacre. During that hot summer night of St Bartholomew's Eve about 3,000 Hugs were murdered, and through the following autumn the rage spread to the prov cities, where about 10,000 more are said to have been killed. Henry of Navarre saved his life by turning R C.

The Massacre of St Bartholomew was a watershed, and the years immediately after brought important changes in the nature of the wars. (1) The Q Mother's days as a conciliator were over: for as the prisoner of the Guises she was opposed by Hug and *Politique* alike. (2) The Hugs were now too weak to aim at turning France into a Prot country, and lowered their sights to the achievement of security and toleration within an R C state. Moreover, their political theory changed. Before, they had been theoretically fighting for the K against his evil advisers. Now, under the influence of Beza's book *Du Droit des Magistrats sur leurs Sujets* (1574) and Du Plessis-Mornay's *Vindiciae contra Tyrannos* (1579), they made the breakthrough into the unashamed philosophy of resistance to tyranny by force. Putting theory into practice, they organized a Hug State in the S, stretching across from Dauphiné in the E through Provence, Languedoc, Béarn, Guyenne and Poitou as far as La Rochelle in the W. Under the Gov of Languedoc, the D de Montmorency-Damville, a *Politique* careerist, they formed their own army, law courts, Estates and taxation system, and were joined by all opponents of the Guises, Prot and R C alike, eg Condé (1574) and Navarre (1575), now Prot again, and the K's youngest brother, Alençon. (3) The *Politique* party, who regarded political unity under the Crown with religious toleration as more important than uniformity of worship, grew in numbers, influence and confidence, fortified as it was by Bodin's *Six Books of the Republic* (1576), which argued the necessity of passive obedience to the sovereign. (4) The Catholic League was formed (1576), a national association of hitherto local leagues of fanatical R Cs, who distrusted the Q Mother and the new K, Henry III, as defenders of the Ch, and who now put themselves on a military footing to wipe out heresy. Headed by Henry, D de GUISE, it incorporated 2 ultimately antagonistic wings: noble clientage connections on the one hand, and city magistrates, clergy, lawyers and artisans on the other; apart from demanding vigorous war on the Hugs in conjunction with help from Rome, Savoy and Spain, it also put out an anti-absolutist programme, calling for the defence of prov liberties and representative institutions.

The 4th War (Dec 1572–June 1573) involved risings in S towns such as Sancerre, but consisted mainly of the unsuccessful siege of La Rochelle (Dec 1572–June 1573) by Anjou, the future K Henry III. This port was a base for the Dutch Sea Beggars and the Hug privateers, and under François de La Noue refused to admit the royal Gov. Anjou besieged it until he heard that he had been elected K of Poland (May 1573), news which made him concede in the Tr of La Rochelle (June 1573) the conditions of St Germain once more.

The 5th War (Dec 1575–May 1576) was a confrontation between Anjou and Montmorency-Damville. On the death of K Charles IX on 30 May 1574, Anjou slipped out of Poland, and back to France via Italy, where he caught a touch of the crusading ardour of the COUNTER-REFORMATION. As K Henry III, he could not stand for Montmorency-Damville carving out a S Kdom for himself and turning it into a practically independent State after the joint general assembly of Hugs and *Politiques* at Nîmes, Languedoc, in Dec 1574. Henry D de Guise beat the English-financed German army under John Casimir at Dormans on the Marne (10 Oct 1575) as it was marching W to the aid of the Hugs; but Henry III, fearful of raising Guise's prestige further, and unable to crack Damville's defences, granted the biggest concessions so far in the Tr of Monsieur (May 1576), negotiated by Alençon, who was known as 'Monsieur'. Hugs were granted freedom of worship everywhere except at Court and within 2 leagues of Paris. They could also garrison 8 *places de sûreté*, and were allowed special courts in all PARLEMENTS (known as *chambres-mi-parties*) for judging cases in which Prots were involved.

The 6th War (Mar–Dec 1577) arose out of R C disgust with these concessions. Guise formed the Holy League (1576) which dominated the Estates-General of Blois (Dec 1576), a meeting at which a large majority voted the cancellation of the concessions of Monsieur. Outmanoeuvred, Henry III placed himself at the head of the League (Jan 1577) in order to control and use it, and launched out on an anti-Hug crusade. This was fairly successful, since the Prots received no help from Damville; and by the Tr of Bergerac (Sept 1577), confirmed by the Edict of Poitiers, they lost many of their recent gains, being restricted to the suburbs of 1 town in each judicial district.

Henry now ordered the dissolution of all religious leagues, and the period 1577–84 was comparatively peaceful except for the 7th War, or Lovers' War (Nov 1579–Nov 1580), in which Navarre took Cahors, Quercy (31 May 1580), and at the end of which the Tr of Fleix (Nov 1580) repeated the terms of Poitiers. One factor in this peaceful period was the tireless negotiating with Hug and *Politique* leaders by the Q Mother.

The 8th War (Mar 1585–Aug 1589) or 'War of the 3 Henries' (ie Henry III, Navarre and Guise) resulted from the death of Alençon (10 June 1584) which made Navarre heir to the throne, and recognized as such by the K and the Q Mother. It was a reversal of positions which turned the Hugs into supporters of divine-right monarchy, and caused the R Cs to begin talking about the sovereignty of the people. Guise signed the secret Tr of Joinville with Spain in Dec 1584, whereby Navarre was set aside as heir in favour of his old uncle, Charles, Card de Bourbon; and the Guises undertook to wipe out heresy with the help of 50,000 *escudos* a month. Guise also revived the League (1585), which was still an uneasy alliance of nobles and urban radicals. In Paris and other cities of the centre, N and E, a more or less spontaneous movement broke out which Guise hoped to exploit to his own advantage. There was much discontent among the masses, caused partly by heavy taxation and economic depression, and partly by the spread of hereditary office-holding in the civil service which had the effect of blocking the upward social mobility of the urban patriciates. Paris differed somewhat from the prov cities, where the city fathers who led the League kept the artisans and clergy of the rank and file in order. In Paris, however, the League was more extremist: it was a revolt of lawyers, clergy and artisans against the municipal authorities. Moved by economic hardship, social envy and religious enthusiasm, the League governed Paris in a secret council – the Sixteen – representing the sections into which they had divided the city. They also sent out agents into the provs to co-ordinate the movements there. In the end, K Henry III could not stand up to this treasonable alliance of the aristocracy, the mob and the Spanish; in the Tr of Nemours (July 1585) he capitulated, accepting the Card de Bourbon as his heir, and revoking all concessions to the Hugs. Soon after, in Sept 1585, Navarre was excommunicated by Pp Sixtus V. Navarre now had no alternative but to fight. He had 2 armies in the field, his own in Poitou and mercenaries marching in from Germany, paid for by England. K Henry III's army under the favourite Joyeuse was beaten by Navarre at Coutras, near Bordeaux, on 20 Oct 1587; but Guise's army defeated the Germans at Auneau, nr Chartres, on 24 Nov 1587. To the plaudits of the League, Guise acted as if he were K, while Henry III lost control of events, even in his own capital. Under orders from the Spanish ambassador, Guise used the League to prevent the K coming to the aid of England, now threatened by the Spanish ARMADA. Defying the K's instructions, Guise entered Paris on 9 May 1588. Henry brought in royal troops but, beginning in the Latin Quarter, the Sixteen revolted on the celebrated Day of Barricades (12 May 1588), forcing the K to flee to Chartres. Further humiliations followed. By the Edict of Union (July 1588) he once more gave in to the League, making Guise the Lieut-Gen of the realm, and recognizing Card de Bourbon as heir to the throne. In Italy, the French fortress of Saluzzo, Piedmont, was taken by Charles Emmanuel I, D of Savoy (1588). And in the Estates-Gen of Blois, called in Oct 1588 to grant revenue, the obstreperous speeches of the League deputies convinced the K that he must eliminate the Guises. On 23 Dec 1588, Guise was summoned to an audience at the château in Blois, and there murdered. His brother, Louis, Card of Lorraine, was killed the next day, while Card de Bourbon was arrested. It was no solution, however, for the League leadership now devolved on Guise's brother, Charles, D de Mayenne; one after another the League cities rebelled against the royal Gov, citing the arguments justifying tyrannicide worked out by the Hugs. With France now controlled either by the Hugs or the League, and with his forces in charge of only a few strongpoints on the Loire, Henry III now joined Navarre in an attack on Paris (Apr 1589), but was himself assassinated at St Cloud on 2 Aug 1589 by Jacques Clément, a keen young Dominican friar who had been promised canonization as a reward.

The 9th War (Aug 1589–May 1598) consisted of the successful struggle of Navarre – now K Henry IV – to defeat or buy off the forces of the League, and to head off the now vigorous attempts of Philip II to turn France into a Spanish satellite. He had the enormous advantage over the League that he was the legitimate K of France – especially after the death in May 1590 of Card de Bourbon, who had been recognized by the League as K Charles X. Moreover, Henry had skill enough to exploit two further weaknesses in the Guise position: (a) mob rule in Paris and other League cities mobilized the middle and upper classes behind Henry IV, as the guarantor of the social order, the more so as Mayenne proved less capable than Guise of maintaining harmony between the aristocratic and proletarian wings of his movement; (b) the League depended upon Spanish money and troops, a taint which enabled Henry IV to appeal to French patriotism, in spite of the fact that he enjoyed English aid (1590–94). The League seemed especially disloyal when Philip II claimed the French throne for his daughter, the Infanta Isabella Clara Eugenia, granddaughter of Henry II and Catherine de Medici. To balance these advantages, Henry had one weak spot: he was a Prot; but he was *Politique* enough to put that right when the appropriate moment came.

At the start his task seemed impossible, as most of France was in hostile hands. Charles Emmanuel I of Savoy invaded Dauphiné and Provence; the D de Lorraine invaded Champagne; the D de Mercoeur ruled Brittany for the League; and Mayenne controlled Burgundy and Normandy. Operating from Tours on the Loire, Henry advanced into Normandy and beat the Leaguers at Arques, nr Dieppe, on 21 Sept 1589, and then at Ivry on the border between Normandy and the Ile de France on 14 Mar 1590. He now laid siege to Paris, but just as the starving Sixteen were about to surrender Henry was driven off by FARNESE whom Philip had ordered to abandon for the moment the REVOLT OF THE NETHERLANDS. Spanish troops also landed in Brittany in Oct 1590; invaded Languedoc in Mar 1591; and intervened a 2nd time under Farnese to relieve Rouen, Normandy, which was under siege from Henry (Apr 1592), and to put a garrison in Paris. In the capital, however, the honeymoon was over for the 2 wings of the League. The fanatical Sixteen hanged 3 moderate members of the Parlement of Paris (Nov 1591). Mayenne hanged 4 of the Sixteen and disbanded the rest (Dec 1591). At the Estates-Gen of Paris in Jan 1593, called at Philip II's request to change French law in favour of the Infanta, only fanatics were prepared to let Spain choose the French monarch, while the moderates – the majority – favoured a deal with Henry IV. The Parlement of Paris took the same view; and for Henry IV the moment had arrived. He became an R C again at St Denis on 25 July 1593, and entered Paris in Mar 1594, receiving absolution from Pp Clement VIII in Sept 1595, and submission from Mayenne in Oct 1595. A Tr of Jan 1596 with Mayenne dissolved the League; and Henry spent the next 3 years reconciling the nobility with money, offices and privileges, and fighting off the foreign invaders. He declared war on Spain in Jan 1595. One Spanish force supported Mercoeur in Brittany; another operated from Marseilles; a 3rd invading from Milan was beaten by Henry at Fontaine-Française, Burgundy, on 5 June 1595; a further Spanish expedition from the Netherlands took Doullens and Cambrai in Picardy (1595), as well as Calais in Apr 1596 and Amiens in Mar 1597 – the last retaken by Henry 7 months later. In Mar 1598, Mercoeur at last submitted, and the Wars came to an end with the Edict of Nantes (13 Apr 1598), the truce with the Hugs, and the Tr of Vervins (2 May 1598), the settlement with Spain.

By the Edict of Nantes, Prots could worship privately in great nobles' houses, and publicly in the towns designated by the earlier Edict of Poitiers, with 1 or 2 additions in each judicial district. The Prots could hold synods from time to time and enjoyed equality with R Cs in public offices and education. They controlled the universities of La Rochelle, Nîmes and Montauban; and special mixed courts were set up in the Parlements of Paris, Toulouse, Bordeaux and Grenoble to try cases in which Prots were involved. Finally, they were allowed to hold about 100 *places de sûreté*, garrisoned at royal expense. By the Tr of Vervins, Spain gave up her French conquests except Cambrai, and the *status quo* of the Tr of Cateau-Cambrésis was restored.

Frobisher, Sir Martin (*c* 1539–22 Nov 1594) Leading mariner under Q ELIZA-BETH I of England, and one of the chief commanders against the Spanish ARMADA.

Son of Bernard Frobisher of Altofts, nr Wakefield; ed in the household of his maternal uncle, Sir John York, City of London merchant and Master of the Mint; m 1st Isabel, widow of Thomas Riggett; m 2nd (1591) Dorothy, widow of Sir W. Widmerpoole. In the 1550s he crewed on several voyages to the African coast, and in the 1560s and 1570s was a pirate in the employ of such Prots as Louis, Pr de CONDÉ, and WILLIAM the Silent. Thereafter he made 3 voyages in search of the NW Passage, financed by the Q and leading City and Gov men: 1st (June–Oct 1576) which found Frobisher Strait and brought back an Eskimo and some black rocks thought to contain gold; 2nd (May–Sept 1577), which brought back 200 tons of black rock (eventually used to repair a road in Dartford, Kent), and a native man, woman and child who soon d; 3rd (May–Oct 1578) which brought back a box of nails, showing perhaps that other Europeans had preceded him to Greenland. Frobisher was a lion-hearted and masterful man of action, and a strong and rough-hewn leader of men; but he became permanently disgruntled by the failure of his voyages and by the lack of recognition he received in comparison with DRAKE. He saw naval and military action (1579–80) against the Fitzgerald rebellion in Ireland, as well as some more piracy, before becoming Vice-Admiral and commander of the *Primrose* on Drake's W Indies invasion of Sept 1585–July 1586. In 1587 he was in command of the Channel fleet preparing for the Spanish invasion, and during the Armada battle he captained the *Triumph* and led one of the 4 squadrons under Howard of Effingham, who knighted him during the action. Between 1589 and 1592 he made 3 expeditions to the Azores and captured valuable Spanish ships; and in 1594 with Sir John Norris he commanded a unit sent to aid the Hugs at Brest. He was fatally wounded during the attack on nearby Crozon (Nov 1594).

Frondes, The (1648–53) A series of civil wars in France during the minority of K LOUIS XIV, when France was ruled by the Regent, Anne of Austria, and MAZARIN (*fronde* meaning a sling that children played with in the streets).

The causes were complex. As usual during a royal minority and under the regency of a foreign Q Mother (cf CATHERINE DE MEDICI and MARIE DE MEDICI) the Prs of the Blood, at the head of their noble clientage networks, fought one another and the Court, in an attempt to capture the Gov, believing they had more right to it than the Q Mother. At the same time, the Robe, headed by the PARLEMENT of Paris and supported by the office-holders, and often fortified by the emotions of prov separatism, rebelled against the policies of centralized absolutism pursued by RICHELIEU and continued by Mazarin, particularly objecting to the use of new agents, the Intendants, to supervise their work. The THIRTY YEARS WAR (1618–48), prolonged into the Franco-Spanish war which lasted till 1659, not only made armies easily available to support one side or the other, but also imposed an intolerable strain on all classes, as Mazarin used old-fashioned taxation and new forms of fiscal manipulation to squeeze money out of each section of society in turn. The economic crisis – severe when the bad harvests of 1647–51 brought starvation to the masses and bankruptcy to business – brought these discontents to a head.

The civil wars consisted of a tangled series of urban riots, peasant revolts, skirmishes and battles, with *coups d'état* at Court and Spanish invasions on the frontiers, amongst which two principal themes can be discerned: the Revolt of the Parlements, and the Revolt of the Princes.

The Revolt of the Parlements (1648–9) was led by the Parlement of Paris against the absolutist measures of Mazarin, particularly the use of Intendants and the imposition of high taxation. From 30 June to 12 July 1648 it debated reform in the Chambre St Louis along with the 3 other sovereign courts, the *Chambre des Comptes*, the *Cour des Aides* and the *Grand Conseil*, and backed by the prov Parlements and the whole body of the office-holders. The Q Mother waited for the military victory over Spain at Lens, Artois, on 20 Aug 1648, and then, against Mazarin's advice, arrested 3 leaders, including the popular Pierre Broussel (26 Aug 1648), a move which precipitated 2 days of rioting on the part of the municipality and the urban radicals, incited, for his own purposes, by de Retz, the nephew of the Archbp of Paris. Prs of the Blood such as HENRY IV's bastard grandsons, the D de Beaufort, and the Dss de Chevreuse (just back from exile) put themselves at the head of the rabble to advance their own cause; while similar risings occurred in the prov capitals, where Prs of the Blood, the Sword and the Robe, the bourgeoisie, the urban radicals, the peasants and the Spanish fought one another in various changing combinations. Mazarin had to release Broussel, the Court had to flee Paris and then issue the Declaration of St Germain (Oct 1648), accepting the demands of the Chambre St Louis, which, if Mazarin had enforced them, would have turned France into a constitutional monarchy, with the Parlement of Paris purporting to be the equivalent of the English Parl, at that time at war with CHARLES I – a false claim since the members of the Parlement represented no one but themselves. The leading Prs of the Blood – the D of ORLÉANS, the Pr of Condé, his brother, Conti, and his sister and her husband, the D and Dss of Longueville – for the moment backed the Court. They besieged Paris, where events now passed beyond the control of the Parlement into the hands of Beaufort and de Retz at the head of the mob, a turn of events which prompted the Parlement to make a deal with the Court, for they had no wish to encourage either the lawlessness of the Prs or the violence of the citizenry. Peace was signed in the Tr of Reuil (Mar 1649) which confirmed the Declaration of St Germain, and thus the Parlement's victory. The Court now returned to Paris, but as Condé and his allies now began to aim at supreme power, Mazarin and the Q Mother joined the weaker side of Beaufort and de Retz; with the help of the Dss de Chevreuse they persuaded Orléans to go along with them. On 18 Jan 1650, Condé, Conti and Longueville were arrested, and the Princes' Fronde began.

The Fronde of the Princes (1650–53) was a series of riots and skirmishings involving Paris, the provinces (especially Bordeaux) and the Spanish. The various social groups continued to form and re-form their alliances. Mazarin slipped abroad to Cologne (Feb–Dec 1651) to raise an army and give his enemies a chance to quarrel amongst themselves. France's 2 greatest generals – Turenne and Condé – fought one another for Paris (Apr–July 1652), the latter eventually winning the capital at the battle of Porte St Antoine (2 July 1652). Condé was a military genius but an irritable, political blunderer, however, and he ruined his victory by massacring the Assembly of Notables sitting in the Hôtel de Ville on 4 July 1652. Unable to find a satisfactory power-base in France, Condé joined the Spanish in the Netherlands in Aug 1652. Mazarin went into exile again (Aug 1652–Feb 1653) to facilitate peace-making. The great body of Frenchmen, nauseated by anarchy, rallied round the young K who, having been declared of age on 7 Sept 1651, made a triumphant entry into Paris on 21 Oct 1652. The next day in a *lit de justice* the Parlement was ordered henceforth to register the K's wishes without interfering in political or revenue matters. Mazarin returned to Paris in Feb 1653, and soon restored order in the provs. By Aug 1653 when the royal troops took Bordeaux the Frondes were over. They had demonstrated how impossible it was for the diverse enemies of centralized absolutism to co-operate together. K and Card now embarked on a programme of strong Gov hardly dreamed of by their predecessors; and the support which the mass of Frenchmen gave them is a measure of the horror they felt at the anarchy of the Frondes.

Gama, Vasco da (*c* 1460–24 Dec 1524) Portuguese pioneer of the sea-route to India.

Son of an admiral, he was employed by K Manoel I (1495–1521) to follow up the voyage of DIAS round the Cape of Good Hope. Sailing from Lisbon on 8 July 1497 with 4 ships and 160 men, he rounded the Cape in Nov 1497, reached the coast of Natal in Dec 1497, and put in at Mozambique in Mar 1498, where the Sultan provided a pilot. Calling at Mombasa and Malindi on the coast of E Africa, he crossed the Indian Ocean, reaching Calicut on the Malabar coast in May 1498. Here he failed to secure a Tr with the Hindu ruler, because of the opposition of Arab and Indian Moslem merchants; and eventually he had to fight his way out of the harbour, somewhat disappointed that the ruler was not some kind of Christian heretic, as he at first thought. His return journey, beginning in Aug 1498, took in Malindi and Mozambique, and the 1st ship reached Lisbon in July 1499, while he himself arrived on 9 Sept 1499. His fleet was laden with pepper, ginger, cloves and other precious spices; and the K rewarded him with an estate and the rank of noble. His 2nd expedition, which left Lisbon in Nov 1502 with 15 ships (and 5 to follow later), included warships, for he had military and political duties in view as well as trade. His main tasks were to punish Calicut (where the men whom CABRAL had left behind had been murdered); to provide protection for friendly Indian rulers against the Arabs (who, apart from being hostile to Christianity, naturally resented this intrusion into their trading network); and generally to steer the Indian spice trade along the Cape route, and away from the Red Sea. Gama bombarded Calicut and signed a Tr with the ruler of Cochin to the S. He reached Lisbon again in Sept 1503, having made an important contribution to the establishment of the Portuguese Emp in the E. Created Count of Vidigueira (1519), and Viceroy of India (1524), he d at Cochin.

Gardiner, Stephen (?1490–12 Nov 1555) Bp of Winchester (1531–51, 1553–5), Chancellor (1553), career-prelate who supported the REFORMATION under K HENRY VIII of England, but opposed moves in the direction of Protestantism under K EDWARD VI, and supported the RC reaction under Q MARY I.

Son of a cloth merchant; ed in law at Cambridge, became Master of Trinity Hall (1525–49), tutor to the household of the 3rd D of NORFOLK, Sec to WOLSEY (1525), and K's Sec (1529–34), being employed on numerous diplomatic missions, especially in connection with Henry VIII's divorce from Q CATHERINE OF ARAGON. He was made Bp of Winchester, but then lost ground to Thomas CROMWELL, who became the K's chief minister (1533–40), and to CRANMER, who became Archbp of Canterbury (1533–53). For the rest of this reign Gardiner and Norfolk led the conservative faction on the Council. He supported the divorce, the breach with Rome and the Royal Supremacy; his book· *De Vera Obedienta* (1535) just as strongly favours a Divine Right view of the monarchy and Erastian view of the Ch as did his enemies, the Cromwellians. He even wrote a pamphlet justifying the execution of John FISHER. On the other hand, he opposed changes in the direction of Protestantism favoured by Cromwell and Cranmer, and he supported the conservative Act of Six Articles of 1539. On the fall of Cromwell and the divorce from Anne of Cleves, he successfully aided Norfolk in dangling Norfolk's niece, Catherine Howard, before the K, and the Norfolk party attained temporary supremacy till Catherine's execution in 1542. His influence declined during the following years, under Catherine Parr, a Q with Prot sympathies, and while his ally, Norfolk, was attainted for treason. The dying Henry VIII struck Gardiner out of the Council of Regency which his will provided to advise the boy K Edward VI, probably because he doubted his steadfastness over the Royal Supremacy. A scheming, arrogant, rough-mannered power-seeker, he had already been worsted by Cromwell and Cranmer: he was now overtaken by Edward SEYMOUR and John DUDLEY and the new generation that came to power in the new reign. As an opponent of their religious changes he was placed in the Tower in June 1548 for the rest of the reign and deprived of his Bpric (Feb 1551). Under Mary I he was restored (Aug 1553) and appointed Chancellor; and he took a leading part in organizing the return to Rome, the persecution of the Protestants and, reluctantly, the marriage of Mary to the future K PHILIP II of Spain.

George I (28 May/7 June 1660–11/22 June 1727) (George Lewis, El of Hanover), K of Great Britain (1 Aug 1714), whose reign under WALPOLE and the other Whig ministers overcame the 'FIFTEEN' and survived the 'SOUTH SEA BUBBLE', and, bringing peace and prosperity, established the Hanoverian dynasty in Britain.

Son of Ernest Augustus, El of Hanover (d 1698) and his wife, Sophia (daughter of Elizabeth of the Palatinate and granddaughter of K JAMES I of Britain), who had been declared heiress to the British throne after Q ANNE by the Act of Settlement, 1701; m (1682) Sophia Dorothea of Celle, his cousin, whom he divorced (1694) for infidelity and locked up in the castle of Ahlden till her death 32 years later. A short, stubborn, irritable man, brave but retiring, domineering but lazy, he arrived at Greenwich (Sept 1714) with his German advisers (von Bothmer and von Bernstorff), his 2 German mistresses (bony Baroness von Schulenberg, later Dss of Kendall, and corpulent Baroness Kielmannsegge, later Countess of Darlington), and his 2 servants whom he had captured during a campaign against Turkey. There was mutual antipathy between George and the English, and he returned to Hanover as often as he could.

1714–17: At home, he began with a ministry dominated by 4 of the new generation of Whigs: Charles STANHOPE, the 3rd Earl of Sunderland, the 2nd Vt Townshend and Robert Walpole – but also including the pro-Hanoverian Tory, the 2nd Earl of NOTTINGHAM. (Of the remaining Tory leaders of Anne's reign, BOLINGBROKE and Ormonde had fled abroad, and HARLEY was in the Tower.) This ministry defeated the Jacobite invasion known as the 'Fifteen', after which Nottingham was forced to resign because he favoured clemency to the rebel leaders (Feb 1716). For the rest of C18, TORIES were permanently in the opposition, branded by Walpole and the Whigs as Jacobites, and party warfare was limited to struggles between various factions of Whigs. Because of this crisis, the Gov passed the Septennial Act (May 1716), prolonging the life of the existing and future Parls from 3 to 7 years – a measure which consolidated the Whigs' grip on office and strengthened the position of all the powerful men who controlled constituencies. The foreign policy of Sec of State Stanhope – who, under the K, dominated this Gov – aimed at peace through the Anglo-French alliance (Sept 1716) which became the Triple Alliance when Holland joined (Jan 1717). Stanhope's diplomatic and military interventions ranged far and wide, staving off conflict between Austria and Spain in the Med, and striving to bring peace to the Baltic, where the GREAT NORTHERN WAR (1700–21) threatened to bring first Swedish, then Russian domination of this trading area vital to Britain. The ministry split over foreign policy, for while Stanhope and Sunderland were with the K in Hanover (July 1716–Mar 1717), the more insular Townshend and Walpole opposed this forward policy, which seemed to the English to be only in Hanover's interest, and which created great difficulties for the ministers in Parl, where the revenue for these policies had to be raised. Personal rivalries also played their part; and when George dismissed Townshend (Apr 1717), Walpole and his friends resigned the next day in sympathy.

1717–20: At home, the split in the ministry was paralleled by a split in the royal family. The K and the Pr of Wales (the future GEORGE II) loathed each other, and as the result of an angry quarrel the Pr was expelled from St James's Palace (Dec 1717). It was a family rift frequently found in England and Europe in C 18. On the whole, the general tendency of this reign was to strengthen the ministers as against the Crown, but this must not be exaggerated. George spoke some English, and attended Cab meetings. He was the master, and the Cabinet – which he chose – could do nothing without his consent. Pr George and his wife, Caroline of Ansbach, set up an opposition Court at Leicester House, which was frequented by Townshend, Walpole and their friends. In Parl they deliberately whipped into action all the various elements in the opposition (Tories, Jacobites and Whig Outs), playing upon whatever Country prejudices they could, even opposing measures they approved of, such as Stanhope's repeal (1718) of the Occasional Conformity Act of 1711 and the Schism Act of 1714 – both attacks on the Dissenters brought in by Q Anne's Tories. Under Walpole's leadership the opposition succeeded in defeating the Peerage Bill (Dec 1719), which would have drastically limited the Crown's right to add to the H of L. Abroad, where the Austro-Spanish quarrel had become war, Stanhope continued to intervene actively in order to reconcile differences and restore peace. In the Med, where the Spanish had attacked Sardinia (Aug 1717) and Sicily (July 1718), a British fleet under Admiral George Byng wiped out the Spanish fleet off Cape Passaro, Sicily, on 31 July/11 Aug 1718. Austria was brought into the Triple Alliance, making it Quadruple (July/Aug 1718). A Spanish-backed Jacobite invasion fleet under the D of Ormonde was destroyed by a storm off Finisterre, Spain, on 18 Mar 1719, and Spain eventually accepted peace (Jan 1720) on the terms of the Quadruple Alliance. In the Baltic, where he had sent a British fleet under Admiral Sir John Norris, Stanhope secured the transfer of Bremen and Verden from Sweden to Hanover in the Tr of Stockholm (Nov 1719), one of the settlements which were ending the Great Northern War. In Parl it was not difficult for the opposition to represent this as a misuse of British resources for the sake of Hanover; and in the end the campaign of Townshend and Walpole succeeded: they forced the Gov to take them back in.

1720–27: At home, as part of the same deal, Walpole brought about the reconciliation of the Pr of Wales and the K – cold and formal though it was (1720). Walpole became Paymaster-Gen of the Forces (June 1720) and Townshend became Ld President of the Council (June 1720) at the peak of the financial boom known as the 'South Sea Bubble'; but when the bubble burst Walpole was promoted to the offices of 1st Ld of the Treasury and Chancellor of the Exchequer (Apr 1721) as the only man capable of both restoring business confidence and shielding the Court and most of the ministers from a Parl inquiry. Townshend became Sec of State (N) in Feb 1721. Within a year or two, Walpole established himself firmly with the 2 centres of power: K and Parl. The opportune deaths of his 2 rivals – Stanhope on 5 Feb 1721 and Sunderland on 19 Apr 1722 – aided him in both areas. The K by this time had learned confidence in his English rather than his German advisers – at least in English affairs – while in Parl Walpole employed all the techniques of management with unprecedented ruthlessness. Tories were systematically replaced by Whigs in all offices where the Gov had control; while Atterbury's Jacobite plot (1722–3) gave Walpole a further opportunity of fixing the stigma of treason on the whole party. Inside the Cab, Walpole demanded complete obedience, and forced the resignation of the independent-minded CARTERET from the office of Sec of State (S) (Apr 1724). In the reshuffle of 1724, Walpole gave no post to his old ally, William Pulteney, who had earlier followed him into opposition – he feared him also as a rival. Instead, he promoted the more amenable Pelhams, ie the D of NEWCASTLE, his brother, Henry PELHAM, and their friend, Philip Yorke, later Earl of Hardwicke. Abroad, George and his ministers continued Stanhope's policy of European peace based on the Triple Alliance in order to foster trade and keep down taxation – and therefore maintain Parl support. Unfortunately, the old enemies, Spain and Austria, revolutionized the situation by coming together in the 1st Tr of Vienna (Apr and May 1725), an alliance which appeared threatening to Britain, since Austria's Ostend Co competed with the East India Co, while Spain was objecting to the British economic penetration of the Spanish colonies and was demanding the return of Gibraltar and Minorca. Townshend reacted – over-reacted in Walpole's view – by organizing Britain, France, Hanover and Prussia into the Tr of Hanover (Aug/Sept 1725), later joined by Holland, Sweden and Denmark. At the same time Russia joined up with Austria. These anti-Austrian war preparations of Townshend embarrassed Walpole in Parl, where taxes had to be voted and charges of acting in the interests of Hanover could be flung; but by the end of the reign Walpole's policy of conciliation was beginning to have effects. The danger of war blew over with the signing of the peace Preliminaries of Paris in May 1727, whereby the Emp CHARLES VI agreed to suspend the operation of the Ostend Co for 7 years. When George d he left the Hanoverian succession firmly entrenched in Britain, and Britain in a strong position in the world.

George II (30 Oct/10 Nov 1683–25 Oct 1760) (George Augustus, El of Hanover) K of Great Britain (June 1727), in whose reign constitutional monarchy firmly established itself and the Hanoverian political system – where the K shared power with the WHIGS – reached its maturity in the ministries of WALPOLE and PELHAM. Under these PMs, the K – who spoke English – ruled as well as reigned; but in his old age under NEWCASTLE his control crumbled, and his last ministries, dominated by PITT the Elder, were forced on him against his will. During his reign Britain enjoyed long periods of peace, but also survived the difficulties of the WAR OF THE AUSTRIAN SUCCESSION, overcame the dangers of the 'FORTYFIVE' rebellion, and enjoyed the glories of the SEVEN YEARS WAR, when the 1st British Emp was won. George's reign was also characterized by economic growth, social reform and ideological torpor.

Son of K GEORGE I and his wife, Sophia Dorothea of Celle; ed in Hanover; m (1705) the very comely and clever Caroline of Ansbach (d 20 Nov 1737); as Pr of Wales he soon quarrelled with his father (1717) and set up a rival Court at Leicester House, which became the HQ of the opposition (*see* GEORGE I), till Walpole reconciled father and son in Apr 1720. A short, obstinate, precise and irritable man, he loved opera, but disliked 'boetry' and 'bainting'. He fought at Dettingen (16/27 June 1743), the last British K to command in battle. He was unpopular in England, and he in turn much preferred Hanover, which he often visited for months at a time, and where he felt free of the constitutional limitations which shackled him as K of Great Britain. Not that he was a do-nothing K in London; on the contrary, he had strong views and marked preferences, and his consent was required for all men who were appointed and all measures which were adopted, even if that consent was wrung from him by a brow-beating PM or a nagging Q. On his father's death, he dismissed Walpole and told his favourite, Sir Spencer Compton, to form an admin; but within 24 hours Walpole was back in office again, for C18 Gov required the support of Parl as well as the consent of the K, and only Walpole and his Old Corps of Whigs could achieve that. This was a constitutional restriction which George many times tried to evade, only to climb down in the end. During the period covered by the ministries of Walpole and Pelham (1727–54), foreign policy – the K's special interest – often caused quarrels, because George favoured an active, pro-Austrian diplomacy, involving elaborate systems of Continental alliances, paid for by English subsidies – all for the defence of Hanover – while the PMs – with the Land Tax and their Parl majorities in mind – tried to keep as clear as possible of European entanglements. It was on these grounds that Walpole forced Townshend out of office in May 1730. Moreover, the difficulty of controlling the H of C increased when George and Caroline, in their turn, quarrelled with their son, Frederick, Pr of Wales, whom they heartily detested. Frederick fled from the Court in July 1737, and his separate household formed the opposition's HQ until he was reconciled with his father after the fall of Walpole in Feb 1742. An unstable period (1742–6) followed the resignation of Walpole, which had been forced on the K by a hostile H of C. At first, George promoted one of the opposition factions to reinforce Walpole's friends, the Old Corps of Whigs. This consisted of CARTERET and Pulteney and their friends: the New Whigs. Carteret was a minister after the K's own heart with his vast knowledge of European diplomacy, and his belief in a policy of Continental alliances; but Henry Pelham – Walpole's successor as 1st Ld of the Treasury and leader of the Old Corps – had him removed in Nov 1744. In the consequent reshuffle, the Old Corps were reinforced by the other opposition faction – the New Allies – to form the so-called Broad Bottom Admin, though George refused to accept Pitt, who had wounded him too often with his virulent attacks on Hanover. Even at this stage George tried to evade the Old Corps' clutches: he took advice from Carteret and Pulteney (now Granville and Bath), even though they were not in office. To scotch this interference 'behind the curtain', the Pelhams resigned in a body (Feb 1746), and George once more discovered the importance of controlling the H of C. He not only had to recall the Pelhams, he also had to give an office to Pitt, who became Joint Vice-Treasurer of Ireland (Feb 1746) and then Paymaster-Gen (May 1746). George had to learn to live with the Old Corps till Pelham's death in 1754. This ministry followed a policy of peace abroad and social reform accompanied by economic growth at home. It covered a period of stable co-operation between K, Cabinet, Parl and the constituencies, which was not seriously upset by Pr Frederick's revival of his quarrel with the K in early 1747, when his household became the opposition centre once more until his unexpected death on 20 Mar 1751. After the death of Pelham himself (6 Mar 1754), a further period of instability ensued in which ministers were appointed and dismissed against the K's wishes, as a result of the power of factions in Parl. It was at this time that the myth of George as the 'king in toils' arose. This apparent weakness of the Crown was due to the political ineptitude of George and Newcastle (the Old Corps leader) in their old age; to their failure once more to learn the lesson of C18 politics that Govs required not only the support of the K but also the backing of both (and not just one) of the main elements in Parl – ie the political factions on the one hand, and the backbench gentry on the other. (These were political misjudgments on the part of George and Newcastle, but unfortunately for K GEORGE III when he acceded (Oct 1760) they were dressed up by his Whig opponents as constitutional precedents so that, when the new K tried to exercise his choice of ministers and policies, he was accused of overturning the constitution.)

The last 6 years of George's life, then, saw 3 different govs: the Newcastle admin (1754–6), the Devonshire–Pitt (1756–7) and the Newcastle–Pitt (1757–61). It was also a period of exceptional international crisis involving the DIPLOMATIC REVOLUTION (1749–56) and first the defeats, then the victories, of the Seven Years War (1756–63). In the Newcastle Gov, the D of Newcastle became 1st Ld of the Treasury (Mar 1754), and made the mistake of trying to run the Gov from the H of L, leaving the H of C under the management of a docile diplomat with no political experience, Sir Thomas Robinson, who became Sec of State (S) in Mar 1754. The 2 H of C giants – Pitt the Elder and Henry FOX – were left in subordinate positions – as Paymaster-Gen and Sec-at-War, respectively – and it was only natural that they should challenge the Gov and jeopardize its majority. The only hope for Newcastle was to promote one or both of them to important posts in order to neutralize them. Pitt, however, would serve only under conditions which George refused to accept, and so he was dismissed on 20 Nov 1755. Fox, on the other hand, became Sec of State (S) on 14 Nov 1755, though he was expected to manage the H of C without full control over patronage. Military disasters accumulated – the Black Hole of Calcutta, the loss of Minorca, the capture of Oswego – and Pitt's attacks intensified till Newcastle was forced to resign (Nov 1756). In the Devonshire–Pitt Gov the D of Devonshire was 1st Ld of the Treasury (Nov 1756) and Pitt was forced on the K as Sec of State (S) in Dec 1756. They had backbench support, but insufficient backing from the Whig groups and no confidence from the K. Under the persuasion of his brother, the D of Cumberland (Fox's leader), George dismissed Pitt in Apr 1757, and condemned himself to 3 months of further bargaining until at last he was prepared to look political reality in the face and accept the coalition of the 2 men who were indispensable to any Gov at that time: Newcastle, who became 1st Ld of the Treasury (July 1757), and Pitt, who became Sec of State (S) in June 1757. This was a strong administration which enjoyed the support of the K (however reluctant) and the majority of both the corrupt and the uncorrupt parts of the H of C. With Newcastle managing Parl and Pitt winning the victories, the reign of George II ended in glory abroad, but with a new K at home who had to learn these political lessons all over again.

George III (24 May/4 June 1738–29 Jan 1820) K of Great Britain (Oct 1760), in whose reign abroad Britain emerged victorious from the SEVEN YEARS WAR, lost the WAR OF AMERICAN INDEPENDENCE, and won the wars against France under the French Revolution and Napoleon; at home the INDUSTRIAL REVOLUTION began, while in politics the RADICALS flourished, and there was a struggle between the K and the politicians, a decline in the power of the Crown, and a rise in the importance of parties.

Eld son of Frederick Louis (Pr of Wales and son of K GEORGE II) (d 20 Mar 1751) and his wife, Augusta of Saxe-Gotha (d 8 Feb 1771); ed inadequately by

Dr Francis Ayscough and other tutors, as well as by BUTE, who came to dominate the heart and mind of the intellectually backward but deeply impressionable young Pr to such an extent that George looked on him as the model of all the virtues, and addressed him as his 'dearest friend'; m (1761) Charlotte Sophia of Mecklenburg-Strelitz (d 17 Nov 1818). Over-protected and under-developed in the Leicester House circle of his parents, George imbibed the ideals and prejudices of the Country opposition and the TORIES, as developed by BOLING-BROKE in his *Patriot King*, which George may have read. As a result, the over-conscientious, diffident, determined young man set himself the task of ending what Plumb has called 'single-party Gov', by removing NEWCASTLE and the Old Corps of Whigs who had corruptly, he thought, reduced George II to a mere cipher, and replacing them with Bute and other non-party ministers who would abolish corruption and institute general happiness. A Court dominated by the philosophy of the Country was bound to upset the political stability which had marked the previous 40 years under WALPOLE, PELHAM and Newcastle, especially as the K chose Bute as his PM, a man with no political experience, and not even a seat in either House of Parl. Moreover, George himself was 'a conscientious bull in a china shop', as Namier called him. Idealistic, ingenuous and industrious, he persisted obstinately in the course he set himself, learning from his mistakes only very slowly. At the same time, he could do more damage because favourable circumstances gave him more freedom of action than George II had enjoyed. His choice of ministers was not narrowed by the existence of a 100-strong party of TORIES, incapable of office. Moreover, until 1783, there was no Pr of Wales round whom the opposition could rally; while the WHIGS were breaking up into warring factions incapable of continuing the closed-shop policy they had forced on George II. His reign, as far as C18 is concerned, falls into 3 periods: 1760–70, a time of political conflict and frequent changes of Gov; 1770–82, the NORTH admin; 1782–4, further struggle and instability until the consolidation of the 1st admin of Pitt the younger, 1783–1801.

1760–70: (a) George inherited the Newcastle–PITT admin (1757–61), a broad alliance, to run the Seven Years War, of Old Corps Whigs and followers of Pitt the Elder, backed by Country and Tory elements in Parl. He failed to see that this all-party Gov backed by the nation was just what he was seeking, and with his mind running on the lines laid down by Leicester House he ousted Pitt and Newcastle in favour of Bute. (b) The Bute admin (1761–3) employed Henry FOX to lead the H of C, to secure the passage through Parl of the Tr of Paris ending the war, to carry out the 'Massacre of the Pelhamite Innocents', and introduce a new excise duty, the Cider Tax; but Bute resigned under the ensuing opposition campaign and popular execration, in which WILKES played an important part. (c) The GRENVILLE admin (1763–5) ensured future trouble for George with their policies – which the K backed – towards Wilkes and America. They roused the Radicals by arresting Wilkes under a general warrant; they incensed the colonists with the Proclamation of 1763 and the Stamp Act of 1765. At the same time, the K – who could not bear Grenville personally – consulted Bute 'behind the curtain', and cast about continually for a new PM, failing to persuade Pitt, and falling back in the end on ROCKINGHAM, the new chief of the Old Corps. (d) The Rockingham admin (1765–6) – deeply suspecting that George was sabotaging their ministry by consulting Bute (which he was not) and by swaying Cab and Parl with the King's Friends (ie the Court and Treasury party) – enacted in office what they had proclaimed in opposition. They condemned general warrants by a H of C resolution; they repealed the Cider Tax; they repealed the Stamp Act, but passed the Declaratory Act. After several attempts, George succeeded in persuading Pitt to serve. (e) The Pitt admin (1766–8) – a mixed, non-party collection of individuals such as George had been seeking – passed the Townshend duties, but soon became ineffective as Pitt fell ill and by Mar 1767 had ceased to control affairs. GRAFTON, the 1st Ld of the Treasury, was left to head a group of ministers who went their own way. (f) The Grafton admin (1768–70) – Pitt having resigned in Oct 1768 and gone into opposition – bore the brunt, along with the K, of the most intense campaign of Parl and popular vilification yet seen. This was the time of the repeated elections of Wilkes as M P for Middlesex, followed by his regular expulsions, accompanied by widespread petitioning and other well-orchestrated Radical campaigns. It was also a time of economic depression; a period of increasing militancy in America and Ireland. It saw the savage letters of *Junius* and the putting together of the new Rockingham Whig philosophy in Burke's *Thoughts on the Cause of the Present Discontents* (1770). The Whigs painted a picture of George which persisted in history books till C20. They accused him of upsetting the balance of the constitution and trying to revive Stuart absolutism. He had appointed his favourite as PM, they said, and after his removal had still consulted him and other K's Friends 'behind the curtain': employing, in other words, a double Cab, an official one with no effective power, and a secret one to which the K gave all his confidence. In aid of his tyrannous schemes, George was supposed to have so corrupted Parl through the K's Friends that it was no longer responsive to the wishes of the people. Evidence of his ambition was the 'Massacre of the Pelhamite Innocents', the persecution of Wilkes, the attack on the press, the taxation of America, the effective disfranchisement of Middlesex and the use of the military against the Radicals. It is generally accepted now, however, that George was not acting unconstitutionally. Like George II, he exercised his undoubted right to choose his ministers, and like him he accepted the measures they proposed and for which they were responsible before Parl. Moreover, the K's Friends were simply the old Court and Treasury party, whose support was necessary – but not sufficient – to give any PM a majority. What can be questioned is George's wisdom, especially in appointing Bute; and what can be conceded is that George III in his youth was more domineering than George II in his dotage.

1770–82: In the North admin George formed a Gov which had the ingredients to revive the stability of Walpole's and Pelham's day: ie the support of both K and Parl. This Gov followed a policy of financial retrenchment; made the 1st Gov intervention into the E India Co's rule in India; made economic concessions to Ireland, but too little and too late to head off the demand for self-Gov; followed an isolationist policy in Europe; and, above all, provoked and lost the War of American Independence. The loss of America was no more George's fault than that of the Gov, or Parl or the nation, though he followed an authoritarian policy throughout, stiffening the resolution of the faint-hearted North, refusing his requests to resign, acting almost as his own PM at times, and prolonging the war until 1782, when North had accepted that American independence was inevitable by 1779. After the surrender at Yorktown (19 Oct 1781) the backbenchers deserted the Gov. North's majority crumbled, and George at last accepted his resignation.

1782–4: a second period of instability, when George even contemplated abdication. (a) The 2nd Rockingham admin (1782) was forced on him because Shelburne – whom the K wanted as P M – was unable to achieve a majority without the co-operation of the Rockinghams. (Shelburne, an individualistic and politically inept follower of Pitt the Elder, was a creative intellectual and radical reformer who nevertheless suited George since he disbelieved in party and asserted the K's right to choose his ministers. Moreover, he did not support independence for America, but favoured instead an idealistic voluntary federal Emp with free trade between the members.) It was a split Gov in which Shelburne and the supporters of the K gave no help to the Rockinghams in enacting their programme of independence for America, Economical Reform and legislative independence for Ireland. On the sudden death of Rockingham, George appointed Shelburne. (b) The Shelburne admin (1782–3) proved again that, though necessary, the support of the K's Friends was insufficient without the backing of one of the parties in the H of C, especially as Shelburne himself lacked a following, as well as any talent for political manoeuvre. The notorious Fox–North coalition defeated Shelburne's peace terms, and forced his resignation (Feb 1783). (c) The Portland admin (1783) – ie the Fox–North coalition – saw George at his most humiliated. He had to allow Portland to choose his own junior ministers after – instead of before – he had become PM: a constitutional innovation. But the coalition was just as weak as Shelburne's had been. Being a party Gov without the K's support, it lacked staying power. In fact, it was dismissed (Dec 1783) when Fox's India Bill was defeated in the H of L, thanks to a message which George allowed to be circulated that 'whoever voted for the India Bill was not only not his friend, but would be considered by him as an enemy'. The K could afford to take this step for he had found his new PM: Pitt the Younger. Moreover, he had the public with him, for the India Bill seemed designed simply to hand over the vast patronage of the E India Co to Fox and a few friends in perpetuity. (d) The 1st Pitt admin (1783–1801) proved to be another case of political stability resulting from a Gov supported by both K and Parl, though it took Pitt till Mar 1784 to achieve the latter. George appointed the 24-year-old Pitt as 1st Ld of the Treasury (Dec 1783) at a time when the Fox–North alliance controlled the H of C, and Fox was accusing the K of unconstitutional interference with the legislature. George held his ground, and Pitt stood firm. Pitt was a new man with a famous name, unsullied by past errors, and gifted with courage and precocious political skill. He became the rallying point not only of the K's Friends, but also of many followers of North and Fox, once they saw which way the wind was blowing. By Mar 1784 he had converted his minority into a majority, and the Gov's preparations for a general election were complete. Pitt benefited from the general C18 tendency for all Govs to win general elections, but he was also aided by the wave of public revulsion from the Fox–North coalition and their India Bill. His overwhelming victory was also a public endorsement of the K's political judgment in dismissing the coalition even though it had a majority in the H of C.

In spite of this royal victory, the rest of George's reign saw a general diminution in the power of the Crown. This was due mainly to general historical developments which were stripping the K of his patronage and other means of influencing Parl, and leading to the formation of disciplined parties through which organized public opinion, not the K, would choose PMs. But it was also due to the decline in George's capacity to rule, brought on by what has been diagnosed as porphyria. At least from 1788 onwards this rare disorder afflicted the K with many very unpleasant symptoms, including intermittent mental derangement.

George William (13 Nov 1595–1 Dec 1640) El of Brandenburg (1619), whose indecisive behaviour and weak position at home, where the Estates were in control, led to a spineless foreign policy during the THIRTY YEARS WAR, as a result of which his territories were very severely devastated by the soldiery of both sides, and the power of the Crown dropped to its lowest point.

Eld son of El John Sigismund and his domineering Lutheran wife, Anna of Prussia; m (1616) the Calvinist, Elizabeth Charlotte (d 1660), sister of Frederick V, the El Palatine; while his sister, Maria Eleonora, m GUSTAV II ADOLF the Lutheran K of Sweden. George William was a pious Calvinist and a greedy gourmandizer. According to his descendant FREDERICK II (the Great), he was 'utterly unfit to rule'. He vacillated between opposing factions and policies, unable to make up what little mind he had. On the one hand, the defence of Protestantism and the political independence of the German Prs – as well as his family ties with Frederick V – required him to fight the Emp. On the other, feudal loyalty to the Emp, and to the K of Poland (whose vassal he was for E Prussia) made him lean towards the imperial side. But as the Gov in each of the 3 sections of his state (Brandenburg, E Prussia and Cleves-Mark) was dominated by the Estates whose votes fixed the level of taxation and size of the army – keeping both very small – he was in no position to help either side effectively. During the 1st part of his reign (1619–31), when his chief minister was Count Adam von Schwarzenberg, a pro-Habsburg Austrian Cath, he remained neutral and took no part in the Bohemian, Palatinate or Danish Wars. During the Swedish War (1630–35), his brother-in-law, Gustav Adolf of Sweden, invaded Brandenburg and trained his guns on the royal castle in Berlin, forcing George William to join the Prot side whether he liked it or not (June 1631). Schwarzenberg had to retire, and troops from Brandenburg fought alongside the Swedes. This was far from what George William wanted, however, for, like other German Prs, however much he opposed the Emp's attempts to achieve absolute power, he was chary of calling in foreign aid for the purpose. Moreover, he was about to inherit Pomerania from its childless D Bogislav XIV (d 10 Mar 1637), while Sweden was occupying it and showing every intention of keeping it. During the 3rd period (1635–40), Schwarzenberg returned to office and George William adhered to the Tr of Prague (May 1635), bringing peace with the Emp. George William and his minister both hoped to use the aid of the Emp to break the power of the Estates and to drive Sweden out of Pomerania. Neither scheme was successful, and Brandenburg simply served as the battleground for Swedish and imperial troops to fight on. George William's revenues fell by over seven-eighths; in 1638 he transferred himself to Königsberg in E Prussia. When he d there of dropsy, he left his son, the El FREDERICK WILLIAM I (the Great Elector) a State and people exhausted, terrorized and at the end of its tether.

Gilbert, Sir Humphrey (?1539–disappearance 9 Sept 1583) Soldier and mariner under Q ELIZABETH I of England, who provided scholarly backing for attempts to find the NW Passage and colonize America, and made unsuccessful tries himself.

2nd son of Sir Otho Gilbert. On his father's death in 1547 his mother m Walter Ralegh of Hayes, Devon, and became the mother of the future Sir Walter RALEGH, who was thus Gilbert's half-brother; ed at Eton and Oxford; m wealthy Anne Aucher of Otterden, Kent (1570). His early military experiences included aiding the Hugs in the FRENCH WARS OF RELIGION (1st War, 1562–3); suppressing Shane O'Neil's rebellion in Ulster, Ireland (July–Nov 1566); and terrorizing the Fitzgerald rebels in Munster, Ireland, with widespread slaughter (1569–70). For this last service he was knighted in Jan 1570. He was MP for Plymouth in the 1571 Parl and suffered a slashing attack from Peter WENT-WORTH for kowtowing to the Crown. During the Anglo-French rapprochement enshrined in the Tr of Blois (Apr 1572) he commanded a party of ostensible volunteers which landed in the Netherlands (July 1572) to aid the Prots, but which had secret orders from the Gov to take Flushing in order to deny it to the French. This expedition was a failure. Gilbert was an irritable leader of men, incapable of inspiring loyalty. His real flair was in the production of bold and original ideas. His *Queen Elizabeth's Academy* (1564) contained educational plans for the nobility and gentry centuries ahead of its time, advocating practical subjects such as mathematics, medicine, navigation, politics and modern languages to vary the exclusive diet of Latin and Greek. Similarly, his mind was fertile with adventurous schemes for exploiting the geographical discoveries by breaking up the Spanish Emp, finding the NW Passage, colonizing America etc. His writings, such as the *Discourse for a Discovery of a New Passage to Cathay* (1566, revised 1576) and *How her Majesty might annoy the King of Spain* (1577), provided the inspiration and the knowledge for many a transatlantic trip. He himself was a failure in the practical field. He lacked the right touch with the self-seeking skippers and their brawling crews. In Nov 1578 he and Ralegh set sail with 7 ships to seek suitable spots for colonizing America, for which he had a royal patent – the 1st English attempt. Unfortunately, his fleet became dispersed before getting very far. In June 1583 he set off again with 5 ships in an attempt to settle Newfoundland. He landed at St John's and annexed the territory to England for 200 leagues in all directions (Aug 1583); but then unwisely sailed S to find similar plots in America. This coast was uncharted, the ships lost one another, the crews mutinied. Gilbert decided to return home but, in his tiny 10-ton frigate the *Squirrel*, he disappeared somewhere N of the Azores and was never seen again.

Godolphin, Sidney Godolphin, 1st Earl of (June 1645–15 Dec 1712) Political 'manager' and leading Treasury minister under Ks CHARLES II, JAMES II, WILLIAM III and Q ANNE.

3rd son of Sir Francis Godolphin, a prominent landowner, and his wife, Dorothy Berkley; ed at Oxford and at Court, as Page of Honour to the K, 1662–72; m (1675) Margaret Blagge, Maid of Honour to the Dss of York (d 1678). His main interest outside politics was gambling, and he pioneered horse-breeding at Newmarket, Suffolk. Under the patronage of the 2nd Earl of SUNDER-LAND he voted for the exclusion of the future K James II; yet was made a Commissioner of the Treasury (Mar 1679), Sec of State for the N (Apr 1684), becoming Bn Godolphin, and Commissioner of the Treasury (1684–9), showing exceptional admin and financial gifts. A non-party careerist, patient and methodical, he was a civil servant rather than a politician; and yet he very skilfully played the role of 'manager' for William III and Anne, mediating between the Crown and the parties, and harnessing in Gov very diverse groups. During the REVOLUTION OF 1688 he served James II until the last minute, representing him as one of the 3 commissioners (along with NOTTINGHAM and HALIFAX) who met William of Orange at Hungerford, Berks, on 8 Dec 1688, as he was advancing on London. When Godolphin returned to the capital he found that James had fled; in the subsequent debates over the revolutionary settlement Godolphin favoured retaining James as K, but with his powers exercised by a Regency. Under William III he was once more appointed a Commissioner of the Treasury (1690–96) in the mixed ministry which opened the reign and which brought in the important measures of the 'financial revolution': the National Debt (1693), the Bank of England (1694) and the recoinage (1696). He resigned after being implicated by one of the conspirators in the Jacobite plot to assassinate the K revealed in Feb 1696. In any case, he had been unhappy with the Whig Junto who had joined the Gov in 1694, and he thenceforth co-operated with HARLEY who was at that time creating the New Country Party in the opposition. Godolphin was 1st Commissioner of the Treasury (Dec 1700–Dec 1701) in the short Tory Gov near the end of William's reign. Under Anne he reluctantly became Ld Treasurer in May 1702 in the ministry dominated by the triumvirate of himself, MARLBOROUGH and Harley, his principal achievements being the UNION WITH SCOTLAND (1707), and the successful management of the Treasury and Parl so as to provide the finance for the War of the Spanish Succession (1702–13/14), becoming Earl in 1706. The ministry was reshuffled in 1708, shedding Harley and taking in the pro-war Whig Junto; but when the Q and the war-weary nation turned to the Tories in 1710 Godolphin's career was over.

Grafton, Augustus Henry Fitzroy, 3rd D of (28 Sept 1735–14 Mar 1811) Reluctant and mediocre PM of Great Britain (1768–70) under K GEORGE III, during a difficult phase of the quarrel leading to the WAR OF AMERICAN INDEPENDENCE, and during a fierce period of opposition and RADICAL activity over WILKES and the Middlesex elections.

Eld son of Ld Augustus Fitzroy and his wife, Elizabeth; succeeded his grandfather, Charles, 2nd D of Grafton, in May 1757; ed at Hackney, Peterhouse, Cambridge (1751–3), and on the Grand Tour; m 1st (1756) Hon Anne Liddell, daughter of Henry, 1st Ld Ravensworth (divorced Feb 1769); m 2nd (1769) Elizabeth, daughter of Rev Sir Richard Wrottesley, Bart, Dean of Windsor; as MP (1756–7), he belonged to the younger generation of the Old Corps of WHIGS led by NEWCASTLE; made Lieut of Suffolk (1757–63), he was one of those whom George III dismissed for not backing the BUTE admin (1761–3) and the peace Tr of Paris. Shy and serious, but difficult and ill-at-ease in public, he was a useful debater and efficient administrator – with liberal views – but not suitable for high office. Preferring horses, crops and books to Court ceremonial, and lacking a following, he was kept in public office only by a strong sense of duty. He became Sec of State (N) in July 1765 in the ROCKINGHAM admin (1765–6), but resigned in May 1766 when Rockingham failed to recruit PITT, who by then was Grafton's idol. He became 1st Ld of the Treasury (Aug 1766) in the Pitt admin (1766–8), becoming in effect PM when Pitt's illness incapacitated him from Mar 1767 onwards, and in theory as well when Pitt resigned in Oct 1768. His Gov was a non-party hotch-potch of individualists with no effective leader in the H of C, and with no one in charge, unless it was the K, to whom Grafton transferred his loyalty, disgusted with Pitt's behaviour. Grafton lacked the intellectual power and force of character to shape the Gov's policy, especially after the entry of the Bedfords (winter 1767/8) introduced a hard-line majority on the 2 chief questions of the day: Wilkes and America. It was against his wishes that the Cab and the H of C decided to expel Wilkes from Parl and thus set in train the Middlesex elections frenzy; and he was overruled in Cab (May 1769) when it was decided to repeal the Townshend duties except for that on tea, in order to enforce the principle. The ensuing Radical campaign in England (1769–70), the mounting militancy in America, the machinations of the opposition, and the fierce satire of the letters of *Junius* (1769–72) unnerved Grafton, and he resigned in Jan 1770. Thenceforth he remained in politics, but not in the firing line. He became Ld Privy Seal (June 1771–Oct 1775) in the NORTH admin (1770–82), but resigned over war in America. He also became Ld Privy Seal (Mar 1782–Feb 1783) in Rockingham's 2nd admin (1782–3).

Granvelle, Antoine Perrenot de (20 Aug 1517–21 Sept 1586) Archbp of Malines, Netherlands (1560), Card (1561), Archbp of Besançon, Franche Comté (1584), who was leading minister of K PHILIP II of Spain in the Netherlands and unwilling executant of policies which provoked the REVOLT OF THE NETHERLANDS, and whose advice might have avoided it. Later he became chief minister in Madrid and organized the conquest of Portugal.

Son of Nicolas Perrenot de Granvelle, a notary who became Sec of State to the Emp CHARLES V; ed in law at Padua and Louvain; became priest, then Bp of Arras; in the 1550s went on diplomatic missions for the Emp, eg negotiating the wedding of the future K Philip II and Q MARY I of England (July 1554), and going as a Spanish delegate to the peace conference at Cateau-Cambrésis (Feb–Apr 1559), where his linguistic skill made him a valuable interpreter. When Philip left the Netherlands for ever in Aug 1559, he appointed Granvelle to the Council of State there, made him the chief adviser to the Regent, Margaret of Austria, and elevated him to the Archbpric of Malines. One of the wisest and most gifted administrators in the Europe of his day, he favoured Charles V's policy of the cautious centralization of the Gov of the Netherlands; and, being a product of HUMANISM rather than of the COUNTER-REFORMATION, he favoured a pragmatic approach to the spread of heresy there. Nevertheless, while advising against Philip's absolutist and persecuting measures, he loyally enforced them and heaped on his own head all the odium they provoked among all classes in the Netherlands, especially among WILLIAM I of Orange, Count Egmont and other members of the Flemish high nobility, whose bitter complaints eventually led Philip to dismiss him in Jan 1564. He then served Philip in another part of his emp: Italy. He helped to negotiate the Holy League of Spain, the Pp and Venice against Turkey in May 1571, and to organize the naval victory of Spain over Turkey at Lepanto on 7 Oct 1571. He was Viceroy of Naples (1571–5), after which he worked at the Spanish embassy at Rome. In Mar 1579, when the Portuguese war was looming, and Philip wished to replace PÉREZ as his chief adviser, Philip summoned Granvelle to Madrid as Pres of the Council of Italy and in practice as chief minister of Spain. In this capacity he organized the diplomatic and military offensive against Portugal, and advised the K to recall ALBA to take charge of the fighting. In the Netherlands and in Europe generally, he now fortified Philip's hardline policies, suggesting the outlawry of Orange which was proclaimed in June 1580, and urging war against France and England in the 1580s.

Great Northern War, The (1700–21) In which K CHARLES XII of Sweden was attacked by a coalition of PETER I of Russia, Christian V of Denmark, and Augustus II of Saxony-Poland.

1700–6: Charles XII defeated each of these in turn, took control of Poland with his own puppet-K – Stanislas Leszczyński – and forced Augustus to resign the Polish Crown and make peace. 1707–9: This left Charles XII free to invade Russia, where Peter had used the interval to reconstruct his armed forces. Charles was defeated at Poltava (1709). 1709–14: Charles took refuge in Turkey while Russia, Denmark and Saxony overran practically all the Swedish possessions on the Baltic and N German coasts. Meanwhile, Charles urged Turkey to attack Russia, and he himself made long-distance efforts to galvanize the Swedish admin and raise a new army. 1714–18: Back on Swedish territory, Charles prepared his counter-attack while trying to deceive his enemies – joined by Brandenburg and Hanover – with peace negotiations; till he was killed at the start of his invasion of Norway. 1718–21: The anti-Swedish coalition broke up through mutual rivalry and the general realization that Russia, not Sweden, was the real menace. Peace was made in a series of Trs (1719–21) which marked the fall of Sweden from great-power status, and left Russia firmly entrenched on the Baltic and fully involved in European power politics for the 1st time.

1700–6. The anti-Swedish coalition of Denmark, Saxony-Poland and Russia was formed (1697–9) to topple the over-extended Swedish empire when it was inherited by the 15-year-old K Charles XII. K Christian V of Denmark and his son, K Frederick IV, aimed at regaining Scania and other territories on the Swedish mainland which Denmark had lost earlier in C17. They also wanted to remove Swedish troops from the Swedish satellite Duchy of Holstein-Gottorp, which gave Sweden a back-door entry into Denmark from the S. Augustus the Strong of Saxony-Poland (ie El Frederick Augustus I of Saxony, who was elected K Augustus II of Poland in June 1697) wished to conquer Livonia from Sweden; with his ambitious plans for the economic development of his double State – based on Polish raw materials and Saxon industry – he was a threat to Sweden's commercial dominance in the Baltic. At the same time, Peter I of Russia was determined to realize the ambitions of his ancestors and secure a Russian foothold in the Baltic, an advance which could be made only at Sweden's expense for she blocked Russia's path with her possession of Karelia, Ingria and Estonia. J. R. von Patkul and other anti-Swedish noblemen in Livonia played an important part in knitting this alliance together. The war was soon over as far as Denmark was concerned. The Danes invaded Holstein-Gottorp (Mar 1700), but the Swedes – helped by the presence of the Anglo-Dutch fleet, as well as their own ships – invaded Zealand and threatened Copenhagen. Denmark withdrew from the war by the Tr of Traventhal (Aug 1700). Meanwhile Augustus had invaded Livonia, but he withdrew when Charles XII transferred his army there from Denmark. The Swedes therefore turned against the Russians who were besieging Narva, Ingria. Here 8,000 Swedes totally defeated 23,000 Russians (19/30 Nov 1700), establishing the 18-year-old Charles's European reputation as a legendary hero, and confirming established opinion about Russia's backwardness. Deciding not to invade Russia until he had established a firm base in Poland from which to do so, Charles XII spent several years campaigning there and building up a confederation of anti-Saxon, anti-Russian Polish nobles. He took Warsaw (May 1702), defeated a Polish-Saxon army at Kliszów (June/July 1702), captured Thorn (Toruń) after a long siege (Mar–Nov 1703), organized the election of Stanislas Leszczyński as K of Poland (July 1704), signed the Polish-Swedish Tr of Warsaw for peace and commerce (Nov 1705), and defeated Saxony once more at Fraustadt (Wschowa) in Poznania (2/13 Feb 1706). By this time he was in control of Poland, having pushed out the Saxons to the W and the Russians to the E. He was ready to invade Saxony. Moreover, the W allies were now beating France in the War of the Spanish Succession, 1702–14 (*see* LOUIS XIV) and no longer objected to his penetrating the HR Emp. In fact, he had only to strike through Silesia at the Saxon border, and Augustus gave in. By the Tr of Altranstädt, nr Leipzig (Sept 1706), Augustus recognized Stanislas as K of Poland, handed over Patkul to be broken on the wheel, and allowed the Swedish army to winter in Saxony. Peter I meanwhile was reforming his admin, rebuilding his army, helping Augustus with men and money, and invading the Swedish provs on the Baltic. He laid the foundations of St Petersburg (May 1703), and took Dorpat, Ingria (13/24 July 1704), and Narva, Ingria (9/20 Aug 1704). By the time of the Tr of Altranstädt, however, Peter was so apprehensive of the victorious Charles XII that he was prepared to cede most of his Baltic conquests in order to make peace. Nevertheless, over-confident Charles XII refused all concessions, and prepared to strike at Moscow itself.

1707–9. While making feints to confuse the enemy, Charles decided to invade Russia by the 2nd most northerly route via Smolensk, while one of his generals, Count A. L. Lewenhaupt, marched S from Riga, Livonia, to join him with reinforcements. As Charles marched E through Poland during late 1707 and early 1708, Peter withdrew before him at Grodno and Minsk, making his 1st stand at Holowczyń on the R Vabich, where Sweden gained an expensive victory (3/14 July 1708). As Peter withdrew into the Russian interior, devastating the land as he went, Charles made the fateful decision to postpone his invasion and winter in the more congenial Ukraine. A further reason for turning S in Sept 1708 was the hope of help from I. S. Mazepa, the Hetman of the Ukraine Cossacks, who continued the traditional policy of playing off Sweden, Poland and Russia against one another with a view to building an independent Cossack state. Further S still, he hoped for the help of the bellicose anti-Russian Khan of the Crimea, Devlet-Girei II. Unfortunately, a series of disasters struck Sweden at this point: (a) Devlet-Girei was forced to remain neutral by his master, the Sultan of Turkey; (b) Mazepa was far from ready for action, having had his HQ captured by the Russians; (c) the winter of 1708/9 was one of the harshest on record; (d) Lewenhaupt's march S was blocked by the Russians at the battle of Lesnaya (28 Sept/9 Oct 1708), where he lost his supply column. It was thus with a depleted, demoralized and under-equipped army that Charles determined to strike a convincing blow at Russia. As a further disadvantage, he had to supervise the attack from a stretcher, having been shot in the foot in a skirmish. The result was a turning point in history. Charles's assault on the Russian camp at Poltava (27 June/8 July 1709) was beaten off with crippling losses, while the bulk of the remaining Swedes surrendered to the Russians 3 days later as they were trying to cross the R Dnieper at Perevolochna. Charles XII and Mazepa had already crossed and found refuge in Turkey. As for Peter, he had revolutionized international relations, making Russia thenceforth a major European power.

1709–14. With the Habsburg frontier closed because of plague, Charles stayed in Turkey at Bender, Bessarabia, plotting his comeback. In the N, Denmark, Saxony and Russia revived the anti-Swedish coalition. Denmark invaded Scania, but was thrown back (Mar 1710). In Poland, Augustus once more became K, while Stanislas took refuge with the Swedes. Meanwhile, Russia continued her conquest of the Baltic provs and Finland (1710–14), defeating the Swedish navy at Hangö (Hangut) on 27 July 1714, and threatening the Swedish mainland. Eventually, the Swedish Council, cowed by their distant K, raised a new army and transferred it to N Germany for an attack on Poland. (Sweden could still not afford to mobilize her army except for immediate action abroad.) Unfortunately, Denmark isolated it by destroying the Swedish sea-transports, and ultimately the army surrendered to a combined Russian–Saxon–Danish army at Tonning, Holstein, in May 1713. In Turkey, with Devlet-Girei II, Charles laboured at the faction-ridden Court to bring about a Swedish-Turkish attack on Russia. In fact, the Swedish prong of the attack did not materialize, but a large Turkish army surprised and surrounded Peter and his troops on the R Pruth, forcing him to hand back Azov and his Black Sea naval base (July 1711). Three times more, under Swedish pressure, Turkey declared war on Russia, but without materially changing the situation; which was recognized in the 25-year Tr of Adrianople (June 1713).

1714–18. Having long outstayed his welcome in Turkey, Charles galloped home incognito in 14 days and nights, reaching Stralsund, Pomerania, in Nov 1714. This and Wismar were his only remaining possessions in N Germany. He spent his last years desperately prolonging contradictory negotiations with friends and enemies alike, hastily rebuilding his forces for a counter-attack, determined to concede nothing but to reconquer everything, and increasingly divorced from reality. During 1715 the anti-Swedish alliance was refurbished, with the El of Hanover, who had become K of Great Britain on 1 Aug 1714, as the chief organizer. Two new combatants joined the old: Brandenburg declared war in Apr 1715 and Hanover in Oct 1715. Stralsund fell on 12/23 Dec 1715 and Wismar on 4/15 Apr 1716. Back in Sweden, Charles continued his separate peace negotiations with Britain and Russia while he put together his new army. In 1718 he was ready with 60,000 men. He invaded Norway, only to be killed at the siege of Fredriksheld, just inside the border (30 Nov/11 Dec 1718).

1718–21. The anti-Swedish coalition broke up through mutual distrust, which grew especially deep when the W members began to appreciate the new situation. Sweden had been replaced by an aggressive Russia with designs on Mecklenburg, Holstein-Gottorp and other parts of N Germany and the Baltic. Fearing for her supplies of Baltic naval stores, Britain took the lead, with French help, in isolating Russia and negotiating peace between Sweden and her enemies. By the Tr of Stockholm (Nov 1719) between Sweden and Hanover, Sweden ceded Bremen and Verden to Hanover in return for financial and naval support. By the Tr of Stockholm (Jan/Feb 1720) between Sweden and Brandenburg, Sweden ceded Stettin, the S part of Pomerania and the islands of Usedom and Wollin in return for money. By the Tr of Fredriksborg (July 1720) between Sweden and Denmark, Sweden gave up her exemption from the Sound dues, and also her connection with the Duchy of Holstein-Gottorp. With Russia the war continued but, not receiving expected naval help from Britain, Sweden was forced to sue for peace. By the Tr of Nystad (Aug/Sept 1721) Sweden ceded to Russia Livonia, Estonia and Ingria, while Russia returned Finland except for Kexholm and part of Karelia. Peace between Sweden and Poland was not signed till 1731, but before that Russia had established a firm grip on Polish internal affairs.

Grenville, George (14 Oct 1712–13 Nov 1770) PM of Great Britain under K GEORGE III, he initiated the prosecution of John WILKES, and took the 1st of the economy measures which ultimately provoked the WAR OF AMERICAN INDEPENDENCE.

2nd son of Richard Grenville, a Whig MP, and his wife, Hester, daughter of Sir Richard Temple, also a Whig MP; ed at Eton (1725–8), Christ Ch, Oxford (1730), the Inner Temple (1729), Lincolns Inn (1734); m (1749) Elizabeth, daughter of Sir William Wyndham, Tory leader; practised law until he became MP for Buckingham, the family pocket borough (1741–70).

Under GEORGE II, he began his Parl career as one of Cobham's Cubs (or the Boy Patriots): an opposition faction of the younger generation which included his brother, Richard (later Earl Temple), his cousin, George Lyttelton, and their school friend, William PITT the Elder. Preaching Country doctrines, they helped to overthrow WALPOLE in Feb 1742, and achieved office under PELHAM. Grenville was a Ld of the Admiralty (1744–7), then a Ld of the Treasury (1747–54) in the Pelham admin (1744–54). In the NEWCASTLE admin (1754–6) he was Treasurer of the Navy (1755) until he was dismissed along with Pitt. He was again Treasurer of the Navy (Dec 1756–Apr 1757) in the Devonshire–Pitt admin (1756–7), resigning when Pitt was dismissed; then he returned as Treasurer of the Navy (June 1757–May 1762) in the Newcastle–Pitt admin (1757–61), this time staying in office when Pitt resigned in Oct 1761. By this time he had broken with Pitt and Temple, for the accession of George III – whose favourite, BUTE, admired him – at last presented the opportunity of advancement above the lowly level at which the Grenvilles had so far kept him.

Under George III in the Bute admin (1760–63) Grenville was promoted to the post of Sec of State (N) (May–Oct 1762) and leader of the H of C, though Bute kept all control of the patronage. Always keen to save revenue, Grenville supported Bute in cutting off the subsidy to Prussia, a change in policy which led to the resignation of Newcastle in May 1762. Grenville was a dull but honest man of high principles. An efficient administrator with iron determination and a good head for details, he lacked imagination, long views and political finesse. He soon quarrelled with Bute over patronage and the preliminaries of the peace Tr ending the SEVEN YEARS WAR (which he thought conceded too much to France). Bute replaced him as leader of the H of C with Henry FOX (Oct 1762), who had the job of getting the preliminaries through Parl. Grenville's place as Sec of State went to Halifax, while he was demoted and given Halifax's post as 1st Ld of the Admiralty (Jan 1763). Bute was soon driven from office (Apr 1763), and the K appointed Grenville in his place, as the least of several evils. Pitt and Fox had refused to serve, and the K had no desire to fall back on Newcastle and the Old Corps of Whigs.

The Grenville admin (1763–5) was a triumvirate with no real PM at first: with Grenville as 1st Ld of the Treasury (Apr 1763), Egremont as Sec of State (S) (Oct 1761), and Halifax as Sec of State (N) (Oct 1762). It lacked the confidence of the K, who took advice from Bute 'behind the curtain', and it was opposed by Newcastle and the Old Corps, as well as by Pitt and Temple. In Aug 1763, on Egremont's death, the K tried to persuade Pitt to replace Grenville, but failed; Grenville used this opportunity to make himself a real PM. He forced the K to agree not to consult Bute, but to regard Grenville as his sole source of communication. At the same time, several of the Bedfords were given office, thus ensuring a hard line from the Gov on the 2 big issues which faced it: the Wilkes affair and the early rumblings of the War of American Independence. In the Wilkes affair, it was Grenville's colleague, Halifax, who issued the general warrant (Apr 1763), and presented the opposition with a stick with which to beat the Gov: in the courts, on the streets and in the press, but not in Parl, where Grenville's strategy managed to maintain anti-Wilkes majorities. American rebelliousness was one of the consequences of Grenville's policy of rigid Gov economy designed to reduce taxation. He cut down the army and the navy, and followed an isolationist foreign policy. His colleague Halifax issued the Proclamation of Oct 1763 limiting the Wward expansion of the American colonists. Moreover, Grenville reduced the duty on imported sugar from 6d to 3d, but enforced its collection with an unprecedented thoroughness. Likewise, the Stamp Act (Mar 1765) formed another part of Grenville's scheme to save the taxpayer money, by making the Americans pay more of their own expenses. These economy measures were well received in Britain, but that was not sufficient to endear Grenville to the K, who said he would rather see the devil in his closet than Mr Grenville. In May 1765 the K made another attempt to persuade Pitt to serve, as a result of the failure of which Grenville was able to make the K dismiss Fox and Bute's brother-in-law. Nevertheless, the K continued his search for an alternative and eventually even accepted the Old Corps of Whigs under their untried new leader, ROCKINGHAM. Grenville was dismissed in July 1765. He spent the rest of his life out of office, though he succeeded in carrying as an opposition measure – for he had then become a respected elder statesman – the so-called Grenville Committees Act (Apr 1770). This very salutary measure transferred the trial of disputed elections from the whole H of C – where Gov pressure could sway the issue – to committees carefully chosen by ballot.

Grenville, Sir Richard (15 June 1542–prob 12 Sept 1591) Soldier and sailor under Q ELIZABETH I of England, famous for his heroic death on the *Revenge*.

Son of Roger Grenville of Cornwall and his wife, Thomasine Cole of Slade, Devon gentry; ed at the Inner Temple (1559 onwards); m Mary, daughter of Sir John St Leger. He divided his life between overseas warfare, attempts at colonization, and Parl and local Gov in Cornwall. He fought for the HR Emp Maximilian II against the Turks in Hungary (1566–8); he belonged to a syndicate which unsuccessfully tried to colonize Munster, Ireland (1568–70); he became an MP. In 1574 he planned to lead the 1st English expedition to reach the E through the Straits of Magellan, to search for the *Terra Australis*, and then return by the NW Passage in a westerly direction. Unfortunately, the Gov withdrew permission to sail in deference to Spanish objections; when the scheme was taken up again later, the well-connected DRAKE got the command and sailed round the world, much to Grenville's resentment. In 1585 he led RALEGH's colonizing expedition to what became N Carolina. He left 100 men on Roanoke Island and returned home, capturing the valuable Spanish prize, the *Santa Maria*, on the way. Next year he went back with supplies only to find that Drake had picked up the men a few days before. He left 15 men on the island, but they were never seen again. He was planning a 3rd trip when the Spanish ARMADA interrupted him, though it is not known what he did during 1588. In 1591 he was recalled from another attempt at settling colonists in Munster to become vice-admiral of a small expedition under Ld Thomas Howard aiming at waylaying the Spanish silver fleet at the Azores. Unfortunately, Spain had adopted a new policy of convoying the treasure-ships with warships, and these caught the English by surprise at Flores in the Azores. Howard and 5 ships successfully retreated, but Grenville on board the *Revenge* – for what reason is not known – stayed on and fought 53 Spanish ships for 15 hours (9–10 Sept 1591). His crew surrendered only when he was dying and too weak to stop them. He had wanted instead to blow up the ship. He d on the Spanish flagship.

Grindal, Edmund (*c* 1519–6 July 1583) Archbp of Canterbury (1575) who sympathized with the Puritans and was suspended by Q ELIZABETH I.

Son of a prosperous farmer; ed at Magdalene, Christ's and Pembroke, Cambridge, where he imbibed the prevailing Protestantism; became Fellow of Pembroke (1538), ordained (1544), Chaplain to Nicholas RIDLEY, Bp of London (1550), Chaplain to K EDWARD VI (1551). Under the Cath Q MARY I he fled to Strassburg, then Frankfurt. Under Q Elizabeth I he became Master of Pembroke and Bp of London (1559). In the latter role he was less assiduous in enforcing uniformity in vestments and ritual than Archbp PARKER would have liked; but as Archbp of York (1570) he had the more congenial task of rooting out Catholicism. He was made Archbp of Canterbury in the hope that he would be able to reconcile the moderate Puritans and isolate the Presbyterians, but the spread of 'prophesyings' upset all calculations. These were unofficial lay and clerical bible-classes, which in Grindal's eyes improved the educational level of the clergy (more important to him than vestments), but which appeared to the Q as nothing less than Presbyterian cells – she was probably right. She ordered him to suppress them (1576), but he refused in a sharply worded letter: '... remember, madam, that you are a mortal creature ... And although ye are a mighty prince, yet remember that he which dwelleth in heaven is mightier.' She suspended him from his temporal duties (June 1577) until his death.

Guise, François de Lorraine (17 Feb 1519–24 Feb 1563) 2nd D de (1550), out-standing general under K FRANCIS I and K HENRY II of France, who became an over-mighty subject, and leader of the RC side at the start of the FRENCH WARS OF RELIGION.

Eld son of Claude de Lorraine, 1st D de Guise, and Antoinette de Bourbon; m (1549) Anne d'Este, granddaughter of K LOUIS XII of France. He belonged to the junior branch of the ruling house of Lorraine, but he and his brother, Charles, the Card of Lorraine, rose high and prospered exceedingly in the military, diplomatic and ecclesiastical service of the Ks of France. Moreover, their sister, Mary, m K JAMES V of Scotland (1538), and their niece, MARY, Q OF SCOTS, m the future K FRANCIS II of France (1558). Guise himself played a leading part in the 9th HABSBURG–VALOIS WAR (1552–9), successfully defending Metz against the Emp CHARLES V (Nov 1552–Jan 1553); then invading Italy to take Naples (1557) till he was forced to withdraw by the Spanish victory over the French at St Quentin, Picardy, on 10 Aug 1557; then taking Calais from England on 7 Jan 1558. His brother the Card was a French representative at the nego-tiations which produced the Tr of Cateau-Cambrésis (Apr 1559). Thus when the death of Henry II ushered in a period of weak Gov, with under-age Ks, and a foreign Q Mother, CATHERINE DE MEDICI, Guise was in a position to aim at supreme power. He headed a vast clientage network whose chief elements were his control of the royal army, his niece's position as Q consort, and his family's possession of rich landed estates and ecclesiastical benefices in E France. Under K Francis II, the Guises replaced the Montmorencies in the chief offices; and when the Bourbons – the 3rd of the big 3 families – led by Louis I de Bourbon, Pr de CONDÉ, tried to destroy them and capture the K at the Conspiracy of Amboise (16/17 Mar 1560), Guise arrested Condé and sentenced him to death. On the death of the K, however, on 5 Dec 1560, the Q Mother as Regent for CHARLES IX released Condé and promoted him as a counter-weight to the Guise faction; while Guise joined his old rival, MONTMORENCY, and his ally, the Maréchal de St-André, in Apr 1561, forming the so-called Triumvirate. Mean-while, the political rivalry took on the tones of religious war as Condé made himself the military protector of the Hugs, and Guise declared himself an in-transigent opponent of concessions to heresy. Retiring from Court in protest against the Q Mother's attempts at RC–Prot reconciliation (Colloquy of Poissy, Sept–Oct 1561, and the January Edict, Jan 1562), Guise put himself on a war footing and marched on Paris (15 Mar 1562), having first massacred a Hug congregation at Vassy, Champagne (1 Mar 1562), killing over 70 and wounding over 100. The Wars of Religion now began, and the royal family were forced to join Guise in Paris (Apr 1562), Condé incompetently having failed to take them under his protection. Guise now laid siege to Orléans, the HQ of Condé, but was shot by a Hug fanatic, Jean Poltrot de Méré, on 18 Feb 1563, dying 6 days later.

Guise, Henri de Lorraine (31 Dec 1550–23 Dec 1588) 3rd D de (1563), leader of the Cath League in the FRENCH WARS OF RELIGION.

Son of François, 2nd D de GUISE, and Anne d'Este; m (1570) Catherine de Clèves, daughter of the D of Nevers. He was a daring and skilful soldier, whose good looks survived the face-wound he received in battle. On his father's assassination, he inherited the largest clientage network in France, rich in land, Ch benefices, Gov offices, military commands, royal relatives and political pretensions; though he emerged as its leader only on the death of his uncle, Charles, Card of Lorraine, on 26 Dec 1574. He fought in the Wars of Religion from the 2nd War (Sept 1567–Mar 1568) onwards; and helped to organize the Massacre of St Bartholomew and the murder of COLIGNY (23/24 Aug 1572), whom he believed to have been behind the murder of his father. In the 4th War he was with the future K HENRY III at the unsuccessful siege of the Hug stronghold of La Rochelle (Nov 1572–June 1573), and in the 5th War he defeated John Casimir's pro-Hug Anglo-German expedition at Dormans on the Marne (Oct 1575), where he received the wound which gave him his nickname 'Scarface' ('Le Balafré'). Fearing Guise's growing reputation, K Henry III moved over towards the Hugs, granting them big concessions in the Tr of Monsieur of May 1576. Guise's response was to form the Holy League (1576): a union of noble conservatives and urban radicals to defend France against the menace of Protestantism; and in the 6th War (Mar–Aug 1577) the K was forced to fight on the League's side. A period of peace ensued till the death of Alençon (10 June 1584) left Navarre – the future K HENRY IV – heir to the throne, and recognized as such by the K. Guise was already in Spanish pay, and in Dec 1584 he signed the secret Tr of Joinville with PHILIP II, whereby Navarre was set aside in favour of his old uncle, Charles, Card de Bourbon, and Guise undertook to eliminate heresy in France, aided by 50,000 Spanish *escudos* a month. He was also involved in the planning of the so-called Enterprise of England – a crusade to rescue his cousin, MARY, Q OF SCOTS, and Christianity, from Q ELIZABETH I of England. The resulting 8th War, the War of the 3 Henries (Mar 1585–Aug 1589), was essentially a struggle between Henry of Guise and Henry of Navarre for the succession, with K Henry III vainly trying to play an independent and kingly role in between. Guise's resounding victory over another pro-Hug German army at Auneau near Chartres on 24 Nov 1587 enabled him to act as if he were K already. He stopped Henry III from aiding England against the Spanish ARMADA (1588) and, despite the K's orders, he entered Paris on 9 May 1588 and there played the dangerous game of encouraging the RC fanaticism of the proletarian wing of the League, the Paris mob, which, on the Day of Barricades (12 May 1588), forced the K to flee his own capital. In July 1588, the K once more had to submit to the League and recognize Guise as Lieut-Gen of the realm; but, tried beyond endurance by Guise's pretensions, by the humiliating loss of Saluzzo in Piedmont to Savoy (1588), and by the radical speeches in the League-packed Estates-Gen of Blois (Oct 1588), the K adopted desperate measures. He summoned Guise to an audience in his château in Blois, and had him murdered in an antechamber. Guise's brother, Louis, Card of Lorraine was murdered the next day.

Gunpowder Plot To blow up the English Parl on 5 Nov 1605, was originated by Robert Catesby of Lapworth, Warwicks, a strong leader of men and zealous Cath idealist, who had backed the rebellion of ESSEX (Feb 1601), and who was deeply angry at the failure of K JAMES I to improve the position of the Caths in England as he had promised. He began with a nucleus of relatives and friends: Thomas Winter, his cousin, and Thomas Percy, John Wright and Guy Fawkes, the last a brave Yorks gentleman, fanatical convert to the Cath Ch, and Capt in the Spanish army in the Netherlands. There appear to have been 2 main aims in the 'Powder Treason', as it was known to contemporaries: (a) to blow up the Palace of Westminster on the opening day of Parl when the K and Q, Pr of Wales, Privy Council, and both Houses would be assembled for the ceremonies; and (b) to launch a Cath rising in the Midlands, capture Pr CHARLES and Prss Elizabeth, and place one or other on the throne. They hired a house adjoining Parl in May 1604 and dug a passage from the cellar to a point under the H of L (Dec 1604). Then in Mar 1605 they managed to rent the cellar next door, directly under the Palace of Westminster, and joined the 2 cellars by a passage. Led by Fawkes, they stored about 20 barrels of gunpowder – with iron bars on top for greater impact – all concealed under firewood and coal, which Fawkes looked after under the name of John Johnson. At the same time, Catesby planned a hunting party at Dunchurch, Warwicks, which apparently was to be the venue of a Cath rising to capture the royal children who lived nearby. Unfortunately, 8 further plotters were let into the secret, and one of them, Francis Tresham, sent a cryptic letter of warning to his Cath brother-in-law, Ld Monteagle, who would have been present at Westminster and possibly killed. The latter showed it to his servant and also to Ld SALISBURY, the chief minister (26 Oct 1605), who later informed the K. On 4 Nov 1605, the day before the opening of Parl, the buildings were thoroughly examined by 2 search-parties. The 1st, in the afternoon, discovered Guy Fawkes and his faggots; the 2nd, at 11 p.m., discovered the powder, and arrested the steadfast Fawkes, the only conspirator present. Catesby and 3 others d resisting arrest at Holbeche, Staffs, on 8 Nov 1605, but the remainder were caught. Tresham d in gaol, but the remaining 8 were tried before Edward COKE on 27 Jan 1606 and executed on 30 and 31 Jan 1606. An Act of Parl of Nov 1605 named 5 November as a day for the nation to give thanks for its deliverance, which they did until mid C19, since when the occasion has been marked by bonfires and fireworks.

Gustav I Vasa (12 May 1496–29 Sept 1560) K of Sweden (1523) and founder of the highly successful Vasa dynasty.

Son of Erik Johansson (Vasa) and his wife, Cecilia Mansdatter; m 1st (1531) Catherine of Saxe-Lauenburg (d 23 Sept 1535), by whom he had one son (later K Eric XIV, 1560–68); m 2nd (1536) Margereta Leijonhufund (d 26 Aug 1551, leaving among others the future Ks John III, 1568–92, and Charles IX, 1604–11); m 3rd (1552) Katarina Stenbeck. He established Sweden's national independence, founded a strong monarchy, and carried through the REFORMATION.

National independence was achieved by the break-up of the Union of Kalmar (1397–1523) in which Sweden, Norway and Denmark were jointly ruled by one monarch, and in which Sweden took 2nd place to Denmark. There was always a strong opposition movement to the Union, supported by nobles, free peasants and miners, and based on the sentiments of aristocratic hostility to a strong monarchy, and Swedish nationalism. The admin of the Ks of Denmark thus never effectively penetrated inside Sweden. Instead, Denmark had to rely on native admin headed by the Regent who, from the late C15 onwards, was a member of the powerful Sture family. Under K Christian II of Denmark, Sten Sture the Younger (leader of the family, 1512–20) led a rebellion against Denmark, fired by aristocratic hostility to Christian's would-be bureaucratic absolutism, and supported by anti-clerical discontent with Gustav Trolle, Archbp of Uppsala, his ecclesiastical agent, who co-operated with Denmark. In this war (1517–20) Gustavus Ericsson Vasa, a young Swedish noble, took part; when Sten Sture was defeated and killed by Christian at Lake Åsunden (20 Jan 1520), he took over the leadership of the Sture party. After this victory, Christian had himself crowned hereditary K of Sweden (4 Nov 1520), granting an amnesty to the rebels which he immediately broke with the 'Stockholm Bloodbath' (8 Nov 1520) in the course of which over 80 leading members of the Sture party (nobles and bps) were slaughtered, including Gustavus Vasa's father and 2 uncles. Gustavus now led a further rebellion against Christian II, based on the national revulsion against this crime, and (more important) on the financial and naval backing of the city of Lübeck which, as a member of the HANSEATIC LEAGUE, was always ready to weaken its commercial rivals, the Danes. Gustavus was elected Administrator of Sweden by an assembly at Vadstena (Aug 1521), then made K Gustavus I Vasa by the Estates (*riksdag*) at Strängnäs (June 1523). Meanwhile, the ships of Lübeck helped in the reconquest of Stockholm (1523), as well as, in Denmark itself, in the overthrow of Christian II (Apr 1523) by his uncle, who now became K Frederick I (1523–33). As joint enemies of Christian, Gustavus and Frederick now co-operated; and with the latter's recognition of Gustavus as K of Sweden (1524), the Union of Kalmar was really at an end. Unfortunately, Sweden was not yet completely independent, for Lübeck now had a stranglehold on the Swedish economy – the result of the concessions she had received (customs exemptions, commercial monopolies etc) in return for helping Sweden against Denmark; and Gustavus did not manage to loosen their grip until the Counts' War (1534–6), in which Sweden and Denmark jointly defeated the attempt of Lübeck to restore Christian II to the Danish throne. Henceforth, Gustavus pursued a cautious foreign policy, joining Denmark in the alliance of Brömsebro (1541) (which brought him into indirect contact with the League of Schmalkalden); and fighting a not very bloody war with Moscow (1554–7). His main concern was the internal consolidation of Sweden, and the establishment of his own supremacy in it.

A strong monarchy was built in typical Swedish fashion: ie by the alliance of the K with the 4 Estates of the comparatively new *riksdag* (especially the peasants, the burghers and the clergy) against the traditional organ of aristocratic opposition, the *riksråd* (Council of the Realm). In this struggle between demagogic absolutism and noble oligarchy, Gustavus was ruthless and violent, but also shrewd and statesmanlike, possessing that precious ability to communicate with the common man which enabled him to encourage the activities of the *riksdag* to strengthen his own position (eg in enacting the Succession Pact at Västerås in 1544, which made the monarchy hereditary instead of elective) while letting the *riksråd* decline in significance. His power was based on his family lands (later supplemented by those of the Ch) which, carefully administered to extract the maximum profit, made him the largest economic entity in the State, in agriculture, forestry, mining and commerce; and he used it to create a national army fed by the conscription of all males from the age of 16 to 60 (1544); to reorganize the navy and give it modern ships; to modernize the economy (about 500 years behind that of the contemporary W) by exploiting Sweden's ironfields and forests, and by thrusting into the vast potential of the Baltic trading area. The aristocracy had been weakened by the Stockholm Bloodbath, and were now reduced further in power by another *riksdag* at Västerås (1527), which carried through the break with Rome, one effect of which was to eliminate the episcopate from the *riksråd*.

The Reformation had similarities with that of K HENRY VIII of England. Although Lutheran ideas were already being diffused in Sweden by missionaries from Prussia (and especially by 2 Swedish products of the Univ of Wittenberg, Saxony: the brothers Olavus and Laurentius Petri), they found acceptance at first only in cities where German merchants were numerous, and the Swedish break with Rome was more political than doctrinal. By threatening to abdicate, and by promising the nobles they could take back all the land their families had given to the Ch since 1454, Gustavus persuaded the *riksdag* of Västerås to agree that the Crown could confiscate bps' palaces and 'superfluous' property, as well as all the property of the monasteries and cathedral chapters. At the same time, the *riksdag* permitted the preaching of Lutheranism. Gustavus was a *politique* to the fingertips, and tolerated both Caths and Prots so long as they preached the 'pure word of God' – a vague phrase typical of the doctrinal side of the Swedish Reformation. Under the leadership of the Petris, the beliefs and practices of the Swedish Ch were now changed in a Lutheran direction, as follows: the appointment of Laurentius as Archbp of Uppsala in 1531; the publication of Olavus's Swedish Bible (1526) and Swedish Mass (1531); the Synods of Örëbro (1529) and Uppsala (1536); the replacement of the Petri brothers by the German, George Norman (1539–44), who vigorously brought all aspects of the Ch under State inspection and control (whereas the Petris had envisaged an independent Ch, and were moreover too fond of criticizing lay morals, including the K's); the revolts against these changes (coloured also by the economic grievances and prov separatism of the peasants and miners) in Västergötland (1529), Dalarna (1531) and, most serious of all, in Smaland and Blekinge (1542–3); the *riksdag* of Västerås (1544) which officially declared Sweden to be an Evangelical Kdom; followed by a return to the more moderate methods of the Petri brothers, and a more systematic opposition to R C practices. The Swedish Reformation had profounder effects on the language and culture of the people than in any other European country, partly because Christianity had arrived there late (500 years behind St Augustine's mission to England); and the great accession of power and wealth it brought to the K gave the monarchy a new firmness and stability (though not at the expense of the rule of law or representative institutions) which enabled it to lead Sweden to European greatness.

Gustav II Adolf (9 Dec 1594–6 Nov 1632) K of Sweden (1611), the greatest Swedish K and one of the greatest statesmen in European history, who raised Sweden in a dramatic way from a position of weakness and insecurity to the status of master of the Baltic and greatest military power in Europe. As well as initiating important reforms in all areas of Swedish life, he defeated Denmark, Poland and Russia, and intervened decisively on the Prot side in the THIRTY YEARS WAR, till he met his death in a battle which was otherwise a victory.

Eld son of K Charles IX and his 2nd wife, Christina of Holstein; ed by his tutor, Johan Skytte; m (1620) Maria Eleonora, the neurotically possessive daughter of the El John Sigismund of Brandenburg, having 1 daughter, the future Q CHRISTINA. Tall, blond and broad-shouldered, he had the Vasa brilliance at public speaking and their mysterious power over the common people; but, though he radiated a cheerful charm in public, he was basically reserved, and capable of bad-tempered outbursts. Built on a heroic scale, with an immense capacity for hard work and a deep religious faith, he was at once a far-sighted statesman and outstanding military commander, whose original vision quickly transformed Sweden's obscure position in the world. On his accession, he inherited a weak position at home and abroad. At home, he was a minor and in the hands of the Council (*riksråd*), the chief institution of the high nobility, who were reasserting themselves after the strong Gov of Charles IX. They made the young K accept an Accession Charter (Jan 1611), in which he promised to give the chief offices only to the high nobility and to conduct all his home and foreign policy in consultation with the Council. But this humiliation was to be neither the prelude to a period of aristocratic constitutionalism, nor its opposite, absolute rule in conjunction with the Diet (*riksdag*) – the two extremes between which the Swedish constitution usually oscillated. In fact, the ancient struggle between the Crown and nobility was laid aside for the whole of this reign, the chief cause of the harmony being the friendship between the K and the leader of the high nobility, Axel OXENSTIERNA, Chancellor from 1612 onwards. Together, they were able to remodel Sweden in all departments. Moreover, the K, as a sincere Lutheran, enjoyed the enthusiastic backing of the whole Swedish nation who, in their fully representative Diet and conscripted national army, participated in their K's heroic adventures in a way which was rare in C17 Europe. Abroad, Gustav Adolf inherited a critical situation: 3 wars in which his own position on the throne and the national independence of Sweden were both at stake. But, guided in diplomacy and war by the varied talents of the K and Oxenstierna, and drawing strength from the reforms they instituted, Sweden survived the crisis to become the leading power in the Baltic, and then the head of the Prot states of Europe in the Thirty Years War.

At home, Gustav Adolf and Oxenstierna made important reforms in (a) the Gov, (b) the armed forces, (c) the economy, and (d) education.

(a) The Gov. Led by Oxenstierna, and shaped by the many ordinances he drafted, the Council developed into the highest organ of the central Gov, instead of being the spear-head of aristocratic opposition. In the past, it had met irregularly on the K's orders, wherever he happened to be; but now it sat permanently in Stockholm, making decisions of high policy in the absence of the K on campaign, and organizing its work rationally on bureaucratic lines. The 5 chief officers of state – Chancellor, High Steward, Treasurer, Admiral and Marshal – ceased to be ceremonial dignitaries to become working heads of Gov departments. One by one they were given collegial organization and regular procedures, worked out in such measures as the Judicature Ordinance (1614) for the High Steward, the Exchequer Ordinance (1618) for the Treasurer and the Chancery Ordinances (1618 and 1626) for the Chancellor. To complete the reforms, the Admiral and Marshal were given boards in the so-called Form of Gov of 1634, a constitutional document put into force after Gustav Adolf's death. During the reign, the Diet developed into a regular participant in Gov, co-operating with Gustav Adolf in its old role as the K's ally against the high nobility of the Council, but also developing the regular procedures, firm outline and self-confidence which enabled it later in the century to replace the Council as the constitutional opposition to the Crown. Oxenstierna's *Riksdag*-Ordinance (1617) fixed the number of the Estates at 4: nobles, clergy, burghers, peasants; and the Diet's support of the K's foreign enterprises fed them with strength drawn from the broad masses of the whole nation. At the same time, prov and local Gov was reorganized on the basis of 23 admin districts, each governed by a royal officer and his staff in accordance with the K's Instruction of 1624.

(b) The armed forces were completely transformed by Gustav Adolf – a commander of the highest gifts, who profited from improvements in the art of war made by others, especially MAURICE of Orange, and who also introduced new features of his own. He reorganized the system of recruitment, based on universal conscription, to form the first truly national army in Europe though, as his foreign ambitions expanded, he had to resort to mercenaries too. These native troops, who had the morale and discipline of men who knew what they were fighting for, also felt the *esprit de corps* derived from the fact that each unit was recruited from its own local district. They were paid regularly, were highly trained and fully equipped with the latest weapons, which gave them a rare mobility, a high rate of fire and a devastating impact. Gustav Adolf also broke up the deep massed formations usual with the Spanish *tercios* into small units, fighting in line, with groups of pikemen, musketeers and cavalrymen intermingled; for the first time, artillery which was light enough to be manoeuvred swiftly was used on the field of battle. In addition, the cavalry abandoned the *caracole*, instead smashing the enemy with the shock of their charge, followed by hand-to-hand fighting. The K also increased and reformed the navy until it was fit enough, not merely to transport his armies to the battlefields of Poland and Germany, and protect the ports and sea-lanes of the Baltic which provided him with such a big proportion of his revenues, but also ultimately to challenge Denmark for the command of that sea itself.

(c) The economy, and consequently the revenues, were developed to finance these great undertakings. Foreign capital, businessmen and artisans were attracted to develop Sweden's natural advantages, especially in iron and copper; the most outstanding figure being the Dutchman, Louis de Geer, who headed the armaments industry. Gustav Adolf also drew much revenue in the form of subsidies from France, and the takings of the Prussian ports whose customs duties he enjoyed as a result of his victories over Poland. Nevertheless, even with this access of income, Sweden could still only finance its army's part in the Thirty Years War so long as the troops could live off the land abroad, and not be a burden at home.

(d) Education benefited greatly from Gustav Adolf's championship and generosity. He made the chief contribution to the foundation of Sweden's grammar-school system, and more or less restarted the ailing Univ of Uppsala, ending its old disputes, and providing it with a new admin structure and lavish endowments. He was the greatest benefactor of education before Alfred Nobel.

Abroad, Gustav Adolf inherited 3 Baltic struggles: (a) the Kalmar War with Denmark, (b) the Russian War and (c) the Polish wars. He eventually laid these aside in order to conquer a wider territory in (d) the Thirty Years War.

(a) The Kalmar War (1611–13) was a struggle with K Christian IV for the supremacy of the Baltic, in which Sweden lost Älvsborg (May 1612), the fortress which defended her only access to the Atlantic. On the other hand, Christian failed to conquer Sweden and thus recreate the Union of Kalmar; his aggressiveness threw Holland and the HANSEATIC LEAGUE on to the Swedish side. By the Tr of Knäred (Jan 1613) Sweden had to pay a large ransom for Älvsborg (which she succeeded in doing by 1619), but maintained her exemption from the dues which the ships of all other States had to pay on sailing through the Danish Sound.

(b) The Russian War (1611–17) resulted from Sweden's hopes of taking advantage of Russia's weakness during the TIME OF TROUBLES to block her Wward advance towards the Baltic, and to stop Poland from acquiring the Russian throne. It was Gustav Adolf's 1st experience of warfare and it was very successful. By the Tr of Stolbovo (Feb 1617) Sweden gave back Novgorod but gained Ingria and Karelia, territories which linked Finland with Estonia, her possessions on each side of the Gulf of Finland, and which blocked Russia from advancing further W than Lake Ladoga.

(c) The Polish Wars (1617–18, 1621–2, 1625–9) with K SIGISMUND III (who had also been K of Sweden until his deposition by Gustav Adolf's father in 1599) were partly caused by Sigismund's continued claim to the Swedish throne, but principally by Gustav Adolf's desire to capture the ports of the Livonian and Prussian coasts in order to collect their valuable customs duties. On 15 Sept 1621 he took Riga, then conquered Livonia (1625) and in 1626 took the cities of Polish Prussia: Memel, Pillau, Elbing and others. By the 6-year Tr of Altmark (Sept 1629), negotiated by RICHELIEU to release Gustav Adolf for action in Germany, Sweden kept these ports, whose customs brought in more income than the whole of Sweden's inland revenue.

(d) The Thirty Years War became a vital interest of Sweden when the Cath armies of Tilly and WALLENSTEIN defeated the Prot alliance headed by Denmark in the Danish War (1624–9). Wallenstein and the armies of the HREmp then conquered Mecklenberg and Pomerania on the N German coast, and, in alliance with Poland, began to build a fleet in pursuit of a Habsburg and Cath plan for the naval and commercial domination of the Baltic. Gustav Adolf's landing on the N German coast thus began as a limited measure for the defence of Sweden, partly with the aim of stimulating the German Prots to defend themselves against Wallenstein, and thus save Sweden from attack. As his invasion prospered, however, so did his war aims magnify, and he played with schemes for turning the Baltic into a Swedish lake, for holding the mouths of all the N German rivers, for forming a League of German Prs with himself at the head, possibly for becoming HREmp and partitioning Poland with Russia. He landed at Peenemünde, Usedom, on 26 June/6 July 1630; signed the 5-year Tr of Bärwalde with France (Jan 1631), whereby France paid his expenses; forced the Prot Prs – including, eventually, Brandenburg and Saxony – unwillingly into an alliance; defeated Tilly and the Cath League at Breitenfeld, Saxony (7/17 Sept 1631); swept S and W through Swabia and Franconia as far as the Upper Rhine, from which base he turned E, invaded Bavaria, and threatened Vienna. Unfortunately, he now allowed himself to be diverted N into Saxony by Wallenstein's strategy and, at Lützen nr Leipzig, the Swedes beat the imperial army, but Gustav Adolf himself was killed at the head of a cavalry charge.

Habsburg–Valois Wars, The (1494–1559) A series of wars, fought at first mainly in Italy but spreading N later, between the chief powers of Europe: the Emp, Spain and France, and their allies. Their chief causes were: (1) mutual dynastic rivalry and fear; (2) territorial disputes between (a) France and the Duchy of Burgundy (Holland and Belgium) over Flanders, Artois and the French duchy of Bourgogne, (b) France and the Emp over Milan, (c) France and Spain over Naples, Roussillon and Cerdagne; (3) the attractions of Italy, the most advanced part of Europe economically and culturally, the home of another big power, the Papacy, and the scene of continuous rivalry between 5 leading states: Milan, Venice, Florence, the Papacy and Naples – who invited the bigger powers to intervene in Italy from time to time.

1494–5: K CHARLES VIII of France began these wars by invading Italy in 1494 to back up his remote claim to Naples and his woolly plans for a crusade. Invited in by Ludovico SFORZA, D of Milan, he upset the peaceful balance of power that had existed since the Tr of Lodi of 1454. His army marched through Milan, Pisa, Florence and Rome, and took Naples without a battle on 22 Feb 1495. This success united his enemies: Pp ALEXANDER VI, who was anxious to keep Italy as a papal preserve; the Emp MAXIMILIAN I, who hoped to reimpose Imperial authority there; and FERDINAND II of Spain, who as K of Aragon already owned Sicily and wished to add Naples to it, as well as to gain lands from France in the Pyrenees, ie Roussillon and Cerdagne. Along with Milan and Venice, they formed the Holy League of Venice on 31 Mar 1495 and forced Charles VIII to retreat. He fought the inconclusive battle of Fornovo, Parma, with the League on 6 July 1495, but got his army safely back to France.

1499–1505: K LOUIS XII of France invaded Italy in 1499 to support his family claim to Milan. He took possession of the city on 6 Oct 1499, defeated D Ludovico Sforza's troops at Novara on 8 Apr 1500, taking him back to France a prisoner. The Emp Maximilian I recognized French rule in Milan by the 1st Tr of Blois (1504). Louis then partitioned Naples with K Ferdinand II of Aragon by the Tr of Granada (1500), but when they quarrelled over the boundary Louis was defeated at Cerignalo on 28 Apr 1503 and on the R Garigliano on 27 Dec 1503; and by the 2nd Tr of Blois of 1505 renounced his claim to Naples, leaving Ferdinand effectively in control.

1508–14: Louis and Maximilian formed the League of Cambrai in Dec 1508 for a joint attack on Venice, and were joined by Pp JULIUS II and Ferdinand II, but the great French victory over Venice at Agnadello on 14 May 1509 led to the formation of the anti-French Holy League in Oct 1511. The French fought well at Ravenna on 11 Apr 1512, but when their general Gaston de Foix was killed they had to retreat; and on 6 June 1513 at Novara another French attack on Milan was repulsed leaving the Sforzas in control once more. The League now invaded France on all sides. K HENRY VIII of England and Maximilian defeated the French at the battle of the Spurs in Artois on 16 Aug 1513. A Swiss army invaded Bourgogne as far as Dijon. An Anglo-Spanish force made an unsuccessful invasion of Aquitaine (1512), and Ferdinand overran Navarra (1512). Fortunately, Louis was able to make separate peace Trs with the very loosely allied members of the League, but all his efforts in Italy had achieved nothing. Neither had those of Maximilian. Only Ferdinand had gained.

1515–16: Soon after his accession K FRANCIS I invaded Milan, defeating the

Swiss at nearby Marignano on 13/14 Sept 1515, thus ending Imperial attempts under Maximilian I to control Italy, and finishing the Swiss as a power in the peninsula. French success was recognized by the signature of the Concordat of Bologna with Pp LEO X in Aug 1516, giving the Crown more control over the French Ch; and by the Tr of Noyon with Spain in Aug 1516 whereby French rule in Milan was recognized by the future Emp CHARLES V.

1521–6: The election of Charles as K of the Romans on 28 June 1519 – and therefore as Emp designate – raised the temperature of the Habsburg–Valois hostility because Charles was also K of Spain, and France felt encircled. Francis declared war on 22 Apr 1521, and Charles, in alliance with Pp Leo X and K Henry VIII of England, recaptured Milan on 19 Nov 1521, and defeated the French at nearby Bicòcca on 24 June 1522. In 1523 the aggrieved French D de Bourbon joined Charles and invaded Provence as far as Marseilles, but, failing to take it (Aug–Sept 1524), retreated back into Italy. The French retook Milan on 26 Oct 1524, but were defeated at nearby Pavia on 24 Feb 1525 where Francis was taken prisoner. In Spain he signed the Tr of Madrid (Jan 1526), whereby he swore (a) to give up the suzerainty over Flanders and Artois; (b) to give up French claims in Italy to Naples, Milan, Genoa and Asti; (c) to cede Bourgogne to Charles V; and (d) to restore the D de Bourbon to his lands and titles.

1526–9: Released from Spain in Apr 1526, Francis I broke the Tr of Madrid – signed under duress in his opinion – by forming the League of Cognac (May 1526) against Charles V with Pp CLEMENT VII, Venice and Francesco Sforza of Milan. In the ensuing war, Charles V's army under Bourbon, mutinous through lack of pay, perpetrated the Sack of Rome (6 May 1527 onwards); the French army in Naples surrendered after the death of its commander, Odet de Lautrec (16 Aug 1528); the French army in Milan was defeated at Landriano (21 June 1529). By the Tr of Cambrai of Aug 1529 (known as the Ladies' Peace because it was negotiated by Margaret of Austria and Louise of Savoy) the terms of the Tr of Madrid were repeated, except that Charles V renounced his claims to Bourgogne, Provence and Languedoc.

1536–8: The sudden death without heirs of Francesco Sforza on 1 Nov 1535 re-opened the question of Milan. In alliance with the Ottoman Emp and the German Prot Prs, Francis I invaded Savoy and took Turin on 3 Apr 1536. In his turn, Charles V invaded Provence from Piedmont, but had to retire before Marseilles in July 1536. Pp PAUL III then negotiated the 10-year Truce of Nice (June 1538), later confirmed by a personal meeting of Charles and Francis at Aigues-Mortes in the Camargue in July 1538.

1542–4: Francis I in alliance with Cleves, Denmark, Sweden and the Ottoman Emp struck out in all directions except in Italy: in Luxemburg, Brabant, Roussillon and Navarra. Moreover, a Franco-Turkish fleet took most of Nice on 6 Sept 1543 and sacked it, and from Sept 1543 to Feb 1544 the French evacuated Toulon and handed it over to the Turkish fleet as winter quarters. Charles V's alliance with Henry VIII led to their simultaneous attack on France: Henry took Boulogne on 18 Sept 1544, and Charles struck at Paris, getting as far as Soissons (12 Sept 1544). Charles and Francis then signed the Tr of Crépy-en-Laonnois in Sept 1544, consisting of (a) a public part in which the territorial arrangements of the Trs of Madrid and Cambrai were broadly confirmed, Habsburg–Valois marriages envisaged, and French help against Turkey promised; and (b) a secret part in which France promised to help Charles to reform the Ch, organize a Ch Council, and bring the German Prots back into the fold. Henry VIII and Francis made peace by the Tr of Ardres (or Guines) in June 1546, whereby Boulogne was to return to France in 8 years' time on payment of 2 million crowns.

1552–9: During the last years of Francis I, the Emp Charles V achieved such a strong position inside Germany by his victory over the Schmalkaldic League at Mühlberg on 24 Apr 1547 that HENRY II, the new French K, signed the Tr of Chambord (Jan 1552) with MAURICE of Saxony, representing the German Prots, whereby France was allowed to occupy the 3 Imperial Bprics of Metz, Toul and Verdun in return for giving financial help to the Prots. The resultant revival of Prot strength led ultimately to Charles's abandonment of all attempts to defeat them – symbolized in the PEACE OF AUGSBURG of Sept 1555. Moreover, Charles tried in vain to retake Metz (Nov 1552–Jan 1553). He obtained the alliance of England by the marriage of his son – the future K PHILIP II – to Q MARY I (25 July 1554); and he then resigned the sovereignty of the Netherlands and Spain to him (Oct 1555 and Jan 1556). Philip made the Truce of Vaucelles with Henry II in Feb 1556, but a year later in alliance with Pp PAUL IV Henry broke it. Francis, D de GUISE, invaded Italy to conquer Naples (1557), but a Spanish invasion of France from the Netherlands decisively defeated the French at St Quentin, Picardy, on 10 Aug 1557, and forced his withdrawal. Though he took Calais on 7 Jan 1558, and other towns, Henry II was too plagued by bankruptcy and heresy to continue the wars. And as Philip was similarly placed, the wars came to an end with the 2 Trs of Cateau-Cambrésis. The 1st, signed on 2 Apr 1559 by England and France, allowed France to keep Calais for 8 years (in the event, for ever). The 2nd, signed by Spain and France on 3 Apr 1559, established Spanish supremacy in Italy by leaving her in control of Sicily, Sardinia, Naples, Milan and 5 fortresses on the coast of Tuscany. France had to evacuate her Italian positions except for Saluzzo and a few other fortresses. She was made to return Piedmont and Savoy to Philip II's general, Emmanuel Philibert, who created an important new Alpine state out of them. France was tacitly left in control of the 3 Bprics.

Halifax, George Savile, 1st Marquis of (The 'Trimmer') (11 Nov 1633–5 Apr 1695) Individualistic, pragmatic, middle-of-the-road politician and pamphleteer under Ks CHARLES II, JAMES II and WILLIAM III, who helped to defeat the Exclusion bills of SHAFTESBURY and, though a reluctant rebel, played a leading part in the REVOLUTION OF 1688 and its subsequent settlement.

Eld son of Sir William Savile, Bart, a prominent Royalist, and his wife, Anne, daughter of Thomas, Ld Coventry; succeeded as 4th Bart in 1644; ed at Shrewsbury Sch (1643–?45) and by private tutor and Grand Tour (1647–?54); m 1st (1656) Dorothy, sister of the 2nd Earl of SUNDERLAND (d 16 Dec 1670); m 2nd (1672) Gertrude, daughter of William Pierrepoint; under the patronage of the 2nd D of Buckingham, MP in the Convention Parl (Apr–Dec 1660); made Bn Savile of Eland and Vt Halifax (1668). Gifted with high intellectual powers and a biting wit, he was hampered in the political world by his ability to see both sides of a question. He was too independent-minded, too detached from party prejudice, too unpredictable in his views, too impatient of the humdrum chores of political strife and Gov office to become a successful statesman, though his occasional writings, composed in the heat of the battle, give him a place in English literature and the history of political thought.

Under Charles II, apart from a period in the Privy Council, though not in office (1672–4), he was in opposition, criticizing the pro-Cath policies of the Cabal (1667–73) and the pro-Anglican reaction of DANBY's ministry (1673–9). During the Exclusion crisis (1679–81) he steered a middle course between the 2 extremes he hated: the Cath absolutism of the D of York (future K James II) and the republican resistance of SHAFTESBURY and the WHIGS. He favoured the alternative to Exclusion: the policy of 'limitations' on the powers of the Crown. He joined the remodelled Privy Council in Apr 1679 and spoke 16 times in the H of L debate on the 2nd Exclusion Bill, being mainly responsible for its defeat (Nov 1680), becoming Earl of Halifax (1679) then Marquis of Halifax (1682) as his reward. In Oct 1682 he became Ld Privy Seal (his 1st office) in the Gov which served Charles in the last years of his reign (1681–5), but he was not privy to its pro-absolutist, pro-French policies, though his reputation was nevertheless tarnished with them. His publication in manuscript of his *Character of a Trimmer* in 1684 – an appeal to the K to avoid extremist measures – failed to arrest the decline of his influence.

Under James II he was made Ld President of the Council in Feb 1685, but was soon dismissed (Oct 1685) for his resistance to the K's pro-Cath policies. From 1686 onwards, in retirement, he was in correspondence with Pr William of Orange; and he wrote 2 of his most famous pamphlets at this time: the *Letter to a Dissenter* (1687), warning Prot nonconformists not to be taken in by the K's promises of toleration, and the *Anatomy of an Equivalent* (1688), opposing the replacement of the Test Act by an Act guaranteeing the Anglican Ch. While no supporter of the Revolution of 1688, he was one of the 3 mediators (with NOTTINGHAM and GODOLPHIN) sent by James to negotiate with William of Orange at Hungerford, Berks (Dec 1688), throwing in his lot with William when he returned to London and found that James had fled. He became chairman of the Guildhall Committee (Dec 1688) which governed England while the Convention Parl was called; and Speaker of the H of L in the Convention (22 Jan 1689), backing the policy, enshrined in the Bill of Rights, of offering the Crown to William and Mary, and acknowledging them as 'rightful and lawful' monarchs.

Under William III he became Ld Privy Seal (Feb 1689) in the mixed ministry with which the like-minded 'trimming' K opened his reign. Although deep in the K's confidence, he was constantly under attack, an aloof, non-party loner, whose past actions rankled with both Whigs and TORIES. He resigned on 8 Feb 1690, and spent the remainder of his days disillusioned in opposition, supporting Country measures and expressing his fears that the post-Revolution wars, together with the 'financial revolution' and the increased executive power over Parl provided by party and patronage, would make the monarchy absolute.

Hampden, John (1594–?24 June 1643) Leading opponent of K CHARLES I of England, who achieved fame as a result of his trial for refusing to pay Ship Money.

Eld son of William Hampden, wealthy gentleman of Hampden, Bucks, and Elizabeth, daughter of Sir Henry Cromwell of Hinchingbrooke, Huntingdonshire – and sister of Oliver CROMWELL's father; ed at Ld William's Grammar,

Thame, Magdalen, Oxford, the Inner Temple; m 1st (1619) Elizabeth Symeon (d 1634); m 2nd Lady Letitia Vachell.

In the 2nd Parl of Charles I (Feb–June 1626) he co-operated with his friend ELIOT in the impeachment of BUCKINGHAM, and after the dissolution he was one of those who were arrested for refusing to pay the Forced Loan (1627). He also played an active part opposing arbitrary taxation in the 3rd Parl (Mar 1628–Mar 1629) and, when Eliot was imprisoned, took care of his children. During the 11 years' Personal Rule he was a member of the group (including the Earl of WARWICK, Ld Saye and Sele, Ld Brooke and John PYM) which founded the Providence Island Co and other schemes for settling Puritans in America, and which used their board meetings to plan joint action against the K. One such piece of agitation was the refusal of some of them to pay Ship Money when it was extended to the inland counties (1635). It so happened that the Gov selected Hampden to be the test case; though the judges found against him by 7 to 5, the narrowness of the majority cast serious doubts on the legality of the K's attempt to raise money without asking Parl, under pretence of a national emergency, and henceforth the receipts declined as the taxpayers went on strike. In the Short Parl (Apr–May 1640) and the Long Parl (1640) he consolidated his position as a leader on the Parl side. No great orator, but a skilled negotiator and conciliator, courageous and incorruptible, he stood out as a supporter of Pym's middle group in their attack on the K's ministers and prerogatives during the run-up to the Civil War, being one of the 5 members whom the K tried to arrest on 4 Jan 1642, and one of the 10 commoners of the Committee of Safety, appointed on 4 July 1642 to co-ordinate Parl and its armed forces. He raised a regiment of foot in Bucks, and served under ESSEX at Edgehill (23 Oct 1642); but next year, during the advance on Oxford – the K's HQ – he was mortally wounded in a skirmish with Pr Rupert's cavalry at Chalgrove Field, nr Thame (18 June 1643).

Hanseatic League, The A loose confederation of mercantile communities in N Germany and elsewhere, trading in the Baltic and North Seas, with the purpose of acquiring monopolies and other privileges, and of taking common measures against pirates, bandits and other menaces to commerce. Beginning in C13, the League reached its highest point of influence in the mid C14 when over 100 towns belonged to it (including Lübeck, Bremen, Hamburg, Cologne, Riga and Danzig), not counting depots of Hanseatic members – *Kontors* – in other towns, such as London, Bruges, Bergen and Novgorod. The League declined with the emergence of the monarchies and principalities of the modern era, and especially with the invasion of Baltic and North-Sea trade by the Dutch and English. Far from presenting a united front to these threats, the towns quarrelled among themselves and each tried to take individual advantage of the new situation. With the Geographical Discoveries and then the THIRTY YEARS WAR, their fate was sealed; and at the last meeting of the League's assembly (1669) only nine members were present.

Harley, Robert (5 Dec 1661–21 May 1724) Earl of Oxford (1711), Puritan-Whig, Country-type politician who became Tory leader and chief minister under Q ANNE; Speaker (1701–4), Sec of State (1704–8), and Ld Treasurer (1711–14).

Son of Sir Edward Harley, moderate Puritan and Parl supporter during the

CIVIL WAR, and his 2nd wife, Abigail Stephens; ed as a Puritan by tutors, the Haymarket Dissenting Academy and the Middle Temple (1682); m 1st (1685) Elizabeth, daughter of Thomas Foley, Worcester's iron-master (d 1691); m 2nd (1694) Sarah, daughter of Simon Middleton. He took part in his father's capture of Worcester for WILLIAM III in the REVOLUTION OF 1688, and was one of the 1st to welcome the new K.

Under William III he joined the backbench Whigs with whose Country outlook he was completely in sympathy. An ordinary, shy, country squire and a sincere, if moderate, Puritan, he was suspicious of the Crown, the City of London and political parties; of anything which smacked of corruption and frustrated honest, open, cheap Gov. At the same time, he was no ordinary backbencher, for he enjoyed political activity and worked hard at it. He was highly skilled in political manipulation, and expert in constitutional history and Parl procedure. He was soon elected to the chief opposition institution, the Public Accounts Commission (Dec 1690), and by 1695 was its acknowledged leader. He and his backbench Whigs coalesced with the Tories, who had their own reasons for opposing William III's ministers, to form the New Country Party, the basis of the Tory Party of Q Anne's reign. The opposition split into its Whig and Tory elements in 1696, but by 1698 Harley had rebuilt it again, and with it he was able to break up the Whig Gov (1699–1700), and force the K to form a new Gov, with the backing of the New Country Party and Harley as Speaker (Feb 1701).

Under Anne (1700–8) Harley formed the triumvirate with MARLBOROUGH and GODOLPHIN which, with Tory backing, headed the Gov and ran the War of the Spanish Succession (1702–13/14). Marlborough was the C-in-C; Godolphin as Ld Treasurer provided the administrative skill; Harley provided the political leadership, 1st as Speaker, then as Sec of State (N). He recruited a vast network of spies and informers – notably Daniel Defoe, an informer and a shaper of public opinion all in one – and was perhaps the best-informed politician of his day. With great political flair he defeated 3 high-flying Tory attempts to pass the Occasional Conformity Bill (1702, 1703, 1704), which would have stopped Dissenters from taking Anglican communion now and then just to qualify for public office. He helped pilot through Parl the Tr of UNION WITH SCOTLAND (Mar 1707). Most important of all, he regularly rallied enough support from reluctant Tories to finance the war effort. To strengthen the Gov's position in Parl, he took in moderate Tories (Henry St John, future Viscount BOLINGBROKE, became Sec-at-War, Apr 1704), and moderate Whigs (D of Newcastle becoming Ld Privy Seal, Apr 1705), while Harley himself became Sec of State in place of the Tory, NOTTINGHAM. Harley was a typical, non-party 'manager', who feared the growth of parties as a kind of trade-union limitation on the freedom of the Q to choose her ministers. Marlborough and Godolphin were similar 'managers'; but during the years 1704–8, with Nottingham and the high-flyers in opposition, and Whigs supporting the Gov (though not in it), Harley differed from them over political tactics. They favoured taking in the Whigs; he feared alienating the Tories, and favoured wooing moderates of both parties, as well as non-party men. They suspected he was undermining their position with the Q through his distant cousin, Mrs Masham, a Woman of the Bedchamber with great influence over Anne. In Feb 1708 they secured his sudden dismissal.

1708–10 was another period in opposition for Harley, perhaps his most congenial role. If he was an isolated individual in 1708, by 1710 he was the leader of all those who opposed the Whig Junto, whether Tories, Country Whigs, disappointed Whig Outs, or valuable journalist allies such as Swift. He rallied them against targets which had once roused Country ire, but which by this time were typical objects of Tory attacks: high taxation, placemen and other forms of influence which corrupted Parl, the Bank of England and the 'money'd' interest in the City, standing armies, Continental warfare and foreigners. In particular, they criticized the Whigs for prolonging the war to serve Dutch interests (eg by supporting the demand for a Barrier Tr) and for losing the opportunity to make peace in 1709 by insisting that LOUIS XIV should help the allies drive his grandson, PHILIP V, out of Spain (the policy of 'no peace without Spain'). By 1710 the majority of the war-weary nation was on their side; when the Whigs made the error of prosecuting Henry Sacheverell for preaching a high Tory sermon on the 21st anniversary of the Revolution of 1688, public opinion exploded in his favour. Moreover, Harley – a master of backstairs intrigue – had by this time persuaded the Q. Seeing which way the wind was blowing, Anne dismissed Godolphin in Aug 1710, then gradually replaced the Whigs with Tories during 1710, called a general election which backed them with a Tory majority (Nov 1710), and dismissed Marlborough on 31 Dec 1711.

1710–14 saw Harley at his peak, in effect, P M of a Tory Gov backed by a Tory H of C. He served as Chancellor of the Exchequer (Aug 1710), then Ld Treasurer (May 1711). His popularity enormously increased after the attempt of a French émigré, Antoine de Guiscard, to assassinate him by stabbing him twice in the chest (8 Mar 1711); and the Q made him Earl of Oxford in May 1711. His 2 great achievements in this period were the restoration of credit at home and the negotiation of peace abroad. At home, in spite of the Bank of England's early hostility, he steered the Gov through a dangerous financial crisis with such success that he convinced the City that Tories could manage finance as well as Whigs could. One of his innovations was the Tory South Sea Co (1711) which had the monopoly of S American trade and the task of managing part of the public debt. Abroad, he withdrew Britain from the war in 1711, drafted the peace terms, got them through the Whig H of L by inducing the Q to create 12 new peers (Dec 1711), and controlled their negotiation with the other powers, eventually achieving the Tr of Utrecht with all its great advantages to Great Britain – even though it left Catalonia and Austria in the lurch and forced the United Provinces to make do with less than they wanted (Mar/Apr 1713). Nevertheless, by the summer of 1714, Harley had been dismissed, and the Tory party doomed to the wilderness for the rest of C18.

1714–24 saw a personal deterioration in Harley, partly caused by the strain of surviving in an increasingly hostile political environment. At the same time, this weakening political situation was due to his own inability to inspire party loyalty. At heart a non-party Country backbencher, and ill at ease as the 'manager' of a party admin, he was too moderate to hold his following together in the renewed party warfare that marked Q Anne's reign. Perhaps it would be truer to say that he alienated party support by being a too-subtle Court manipulator. In the H of L, Nottingham and his High Ch Tories let him down by voting for the Whig 'no peace without Spain' doctrine in return for Whig support for the Occasional Conformity Act (Dec 1711). In the H of C, a pressure group of about

150 Tory backbenchers – the October Club – moved into opposition (1711–12); while another group – the Whimsical or Hanover Tories – suspected Harley of Jacobite loyalties because of his peace negotiations with France. Exploiting these divisions was his personal rival, the ambitious Henry St John, dissatisfied at being promoted only Viscount Bolingbroke, and determined to replace Harley as the leader of the Tories. The session of 1714 showed how little of a party leader Harley was, for the High Ch Tories, egged on by Bolingbroke, were able to pass their Schism Act (June 1714) against his wishes. Its aim was to eliminate the Dissenters (one source of Whigism) by closing their academies – in one of which Harley had been educated himself. By this time, Harley was drinking far into the night, neglecting his work, speaking unintelligibly, and showing disrespect to the Q. She dismissed him on 27 July 1714, only 5 days before her death, a period too short for Bolingbroke to rally the divided Tories and prevent the Hanoverian succession and the Whig triumph. With typical courage, Harley did not flee abroad like some other Tory leaders. He was impeached, and spent 2 years in the Tower (1715–17) before being acquitted (July 1717) and allowed to return to the H of L (but not the Court). He busied himself as an improving landlord on his Hereford estates, and as the collector of a famous library of books and manuscripts.

Haro, Don Luis Méndez de (1598–26 Nov 1661) Chief minister (1643–61) of K PHILIP IV of Spain, under whom the Grandees enjoyed power again and the DECLINE OF SPAIN quickened, with military defeat abroad and economic collapse at home.

Son of Diego López de Haro, Marquis of Carpo y Sotomayor, and his wife, Francisca de Guzmán, sister of OLIVARES; he rose in the service of the Court under the patronage of his uncle, on whose fall he became chief minister. The K had piously vowed to rule himself without a favourite, but by 1647 Haro was in full control of all business. Suave and protean, with a deceptive air of carelessness, he soon mollified the aristocracy into forgetting whose nephew he was by abandoning Olivares' *juntas*, and giving the Grandees back their former powers and perquisites. Faced with essentially the same problems as his predecessor, he followed his example where he had been mistaken, and rejected it where he had been right.

Abroad, his chief problems were (a) the last few years of the REVOLT OF THE NETHERLANDS, to which he brought a humiliating end for Spain with the Tr of Münster (1648), recognizing the independence of Holland, handing over to her certain border strongpoints in addition, and allowing her to close the R Scheldt, ie to bottle up her rival Antwerp, thus ruining Belgian trade and hastening Spain's decline. (b) In the last few years of the THIRTY YEARS WAR, Spain collaborated less with Austria, which was mainly interested in fighting Sweden, and concentrated unsuccessfully on fighting the France of MAZARIN, which inflicted a catastrophic defeat on the Spanish army at Rocroi, Ardennes (19 May 1643), stopped an Austro-Spanish invasion of France at Lens, Artois (20 Aug 1648), and in the Tr of Westphalia (1648) blocked the Spanish Road by taking Alsace, and opened a gateway into Italy by keeping Pinerolo, Piedmont. (c) The Franco-Spanish war did not end in 1648 but continued till 1659 in N Italy and NE and SW France (*see* MAZARIN), with France helping the REVOLT OF CATALONIA and the REVOLT OF PORTUGAL against Spain. The situation deteriorated for Spain when the aggressively Prot and colonizing England of Oliver CROMWELL took Jamaica from Spain (May 1655), captured part of 1 silver fleet in Sept 1656, and destroyed another in Apr 1657, and then joined France in attacking the Spanish Netherlands, winning the Battle of the Dunes (14 June 1658) and capturing Dunkirk (24 June 1658). Spain was forced to concede victory in the Tr of the Pyrenees (Nov 1659), negotiated by Haro himself on the Isle of Pheasants in the R Bidassoa (*see* MAZARIN).

At home, Haro dealt slowly but successfully with the Revolt of Catalonia (1640–52), but totally without success with the Revolt of Portugal (1640–68). At the same time, all the other symptoms of the Decline of Spain grew more envenomed as the wrong treatment was applied. Back in power, the Grandees held the Court and community to ransom. Economic decline and popular distress were exacerbated by the harvest failure of 1647 and the plague of 1648–9. Desperate for ready cash, the Gov of Haro punctuated periods of debasement with sudden bursts of deflation which played havoc with business confidence. He also repeated all the other shifts of Olivares. He sold honours, lordships, jobs and Gov land. He extorted forced loans and grants from the nobility and clergy. He extended the *millones* – taxes on the daily purchases of the mass of the people. He went bankrupt in 1647 and 1653. Moreover, his exactions helped to cause the rebellion in Naples and Sicily (1647–8) and the D of Hijar's plot, discovered in Aug 1648, which aimed at an independent Aragon. He was fortunate that Spain's provs never aided one another in their rebellions, and so with the exception of Portugal could be reconquered. The Spanish monarchy was too inefficient to be oppressive, and provs would rather live under its protection than risk independence in a dangerous international world. Thus, when Haro d Spain was on its knees but not flat on its back.

Hawkins, Sir John (1532–12 Nov 1595) Leading mariner and naval administrator under Q ELIZABETH I of England, who established the navy which defeated the Spanish ARMADA, and made important invasions into the Spanish sea-going emp.

2nd son of William Hawkins, prosperous trader with Africa, and mayor of and MP for Plymouth. Hawkins and his brother joined their father's business and traded in African slaves with America until 1560 when they separated and Hawkins moved to London; m 1st (1559) Katherine, daughter of Benjamin Gonson, Treasurer of the Navy (d 1591); m 2nd Margaret Vaughan. He made 3 slaving voyages from Africa to America: 1st (Oct 1562–Aug 1563) for a consortium of London merchants; 2nd (Oct 1564–Sept 1565) for a similar group, which included the Q; 3rd (Oct 1567–Feb 1569) in a composite affair, part joint-stock venture, part foreign-policy strike, which was a complete failure. On it, Hawkins took shelter in the harbour of San Juan de Ulúa (Vera Cruz, Mexico) in order to refit the dilapidated Q's ship, the *Jesus of Lubeck*, and here, in spite of an agreement made with the Spanish Viceroy, Don Martin Enriquez, he was attacked by the Spanish (Sept 1568). Only 2 ships got away: the *Judith* with DRAKE aboard (Drake appears to have left Hawkins in the lurch), and the *Minion* commanded by Hawkins. Back in England, Hawkins became MP in 1571, and succeeded his father-in-law as Treasurer of the Navy in 1577. In the latter capacity he was chiefly responsible for the quality of the navy which defeated the Armada. He encouraged the construction of fast, streamlined ships, well-armed with guns, and in battle relying on broadsides instead of boarding. He also raised the pay of seamen, and reduced losses through corruption by reforming naval admin. In the Armada battle he was 3rd in command after Howard of Effingham and Drake, and commanded the *Victory*, on which he was knighted off the Isle of Wight on 26 July 1588. He strongly favoured an aggressive anti-Spanish policy, sending out expeditions to intercept the silver fleets at their source in the W Indies or nearer home in the Azores; but his greatest and last venture of this kind sailed in Aug 1595 into complete disaster. It was a mistake to place the fleet under the joint command of Hawkins and Drake. They were too old, and could not agree. Hawkins d off Puerto Rico the night before their unsuccessful attempt to capture a disabled silver ship, while Drake d 11 weeks later.

Henry II (31 Mar 1519–10 July 1559) K of France (1547), whose reign was important in foreign affairs for the continuation and end of the HABSBURG–VALOIS WARS; and in home affairs for the continued growth of absolutism, and for the intensification of the measures against the HUGUENOTS, who nevertheless grew in numbers.

2nd son of K FRANCIS I and Q Claude; he was in Spain with his elder brother from 1526–30 as hostage for his father; m (1531) CATHERINE DE MEDICI, daughter of Lorenzo de' Medici, D of Urbino, and great-niece of Pps LEO X and CLEMENT VII; they had 4 sons: the future FRANCIS II, CHARLES IX, HENRY III and François, D d'Alençon; and 3 daughters: Elizabeth, Q consort of Spain; Claude, Dss of Lorraine; and Margaret, Q consort of Navarre. Far from cheerful or competent, Henry was dominated by his mistress, Diane de Poitiers, and by Francis, D de GUISE who, along with the Constable, Anne de MONTMORENCY, controlled policy-making.

In foreign affairs: Henry fought the 9th and last war against the Habsburgs (1552–9), in which he allied with the German Prot Prs (receiving the Imperial Bprics of Metz, Toul and Verdun as reward), so strengthening them that the Emp CHARLES V abandoned his struggle to unite Germany and stamp out heresy. By the Tr of Cateau-Cambrésis (Apr 1559) Henry abandoned French claims in Italy, but kept the 3 Bprics, as well as Calais, which he had taken from Q MARY I of England in Jan 1558.

In home affairs: Henry continued the trend towards absolutism. Specialization of function increased among the different courts which the Royal Council was spawning, and the chief of these, the *Grand Conseil*, continued to extend its grip on prov and local judicial admin. At the same time, the importance of the royal Secs was increasing. Four were appointed in 1547, to act as links between the K and the Councils, and between the central Gov and the provs. In the provs, the legal representatives of the Crown, the *baillis*, became bureaucratized into courts instead of remaining individual local worthies like the English JPs; and between the *Bailliages* and the PARLEMENTS an intermediate layer of appeal courts was inserted: the *Présidiaux* (1552). Meanwhile, *Commissaires* – ancestors of the Intendants – were sent out from time to time to supervise admin at the prov level. At the same time the Gov intensified its persecution of the Prot movement. The Edict of Fontainebleau (Dec 1547) handed control of the book trade over to the Sorbonne. The *Chambre Ardente* – a special central court created by Henry to take criminal cases away from the Parlement of Paris – was given the monopoly of heresy cases (1547–50); until these were later handed over to the new *Présidiaux*. The Edict of Ecouen of June 1559 announced a determined effort to eliminate 'the damned enterprises of the heretical enemies of our faith' – a move now possible since the Tr of Cateau-Cambrésis had been signed and there was no longer any need to conciliate the Prot Prs of Germany. On the other hand, attempts, backed by the Crown, to establish a Jesuit college in Paris were for the time being frustrated by the opposition of the Paris Parlement and the Sorbonne. Meanwhile, Calvinism spread, not so much in the now-declining inland cities – where heresy had first taken root – as in the ports of the Atlantic, now in the van of economic growth. About 34 churches with ministers existed by 1558; and in May 1559 the 1st National Synod met in Paris, at which 72 congregations were represented. This polarization between COUNTER-REFORMATION Catholicism and Geneva-based Calvinism generated much of the tension which provoked the FRENCH WARS OF RELIGION after Henry's death.

Henry III (19 Sept 1551–2 Aug 1589) K of Poland (1573), K of France (1574) during the FRENCH WARS OF RELIGION, whose character and policies led to the practical extinction of royal authority by the competing RC and Prot factions. He was the last of the Valois dynasty.

3rd son of K HENRY II and CATHERINE DE MEDICI (and her favourite child), he became D of Anjou and fought on the RC side in the Wars of Religion, defeating Louis, Pr de CONDÉ, at Jarnac in Poitou (13 Mar 1569) and COLIGNY at Montcontour in Brittany (3 Oct 1569), victories which gave him a reputation for martial valour quite out of keeping with his effeminate nature. He was intelligent and artistic, but unstable and extravagant, oscillating between bouts of COUNTER-REFORMATION religiosity and orgies of wasteful indulgence with his male harem, his *mignons*. When his brother, K CHARLES IX, came under the influence of the Hug leader, Coligny (1570–72), Henry placed his weight on the RC side, and encouraged the Q Mother in her adoption of the desperate measures which brought about the Massacre of St Bartholomew (23/4 Aug 1572). In the consequent 4th War of Religion (Dec 1572–June 1573) he laid siege to the Hug port of La Rochelle, Poitou, until he received news of his election as K of Poland. There he had to agree to limitations on the power of the Crown which turned Poland in effect into an aristocratic republic in which all religious faiths were tolerated, as far as the nobles were concerned; and he was glad to escape from these humiliations (June 1574) as soon as he received news of the death of Charles IX, returning to France via Germany and Italy. He was crowned at Rheims on 11 Feb 1575, and m Louise de Vaudémont, cousin of Henry, D de GUISE, on 14 Feb 1575: both ceremonies being financed by a loan from an Italian merchant at Avignon. As K of France he planned far-sighted reforms, but lacked the industry and firmness to carry them through, or even to maintain the prestige of the Crown and prevent its power being nullified by the 3 rival magnates who were competing for the control of the country. These clientage connections were (a) the Hugs, led by Navarre, the future K HENRY IV, (b) the Catholic League, led by Henry, D de Guise and (c) the *Politiques*, led by the D de Montmorency-Damville. Henry laboured under the disadvantage that, if he defeated one group, its effect was to strengthen the other 2, and only weaken the Crown; in any case, what little success he did achieve was due mainly to the diplomatic skill of his mother. In the 5th War (Dec 1575–May 1576), he failed to defeat the semi-independent Hug-*Politique* State-within-a-State in the S, and conceded the most favourable terms so far achieved by the Hugs in the Tr of Monsieur. In revenge, Guise formed the Catholic League (1576). Henry in his turn placed himself at its head (Jan 1577), in the hope of turning it to his own advantage, and launched out on the fairly successful 6th War (Mar–Sept 1577), at the end of which, by the Tr of Bergerac (1577), the Hugs lost most of their recent concessions. Henry then ordered all religious leagues to break up and, with the help of his mother's negotiations with the Hug and *Politique* leaders, he managed to maintain peace in France from 1577 to 1584, except for the short and trivial 7th War (1579–80). However, the death of his younger brother, François, D d'Alençon (now called Anjou), on 10 June 1584 transformed the situation by making the Hug leader, Henry of Navarre, the heir to the throne. Henry recognized him as such, but Henry, D de Guise, refused. The revival of the Cath League led to the 8th War (War of the 3 Henries, Mar 1585–Aug 1589), in which Henry lost control of most of his Kdom, occupied as it now became by the other 2 Henries and their foreign allies. By the Tr of Nemours (1585) he backed the League and recognized the League-backed Card of Bourbon as his heir. His military failure, however, placed him again at the Guises' mercy. On the Day of Barricades (12 May 1588) he was forced by the Paris mob – the proletarian wing of the League – to flee from his own capital; but with Guise in military control of the capital Henry was forced to capitulate once more, joining the League by the Edict of Union (1588). At the Estates-Gen held at Blois in Oct 1588, the radical impertinences of the League deputies turned Henry to desperate measures. He had Guise murdered in the royal antechamber while paying him a visit; and the next day he had Guise's brother, Louis, killed. These acts of violence did nothing to improve Henry's situation, for a 3rd Guise brother, Charles, D de Mayenne, now assumed the leadership. Left with only a few castles on the Loire, Henry swung to the other extreme and joined Navarre in an attack on Paris (Apr 1589), only to be assassinated in his turn at St Cloud by Jacques Clément, a young Dominican friar.

Henry IV (14 Dec 1553–14 May 1610) K of France (1589), K Henry III of Navarre (1572), the 1st of the Bourbon dynasty and 1 of France's greatest Ks, who brought France successfully out of the FRENCH WARS OF RELIGION, and in his post-war reconstruction made important contributions to the build-up of French absolutism and the anti-Habsburg tendency of French foreign policy.

Son of Antoine de Bourbon, D de Vendôme, and Jeanne d'Albret, Q of Navarre and cultivated daughter of Marguerite d'Angoulême; baptized R C, but ed as a Calvinist mainly under his mother's supervision; m 1st (1572) Marguerite de Valois, daughter of K HENRY II and CATHERINE DE MEDICI; and after their divorce (1599) m 2nd (1600) MARIE DE MEDICI, daughter of Francesco de' Medici, Grand D of Tuscany, by whom he had the future K LOUIS XIII. A stocky, scruffy, impetuous, outdoor type, full of spirit and humour, keen on hunting and excessively fond of the ladies, he was known as the *vert galant* – the gay spark, who got on well with the common people, and had at least 56 mistresses. He was involved principally in (1) the Wars of Religion, (2) the post-war reconstruction and (3) the anti-Habsburg foreign policy.

The French Wars of Religion soon involved him, as a leading Prot noble; and he 1st saw action under COLIGNY in the fierce 3rd War (Aug 1568–Aug 1570) and distinguished himself at the battle of Arnay-le-Duc, Burgundy, on 25 July 1570. His marriage to the daughter of the Q Mother was part of the policy of R C–Prot reconciliation conducted by Coligny during his ascendancy at Court, 1570–72; but Catherine de Medici used the opportunity, when the leading Hugs were all gathered in Paris for the wedding, to perpetrate the Massacre of St Bartholomew (23/4 July 1572). He was imprisoned in the Louvre, but saved his life by turning R C, till he escaped in 1576 and recanted again. During the ensuing civil wars he fought with the Hugs and *Politiques*. One by one the leaders of both sides were eliminated until, with the death of the Q Mother's youngest son, François, D d'Alençon, on 10 June 1584, he became recognized as heir to the throne by K HENRY III himself; though the Cath League with the backing of Spain recognized Henry's uncle, Charles, Card de Bourbon, by the secret Tr of Joinville with Spain (Dec 1584). The Pp, Sixtus V, gave this latter view backing when he excommunicated Henry in Sept 1585. Forced to fight for his inheritance, Henry played a leading part in the 8th War – the War of the three Henries (Mar 1585–Aug 1589) – in which the other 2 Henries, Henry, D of Guise, leader of the League and Henry III, K of France, were both assassinated, leaving Henry as K of France. During the 9th War (Aug 1589–May 1598), Henry successfully exploited 4 great advantages he possessed. Firstly, he was the legitimate K of France, the object of the instinctive loyalties of the mass of Frenchmen. Secondly, the League was split between its aristocrat leaders on the one hand, and the radical urban masses it had stirred into action on the other; and the body of the nobility and bourgeoisie soon looked to Henry to save them from social revolution. Thirdly, the League was patronized by K PHILIP II of Spain, the national enemy, who thus rallied French patriotism behind Henry. Fourthly, the war-weary masses of the French peasantry looked to their K to deliver them from the exploitations of the warring nobility. And, with very careful timing, Henry now added 3 more advantages: he became an R C again (July 1593), he entered Paris, the fanatical mob now admitting him (22 Mar 1594), and he received absolution from Pp Clement VIII (Sept 1595). Henceforth it was a question of defeating or reconciling the leaders of the League, and driving out Philip II and all the other foreigners who had invaded France in her weakness, while at the same time not losing the backing of his Hug supporters. Henry was gifted with sufficient political skill and personal charm to achieve all his objects, his success being chiefly enshrined in the 2 great settlements of 1598: the truce with the Prots in the Edict of Nantes (Apr 1598), and the peace with Spain in the Tr of Vervins (May 1598).

His reconstruction of France after the wars was not brought about by fundamental Gov or economic reform based on sophisticated theory; but mainly consisted of *ad hoc* measures to restore law and order, so as to allow the natural powers of recovery of the French people to assert themselves. As far as the Gov was concerned, Henry was able to establish a balance between the centralizing monarchy on the one hand, and the forces of resistance on the other: the great nobles, the Hugs and the provs. He succeeded not by new constitutional devices, but by persuasion, bribery and brute force. Consulting daily with his *Conseil des Affaires*, a 6-strong inner ring of ministers, he issued oral as often as written orders, and insisted on being obeyed. He sent out Intendants to bring the wishes of the monarchy to bear more closely on prov Gov. He reduced clientage and brigandage. He executed the over-mighty D de Biron, who led a conspiracy against him involving discontented Prots, separatist provs and at least 2 foreign powers. He called no Estates-Gen, and only once asked for money from a carefully selected Assembly of Notables held at Rouen, Normandy, in 1597. In general, he did not aim to suppress the nobility, but rather to foster them as agents of the central Gov, instead of enemies of it. Above all, his economic and financial measures, carried out mainly by his chief minister, SULLY, but inspired by Henry's own knowledge and concern, gradually put France once more in a position to defend her frontiers and even aspire to extend them. In sum, he constructed the base from which RICHELIEU, MAZARIN and LOUIS XIV were able to enforce really radical policies of centralization and absolutism in their turn, policies which he himself would undoubtedly have followed, but for his untimely assassination.

In foreign affairs, Henry pursued the traditional French policy of hostility to the 2 branches of the House of Habsburg, Spain and Austria, and thus of friendship with the Ottoman Emp, with the Pp, Venice and Tuscany in Italy, with the Prot Prs of Germany, and with the Dutch, whom he continued to support until their Truce with Spain (Apr 1609). During the French Wars of Religion, Charles Emmanuel I, D of Savoy, had captured the Piedmontese fortress of Saluzzo (1588), which had hitherto provided France with a means of access to Italy; and then had invaded Dauphiné and Provence (1590). In Aug 1600, Henry successfully invaded Savoy to make the D give Saluzzo back, but in the ensuing Tr of Lyons (Jan 1601) he allowed Savoy to keep the fortress, while France gained Bresse, Bugey, Valromey and Gex – a valuable stretch of land N of Lyons between the Rhône and Saône. In Germany he did all he could to get the Prot Prs to act together and join Holland and France in war against Spain and the Emp. In 1609, when the D of Jülich and Cleves, 2 duchies on the lower Rhine bordering the Netherlands, d without heirs, the Emp RUDOLF II sent in Spanish troops to keep out the Prot claimants. Seeing this as an opportunity to strike at the Habsburgs – and also to punish the Pr de CONDÉ, who had fled to Brussels with his wife, Charlotte de Montmorency, Henry's latest passion – he signed the Tr of Schwäbische Halle with the Prot Prs in Feb 1610; and the Tr of Brussolo with Savoy for an attack on Milan (Apr 1610). He was thus about to embark on a large-scale war when a fanatical RC schoolmaster, François Ravaillac, who was scandalized by the K's traffic with heretics, stabbed him to death in his coach as it was caught in a Paris traffic-jam. The ensuing breakdown of royal authority during the minority of his son Louis XIII shows that the authority of the Crown in France was still personal and not yet institutionalized.

Henry VII (28 Jan 1457–21 Apr 1509) K of England (1485), the 1st Tudor, who firmly established the new dynasty on the throne.

Son of Edmund Tudor, Earl of Richmond (whose father m the widow of Henry V) and Margaret Beaufort (heiress of John of Gaunt's second marriage, the heirs of the first, ie the Lancastrians, having died out) – a descent which made him the chief Lancastrian claimant to the throne. As his father d (3 Nov 1456) before he was born (leaving his mother a 14-year-old widow), Henry, known as the Earl of Richmond from birth, was brought up by his guardian William Herbert at Pembroke Castle (1457–69). In 1471, when the Yorkist Edward IV became K, and the deaths of Henry VI and his son made him the Lancastrian heir, he was taken by his uncle, Jasper Tudor, to exile in Brittany, in case Edward IV tried to eliminate him. There he collected a nucleus of exiles, Yorkist as well as Lancastrian, magnates as well as civil servants, including John de Vere, Earl of Oxford, Morton, Fox POYNINGS, and Bray. The 1st attempt at a coup (led by Henry Stafford, 2nd D of Buckingham, and organized by Morton and Bray, 1483) was a failure: Buckingham was captured and executed, while Henry's fleet was scattered by a storm without landing. The 2nd attempt succeeded. Leaving Harfleur, Normandy, on 1 Aug 1485, Henry's expedition of c 2,000 men landed at Milford Haven, S Wales (7 Aug 1485), marched into England via Shrewsbury and defeated and killed the then K Richard III at Bosworth, Leics, on 22 Aug 1485 (God thus showing, it was believed, who was rightful king). He was crowned on 30 Oct 1485, and confirmed by Parl statute (Nov 1485). He further strengthened his position by m Elizabeth of York (1486).

Shrewd and calculating, aloof and industrious, though fond of music and games, moderately uxorious and unusually pious, Henry was a working monarch and his own chief minister who grew into one of the greatest statesmen to occupy the English throne. He set himself the same goals as the Yorkists, and in time learned to use the same methods. The goals consisted of restoring the authority and prestige of the Crown by (1) ending its bankruptcy; (2) disciplining the nobility and stamping out private warfare, and reviving the effectiveness of the royal courts of justice in order to eliminate the danger to law and order posed by bastard feudalism; and (3) achieving such a secure international position that internal rebellions no longer enjoyed foreign aid. Such problems were endemic in all late-medieval societies, and in England had been seriously aggravated by the WARS OF THE ROSES; but Henry, by the time of his death, had effectively solved them, not by means of new techniques, but by dint of meticulous day-to-day personal management imparting new drive to the old machinery of gov.

The royal bankruptcy is illustrated by the fall in the average annual revenue from £120,000 in the late C14 to £50,000 in the late C15. Henry VII raised it to £140,000 by the end of his reign, and also left a modest treasure (though not a fortune), by gradually adopting the Yorkist method of paying all his different revenues into the Chamber – a part of the Household which was the K's private treasure – where they could be audited by K and Council instead of getting lost in the Exchequer – a Gov department. Thus, in the first place, he made sure he got what was due to him. In the second place, he increased what was due to him by techniques of management which had been developed on private estates, and by enforcing his rights down to the last farthing. His income from the royal domain (swelled by the resumption of previously alienated estates and by the confiscation of the property of attainted Yorkists) rose by 45%; his income from the customs rose by over 20% (helped, of course, by the general upturn in economic activity which occurred just before his accession); his agents such as Morton, Bray, EMPSON and DUDLEY, by patient investigation and harsh legal enforcement, increased the yield from benevolences, forced loans, parl taxes and, especially, feudal dues (wardship, marriage etc), often long 'concealed', but now resuscitated.

Law and order were improved by Yorkist methods also: ie by the effective use of the medieval K's council (chosen by the K and subordinate to him, not forcing themselves on him, as under Henry VI) to ensure that the common-law courts handed down and enforced impartial verdicts; that the law they enforced did not fall behind the times; and that these judicial processes were not perverted by 'maintenance' (a magnate intervening to get a favourable verdict for his retainer) or bypassed altogether in rioting and private warfare. Paucity of records makes precise description of conciliar Gov difficult, but Henry's council was similar to that of the Yorkists, even containing the same ministers and civil servants. Of about 200 members (half prelates and peers, half lower clergy, gentry and middle class) only about 20 were active at any one time; much of the council's work was delegated to small temporary or permanent committees of perhaps 4 or 5 members, such as the Council Learned in the Law (to exact payment of royal dues); the Council (set up in 1487 by a statute since given the erroneous title of *Pro Camere Stellata*) to put down 'livery' (private armies of retainers) and 'maintenance' (supporting them in court); the Court of Requests (for poor men's causes); the Star Chamber (ie the council acting as a very swift and powerful court reinforcing the whole common-law system, sitting in a room at Westminster decorated with stars); the Council of the North and the Council of Wales (to enforce the law in the border regions). And if these councils formed the arms and hands of the K's justice and admin, the sheriffs and the JPs (local gentry) were the fingers working in the localities. The whole structure answered the deepest yearning of the mass of Englishmen for relief from baronial brigandage and endemic violence, and was a great success, judging by such signs as the expansion of economic activity, the spread of learning, the extension of literacy, the reception of HUMANISM, the failure of the Cornish Rising, the defeat of SIMNEL, WARBECK and other men trying to revive the disorder of the Wars of the Roses.

In foreign affairs, Henry wisely bore in mind the weakness of England compared with the great powers of France, Spain and the HREmp; the precariousness of his own hold on the throne; the weak financial position of the English Crown; the importance of the Netherlands to English trade; and (following the Yorkist precedent) he made no anachronistic attempt to make good the claims of English Ks to the throne of France, but by a policy of peace and flexible diplomacy managed to achieve non-involvement without isolation, and increased prestige without war – as well as the destruction of the Yorkists. Up to 1492, French designs on Brittany and support of the Yorkists led to Henry's alliance with Spain in the Tr of Medina del Campo (Mar 1489), the terms of which included plans for the marriage of Pr Arthur and CATHERINE OF ARAGON; and two attempts to invade France: first, an expedition to Brittany (Apr 1489); second, an expedition to Calais (Oct 1492), an unsuccessful siege of Boulogne (Oct 1492), and the Tr of Etaples (Nov 1492), by which K CHARLES VIII of France (about to invade Italy) bought peace by promising Henry a payment of 745,000 gold crowns in annual instalments. From this time forward, Henry's position in England, and England's position in Europe grew more and more secure, thanks to good luck and astute diplomacy. True, for a time Perkin

Warbeck seemed a serious menace as many powers supported him; and because of him Henry broke off trading relations with the Netherlands (Sept 1493) and repelled two Scottish attacks (Sept 1496, and July–Aug 1497). However, Charles VIII's invasion of Italy (1494) and the consequent formation of the anti-French Holy League of Venice (Mar 1495) turned Henry into an ally desirable to both sides, and enabled him to keep the peace with everyone. He even, by means of Poynings, achieved the miracle of a *modus vivendi* with Ireland. He revived trade with the Netherlands (*Magnus Intercursus*, Feb 1496); joined the Holy League (July 1496), though with no commitment to fight; renewed the Tr of Medina del Campo with Spain (Oct 1496); signed a 7-year truce with the Scots at Ayton (Sept 1497), which later blossomed into the marriage of his daughter Margaret with K JAMES IV (1503); and renewed the Tr of Etaples with the new K of France, LOUIS XII (July 1498). This peaceful outcome lasted till the end of his reign, though when K FERDINAND of Spain (on ISABELLA's death) suddenly switched to a French alliance (Oct 1504), Henry was forced to ally with MAXI-MILIAN I and PHILIP I (the Handsome) (Tr of Windsor, Feb 1506; *Intercursus Malus*, Apr 1506), neither of which pacts had any effect, though the Anglo-Spanish tension delayed the marriage of the future K HENRY VIII with Catherine of Aragon till after Henry's death. In foreign affairs perhaps lay Henry's greatest achievement, as a comparison between the success of his shrewd diplomacy and restrained militancy with the failure of Henry VIII's irrelevant and unrealistic crusades shows. But the curbing of aggressive patriotism in foreign affairs and the taming of baronial loutishness at home, by stern and unremitting daily toil, does not bring popularity. Henry was unpopular, especially in his last years of failing health and faltering judgement. He lacked the common touch, the martial glamour, the charisma of the hero; and when he d, consumptive and over-worked, his people were not sorry to see him go.

Henry VIII (28 June 1491–28 Jan 1547) K of England (1509), a handsome, accomplished and ruthless tyrant, he carried through revolutionary political and religious changes, but handed on a fundamentally sound and stable State to his successors.

3rd child of K HENRY VII and Q Elizabeth of York; ed in HUMANISM; m CATHERINE OF ARAGON (1509), after first obtaining a dispensation from Pp JULIUS II, as she was the widow of his deceased elder brother, Arthur, Pr of Wales. She provided him with a daughter, the future Q MARY I (b 18 Feb 1516). His reign falls into 3 periods: (1) 1509–29, with WOLSEY as chief minister and foreign affairs the main activity; (2) 1529–40, when Thomas CROMWELL emerged as chief minister and the momentous Henrician REFORMATION was carried through; and (3) 1540–47, when there was no chief minister and foreign affairs again predominated.

1509–29: After an initial period of aristocratic resurgence following the death of the absolutist K Henry VII, strong Gov was re-established partly by measures to conciliate the nobility, such as the judicial murder of Richard EMPSON and Edmund DUDLEY, the rapacious financial ministers of the late K; but mainly by the rise to power of the base-born but awe-inspiring Thomas Wolsey, who was chief minister from 1514 to 1529. He tamed the nobility (executing, eg, Edward Stafford, 3rd D of Buckingham) and controlled all aspects of Gov in its day-to-day detail. This left the young K free to enjoy his sport and music and other diversions, including theology. He wrote a book *Assertio Septem Sacramentorum* in 1521 against LUTHER'S *De Captivitate Babylonica* of 1520, for which Pp LEO X named him *Defender of the Faith* (1521), a title permanently annexed to the Crown by Act of Parl in 1543. In Gov, though, as ever, he was no *roi fainéant*, but controlled overall policy, and made and broke ministers. In foreign affairs he anachronistically revived the chivalric spirit of the Hundred Years War (partly again to appease the nobility by giving them a chance to let off steam abroad instead of at home), and wasted much blood and treasure in pointless attempts to conquer France, sway the issue in the HABSBURG–VALOIS WARS, and dominate European diplomacy at a time when Henry VII's policy of peace and commercial expansion was more in keeping with English resources and long-term needs, and when the great Continental powers, France, Spain and the Emp, though glad of the English alliance, were quite strong enough to leave Henry entirely isolated and ignored at critical moments. He fought France (1511–14) as a member of the Holy League in a war involving (a) the unsuccessful Anglo-Spanish attack on Aquitaine in 1512; (b) the invasion of France (Henry was there from June to Oct 1513), the joint victory with the Emp MAXIMILIAN I at the Battle of the Spurs on 16 Aug 1513 (a cavalry action near Guinegate), the capture of Thérouanne on 24 Aug and Tournai on 24 Sept 1513; (c) the battle of Flodden on 9 Sept, where K JAMES IV of Scots was defeated and killed while invading England in alliance with France; and (d) the Anglo-French peace Tr of Aug 1514, whereby Prss Mary Tudor m K LOUIS XII of France. For the next 7 years – 1515–21 – England's role was diplomatic: the organizing by Wolsey of the European peace of 1518 in the Tr of London, the negotiations with K FRANCIS I of France at the Field of the Cloth of Gold, June 1520, the negotiations with the Emp CHARLES V in England in May 1520 and at Gravelines on the coast of Flanders in July 1520. During the 2 periods of war between Charles V and Francis I (the 5th and 6th Habsburg–Valois Wars, 1521–6 and 1526–9) Henry first tried to mediate in 1521. Then he joined Charles V and the D de Bourbon and fought France in a war which involved his 2nd major invasion of France (Aug–Oct 1523), his unsuccessful siege of Boulogne, and catastrophic thrust towards Paris; after which, through lack of money, he was limited to diplomacy again, belatedly switching to the French side from 1526 to 1529, and in general witnessing the triumph of Charles V in the battle of Pavia in 1525, the Sack of Rome and the capture of the Pp in 1527, and the battle of Landriano in 1529. Charles made peace with the Pp (Tr of Barcelona, 1529) and with France (Tr of Cambrai, 1529) behind Henry's back, and was then in a position to use his control over the Pp to block Henry's divorce from Catherine of Aragon, who was his aunt.

1529–40: During these years Henry carried through momentous changes under the guidance of Thomas Cromwell, who replaced Wolsey as chief minister, and Thomas CRANMER, who was Archbp of Canterbury from Mar 1533 onwards. As far as the K personally was concerned, this period saw his divorce from Q Catherine of Aragon (May 1533) and his marriage to Q Anne Boleyn (Jan 1533). The latter provided Henry with a daughter, the future Q ELIZABETH I, on 7 Sept 1533, and was executed for treasonable adultery (19 May 1536). He m his 3rd wife, Q Jane Seymour, on 30 May 1536, but she d on 24 Oct 1537, shortly after giving birth to the future K EDWARD VI on 12 Oct 1537. His 4th marriage to the homely Q Anne of Cleves (Jan 1540) was but one element in Cromwell's political alignment with the Protestant German Prs, which had been made necessary by the temporary alliance in 1538–9 of the usually warring Emp Charles V and K Francis I of France. This marriage was not consummated, but was declared null and void (July 1540), as soon as the foreign crisis was over. In public affairs, the need for a divorce from Catherine of Aragon released the log-jam of the English Reformation, a complex development whose main elements were: (a) the breach with Rome (enacted in the Act in Restraint of Appeals of 1533 and the Act in Restraint of Annates of 1534); (b) the establishment of the K as Head of the Ch of England (Act of Supremacy of 1534); (c) the DIS-SOLUTION OF THE MONASTERIES (1536–40). These changes, which had pro-found cultural, social, economic and political consequences in English history, were effected by Acts of Parl, and formed part of Cromwell's revolutionary policy of making Crown and Parl the sovereign authority in England, and of establishing the omnicompetence of statutes. These years also saw Cromwell's important admin reforms in the royal Council, the Council of the North, the Exchequer, and the royal Household; as well as the incorporation of Wales into the English system of gov, and the start of the Poor Law. Moreover, the period saw the resolute enforcement of the Reformation on the country at large and the vigorous suppression of opposition: eg the execution of Bp John FISHER and Sir Thomas MORE, and the suppression of the most dangerous revolt of the reign, the Pilgrimage of Grace, which set aflame the northern counties in 1536 and 1537. At this stage Henry regarded the Reformation as simply a series of political changes, and in the Act of 6 Articles of 1539, and in other measures, he set his face against any doctrinal drift in the direction of Protestantism. And this shift to the religious right was one move in the obscure political game which now led to the downfall and execution of Cromwell on 28 July 1540, and the rise to power of the conservative group led by the 3rd D of NORFOLK, and Bp Stephen GARDINER. Henry was displeased with Cromwell's policy of joining the German Prs, and especially its side-effect, the marriage to Anne of Cleves. On the other hand, he was very pleased by Gardiner's theological restraint, and by Norfolk's attractive niece, Catherine Howard, who was now brought to Court to become the K's 5th wife on the day of Cromwell's execution.

1540–47: During this period the egotistical Henry held the mistaken belief that he was old and wise and industrious enough to govern the country by him-self. He thus had no chief minister. Instead, the Privy Council was in day-to-day charge, executing the broad policy decisions of the K. These years also brought the adulteries of Q Catherine Howard, her execution (13 Feb 1542), and Henry's 6th marriage, to Q Catherine Parr, who survived him. They also witnessed the continuation of the Reformation, with Henry holding a middle position between the conservatives, led by Norfolk and Gardiner, and the radicals, led by Cranmer. At the same time, a new generation of leaders emerged, led by Edward SEYMOUR and John DUDLEY, who were to dominate the next reign. In foreign affairs, Henry took an aggressive part again, now that the Reformation crisis was past, Cromwell dead, and Charles V and Francis I at war again. His main difficulties were with Scotland and France. Scotland occupied him greatly as he tried and failed to turn it into a satellite. He began by trying to browbeat K JAMES V, then he tried diplomacy (1541), then sent Norfolk in Oct 1542 to raid the country as far as Kelso, an invasion which roused a Scottish counter-attack which was defeated at Solway Moss, Cumberland, on 24 Nov 1542. Henry was now sucked deeper into the hopeless task of dominating Scotland by forming, under the 2nd Earl of Arran, a pro-English, Prot party in order to oust Card Beaton and the Pro-French, Cath party. Henry forced the Scots to accept the Tr of Greenwich (July 1543), which was supposed to bring peace and the marriage of the infant MARY, Q OF SCOTS and the future K Edward VI. On the successful coup of Beaton and the Franco-Catholics, however, Henry sent Seymour on a punitive raid as far as Edinburgh in May 1544, a mistake which made the Scots more anti-English than ever. Probably Henry's chief motive in thus becoming involved in Scottish affairs was his desire to head off the Scots from coming to the aid of his chief preoccupation, France. France was involved in the 4th Habsburg–Valois War of 1542–4, and Henry now invaded her for the 3rd time. In accordance with his alliance with Charles V (Feb 1544), he dispatched a large army to Calais in June 1544, and followed himself on 14 June 1544. He captured Boulogne on 18 Sept 1544, but failed to take Montreuil, or advance on Paris (as he had promised the Emp). The latter now made the Tr of Crépy with France, behind Henry's back (Sept 1544). After the failure of French attempts to retake Boulogne from the sea (1545), peace was brought by the Tr of Ardres (June 1546), whereby Boulogne was to return to France in 8 years' time on payment of 2 million crowns. This was small compensation for the ruinous expense of the war which had led Henry to undo the work of Cromwell and K Henry VII by debasing the coinage, contracting high-interest loans at Antwerp and squandering the gains of the Dissolution of the Monasteries. By this time, though planning further Continental involvement, Henry was past leading armies. Grossly overweight and suffering from varicose ulcers (or osteomyelitis – the scanty evidence points to either) he was carried about in a chair and hauled upstairs by machinery. Beset by recurrent fevers, he d in the Palace of Westminster.

Humanism The name given to the ideas of the Humanists: ie the C15 and C16 scholars who studied and taught the humanities (grammar, rhetoric, history, poetry and moral philosophy), in part by reading the standard Latin and, to a lesser extent, Greek authors. In other words, in place of medieval scholasticism, the humanists made classical antiquity the basis of the W European educational system and cultural outlook for the next four centuries. They did not have a coherent philosophy, but the main feature of their outlook (which developed first in Renaissance Florence) was enthusiasm for the dignity of man, and for the discovery of man through history and contemporary affairs. Preferring the active to the contemplative life, they became involved in Gov as jurists and diplomats, and produced works of political theory and history characterized by clear analytical powers and down-to-earth political and psychological realism. In the religious field, where the classical authors were regarded as a source of wisdom on a level with the Bible and the Fathers, and where the Christian texts were rescrutinized in the light of the humanists' new knowledge of language, literature and history, there was a shift of interest away from the abstractions of theology to the problems of leading the good Christian daily life, and from relics, pilgrimages, the invocation of saints, indulgences and other popular routes to eternal salvation, to the individual's direct relationship with God. Moreover, their belief in the fundamental similarity (beneath the apparent diversity) of all religious beliefs (Christian or not) led to their support for toleration and the quest for international peace. Humanism flourished in the advanced urban centres, and was as much a lay as a clerical movement; it represents the invasion of laymen into scholarship and culture, hitherto a clerical monopoly, and helped to prepare the way for the CATHOLIC REFORMATION and the REFORMATION. Humanists were strongly critical of the ignorance and corruption of the clergy; and their more accurate texts of the sources of Christianity provided them with ammunition against the conservatism of the Ch authorities. On the other hand, the humanists were not modern rationalists or natural scientists; they were much involved with Platonic mysticism and Christian piety (especially in N Europe); they must also be distinguished from those C20 believers in a non-theistical morality also called 'humanists'. (*See* MORE, COLET, ERASMUS, LEFÈVRE D'ÉTAPLES etc.)

Hutten, Ulrich von (21 Apr 1488–29 Aug 1523) German Humanist, poet, satirist of the clergy, and leader in the KNIGHTS' WAR.

ed at the Benedictine monastery at Fulda, but abandoned the monastic life to become a wandering scholar and poet. Visited Italy, 1512–17 to study law, adopted HUMANISM, and became a German patriot, a pro-Lutheran pamphleteer, and ideologist of the Knights. A supporter of Reuchlin, he contributed to his *Letters of Obscure Men*, 1515–17, a sharp satire on Dominican and other clerical enemies of Humanism; and then in 1520 he came under the protection of Franz von SICKINGEN, the robber-knight and military protector of Protestantism. As a result of defeat in the Knights' War, 1522–3 – which he helped to inspire – he fled to Basle, then to Zurich in Switzerland, where ZWINGLI sheltered him.

Independents (Congregationalists) English PURITANS who followed CALVIN's teachings except for their insistence on the autonomy of each congregation, and therefore on the necessity for toleration; though many of them were not against forming a federation of Independent congregations so long as it did not possess disciplinary powers. They believed that each congregation should support its clergy by voluntary contributions. Coming mainly from the lower middle classes, they struck fear into the property owners by their desire to abolish tithes and patronage. Only a minority in the Westminster Assembly under Oliver CROMWELL's rule, they opposed the Presbyterian system there worked out, and spread their influence strongly among the lower classes, especially among the rank and file of the New Model Army, where they received Cromwell's support. They must be distinguished from the 'Independents', a political grouping in the Long Parl (*see* CHARLES I).

Index Librorum Prohibitorum A list of forbidden books published in 1559 by Pp PAUL IV, and enforced by the INQUISITION as an important agent of the COUNTER-REFORMATION. Revised from time to time, it was suppressed in June 1966.

Indulgences Strictly, were granted only by popes, and only to sinners after confession and absolution; they remitted the temporal penances incurred by the sin. In the later Middle Ages there developed the doctrine of a 'treasury of merit' (accumulated by Jesus and the saints out of their superfluity of good works) on which the Pp could draw to reduce – by granting indulgences – the time the sinner would spend in Purgatory, and even to shorten the sufferings of souls already there. By LUTHER's time the general public were receiving indulgences simply by paying cash down, without real repentance; while the Ch was using them primarily as a money-raising racket. It was against the indulgences which Tetzel was peddling that Luther wrote his 95 Theses, thus launching the German REFORMATION.

Industrial Revolution, The The breakthrough into a sustained acceleration in the growth of the total output of manufactured goods – based on steam-power, machinery and factories – which occurred 1st in Britain from c 1780 onwards, and which opened a new epoch in human history. Britain seems to have experienced moderate economic growth, 1714–45; faster growth, 1745–60; a slowing down, 1760–80; and a sharp upswing in all the leading sectors, 1780 onwards. Historians and economists continue to debate the causes of these phenomena but, though there is no universally agreed explanation, it is possible to point to factors whose importance is generally accepted. It seems that the more commercialized economies of W Europe were exposed in the late C18 to a rise in demand for increased output, and that, of these, Britain was not only the most responsive to this demand, but also in a position where her response had to be in the form of the Industrial Revolution, since further expansion of the traditional economy was impossible. This rising demand was due to rising population and the increasing prosperity of that population in Europe, and especially in Britain. It was also due to expanding trade with America, Africa and Asia, sometimes called the Commercial Revolution. Moreover, this rising demand was one for the cheap, mass-produced, standardized articles with which Britain was familiar in the putting-out system, and for which machine production was at that time technically possible. Moreover, the demand could only be supplied by machinery because the 2 alternatives were not possible: that is, the industrial labour force could not be sharply increased because Britain no longer had untapped sources of spare peasant labour; while the output of this labour force could not be increased by wage incentives since higher wages at that time usually resulted in reduced hours of work and lower output. The response to the demand thus had to be in the form of factories, and Britain was well provided with the necessary qualifications. She was well placed geographically to participate in European and world trade; and well endowed with a temperate climate, useful raw materials, good internal transport round the coast, and a national market, unhindered by internal customs barriers. British society was highly diversified, socially mobile, intellectually flexible and long habituated to empiricism, politically secure, peaceful and free, with institutions which did not hamper enterprise or block change. The limited monarchy which resulted from the REVOLUTION OF 1688 ensured that the powerful economic interests in the community could exert their influence over Gov policy. In addition, the technical skill necessary for the invention and use of early machinery (eg that possessed by clock-makers) seems to have been more abundant in Britain than elsewhere, since Continental economies, when they industrialized decades later, were at first dependent upon the importation of British technicians. Capital was also available in large quantities (the rate of interest was low) thanks to the National Debt, the banking system, and the other institutions associated with the 'Financial Revolution'. Moreover, the enclosures and other improvements in agriculture – which would have amounted to an Agrarian Revolution if they had not been spread over several centuries – made their contribution by providing food for the rising population, labour for the factories, and some of the raw materials needed by industry. Finally, the innovations that the textile industry adopted to meet the rising demand were such that changes in this sector – cotton rather than wool – had repercussions over the whole economy. Spinning was revolutionized by James Hargreaves' spinning-jenny (1766), which enabled one hand labourer to spin many threads at a time; and by Richard Arkwright's water-frame (1769) and Samuel Crompton's mule (1779), which replaced hand labour altogether, and required power to drive them: first water-power, then steam. In weaving, John Kay's flying shuttle (1733) doubled the width of cloth that one person could weave (though it did not come into general use until after 1760); while Edmund Cartwright's power loom (1784) eventually enabled weaving to catch up with spinning. Because of the size of the textile industry, these changes set up chain reactions in other sectors which soon affected the whole economy. Steam power was developed first by Thomas Newcomen with his atmospheric steam-engine whose reciprocating motion made it suitable for pumping the water out of mines (1708); then by James Watt, whose many improvements (1765) produced a very efficient steam-engine with a rotary motion that could be applied to textile and other machinery. Iron production could also expand, thanks to Abraham Darby's discovery (1709) of a method of smelting the ore with coke, which, when it spread (1760 onwards), freed smelting from its dependence on shrinking supplies of timber, and located it on coalfields instead of in forests. Similar developments occurred in the forging side of the iron industry when improvements such as Henry Cort's puddling and rolling processes (1784) enabled vastly increased quantities of high-quality iron to replace wood and stone in many sectors of the economy – to such a degree that the last decade of the century saw a veritable 'iron mania'. As factories went up on the coalfields and industrial cities grew, the changes in these chief industries brought changes to one another, to transport (eg road and canal construction), and to all sectors of the economy, accelerating that mutual interaction which still continues, and which has since revolutionized life in all its aspects.

Inquisition, The Roman A court similar to the Spanish INQUISITION set up to drive out heresy, established by Pp PAUL III (by the Bull *Licet ab initio* in July 1542) under the enthusiastic leadership of Gian Pietro Caraffa (later Pp PAUL IV), who had admired the work of the Inquisition in Spain. An important agent of the COUNTER-REFORMATION, this court centralized in Rome what hitherto had been the inquisitorial powers possessed by all bps in their dioceses. It eliminated Protestantism in Italy, and with less success tried to ward off intellectual threats to the R C Ch's world-picture, such as those posed by the pantheism of Giordano Bruno (burned 1600) and by the heliocentric theory of the universe supported by Copernicus and Galileo (declared heretics in 1616 and 1632).

Inquisition, The Spanish A council to combat heresy, authorized by papal bull (Nov 1478) and established by K FERDINAND II and Q ISABELLA (Sept 1480), as responsible to the Crown, not the Ch. Using secret procedures and judicial torture, and burning its victims in public ceremonials, it was established to wipe out heresy, first among the *Marranos* (baptized Jews) and *Moriscos* (baptized Moors), then to attack the supporters of HUMANISM, the Prots, and the intellectual deviants among the RCs (eg the Jansenists, and the supporters of the Enlightenment), thus becoming an important arm of the COUNTER-REFORMATION. Its powers were widened and its efficiency increased under the rule of Torquemada (Inquisitor-Gen, 1483–98) and XIMÉNEZ (Inquisitor-Gen, 1507–17); and its authority was extended to the Spanish colonies, to Sicily, and to the Netherlands. With its independence from papal interference, the Inquisition soon became an important instrument of the Spanish Crown's build-up of absolute power in C16 and C17, cruelly eliminating not merely religious dissent but every kind of deviation from Spanish political, social, racial, or cultural norms; it was finally abolished in 1834.

Ireton, Henry (3 Nov 1611–26 Nov 1651) Leading commander under Oliver CROMWELL in the English CIVIL WAR, who provided the chief political thrust and theory leading to Pride's Purge and the execution of K CHARLES I.

Eld son of German Ireton, a Puritan gent; ed at Trinity, Oxford (1626) and the Middle Temple (1629); m (1646) Bridget, daughter of Cromwell. During the Civil War (1642–6), as a competent general and convinced Puritan idealist, he fought on the Parl side at Edgehill, nr Warwick (23 Oct 1642); helped Cromwell establish Parl control over E England (1643–4); fought at Marston Moor, nr York (2 July 1644) under MANCHESTER, whom he criticized for his faint-hearted generalship; commanded the left wing of the cavalry at Naseby, Northants (14 June 1645), where he was charged off the field by Pr Rupert and taken prisoner, till Cromwell's charge rescued him; fought with FAIRFAX in the SW campaign (1645–6) culminating in the siege and surrender of Oxford, the K's HQ (24 June 1646). He was elected MP in the Long Parl (Oct 1645); but, with the emergence of the numerous political groups during the post-war negotiations with the K (1646–9), he threw in his lot with the Army and became the leading policy-maker and negotiator for the Grandees (the generals). He drew up the *Heads of the Proposals* (published 1647) a settlement which would have brought about a moderate purge of the Royalists, religious toleration, biennial Parls, a Council of State, Parl control of the militia and offices of State for 10 years, and a reform of the constituencies, but no democratic extension of the franchise. It was the most reasonable offer the K received, but he rejected it. The Agitators – Leveller-influenced representatives of the rank and file – also opposed it, and Ireton took a leading part in the Putney Debates (Oct–Nov 1647) on their scheme, the *Agreement of the People*. He resisted their proposals to extend the franchise to non-property holders – those that had in his view 'no permanent fixed interest in the kingdom' – and very shortly these democrats were dispersed by force. Ireton fought in the 2nd Civil War in Kent and Essex, mercilessly executing the rebel leaders; and while Cromwell unaccountably lingered in the N mopping up resistance long after he had defeated the Scots at Preston, Lancs (17–19 Aug

1648), Ireton in London, with a clear-eyed appreciation of political realities and the will for decisive action, took the courageous decisions to capture the K (30 Nov 1648), and use force against Parl (Pride's Purge, 6 Dec 1648) which transformed the political situation. Cromwell acquiesced, and then Ireton provided the drive behind the revolutionary moves to put the K on trial and execute him (Jan 1649). Soon after, Ireton was Cromwell's 2 i/c in Ireland (1649–51), but d soon after capturing Limerick after a prolonged siege.

Isabella I (22 Apr 1451–26 Nov 1504) Q of Castile (1474), whose marriage to K FERDINAND of Aragon (1469) united the 2 Kdoms later known as Spain, the 2 rulers being known as the 'Catholic Kings', the title given them by Pp ALEX-ANDER VI (1494).

Daughter of K John II of Castile and his 2nd wife, Isabella of Portugal. She and her husband ruled jointly in both Kdoms (*see* FERDINAND II).

Ivan III (The Great) (22 Jan 1440–27 Oct 1505) Grand Pr of Moscow (1462), who played a leading part in the build-up of the Principality of Moscow, the basis of modern Russia.

Son of Vasily II, Grand Pr of Moscow; m 1st (1452) Prss Maria Borisovna of neighbouring Tver (d 22 Apr 1467, leaving a son, Ivan Molodoi); m 2nd (1472) Sofia (or Zoe) Palaeologa (niece of the last E Roman Emp and ward of Pp Paul II), by whom he had the future VASILY III.

Tall, thin and round-shouldered, Ivan was ruthless and painstaking in the pursuit of his vision of Russia as a great united State under an absolute ruler: a conception beyond the imagination of any of his brothers or rival Prs. He greatly accelerated the process of the 'gathering of Russia' which his predecessors had initiated, increasing Moscow's territory from the mere 600 square miles of the 1340s to the 15,000 of the 1460s. This in-gathering was necessary because early medieval Russia – Kievan Russia – had been overrun by the Mongol invaders of the Golden Horde (1240), and its people had been broken into 3 main fragments: the Great Russians, the Ukrainians and the White Russians. The Great Russians (unlike the other 2) became cut off from W Europe, broke up into a large number of small appanages, regressed into subsistence agriculture, and survived by paying tribute to the Khan of the Golden Horde. One of these appanages, Moscow, beginning as 'a minor plunderer, lying around a corner in ambush for his neighbours' (Klyuchevsky) eventually took the lead. Favoured by good fortune, aided by a central position at the cross-roads of the Russian road- and river-system (bringing both economic and military advantages), but above all driven on by a line of dynamic Grand Prs, Moscow absorbed its Great Russian neighbours one by one till it was powerful enough to assume the political and religious leadership of all the Russians, and in addition to lay claim to the rest of the Kievan inheritance: the Ukrainians and the White Russians. This involved conflict with the remaining Great Russians, struggles with the Golden Horde to the E and S, wars with Lithuania and the Livonian Knights to the W, and the build-up of autocracy inside Moscow itself. The reign of Ivan III brought progress in all 4 fields.

In Great Russia he purchased the principality of Yaroslavl (1463), and the remaining half of the principality of Rostov (1474). In 2 campaigns (1471, 1477) he conquered the great mercantile republic of Novgorod, and in a 3rd (1485) subdued the principality of Tver – thus absorbing Moscow's 2 biggest rivals. Later (1489) he suppressed the wild horsemen of the republic of Vyatka, and inherited half of the principality of Ryazan (c 1500). He ensured the subservience of these new provs by executing the leaders or resettling them elsewhere, and replacing them with reliable subjects from Moscow; and by the end of his reign he ruled all the Great Russians, except the other half of Ryazan and the republic of Pskov, both of which, however, obeyed his commands, since they needed his help to defend them against their W enemies, the Lithuanians and the Livonian Knights.

The Mongol Emp had broken up into the 3 Khanates of the Golden Horde, Kazan and the Crimea. The rulers of Moscow had hitherto paid tribute to the Khans, and received their title of Grand Pr from them, but Ivan subdued Kazan in 4 campaigns (1467–9), and later established his suzerainty over it (1487), though the Mongols often rebelled. Moreover, Ivan won great renown (in alliance with the Crimean Khan) by beating off (1480) a powerful invasion by Khan Ahmad of the Golden Horde in alliance with Lithuania (whose troops arrived too late). Henceforth, the Grand Pr of Moscow ceased to be a vassal of the Mongols, and Ivan had thus brought his State through a crucial stage of its history.

Lithuania also claimed to be the heir of Kievan Russia, and Ivan was in conflict with it for much of his reign. In the early stages, he stirred his allies in the Crimea to raid Lithuania and, spinning a network of negotiations as far afield as Turkey, Moldavia, the Emp and Denmark, he contested Lithuania's sovereignty over the Prs on the borders of their two States. At the end of this first bout (1494), Alexander, the Grand Pr of Lithuania, not only recognized Ivan's conquests, but also m his daughter Elena (1495). In the 2nd bout (1500–3), Ivan won an important victory on the Vedrosha River (14 July 1500), and by the 6-year truce (1503) kept all the lands he had conquered. He did not succeed in taking Smolensk, his main objective, but he left Moscow in a very favourable position to take it later – as well as Kiev.

At home, Ivan continued his predecessors' policy of integrating the added appanages with Moscow into a centralizing and absolutist monarchy. In 1497, an important stage was reached when he issued the *Sudebnik*, a code of law applicable to all his lands. This judicial system did not apply, however, in the vast private estates of the Prs and *boyars* (aristocrats); nor did it operate in the Ch and monastic lands. These all continued to be admin in the traditional fashion, independently of the Grand Pr. Moreover, Ivan was too dependent for his comfort on the princely retinues for his armed forces. What he wished to do was to oust the magnates from power and influence, and replace them as army officers and civil servants with new men dependent on himself; but he was strong enough to do this only in lands taken by force, eg in estates taken from his brothers and other relatives, or in lands (including Ch lands) in conquered provs. Here he steadily created a civil and military structure manned by serving nobility (*dvoryane*), whom he paid by granting them estates for life (*pomestya*), cut out of the confiscated territories. He thus initiated a system of gov which later spread to all Russia, and lasted until the Revolution. Another important factor in the creation of the autocracy, and in the rise of Moscow to all-Russian leadership, was the Ch, the leader of which, the Metropolitan, fixed his headquarters in Moscow from 1328 onwards. When Constantinople (the 2nd Rome) recognized the supremacy of the Pp (Council of Florence, 1439), Moscow took an independent line; and when Constantinople fell to the Turks (1453), Moscow regarded herself as the 3rd Rome, the centre of Christianity. Ivan, for his part, assumed by his marriage to Sofia the leadership of the whole Orthodox Ch, and, possibly under her influence, employed Italian architects and other W experts, and adopted the elaborate Byzantine court ceremonial. Moreover, he advertised the range of his ambitions by calling himself by the Greek and Roman titles of 'Autocrat' and 'Tsar' of 'All Russia', and by using as his crest the double-headed eagle of Byzantium.

The succession question caused much trouble in the period from the death of his eldest son Ivan Molodoi to the end of the reign, giving rise to a fierce struggle between Ivan Molodoi's wife, Elena (backing their son Dmitri) and Ivan III's 2nd wife, Sofia (backing their son Vasily). As there was no established rule to guide him in his choice between his grandson by his 1st wife and his son by his 2nd, Ivan hesitated to pronounce, especially as the parties led by the 2 mothers were tied up with clashes over foreign policy, struggles between magnates and *dvoryane*, and disputes over a heretical movement in the Ch known as the Judaizers. Ivan's old age was thus plagued by treasonable conspiracies and incipient civil war, while his former cunning was blunted by alcohol. He first crowned Dmitri as Grand Pr (Feb 1498), but later switched to Vasily (Apr 1502). Dmitri and Elena were arrested (Apr 1502) and later suffered violent deaths, while Vasily III succeeded without trouble.

Ivan IV ('The Terrible') (25 Aug 1530–18 Mar 1584) Grand Pr of Moscow (1533), Tsar of Russia (1547), who conquered Kazan, Astrakhan and Siberia from the Mongols, but failed to establish Russia on the Baltic, in spite of strenuous efforts. Notorious for the pathological savagery of his methods, he made important contributions to the build-up of autocracy, trampling on the Prs and magnates (*boyars*), consolidating the serving nobility (*dvoryane*), and reforming the admin and the army; though leaving Russia in a state of thorough exhaustion, the prelude to the TIME OF TROUBLES.

Eld son of VASILY III and his 2nd wife, Elena Glinskaya; ed in the traditional religious manner, he seems to have been warped by the fear and neglect in which he was left as a boy, especially after the sudden death (possibly by poison) of his mother (3 Apr 1538). After a period of misrule by alternating factions of *boyars* he was crowned 'Tsar and Grand Pr of all Russia' – the 1st such – on 16 Jan 1547, taking charge of the Gov himself. He m 1st (1547) Anastasia Romanovna Zakharina-Yurieva, whom he picked from a short-list of beauties from all over Russia. (Her brother, Nikita Romanov, was the grandfather of Tsar MICHAEL, the 1st of the Romanov dynasty.) This love-match produced 3 sons, Dmitri (d in childhood), Ivan and THEODORE; but she d, to his intense grief, on 7 Aug 1560. He m 2nd (1561) a Circassian beauty, Maria Temryukovna (d 1629); 3rd (1571) Marfa Vasilievna Sobakina (d 1571); 4th (1572) Anna Alekseevna Koltovskaya (divorced 1575, d 1626); 5th (1575) Anna Vasilchikova (divorced 1576); 6th Vassilissa Melentievna; 7th (1580) Maria Fedorovna Nagoi (d 1612), by whom he had a son, Dmitri. (The last 4 were essentially mistresses, as they lacked the formal blessing of the Ch.) Uncontrollably agitated by extremes of violent passion, he oscillated between drunken sensuality one day and morbid religiosity the next; between cruelty and tender affection; between paranoiac aloofness from his Prs and *boyars* and fiery eloquence before the assembled masses. His Russian nickname, Ivan Groznyi, is better translated as 'the Dread' or 'the Awe-Inspiring' than 'the Terrible'.

His Minority, 1533–47, was haunted by the bloody rivalries of *boyar* factions intent on castrating the autocracy and plundering the community, while anarchy and poverty stalked the land. At first his mother's family, the Glinskys, were in the saddle; after her death, the Belskys alternated with the Shuiskys. Ivan, aged 13, suddenly intervened in Dec 1543 and had Andrei Shuisky torn limb from limb by a pack of hounds, a coup which brought the Glinskys back into power again. His terrorized childhood, which he somehow survived without being murdered, not only damaged his psyche. It also showed him his main political task at home: the destruction of the Prs and *boyars*.

His 'Good' Period, 1547–63, was characterized by reforms at home and successful aggression abroad.

At home, (i) he ran the central Gov with the advice of an informal inner ring known as the Chosen Council (*izbrannaya rada*), the leaders of which were 3 favourites: his confessor, Silvester; a household official, Alexei Adashev; and the Metropolitan, Makary. The overall tendency was to continue the policies of IVAN III and VASILY III: ie to strengthen the centralizing autocracy by replacing the independent Prs and *boyars* with serving nobles (*dvoryane*). (ii) He summoned the 1st Assembly of the Land (*zemskii sobor*) – the equivalent of the Parls and Estates of the W – and harangued it on Red Square in Feb 1549, seeking wide support for his projected reforms in law and local Gov. (iii) In the Legal Code (*sudebnik*) of June 1550 he substantially revised and expanded the Sudebnik of Ivan III (1497) in the fields of property-relations, local gov and military procedure; in particular confirming the law that peasants could leave their masters only on or about St George's Day (26 Nov), and only if they had paid their dues. (iv) In local gov, his aim was to reduce the oppression inflicted on the public by his District Govs (*nastavniky*) and Local Govs (*volostely*) by encouraging the appointment of Sheriffs (*gubnie starosty*) and other elected local officials, to put down crime, collect taxes and supervise the bureaucrats from Moscow. A start was also made on the replacement of the *kormlenie* system – literally, 'feeding' – whereby the unpaid Govs extorted their incomes from the unfortunate population under their care – by direct payments from the Treasury. (v) In the Ch, the so-called Hundred-Chapter Council (*stoglavnii sobor*) of 1551 approved the *Sudebnik*, reformed many abuses, merged all the regional saints into one all-Russian calendar, and successfully resisted schemes to subject the Ch to the State and take away its property. (vi) In the army (1550) a regular, paid and privileged unit of musketeers called the *Streltsy* (or 'shooters') was formed, eventually numbering 20,000 men, garrisoned in towns all over Russia. Moreover, a decree of 1556 compelled every lord – whether his land was a hereditary holding (*votchina*) or conditional upon service (*pomestie*) – to provide and equip a man and a mount for every unit of land he held. At the same time, the top command structure was greatly unified and discipline tightened by the partial abolition of *mestnichestvo*, a gradation of ranks which had hitherto frozen the *boyars* in an unalterable hierarchy and made the promotion of military talent difficult and the prompt execution of orders impossible. (vii) In society, the effect of most of the above changes was to raise the *dvoryane* at the expense of the *boyars* above and the peasants below – a social change which the economic development of Russia reinforced. As the economy advanced beyond subsistence farming into an era of national and international trade, industrial production and new agricultural methods, the feuding *boyars* clinging to tradition were outpaced by the *dvoryane* – new men keen to exploit the new possibilities. At the same time, economic change and State policy were increasingly enserfing the peasantry. Indebtedness was placing the peasants in the power of their lords, and driving them to attempt flight into the empty border regions; the State did all it could to pin them down on their manors. The State, after all, depended on the services of the *dvoryane*, who could not provide it without peasants.

Abroad, Ivan continued the 'gathering of Russia' with successful counter-attacks on the Mongols. (i) On the Khanate of Kazan on the middle Volga he made 3 unsuccessful attacks (1545, 1547–8, 1549–50), and then took the city by storm after a land and water siege from 20 Aug–2 Oct 1552 – a triumph which has an important place in the creation of the Russian national consciousness. (ii) The Khanate of Astrakhan at the mouth of the Volga was then annexed in 1556, giving Russia the whole length of the river for trade down to the Caspian. (iii) The 3rd of the Mongol hordes – the Khanate of the Crimea – was in Ivan's view too far away across the steppe and too strongly backed by the Turkey of SULAIMĀN II to permit of a successful attack by Russia. Instead, he fought (iv) the Livonian War (1558 onwards). Though some of his advisers pressed for an attack on the Crimea, he decided to wrest the Baltic coastline from the decadent Livonian Knights in order to make commercial and technological contact with the W, the advantages of which he was fully aware of, if only since the voyage of Richard Chancellor to Moscow (1553) and the formation of the Muscovy Co (1555). His attacks were at first successful. He took Narva (11 May 1558) and many other towns. The Livonian Order first allied with Poland (Sept 1559) and then merged with it (Nov 1561), the Grand Master becoming the D of Courland; yet Russia still made successful inroads, taking Polotsk on 15 Feb 1563, a victory which gave her control of the W Dvina.

The reign of terror (1564–84) arose out of his deteriorating mental condition and the worsening political situation. On the personal side, his persecution mania grew fat on lost battles, defections to the enemy, criticisms in council and clashes over policy. His mind had been incurably poisoned against the *boyars* from early childhood, and in Mar 1553, when he fell seriously ill and was expected to die, he was deeply offended to observe how his closest counsellors battled for power round his sick-bed, ignoring his wishes to support his wife and son. The destruction of Moscow by fire and other calamities fed his suspicions. In 1560, he broke with his closest advisers, Silvester and Adashev. They left court, and he executed many of their supporters. The same year his wife Anastasia d, clouding his mind with further suspicions. His days and nights became filled with orgies of drink, sex, sadism and prayer. In the political field, his 2 main tasks – consolidating the autocracy and extending the frontiers – required an ever-expanding force of servitors in the army and the bureaucracy. But the *dvoryane* could not serve the State unless provided with estates and peasants, and in the chronic shortage of both only the *boyars* could provide (the Ch being too strong to be despoiled at that time). Thus personal drives and political necessities conspired to produce the notorious *Oprichnina*.

The Oprichnina (1564–75) – a separate royal State within the State, manned by *oprichniky*, a specially selected guard – was created out of *boyar* estates. It seems to have been *boyar* treacheries in the Livonian War, capped by the defection to Lithuania (Apr 1564) of his close friend and leading gen, Pr A. M. Kurbsky, that finally unhinged the Tsar's mind. On 3 Dec 1564 he took his household to Alexandrovsk (100 km N E of Moscow), announcing his abdication. The terrified citizens of Moscow, led by their clergy, begged him to stay at their head (Jan 1565), and he agreed on condition he was given despotic powers. He returned to the capital on 3 Feb 1565, prematurely bald and old, the victim of a psychological crisis. Henceforth he cut himself off from normal society, surrounding himself with his élite, the *oprichniky*. Dressed in black and riding black horses, they eventually numbered 6,000 and the land they ruled occupied half the kingdom. (The other half – called the *zemshchina* – continued to be governed by the *boyars'* *duma* and other traditional organs.) In order to provide for the *oprichniky*, Ivan brutally uprooted about 12,000 *boyars* from their estates that winter and forced them to colonize new land on the frontiers. Any sign of opposition was dealt with in a similarly arbitrary fashion. Philip, the saintly Metropolitan, who dared to criticize the way the *oprichniky* terrorized the public, was defrocked, and then strangled in Dec 1569. When Ivan suspected the city of Novgorod of planning to defect to Lithuania, he destroyed it and killed about 60,000 inhabitants, an orgy of cruelty in which he took a personal part (Jan–Feb 1570). Later, on 25 July 1570, he tortured and killed over 200 citizens of Moscow – including close advisers – whom he suspected of supporting Novgorod. Unfortunately for Ivan, defeats by the Mongols and the Lithuanians soon showed the *Oprichnina* to be a failure, and from 1572 to 1575 he wound it up, merging the *oprichniky* with the army, and returning at least some of the confiscated estates.

Abroad, (i) the Crimean Khan invaded Russia and on 24 May 1571 put all Moscow to the flames except the Kremlin, taking away about 100,000 prisoners. (ii) In the Livonian War his enemies, Lithuania and Poland, merged into one State (Union of Lublin, 1569) and on 14 Dec 1575 elected the able Stephen Báthory, Pr of Transylvania, as their K. Ivan at first had success, conquering the whole of Livonia except Riga and Reval (1576), but Báthory, as well as Sweden, was soon ready for the counter-attack. Sweden wiped out the Russian army at Wenden, Livonia (21 Nov 1578) and then drove the Russians out of Karelia and Narva (1580). Stephen Báthory retook Polotsk (30 Aug 1579), captured Velikie Luki (4 Sept 1580), and then attacked Pskov (26 Aug 1581), but failed to take it. Amidst these disasters, Ivan was forced to abandon his prime object, a foothold on the Baltic. In fact, it was an ambition that Russia had to postpone till the reign of PETER I. In the Tr of Jam-Zapolsky with Poland-Lithuania (Jan 1582) and in the Tr of Pliussa (May 1583) with Sweden, he gave up all his Baltic conquests. (iii) In Siberia he was more successful. Here the great trading and colonizing family of Stroganov, employing a Cossack band under Ermak Timofeev, crossed the Urals and defeated the Siberian Khan on 23 Oct 1581, taking the capital, Isker, 3 days later. The Khanate was annexed to Russia.

The end took place amid total disaster. On 15 Nov 1581, Ivan had a sudden fit of anger with his son Ivan. Beside himself, he struck him in the face with the spear-like staff he always carried, and his gifted heir d 4 days later. Thus, when the Tsar himself d, he not only left his country on the brink of anarchy, and humiliated by defeat: he also left in Theodore, his next son, a totally incapable successor. The Time of Troubles was at hand.

James IV (17 Mar 1473–9 Sept 1513) K of Scots (1488) son of K James III, he participated in a rebellion of nobles against his father who was defeated at the battle of Sauchieburn (nr Stirling) and killed as he fled from the field (11 June 1488). As K, James was vigorous, imposing and popular, if extravagant and pleasure-bent. He ruled the country himself, extended the power of the Crown (taking over, eg, as Lord of the Isles in 1493), improved law and order, increased the army and navy and encouraged Renaissance learning: eg, the poet William Dunbar flourished at his Court, and King's College, Aberdeen, was founded under his auspices. James also counted in European diplomacy. He joined the 'auld alliance' with France, supported Perkin WARBECK, and made 2 attempts to invade England on his behalf (Sept 1496, July–Aug 1497), though he favoured peace with England and signed a Tr with K HENRY VII (1502) whereby he m Henry's daughter Margaret (1503). When the next English K, HENRY VIII, invaded France, James renewed his French alliance and invaded England (Aug 1513). He was defeated at Flodden, Northumberland, where he and most of his nobles were killed.

James V (10 Apr 1512–14 Dec 1542) K of Scots (1513).
Succeeded when his father, JAMES IV, was killed at Flodden. His Regents were, 1st his mother, Margaret Tudor (1513–14), then John Stewart, Earl of Albany, his cousin and heir presumptive (1514–24). The Scottish nobility were divided into competing pro-English and pro-French parties, led respectively by Margaret's 2nd husband, Angus, and French-speaking Albany; and it was a victory for the former when James was proclaimed K (1524) in his own name, to become the puppet of Angus and be confined to Edinburgh (1524–8). Escaping from prison to Stirling in 1528, James henceforth was his own master, becoming a powerful and popular K, who extended the territorial sway of the Crown and mixed easily with the common people. In foreign affairs he resisted the wiles of K HENRY VIII of England, and refused to join him in his anti-papal and anti-French policies. Going to Paris (Dec 1536), he m Madeleine, daughter of K FRANCIS I (1537). She d soon after, however (1537), but James continued his pro-French policy by taking as his 2nd wife Mary de Guise, daughter of the D de Guise (1538). The breach with Henry VIII led to war in which James's army invading England was heavily defeated at Solway Moss on 24 Nov 1542. With 1,200 Scots dead to 7 English, this was a disaster which is said to have brought on James's sudden death soon after. His only legitimate offspring was MARY, Q OF SCOTS, b only a few days before.

James VI and I (19 June 1566–27 Mar 1625) K of Scots (1567), K of Great Britain and Ireland (1603), who in Scotland strengthened the power of the Crown over the Prot and Cath noble factions as well as over Parl and the Kirk; but who in England, after uniting the 2 Crowns, reduced the effectiveness of

England abroad, and weakened the monarchy at home in its constitutional powers, religious authority, financial health and popular prestige.

Son of MARY, Q OF SCOTS and her 2nd husband, Darnley; and in 1567 proclaimed K on the enforced abdication of his mother; ed under the hardhearted Puritan tyranny of George Buchanan and Peter Young (who had studied under Beza at Geneva), he emerged fluent in English, Latin and French, and competent in Italian, with an insatiable thirst for theology, a dreary penchant for pedantry, and a number of character defects which were fatal in a ruler.

In Scotland during his childhood and youth he was a pawn in the primitive power-game of Cath and Prot over-mighty subjects – a loveless orphan whose taste for men was encouraged for their own political ends by the D of Lennox and other leaders; an erring sinner who was lectured at by Andrew Melville and other leaders of the Kirk with no respect for monarchy. He m (1589) Anne, daughter of Frederick II, K of Denmark, by proxy in Copenhagen, after which he romantically sailed the seas to bring her home, arriving at Leith in May 1590. She was blonde and graceful but shallow and frivolous, causing difficulties by turning Cath in the 1590s. She d on 2 Mar 1619 of dropsy. James gradually strengthened the Crown by balancing one faction against the other; by encouraging the moderates in the Kirk, the lairds in the villages and the middle-classes in the burghs; by drawing strength from his Tr of Berwick (July 1586) with Q ELIZABETH I of England and from his expectation of succeeding her; and by manipulating the Parl and appointing effective ministers such as Sir John Maitland, his Chancellor, 1587–95. The Scottish central admin was extended over the Highlands, the Western Isles and the Border, and the nobles were taught the advantages of looking to the Crown instead of feuding with one another. The revenues were increased, thanks to the work of an 8-man team, the Octavians (1596), and trade was encouraged. An unsuccessful attempt was made to colonize Nova Scotia; but the plantation of Ulster at the expense of the Irish tribesmen was only too successful. In the Kirk he encouraged the moderates and excluded the extremists, and gradually browbeat the Gen Assembly and Parl to accept Anglican institutions, such as Bps and a Court of High Commission, and rites, such as episcopal confirmation and kneeling at communion. These successes were only external, however, and the Kirk remained solidly Presbyterian and ready to resist further interference. In all these fields, and others, the power of the Scottish Crown gained greatly from James's accession to the throne of England, so long hoped for and so deeply apprehended, and yet so smoothly accomplished, thanks to the preparations of Robert Cecil, later Earl of SALISBURY, with whom James secretly corresponded from 1601 onwards. Within 8 hours of the Q's death James was proclaimed K in London; 2 days later he received the news in Edinburgh; 10 days after that he left on his journey S (5 Apr 1603), never to see Scotland again except for one short visit (May–Aug 1617). On his way through England he created 300 knights – a warning of what was to come.

In England – the 'promised land', as he called it, 'where he sat amongst grave, learned and reverend men, not as before, elsewhere, a king without state, without honour, without order, where beardless boys would brave him' to his face' – circumstances beyond his control were tending towards a struggle between K and Parl, but his character, his ideas and his methods gave them plenty of help. As well as having a long, weedy body, skinny legs, slovenly eating habits, an immoderate taste for sweet wines and deep fear of soap and water, he suffered from the disadvantages of being a Scot who fancied himself as an intellectual. Too conceited to appreciate the disastrous effect he created, he garrulously lectured all and sundry with a mixture of dirty jokes and learned references in a strong Scots accent, and went into print at the slightest excuse, eg his *Demonology* (1597) – an attack on witchcraft – *The Trew Law of Free Monarchies* (1598) and *Basilikon Doron* (1599) – both giving his political ideas – and *Counterblaste to Tobacco* (1604), in which he denounced smoking as 'a custom loathsome to the eye, hateful to the nose, harmful to the brain, dangerous to the lungs, and in the black stinking fumes thereof nearest resembling the horrible Stygian smoke of the pit that is bottomless'. Unfortunately, his preposterous vanity and his elevated view of the rights and duties of monarchs were not backed up by solid effort. Work-shy and pleasure-bent, he governed Britain by correspondence, moving about the Home Counties stag-hunting, bear-baiting, horse-racing and banqueting – only dropping in to London for a few days at a time. Though he had a quick and penetrating mind, he was too much under the sway of his emotions to resist the flattery of courtiers, and he was putty in the hands of men he loved, such as CARR and BUCKINGHAM. 'The King,' wrote Sir John Oglander, 'loved young men, his favourites, better than women, loving them beyond the love of men to women. I never yet saw any fond husband make so much or so great dalliance over his beautiful spouse as I have seen King James over his favourites, especially Buckingham.' And thus it was James himself, and his manner of life, that roused the opposition of the ruling classes, rather than his views on Gov, which were part of the intellectual furniture of Europe at that time. Instead of concentrating on getting his way over particular issues, he irritated an unnecessarily broad spectrum of opinion by reiterating his divine-right views in broad theoretical generalizations, such as in his well-known speech to the H of C on 21 Mar 1610, when he said: 'The state of monarchy is the supremest thing upon earth; for kings are not only God's lieutenants upon earth, and sit upon God's throne, but even by God himself they are called gods.' His reign divides into 2 periods: 1603–12, when Salisbury's leadership restrained decay, and 1613–25, when the rule of favourites brought deterioration.

1603–12: As Principal Sec from the start of the reign and Ld Treasurer from 1608, Salisbury supervised all aspects of Gov, but he was not able to prevent the growth of distrust between K and Parl. For one thing, he could not control the actions or the words of the K; for another, as a member of the H of L, he could no longer manipulate the business of the Commons as Elizabeth and her ministers had done, and, in the absence of Gov leadership, opposition spokesmen made the running. Accustomed since the REFORMATION under HENRY VIII to participate in Gov, the H of C had by this time developed efficient procedures and an *esprit de corps*, and its members had grown wealthy, confident and assertive, as Elizabeth often discovered. The 1st Parl (Mar 1604–Feb 1611) clashed with the K over its privileges, over the Ch, and over the revenue. Foreign policy was not at this stage a burning issue, and the K's skirmishes with COKE and the Common-Law Courts were still separate from the Parl struggle. The privileges of the H of C were involved in a clash over the Buck selection (*Goodwin v Fortescue*, 1604) in which the H of C in practice confirmed its privilege of deciding upon disputed elections. In the Church, the H of C took up the case for further reform. The

K at first dealt sympathetically with the Puritans, responding to their Millenary Petition of 1603 for moderate reform with the Hampton Court Conference (Jan 1604), losing his temper only briefly in defence of Bps – 'No bishop, no king,' he shouted – and setting up a team of 54 scholars to provide a new translation of the Bible (the Authorized Version, 1611). Unfortunately, the enforcement of Convocation's Canons of 1604 by Archbp BANCROFT led to the expulsion of about 90 Puritan clergy from their livings; and MPs supported the Puritan grievances and demands for reform, and objected to the Canons of 1604 as a non-parl change in the law and an invasion of Englishmen's rights. Shortly after, the GUNPOWDER PLOT (5 Nov 1605) caused Parl to demand strict enforcement of the laws against Caths, to whom MPs suspected James was sympathetic. The revenue was inadequate to meet James's needs partly because of inherited circumstances – Q Elizabeth's debt, the mounting costs of Gov, the inflation, the out-of-date tax assessments, and the refusal of Parl to vote extraordinary revenue for ordinary peace-time purposes – but partly also because of the indulgent way he showered gifts on his favourites who lined the pockets of their relatives and friends. Incapable of cutting James's expenditure, Salisbury increased his income – to the annoyance of the parl classes – by the Great Farm of the customs (1604), by seeking out concealed alienated royal estates, by discovering old debts to the Crown, by more efficient admin of the royal domain, by a new Book of Rates for the customs, and by impositions. The decision of the Court of Exchequer in Bate's Case (July 1606), that the Gov could impose extra customs duties – impositions – without recourse to Parl if the purpose was not to raise revenue but to regulate trade, was seized on to raise revenue from a wide range of imports, causing a running battle with Parl for the rest of the reign. Very sharp words were uttered on both sides in the session of Feb–July 1610. It was not simply that James had neglected to manage the H of C through a 'front bench' of councillors: his provocative phraseology and outbursts of rage disarmed would-be supporters, and allowed the extremists to take the bit between their teeth. As a result, Salisbury's statesmanlike scheme to replace purveyance, wardship and other feudal irritants, by an annual Parl grant – the Great Contract, 1610 – failed to pass the House before the K dissolved Parl.

James's foreign policy of peaceful neutrality fed his illusion that he was the great European father-figure reconciling the warring powers and creeds, and did not antagonize important sections of opinion at this stage. On the one hand there was peace with Spain (Tr of London, Aug 1604), mediation between Spain and Holland (12-year Tr, Apr 1609), and tentative discussions of a Spanish marriage for Pr Henry; balanced, on the other, by James's association with the alliance created by K HENRY IV of France in the Jülich-Cleves Succession Crisis (1609–14), his alliance with the German Prot Union (Apr 1612), and the marriage of his daughter, Elizabeth, to Frederick V, the Elector Palatine in Feb 1613. The Common-Law Courts, under their leader Coke, opposed the High Commission and other prerogative courts (but not the Star Chamber), and rejected James's high view of the powers of the Crown as supreme law-maker, exemplified in his claim that 'Kings are properly judges, and judgment properly belongs to them from God: for kings sit in the throne of God and thence all judgment is derived.' Such a remark was typical of James's words rather than his deeds, and in practice he always kept scrupulously within the bounds of the Common Law. He eventually dismissed Coke for his opposition (Nov 1616); but this struggle was as yet only parallel to the struggle with the H of C. The two did not fuse until Coke became an opposition MP in the 3rd Parl (1621–2).

1613–25: saw James entering upon premature senility and possibly suffering from porphyria. He not only slobbered in public over 2 handsome favourites in turn – Carr and Buckingham – but also allowed them to filch supreme political power, an indulgence which had disastrous consequences for the Crown's solvency and its relations with Parl. And these two defects brought impotence in foreign policy. In foreign affairs James continued his pacific role and sought to balance his daughter's marriage to a German Prot with his son CHARLES's marriage to a prss from Cath Spain, a fantasy which possessed the added attraction that her dowry would save the Crown from bankruptcy. He was encouraged in the pursuit of this mirage by the Howard faction which dominated the Court until 1618 and then by Buckingham who replaced them. The persuasive Count Gondomar, Spanish ambassador to London 1613–18 and 1620–22, and carousing companion of the K, craftily encouraged James in his delusions, though it was most unlikely that the Spanish K would ever sacrifice his daughter to a heretic land. Moreover, James persisted in his pro-Spanish stance even after the outbreak of the THIRTY YEARS WAR (1618–48), when he should have refashioned his strategy. At a time when powerful interests in England were clamouring for the kind of sea-going, colonial crusade against Spain that characterized the reign of Elizabeth I, James still imagined that it would be possible not only to persuade Spain to restore the Rhenish Palatinate to his son-in-law, Frederick, but also to coax Spain to cajole the HR Emp into doing the same with the Upper Palatinate. This foreign policy had unfortunate repercussions on his relations with the Ch, on his revenues, and on Parl. In the Ch, the pro-Spanish alignment aroused the suspicion that James was a crypto-Cath, especially when he executed RALEGH in deference to Spanish wishes (29 Oct 1618). Furthermore, Puritan consciences were upset by the Book of Sports of May 1618, which allowed certain recreations on Sundays after divine service. They particularly disliked having to read out these concessions from the pulpit. On the other hand, it must be said that the appointment of the mildly Puritan ABBOT as Archbp of Canterbury (Mar 1611) did have a calming effect on religious controversy. The revenues were totally inadequate for an active foreign policy, especially one that Parl opposed and refused grants for. In consequence, James fell back on more and more dubious financial expedients. He sold monopolies, royal lands, offices and peerages. The new title of 'baronet' was created for quick sale at £1,095 a time, till the market became saturated. He also continued to collect impositions without Parl approval; and embarked on the Cockayne Project (1614–15) – a scheme of the dubious financier, Alderman Sir William Cockayne, to raise customs revenues by granting him the right to export dyed cloth instead of undyed, which the Merchant Adventurers had monopolized hitherto. The project failed and had to be abandoned. Ld Treasurer CRANFIELD could have reformed the revenues, but James lacked the grit to force painful measures through – for reform was possible only at the expense of his favourites and their satellites who battened on corruption. 'If I were to begin to punish those who take bribes,' he said, 'I should soon not have a single subject left.' Parl, to which James had desperate recourse, would vote revenue only if it could control the men who spent it and the purposes for which it was spent: in other words, if it could intervene in foreign policy, and in the appointment (or, more strictly, the dismissal) of ministers. The 2nd Parl (Apr–June 1614) came to be called the Addled Parl as it passed no measures. It refused to vote taxes till its grievances had been redressed, among which impositions loomed large, as well as the deprived clergy of 1604, and the accusation (untrue) that the Court had influenced the elections on an unusually large scale. The 3rd Parl (Jan 1621–Jan 1622) revived the medieval procedure of impeachment, not used since 1449, to bring down first of all the monopolists, Mompesson and Mitchell – satellites of Buckingham – and then Ld Chancellor BACON on a charge of bribery. It also criticized the Spanish marriage policy, causing a wrangle in which the K forbade them to meddle in the affair. Parl protested at this abridgement of its 'ancient liberty', but James replied that their privileges were not an 'ancient right' but only 'derived from the grace and permission of our ancestors and us'. Parl's reply was the Protestation of 18 Dec 1621, asserting that its privileges were 'the ancient and undoubted birthright and inheritance of the subjects of England'. James tore it out of the H of C Journals with his own hands on 30 Dec 1621. Buckingham and Pr Charles then made their marriage expedition to Madrid (Feb–Oct 1623), the failure of which brought about a complete reversal of policy and war against Spain, which in its turn meant the calling of the 4th Parl (Feb 1624–Mar 1625). James formed alliances with Holland and Denmark, and an expedition under Mansfeld was dispatched to intervene in the Danish War phase of the Thirty Years War – an ill-equipped rabble, three-quarters of which perished while still aboard ship off Flushing – thanks to Parl's refusal to finance a land war. By this time, the besotted K had abandoned affairs to his favourite and his heir. He allowed Parl to debate foreign policy, to vote revenue on condition it was spent as Parl wished, to pass the Monopolies Act (1624) making monopolies illegal except in the case of new inventions, and to bring down a minister by impeaching Cranfield, the opponent of the war and the enemy of extravagance. It would be inaccurate to picture Parl under James as embarking on a revolutionary career, for that would be to anticipate the next reign. Under him, however, the vices of the Stuart system of Gov were fully exposed to view. Parl already had the intention of reforming them, and the appropriate weapons had been found.

James VII and II (14 Oct 1633–6 Sept 1701) K of Great Britain and Ireland (1685) who tried to turn the country into a Cath absolutism, and consequently lost his throne in the REVOLUTION OF 1688.

2nd son of K CHARLES I and his Q consort, Henrietta Maria; ed in the arduous times of the CIVIL WAR, and then (1648 onwards) in exile abroad where he fought in the French and Spanish armies.

As D of York under the rule of his eld brother, CHARLES II, he m 1st (1660) his pregnant mistress, Anne Hyde, daughter of CLARENDON (d 1671 leaving 2 children: the future Q Mary II and Q ANNE); m 2nd (by proxy, 1673) Maria Beatrice d'Este, daughter of Alfonso IV, D of Modena – a wedding negotiated by France, by which he had 1 son, James Edward, the Old Pretender. Slow, dull-witted, solemn and humourless, he lacked the flexible pragmatism of his eld brother. He was crippled in the world of politics by the sincerity with which he held his beliefs and the honesty with which he expressed them. He stood firm to the principles he had picked up in his youth: devotion to his father's memory and to the Catholicism and absolutism he so admired in France and Spain. He was convinced that rigid authoritarianism was the only way to deal with the English Parls and their Dissenting allies. During the reign of his brother, as Ld High Admiral, he presided over the expansion of the fleet and the reform of its admin and training which made this period a turning-point in naval history. He commanded the fleet during the 2nd and 3rd Anglo-Dutch Wars (1665–7, 1672–4), showing courageous leadership, if not brilliant strategy; and he continued to work closely with the Admiralty even after the Test Act drove him from his offices (June 1673) and into temporary exile in Brussels and Scotland. Received into the Cath Ch in 1669, he had ceased to attend Anglican communion from Easter 1672 onwards; since he was the heir to the throne he became the centre of the political storm brought on by the POPISH PLOT and the Exclusion Crisis (1678–81), though in the end K Charles outmanoeuvred his Whig enemy, the Earl of SHAFTESBURY.

As K of Great Britain and Ireland his programme expanded from an early hope of securing toleration for Caths, into a wholesale scheme of establishing absolute rule and the Catholic Ch, if necessary by violence. At first he inherited the popularity which Charles II had ultimately won for the monarchy, as was shown by the generosity with which his Parl (May 1685–July 1687, but prorogued Nov 1685) granted him the largest revenue of any Stuart, and by the absence of any support for the invasion of Argyle in Scotland (June 1685) and that of MONMOUTH in SW England (June–July 1685). When this Parl objected to his appointment of Cath officers in the army (which he was enlarging and re-organizing on French lines, and training in summer camps on Blackheath and Hounslow Heath), he prorogued it; and during 1686 he embarked on a programme of 'closeting' – attempting to persuade Anglican clergy and Tory politicians, as well as Prss Mary and Prss Anne, to join with him in swaying Parl to repeal the Test Act and the Penal Laws. At the same time he used his dispensing power to promote Caths in the civil service, local Gov and Oxford and Cambridge, as well as the armed forces. In the collusive action of *Godden v Hales* (June 1686) a purged Court of K's Bench gave legal recognition to this use of the dispensing power. Moreover, to tame the Anglicans he created the Commission for Ecclesiastical Causes (July 1686), in spite of the fact that prerogative courts had been banned by the Long Parl in 1641; and one of the uses to which he put it was to expel the Fellows of Magdalen, Oxford, and turn the college into a Cath institution (1687). Further radical measures followed during that year: a break with the Anglicans and Tories, and an alliance with the Dissenters. At Court, Rochester and Clarendon and their supporters were dimissed (Jan 1687), leaving SUNDERLAND and the Caths dominant. In Ireland, the Cath Earl of Tyrconnel was made Ld Deputy (Jan 1687) and the traditional pro-Prot policies reversed. Advised by William Penn, the Quaker leader – who thought that Anglicans were a bigger danger to Dissent than Caths – James issued the 1st Declaration of Indulgence (Apr 1687), suspending the operation of the Penal Laws in favour of both Caths and Dissenters. On 2 July 1687 he dissolved Parl, and embarked on the operation central to all his efforts: the election – in alliance with Dissenters, Caths and ex-Whigs against Anglicans and Tories – of a packed Parl which would do his will. Under Sunderland's central control, he used paid agents led by Robert

Brent and Sir Nicholas Butler to canvass the gentry in the counties and the middle classes in the boroughs, to fill the offices of Ld Lieut, Deputy Lieut and J P with supporters, and to remodel the admin of the boroughs. The aim was the election of a Parl which would rubber-stamp his programme and give legal recognition to centralized absolutism. Moreover, with the pregnancy of the Q (Sept 1687) his religious plan grew more ambitious. He no longer limited himself to making the Cath position secure in the reigns of his Prot heirs, Mary and Anne; for a male heir could make Cath rule permanent and the reCatholicization of England possible. In this campaign, James was appealing to social groups below the nobility and gentry – the 'natural' local leaders – to middle-class Dissenters and erstwhile Whigs, the same groups from which Shaftesbury had formed the original Whig party, and using the same methods. James found the boroughs co-operative, but the counties resistant.

In Apr 1688 he reissued the Declaration of Indulgence, instructing the Bps to order all clergy to read it to their congregations on 2 successive Sundays. Seven Bps petitioned against it (May 1688); and he lodged them in the Tower and tried them for seditious libel. It was essentially a trial of his use of the suspending power, and the acquittal of the Bps amid popular rejoicing (30 June 1688) was a serious blow to his cause. Moreover, the birth of a male heir, James Edward, on 10 June 1688 had already transformed the situation. The Cath threat was no longer limited to James's lifetime, but stretched forward indefinitely into the future. On the day of the acquittal, the famous all-party Invitation was dispatched to William of Orange, signed by 4 who could be called Whigs (Admiral Edward Russell, Henry Sidney, the 4th Earl of Devonshire and the 12th Earl of Shrewsbury) and by 3 who could be called Tories (the Earl of DANBY, Baron Lumley and Henry Compton, Bp of London). It was an association rather than an invitation, for William had already decided to invade England. Once James realized this, and found the initiative snatched from him, he went to pieces. He called a halt to all his preparations, in a desperate effort to rally support – which made him seem all the more devious. The election was called off (Sept 1688); the Ecclesiastical Commission was abolished (Oct 1688); London had its old charter restored (Oct 1688); Magdalen had its Fellows restored (Oct 1688); the attack on the borough charters was suspended (Oct 1688). It was all too late, however, and, when William landed at Torbay, Devon (5/15 Nov 1688) and began his stately advance on London, the local risings in his favour (eg Ld Delamere rose in Cheshire on 15 Nov, the Earl of Devonshire seized Nottingham on 21 Nov, Danby took York on 22 Nov) and the defections from the army (eg that of John Churchill, the future MARLBOROUGH on 24 Nov), as well as the flight from London of Prss Anne on 25 Nov, showed how far James had alienated the nobility and gentry. He advanced as far as Salisbury, Wilts, to meet William (19 Nov 1688); retreated back to London (26 Nov); issued a proclamation for a Parl and a general pardon (28 Nov); sent the Q and his son to France (9 Dec); followed himself on the night of 10/11 Dec, but, being recognized at Faversham, Kent, was brought back to London. William allowed him to make a 2nd and successful escape on 23 Dec, and he landed at Ambleteuse, Pas de Calais, on 25 Dec 1688, to become a pensioner of Louis XIV. In England, the Bill of Rights declared that James had abdicated the throne, and offered it to William and Mary. From France, James landed in Ireland with French troops in Mar 1690 in an unsuccessful campaign to regain his throne, marked by the heroic success of Londonderry in withstanding a long siege (Apr–July/Aug 1690), and James's defeat by William at the battle of the R Boyne (1/11 July 1690), after which he hurriedly returned to France and a pension of a million *livres* a year from Louis XIV. There he remained till his death, gloomy and penitent, and mystified by the ways of God, whose agent he believed he was.

Jesuits (Society of Jesus) A new religious order of priests who became the shock-troops of the COUNTER-REFORMATION. Founded by Ignatius LOYOLA and his 8 companions in the Chapel of St Denis, Montmartre, Paris (15 Aug 1534), the Order received papal recognition in PAUL III's Bull *Regimini militantis ecclesiae* (27 Sept 1540). Unlike the semi-democratic medieval orders, the Society of Jesus had an absolutist structure (based on Loyola's *Constitutions*, 1547–50) in which the members owed unquestioning obedience to the Gen – the 1st of whom, with great reluctance, was Loyola himself (Apr 1541). Whether as scholars, preachers, confessors, secondary-school teachers, or univ lecturers, the Jesuits rapidly exercised a profound influence on Italy, Spain, Portugal, S Germany and Austria, as well as sending out missionaries to N and S America, India, the Philippines, China and Japan. Unencumbered by monastic dress or the need to chant offices, they mixed freely in the world and were modern in their methods. Their schools were soon opened to laymen as well as seminarists. They taught humanistic subjects, and used competition rather than punishment as a means of stimulating effort. They shaped the outlook of the ruling classes in all Cath countries. Many of them became confessors to Ks and thus had their say in diplomacy and Gov. Their success aroused the hostility of Dominicans, Jansenists and others, who accused them of being too permissive towards the weaknesses of the masses (encouraging their semi-pagan carnivals etc) and too accommodating towards the worldly necessities of the time and place in which they worked – eg, adjusting Christianity to suit the Chinese outlook. They were expelled from Portugal (1759), France (1764) and Spain (1767); and under pressure from these States Pp Clement XIV suppressed the Order on 21 July 1773. The Order was revived by Pp Pius VII on 7 Aug 1814.

John of Austria, Don (24 Feb 1545–1 Oct 1578) Spanish general and admiral, who defeated the Turkish fleet at Lepanto, but who was unsuccessful as Gov-Gen during the REVOLT OF THE NETHERLANDS.

Illegitimate son of the Emp CHARLES V and Barbara Blomberg, a burgher's daughter; ed in Spain at Alcalá and at Court; recognized by K PHILIP II as his half-brother in 1559, he was appointed C-in-C of the Spanish navy in 1568 and then in Mar 1569 given command (under the supervision of Requesens, which he resented) of the troops suppressing the revolt of the Moriscos in Granada (Dec 1568–May 1570). After supervising the forceful removal of the Moriscos from Granada, he was given command – still under Requesens – of the fleet of the Holy League of Spain, Venice and the Pp, which more or less destroyed the Turkish navy off Lepanto on 7 Oct 1571. On the break-up of the League, Philip decided to attack Islam in N Africa, and Don John, sailing across from Sicily, conquered Tunis fairly easily (Oct 1573) – rather uselessly leaving a garrison there which soon capitulated to the Turks (Sept 1574). In Nov 1576 Don John arrived in the Netherlands to take up his new post as Gov-Gen, left vacant by the death of Requesens on 5 Mar 1576. By now an attractive and glamorous hero celebrated for his victories over Turkey, he was out to compensate for his illegitimacy by winning a throne. His plan was to invade England, rescue MARY, Q OF SCOTS and marry her, and replace Q ELIZABETH I on the throne; but, dashing and impetuous as he was, he was too naïve to worst Philip II and his wily secretary, PÉREZ, who were writing quite a different scenario for him. His instructions were to be as conciliatory as possible to the Netherlands, except, of course, in the key matters of Spanish sovereignty and the RC religious monopoly. Unwillingly, then, this soldier signed the Eternal Edict with the S nobles (Feb 1577); but, impatient of peace-making, he suddenly captured Namur on 24 July 1577, jettisoning thereby what confidence the S had in him. The States-Gen rejected him as Gov-Gen and accepted the Archd MATTHIAS instead. His reply was to attack and defeat the N army at Gembloux, Brabant on 31 Jan 1578. Meanwhile, he had sent his secretary, Juan de Escobedo, to Madrid to plead for authority and troops for a more warlike policy. Pérez, the leader of the doves, persuaded Philip that Don John, led astray by Escobedo, was about to commit treason. Philip approved of the murder of Escobedo in the streets of Madrid on 31 Mar 1578, though when Don John d of typhus near Namur a few months later and his papers became available, Philip realized that he had made a mistake, and that Don John was no traitor.

John II Casimir Vasa (22 Mar 1609–16 Dec 1672) K of Poland (1648–68), under whom the constitutional powers of the magnates blocked all moves for strengthening the monarchy and thus hindered his attempts to defend Poland from the invasions of Russia, Sweden, Transylvania and the Crimean Tatars – to such an extent that he abdicated.

Younger son of K SIGISMUND III and his 2nd wife, Constance of Styria; saw military service with the Habsburgs (1635 onwards), and became a Jesuit novice and a Card before being elected K on the death of his brother, WLADYSLAW IV; m his brother's widow, Marie Louise de Gonzague-Nevers (d 1667), who brought a French dowry and considerable diplomatic intervention in Polish affairs by LOUIS XIV. At home and abroad he faced overwhelming problems – known in Polish tradition as 'the deluge' – but he lacked the force and decisiveness to solve them.

At home, the Gov deteriorated, the monarchy becoming more limited, and the admin becoming more decentralized, than under his predecessors. In 1652 occurred the 1st use of the *liberum veto*, when the adverse vote of one member of the Seym (Diet) dissolved it. A reform group introduced plans in 1659 for changing to a two-third's majority system of voting with a secret ballot, and for setting up a regular means of taxing the nobility, but with no success. Similarly, plans to elect a new K during the lifetime of the old – supported by Louis XIV who hoped to have a French K of Poland – were rejected as tending towards absolute – even hereditary – monarchy. The opponents were supported by Austria and Brandenburg, who had no wish to see a strong Polish monarchy. One magnate, Jerzy Lubomirski, felt justified in mounting an armed rebellion (1665–6) against these threats to his 'Golden Freedom'. In other words, the K was helpless before the magnates with their latifundia, their vast labour force of serfs, their clientage networks of gentry, their private armies, and their political control over the prov diets, the Seym and the ministries. In the Ch, the Cath hierarchy were the best organized pressure-group in the country, and the COUNTER-REFORMATION continued to prosper. It was helped by the devastating Swedish invasion (1655–60), which was seen by the pious as a visitation from God for harbouring Prots, and during which Protestantism came to be identified with treason. In the middle of the crisis, John Casimir solemnly dedicated himself and his Kdom to the Virgin Mary; while the Seym banished one Prot sect – the Socinians (Unitarians) – in 1658, and in 1668 imposed the death penalty on Caths who became Prots. In the economy, Poland fell from her earlier prosperity, though it is a disputed point whether 'the Deluge' was the cause, or whether Poland's role as a producer of grain, timber and other raw materials in exchange for the industrial and colonial products of the W was a long-term drain, enriching businessmen in England, Holland and Sweden, and benefiting Polish magnates, but impoverishing Polish merchants, artisans and peasants. In John Casimir's time the grain exports down the Vistula dwindled, the population fell, the currency was debased, the cities declined and enserfment spread.

Abroad, his problems were triggered off by an internal revolt which had begun just before he became K. The Cossack Rebellion (1648–57) of Bohdan Chmielnicki was serious enough as a Polish affair, stirring religious and national minorities into violence as well as infecting Polish peasants and townsmen, but catastrophic as an international conflict. The Ukrainian Cossacks had long been restive as the tide of Polish colonization crept over their steppes, regimenting their freedom-loving brotherhood, enserfing the peasants and persecuting the Orthodox; and disappointment with the policies of Wladyslaw IV brought them out in open rebellion in 1648. In Chmielnicki the Cossacks chose a Hetman (leader) with burning grievances of his own against the agent of a Polish magnate who had confiscated his property and his wife – but also with the vision and skill to play off Poland, Russia, Sweden, Turkey and the Crimean Tatars against one another in an attempt to elevate the Ukraine into a sovereign State. Starting in Apr 1648 in alliance with the Tatars, he invaded Poland from his base on the lower Dnieper, beating John Casimir's troops at Zólty Wody, Korsuń (6/16 May 1648) and Pilawce (11–13/21–23 Sept 1648), and raising mass revolts in his wake. Then, abandoned by the Tatars, he made the Tr of Zborow (Aug 1649) with John Casimir, the new K, who was ready to compromise. War then restarted, and Chmielnicki, with the fickle Tatars once more not pulling their weight – they did not want the Cossacks to be too successful – was defeated at Beresteczko (18–20/28–30 June 1651). As a result he sought help from ALEXIS of Russia, with whom he had been negotiating since June 1648 and on whom he now applied pressure by threatening to join up with Turkey. By the Tr of Perejaslaw (Pereyaslavl) (Jan 1654), the Ukrainian Cossacks were incorporated into Russia, but allowed to keep their form of Gov, legal system, social structure and other peculiarities. The Russian War (1654–6) immediately followed as Alexis took Smolensk (Oct 1654) and other towns, penetrating deep into Poland and Lithuania. However, when the Northern War (1655–60) broke out, Russia decided to make peace (Tr of Vilno, Oct/Nov 1656) in order to concentrate on CHARLES X GUSTAV of Sweden. By the Tr, Poland lost much of White and Little Russia. The Northern War (1655–60) – 'the Deluge' – submerged Poland as Charles X himself conquered W Poland and the Vistula valley, taking Poznań, Warsaw (29 Aug/8 Sept 1655), and Cracow, while another army invaded Lithuania from Riga, Livonia. The self-centred Polish magnates were ready to save their own skins at any cost, even the integrity of Poland, and many (eg Boguslaw Radziwill of Lithuania) accepted Charles as their sovereign, while John Casimir fled into Habsburg Silesia. The K returned in Jan 1656 to head a national revival of disillusioned magnates and Cath masses against the Swedish Prots. He retook Warsaw (20/30 June 1656) but lost it again after a 3-day battle against Charles X, now joined by FREDERICK WILLIAM the Great Elector of Brandenburg (18–20/28–30 July 1656). György II Rákóczy, Pr of Transylvania – a Calvinist who expected the 2nd Coming, and hoped it would make him K of Poland – invaded with Cossack help (1657) but had to turn back at Warsaw with his army in shreds, and Charles himself at this stage had to abandon Poland. The war had widened as Denmark attacked Sweden, and John Casimir made alliances with Denmark, Austria and Holland, and in the Tr of Welaw (Wehlau) (Sept 1657) got Brandenburg's help in return for recognizing the Great Elector as sovereign in E Prussia and no longer his vassal. The sudden death of Charles X (23 Feb 1660) allowed the Tr of Oliva (Apr/May 1660) to be signed between Sweden on one side, and Poland, Brandenburg and the Emp on the other. Sweden gave up her conquests in Poland; John Casimir renounced his claim to the Swedish throne (which he had inherited from Sigismund III); Brandenburg was recognized as sovereign of E Prussia. The Russian War (1658–67) broke out again when Alexis made peace with Sweden (Tr of Kardis, June 1661) in order to consolidate his hold on the Ukraine; but peace became essential here also when it became clear to the mutually exhausted combatants that the Cossacks, who had no real wish to become full Russian subjects, were joining up with Turkey against them both. By the Tr of Andruszów (Andrussovo) (Jan/Feb 1667) Poland regained some of her losses of Vilno, but had to give up Smolensk and the E bank of the Dnieper, as well as Kiev on the W bank. The 2 powers – with Russia the stronger, a great change since the TIME OF TROUBLES – now planned a joint defence against Turkey. A Cossack–Tatar invasion was stopped by Hetman John III Sobieski (the future K) at Podhajce (1667) – the prelude to much bigger Turkish onslaughts. Distressed by his failure and the death of his wife, John Casimir abdicated (16 Sept 1668) and lived in France where Louis XIV gave him the revenues of 8 abbeys. He d at Nevers. That his Kdom survived his reign without being shared out among its neighbours was due less to him than to the rivalries between the would-be partitioners.

John George I (5 Mar 1585–8 Oct 1656) El of Saxony (1611), who attempted to follow a middle course during the THIRTY YEARS WAR, between the Emp and the Prs, and between the Caths and the Prots, and who tried to prevent foreign powers intervening in Germany. Had he pursued that course in a statesmanlike way, Germany might have been spared much of the War; but he was indolent, inept and out for what he could get, though as honest as it is possible for a ruler in his circumstances to be. Under his Gov Saxony ceased to be the leading German State, ceding that place to the Brandenburg of FREDERICK WILLIAM I, the Great Elector.

Younger son of the El Christian I, and brother of the El Christian II; ed as a

Lutheran; m 1st (1604) Sibylla Elizabeth of Württemberg (d 1606); m 2nd (1607) Magdalena Sibylla of Brandenburg (d 1669). Hard-drinking, irresolute and acquisitive, he was not fitted by character or policy to be the leader of the German Prots during the Thirty Years War – a role which the great power of Saxony thrust upon him. During the Bohemian and Palatinate Wars (1618–23) he supported the Emp, invading Lusatia and Silesia; for, though a German Pr, he opposed rebellion against the Emp's authority, and, as a Lutheran, he hated the Calvinists and, in any case, could not sit idly by while Frederick V, the El Palatine, became also the K of Bohemia – and thus the greatest Prot power. Moreover, the Emp had also promised him Lusatia. During the Danish War (1624–9), he again followed his bent of loyalty to the Emp and hostility to foreign interference; but during the period of the Emperor's pride and fall (1629–30) he backed the other Prs in objecting to WALLENSTEIN's pretensions and the Edict of Restitution at the Regensburg Electors' Meeting (July–Aug 1630). During the Swedish War (1630–35), he again refused to support foreign interference in German affairs. At the Leipzig Meeting of Prot Prs and cities (Feb–Apr 1631) he tried to form a 3rd force between the Emp and Sweden, a project which foundered on FERDINAND II's refusal to withdraw the Edict of Restitution. John George nevertheless refused to join GUSTAV ADOLF's invading Swedish army until the invasion of his State by Tilly and the Cath forces made him reluctantly change his mind. He allied with Sweden by the Tr of Coswig of Sept 1631; and the joint armies defeated Tilly at Breitenfeld on 7/17 Sept 1631, though John George galloped off the field in mid-battle. While Gustav Adolf was sweeping through SW Germany to the upper Rhine, the Saxon army invaded Bohemia and took Prague from Wallenstein on 10 Oct 1631, and with John George's approval its general, Arnim, engaged in secret peace negotiations with the enemy. When Wallenstein was recalled to command the Emp's army, however, he drove the Saxons out of Prague (25 May 1632) and invaded Saxony itself, where at Lützen on 6/16 Nov 1632 the Swedish army defeated him, though Gustav Adolf was killed. At this juncture John George tried to negotiate a German peace settlement, but he was out-manoeuvred by the dead K of Sweden's Chancellor, OXENSTIERNA, who rallied the Prot side into the League of Heilbronn (13/23 Apr 1633). When this was defeated by the Cath armies at Nördlingen on 26–7 July/ 5–6 Aug 1634, however, John George helped to break up the League by abandoning his allies in a separate peace with the Emp – the Tr of Prague (May 1635), which confirmed him in the possession of Lusatia and ceded the Archbpric of Magdeburg to one of his sons. During the Franco-Habsburg War (1635–48), John George continued his dilatory policy of appeasing whichever side was in a position to inflict the most damage on him. He supported the Emp (1635–45) during the period when Sweden regained control of N Germany and defeated a joint army of imperialists and Saxons at Wittstock, Brandenburg, on 4 Oct 1636. When the Swedes invaded Saxony, John George abandoned the Emp and made a truce with Sweden in Sept 1645. By the Trs of Westphalia he kept Lusatia, but not Magdeburg. This went to Brandenburg, now taking Saxony's leading place in German politics.

Joseph I (26 July 1678–17 Apr 1711) Head of the Austrian Monarchy (1705) and H R Emp (1705) during the War of the Spanish Succession against LOUIS XIV.

Eld son of LEOPOLD I and his 3rd wife, Eleanora Magdalena of Pfalz-Neuburg; m (1699) Wilhelmina Amalia of Brunswick-Lüneburg (d 1742). Talented musically like several of his family, but more cheerful and worldly and less Jesuit-ridden than most Habsburgs, he spent his short reign subduing the Hungarian rebellion (1703–11) under Ferencz II Rákóczi, and fighting in the War of the Spanish Succession (1702–13/14). His sudden death from smallpox transformed the war situation, for his younger brother – whom the allies were fighting for as K 'Charles III' of Spain – became the Emp CHARLES VI; and the allies, who had hitherto fought to keep France and Spain separate, could not now be expected to upset the balance of power by allowing Spain to join Austria.

Joseph II (13 Mar 1741–20 Feb 1790) Co-Regent with MARIA THERESA of the Austrian Monarchy (1765), HREmp (1765), Head of the Austrian Monarchy (1780), a leading ENLIGHTENED ABSOLUTIST, who abroad pursued an expansionist policy which alerted rival powers and failed; and at home tried to frog-march Austria into modernity with a revolution from above, which antagonized traditionalists, and kindled the radicals, to such a degree that it had to be abandoned.

Eld son of Maria Theresa and her husband, Francis Stephen, D of Lorraine and future HREmp Francis I; ed by strict tutors who crammed him with information in preparation for his future career; m 1st (1760) Isabella, Dss of Parma, whom he loved deeply and whose early death (1763) embittered him; m 2nd (1765) Maria Josepha of Bavaria, whom he treated with contempt (d 1767). Gifted intellectually, hungry for power and well-read in politics and economics, he drove himself to an early grave, and expected similar self-sacrifice from ministers and civil servants. He was an over-clever, short-tempered, sharp-tongued autocrat. Logic was his guiding star, and if his methods were despotic, in his view it was nature, not himself, that was the tyrant. He was too unworldly and philosophical; he adopted a take-it-or-leave-it attitude towards his subjects whose co-operation he should have invited; and he was naïve in his over-estimation of what rulers can do to change things as they are. He aimed to perfect the machinery of centralized absolutism in Austria, eliminate all the peculiarities of language and religion, custom and habit, locality and class, with which history had littered the monarchy; and mobilize Austria's resources to the full, and achieve European dominance – his prime object. During the Co-Regency (*see* MARIA THERESA) his mother kept his feet near the ground; after her death he was at the mercy of theory.

At home in Austria-Bohemia he issued long edicts from his desk at the average rate of 2 a day. (a) The gov of these provs was streamlined in the interests of economy. In the capital, the *Staatsrat* (Council of State) was reduced from 6 to 4; while the Treasury was merged with the United Chancellery, which itself was reorganized into 13 departments. In the provs, neighbouring *Gubernia* (Govs) were joined together, thus halving their number. The permanent committees of the Diets were suspended, and their work given to civil servants (1783). Municipalities lost their independence and were brought under the purview of the bureaucrats. Dossiers were kept on àll civil servants, and the police spied on them on the Crown's behalf. (b) Law reform continued. The Order of Civil Procedure (1 May 1781) enlarged the powers of the State to protect the masses against the privileged, by supervising the judgments of the manor, municipal and Ch courts. Appeal courts were provided at local and prov level, all under the Supreme Office of Justice at Vienna. The 1st volume of the new Civil Code appeared in Nov 1786; while criminal justice was improved by the Penal Code (1781) and the Code of Criminal Procedure (1788). The death penalty was abolished, except in the army. Joseph considered that a flogging followed by hard labour was more productive. (c) The Ch also underwent Joseph's scrutiny to eliminate waste. Economic motives were behind the Patent of Toleration (Oct 1781), which gave civil equality and freedom of worship to Lutherans, Calvinists and Orthodox Christians, so long as their services were held discreetly. All purely contemplative monasteries not engaged in educational or welfare work were dissolved and their property sold to form a fund (the *Religionsfond*) with which Joseph reorganized the Ch. Foreign bishops lost their authority inside Austria; large dioceses were divided up; new parishes were marked out: the whole reform aiming to provide each person with a Ch not more than one hour's walk from home. Joseph was less concerned with salvation after death than with behaviour during life; and he took the education of the clergy out of episcopal and monastic hands, and gave it to State-run Gen Seminaries, which trained priests as public servants, charged with the duty of moulding upright and hard-working citizens. The Emp interfered also in the minutiae of religious life. Holidays, processions and pilgrimages were cut, as they wasted time and labour. Music, candles, images – all came under Joseph's scrutiny. He introduced civil marriage; allowed the interment of Prots, Jews and suicides in the cemeteries; ordered burials to be in sacks instead of extravagant coffins. Moreover, further limits were placed on papal power inside the monarchy, and even the visit of Pp Pius VI to Vienna in 1782 – the 1st descent of a Pp on Germany since 1414 – failed to modify Joseph's strong regalism. (d) In education he continued his mother's policy, though in a more utilitarian manner. He encouraged practical knowledge, not pure science or fine arts. All univs except 4 were reduced to the rank of high-school; and univ admissions were made to fit vacancies in the civil service. (e) The censorship of the press was used by Joseph to encourage the Enlightened views of the middle-class intellectuals – journalists, univ teachers and bureaucrats – who provided him with arguments against the traditionalism of his chief opponents, the nobility and clergy. (f) The social order of lord and serf was one of the chief objects of his reforms. He wished to improve the legal and economic position of the peasantry so as to boost their productivity and thus their taxable capacity. The Patent to Abolish Serfdom (1781) freed serfs to marry as they wished, leave the manor and take up whatever jobs suited them. The Land Purchase Patent (1781) gave Gov support and security to peasants who bought land. The Patent concerning Subjects (1781) provided effective machinery to enable a peasant to appeal from his lord's court to a State court. The Penal Patent (1781) limited the lord's rights of punishment. These reforms seriously undermined tradition, but they were not so revolutionary as Joseph's attempts to abolish *Robot*, the serf's compulsory labour. He speeded up the process, which had begun under Maria Theresa, of breaking up feudal relationships on Crown lands, municipal lands and lands forfeited by Jesuits and monasteries. All through his reign commissioners and surveyors laboured on these estates to wipe out *Robot* and divide up the demesne-lands among the peasants. On private land, Joseph aimed to abolish *Robot* in a wholesale tax reform. Against fierce noble opposition, a census of the population and a register of landed property were painfully undertaken, until in 1789 the Tax and Agrarian Regulation was promulgated. It covered both State taxes and feudal dues, and applied to the better-off peasants – about one-fifth of the whole. By it, peasants were to pay a single tax of 30% of their income (instead of about 70% as before), of which $12\frac{2}{9}$% went to the State, and $17\frac{7}{9}$% went to the lord and the Ch, in lieu of *Robot* and tithes. Naturally, the nobles and clergy condemned these proposals in their Diets, and obstructed their application on their estates; but the peasants resisted also. Badly informed and deeply suspicious, they resorted to arson, assault and full-scale rebellion. (g) The economy flourished in the laissez-faire conditions provided by Joseph's decrees, especially in Bohemia and around Vienna. He believed in tariffs at the frontiers, and liberalism inside them. Like the Physiocrats, he used the State to clear away all obstacles to the natural economic order. He liberated industry from gild restraints and bureaucratic interference, and let it have its head. The statistics tell their own story. The population rose from $18\frac{1}{2}$ to 21 million; the revenue from under 63 million florins to over 87 million; the army from 108,000 to 300,000.

In Milan, Belgium and Hungary, which had been left by Maria Theresa to stew quietly in their constitutional privileges, Joseph stirred up serious trouble for himself. As a devotee of logical consistency, he was incapable of benevolent neglect. In Milan (1786) he abolished the Council of Sixty and the Senate of Lombardy, and then divided the prov into new admin districts manned by bureaucrats responsible to Vienna. With these he launched a programme of law codification and judicial reform, and set in train a scheme to rationalize the tax system by eliminating noble and clerical privileges. In Belgium, where the 10 provs were not even centralized under Brussels, let alone Vienna, he began to create (1781) a rational judicial and admin system which worked under orders from Vienna, and side-stepped the traditional authorities of the prov Estates, town councils and manor houses. Not surprisingly, the nobles, clergy and city-fathers grew restive at his measures to dissolve monasteries, abolish torture, undermine the gilds, and inspect the Univ of Louvain. They began to refuse taxes and vote remonstrances, until in 1789 each prov voted its own declaration of independence. In Hungary he moved the crown of St Stephen from Budapest to Vienna (1784) as a sign of his intention to snuff out Magyar independence. Already the Patent to Abolish Serfdom, the Toleration Patent and the reorganization of the Ch applied to Hungary, but their practical application was impeded by the passive resistance of the central and county Diets. To eliminate these obstacles, Joseph applied the Haugwitz-Kaunitz admin reforms which Maria Theresa had given to Austria-Bohemia. Hungary, Croatia and Transylvania were merged into one *Gubernium* (Gov) divided into *Kreise* (districts) and placed under the United Hungarian–Transylvanian Chancellery in Vienna (1785). The new boundaries were based on reason, and owed nothing to the old counties, whose Diets and officials were suppressed. Using this new hierarchy of officials Joseph began to count the population and survey the land to provide the basis of a new tax-system based on wealth. In addition, he introduced conscription instead of the feudal levy, and new Austrian courts in place of the Hungarian private courts. German replaced Latin as the language of Gov, and Magyar as the language of education. Resistance by the Hungarians merely stiffened Joseph's determination of course, and by 1789 the prov was ready to burst into armed revolt.

Foreign-policy failures eventually brought these multiform discontents to a crisis, as he persisted with the expansionist policies he had initiated under Maria Theresa. (a) Over the R Scheldt – which he wished to re-open after it had been closed to non-Dutch shipping since 1648 – he made provocative lunges at Holland (1781–5). His allies, France and Russia, failed to back him, however; and he eventually had to recognize his failure in the Tr of Fontainebleau (1785). (b) His Bavaria–Belgium exchange scheme also failed (1785). Russia was indifferent, but France opposed, and FREDERICK II of Prussia led the opposition inside Germany by creating the *Fürstenbund* (League of Princes) to resist Austrian aggressiveness. (c) The Austro-Turkish War of 1788–91 was the last act of Joseph's tragedy. His ally, CATHERINE II of Russia, embarked on her Russo-Turkish War (1787–92) before Joseph was fully prepared; but he insisted on joining in, nevertheless, in case she won more than her fair share of the spoils. Not only was Turkey temporarily rejuvenated, however, but Joseph was an incompetent general, and in poor health into the bargain. His disastrous campaigns brought all his troubles to a head.

Rebellion and retreat marked his last year, when military failure was joined by bad harvests and economic depression at home, and the French Revolution abroad. The year 1789 was not the best moment to try to revolutionize an Emp from above. Everywhere he was opposed by those he tried to help as well as by those whose privileges he had tried to abridge. Against him rose peasants as well as landlords, urban radicals as well as aldermen, the Enlightened as well as the conservative. In his weak physical condition – plagued with varicose veins, erysipelas, weak lungs and bad digestion – he sounded the retreat; and the Crown joined the nobility once more, to sink or swim together. In Austria-Bohemia the secret police received orders to back the nobility and tradition; while Joseph postponed his new law on taxation and the *Robot*. In Hungary he returned the crown of St Stephen, and cancelled all his decrees except those granting toleration, Ch reform and the abolition of serfdom. But it was all too little and too late. When Joseph d disorder was rampant everywhere. It was left to his brother and successor – the Enlightened but pragmatic Leopold II – to make the real concessions and restore order. He re-established the independence of the Treasury, restored the tithes, and abolished the Gen Seminaries. He cancelled the single land-tax, and brought back the *Robot*. In Lombardy he restored the Senate and the Council of 60. In Belgium he offered the full restoration of the Estates. In Hungary he ordered a complete return to the pre-Josephinian situation. He made peace with Turkey in the mildly profitable Tr of Sistowa (Aug 1791). Nowhere, however, could he wipe the slate clean, for Joseph's work had made indelible marks on Austrian life. His legacy was a strengthened State machine opposing change on the one hand, and its chief opponents on the other: liberalism and nationalism.

Julius II (Giuliano della Rovere) (5 Dec 1443–21 Feb 1513) Pp (1503) who played an unusually warlike role in the HABSBURG–VALOIS WARS, extending and consolidating the Papal States, and who surpassed all other Pps in the employment of Renaissance artists to beautify Rome.

Son of a modest family, he rose rapidly in the Ch, thanks to the favours of his uncle Pp Sixtus IV (1471–84), who made him a Card (1471) and showered him with 1 archbpric, 7 bprics, several abbacies and other benefices. On 1st standing for the papacy, he was beaten by his Borgia rival, Pp ALEXANDER VI (Aug 1492), and he went to France to encourage K CHARLES VIII to invade Italy to depose him. As an extraordinarily vigorous and militant Pp – *papa terribile* – he was concerned mainly with: the Habsburg–Valois Wars; the extension and unification of the States of the Ch – rather than those of his family – into a viable political unit which lasted till C19; and the establishment of Rome as the centre of the High Renaissance.

He completed the ruin of Cesare BORGIA by taking over his conquests in the Romagna – though Venice occupied Rimini, Cesena and Faenza. Julius conquered Perugia and Bologna at the head of his army (1506); then took part in the 3rd Habsburg–Valois War of 1508–14 with a view to making Venice disgorge her share of the Borgia booty. The Emp MAXIMILIAN I and K LOUIS XII of France had formed the League of Cambrai (Dec 1508) with Venice in mind. Julius joined in Mar 1509, and in Apr 1509 excommunicated the city. The French victory at Agnadello, near the Milan–Venice border, on 14 May 1509, however, enabled Julius to take over Faenza, Rimini and Ravenna, but it put France in such a dominating position in Italy that he withdrew from the League, releasing Venice from excommunication in Feb 1510. The Venetians, for their part, conceded to Rome freedom of commerce and navigation on the Adriatic, and the full recognition of Ch privileges in the Republic. Julius's aim now was to drive the French out of the peninsula, and also to counter their politically-motivated ecclesiastical project: the Council of Pisa of May 1511, designed to reform the Ch and depose him. To achieve the former, he organized the Holy League in Oct 1511 with Spain, the Emp, Venice, England and the Swiss; and the French were beaten at Ravenna on 11 Apr 1512, a victory which enabled him to add Parma and Piacenza to the Papal States. To achieve the latter, he opened the 5th Lateran Council on 3 May 1512, which certainly made the delegates of Pisa – now in Milan – look more spurious than ever, but which went on discussing Ch reform without any practical effect until Pp LEO X closed it down on 16 Mar 1517.

As a patron of the arts, Julius employed Bramante, Michelangelo, Raphael and others, and out-classed all other Pps in his efforts to rebuild St Peter's, the Vatican and Rome in general. It was he who proclaimed the INDULGENCE of 1506 for the rebuilding of St Peter's which ultimately led LUTHER to protest. By the time of his death, Julius had driven the French out of Italy, but at the cost of laying her under the yoke of Spain instead; he had centralized the various Papal States firmly under the control of the Pp: but at the cost of publicizing all those faults in the Ch which led to the REFORMATION.

Knights' War, The (1522–3) An unsuccessful rising of a declining social group in Germany who were self-styled protectors of the followers of LUTHER.

In C16, the Imperial Knights (*Reichsritter*) of SW Germany, proud but impoverished owners of small estates and decaying castles who claimed to be the direct vassals of the HR Emp, were in economic, social and political decay, and were making desperate moves to preserve their archaic independence in the face of the rising power of the ecclesiastical and lay Prs, and of the cities, with whom the future lay. They often resorted to private warfare and banditry; and, led by Franz von SICKINGEN (a rich robber-knight who gave unwelcome backing to the Lutherans) and Ulrich von HUTTEN (a Humanist idealist) they attacked the city of Trier in Aug 1522, partly out of a personal vendetta against the Archbp, and partly in aid of a wild scheme to shore up the fortunes of the whole knightly class by sharing out ecclesiastical land among them. Failing to receive mass support – the Lutherans would not bite, and the peasants (whom the Knights exploited) were indifferent – they were easily defeated by the forces of the Swabian League (the joint army of the SW German Prs), which then proceeded to demolish their castles in the interests of law and order.

Knox, John (*c* 1505–24 Nov 1572) Inflammatory leader of the Scottish Reformation.

Son of William Knox and his wife, possibly farmers; ed either at the Univ of St Andrews or Glasgow; m 1st (1555 or 1556) Marjory, daughter of Sir Richard Bowes (d 1560); m 2nd (1564) Margaret Stewart, daughter of Ld Ochiltree.

His early career is thinly documented. He became a priest and a lawyer, and by 1545 was tutor to the children of 2 Prot nobles who were the protectors of George Wishart, the Prot preacher. In Scotland the Reformation had been making headway since the 1520s, closely identified with anti-French nationalism. Knox became converted, thanks to the influence of Wishart; and after the latter was burnt at the stake for heresy (1 Mar 1546), he joined the rebel nobles who had murdered Card Beaton, the Archbp of St Andrews (29 May 1546). Besieged in St Andrews Castle for 3 months, he proved himself a powerful preacher. A later observer said that he inspired like the noise of 500 trumpets and 1,000 drums. Far from willingly – for he was an academic type – he was elected to lead the Scottish Prots, and when the French broke the siege in June 1547 he spent 18 months as a prisoner on a galley until he was released through the good offices of K EDWARD VI of England (Feb 1549). In England (1549–53), he became a leading Prot preacher, breathing fire against Rome, helping CRANMER with his *42 Articles* and 2nd Prayer Book (1552), but refusing Ch preferment. On the Continent (1553–9), where he fled during the reign of MARY I, he ministered to the more extreme Calvinist refugees from Britain, ie the 'Knoxians' at Geneva as distinct from the 'Coxians' at Frankfurt. Like Beza, he went further than CALVIN in approving of armed resistance to ungodly rulers (eg in his *Appelation*, 1558); while his *First Blast of the Trumpet Against the Monstrous Regiment of Women* (1557), attacking the female Cath rulers of Scotland, France and England, came out just as ELIZABETH I acceded and barred England to him – though it was not meant for her, and she allowed him to pass through England to lead the Prot rebellion which ensued in Scotland. In Scotland (1559–72), where he arrived in May 1559, his sermons inspired the Lords of the Congregation – the rebel Prot nobility – who with English military aid forced the French out of Scotland (Tr of Edinburgh, July 1560) and carried through the Scottish Reformation. Knox became minister of St Giles, Edinburgh, and was closely involved in the *Scots Confession* and the *1st Book of Discipline*: the body of beliefs and the Presbyterian organization adopted by the Kirk from 1560 onwards. The rule of MARY,

Q OF SCOTS (1561-7) led to further civil war, and before she fled to England she felt the rough edge of Knox's tongue on at least 4 occasions.

Lambert, Maj-Gen John (17 Sept 1619–winter 1683/4) Successful commander under Oliver CROMWELL in the English CIVIL WAR, who, with political ambitions of his own, unsuccessfully opposed the restoration of CHARLES II and spent the rest of his life in prison.

Son of recent gentry; ed at Trinity, Cambridge, and at one of the Inns of Court; m (1639) Frances, daughter of Sir William Lister.

On the outbreak of the Civil War (1642–6), Lambert became a cavalry capt in FAIRFAX's Yorks army, rising rapidly through his unusual military abilities, displayed at Nantwich, Cheshire (24 Jan 1644) and Marston Moor, nr York (2 July 1644), to become third after Cromwell and IRETON in the Parl side's hierarchy. He helped Ireton to draw up the *Heads of the Proposals* (Aug 1647), and Cromwell to defeat the Scots during the Second Civil War at Preston (17–19 Aug 1648); though he was out of London in the field during Pride's Purge (6 Dec 1648) and the trial and execution of the K (Jan 1649). He was 2 i/c to Cromwell in the campaigns which led to the defeat of the Scots at Dunbar (3 Sept 1650) and Worcester (3 Sept 1651), and on Ireton's death (26 Nov 1651) became the most powerful soldier after Cromwell, and in many eyes – including his own – his likely successor. He was a member of Barebone's Parl (July–Dec 1653), though he had opposed the whole idea and was one of the conservatives who voted its dissolution. He was chiefly responsible for the new constitution – the *Instrument of Gov*, Dec 1653 – which made Cromwell Ld Protector. He then largely devised the Major-Generals (Aug 1655–Jan 1657), but at this stage he began to break with Cromwell, acting like an over-mighty subject, nourishing ambitions of succeeding him, but lacking the religious idealism, statesmanlike vision and political skill of the Protector. Lambert opposed Cromwell's imaginative foreign policy; he opposed proposals to make Cromwell K; he opposed the *Humble Petition and Advice* (May 1657), constitutional amendments which gave Cromwell the right to name his successor. On 13 July 1657, Cromwell made Lambert resign all his commissions, and he retired to private life and tulip-growing until the anarchy which succeeded Cromwell's death (3 Sept 1658) gave him a further chance to reach supreme power. With the overthrow of Richard Cromwell (Oliver's unwilling successor) and the recall of the Rump, he was given back his commands, and sent to put down Sir George Booth's Royalist rising in Cheshire in Aug 1659. He and the other generals then quarrelled with the Rump. On 12 Oct 1659 the Rump cashiered them; the next day Lambert dispersed the Rump, and began to rule with a Committee of Safety in alliance with City Republicans. Lambert was simply a skilful general, with no political following and no instinct for the way things were going. MONCK, the commander of the Army in Scotland, crossed into England on 2 Jan 1660, and Lambert marched N to oppose him. He discovered that the people wanted an end to military rule, and under the pressure of public opinion his army melted away. With the restoration of Charles II, which Monck organized, Lambert's career was finished. He was arrested, but escaped from the Tower in Apr 1660, in a desperate attempt to rally resistance in the Midlands. Easily recaptured, and now a broken man, he was put on trial (1662) and imprisoned for life in various isolated fortresses, including Guernsey and St Nicholas Island, Plymouth Sound.

Latimer, Hugh (*c* 1485–16 Oct 1555) Bp of Worcester (1535–9), early Prot, and critic of social evils, who was burnt at the stake by Q MARY I.

Son of a yeoman; ed at Cambridge (1506 onwards), where he joined the first generation of English Prots who discussed the doctrines of LUTHER at the White Horse Tavern. Converted by Thomas Bilney in 1524 into a believer in justification by faith alone, he was often in trouble with the hierarchy for his sermons against mere works, but gained royal favour for his support of K HENRY VIII's divorce from Q CATHERINE OF ARAGON and marriage to Anne Boleyn. Made Bp of Worcester, he supported CROMWELL and CRANMER against NORFOLK and GARDINER, and resigned his see on the passage through Parl of the Act of 6 Articles in 1539. Under K EDWARD VI he preached vigorous and earthy sermons against absentee Bps, the exploitation of the poor by the rich, and other social evils denounced by the 'Commonwealth Men'. Under Q Mary I he was arrested on 13 Sept 1553 – after refusing a chance to escape – and examined at Oxford along with Cranmer and RIDLEY by a delegation appointed by Convocation. Refusing to recant, he was found guilty of heresy (Apr 1554). He was then condemned to death at a trial in Oct 1555, and burned at the stake at Oxford, chained along with Ridley, on 16 Oct 1555. Their astonishing fortitude immeasurably encouraged English Prots and other opponents of authority.

Laud, William (7 Oct 1573–10 Jan 1645) Archbp of Canterbury to K CHARLES I of England, whose authoritarian enforcement of High Ch innovations, whose exaggerated notions of the extent to which the clergy could interfere in lay life, and whose vigorous support for the prerogatives of the Crown did much to provoke the CIVIL WAR, and led to his own execution.

Son of William Laud, clothier: ed at Reading Grammar and St John's, Oxford, of which he became President (May 1611). He did not marry. He attached himself to the Arminian Bp Neile of Rochester, becoming his chaplain in 1608; but promotion was slow under K JAMES I and his Puritan Archbp ABBOT, though eventually Laud's qualities as a theologian impressed themselves on the favourite BUCKINGHAM, who promoted him at Court and persuaded the K to make him Bp of St David's (Nov 1621). James was full of misgivings, and his opinion of Laud was borne out by events: 'He hath a restless spirit,' he said, 'and cannot see when matters are well, but loves to toss and change, and to bring things to a pitch of reformation floating in his own brain.' Laud was small, rosy-cheeked, austere, irritable and sharp-tongued; entertaining no doubts about the correctness of his own views, and entirely lacking the politician's flair for compromise he did more, perhaps, than any other single man to provoke the Civil War. Unfortunately, Charles I had the same qualities, and under him preferment came more swiftly. He became Bp of Bath and Wells (June 1626), Bp of London (July 1628) and Chancellor of Oxford University (Apr 1630); and, though he had to await Abbot's death before he could become Archbp (July 1633), he was in effect the head of Charles's Ch and much of the State besides from 1628 onwards, sitting regularly in Star Chamber and High Commission, serving as a Treasury Commissioner and member of the Privy Council committee on foreign affairs; with STRAFFORD, dominating every aspect of Gov during the 11 years' Personal Rule. His chief aim was to stop the rot in the Ch of England: to recover its alienated revenues, to rebuild its decaying churches, to discipline the presses and the univs, to educate the clergy, to clean up the ecclesiastical courts and to enforce uniform worship according to the Prayer Book, suppressing all traces of Puritanism. Along with a small group of like-minded ARMINIANS, whom the K also promoted (eg Neile, who was made Archbp of York in 1632), he used ecclesiastical visitations, Ch courts, High Commission and Star Chamber to carry out a revolution from above, sometimes using stern punishments, such as whipping and ear-cropping. The Laudians placed great stress on Ch services, vestments, Ch decorations, lights and music, kneeling and bowing. They caused great offence by turning the communion table into an altar at the E end of the Ch and then railing it off; and by reissuing the Book of Sports (1633) and not observing Sunday in the Puritan manner. They suppressed Puritan lecturers and pamphleteers. They disbanded the Feoffees for Impropriations (1635) – a Puritan trust for buying up impropriated tithes from laymen and using the income to finance lecturers. They looked on Bps, not as an admin convenience, but as a divinely appointed essential element in the Ch; and nothing offended the nobility and gentry so much as Laud's puffed-up notions of clerical authority over the laity – especially as the Bps had all risen from lowly origins. By the end of the 11 years' Personal Rule (1629–40), the laity and the Puritans together formed a vast phalanx of opposition, many of them suspecting Laud of planning to turn the Ch over to Rome once again, though in fact he strongly opposed the Cath influences at Court. Not content with this, Charles and Laud provoked an anti-English, anti-Anglican revolt in Scotland, where they tried to enforce a new Prayer Book (1638), touching off a trail of consequences which led to the Bishops' Wars, the Long Parl, Laud's imprisonment and impeachment (Dec 1640), and then his trial which lasted most of 1644. Unable to prove treason, the H of C passed an Act of Attainder, the H of L concurring in Jan 1645. Laud was beheaded on Tower Hill.

Lefèvre d'Étaples, Jacques (c 1450/5–1536 or 1537) Leading French exponent of HUMANISM.

Ed at Paris, where he also taught. His journeys to Italy in 1492 and 1500 brought him into contact with the humanistic scholarship to which he devoted the rest of his life. From 1507 onwards he worked as librarian at the Abbey of St Germain-des-Prés in Paris, and brought out works aimed at revealing to the educated public what the Scriptures actually said. He favoured reforms in the Ch, not a REFORMATION, yet his studies brought him to conclusions which anticipated some of those of LUTHER. Harassed by the Sorbonne, he moved to Meaux in 1520; here, with a circle of like-minded reformers, he took part in removing the abuses in the diocese, and in publishing works of Humanism which the conservatives of the Sorbonne and the Paris PARLEMENT mistook for Lutheranism. When genuine Protestantism began to spread, and persecution increased during K FRANCIS I's imprisonment in Madrid, Lefèvre fled to Strassburg (1525), then to Blois under the K's protection, and ultimately (1531) to the court of Marguerite d'Angoulême at Nérac in Gascony, where he d.

Leicester, Robert Dudley, Earl of (24 June 1532 or 1533-4 Sept 1588) Favourite and leading minister of Q ELIZABETH I of England. She would probably have m him had not statesmanship forced her to deny her feelings. He was a political rival of BURGHLEY and the 4th D of NORFOLK, and, like WALSINGHAM, he favoured an active pro-Prot, anti-Cath home and foreign policy, to which he gave practical form in leading a disastrous expedition to the Netherlands to aid the Dutch in their REVOLT against Spain.

Son of John DUDLEY, D of Northumberland; ed in HUMANISM; m (1550) Amy Robsart, only daughter of Sir John Robsart of Norfolk. His grandfather, Edmund DUDLEY, had been executed by K HENRY VIII, and his father was executed by Q MARY I for his treason in the Lady Jane Grey affair; Leicester himself was sentenced to death, but pardoned in 1554. He fought in the battle of St Quentin, Picardy, when the Spanish defeated the French (10 Aug 1557), and Q Mary restored him to his rank of duke's son (Mar 1558). Under Q Elizabeth he made swift political progress. He was tall, handsome, athletic and gifted; and she seems to have fallen in love with him. He was appointed Master of the Horse (1559), made Knight of the Garter (1559), brought on to the Council (1562) and made Earl of Leicester (1564). He even aimed at marrying the Q, but it is doubtful if she would have committed the political folly of dividing the nation by uniting the Crown with one of the English noble houses. In any case, such a marriage became even more unthinkable when the death of Leicester's wife made it possible, for the countess was found with a broken neck at the bottom of her stairs at Cumnor Place, nr Abingdon, Berks, on 8 Sept 1560. Although the fall was probably accidental, word spread that Leicester had organized her murder. During 1563-4 Elizabeth suggested him as a husband for MARY, Q OF SCOTS, but this was probably merely a political manoeuvre on her part. By this stage their relationship seems to have gradually shed its emotional colouring; though he continued to be her favourite, he also established himself as a leading political figure in his own right, the leader of a faction at Court, a great territorial magnate, and the self-appointed leader of the thrusting PURITANS – as well as the proprietor of James Burbage and his troupe of actors. His special relationship with Elizabeth eased his ascent up the ladder of power, though on the other hand he had to cope with the jealousy he aroused in all his rivals. He eventually accepted that marrying the Q was an impossibility, for he formed an extra-marital liaison with the dowager Lady Sheffield (1573-7), and then secretly m Lettice Knollys in 1577 or 8 – widow of Walter Devereux, 1st Earl of Essex. Both affairs drove the Q to fury, but she forgave Leicester, if not his women.

In politics he diverged sharply from the frigid pragmatism of the Q and the cool conservatism of Burghley. At home, he backed further reforms for the Puritans and severer persecution for the Caths; abroad, he favoured an alliance with France, and active intervention against Spain and the Caths in the Netherlands. He was the leading advocate of the ineffective military intervention in the 1st War of the FRENCH WARS OF RELIGION on the side of the Hugs (1562-3); and when Elizabeth at last gave reluctant sanction for open war in aid of the Dutch, Leicester was placed in command of the expeditionary force, landing at Flushing on 9 Dec 1585. He proved to be an incompetent general: his tactless acceptance from the Dutch of the office of Gov and Capt-Gen (Jan 1586) went clean against the Q's concept of a very limited English involvement in the war.

He was brought back to England in Nov 1586; sent back again because his officers had betrayed Deventer and Zutphen to the enemy; and finally recalled in Dec 1587. He was not in disgrace, however, but was appointed Lieut-Gen of the army raised at Tilbury to oppose the Spanish ARMADA, though he did not see action.

Leo X (Giovanni de' Medici) (11 Dec 1475–1/2 Dec 1521) Pp (1513) who promoted the Renaissance in Rome, pushed the material interests of the Medici family and Papal States, and dealt ineffectively, and without understanding, with the early stages of the German REFORMATION begun by LUTHER.

2nd son of Lorenzo the Magnificent, the ruler of Florence, and Clarice Orsini; ed at Pisa; was made a Card (1589), and after his election as Pp was ordained priest (1513) and consecrated Bp (1513) before being actually enthroned (1513). An enthusiast for HUMANISM, diplomacy and war – though in a more relaxed way than his predecessor, JULIUS II – he switched from side to side in the HABSBURG–VALOIS WARS with the aim of clearing Italy of both great powers. Inheriting the Habsburg alliance of the Holy League (1511), he was on the wrong side when K FRANCIS I of France won the battle of Marignano on 13 and 14 Sept 1515; and in the subsequent conference with Francis at Bologna (Dec 1515) it was he who had to make the concessions. He signed the Concordat of Bologna (1516), yielding the French K substantial rights over the French Ch; and he gave up Parma and Piacenza, in return for a free hand in the Papal States. He used the latter to eject D Francesco Maria della Rovere from Urbino and put his nephew Lorenzo de' Medici there instead (1516) and, when he d in 1516, incorporated the city into the Papal States. During the run-up period to the election of CHARLES V as HR Emp in June 1519, he did all he could to oppose Charles, backing Francis I, even trying to persuade FREDERICK III to stand, and only supporting Charles at the last minute – and in return for the promise of Parma and Piacenza. In the 5th Habsburg–Valois War (1521–6) he changed over to an alliance with the Emp (May 1521) in order to incorporate Parma, Piacenza and Ferrara into the Papal States, but he was dead before he could profit from Charles's victories over the French at Milan (19 Nov 1521) and La Bicocca (24 June 1522). The 5th Lateran Council – called to reform the Ch by Pp Julius II in May 1512 and closed down by Leo in Mar 1517 – continued to pass reforming measures against simony and other forms of corruption; and, except in cases where there was any suggestion that Councils were more important than Pps, Leo continued to confirm them by issuing Bulls. But it is a big step from legislating to executing, and, far from reforming abuses, he spread them. He renewed the INDULGENCE which Julius II had initiated for rebuilding St Peter's and paying the debts – incurred through simony – of Albert of Hohenzollern, Archbp of Mainz; and it was Luther's protest against this that led to the Reformation. Failing to appreciate the profundity of the Prot movement in Germany, he took no effective action until he issued the Bull *Exsurge, Domine* on 15 June 1520, which was too much and too late. It condemned Luther as a heretic. Luther put it on the bonfire. The following year, in Oct 1521, Leo conferred what turned out to be the ironic title of *Defender of the Faith* on K HENRY VIII of England.

Leopold I (9 June 1640–5 May 1705) Head of the Austrian Monarchy (1657),

HREmp (July 1658) who gave up the attempt to turn Germany into a centralized absolutism under the Habsburgs, and concentrated instead on consolidating his position as head of the Austrian Monarchy. He not only extended his grip over Austria and Bohemia, he also reconquered Hungary from the Turks and played a leading part in the W European coalitions which blocked the aggressive designs of K LOUIS XIV of France.

2nd son of FERDINAND III and his 1st wife, Maria Anna, daughter of K PHILIP III of Spain; ed in Spain for the priesthood till his eld brother's death (1654) made him heir to the throne; m 1st (1666) the Infanta Margaret Theresa, 2nd daughter of K PHILIP IV of Spain (d 1673); m 2nd (1673) Claudia Felicitas of Tirol (d 1676); m 3rd (1676) Eleanora Magdalena of Pfalz-Neuburg (d 1720) by whom he had the future Emps JOSEPH I and CHARLES VI. Pious, virtuous, artistic and musical, Leopold was more suited to the Ch than the State. In great measure he was endowed with the tired eyes, hooked nose and underslung jaw of the Habsburgs, and in larger measure even than FERDINAND II or III he took political advice from the JESUITS. Convinced that he was the agent of divine purposes, he eventually took his own decisions, usually late, after painful heartsearching. His election as HREmp was unsuccessfully opposed by MAZARIN, who tried to get the post for Louis XIV. Mazarin did, however, manage to get the German Prs to limit the Emp's power: eg Leopold had to agree not to help Spain in the Franco-Spanish war then raging. With territories strung out from one end of Europe to the other, Leopold was fully involved throughout his reign in the W defending W Germany against Louis XIV and fighting to inherit the Spanish emp, and in the E defending the Emp against a revived Turkey, and then rolling back the Turks in the Balkans with the reconquest of Hungary. Before 1683, Leopold's constant dilemma was whether to listen to those in his Court who favoured action in the W, or those who favoured a crusade in the E. After 1683, he was able to fight on both fronts simultaneously.

Before 1683 Leopold was not capable of blocking Louis XIV's aggression in the Netherlands and along the Rhine because of the constant pressure of a temporarily revived Ottoman Emp. In the E, Turkey was in long-term decline compared with the capitalistic, scientific, bureaucratic W but, under able leaders, she could occasionally stage revivals which shook neighbouring powers: Venice, Austria, Poland and Russia. Such a revival occurred in the reign of Mehmed IV, who left the task of gov (1656 onwards) to a dynasty of Grand Viziers of the Köprülü family. These sometimes attacked one Christian power, sometimes another, but, whether Austria was in the firing line or not, Leopold had to be permanently on watch in Hungary. Leopold was K of Hungary, but one-third of it was under Turkish occupation; of the rest, Transylvania had established itself as an independent Prot principality with Turkish backing, and the ungovernable Prot nobility of Austrian-controlled Hungary sought every opportunity to eject the Austrians. Naturally, Louis XIV did all he could with diplomacy and cash to stimulate all these forces in Turkey, Transylvania and Hungary into anti-Habsburg actions. The trouble began for Leopold when Mehmed Köprülü invaded Transylvania, overthrew Pr György II Rákóczy, and replaced him with a Calvinist puppet, Pr Mihály Apafi (1660–61). When Leopold opposed this move, the next Grand Vizier, Ahmed Köprülü, launched 2 campaigns against Vienna (1663, 1664) the 2nd of which was brilliantly defeated by the imperial general,

Count Raimondo Montecucculi, at St Gotthard on the R Raab (1 Aug 1664). This was a great tonic to W morale, but many thought that Leopold had wasted an opportunity to roll back the Turks once and for all when he signed the truce of Vasvár with Turkey (Aug 1664), handing back his conquests and recognizing Apafi. For his part, Leopold had to bear in mind K Louis XIV, whose aggressions were just beginning. For the next 20 years Turkey made no direct attack on Austria, and Leopold employed the interval trying to extend his Gov over the portion of Hungary under his control. He tried terror and the COUNTER-REFORMATION (1664–81) without making any impression. He tried persuasion (1681–3), called the Diet at Sopron (Ödenburg) in 1681, and restored Hungarian self-Gov and allowed Prot worship, but still the nobles rebelled. These pre-occupations, together with the Turkish capture in Sept 1669 of the Venetian possessions of Candia and the whole of Crete (which they had besieged since 1648); and together with the Turkish attacks on Poland (1672–6) and Russia (1674–81) meant that Leopold could not put up any opposition to Louis XIV.

In the W, Leopold left France free to launch the War of Devolution (1667–8). He even jeopardized his claim to the Spanish inheritance by signing the Partition Tr with France (Jan 1668) envisaging the division of the Spanish Emp between France and Austria, should the weakly CHARLES II die without issue. At the start of the Franco-Dutch War (1672–9), Leopold was neutral; but the French onslaught on the United Provinces made Leopold form the Grand Alliance (1673/4) and come to the defence of his own territories along the Rhine. Of course, he was never able to rally effective German opposition to the French, for, as ever, there were Prs who supported Louis XIV in order to keep the Emp weak, or to avoid French brutality or to gain French bribes. He took Philippsburg (Sept 1676), though the French took Freiburg (Nov 1677); and at the Tr of Nijmegen (Feb 1679) Leopold kept Philippsburg, but France kept Freiburg and Breisach.

In the E, the last major Turkish invasion of Austria, the siege of Vienna by Kara Mustafa (July–Sept 1683), now fully occupied him, though he personally sat it out upriver at Passau. The Austrian army under Charles of Lorraine had been too small to hold back the Turkish horde; but, reinforced by the troops of the coalition which Leopold now formed with Poland, Bavaria, Saxony and other German States, they crashed down on the besiegers from the heights of the Kahlenberg which overlook the city (12 Sept 1683), and forced them into a hurried retreat into Hungary.

In the W, this was the period of Louis XIV's *Réunions* (1679–84), and Leopold was forced by the Turkish invasion not merely to do nothing while France annexed Strasbourg and Casale in 1681, and Luxemburg in 1684, but even to sign the 20-year Truce of Regensburg (Aug 1684) recognizing French gains.

After 1683 Leopold operated with a new vigour, both E and W. His horizons had expanded along with his successes, and by this stage he was against any partition of the Spanish inheritance and determined to inherit the whole himself. Also he was bent on undoing the Trs of Westphalia (1648), and reviving the vast emp of CHARLES V. It can even be argued that, as early as the later stages of the Franco-Dutch War and the *Réunions*, it was he who took the initiative and Louis XIV who was acting defensively to head off his aggressions.

In the E, with his new army under D Charles of Lorraine, and later under Pr

Eugen, he pursued the retreating Turks, who now suffered from a series of incompetent Grand Viziers. He took Buda on 2 Sept 1686, and defeated the Turks heavily nr Mohács on 12 Aug 1687. These victories enabled him to revert to a tougher line in Hungary. At the Diet of Pozsony (Pressburg or Bratislava) in Sept 1687 the Hungarians were forced to declare the Crown hereditary in the male Habsburg line (and no longer elective) and to abandon their ancient 'right of resistance'. On 6 Sept 1688 Belgrade fell; on 19 Aug 1691 Turkey was heavily defeated at Szalankemen. At this stage the Austrian advance slowed down, as Leopold played his part in the W War of the League of Augsburg (1689–97); but Pr Eugen took command in 1697 and wiped out a Turkish army 3 times the size of his own at Zenta on 11 Sept 1697. By the Tr of Carlowitz (Jan 1699) Turkey recognized Austrian rule in Transylvania and all of Hungary except the Bánát of Temesvár. Gradually, Leopold was able to clamp on Hungary the fetters of Austrian rule and Roman Catholicism, though without ever putting an end to rebellions and guerilla warfare. Hungary was turned into an Austrian colony, and never integrated into an Austrian Prov.

In the W, Leopold and Louis XIV were taking the provocative steps out of mutual fear which led to the War of the League of Augsburg (1689–97). At the end of the war (*see* LOUIS XIV) by the Tr of Rijswijk, which Leopold signed very reluctantly under pressure from WILLIAM III, France gave up all her conquests since 1678 save Strasbourg. At this point the declining health of K Charles II of Spain concentrated the attention of all powers on the question of the Spanish inheritance. Leopold refused to go along with the efforts of William III and Louis XIV to avoid war by the 2 Partition Trs (Oct 1698, June 1699), as he did not wish to abandon his claim to the whole inheritance. (The mothers and wives of both Leopold and Louis were respectively daughters and grand-daughters of K Philip III.) Moreover, Leopold was ready to back his claim with war. Bemused by the dream of reviving the Habsburg emp of bygone days, he was incapable of appreciating the importance of such mundane matters as the BALANCE OF POWER. (For his role in the War of the Spanish Succession (1702–13/14), *see* LOUIS XIV.) In 1703–5 the E and W fields came together as a Hungarian rising under young Ferencz II Rákóczy was co-ordinated with a Franco-Bavarian thrust down the Danube. The hopes of the French and Hungarians to meet from opposite sides on the streets of Vienna were frustrated, however, when MARLBOROUGH and Eugen defeated the French at Blenheim, Bavaria, on 13 Aug 1704, and the Hungarian war of independence subsided into guerilla activity which lasted until 1711. The other scenes of Leopold's activity in this war were N Italy, from which Eugen drove out the French by 1707 (after Leopold's death), and Spain, where Leopold's principal contribution was to send his 2nd son, the Archd Charles (the future Emp CHARLES VI), to be landed at Barcelona by the British and proclaimed K 'Charles III' of Spain (1705), with the backing of the revolutionary Catalans.

Lerma, Francisco Gómez de Sandoval y Rojas, Marqués de Denia, D de (1553–18 May 1625) Favourite and chief minister of K PHILIP III of Spain, who enriched himself at public expense and generally aided the decline of SPAIN.

Son of the 4th Marquis de Denia, of Valencia, and his wife, Isabel de Borja; ed at Seville; m Catalina, daughter of the D of Medinaceli. He rose in the Court of K PHILIP II, became Viceroy of Valencia, and established such a dominating position over the mind of the heir to the throne that the latter handed over full powers to him on his accession (1598). He was thus, until his dismissal in Oct 1618, responsible for the chief developments of Philip III's reign: in foreign affairs mainly inaction because of the economic crisis; in home affairs the expulsion of the MORISCOS (1609–14), and the intensification of the economic crisis by allowing a small group of Grandees (led by himself) to batten on the community for power and wealth, by upsetting the economy with periodic debasements and royal bankruptcies, and by failing to make any reforms. In the end he was overthrown by a faction in the Council of State led by his son, Cristóbal, D de Uceda, supported by Grandees who disapproved of his immense wealth and demanded a more aggressive foreign policy.

Levellers, The A secular radical movement which, flourishing in the City and the Army towards the end of the English CIVIL WAR and during the post-war negotiations (c 1645–9), not only stiffened the resolution of CROMWELL and the war party to bring in the New Model Army (Feb 1645) and the Self-Denying Ordinance (Apr 1645) (thus eliminating the unwarlike generals, ESSEX and MANCHESTER), but also helped to push the 'Independents' in Parl and the Grandees in the Army towards Pride's Purge (6 Dec 1648) and the execution of the K (30 Jan 1649). Consisting mainly of shopkeepers, artisans, apprentices and yeomen, they represented the grievances and aspirations of social groups who had supported Parl against the K, but who by this stage resented the fact that neither the Long Parl, nor the Rump, nor Cromwell and the generals would pay attention to their programme as it threatened the rights of the property-owners. They were led by minor gentry such as John Lilburne (1614–57), William Walwyn (1600–?1680) and John Wildman (?1623–93), who formulated radical plans, supported by arguments from reason and nature, not precedent or religious authority, for the defence of the small entrepreneur rather than the mass of the people. They opposed restrictions, from whatever source: merchants or landlords, Ch or State. In politics, they favoured a republic under annual or biennial Parls, male franchise (except for servants and day labourers), the redistribution of seats, the decentralization of Gov, and freedom of expression. In the Ch, they backed toleration and the self-Gov desired by INDEPENDENTS and sectaries, and opposed a State-Ch – whether Anglican or PRESBYTERIAN – as well as tithes and lay patronage. In the economy, they opposed monopolies and enclosures, customs and excise, and demanded security of tenure for copyholders. In society, they opposed imprisonment for debt, supported free medical aid and demanded cheaper justice, based on a simplification and clarification of the law. The movement began to spread with Lilburne's pamphlet *England's Birthright Justified* (1645), which outlined his main ideas. He was imprisoned by Parl in 1645 and again in 1646–8, but his ideas captured the City of London, and in 1647 spread to the Army when it was clashing with Parl over pay and disbandment arrangements. Cromwell accepted their backing when he decided to support the Army against Parl (June 1647), but only in order to contain them. He allowed the regiments to elect Agitators – or Agents – and he discussed with them their postwar settlement – the Leveller-inspired *Agreement of the People* – in the Putney Debates (Oct–Nov 1647), opposing their democratic ideas as a threat to property, and, at the appropriate moment, disbanding the Agitators and suppressing a mutiny (Nov 1647). The 2nd Civil War (1648), Pride's Purge (6 Dec 1648) and the execution of the K (30 Jan 1649) merely substituted one tyrant for another in Leveller eyes, as Lilburne's pamphlet *England's New Chains Discovered* – presented to Parl in Feb 1649 – made clear; and this year saw another bout of agitation, this time against the Grandees (the generals). 'You have no other way to deal with these men,' said Cromwell, 'but to break them, or they will break you.' In Mar 1649 Lilburne, Walwyn and other leaders were arrested and the City branch of the movement put down; while in May 1649 the Army Levellers were crushed by Cromwell himself at Burford and Banbury. This was the effective end of the Levellers, though not of the grievances which fed them. These henceforth found expression among the religious radicals, especially the FIFTH MONARCHY MEN.

L'Hôpital, Michel de (c 1505–13 Mar 1573) Chancellor of France (1560–68), *Politique* statesman in the early years of the FRENCH WARS OF RELIGION, and early advocate of religious toleration.

Son of a doctor; ed at Toulouse and Padua in law; then practised law, becoming a member of the PARLEMENT of Paris, and rising in the royal service to the rank of Master of Requests, and then Chancellor. During the period of tension between the pro-Cath Guise faction and the pro-Prot Bourbons, which followed the death of K HENRY II (10 July 1559) and eventually led to the Wars of Religion, L'Hôpital was the chief advocate of what became known as the *Politique* point of view of religious compromise. He and the Q Mother, CATHERINE DE MEDICI, tried unsuccessfully to put this policy into force in the Colloquy of Poissy (Sept–Oct 1561), the January Edict (Jan 1562) and the Pacification of Amboise (Mar 1563), which ended the 1st War. He developed the important *Politique* thesis, rarely expressed in C16, that politics was separable from religion, and that the ruler's duty was to enforce toleration of more than one religion if this was the only way to achieve law and order. This was a lesson which the 2 sides were not willing to learn, however, till after the Wars of Religion. He also produced the Ordinances of Moulins (Feb 1566), a sound programme of far-reaching admin and social reform which, like many another attempt to change the *Ancien Régime*, was never put into force because it involved an attack on the Parlements and other privileged groups. When the 2nd War (Sept 1567–Feb 1568) broke out, L'Hôpital retired from Court, and lost his office (1568).

Louis XII (27 June 1462–1 Jan 1515) K of France (1498), whose foreign policy was disfigured by unwise and unsuccessful attempts to win territory in Italy, and whose home policy continued the trend towards centralized absolutism, bringing internal order and economic growth.

Son of Charles, D d'Orléans, and Mary of Cleves, and cousin of K CHARLES VIII of France; succeeded as D d'Orléans in 1465; m 1st (1476) the pious Jeanne de France, daughter of K Louis XI. He was among the aristocrats who rebelled against the Crown during the minority of Charles VIII (1483–92), but was restored to favour in 1491, and took part in Charles VIII's invasion of Italy in 1494 at Genoa, Asti and Novara. On becoming K, he m 2nd (1499) Anne of Brittany, Charles VIII's widow, having had his 1st marriage scandalously annulled by Pp ALEXANDER VI in return for political help which he gave to the Pp's son, Cesare BORGIA. On her death (1514), he m 3rd (1514) Mary Tudor.

In foreign affairs, he began by claiming Milan on the grounds of his grandfather's marriage to Valentina Visconti, member of the family whose leaders had been predecessors of the ruling Sforza family as Dukes of Milan. He invaded Italy, drove Ludovico SFORZA out of Milan, and entered the city in a solemn triumph in Oct 1499. Sforza retook Milan on 5 Jan 1500, but his Swiss mercenaries refused to fight Louis' Swiss mercenaries at the battle of Novara on 8 Apr 1500, and he was taken prisoner to France. Milan was a fief of the H R Emp, and by the Tr of Blois (Sept 1504) the Emp MAXIMILIAN I recognized French rule there as part of a marriage deal between Louis' daughter Claude and Maximilian's grandson, the future Emp CHARLES V. After Milan, Louis followed up the French claim to Naples by signing the Tr of Granada (Nov 1500) with K FERDINAND II of Aragon, whereby they partitioned it between them. (Ferdinand wished to add Naples to his Kdom of Sicily.) But border disputes between the signatories led to warfare, in which the French were defeated by the Spanish general, CÓRDOBA, at Cerignalo on 28 Apr 1503 and on the R Garigliano on 27 Dec 1503. On 1 Jan 1504, Louis yielded Gaeta, his last stronghold in Naples; and by the Tr of Blois (Oct 1505) renounced his claim to Naples in favour of his niece, Germaine de Foix, who was about to become the 2nd wife of Ferdinand (who at that time was passing through a pro-French, anti-Imperial phase). Venice was the next enemy, and Louis and Maximilian formed the League of Cambrai (Dec 1508). Pp JULIUS II joined in Mar 1509, and other members were Ferdinand II, England, Hungary, Savoy, Ferrara, Mantua and Florence; but a reversal of alliances took place when Louis won a great victory over Venice at Agnadello (14 May 1509), dominated Milan once more, and sponsored the Council of Pisa (May 1511) to reform the Ch. Louis' erstwhile allies now formed the Holy League (Oct 1511) with a view to driving him out of Italy. Though the French under Gaston de Foix fought well at Ravenna on 11 Apr 1512, Gaston was killed and the French had to retreat, leaving Milan to be ruled by a Sforza again. The following year, Louis made another attempt to regain Milan, but was defeated by the Swiss at Novara on 6 June 1513. And so Louis had to spend his last year buying off invasions of France by members of the League. Maximilian and K HENRY VIII of England beat him at the battle of the Spurs in Artois on 16 Aug 1513; while the Swiss penetrated as far as Dijon in Burgundy, an Anglo-Spanish army made an unsuccessful incursion into Aquitaine (1512), and Ferdinand overran Navarra (Aug–Sept 1512). It was part of the ensuing peace Trs that Louis m Mary Tudor, the sister of Henry VIII; but his costly Italian adventures had been unwisely embarked upon and incompetently conducted, for he had been outwitted by Julius II and Ferdinand II.

In his home policy, on the other hand, Louis was reasonable, humane, economical and popular, being known as the Father of his People – a title conferred on him by the Estates of Tours in 1506. Under him France continued the main trends established under Charles VIII: economic growth, internal peace (till the last year), and admin consolidation, as the typical governing hierarchies of the *Ancien Régime* were built up. From the centre, the royal Council and the great judicial, financial and military departments – reformed by the Ordinance of Mar 1499 – were pushing out their tentacles over the provs and localities: more prov appeal courts, ie PARLEMENTS, were established, and jurists were steadily codifying the multifarious types of customary law; in the bureaucracy, the disastrous practice of selling offices had already begun; in the Ch Louis' chief minister, Georges d'AMBOISE, was merely the most blatant example of the continuing practice of using the top benefices to provide income for political supporters or family connections; he also encouraged Louis to use Gallican arguments and threats of Ch reform as weapons in foreign policy involving war with Pp Julius II. At the same time, a genuine reform movement was beginning with the spread of HUMANISM, especially exemplified in the work of LEFÈVRE D'ÉTAPLES. Prematurely aged, Louis survived only 11 weeks of married life with his young bride.

Louis XIII (27 Sept 1601–14 May 1643) K of France (1610). During his minority his mother, MARIE DE MEDICI, dissipated practically all the authority and treasure that his father, HENRY IV, had built up after the FRENCH WARS OF RELIGION, giving the magnates their head, and following a pro-Spanish foreign policy. Incapable of ruling himself, but nevertheless keeping the major decisions in his own hands, he ruled through stronger men, notably LUYNES, who ruled 1617–21 after he and the K had organized the assassination of the Q Mother's minister, Concini, and RICHELIEU, who was chief minister 1624–42. His reign was marked at home by the elimination of the political independence of the Hugs, the suppression of the Prs of the Blood and the magnates, the general increase in royal authority by *ad hoc* ruthlessness rather than fundamental reform, and the frequent rebellions of the masses suffering from high taxation and periodic famine; and abroad by the successful role of France in the THIRTY YEARS WAR, denying the Habsburgs victory in Germany, breaking the Spanish encirclement, and gaining valuable border territory.

He succeeded as a minor after the assassination of his father, under the Regency of his mother which was declared by the PARLEMENT of Paris on 15 May 1610. Officially declared of age in Oct 1614, he m (1615) the Spanish Infanta, known as Anne of Austria, as a consequence of his mother's pro-Spanish foreign policy (Tr of Fontainebleau, Apr 1611). It was an unhappy relationship both personally and politically, and it was not until very late in the reign, after 2 miscarriages (1618, 1630) and many years without cohabitation, that the future LOUIS XIV was born as the result of a night which Louis spent in her apartments in the Louvre, probably out of a sense of duty to his Kdom.

Louis himself suffered an unhappy childhood and grew up into a mass of contradictions which have made him difficult to interpret. He was usually modest, reserved and silent, but wilful and ruthless beneath, and capable of sudden, powerful decisions, violent wrath, or cruel deeds. He was deeply religious and highly conscientious; a hypochondriac with weak health who enjoyed leading an army; keen on hunting, a practising artist and craftsman, with a high sense of his position as K of France, but with the gift of appearing at ease with the common people. He was well aware that he lacked the ability and application to rule France, and he left the tedious detail to others; but, as Richelieu well knew, the final choice of men and measures was the K's. His reign can be studied under the names of those who ruled for him – Marie de Medici, Luynes, Richelieu –

and those who rebelled against him – Henry, 3rd Pr de CONDÉ; Gaston, D d'ORLÉANS; Henry, D de ROHAN.

Louis XIV (5 Sept 1638–1 Sept 1715) K of France (1643) in whose long reign France made important progress in the development of centralized absolutism, economic strength, scientific knowledge and artistic style. At the same time, in a series of aggressive wars, he extended the realm and strengthened its frontiers, making France the leading power in Europe, though at the same time stimulating the formation of hostile alliances led by the Emp, the United Provinces and Great Britain, determined to preserve the BALANCE OF POWER.

Son of K LOUIS XIII and his Q consort, Anne of Austria; ed thoroughly in all the physical and mental pursuits suitable to a future K, and taught to be a strong ruler by his experiences in the FRONDES (when he was forced to flee Paris on 3 occasions, and have the mob file through his bedroom while he feigned sleep), and more deliberately by MAZARIN, chief minister during his minority. Gifted with good looks and wonderful health, he was graceful, dignified and awe-inspiring, if humourless. He took himself and his job very seriously, and as K worked 6 to 9 hours each day governing France, as well as indulging vigorously in the elaborate Court life, in all the arts and sciences, hunting and womanizing. He m 1st (1660) Maria Teresa, daughter of K PHILIP IV of Spain, by whom he had 6 children, of whom only the Dauphin, Louis de France, survived. (She d 1683.) He m 2nd (in secret, 1683 or 1684) Françoise, widow of the poet, Paul Scarron, who had brought up his illegitimate children and been created Marquise de Maintenon. His chief – non-political – love affairs were with: 1st (1657–60) Marie Mancini, niece of Mazarin; 2nd (1661–7) Louise de la Vallière (4 children); 3rd (1667–78) Athénaïs de Montespan (7 children, including Louis Auguste, D du Maine, and Louis Alexandre, Comte de Toulouse); followed by a quick succession of several (1676 onwards) until he m Mme de Maintenon. He was declared of age in Sept 1651, but did not begin to rule until the death of Mazarin (8/9 Mar 1661).

His home policy was characterized by the deliberate extension of centralized absolutism, built upon the foundations recently laid by RICHELIEU and Mazarin and justified by political theorists such as Bossuet.

In central gov he ruled France personally, in consultation with individual ministers, and in conference 3 or 4 days a week with his chief Council of 3–5 members: the *Conseil d'en Haut*. His chief ministers in the early part of his reign were Jean-Baptiste COLBERT (Controller-Gen of Finances, among other posts), Michel Le Tellier (Sec of State for War), François-Michel Le Tellier, Marquis de Louvois (Sec of State for War), Hugues de Lionne (Sec of State for Foreign Affairs). The ministers in the later part of the reign, when the K dominated affairs more completely, were the sons and nephews of this 1st generation. Both the ministers and the members of the other central Councils were members of the Robe or bourgeois career administrators: he deliberately excluded the Prs of the Blood and the nobility from political power, and successfully kept the PARLE-MENTS subdued.

In prov and local gov, he greatly extended the number and functions of the Intendants – middle-class agents sent from Paris to supervise the chaotic traditional admin (in finance, justice, police, economic planning etc). This system was still manned by remnants from feudal times, or by the more recently developed *officiers* (office-holders who had bought their jobs) or even (as in the *pays d'états*) by independent prov administrators, responsible not to Paris but to their prov Estates.

In the law he made codifications and reforms which formed the basis of French justice till the *Code Napoléon*: the Civil Code (1667), the Criminal Code (1670), the Maritime Code (1672), the Commercial Code (1673) and the *Code Noir* for slaves in the colonies (1685).

The army was enlarged from 80,000 native Frenchmen to 350,000 at the end of his reign. It was also greatly improved and, most important, subordinated to the State. Clientage was gradually eliminated, and the great feudal lords, who in the past, with considerable independence, had raised their units on a semi-feudal, semi-commercial basis, were brought under the close supervision of the Sec of State for War and his Intendants, who henceforth controlled appointments, promotions, recruitment, discipline and provisioning. Likewise, the prov Govs, whose military power in the past had as often been used against the Crown as for it, were posted from prov to prov frequently, while their responsibilities shrank to ceremonial functions as the real work was increasingly performed by less aristocratic Lieut-Gens sent from Paris.

The navy was created by Colbert, for he found only 2 or 3 serviceable ships at the start of the reign. The merchant marine was expanded also, and France increasingly followed a deliberate policy of colonization and commercial aggression.

In religion, the K's policies were mainly motivated by his view of the Ch as an essential agent of order and unity in France, and by his suspicion of unorthodoxy as divisive, even rebellious. In the 2nd half of the reign, as he grew older and fell under the influence of Madame de Maintenon and his Jesuit confessors, he enforced uniformity more harshly, possibly because he became more pious himself, more likely because of the necessity of appearing more pious to a France and a Europe which were aware that he had done nothing to help save Vienna from the Turks in 1683. (a) *The French Church* usually toed his line in the General Assembly of the Clergy (for he limited appointments in the hierarchy to Robe and bourgeois clerics). They backed him financially, and supported his Gallican position when he quarrelled with the Pp, as he did from time to time, over international politics and over the ultramontane claims of the Pp to rule the French Ch. The most acrimonious example of the latter was the *régale* dispute. In this both K and Pp claimed the right to enjoy episcopal revenues and patronage during a vacancy in those 59 dioceses which had been added to France since 1516, and which were not covered by the Concordat of Bologna (1516), which had granted the others to the K. By 1688, 35 dioceses were without a Bp, and in Mar 1682 the Assembly issued the Four Articles spelling out the firm Gallican position. In 1693, with a new Pp and a new international situation, the quarrel was called off with a compromise which gave Louis more or less victory in the *régale* dispute, while he soft-pedalled over the Four Articles. (b) *Jansenism* was persecuted through most of the reign, except during the so-called 'peace of the Church' (1668–79), when he was at war with the Pp. An independent-minded puritanical movement believing in predestination, Jansenism was strong in the 2 convents of the Port-Royal in Paris and the Port-Royal-des-Champs nearby. Louis hated it for its rebellious role in the Frondes and its hostility to the Jesuits. In 1661 he enforced the papal Bull *Cum Occasione* (1653), condemning 5 Jansenist beliefs as heresy. He expelled their novices (1661) and the 12 chief nuns (1664), and placed the convents under military guard. Renewing the persecution in the 1680s, he exiled the leaders, then arrested the nuns (1709) and distributed them forcibly among anti-Jansenist convents. In 1710 he destroyed Port-Royal-des-Champs and ploughed up its cemetery. In 1713 he got the Pp to publish the Bull *Unigenitus* condemning Jansenist views. (c) *Quietism* was also persecuted. This mystical movement, originating in Spain and Italy, led by the hysterical Mme de Guyon, and supported by Fénelon, a royal tutor and leading prelate, was suspect in the eyes of Louis and Bossuet because its emphasis on the mindless ecstasy of the love of God placed believers above the necessity of ceremonies and works – made them independent of the Ch, in fact. He locked up Mme de Guyon in Vincennes (Dec 1695), backed Bossuet in his bitter debate with Fénelon, and got the Pp to condemn the movement as erroneous, though not heretical (Mar 1699). (d) *The Hugs* – a minority of some $1\frac{1}{2}$ to 2 million – were harassed by Louis from 1666 onwards in a campaign designed to drive them back into the Ch. The courts reduced their privileges by strictly interpreting the Edict of Nantes (1598). Decrees were issued restricting their entry into public office and the liberal professions. Some converts received cash payments to encourage others; while in some areas Hugs had troops billeted on them (the 'Dragonnades'). Finally in Oct 1685 the Edict of Fontainebleau was issued, revoking the Edict of Nantes. Henceforth it was illegal to be a Prot, and about 200,000 fled the country, though emigration was also illegal. Exactly why the K wounded France by the harsh treatment of a loyal, talented and industrious group is not easy to establish. Though no theological enthusiast himself, he came under the influence of Mme de Maintenon and her *dévot* allies from 1679 onwards; probably this made him more sensitive to the clamour of the Assembly of the Clergy, which had been pressing him to punish heresy since 1665. Moreover, he needed to demonstrate his orthodoxy to Europe at large. He was practically at war with Pp Innocent XI, and in 1683 Vienna was saved from the Turks by an allied campaign which notoriously had received no help from France. The consequences of the Revocation are also difficult to assess; at least in the short term, France suffered economically from the emigration of a proportion of her skilled manufacturers to rival states such as Brandenburg, the United Provinces and Britain. She also suffered militarily by the injection of ideological fervour into the power-politics determination of Britain, the United Provinces and their allies to stop France's attempt to dominate Europe.

In financial and economic affairs the Controller-Gen of Finances, Colbert, increased the royal revenues by reforms in the tax-collecting system, though without eliminating royal indebtedness or eradicating the basic weakness of the *Ancien Régime*: that taxes were paid in inverse proportion to wealth because of the immunities secured by the nobility, the clergy and the office-holders. The taxable capacity of Frenchmen was increased, however, by Colbert's efforts to stimulate commerce and industry. In a long period of European economic depression, France captured more than her fair share of world trade, and established for good her reputation for fine craftsmanship.

In the arts, crafts and sciences also, Colbert created a cultural absolutism.

267

Through the Univ, the schools, the Academies, the Court, the censorship and the official press, an all-pervading Louis XIV style was imposed on all products of the human spirit, whether it was Versailles, a château, an opera, a firework display, or an inscription on a medal. Bernini was invited to design the E front of the Louvre (1665), only to have his curves rejected in favour of Perrault's classicism: a sign that France had replaced Italy as the centre of European art.

In foreign affairs, Louis used his overwhelming military power and his clever and brutal diplomacy for purposes which at first could be shown to be in France's interests, but which later can only be explained by the vainglorious psychology of the K and also by the following motives, singly or in various combinations: the search for safer frontiers, the lust for European dominion, economic expansion, the defence of the Trs of Westphalia and the Pyrenees from the vengeful Emp LEOPOLD I, the pursuit of his legal claim to the Spanish emp, or the need to find employment for otherwise discontented nobles. What is clear is that the prudent thrusting up to about 1678 turned into a megalomania so excessive that WILLIAM III and MARLBOROUGH were able to organize their European coalitions to restore the balance of power. In addition to ruling the largest centralized state in Europe, Louis enjoyed other advantages over his enemies. In E Europe the Emp was also fighting the Turks and the Magyars in the Balkans; in the W, Spain in decline was preoccupied with the REVOLT OF PORTUGAL. Louis, moreover, exercised a unified command while his enemies were a coalition kept together with great diplomatic difficulty. He was an absolute monarch, while the Govs of Sweden, the United Provinces and Britain were often hamstrung by federal and constitutional opposition. Louis' chief wars were (a) The War of Devolution (1667–8), gaining Lille and 11 other fortified towns on the Belgian border (Tr of Aix-la-Chapelle, 1668); (b) The Franco-Dutch War (1672–9), gaining Franche Comté (Trs of Nijmegen, 1678/9); (c) The *Réunions* (1679–84), a period of legalistic aggression and diplomatic intimidation, gaining Strasbourg, Luxemburg and Casale in Italy (Tr of Regensburg, 1684); (d) War of the League of Augsburg or Nine Years War (1689–97) in which he kept Strasbourg, but ceded Pinerolo, Casale, Nice, Lorraine and Luxemburg (Tr of Rijswijk, 1697); (e) The War of the Spanish Succession (1702–13/14), keeping his main European gains and putting his grandson on the throne of Spain (Trs of Utrecht etc, 1713/14).

(a) The War of Devolution began as an attack by Louis (24 May 1667) on the Spanish Netherlands after the death of K PHILIP IV of Spain (1665). Louis used the argument that the law of devolution in Brabant private law gave his wife, Maria Teresa – who was Philip's daughter by his 1st wife – a better claim than that of K CHARLES II of Spain – who was Philip's son by his 2nd wife. Louis was in alliance with Great Britain (who sold him Dunkirk, 1662), Johan de WITT of the United Provinces (Tr of 1662), and the League of the Rhine (Tr of 1663), ie German Prs who opposed the Emp Leopold. Britain and the United Provinces were fighting the 2nd Anglo-Dutch War (1665–7). Leopold, threatened from the E, was unable to offer any resistance to France, and agreed in a secret Tr with Louis (Jan 1668) to the ultimate partition with France of the whole Spanish inheritance. With France backing the Portuguese revolt (Tr of 1667) Spain was effectively isolated: a triumph of diplomacy. In a war of sieges, Turenne, Vauban and Louvois swiftly took Lille and 11 other Belgian fortresses, sometimes in the presence of Louis and his Court, while Condé invaded Franche Comté. The inevitable reaction occurred. Britain made peace with the United Provinces (1667). The two States formed an alliance (Jan 1668), which became the Triple Alliance when Sweden joined in Apr 1668. Louis decided on peace, which was signed at Aix-la-Chapelle (May 1668). France returned Franche Comté to Spain, but kept the 12 Belgian fortresses, greatly strengthening the frontier in that area.

(b) The Franco-Dutch War arose from Louis' indignation at the United Provinces' adhesion to the Triple Alliance, fortified by Colbert's wish to loosen the hold that the Dutch entrepreneurs had on the French economy and to capture their world trade. Colbert erected a prohibitive tariff against the United Provinces in 1667, and imposed high sugar duties in 1670–71. The European powers seemed paralysed by French power and money, and one by one they succumbed: Britain (secret Tr of Dover, May/June 1670), Bavaria (Feb 1670), various W German Prs (1671) and Sweden (Apr 1672); even Leopold had to promise neutrality (Dec 1671). The only power to support the United Provinces was FREDERICK WILLIAM, the Great Elector of Brandenburg (Feb 1671). The war began with a double onslaught on the Dutch. By sea, England treacherously started the 3rd Anglo-Dutch War (1672–4) without much success. By land, the French army passed through Cologne, crossed the Rhine, thrust W into Holland, took Utrecht, but made no further progress as the Dutch took 2 extreme measures: they opened the dykes and flooded Holland, and they overthrew de Witt and rallied behind WILLIAM III. Abandoning neutrality, Leopold formed the Grand Alliance of the Emp, the United Provinces, Spain, Lorraine and Brandenburg (1673–4); henceforth the war broadened out to involve campaigns in the Spanish Netherlands, Alsace, Lorraine and Franche Comté. France took Maastricht (June 1673), conquered Franche Comté, struck into W Germany, and drove the enemy out of Alsace (1674). It then broadened still further, for Louis' ally Sweden fought Denmark over Scania, and Brandenburg over Pomerania, the Great Elector defeating the Swedes at Fehrbellin (28 June 1675). In the Med, the French navy backed Sicily against Spain, and twice defeated the Dutch. In Spain French troops invaded Catalonia. Further afield still, the Dutch attacked French colonies in the W Indies and the Indian Ocean. On the Rhine, Leopold took Philippsburg (Sept 1676) and France took Freiburg (Nov 1677). In 1678/9, France signed the Trs of Nijmegen: (i) with the United Provinces, whereby France returned Maastricht and other conquests and also cancelled the tariff of 1667; (ii) with Spain, whereby France kept Franche Comté and gave up some fortresses in the Spanish Netherlands in exchange for some better ones so as to make an impregnable frontier; (iii) with the Emp whereby France kept Freiburg, Leopold kept Philippsburg, France gave Lorraine back to D Charles on terms which he refused to accept, leaving France in occupation. In the Tr of St Germain-en-Laye (June 1679), France forced Brandenburg to return his conquests in Pomerania to Sweden. In the Tr of Fontainebleau (Sept 1679), Denmark likewise had to return her Scanian conquests to Sweden. It was the high point of French foreign policy, and for the next few years, with bribery and intimidation, Louis was able to have his way with a Europe in disarray.

(c) The *Réunions* (1679–84) saw Louis using his dominating position to make territorial gains without striking many blows. Tribunals called *Chambres de Réunions* were set up in Metz, Alsace, Flanders and Franche Comté to extend

French possessions round the numerous towns in these areas which she had gained by Trs from 1648 onwards. At this stage, Louis could exercise his superiority with impunity, for Spain was in full decline, Charles II of Britain was in his pay, William III of the United Provinces was at loggerheads with the Regents of Amsterdam, and the Emp Leopold was locked in conflict with the Turks (Siege of Vienna, 1683). The tribunals interpreted uncertain wording in the Trs in France's favour, and where necessary force supplemented judicial process. On 30 Sept 1681 Louis' troops took Strasbourg, Alsace and Casale, Piedmont; in June 1684 they took Luxemburg and other strong points in the Spanish Netherlands. Then by an agreement with Spain (1684) and the Truce of Regensburg with the Emp (Aug 1684), these gains were recognized for 20 years. It was the furthest extent of French expansion.

(d) The War of the League of Augsburg or Nine Years War (1689–97) resulted from the exhaustion of Europe's patience at the continued acts of violence by Louis, who was just as aggressive after the Tr of Regensburg as before. In May 1684 he destroyed three-quarters of Genoa in a 6-day bombardment and forced the Doge to visit Versailles to apologize for helping Spain. On the death of the El Palatine (1684) he demanded territory for his sister-in-law, the Dss of Orléans, to pay for her supposed claims. He intervened in Cologne to secure the election of his candidate as Archbp-Elector instead of the one backed by the Pp and the Emp (10 July 1688). Meanwhile the Emp and some of the German Prs formed the defensive League of Augsburg (July 1686), to which Sweden and Spain also belonged by virtue of their German territories. Moreover, the general situation which had long favoured Louis was changing. Leopold was having success against the Turks: eg the capture of Buda (2 Sept 1686), the victory nr Mohács (12 Aug 1687), and the capture of Belgrade (6 Sept 1688). Louis decided on a short sharp campaign to cow Germany and encourage the Turks. He occupied the Rhineland and invaded the Palatinate (Sept 1688); but instead of intimidating his enemies, he further united them. He also allowed William III the opportunity to invade England, carry out the REVOLUTION OF 1688, and thenceforth become the leader of the great anti-French alliance. To limit his battle fronts, Louis retreated from the Palatinate, having first devastated it in order to cripple it as a base for invading France. Heidelberg, Mannheim, Speier and Worms were put to the sack and the countryside turned into a desert. The war, which now started, was fought (i) at sea, (ii) in the Netherlands, (iii) in N Italy, (iv) in Spain and (v) in the colonies. Neither side achieved superiority, and peace was signed in (vi) the Tr of Rijswijk (1697). (i) *At sea*, the French landed JAMES II in Ireland (Mar 1690), and then evacuated him when he was beaten at the Boyne (1/11 July 1690). They also beat the Anglo-Dutch fleet off Beachy Head (30 June/10 July 1690). A French plan to invade England and restore James II was frustrated by the Anglo-Dutch victory at La Hogue (19/29 May 1692); though the French captured the Anglo-Dutch Smyrna fleet off Lagos (1693). (ii) *In the Spanish Netherlands*, the French beat William III at Fleurus (1 July 1690), Steenkirk (3 Aug 1692) and Neerwinden (29 July 1693), capturing Mons (Apr 1691) and Namur (June 1692); though William began to restore the balance by his 1st land victory, retaking Namur on 5 Sept 1695. (iii) *In N Italy*, the French overran Savoy and Nice (1690–91) and invaded Piedmont, thrusting at Turin (1693) until the D of Savoy, Victor Amadeus II, changed sides and backed France. Louis paid a high price, ceding Casale, Pinerolo and Nice (Tr of Turin, Aug 1696). (iv) *In Spain*, the French invaded Catalonia (1689) and in conjunction with their fleet laid siege to Barcelona, until the arrival of the English fleet relieved it (1694). Later, on the withdrawal of the English navy, the French took Barcelona (1697). (v) *In the colonies*, the normal peace-time skirmishing intensified. In America, the French at Quebec and the English at Boston and New York raided one another and fought over Nova Scotia, Newfoundland and Hudson Bay, while the English unsuccessfully attacked the French W Indies. In W Africa, the French lost and regained Goree and the R Senegal. In India, the United Provinces captured Pondicherry from the French (1693). (vi) *The Trs of Rijswijk* (1697) showed that the ageing Louis was chastened, realistic and moderate. With his treasury empty and his people suffering the pains of forced recruiting, heavy taxation and bad harvests, the K was prepared to make peace without gaining any of his war aims. He returned all his conquests since Nijmegen (1678) except Strasbourg, ceding Luxemburg, Mons and Catalonia to Spain, and Philippsburg, Freiburg, Breisach and other conquests on the German side of the Rhine to the Emp. He also returned Lorraine to its D, abandoned his candidate for Cologne, and gave up the Orléans claim to the Palatinate. He recognized William III as K of Great Britain and Ireland. He allowed the Dutch to fortify certain barrier fortresses in the Spanish Netherlands. The moderation of Louis was remarkable, but there was another good reason for it: CHARLES II, of Spain was at last about to die, and Louis was anxious for as big a share of the inheritance as possible.

(e) The War of the Spanish Succession (1702–13/14) broke out because the balance of power would have been seriously upset had one or other of the chief heirs received the whole inheritance: ie the Emp Leopold and Louis XIV, each with a Spanish mother and wife. To avoid war, Louis (but not Leopold) was prepared to share out Spanish possessions in 2 Partition Trs with Britain and the United Provinces: Oct 1698 and June 1699. The Spanish not unnaturally wanted the inheritance kept intact, and in his will Charles II made Louis' grandson, Philip of Anjou, his sole heir. On Charles's death (1 Nov 1700), Louis abandoned the Partition Trs and accepted the will – his wisest course. William did likewise for Britain and the United Provinces. War was bound to ensue with Leopold, but certain provocations of Louis enabled William (who also favoured war) to form a strong anti-French coalition. Louis ceremonially safeguarded Philip's right to inherit the French throne (Dec 1700); occupied fortresses in the Spanish Netherlands from which William had to withdraw (Feb 1701); gained for France the *Asiento*, or monopoly of importing African slaves into the Spanish colonies (Aug 1701); and recognized the Old Pretender as K James III of Great Britain (Sept 1701). In reply, Britain, the United Provinces and the Emp formed the Grand Alliance by the Tr of the Hague (Sept 1701); while Louis was supported by Bavaria and Cologne, and to a lesser extent by Savoy and Portugal. The war was fought (i) in Italy, (ii) in Germany, (iii) in the Netherlands and (iv) in Spain; and it ended with (v) the peace Trs of Utrecht (1713), Rastatt and Baden (1714). (i) *In Italy*, where fighting began in 1701, before the allied declaration of war (15 May 1702), the French occupied Milan, and Pr Eugen descended from Austria to drive them out. His task was facilitated when Victor Amadeus II of Savoy changed sides (Oct 1703). Eugen defeated the French at Turin (7 Sept 1706), and the war ended in this theatre with the Convention of Milan (Mar 1707) between

France and the Emp. (ii) *In Germany*, the armies of the Emp and the Prs were kept out of Alsace by the French victory at Friedlingen, Black Forest (14 Oct 1702). The French and the Bavarians were thus in a position to strike down the Danube at Vienna, having beaten the Germans once more at Höchstädt, Bavaria, on 20 Sept 1703. With Hungarian rebels menacing Vienna from the E, Leopold was in grave danger, but the allied commander in the Netherlands, Marlborough, swiftly marched up the Rhine and into Bavaria, joining the imperial commander, Pr Eugen. Together they beat the French at the celebrated battle of Blenheim, Bavaria (2/13 Aug 1704), forcing the French to stay on the defensive W of the Rhine for most of the rest of the war, though they made a short incursion into SW Germany in May–Sept 1707. (iii) *In the Spanish Netherlands*, Marlborough pushed the French from their advanced positions (1702) and conquered the territory of Louis' ally, the Archbp of Cologne, taking Bonn on 7/18 May 1703. Then, managing to squeeze a little more freedom of action from the cautious Dutch Gov, which placed commissioners with the armies, hampering their movements, he defeated the French at Ramillies (12/23 May 1706). This enabled him gradually to overrun Flanders and Brabant, leaving only the extreme, Walloon, S Netherlands in French hands. The French counter-attacked, but Marlborough defeated them at Oudenarde (31 July/11 Aug 1708) and took Lille (11/22 Oct 1708). The allies were at this stage in a position to march on Paris, but were so mauled by their costly victory over the French at Malplaquet (31 Aug/11 Sept 1709) that they had to content themselves with a few more fortresses: Tournai, Mons and Douai. (iv) *In Spain*, the allies unsuccessfully tried to oust Philip of Anjou – K PHILIP V – from his throne. He was powerfully supported by the Castilian people as well as a big French army. The allied candidate, Leopold's 2nd son, the ArchD Charles, was backed by the breakaway Catalans as 'K Charles III', and he was supported by the British navy. The allies first landed at Cádiz, but had to withdraw (Aug–Sept 1702), compensating themselves with the capture or destruction of the Spanish treasure fleet at Vigo Bay, Galicia, on 12/23 Oct 1702. The following year they succeeded in opening a W front by detaching Portugal from France with the 2 Methuen Trs, one of alliance (May 1703), one of commerce (Dec 1703). Until 1704 Philip had a good opportunity of establishing himself, but the British navy changed the situation by capturing Gibraltar (24 July/4 Aug 1704) and taking command of the sea along the Med coast. 'Charles III' was deposited in Catalonia (1705) where he was enthusiastically received by the people who were re-enacting the REVOLT OF CATALONIA (1640–52). In 1706 Aragon and Valencia also rebelled with allied support, but with short-lived success. The Castilians were solidly behind Philip V, and with French help he recovered Madrid (though he lost it again more than once), beat the allies at Almansa, nr the border of Valencia (14/25 Apr 1707), and subdued Aragon and Valencia. In Sept 1708 the allies took Minorca, but they failed to loosen Philip's hold on Spain. They beat him at Zaragoza (8/19 Aug 1710), then took and lost Madrid, then retreated back to Catalonia to be beaten at Brihuega (28 Nov/8 Dec 1710) and Villaviciosa (30 Nov/10 Dec 1710). (v) *The peace Trs* were arrived at after a long process of bargaining which began in the middle of the war. France was so exhausted by 1709 that Louis offered humiliating concessions (May 1709) whereby Philip should give up Spain and be limited to Naples and Sicily, while he himself would give up Alsace and Franche Comté, and generally go back to the settlement of 1648. In addition, he was prepared to allow the United Provinces to have a line of barrier fortresses in the Spanish Netherlands, to recognize the Hanoverian succession in Britain, and to expel the Old Pretender from France. Led by the Emp and the United Provinces, the allies refused, and insisted that Louis should declare war on his grandson and help to drive him out of Spain – the policy of 'No peace without Spain'. Louis indignantly refused, and was backed by the patriotism of the French people. Regaining strength, the French made progress in Spain and defeated Pr Eugen and the allies at Denain, Netherlands, on 24 July 1712. At the same time the Grand Alliance began to crack. In Britain, Anne appointed a Tory Gov bent on peace. Moreover, the Emp JOSEPH I – who had succeeded his father in 1705 – suddenly d on 17 Apr 1711, completely changing the situation. K 'Charles III' now became the Emp CHARLES VI, and it was as much against the allied balance-of-power policy to allow Spain and Austria to unite as it was Spain and France. In a series of Trs at Utrecht (1713) between France and Spain and the allies, at Rastatt (Mar 1714) between France and the Emp, and at Baden (Sept 1714) between France and the Prs of the Emp, the following settlement was arrived at. Philip V kept Spain and Spanish America, and renounced his right to succeed to the French throne. The Emp received Milan, Naples, Sardinia and the Spanish Netherlands. Savoy received Sicily and had French conquests in Savoy and Nice returned. France kept Strasbourg, Alsace, Franche Comté and the strong frontier she had conquered in the E and NE, but gave up her possessions E of the Rhine. She agreed to dismantle Dunkirk and fill in the harbour. She recognized the Hanoverian succession in Britain and Ireland, and agreed not to shelter the Old Pretender. The El of Brandenburg was recognized as K in Prussia. Britain gained the *Asiento* and the *navio de permiso* (the right to send one ship each year to trade with Spanish America). She also kept Gibraltar and Minorca, as well as Nova Scotia, Newfoundland and Hudson Bay. The United Provinces resented not having a share in Britain's commercial gains, but in the Barrier Tr (Nov 1715) they achieved one important aim: the right to garrison 7 fortresses in Belgium, three-fifths of the expenses being paid by the Emp.

The last years of Louis – especially 1709 – were filled with humiliation abroad and economic crisis at home. Though fortunes were made, the mass of Frenchmen suffered deeply from royal taxation, feudal exactions, military service, bad harvests, industrial depression, famine and disease. Undernourished and overstrained, they rioted, only to be put down by the sword. At the same time, criticisms percolated through cracks in the censorship, attacking absolute monarchy, military aggression, religious persecution and other aspects of the *Ancien Régime*. It was the start of the Enlightenment. The France of Louis XIV lacked the advantages of the new century which so favoured her new rival, Great Britain: constitutional gov, political liberty, free enterprise, science and reason. Moreover, Louis himself suffered personal tragedies which swept away his family. His only son, the Dauphin, d on 14 Apr 1711. His 1st grandson, the D of Burgundy, succumbed to smallpox on 18 Feb 1712 along with his Dss and eld son. His 2nd grandson, Philip of Anjou, became K of Spain and incapable of succeeding in France. His 3rd grandson, the D de Berry, d on 4 Mar 1714. In consequence, when Louis d his heir was his great-grandson, the 3rd son of the D of Burgundy – the future LOUIS XV.

Louis XV (15 Feb 1710–10 May 1774) K of France (1715), whose personal inadequacies and incompetent leadership (except for a last-minute show of strength) seriously reduced the power and prestige of the French monarchy at home and abroad. At home he failed to settle the issues that divided Frenchmen: notably the enmity between Jesuits and Jansenists; the resistance of the privileged to the Crown's efforts to make them pay their fair share of taxation; the general inflexibility of the institutions of the *Ancien Régime* in the face of a buoyant and prosperous people, rapidly evolving economically, socially and culturally; and the constitutional struggle between the Crown on the one hand, and the PARLE-MENTS and the prov Estates on the other. Abroad he pursued unwise ends with ineffective means, and France became outclassed in the power-politics arena by Great Britain.

3rd son of Louis, D of Burgundy (who was the grandson of LOUIS XIV) and his wife, Marie Adelaide of Savoy; ed by the D de Villeroy and André Hercule Fleury, Bp of Fréjus; m (1725) Marie, daughter of Stanislas Leszczyński, ex-K of Poland (1704–9); became heir of Louis XIV after the deaths in rapid succession of his grandfather, father and elder brothers.

The Regency of Orléans (1715–23) was necessary because the K was under age. Philip, D of Orléans – nephew of Louis XIV and 1st Pr of the Blood – was appointed to the Council of Regency by the will of the old K, along with 2 legitimized bastards, the D du Maine and the Count de Toulouse. Orléans – a debauched and free-thinking soldier and intellectual – had headed the groups who opposed the old K (the Sword, the Parlements and the Jansenists); the Sword especially looked to him to dismantle the apparatus of absolutism and revive the bygone days of aristocratic disorder. With the connivance of the Parlement of Paris – which in return was given back its right of remonstrance – Orléans broke the K's will, ousted Maine and Toulouse, and made himself sole Regent (Sept 1715), a coup confirmed by the K. He ruled as Regent until the young K was declared of age in Feb 1723 and then became *Premier Ministre* (Aug–2 Dec 1723, his death). In government, this helped to revive the pretensions of the Parlements to be a constitutional limitation on absolutism. They tried several times to block his financial measures and in 1720 he exiled the Paris Parlement to Pontoise. The Parlements also opposed the Regent in religious affairs. He insisted on enforcing the papal Bull *Unigenitus* (1713) against the Jansenists, while the Parlements backed the Jansenists, in fact, all anti-Jesuits and all Gallicans (ie those who opposed the extension of the Pp's power over the French Ch). At the same time, he indulged the dreams of the Sword by replacing the Sec of State with 6 councils manned by nobles, both Sword and Robe. The frivolous nobles, however, soon proved themselves unfit for admin drudgery and by 1718 this experiment in nostalgia – the *Polysynodie* – was being wound up. The central Gov reverted to the customs of Louis XIV's day, with departments under Secs of State. The Regent tried different solutions to the main problem – the insolvency of the crown – the chief one being John Law's System which led to a financial panic similar to the contemporary 'SOUTH SEA BUBBLE'. This Scottish financier with faith in the virtues of paper money persuaded the Regent to back his adventurous scheme of credit expansion. Law set up a private *Banque Générale* (May 1716) and then (Aug 1717) the Company of the West (or Mississippi Co) which had the monopoly of trade with Louisiana. The Treasury was involved in both affairs, and by 1719 the Co had absorbed several other colonial trading companies, and the Bank had become a Royal Bank. Law outbid the Farmers-Gen for the farm of the taxes and took over the royal debt. In 1720 the Bank and the Co were united, and Law was appointed Controller-Gen of Finance, after turning Cath. A wave of frantic speculation ensued in which the Co's 500-livres shares touched 18,000 at one point. Then confidence faltered (Feb 1720) and by Oct 1720 the crash was complete and Law had fled the country. Fortunes were made and lost, and the shocked French public took almost a century to shake off their prejudice against a State bank. The economy nevertheless soon revived, and colonial development went forward. At the same time, the Crown's financial crisis deepened. Foreign affairs were in the hands of the Regent's old tutor, the Abbé Dubois, a brilliant careerist who became Archbp of Cambrai (1720), Card (1721) and *Premier Ministre* (Aug 1722–10 Aug 1723, his death). His policy was based on co-operation with the old enemy, Britain. With STANHOPE he negotiated the Anglo-French alliance of Sept 1716, which became the Triple Alliance when Holland joined (Jan 1717). Its aim was the pacification of Europe in general; but as far as France was concerned the 2 chief purposes were to allow the Treasury and the economy to recover from the wars of Louis XIV, and to make sure that – if the sickly Louis XV did not survive – the Crown would go to Orléans, and not to PHILIP V, the Bourbon K of Spain. This involved a short war with a resurgent Spain (1719–20), but in the subsequent peace Tr (Jan 1720) Philip V renounced his claim to the French throne. Franco-Spanish amity was confirmed by the betrothal in 1721 of Louis XV to the Infanta Maria, Philip V's daughter.

Bourbon's admin (Dec 1723–June 1726) followed immediately upon the Regent's death. As 1st Pr of the Blood, the one-eyed, bow-legged, incompetent D de Bourbon became *Premier Ministre*, but in most matters he deferred to the caprices of his seductive but ambitious mistress, the Marquise de Prie. He also had to put up with the sniping of the K's old tutor, Fleury, who also had a seat on the Council. Bourbon continued the policy of peaceful co-operation with Britain. His chief work otherwise was the break-up of the Spanish marriage project and the marriage of the 15-year-old Louis to the 22-year-old Marie Leszczyński. He was in a hurry for the K to sire children, since otherwise the Orléans family would succeed to the throne. The marriage alienated the K of Spain who then upset the European equilibrium (and reasonable expectations) by joining his old enemy, Austria, in the 1st Tr of Vienna (Apr 1725). In the end, Fleury's massive abilities triumphed and the K dismissed Bourbon and put Fleury in his place, though without the title of *Premier Ministre*.

Fleury's admin (June 1726–29 Jan 1743, his death) continued the pacific policies of the Regency, but brought in a period of firmer gov and rising prosperity. A cautious and reserved son of a bourgeois tax official, Fleury had a fine presence, a powerful mind and ruthless ambition, becoming Bp of Fréjus (1698), tutor to the future Louis XV (1714), and Card (1726). He was already 73 when he took office, but he had won the affection and confidence of his pupil – possibly by not setting him too much work – and the K – who always preferred the old faces and hated change – defended him steadfastly against intriguing rivals almost to the end. At home, Philibert Orry, the Controller-Gen (1730–45), balanced his budgets in peacetime, and steadily operated the mercantilist machinery set up by COLBERT.

With efficient and prudent management, avoiding controversial innovation, he presided over a period of steadily rising prices and economic growth. In wartime he revived Louis XIV's direct tax, the *dixième*. The Jansenist controversy broke out again (1721–32), involving further struggles between the Gov and the Parlements. A decree ordering all clergy to accept *Unigenitus* was forced through by a *lit de justice* (1730), but the judges obstructed its enforcement in 1732, and 139 of them were exiled to the provs. Fleury found a formula of appeasement that damped down the issue for the rest of his rule, while he pursued a policy of the steady replacement of Jansenists by their opponents in all the top posts of the hierarchy. The struggle thus became one between the lower and the higher clergy, with the former adopting Richérist rather than Jansenist views (ie the semi-democratic philosophy that power in the Ch resides in all the clergy equally, and not simply in the Pp or the bps). Abroad, he strove for peace based – for as long as it suited France – on the alliance with the Britain of WALPOLE. France's entry into the WAR OF THE POLISH SUCCESSION (1733–5/8) and the WAR OF THE AUSTRIAN SUCCESSION (1740–48) resulted, not from Fleury's wishes, but from the temporary ascendancy at Court of backstairs war-mongers who managed to win over the K through his mistresses. The only profit that France gained from these wars – the eventual acquisition of Lorraine – was more than off-set by the huge Treasury deficit, and the rise of 2 dangerous rivals to France: Prussia on the Continent and Great Britain in the colonies and on the seas.

Louis XV's personal rule (1743–74) made ministerial instability a permanent feature of the rest of the reign. Handsome, dignified and gracious the K may have been, but he was too indolent and self-indulgent to be the practical working monarch he thenceforth pretended to be. Hunting and women so filled his time-table that he lacked the energy, interest, time or application for the day-to-day drudgery that governing requires; while with his diffident and taciturn nature he made but poor and infrequent contributions to Council debates. Moreover, in his choice of ministers and policies, his hesitant judgement (till his last 4 years) was all too often swayed by feeling rather than calculation – by affection, remorse or intermittent piety. His admin lacked leadership and firm direction, each minister going his separate way. Appointments, promotions and dismissals depended upon the backstairs intrigue of shifting factions of courtiers and the proficiency in bed of a succession of rococo mistresses: eg (to name merely the most influential) the Marquise de Vintimille (1739–41), her sister, the Dss of Châteauroux (1742–4), the Marquise de Pompadour (1745–51, though her influence lasted until her death in 1764), and the Countess du Barry (1768–74). Abroad, Louis tried to maintain France's diplomatic and military predominance in Europe, deploying a network of agents in central and E Europe, and becoming tied up in alliances and wars which aimed at the aggrandizement of the royal family's possessions, but hardly served the interests of the French people. At times, he spun his own alternative diplomatic web – the *secret du roi* – stultifying French foreign policy by crossing the purposes of the regular diplomats. In fact, the rise of Russia and Prussia, and the revival of Austria, had snatched the initiative from France, and Louis could no longer call the tune. Moreover, it was no longer in his interest to try. Instead, he should have been preparing for the imminent death-struggle with Britain on the seas and in the colonies. In any case, France no longer possessed the resources to achieve Continental and colonial predominance. The effort to do so simply worsened the Crown's financial crisis, and thus fed the constitutional struggle with the Parlements. The DIPLOMATIC REVOLUTION (1749–56), in which France switched alliances from Prussia to her old enemy Austria, saw Austria taking the lead, and France merely responding to events. In the consequent SEVEN YEARS WAR (1756–63) France was defeated by Prussia in Europe (notably at Rossbach, Saxony, 5 Nov 1757) and by Britain in India, Africa, Canada and the W Indies. Even the D de Choiseul (in power Dec 1758–Dec 1770) – who was a protégé of Pompadour and the nearest approach to a strong PM to be found in this period – could save little from the wreckage, though he gave the French war effort a unity and force it had hitherto lacked, and strengthened France by the alliance with Spain: the *pacte de famille* of Aug 1761. By the Tr of Paris which ended the war (Feb 1763) France suffered the following losses: in America: Canada, Cape Breton Isle and the Middle W as far as the Mississippi to Britain, and Louisiana to Spain; in the W Indies: Grenada, Dominica, St Vincent and Tobago to Britain; in Africa: Senegal to Britain; in India: all effective power to Britain, except for a few unfortified trading posts. As well as losing an emp, France found her power in Europe much reduced. She was unable to prevent CATHERINE II of Russia choosing the new K of Poland in 1764 (Stanislas Poniatowski) and then joining Prussia and Austria in the 1st Partition of Poland (1772). Similarly, France was too weak to help her ally Spain in her quarrel with Ld NORTH and Great Britain over the Falkland Islands (1770–71). This was the issue over which the K dismissed Choiseul. He had favoured war – and he had also incurred the enmity of Mme du Barry. Moreover, the K was at last asserting himself by appointing reforming ministers with the task of attacking just those aristocratic interests that Choiseul represented.

At home, the struggle continued between the Crown and the chief institutions protecting privilege: the Parlements, the prov Estates and the Assembly of the Clergy, all backed by the office-holders in the bureaucracy, who had bought their jobs. The 2 chief sources of conflict were the Jansenists and the financial crisis. *The Jansenists* – and the Richérists – continued to flourish among the lower clergy, and during the 1750s there was a running battle between the K and the Parlements over them. The hierarchy ordered the clergy to refuse the sacraments to people who could not produce a *billet de confession* showing that they had made their confession to a priest who accepted the bull *Unigenitus*. The Jansenists took the clergy to court; when they appealed, the Parlements backed the Jansenists while the Crown supported the hierarchy and the Jesuits. Bitter confrontations interspersed with compromises ensued, with the *Parlementaires* refusing to work, being exiled to the provs, and then recalled. Hostilities became intensified by new taxation proposals (as will be seen), then led to the complete destruction of the Jesuits. The bankruptcy of the Jesuits in Martinique (their trade having been ruined by war) led to court cases in France and an appeal to the Parlement of Paris. For the Parlement this was an excellent opportunity to punish its chief enemy. It suppressed the Jesuits, on the Gallican grounds that it was an alien institution threatening the rights of the French Crown and people (Aug 1762). Because of the financial crisis the K did not dare support his chief ecclesiastical backers, and he decreed their abolition (Dec 1764). *The financial crisis* deepened with the K's expensive and unsuccessful foreign policy. To begin with, the War of the Austrian Succession had had grave consequences for the Gov deficit, and so Jean Baptiste de Machault d'Arnouville (Controller-Gen, 1745–54) introduced a new permanent tax on all classes, the *vingtième* (1749). In Paris, the Parlement had to be forced to register it; in the provs, the Parlements and the Estates obstructed the Intendants; but the chief opponents were the clergy, backed by the *dévots*, the Jesuits and other Court factions. By Dec 1751 the K's will collapsed, and this essential reform was abandoned. The Seven Years War revived the problem once more, and in July 1756 the Paris Parlement was forced to register new financial edicts by the 1st *lit de justice* since 1732, soon followed by others in 1759 and 1760. Consequently, the Parlement steadily advanced its constitutional pretensions, voting remonstrances which claimed that it was as old as the monarchy, and that it represented the whole community in checking royal power. By 1756 it was claiming that all the Parlements formed one body, with the Paris Parlement acting as the head. (In fact, the Parlements were nothing more than courts of appeal, each consisting of a trade union of members of the Robe and Sword who had purchased their offices. They did not possess the representative character of the British Parl, but by publishing their remonstrances and generally excelling the K at public relations they convinced the people that they were defending liberty against tyranny. In fact, they were defending privilege against reform: not only the individual privileges of clergy, nobility and civil servants, but also the corporate privileges of the provinces.) When the Gov tried to solve the post-war crisis by continuing the *vingtième* in peacetime and beginning a land survey in order to reassess incomes (1763), the Paris Parlement accused the K of violating French law; the Toulouse Parlement arrested the Gov of Languedoc; and the Grenoble Parlement tried to arrest the Gov of Dauphiné, but he was saved by his troops. Again the K's will faltered. He dismissed the minister, replaced the Govs, and withdrew the tax (1764). In Brittany, which had taken a leading part in this resistance, the Estates (backed by the Parlement) refused to allow the Commandant and the Intendant to introduce the *corvée* (compulsory labour for building the royal roads). Judges went on strike and were arrested. Remonstrances were passed, one of which asserted that the only authority capable of introducing new taxes was the Estates-Gen. The leader of the Breton Parlement was taken to Paris and tried by a special court. The 12 Parlements made joint protests; and the K held a *séance royale* of the Paris Parlement (Mar 1766) and read them a scathing speech denying the pretensions of the Parlements to form 'a confederation of resistance' and asserting the sovereign power of the K. 'In my person only does the sovereign power rest,' he said. 'To me alone belongs legislative power without dependence or division.' The controversy continued, however, and for another 4 years strikes and lock-outs, denunciations and remonstrances gave the French people a lesson in resisting absolutism. Finally in 1770 the K struck back, and ended his reign in an unaccustomed burst of courageous statesmanship. He dismissed Choiseul, and gave power to his opponent, the Chancellor René Nicolas de Maupeou. In addition to his foreign-office responsibilities, Choiseul had become Navy Minister (1761–6) and War Minister (1766–70), in both of which capacities he had carried out valuable reforms. On the other hand, he had led the war party in the Falkland Islands crisis, he had alienated Mme du Barry, and had supported the Parlements. Maupeou, who became Chancellor in 1763, supported the powers of the Crown, and he brought into the Gov the like-minded Abbé Joseph Marie Terray as

Controller-Gen (1769). It was now possible to begin to solve the central problem of the *Ancien Régime* – the financial crisis – by eliminating the leading opponents of change, the Parlements. In 1771 Maupeou abolished the Paris Parlement and replaced it with a new set of courts serving smaller areas and manned by judges who were appointed and paid by the Crown. Wholesale judicial reform was set in motion; at the same time Terray set about his main task: the redistribution of the tax load in accordance with wealth. He began to increase the yield of the *vingtième* and the *capitation* by inaugurating a new assessment of wealth to replace the old tax rolls. The loud protests of the Sword and Robe, hierarchy and bureaucracy, were a foretaste of the nobles' revolt which ushered in the great Revolution itself, but the K stood firm. Unfortunately, the privileged groups carried the rest of the nation with them, and the K ended his reign amid the execration of a people who could not appreciate the last-minute coup he had struck on their behalf. When he d he bequeathed to LOUIS XVI the unresolved main problems of the *Ancien Régime* – economic, social, cultural and political – it was not his fault if his successor chose to begin the new reign by abandoning what little progress he had made.

Louis XVI (23 Aug 1754–21 Jan 1793) K of France (1774), whose kind heart and good intentions proved inadequate to deal with mounting crisis of the *Ancien Régime*. He was far from possessing sufficient force of character, intellectual power, or political wisdom to inflict the necessary surgery on the privileged groups, and head off the Revolution by adequate reforms. The financial crisis which he inherited from LOUIS XV was deepened by his unwise entry into the WAR OF AMERICAN INDEPENDENCE (1776–83) on the side of the rebels, and by the slump which set in from the late 1770s. In its turn, the slump exacerbated the grievances of the unprivileged members of the social order, who were in any case being dangerously radicalized by the seditious notions of resistance which they were learning from the *philosophes*, the Americans, the Richérist lower clergy and especially from the Sword and Robe and upper clergy. These last aristocratic groups used their political institutions – the PARLEMENTS, the Assembly of Notables, the prov Estates, and the Assembly of the Clergy – to obstruct the financial and judicial reforms of a succession of chief ministers, and to force the K eventually to call a meeting of the Estates-Gen: a device which soon destroyed both them and the K.

3rd son of the Dauphin, Louis (the son of K Louis XV) and his 2nd wife, Maria Josepha of Saxony; ed inadequately under the care of the D de la Vauguyon; m (1770) Marie Antoinette, daughter of MARIA THERESA and the HR Emp, Francis I (she was guillotined, 16 Oct 1793); became heir to the throne on the deaths of his eld brothers and father in the 1760s. Heavy and short-sighted, diffident and vacillating, pious and virtuous, he was an unwilling but conscientious K, who lacked the grasp and the steel which his situation demanded. His shallow, frivolous and extravagant wife established an ascendancy over him which warped what little political judgement he possessed. Inexperienced and indecisive, the young K relied on the advice of the cynical old courtier, Jean Frédéric Phélypeaux, Comte de Maurepas, whom he recalled out of prov exile and appointed Minister of State (May 1764–21 Nov 1781, his death). Maurepas was crafty at Court manoeuvre but inept in the wider world of politics; on his advice Louis tried to buy popularity by dismissing Louis XV's far-sighted ministers, Maupeou and Terray (Aug 1774), abandoning their reforms, and recalling the Parlement of Paris (Oct 1774), the most dangerous enemy the monarchy faced before the Revolution.

Foreign affairs were handed over to the experienced diplomat, Charles Gravier, Comte de Vergennes (1774–13 Feb 1787, his death), whose mainly cautious and pacific policy accorded well with the lack of money in the Treasury. His main preoccupations were with Austria and Britain. Austria under JOSEPH II (France's ally since the DIPLOMATIC REVOLUTION) tried continually to enlist French aid in her aggressive designs, but Vergennes and the K refused all the pleas of the Q to support her brother. In the War of the Bavarian Succession (1778–9), in the period 1781–4 when Joseph made provocative attempts to force Holland to open the R Scheldt (which had been closed to non-Dutch shipping since 1648), and during Joseph's attempt in 1785 to take Bavaria in exchange for the Austrian Netherlands (Belgium), Vergennes successfully restrained Austrian ardour and used French mediation to achieve a peaceful outcome. Great Britain was still the main enemy of France, and the War of American Independence gave France the opportunity to exact revenge for the humiliations of the SEVEN YEARS WAR (1756–63), even though it meant aiding rebels against their rightful sovereign. At first, French aid was secret. Vergennes supplied war materials through what was ostensibly a private co run by the playwright, Pierre Augustin Caron de Beaumarchais. After the British surrender at Saratoga (17 Oct 1777), however, France joined openly in the war, signing an alliance with the Americans – represented by Benjamin Franklin – on 6 Feb 1778. Thanks to the army and navy reforms set in train by Choiseul and continued under Louis XVI, the French forces improved their performance, and by the Tr of Versailles (Sept 1783) France gained Tobago in the W Indies and Senegal, Africa. To offset these precise gains, however, were 2 incalculable losses. The war aggravated the financial crisis, and the American victory gave ideological sustenance to all Frenchmen who resisted absolutism.

Home affairs were dominated by the appointment and dismissal of a string of ministers whose plans to solve the financial problem were frustrated by all those whose privileges would have to be sacrificed in any effective reform: the Sword and the Robe, the upper clergy and the office-holders, individual provs and cities. They blocked all change implacably, either directly, with confrontations in the Parlements, the Assemblies of Notables, the Prov Estates and the Assembly of the Clergy, or more subtly at Court, through the influence of their agents on the headstrong Q and the weak-kneed K.

The causes of this crisis in the *Ancien Régime* were: (a) The financial crisis had never been overcome since it had been inherited from LOUIS XIV. It had been intensified – on the expenditure side – by the extravagant foreign policies of C18 and the conspicuous expenditure of the Court at home. It had been intensified – on the income side – by the wasteful system of tax collection, whether by office-holders (direct taxes) or tax-farmers (indirect taxes); and by the archaic and irrational system of assessment whereby the main load fell on those least able to pay, an absurdity made worse by the inflation of C18. All those who had the pleasure of paying little or no taxation were deeply entrenched behind ancient privileges which were defended – at the legislative level – by their various representative institutions and – at the admin level – by the office-holders who had bought their jobs and were irremovable since no Gov could afford to buy them out. (b) The economy contributed to the crisis by booming from the early 1730s, levelling off in the late 1770s, and diving into a depression in 1788. The good times lifted the urban and rural masses above starvation level on to the arena of political action. Since they were no longer exclusively preoccupied with their next meal, they could entertain ambitions which, when jeopardized by the unemployment and high prices of the late 1780s, turned them into combustible material. (c) The social order as a whole was riddled with aspirations and disappointments which would one day erupt into violence. The Sword and the Robe – no longer enemies – collaborated to secure for themselves the monopoly of all the top posts in the Gov, the civil service, the Ch and the armed forces. The invigorating social mobility of Louis XIV's day had given way to a stagnation which insulted the abilities and halted the progress of the bourgeoisie and the peasantry. The bourgeoisie were dissatisfied, whether they were the falling professional middle class of the bureaucracy whose offices were declining in value, the rising business middle class whose prosperity was threatened by the end of the boom and by the disastrous foreign policy, or the mass of the clergy who could no longer look forward to higher stipends. The country people were divided between those who wished to continue with the traditional communal methods of farming and those who favoured a change-over to individualistic capitalism. They nursed multifarious grievances, whether landless labourers on low wages, small-holders with no surplus with which to profit from the inflation, or farmers with a surplus for which the price-controlled towns gave them less than a fair return. There were also the peasants whose income was battened upon by the State for taxes, by the landlord for feudal dues, and by the clergy for tithes. In the towns there was plenty of scope for radicalism, among labourers suffering from low wages enforced by the police, as well as periodic unemployment, or craftsmen hit by the competition of large-scale industry using the putting-out system. The ideas circulating among these social groups in the 2nd half of C18 roused their resentments and sharpened their intellectual bite. They raised their quarrels from the humdrum level of material interest to the high plane of political principle. The exciting ideas of the Enlightenment were being expounded in the works of Montesquieu, Condillac, Diderot, d'Alembert, Voltaire, Rousseau etc, and popularized by the press, the salons, the public libraries, the reading societies and the academies. They fired the K and his ministers in their attempts to make the Crown absolute and the admin more efficient in order to reduce inequalities and injustices and maximize the people's happiness. They also inspired the opponents of such changes; and resistance was also encouraged by the War of American Independence, which furnished a real example of a successful rebellion and the creation of a new State based on rational principles. The rank-and-file clergy – so potent in their influence over the masses – also fostered resistance to absolutism with their Richérist interpretation of the Ch. The most insidious influence of all in encouraging mutiny among the masses was probably the long campaign of the Sword and Robe in their Parlements and Estates. The remonstrances which they published and circulated were a veritable armoury of concepts highly dangerous to divine-right monarchy: 'natural rights', 'the constitution', 'the nation', 'the citizen', 'patriots', to name but a few. They ultimately proved lethal to its privileged opponents as well.

The reforming ministers also played their part in bringing the crisis to a head, the most notable being Turgot, Necker, Calonne, Loménie de Brienne and Lamoignon. Anne Robert Jacques Turgot – Controller-Gen (Aug 1774–May 1776) – was an austere idealist with much reforming experience as Intendant of Limoges, but too little political agility to vanquish the wily defenders of the *status quo*. A Physiocrat by conviction, he decreed the free circulation of grain inside France (Sept 1774), only to have his experiment in laissez-faire economics ruined by the bad harvest of 1774 and the food riots of Apr–May 1775. His Six Edicts – forced through the Paris Parlement by a *lit de justice* in Mar 1776 – travelled further along the same liberal road by, among other measures, abolishing gilds in most businesses, and turning the *corvée* from compulsory labour into a land tax paid by all classes. The loud outcry of the privileged unnerved the K, and Turgot was dismissed. Jacques Necker – Director-Gen (June 1777–May 1781) – was a cautious and conservative, but very rich, Swiss Prot banker. His reputation enabled him to ease the Crown's financial problem temporarily by borrowing. He headed off criticism by avoiding an increase in taxation and limiting himself to reforms which did not hurt vested interests too much: eg he abolished torture in the courts and serfdom on the royal domain. He also disarmed his opponents by publishing the state of the royal accounts: the *Compte Rendue au Roi* (1781), a best-seller which unfortunately encouraged the opponents of higher taxation by claiming that no royal debt existed. Necker resigned when the K refused to widen his powers. Charles Alexandre de Calonne – Controller-Gen (Nov 1783–Apr 1787) – was a handsome, polished and pragmatic ex-Intendant of Flanders and Artois, who borrowed more money and then unfolded a package of reforms similar to those of Turgot. His programme included a stamp tax and a land tax to be paid by all classes and to be supervised by new prov assemblies representing all owners of land, whether nobles, clergy or commoners. Shying away from confrontation with the Parlements, and refusing to call the Estates-Gen, which they were demanding, Calonne got the K to call an Assembly of Notables, the 1st since 1626. It is from the resistance of this body (sitting Feb–May 1787) that historians tend now to date the start of the Revolution. Consisting of 144 representatives mainly of the Sword and Robe, it failed to rise to the occasion and, like the Parlements, simply brandished its privileges. Calonne appealed to public opinion, but the privileged swayed the K, and Calonne was dismissed. Etienne Charles Loménie de Brienne – Controller-Gen (Apr 1787–Aug 1788) – was Archbp of Toulouse, and one of the chief opponents of Calonne in the Assembly. Nevertheless, he adopted the former's plan for a stamp tax and a land tax, and forced them through with a *lit de justice* on 6 July 1787. The Parlement of Paris protested that only the Estates-Gen had the power to vote new taxes, and demanded it be called. Loménie de Brienne exiled them to Troyes (15 July 1787) where they continued to protest. He then worked out a compromise, but his sterner colleague, Chrétien François de Lamoignon – the Keeper of the Seals – introduced (May 1788) wholesale judicial reform on the lines of the changes initiated in the last years of Louis XV. The Parlement's powers of verifying laws and taxes were to be taken away and given to a new Plenary Court. With these May Edicts, however, the resistance of the Sword and Robe reached such a pitch that historians have labelled this phase the *révolte nobiliaire*. The Assembly of the Clergy passed remonstrances backing the Parlement, and voted one of the smallest taxation grants in its parsimonious history. In the prov capitals the office-holders were unable or unwilling to carry out their orders. In the Parlementary cities the magistrates brought the mob out on to the streets. In Franche-Comté the Estates met for the 1st time since 1678, in Provence for the 1st time since 1639. In Dauphiné the royal troops were stoned in the streets of Grenoble on 7 June 1788, while at Vizille, 8 km away, on 21 June 1788 a spontaneous assembly demanded the reinstatement of the local Parlement, the calling of the Estates-Gen, and the re-assembly of the Estates of Dauphiné, not called since RICHELIEU suppressed them in 1628. With absolutism dissolving into anarchy and the centralized monarchy crumbling into its constituent parts, the over-taxed K gave way once more. On 8 Aug 1788 he called the Estates-Gen to meet on 1 May 1789. It had not met since 1614. Jacques Necker – for the 2nd time Director-Gen (Aug 1788–11 July 1789) – repealed the May Edicts and recalled the Parlements. The whole nation concentrated on the preparations for the Estates-Gen. Until this point, the 3rd Estate, led by the bourgeoisie, had backed the Sword and Robe against the Crown, so successful had the Parlements' propaganda been in portraying the K as a tyrant and themselves as the defenders of the people. The plans for the Estates-Gen changed all this. The 3rd Estate demanded the 'doubling of the 3rd' and 'voting by heads': ie they wanted to have as many representatives as the 1st and 2nd Estates put together; they demanded that votes should be taken by all 3 Estates sitting together, not, as traditionally, each Estate voting separately, thus enabling the two leading Estates to outvote the 3rd. When a new Assembly of Notables (Nov–Dec 1788) and the Parlement of Paris (Sept 1788) both opposed these changes, it became clear to the 3rd Estate – headed by the Patriot Party – that the main enemy was not the Crown but the other two Estates. The K, advised by Necker, agreed to 'double the 3rd' (Dec 1788), but left voting procedure to be decided by the Estates-Gen itself. Meetings began on 5 May 1789 and, as crisis followed crisis in the unfolding drama of the Revolution, the K threw in his lot with the 1st and 2nd Estates, and went to destruction with them. He was guillotined in Paris.

Louis of Nassau (10 Jan 1538–14 Apr 1574) Pr of the Emp, younger brother of WILLIAM I of Orange, and a leader in the REVOLT OF THE NETHERLANDS.

Son of the Lutheran William, Count of Nassau-Dillenburg and Juliana von Stolberg; ed as a Lutheran. Possessing extensive estates in the Netherlands, he led the nobility in their opposition to the absolutist and persecuting policies which K PHILIP II of Spain enforced there in the 1560s. He organized the Compromise, the league of RC and Prot nobles who wrote to Madrid calling for religious toleration; but when Philip replied by sending the D of ALBA with a Spanish army, Louis went into exile to organize resistance. He invaded Groningen in the N Netherlands, defeated the Spanish at Heiligerlee on 23 May 1568; but at this stage of the Revolt the people were too cowed by Alba to rise in his support, and he was defeated by Alba himself at Jemmingen on the Ems on 21 July 1568. Shortly after, he was with his brother Orange's unsuccessful invasion of the S. They crossed the Maas (Oct 1568), but had to retreat for lack of a popular rising in their support. Henceforth he tirelessly tried to organize anti-Spanish support among the German Prs, the French Hugs, and the English war party. In 1570 he was at La Rochelle in France organizing the Sea Beggars, a fleet manned by exiled nobles and commoners from the Netherlands and France, which raised funds for the cause by piracy. COLIGNY, the Hug leader, was in power in France at this time (1570–72), and Louis was in close touch with him at Fontainebleau, as well as with K CHARLES IX and WALSINGHAM, the English ambassador, as they prepared their joint onslaught on the Spanish in the Netherlands. This threat forced Alba to concentrate his forces in the S, a contingency which enabled the Sea Beggars to capture Brill and obtain a firm grip on the towns of Holland and Zeeland. Louis helped to pin Alba down by taking Mons, Hainault, on 23 May 1572 and holding it until Sept 1572. During Dec 1573 he helped to form an anti-Spanish alliance of France, Poland and the German Prs in negotiations at Blamont, Lorraine, with CATHERINE DE MEDICI and her son, the future K HENRY III of France, who was at that time on his way to become K of Poland. The following year he led an army from Germany into the N Netherlands, but was defeated at Mook, nr Nijmegen, on 14 Apr 1574. He and his brother, Henry, were killed.

Loyola, Ignatius (Inigo López de) (1491–31 July 1556) Spanish founder of the JESUITS.

b at Loyola (Guipúzcoa) of a wealthy noble family; ed as a knight, he was wounded in the legs by a cannon-ball at Pamplona (20 May 1521) while fighting for Navarra against France. Reading the lives of the saints and of Christ while convalescing, he underwent a spiritual transformation, then made a pilgrimage to the monastery of Montserrat (Catalonia). Here he spent 3 days confessing his sins (1522); after which he lived for a year (1522–3) as a beggar in a cave at Manresa (nr Barcelona), devoting hours each day to prayer, scourging himself, and tending the poor and sick. Aiming to convert the Moslems, he travelled via Venice to the Holy Land (1523); but, his crusade a failure, he returned to Spain to educate himself, first at the Univ of Barcelona, Alcalá de Henares and Salamanca, then at the Univ of Paris (1528–35). Meanwhile he collected 8 likeminded followers who with him on Montmartre, Paris, took vows of poverty, chastity and obedience to the Pp (15 Aug 1534), dedicating themselves as missionaries to Palestine, if possible. Thus was founded the Society of Jesus, which received recognition from Pp PAUL III on 27 Sept 1540. Loyola was ordained priest in Venice (June 1537), and spent the rest of his life mainly in Rome as the first Gen of the Order. Small, limping and frequently ill, he nevertheless had a will of iron, and an instinctive grasp of the human condition; the success of the Jesuits had much to do with his *Constitutions* (1547–50), on which their militant organization was based, and with his *Spiritual Exercises* (roughed out while he was at Manresa), a course of meditation and self-examination which proved the ideal training-manual for the shock-troops of the COUNTER-REFORMATION. By the time of his death, there were 1,000 Jesuits, organized into 11 provinces, 9 in Europe, 1 in India and 1 in Brazil. He was canonized in 1622.

Luther, Martin (10 Nov ?1483–18 Feb 1546) Leader of the German REFORMATION.

Son of Hans Luther, a prosperous miner and metal worker of free-peasant stock, and Margarete Ziegler; ed Magdeburg (1497), Eisenach (1498), Erfurt Univ (1501–5). Instead of continuing his law course (as his father wanted), he suddenly joined the Augustinian Friars (July 1505), fulfilling a vow he had made to St Anne when he was struck down by a thunderbolt during a violent storm. Ordained priest (Apr 1507), he was posted to the Augustinians at Wittenberg to preach and lecture at the new univ (founded 1502). He visited Italy on Ch business (probably winter 1510/11), and was shocked by the Renaissance style of life of the Roman clergy (though not yet out of his Cathorthodoxy). Taking his doctorate in theology and the Chair of Biblical Theology at Wittenberg (1512), he spent the next 5 years lecturing on the Bible and arriving at an interpretation of it which not only drove out his own spiritual doubts and psychological terrors, but also placed a mine under the whole fabric of Roman Catholicism. As a young man, Luther was assailed by profound depressions during which the sacraments and other 'works' of the Ch did nothing to dispel his sense of guilt or his conviction that God had destined him for eternal damnation. Through years of mental anguish and deep application to the Scriptures he reached the conclusions that gave him peace of mind (1517–18), ie the doctrine (going back to St Augustine and St Paul) that salvation comes through Christ's works (and not through the good works performed by the sinner, or by the clergy on his behalf), and that his faith comes solely from the grace which an all-powerful God confers on the totally corrupt sinner he has chosen to save (who can contribute nothing on his own behalf). This belief in justification (or salvation) by faith alone – the doctrinal lever under the whole Prot Reformation – was taken a stage further than St Augustine or St Paul. According to Luther, justification is not a gradual cleansing of the sinner but an instantaneous sanctification by the merits of Christ, and the good works performed by the justified sinner follow as a result. Thus Luther was not merely attacking the Ch for being corrupt, for not living up to its own doctrine; he was attacking the doctrine itself. The explosive force of the new doctrine of justification by faith alone was due to the fact that, since salvation was a matter of the direct relation between God and the individual, there was no need for the mediation of priests, for everyone was his own priest. (In Luther's eyes, the main job of the clergy was to preach the Word.) In other words, Luther's doctrine of the priesthood of all believers rendered irrelevant all the outward ceremonial which the Ch was so lavishly equipped and manned to perform: pilgrimages, masses for the dead, the invocation of saints, the raising of images, the sale of INDULGENCES. Luther raised the whole issue to the level of public debate by protesting against the sale of indulgences which Tetzel was organizing in Saxony. His 95 Theses nailed to the door of All Saints' Church, Wittenberg (31 Oct 1517) led not merely to the doctrinal disputation he envisaged, but, printed and widely circulated in Latin and German, to the European Reformation itself; for these were germs invading a constitution already seriously undermined by other changes, cultural, political, economic and social. During the following 4 years (1517–20), as public discussion raged and he defended himself before the Ch authorities, Luther unfolded the details of his philosophy in, for example, the Augsburg interview (Nov 1518) with the Dominican Card Cajetan, the papal legate in Germany; in the public discussion at Leipzig (June–July 1519) with Johannes Eck, Prof of Theology at Ingolstadt (Bavaria); in the publication of the papal Bull *Exsurge, Domine* (June 1520) condemning Luther as a heretic, which Luther criticized in his pamphlet *Against the Accursed Bull of Antichrist* (Nov 1520) and which he burned on a public bonfire at Wittenberg

(Dec 1520); in the 24 or so key publications he issued in 1520; in his appearance before the Emp CHARLES V at the Diet of Worms (Apr 1521), when he refused to recant unless convinced by Scripture or reason, and where the Ban of Emp was proclaimed against him, making him an outlaw (26 May 1521); in his translation of the Bible in FREDERICK III (the Wise's) castle on the Wartburg, where he was hidden for safety's sake (1521–2).

In these debates, and also in his tracts, the chief of which were the *Sermon on the Mass* (Apr 1520), *On the Papacy at Rome* (June 1520), *To The Christian Nobility of The German Nation* (Aug 1520), *The Babylonian Captivity of the Church* (Oct 1520) and *The Freedom of a Christian* (Nov 1520), Luther worked out in detail the doctrinal consequences of his courageous stand. (1) Sweeping away practices and beliefs for which there was no Scriptural warrant, he reduced the number of sacraments to three, and then two (Eucharist and Baptism). (2) He used the vernacular for Ch services and translated the Bible into German. (3) In the Eucharist, he believed in communion in both kinds, ie that the participant should drink the wine as well as eat the bread. (4) He condemned the R C doctrine of the Mass as a kind of magical re-enactment of Christ's sacrifice, and denied the doctrine of transubstantiation, ie that the substance of the bread and wine are transformed into the body and blood of Christ by the priest. Without going so far as ZWINGLI or CALVIN, he interpreted Christ's phrase, 'This is my body', as the 'real presence': that is, that through Grace the body and blood of Christ were present to the believer in the unchanged bread and wine. These and other doctrinal changes led Luther into organizational change and thus into politics. When the Pp's agents rejected his beliefs, he had to reject the Pp's authority, falling back ultimately on the authority of the Bible: not the Bible as interpreted by every Tom, Dick and Harry (that road led to the SPIRITUALISTS and ANABAPTISTS and other left-wing deviationists, which he condemned) but as laid down by himself and enforced by the legitimate authority – the Pr, or the city council. In order to avoid being wiped out by the Emp Charles V on the one hand, and swamped in an anarchy of sectarianism on the other, the Lutherans had to rely on the protection of the El Frederick the Wise of Saxony, the Landgrave Philip of Hesse, D Albert of Prussia and other secular rulers. He rejected the proffered aid of the knights in the KNIGHTS' WAR, and preached brutal suppression during the PEASANTS' WAR. Making the distinction (in his 1523 treatise *Of Earthly Government*) between the spiritual realm (where real Christian freedom lies) and the temporal realm (where the Christian's duty is one of obedience to the secular ruler, and where rebellion is a sin) he headed off the potentially liberating force of Lutheranism, and turned it into the support of civil obedience. Similarly, the distinction developed by Lutherans between essentials and inessentials in Christianity, and the inclusion of church order and liturgy as inessentials and therefore appropriate to be left to the State, equally helped to turn Lutherans into supporters of absolutism. Thus Luther's new German-language liturgy, the *Deutsche Messe* (1526), which laid down the ceremonial applications of his doctrinal reforms and which became the basis for Lutheran churches everywhere, were put into force and maintained in Saxony by the Visitation, a committee appointed by the El.

Luther's life from 1520 until his death is bound up in the history of German Lutheranism: its successful struggle to survive first the political, then the military, attempts of Charles V to suppress it; its unsuccessful attempts at compromise with the COUNTER-REFORMATION papacy on its right and the church which followed Zwingli on its left; its implacable hostility to Spiritualism and Anabaptism; its firm rooting across N Germany, and in Denmark and Sweden; its steady accumulation of a distinctive liturgy, doctrine, church-order, hymn-book, educational system etc. Luther himself, passionate, voluble, often coarse and violent, presided over all from his home in Wittenberg. He m (1525) Katherina von Bora, a convert who had left a Cistercian convent 2 years previously, and lived in happy domesticity, producing 3 sons and 3 daughters.

Luynes, Charles d'Albert, D de (5 Mar 1578–15 Dec 1621) Favourite and chief minister of the young K LOUIS XIII of France, who broadly anticipated the policies of RICHELIEU by disciplining the magnates, attacking the Hugs, and following an anti-Habsburg foreign policy.

Son of Honoré d'Albert, of the minor nobility; ed at Court where he joined the service of the future Louis XIII, who became very attached to him; m (1617) the beautiful and tempestuous Marie de Rohan, the future Dss de Chevreuse. During the disastrous Regency of the Q Mother, MARIE DE MEDICI, which followed the assassination of K HENRY IV on 14 May 1610, the power of the Crown was gravely threatened by the Prs of the Blood, led by Henry, Pr de CONDÉ, and the magnates, and by the 'State within a State' of the Hugs in the S and SW, both of which groups, using civil disturbance and foreign aid, grasped the opportunity of a royal minority to reverse the progress towards centralized absolutism achieved by Henry IV and his predecessors. The boy king, resenting the indifference of his mother and the monopoly of power enjoyed by her favourite, Leonora Galigai, and her husband, Concino Concini, co-operated with Luynes in planning the assassination of the latter on 24 Apr 1617, when he was shot at the entrance to the Louvre. Marie de Medici was exiled to Blois and Leonora Galigai was burned as a witch (July 1617), while Luynes assumed control of the gov, becoming Gov of Picardy (1619), Constable of France (1621) and Keeper of the Seals (1621). He also made a fortune and became a D (1619).

In foreign affairs, he was hamstrung by the necessity of using his limited resources to put down noble and Hug rebellions, but he did what he could by diplomacy to hamper the Habsburg side in the THIRTY YEARS WAR. With Spain, he signed the Tr of Madrid (Apr 1621) to keep the Spanish out of the Valtelline – their chief supply route between Italy and Germany. In Germany he negotiated the Tr of Ulm (July 1620) between the Cath League and the Evangelical Union to keep the Spanish out of the Rhine valley, their chief supply route between Italy and the Netherlands. Unfortunately, he was unsuccessful in both missions; his German diplomacy in particular made it easier for the Emp FERDINAND II to defeat the Bohemian rebels at the battle of the White Mountain (8 Nov 1620); this also convinced historians that he was motivated solely by a *dévot*, pro-RC policy to the detriment of French interests, which was not the case.

At home, he embarked on the policy of liquidating the independence of the magnates and the Hugs – the essential precondition of an active foreign policy, as Richelieu appreciated in his turn. He held an Assembly of Notables at Rouen in 1617 in an effort to persuade these privileged groups – the Clergy, the Sword and the Robe – to make a bigger contribution to the revenue so as to avoid over-taxing the masses and risking rebellion; but when he abolished the *paulette* and reduced nobles' pensions in 1618 the magnates revolted (1619–20). Led by the D d'Epernon, they rescued Marie de Medici from Blois (Feb 1619), and rose in Poitou and the S, aided by the Hug nobles, but not the towns. The K defeated the magnates at Ponts-de-Cé, Poitou, 7 Aug 1620; and then made 1620 a turning point in French history by deciding upon an all-out attack on the Hugs. Against the Hugs, preliminary measures had already been taken in June 1617, when Luynes decreed that K Henry IV's theoretically separate and predominantly Prot Kdoms of Navarre and Béarn in the Pyrenees were united with the Kdom of France. Since this order entailed the restoration of RC worship and the return of confiscated Ch lands, the population defied it and planned common action with the Hugs. However, after Ponts-de-Cé, Luynes marched S and forced them to accept the union at a ceremony at Pau, their capital (Oct 1620), after which dissident Prots were harshly treated. Disturbed by this new royal outpost in their rear, the Hugs put themselves on a war footing under the D de ROHAN; but on 25 June 1621 the K took St Jean-d'Angély, a fortress which had covered La Rochelle on the landward side. Luynes laid unsuccessful siege to Montauban, Languedoc (Aug–Nov 1621), but then caught purple fever and d at Longueville, Guyenne. By this time, two-thirds of the Hug 'State' had been reconquered, a good base from which Richelieu completed the job by 1629.

Machiavelli, Niccolò (3 May 1469–21 June 1527) Florentine statesman, political theorist and writer.

Son of Bernardo Machiavelli and Bartolomea Nelli (less wealthy members of a noble family turned bourgeois). His career divides into 2 parts: (a) till 1512, when Florence was a fairly democratic republic for which he worked as a civil servant; and (b) after 1512, when Florence became a narrow oligarchy again, ruled by the Medici, when he was mainly unemployed.

His ed and early life are largely unknown; he was elected to the office of Second Chancellor (1498), in which capacity he worked as Sec to the Ten of War, the committee concerned with diplomacy and war. He m (1501) Marietta Corsini. A keen advocate (from 1503 onwards) of a trained citizen militia (instead of mercenaries), he was put in charge of the organization of Florence's militia (1505–6) and then made Chancellor to the new committee which was created to supervise it: the Nine of the Militia. In these posts he not only saw all the diplomatic papers that passed through his office, but also represented Florence on many diplomatic missions, including 4 to K LOUIS XII of France (1500–1, 1504, 1510, 1511); 1 to the Emp MAXIMILIAN I in Germany (1507–8); 2 to Cesare BORGIA when he was operating in the Romagna (1502, 1502–3), being at Sinigaglia when the celebrated murders took place; 1 to Rome to witness the election of Pp JULIUS II (1503); 1 to Pp Julius during his military operations against Perugia and Bologna (1506); apart from many others to lesser Prs, eg to Monaco (1511).

Machiavelli was dismissed (7 Nov 1512) after the Medici *coup d'état* of Nov 1512. After a period of imprisonment (Feb–Mar 1513), he retired to his farm at Sant'Andrea in Percussina, 7 miles away, until he could get back into favour again. He studied the classics and history, especially of republican Rome; and put together the fruits of his experience and reading to produce a body of work on politics and history which he turned out simply in the hope of getting back into Florentine politics, but which had profound long-term effects on subsequent European statesmen and philosophers in general. Believing that 'the world has always been inhabited by human beings who have always had the same passions', he assumed that general rules of political science could be distilled from history and current affairs which could guide politicians in the pursuit of their aims. Clearing his mind of cant, he introduced a new, realistic understanding of the psychological and other forces at work in politics. 'The gulf between how one should live and how one does live,' he wrote, 'is so wide that a man who neglects what is actually done for what should be done learns the way to self-destruction rather than self-preservation.' The successful Pr is one who is gifted with strength (or *virtù*) and who can seize the opportunities presented by fortune. He is guided, not by religious dogma or moral precepts, but by the strictly utilitarian choice of means appropriate to ends. He can manipulate the laws governing political behaviour and shape the course of events to his own pattern. Machiavelli's chief works were *The Prince* (1513), *Discourses on Livy* (1515–17), *The Art of War* (1519–20), *The History of Florence* (1520–25), and his 2 comedies, *Mandragola* (1518) and *Clizio* (1524–5). By 1520, under the patronage of Card Giulio dei Medici (later Pp CLEMENT VII), he began to receive political office again: minor posts, but sufficient to make him undesirable to the new republican gov which overthrew the Medici in May 1527. Hurt by this rebuff, he d in Florence of a stomach complaint.

Magellan, Ferdinand (Fernão de Magalhães) (*c* 1470–27 Apr 1521) Portuguese leader of the Spanish expedition which was the 1st to circumnavigate the world.

Son of a noble; ed at Court; m (1517) Beatriz Barbosa. He took part in Portuguese empire-building expeditions in the Indian Ocean and SE Asia, serving under ALBUQUERQUE at the capture of Malacca, Malay Peninsula, in 1511. Wounded in a battle in Morocco, he limped for the rest of his life; getting inadequate advancement in Portugal, he joined the service of Spain as commander of an expedition which the Emp CHARLES V was sending to the Moluccas, or Spice Islands. Magellan knew the area well through his service with Portugal, but he now had to approach it via the W route in accordance with the Tr of TORDESILLAS. His 1st task was to find the long-sought way either through or round the Americas. With 5 ships he left Sanlúcar de Barrameda at the mouth of the Guadalquivir on 20 Sept 1519, ran along the coast of Brazil, explored the Rio de la Plata estuary and spent from Mar to Aug 1520 at Port St Julian, Patagonia, where he severely punished a mutiny of Spanish captains, executing one and marooning another. He then discovered the Straits of Magellan, and spent 5 dangerous weeks sailing through them (Oct–Nov 1520), to enter the sea later known as the Pacific with only 3 ships. They endured 14 weeks of hunger, thirst and scurvy crossing this ocean, making their 1st landfall at Guam in the Mariana Islands, which were then called the Ladrones, or Islands of Thieves (6 Mar 1521). They then landed on what were later called the Philippines (Mar 1521), and later at Mactán Island, where Magellan and 40 men were killed in a local war. Now reduced to 2 ships (the *Trinidad* and the *Victoria*), the expedition reached the Moluccas in Nov 1521, established a depot there and loaded up with spices. For the return journey, the *Trinidad* set off the way they had come, and was captured by the Portuguese. The *Victoria*, under its Basque capt Sebastián del Cano, continued on across the Indian Ocean and round the Cape of Good Hope, reaching Spain on 6 Sept 1522, with 18 Europeans and 4 Indians, all extremely weak.

Manchester, Edward Montagu, 2nd Earl of (1602–7 May 1671) Bn Kimbolton (1626), known by his courtesy title of Vt Mandeville until he succeeded to the Earldom (1642); leading opponent of K CHARLES I of England, Parl Gen in the Civil War, and leading 'Presbyterian', who shrank from all-out war.

Eld son of the 1st Earl of Manchester; ed Sidney Sussex, Cambridge; m 5 times; became an important Puritan critic of the K, the only peer whom Charles I tried to arrest along with the 5 members (3 Jan 1642). In the Civil War, as an aristocrat, he was given high command, becoming C-in-C of the Eastern Association army (Aug 1643) with Oliver CROMWELL as his 2 i/c – who soon became his harshest critic. According to a contemporary 'a sweet meek man', Manchester established Parl control over E England, and soundly defeated the K at Marston Moor, nr York, on 2 July 1644. On the other hand, he opposed an all-out attack on the K, and was one of the chiefs of the 'Presbyterian' party in Parl which supported the Scots alliance, favoured negotiations with the K, and feared the religious, political and social radicalism which the war was unleashing. The 2nd battle of Newbury (27 Oct 1644), where his pusillanimous refusal to attack because the K was present allowed the Royalists to break through to their HQ at Oxford, was the last straw for the war party, and Cromwell (who was also his family rival in Huntingdon) criticized him before Parl for 'his backwardness to all action', and his 'unwillingness to have this war prosecuted unto a full victory'. The result was the New Model Army (Feb 1645) and the Self-Denying Ordinance (Apr 1645), placing the Parl cause in more warlike hands. Manchester supported further negotiations with the K, and opposed his trial and execution, receiving his reward at the restoration of CHARLES II with the Garter and the office of Chamberlain of the Household (1661).

Maria Theresa (13 May 1717–29 Nov 1780) Head of the Austrian Monarchy (1740) and wife of the HR Emp, Francis I (1745), whose sound political instincts and humane leadership saved the monarchy from break-up in the WAR OF THE AUSTRIAN SUCCESSION (1740–48), though she lost Silesia to FREDERICK II of Prussia, and failed to regain it in the SEVEN YEARS WAR (1756–63). At home, her admin reforms turned Austria-Bohemia – though not Hungary, Milan or the Austrian Netherlands (Belgium) – into a mainly beneficent centralized absolutism, which succeeded in overriding the nobility, subordinating the Ch, and reducing prov separatism, all in order to give the State the powers to strengthen the army, reform education, stimulate the economy, and improve the lot of the peasant. After 1765, when her son (the future JOSEPH II) became Co-Regent with her, she grew hostile towards his ENLIGHTENED ABSOLUTIST aims, and his aggressive foreign policy. Consequently, she resisted his attacks on the Ch, his involvement in the 1st Partition of Poland (1772), his annexation of the Bukovina (1774), and his participation in the War of the Bavarian Succession (1778–9) – but to no avail.

Eld daughter of the Emp CHARLES VI and his wife, Elizabeth Christina of Brunswick-Wolfenbüttel; ed in a narrow, old-fashioned manner by her governess and Jesuit tutors, who gave her no preparation in politics; m (1736) Francis Stephen, D of Lorraine (d 18 Aug 1765), whom she loved deeply and by whom she had 16 children in 19 years, of whom 10 reached adulthood. A robust, dignified and powerful woman with an iron constitution, she scarcely heeded these pregnancies amidst the daily tasks of ruling a vast Emp; as well as being a devoted wife and mother, she managed to achieve a parental relationship with the millions of her subjects. Blue-eyed, fair-haired and attractive, she lacked the usual Habsburg features; in place of their cold haughtiness, she charmed everyone with her spontaneous friendliness and human warmth. She ruled by instinct rather than theory, and her mind was a rich amalgam of idealism and interest, deep feeling and earthy common sense. Even as a young woman, thrust suddenly into office by the unexpected death of her father, she displayed natural gifts which counterbalanced her lack of training: high courage, shrewd judgement of men, firm loyalty to principle and shrewd appraisal of the possible. Her reign divides into 2 periods: (a) before 1765 when, with her husband as Co-Regent, she fought 2 exhausting wars against Prussia and other aggressors; while, with the aid of her 2 advisers – Count Friedrich Wilhelm Haugwitz, then Pr Wenzel Anton von Kaunitz – she carried through, in a pragmatic and piecemeal way, reforms in Gov and the army which gave the monarchy the strength to survive and fight back; and (b) after 1765 when, with her son Joseph as Co-Regent and Kaunitz as chief minister, she tried to put through social reforms, but resisted in vain their programme of Enlightened transformation at home, and territorial aggression abroad.

Before 1765 her attention was focused on the integrity and security of the provs which made up the Austrian Monarchy: the hereditary Habsburg lands of Upper Austria, Lower Austria, Inner Austria (Styria, Carinthia and Carniola), Tyrol, Vorarlberg and Freiburg-im-Breisgau, as well as the Kdom of Bohemia, the Kdom of Hungary, the Duchy of Milan and the 10 provs of the Austrian Netherlands (Belgium).

Abroad, she was immediately swept up in (i) the War of the Austrian Succession, when Prussia invaded Silesia, and a coalition of Saxony, Bavaria, Spain and France aimed at splitting up the rest of the monarchy among themselves. Prussia conquered Silesia, and the El Charles Albert of Bavaria took Linz and Prague, making himself K of Bohemia (Dec 1741) and being elected H R Emp (as Charles VII, 1742 – the 1st non-Habsburg since 1437). Maria Theresa stirred her father's septuagenarian ministers into action, galvanized the creaking machinery of Gov, and with her celebrated appeal to the Hungarian Diet at Pressburg (Pozsony) on 11 Sept 1741, holding baby Joseph in her arms, roused the chivalry of the ungovernable Magyar nobility. Aided by her ally, Britain (and later by Savoy, and later still by Russia), she fought in E and W Germany, the Netherlands, Italy and even Provence, saving Austria from total dismemberment. By the Tr of Aix-la-Chapelle (Oct 1748) Austria lost Silesia to Prussia, and Parma-Piacenza and Guastalla to Don Philip (son of PHILIP V of Spain). In the meantime, the Emp Charles VII had d (20 Jan 1745) and Francis Stephen had been elected Emp Francis I (1745). (ii) The DIPLOMATIC REVOLUTION (1749–56) was carried through at the instance of Maria Theresa and Kaunitz, who appreciated that a new situation had arisen in which Prussia, not France, was Austria's main enemy, and Britain (immersed in the colonial struggle and not interested in Silesia) was no longer her chief friend, but France. (iii) The Seven Years War saw Austria in alliance with France, Russia, Sweden and Saxony fight Prussia and Britain, but fail to regain Silesia (Tr of Hubertusberg, Feb 1763).

At home, in this period Maria Theresa, Haugwitz and Kaunitz carried out major reforms which enabled Austria to survive till 1918. (i) *The gov* of the Austrian Monarchy was too weak and fragmented to exist in the C18 world of centralized absolutisms. At the centre in Vienna, separate Chancelleries represented the provs, whose interests (rather than monarchy's) they pursued, often at cross-purposes with one another. In the provs, the essential powers of raising revenue, recruiting troops and dispensing justice were still controlled by the nobles in their Diets. The consequence was that the Crown was heavily in debt, the army was in serious decline (since the death of Pr Eugen on 21 Apr 1736, if not before) and the peasants were oppressed by their lords. Maria Theresa thus needed to make the crucial moves towards centralization and absolutism; and she forced them through in the teeth of the last-ditch resistance of the nobles and their Diets. In Vienna the Bohemian and Austrian Chancelleries were merged (May 1749) to become the *Directorium* (Directory), on the lines of the Prussian Gen Directory, which Haugwitz admired. Other boards were set up, separate from it: eg the *Staatskanzlei* (State Chancellery, 1742), for foreign affairs (which was under State Chancellor Kaunitz from 1753); and the *Oberste Justizstelle* (Supreme Office of Justice, 1748). Still other boards were added to it and then taken away again, in a constant search for the right balance between overall control and top-heaviness: eg the Treasury and the Universal Directory of Commerce were added in 1749 and 1753 respectively, and then taken away when Kaunitz took over internal as well as external affairs (1761). He changed the Directory into the United Bohemian and Austrian Chancellery. He also created the 7-man *Staatsrat* (Council of State) to replace the Privy Conference as the chief advisory board to the Crown (1760). In the provs, Haugwitz's key reform was the 10-year tax scheme (Jan 1748), whereby the Diets were to vote taxes (and higher taxes) for 10 years instead of the usual 1 (that is, after they had been persuaded or brow-beaten by the Crown to agree). In addition, their military contributions in kind (horses, forage etc) were converted into a cash payment. Thus nobles and clergy were to pay taxes for the first time, though only half those paid by the peasants. The admin of revenue and army matters (but not justice) was taken from the Diets and given in each prov to a civil-service board called eventually a *Gubernium* (Government), taking orders from the central Directory. At the local level, each *Kreis* (circle or district) was headed by a civil servant, the *Kreis-hauptman* (District Chief) – at first a local landowner, eventually a trained bureaucrat. This bureaucratic pyramid of Directory–Government–District gradually added many other admin matters to its responsibilities: police, roads, schools, poor law, trade etc. It operated in Bohemia and Austria, but not in Hungary, Milan or Belgium, where prov separatism – long sanctified by tradition, and then strengthened under CHARLES VI by the Pragmatic Sanction – was too big a nut for Maria Theresa to crack. The traditional prov and local organs of the Diets were not abolished: they were simply left to fade away as the new machinery expanded its activity. The Crown was thenceforth in a position to impinge more effectively on most aspects of life. (ii) *The army* was expanded into a vast, multi-lingual force, and brought up to date in organization, training and equipment. (iii) *Law reform* was set in train under 2 Commissions (1752), one for civil law, one for criminal law. They aimed at improving and unifying judicial procedure, and producing a code of law based on rational principles. (iv) *The Ch* was brought further under the power of the State in order to increase its efficiency and social usefulness (but not to undermine its influence over the public). Maria Theresa may have been an Erastian in Ch–State relations, but she was otherwise a devoted, somewhat puritanical Cath, who was totally out of sympathy with the anti-clerical views of the Enlightenment, and their proposals for tolerating Prots or Jews. With her short-lived Chastity Commission (1747), she hoped to keep a motherly eye on the moral behaviour of her subjects, male and female. On the other hand, during her reign the leading positions went to Jansenists rather than JESUITS; the State took over the censorship of the press (1753); 24 public holidays were abolished (1745); and the Jesuits lost their stranglehold over education. (v) *The education system* was reformed so that the schools could produce upright and useful citizens, and the univs a good supply of trained bureaucrats. The narrow academic courses of the Jesuits were replaced with modern subjects with a practical slant. Advised by her personal physician, Gerhard von Swieten (a Dutch Prot who became a Cath and a Jansenist) she reformed the Univ of Vienna, beginning with the Medical Faculty (1749). Of especial importance to the growth of the bureaucratic State were the appointments of Karl Anton von Martini to the new Chair of Natural Law (1754) and Joseph von Sonnenfels to the Chair of Political Science (1763). (vi) *The economy* occupied much of the attention of this new bureaucratic machinery, the aim being to use the State to counterbalance the economic disadvantages from which the monarchy suffered (*see* CHARLES VI). Civil servants practised the Mercantilist theories they had been taught at the univ, but only with modest success. Austria and Bohemia became a common market, and a high tariff wall was erected round the whole monarchy. Roads were built and ports developed. The lands conquered from Turkey were colonized, and attempts made to use the Danube as a trade route. Manufacturers who produced for the national and international markets were encouraged with State loans, exemptions from gild regulations, cheap labour, access to raw materials, patents of monopoly and exemption from military service. After the loss of Silesia, Bohemia became the chief centre of industry, some noble entrepreneurs using their serfs as forced labour, as in Russia. In agriculture, the State encouraged experimentation with new methods, new crops and better breeds of sheep and cattle; but little impact could be made on the countryside's adherence to medieval agriculture as long as the social structure of lord and serf predominated.

After 1765, with her husband d – an almost mortal blow to her – and her son, Joseph, as Co-Regent, Maria Theresa devoted herself to hard work more than ever; a sad and gloomy ruler in widow's weeds. While never losing her grip on political reality, and still giving top priority to the security of the Austrian monarchy, she shifted her emphasis towards peace abroad and social reform at home. She was out of sympathy with the amoral egoism of Joseph's political behaviour, and by no means convinced by the rationalizations of the Enlightenment. What happened in this period was usually the result of a struggle between herself on the one side, and the cantankerous Joseph and Kaunitz on the other, with the latter pair progressively gaining the upper hand.

At home, her reforms were motivated by a mixture of utilitarianism and humanitarianism. (i) *Serfdom*, according to the theorists of her day, was not the most productive way to run agriculture. Moreover, it was felt, a less rigid social order would release labour for industry, and also allow the State to take a bigger slice of the peasants' income at the expense of the lords. On Crown lands and lands confiscated from the Jesuits (1773), progress was possible. Councillor Franz Anton von Raab led the way in a programme of commuting *Robot* (forced labour) to money payments, and breaking up estates into small-holdings for lease to peasants on easy terms. No such change was possible on nobles' estates; and here she concentrated on compiling official records (*Urbaria*) of exactly what services the peasants owed, and protecting them from abuses by their lords. At the same time, a campaign was mounted to persuade the prov Diets to reduce peasants' obligations – an arduous and sometimes unsuccessful process. Lower Austria took 10 years before agreeing to limit peasants' *Robot* to 3 days a week. In Hungary, where suggestions for reducing *Robot* were on one occasion received in the Diet with 'uproarious laughter', the nobles resisted any interference from Vienna. Maria Theresa had guaranteed their constitutional liberties as 'an eternal and immutable fundamental law' at that famous Diet at Pressburg when they had come to her aid. Her only chance to help Hungarian serfs was to decree an *Urbarium* above the nobles' heads (Jan 1767) limiting *Robot* to 2 days a week, or 1 day with draught animals. Since Hungary, however, had refused all truck with the Haugwitz–Kaunitz admin reforms, she had no machinery to enforce her views, and it is doubtful if she made much difference to the peasants' lot in practice. In Bohemia, a combination of bad harvests, extravagant hopes of reform, and obstructiveness by the lords led to the peasant revolt of 1775. Joseph drowned it in blood, and at the same time issued the *Robot* Patent (1775), over the heads of the Diet, limiting labour to 3 days a week. These reforms – which covered most provs by the end of Maria Theresa's reign – were a thankless exercise, since they usually antagonized the nobility and failed to satisfy the serfs. (ii) *The Ch* had its power further reduced as Maria Theresa reluctantly fell back before Joseph's campaign to cut down the influence of Rome, and make the Ch more socially useful. A special Commission, the *Giunta Economale*, was set up in Milan (1765) to strip the Ch of its economic privileges. It enforced the policy – later extended to the rest of the monarchy – that all ecclesiastical activity not entrusted by Jesus to the apostles was the responsibility of the Crown. Joseph taxed the clergy, dissolved monasteries, used State courts to supervise Ch courts, sent bureaucrats to inspect Ch property, reduced holidays to save man-hours, forbade the publication of Papal orders without the sovereign's permission and allowed Prots to take degrees at the Univ of Vienna (1778). When the Pp dissolved the Jesuits (1773), Maria Theresa reluctantly complied, and Jesuit property was seized to form the Education Fund. (iii) *In education*, with the Jesuits out of the way, wholesale reform of the schools could be introduced by the General Education Regulation (1774). A network of primary and secondary schools, and training colleges, was set up to form perhaps the best educational system in Europe. (iv) *Law reform* steadily proceeded, though neither the civil code nor the criminal code was complete in Maria Theresa's lifetime, partly because of her disagreements with the Commissions. The criminal code was ready in 1768, except that she refused to go along with the Enlightened view, and abolish the death penalty and torture.

Abroad, she acquiesced in the loss of Silesia, and opposed the expansionist policies of Joseph and Kaunitz. (i) The 1st Partition of Poland (July/Aug 1772) added Galicia to the monarchy, with 2,600,000 new subjects. (ii) The Bukovina was annexed (1774) as Austria's compensation for Russia's gains after CATHE-RINE II's 1st Russo-Turkish War (1768–74); but Maria Theresa solemnly warned Joseph of the dangers of these efforts to partition Turkey. (iii) The War of the Bavarian Succession (1778–9) was again no part of her programme. Joseph was prevented by Prussia (*see* FREDERICK II) from annexing the one-third of Bavaria which he claimed, and he had to be content with the small triangle called the Inn Quarter (Tr of Teschen, May 1779). Just before Maria Theresa d she was filled with misgivings at policies which were allowing Prussia to steal the leadership of Germany which Austria had until then enjoyed.

Marie de Medici (26 Apr 1573–3 July 1642) Q consort of K HENRY IV of France (1600–10), and, after his assassination, Regent for their son, K LOUIS XIII (1610– 2 Oct 1614), during whose minority the Prs of the Blood and the magnates once more made free with the resources of the Crown, while the Hugs consolidated their position against authority, and France abandoned its anti-Habsburg posture abroad.

Daughter of Francesco de' Medici, Grand D of Tuscany, and Joanna of Austria; m (1600) K Henry IV, but became important politically only after his death, when, in accordance with his wishes, the boy K and the PARLEMENT of Paris pronounced her Regent in a *lit de justice*. Incapable of dominating the competing forces that divided France – Henry's old ministers, CONDÉ and the other Prs of the Blood and magnates, and the Hugs organized into a semi-independent republic in the S and SW – she entrusted power to her childhood friend, Leonora Galigai, and her husband, Concino Concini, whom she had brought with her from Florence and made the Marquis d'Ancre. Abroad, they abandoned Henry IV's projected anti-Habsburg war for a pro-RC policy, involving the Tr of Fontainebleau (Apr 1611) for the marriage of the K to the Spanish Infanta, confusingly known as Anne of Austria, and of his sister Eliza-beth to the future K PHILIP IV of Spain. At home, as only a Regent and a foreigner, she was unable to withstand the demands of Condé and his followers except by bribes and offices which bankrupted the treasury and threatened to break up France into a confederation of provs. Insatiable, the Prs and magnates rebelled in Feb 1614, using their offices as prov Govs to raise private armies and force the calling of the last Estates Gen before 1789. At this assembly in Paris (Oct 1614–Feb 1615) nothing positive was achieved, as none of the 3 Estates – the Clergy, the Nobles and the 3rd Estate led by the office-holders – could think more broadly than the protection of their own group interests. Shortly after, in Mar 1615, the Parlement of Paris proposed a subversive plan for placing power in the hands of the leaders of the Sword and the Robe; while Condé and his like tried to start a broadly based prov revolt in conjunction with the Hugs, but without success for, though the Prot nobles joined in, the towns held aloof. The revolt of 1614–16 ended at the Tr of Loudun (May 1616), whereby the magnates were once again bribed into acquiescence. Concini now brought energetic new members into the Council, including RICHELIEU for foreign affairs, locked up Condé at Vincennes, and sent armies and Intendants into the rebellious provs; but, as his measures began to bite, he was assassinated on 24 Apr 1617 outside the Louvre by conspirators approved by the K and led by his favourite LUYNES, who now became chief minister. During his admin, Marie was exiled to Blois, until she was rescued in Feb 1619 by the D d'Epernon. She now joined in 2 periods of revolt against her son, until the latter decisively defeated the magnates at Ponts-de-Cé, Poitou, on 7 Aug 1620. During this period Richelieu was her close adviser and agent, and when the death of Luynes on 15 Dec 1621 left the K without a chief minister, Richelieu negotiated Marie's return to the Council (1622), and she in her turn played an important part in getting her protégé into high office (1624). As chief minister, however, Richelieu disappointed her. True, he completed the destruction of the Hugs' political power, but the Grace of Alais (June 1629), which allowed their Prot worship to continue, was a betrayal of her *dévot* principles. Similarly, Richelieu's determination to concentrate on defeating the Habsburgs in the THIRTY YEARS WAR shocked her pro-Spanish feelings, as it also shocked Marillac, the Keeper of the Seals, and his faction, who considered that active intervention in foreign affairs should be postponed until France had been reformed internally. Marie and the Marillacs plotted Richelieu's destruction, and almost achieved it on the Day of Dupes (10 Nov 1630) when they believed that Marie's emotional blackmail at a meeting with the then convalescent K in her palace, the Luxembourg, had persuaded him to dismiss his minister – only to find they were wrong on 12 Nov when Marillac was arrested, and Richelieu confirmed in supreme power. In July 1631 she was exiled to Compiègne, but escaped into the Spanish Netherlands, spending the rest of her life unsuccessfully plotting against Richelieu with her younger son, Gaston, D d'ORLÉANS.

Marlborough, John Churchill, 1st D of (24 May 1650–16 June 1722) Greatest of English commanders, who was C-in-C of the British forces in the War of the Spanish Succession against K LOUIS XIV of France.

3rd son of Winston Churchill (knighted 1663), a modest Royalist squire who was grossly impoverished by the CIVIL WAR, and his wife, Elizabeth, daughter of Sir John Drake; ed privately and at St Paul's Sch, London, and at Court as page to the D of York (future K JAMES II); m (secretly, prob winter 1677/8) Sarah, beautiful and wilful daughter of Richard Jennings, modest squire, and his wife, Frances Thornhill. Commissioned as an ensign in the Foot Guards (1667), he was no doubt aided in his career by his sister, Arabella, the D of York's mistress, though doubtless his handsome face, graceful figure and irresistible charm played their part. He served in Tangier (1668–70); and in the 3rd Anglo-Dutch War (1672–4) he fought in the English fleet and in the French army. The careers of Marlborough and Sarah advanced together, united as they were in deep affection and in determination to rise above their earlier privations and make their fortune. She became Lady-in-Waiting to Prss Anne (future Q ANNE) at the same time as he became Baron Churchill in the Scots peerage (Dec 1682).

Under James II he was 2 i/c of the army which suppressed the rebellion of MONMOUTH in June–July 1685. He disapproved of the K's pro-Cath politics, and at a crucial moment in the REVOLUTION OF 1688, when he realized that James had lost the will to oppose the rebels, he rode out of the K's HQ to join William of Orange at Axminster on 24 Nov 1688, while next morning Sarah and Prss Anne fled London to join the rebels at Nottingham.

Under William III he joined the Privy Council and became the Earl of Marlborough (1689), but saw only minor service in the War of the League of Augsburg (1689–97), capturing Cork and Kinsale in Ireland (Oct 1690). His progress was delayed by a false accusation of being implicated in a Jacobite plot to assassinate William, as a result of which he lost his offices and spent 6 weeks in the Tower of London (May 1692). Moreover, the quarrel between the K and Q on the one hand, and Prss Anne on the other, militated against Marlborough until the death of Mary in 1694 enabled a reconciliation to take place. When the War of the Spanish Succession loomed (*see* LOUIS XIV), Marlborough, groomed by the K as Capt-Gen of the English troops in the Netherlands and as Ambassador-Extraordinary, negotiated the formation of the Grand Alliance with Holland and the Emp LEOPOLD I which was signed in Aug/Sept 1701; and on William's death (8 Mar 1702) Marlborough took his place as the military and political leader of the allied war effort against the French.

Under Anne he formed with GODOLPHIN and HARLEY the triumvirate which governed Britain during most of the war. In England Marlborough was a timid politician, relying on the management of his 2 partners to secure the necessary legislation for the prosecution of the war. On the Continent he was a soldier of genius who, without innovating, used the strategy, tactics and equipment of his day to perfection, and who performed miracles of organization. He himself campaigned mainly in the Netherlands, but his concern as international statesman ranged over Europe. Moreover, as well as defeating the French in battle and co-ordinating the efforts of a ramshackle union of egotistical allies, he was cool and calculating in pursuit of his own fortune. In the field (*see* LOUIS XIV), his main achievements were the capture of Bonn (7/18 May 1703) and the victories at Blenheim, Bavaria (2/13 Aug 1704), Ramillies, Netherlands (12/23 May 1706), Oudenarde, Netherlands (31 July/11 Aug 1708) and Malplaquet, Netherlands (31 Aug/11 Sept 1709). For these successes and others, the Q made him D of Marlborough in Dec 1702 and granted him £5,000 a year for her lifetime (a grant later made perpetual). The Emp Leopold I made him Pr of Mindelheim in the HREmp (1704), a title the present D of Marlborough still possesses, though Marlborough had to return the little Bavarian town of Mindelheim at the Peace of Utrecht. In Feb 1705 the Q and Parl presented him with the royal manor of Woodstock in Oxfordshire, 16,000 acres on which to build, with the help of further public money, the palace of Blenheim (a home Sarah never liked). From 1708 his political security in England crumbled, however. War-weariness affected the public; and at Court his wife – at 50 a pugnacious and paranoiac termagant – was replaced in the Q's affections by Mrs Masham. In Parl, he and Godolphin relied more and more on the pro-war Whigs, while Harley plotted their overthrow and was dismissed (Feb 1708). In private, Marlborough opposed the Whigs' 'No peace without Spain' demand which wrecked the peace negotiations of 1709; but he said nothing, afraid to risk his career in a quarrel with the Whigs. Unfortunately, he had attached himself to a losing cause. The Q dismissed the Whigs and appointed a Tory ministry bent on peace (1710), a change confirmed by the general election of the same year. Marlborough's time for dismissal came on

31 Dec 1711, and Sarah lost her Court positions at the same time. They travelled abroad in 1712, maintaining contact with the Jacobites as well as the Hanoverians; and in Sept 1714 GEORGE I restored him to all his offices.

Mary I (18 Feb 1516–17 Nov 1558) Q of England (1553), who took England back into the R C Ch and burnt many Prots at the stake.

Daughter of K HENRY VIII of England and Q CATHERINE OF ARAGON; ed in HUMANISM under the supervision of Margaret, Countess of Salisbury, until the divorce of her royal parents on 23 May 1533 completely changed her life. She was not allowed to see her mother after 1531; was declared illegitimate and barred from the throne by the Act of Succession of 1534; and was subjected to innumerable humiliations in an attempt to break her spirit, for she steadfastly refused to co-operate with the new order of things. After her mother d (7 Jan 1536) and Anne Boleyn's execution on 19 May 1536, she consented to go through a form of reconciliation in which she acknowledged the Royal Supremacy over the Ch, renounced the Pp, and agreed that her parents' marriage was 'incestuous and unlawful' (thus acknowledging her own illegitimacy). These concessions (for which she immediately asked papal absolution through the Emp CHARLES V's ambassador) resulted in better treatment, appearances at Court etc; and in the Succession Act of 1544 she was recognized as next in line to the throne after the future K EDWARD VI. In the face of the Prot policies carried out in the latter's reign (Jan 1547–July 1553), she remained unflinchingly R C; and also outmanoeuvred the schemes of John DUDLEY, D of Northumberland, to replace her on the throne with Lady Jane Grey on K Edward's death. Amidst the enthusiasm of the nation she was proclaimed Q on 19 July 1553 and entered London from E Anglia in triumph in Aug 1553. Though generous-hearted, courageous and steadfast, she soon forfeited this early popularity, and ended her reign tragically as 'Bloody Mary'. She lacked the normal Tudor pragmatic gifts, and was guided in her public, as well as in her private, life by an unflinching devotion to duty, from which no considerations of expediency could deflect her. Unfortunately, the two values she treasured most were her R C religion and her Spanish blood, both inimical to the interests of England.

The reconciliation with Rome began with the release and restoration of leading R Cs such as the 3rd D of NORFOLK, GARDINER and BONNER, and the imprisonment and deprivation of leading Prots, such as CRANMER, LATIMER and RIDLEY (1553). Her 1st Parl, meeting in Oct 1553, repealed the Prot legislation of Edward VI, and re-established the situation of 1547 (ie at the end of Henry VIII's reign), except that no heresy laws were passed, there was no restoration of the monastic lands, nor any return to Rome. About 1,500–2,000 married clergy were deprived of their livings – a policy in which Mary took a great personal interest. She concluded a Tr to marry the future PHILIP II, K of Spain (Jan 1554). Wyatt's rebellion, motivated by Prot and nationalistic opposition to these changes, was led by Sir Thomas Wyatt (son of the poet), who at the head of some 3,000 men from Kent tried to seize London. Finding London Bridge closed (Feb 1554), they crossed by Kingston Bridge and marched on the City from the W. The City refused to rise, however, and Wyatt had to surrender on 9 Feb 1554. He and about 100 others were executed; and so were Lady Jane Grey and her husband, hitherto treated with mercy. Philip visited England from July 1554 to Sept 1555, and the fatal marriage was celebrated by Gardiner in his cathedral at Winchester on 25 July 1554. Card Pole returned to England in Nov 1554; under the inspiration of this keen agent of the COUNTER-REFORMATION the restoration of the RC Ch went on apace. In Nov 1554, in the presence of Mary, Philip and both Houses of Parl on their knees, he gave absolution to England, and received her back into the Ch. This same Parl (the 3rd, which had met in Nov 1554) was less difficult to manage than earlier ones, a good deal of Gov pressure having been brought to bear during the elections. It now repealed all the anti-papal legislation that had been passed since 1529 – the start of the REFORMATION in England - except the DISSOLUTION OF THE MONASTERIES. It also revived the laws against heresy and passed a new Treasons Act. Pole and Mary were now able to begin the campaign of Prot persecution in which Latimer, Ridley, Cranmer and about 300 humbler men (craftsmen, peasants, labourers etc) were burned at the stake, while about 800 members of the gentry and middle classes fled abroad. If this did not ensure the failure of the Counter-Reformation in England, then Mary's foreign policy did.

The Spanish alliance with her husband, who became K of Spain in Jan 1556, led her into his war with Pp PAUL IV and K HENRY II of France, who were trying to eject the Spanish from Naples in what were the final campaigns of the last HABSBURG–VALOIS WAR, 1551-9. Philip paid a 2nd visit to England in Mar 1557 to drag the country into a war for which the Gov had no funds, and the people only a deep resentment, and which was certainly not in their interests. The chief consequences were the loss of Calais, the last English foothold on the Continent, on 7 Jan 1558, and the acquisition of a deep hatred of Spain amongst the precociously nationalistic English which lasted out the C16. In spite of Philip's 2 visits, Mary conceived no heir, and she d cursed by the people, her armies at war with the Pp, and with the knowledge that ELIZABETH I would succeed her, that her life's work had failed.

Mary, Q of Scots (8 Dec 1542–8 Feb 1587) Q of Scots (1542), Q Consort of K FRANCIS II of France (July 1559–Dec 1560), and Cath claimant to the throne of England in opposition to Q ELIZABETH I. Exiled from Scotland by a rebellion of Prot nobles, she was imprisoned in England, where she attracted the loyalty of English Caths and discontented magnates, and the support of France, Spain and the Pp – to such a degree that Elizabeth at last reluctantly allowed her to be tried and executed.

Only daughter of JAMES V, K of Scots, and his 2nd Q Consort, Mary of Guise; betrothed to the future K EDWARD VI of England (Tr of Greenwich, July 1543); but then (Aug 1548) sent to be ed at the Court of France as a Cath, under the eye of her uncles, François, D de GUISE, and the Card of Lorraine, who were in power there; m 1st (1558) the future K Francis II of France; m 2nd (1565) Henry Stuart, Ld Darnley (1 son, who became K JAMES VI of Scots and JAMES I of England); m 3rd (1567) James Hepburn, Earl of Bothwell. As her father was the son of Margaret Tudor, daughter of K HENRY VII, she was in Cath eyes the legitimate heir to the English throne in place of Elizabeth I, and on the death of Q MARY I (17 Nov 1558) she began to call herself Q of England. On the death of her 1st husband (5 Dec 1560) she was no longer welcome in the France of CATHE-RINE DE MEDICI, and thenceforth lived first in Scotland, then in England.

In Scotland, where she landed at Leith on 19 Aug 1561, a revolution had recently occurred. The Lords of the Congregation – a party of nobles inspired by aristocratic rebelliousness, anti-French nationalism, and the Calvinist exhortations of John KNOX – had deposed her mother, the Regent, in Oct 1559. (She d on 10 June 1560.) Elizabeth of England grasped this opportunity to break the French grip on Scotland and sent troops to help the Scots expel the French, whose abandonment of Scotland was recognized in the Tr of Edinburgh, July 1560. For a few years Mary sensibly adjusted herself to this anti-monarchical, anti-Cath, anti-French atmosphere. She was gifted with brains and charm, but violent passions clouded her judgement and her inordinate lust after the throne of England led her into political folly. On 29 July 1565 she m Ld Darnley, a good-looking but worthless weakling who, being descended from the 2nd marriage of the same Margaret, daughter of Henry VII, was next in line for the English throne after her. The pair of them antagonized the Scots nobility, leaders of whom fled to England in Sept 1565. Darnley then grew jealous of David Riccio, an Italian singer who rose to be an arrogant Sec to Mary, conducting all her affairs. He was murdered on 9 Mar 1566, receiving 56 stab wounds. Alienated from Darnley, Mary fell in love with Bothwell, an unruly Prot soldier who had served her mother and herself in various military and diplomatic tasks. What followed is far from certain, but Bothwell appears to have organized Darnley's murder on the night of 9/10 Feb 1567 as he lay sick (possibly of syphilis) in a house called Kirk o' Field in the city wall of Edinburgh. The house was blown up, but Darnley was found unsinged but strangled in the garden. Shortly after, Mary convinced everyone of her complicity by marrying Bothwell after waiting for him to get divorced. The Scots lords rebelled again and defeated Mary at Carberry Hill, nr Edinburgh (15 June 1567), and at Langside, nr Glasgow (13 May 1568). She fled to England, landing at Workington, Cumberland, in May 1568; and spent the rest of her life confined in a series of English castles.

In England, Mary became the focus, and eventually the martyr, of a variety of opposition groups. She was supported by many English Prot nobles who were terrified at Q Elizabeth's failure to marry and provide an heir, and who wanted Mary to m the 4th D of NORFOLK and guarantee the succession herself. She was supported by the English Caths, who began a revival at this juncture, marked by the REVOLT OF THE NORTHERN EARLS (Nov–Dec 1569), the Pp's Bull excommunicating and deposing Elizabeth (Feb 1570), and the arrival of the Douai-trained priests (1574 onwards) and the JESUITS (1580 onwards). She was supported by the French who were trying to re-establish themselves in Scotland (1569–73, 1580–86). And she was fortified by the gradually deteriorating relations between England and Spain, leading in 1585 to open war. The Ridolfi Plot (1571–2), the Throckmorton Plot (1582) and the Babington Plot (1586) all had the aim of destroying Elizabeth and placing Mary on the English throne with the help of France, Spain and the Pp; in the last of them the Q's Sec, WALSINGHAM, tricked Mary into providing evidence of her own involvement and approval. She was tried by a commission of 36 at Fotheringay Castle, Northants, beginning in Oct 1586, and found guilty. Elizabeth delayed signing the death-warrant for 4 months while she was urgently pressed to do so by the Council and both Houses of Parl. Eventually, on 1 Feb 1587 she added her signature and gave the document to her Sec, William Davison. Once the Ld Treasurer,

BURGHLEY, got his hands on it, action swiftly followed. Mary was beheaded at Fotheringay, meeting her end with dignity and courage.

Matthias (24 Feb 1557–20 Mar 1619) ArchD of Austria and K of Hungary (1608), K of Bohemia (1611), HREmp (1612), younger brother of the eccentric Emp RUDOLPH II. His ambitions led him 1st to intervene in the REVOLT OF THE NETHERLANDS in the hopes of carving out a Kdom there; and then to overthrow his brother and become a comparatively powerless head of the Habsburg Monarchy and HREmp in the years immediately before the outbreak of the THIRTY YEARS WAR.

3rd son of the Emp Maximilian II and Maria, daughter of the Emp CHARLES V, he was sent to the Spain of K PHILIP II for his education, out of reach of the Prot influences which had entrenched themselves all over the Austrian Monarchy; m (1611) his cousin, Anna of Tyrol. In the Netherlands, where he hoped to compensate for his younger-brother status by winning a throne, he tried to build up a position midway between Philip II and the extremist rebels. Against the wishes of both Philip and Rudolf, he accepted the position of Gov-Gen (theoretically on behalf of Philip) to which the Netherlands Estates-Gen elected him (Jan 1578). A lazy, political lightweight, he failed to command the situation and was simply tossed about like a cork in the heaving waters of the Revolt till the formal Dutch Abjuration of Philip II (July 1581) automatically ended his adventure too. Back in Austria, he was appointed Gov of Austria on the death of his brother, Ernest, in 1595. He supported the attack on the Prots there, and also took part in Rudolf's Turkish War (1593–1606), until his ambitions prompted him to take advantage of the increasingly eccentric behaviour of his brother and take over all his offices. In Vienna in Apr 1606, he and his Habsburg cousins formally recognized Matthias as head of the family with full powers. Against Rudolf's wishes, he made peace with István Bocskay, Pr of Transylvania and Turkish satellite (Tr of Vienna, June 1606), and with Sultan Ahmed I of Turkey (Tr of Zsitva-Torok, Nov 1606). He bribed the Estates of Hungary, Austria and Moravia with religious and political concessions to recognize him as their sovereign instead of Rudolf (Tr of Libeň, or Lieben, June 1608). In Bohemia and Silesia, where Rudolf was still sovereign, Matthias had to wait a little longer. He invaded Bohemia in 1608, but the Czechs preferred loyalty to Rudolf at this stage, and they got their concessions from him (Letter of Majesty, July 1609). However, Rudolf's clumsy attempts to suppress them in Jan 1611 with troops hired from Passau led Bohemia to transfer its allegiance to Matthias, who again invaded Bohemia, this time to be elected K (23 May 1611). In Germany, Matthias became HREmp on the death of Rudolf.

As a result of the Turkish War and the rivalry of the brothers – both of which led to the granting of large concessions to the Estates – Matthias's authority both in Germany and Austria was feeble. In the HREmp, the activities of the Prot Union and the Cath League, and the evolution of the Jülich-Cleves succession crisis – in fact, the general build-up of tension leading to the Thirty Years War – were beyond his control. In the Austrian Monarchy, which was now a constitutional monarchy, if not an aristocratic republic, royal power was at its lowest ebb. It was fortunate for the Crown that the various Estates were incapable of acting together against it, as was demonstrated by the failure of the confederation of all the Estates planned for Prague in June 1615. Rivalries between the provs and rifts between the classes allowed the monarchy to survive. It was a result in no way due to the efforts of Matthias, who left everything to his chief minister, the ageing Card Khlesl. But the latter's statesmanlike efforts to avoid religious war in the Monarchy and the Emp led Spain, the Papacy and the Habsburg family to redouble their efforts to ensure that on his death Matthias would be replaced by someone capable of re-establishing the authority of the Crown and reinforcing the COUNTER-REFORMATION – for Matthias and his brothers were childless. By the Oñate Tr (June and July 1617) – named after the Spanish ambassador to Vienna who dominated the negotiations – Matthias's cousin, Ferdinand of Styria (future FERDINAND II) was named as his successor in the Monarchy and the Emp. K PHILIP III of Spain gave up his claims only in return for a promise that Habsburg fiefs in Alsace and Tyrol and imperial fiefs in Italy would be transferred to Spain. At the same time the Estates of Bohemia voted to 'accept' Ferdinand as K (June 1617) as did the Estates of Hungary (July 1618). In the last months of Matthias's life the Defenestration of Prague (23 May 1618) and the Bohemian rebellion occurred. Matthias's continual search for compromise led Ferdinand, backed by the Spanish party in Vienna and the Bohemian R Cs, to take affairs into his own hands. He arrested Khlesl (July 1618), and prepared to use force against the Czechs; but, as Vienna plunged Europe into the Thirty Years War, it was no longer Matthias's hand on the helm. Incapacitated by asthma, he was a mere spectator till his long-hoped-for death.

Maurice, Count of Nassau (13 Nov 1567–23 Apr 1625) Stadholder (Gov) of Holland and Zeeland (1585), of Utrecht, Overysel and Gelderland (1590); Pr of Orange (1618), after the death of his elder brother, Philip William, who had been imprisoned in Spain for much of his life. He assumed the military leadership of the REVOLT OF THE NETHERLANDS after the assassination of his father, WILLIAM I of Orange, on 10 July 1584; supported by the political head, OLDENBARNEVELT, he modernized the Dutch army and drove out the Spanish. Later he quarrelled with Oldenbarnevelt and organized his political defeat and execution; during the THIRTY YEARS WAR he renewed the fighting with Spain, though without great success.

Son of William I and Anna, daughter of MAURICE of Saxony; ed at Heidelberg, then Leiden, where he studied classics and maths, attending Simon Stevin's lectures on maths and mechanics. With Oldenbarnevelt's help he was appointed Stadholder after his father's assassination, and thus commanded most of the Dutch military forces. Scholarly by inclination, he made a thorough study of warfare in the Roman and modern writers and, aided by his cousin, William Louis, Count of Nassau, who was Stadholder of Friesland, Groningen and Drente, he applied the lessons he learned from them and Stevin to turn the Dutch army into the most advanced in Europe. In place of the Spanish *tercio* he introduced the much smaller battalion of highly-trained infantrymen, fighting in lines rather than squares, and capable of very swift manoeuvres. He also used the latest technology in the design of artillery and fortifications, and paid careful attention to the pay and equipment of his men, as well as their supply by land and water. Aided by these reforms, and other favourable factors (*see* the REVOLT), he drove out the Spanish from the N provs (1588–98); on Oldenbarnevelt's orders, but against his better judgement, he invaded the S, beating the Spanish at Nieuwpoort, Flanders, on 2 July 1600, but did not follow up the victory. He also disapproved of the Twelve Years' Truce which Oldenbarnevelt negotiated (Apr 1609); and the erstwhile partners drew further apart as they headed the emerging 2 sides in what became the classic split in Dutch life (*see* OLDEN-BARNEVELT). Ultimately, when civil war threatened, Maurice outwitted Olden-barnevelt and had him executed on 13 May 1619; nevertheless he failed to use this opportunity of supreme power to make any reforms in the Dutch system of Gov, and thus end its chronic decentralization. In foreign affairs, Maurice sought every opportunity to strike at the Habsburgs so as to relieve pressure on his S frontier; but, though he was diplomatically and militarily committed to support Bohemia in the early stages of the Thirty Years War, the tension with Olden-barnevelt prevented Holland from playing a large military role. His involvement in the war increased when the Truce with Spain expired and neither he nor the new regime in Spain (K PHILIP IV and OLIVARES) was willing to extend it. Maurice gave shelter to Frederick V of the Palatinate, the exiled K of Bohemia, in Apr 1621; but his last years of warfare against Spain were not brilliant. Spinola from the S had already invaded the Rhine Palatinate in July 1620. He now took Jülich (Feb 1622) and invaded Holland. Though Maurice's ally, Mansfeld, fought off his attack on Bergen-op-Zoom, Brabant, in July 1622, Maurice's own powers were in decline; and, a few weeks after his death, the Spanish achieved an important success in the capture of Breda, Brabant, on 5 June 1625. Maurice's work was continued by his younger brother, FREDERICK HENRY.

Maurice, D, then El of Saxony (21 Mar 1521–11 July 1553) A Prot Pr who fought for the Emp CHARLES V against the Prot Schmalkaldic League, which he then joined against the Emp.

Son of Henry, later D of Saxony; m (1541) Agnes, 14-year-old daughter of Philip, Landgrave of Hesse. His family had divided in 1485 into 2 branches: the Electoral and the Ducal. Maurice inherited Ducal Saxony from his Prot father (1541), and he continued his policy of furthering the REFORMATION and using secularized Ch property for charitable and educational purposes. He was not religious, however, but politically ambitious and agile, too; having designs on Electoral Saxony (ruled by the corpulent John Frederick since 1532) as well as on the Bprics of Magdeburg and Halberstadt, he kept a foot both in the Imperial camp and in that of the Schmalkaldic League until he was won over to an alliance with Charles V at Regensburg in June 1546. In the ensuing war the Schmalkaldic League was defeated at Mühlberg on the Elbe on 24 Apr 1547 and the Elector John Frederick was taken prisoner. At Wittenberg, which Charles now entered, John Frederick signed the Capitulation on 19 May 1547, ceding to Maurice the Electoral title and the prov which contained Wittenberg. Maurice changed sides, in disgust at Charles's autocratic behaviour and in disappointment at not getting also Magdeburg and Halberstadt. He and the Prot Prs signed the Tr of Chambord (Jan 1552) with K HENRY II of France, drove Charles S as far as Villach, Carinthia, and by the Tr of Passau which Maurice negotiated with FERDINAND I (Charles's deputy) achieved their aims: religious equality and a guarantee of the separatist political privileges of the Prs. Maurice then campaigned against the

Turks in Hungary on Ferdinand's behalf; then he waged war on Albert Alcibiades, the Margrave of Brandenburg-Kulmbach-Bayreuth, a former Prot ally who had now, Maurice-like, joined the Emp in pursuit of territorial gain. Maurice defeated him at Sievershausen, Solling, the bloodiest battle of the Reformation, on 9 July 1553 – but himself d of wounds 2 days later.

Maximilian I (22 Mar 1459–12 Jan 1519) K of the Romans (1486), H R Emp (1493), whose marriage diplomacy added the Netherlands, and ultimately Bohemia and Hungary to the Habsburg possessions. He made some progress in centralizing the Gov of the Austrian Monarchy, but none in his attempts to reorganize the Gov of the Emp, where the Prs rightly suspected that he intended to use German resources to back Habsburg family interests. Being thus starved of money and men, he was unsuccessful in his attempts to extend the power of the Emp in Italy and to eject the French.

Son of Emp Frederick III and Eleanor of Portugal. Huge, energetic, genial, popular, athletic and scholarly, part knight-errant, part humanist intellectual, writer and patron of the arts, his head buzzed with wild schemes which he had neither the cash nor the constancy to carry out. His main fields of action were The Netherlands, The HABSBURG–VALOIS WARS, The Habsburg provs (Austrian Monarchy) and The H R Emp.

The Netherlands. By marrying Mary, daughter and heiress of Charles the Bold (1477) he added to the Habsburg lands the Duchy of Burgundy, the most powerful state in Europe till 1477, and possessor of multifarious lands and responsibilities: ie the 17 provs which constitute modern Holland, Belgium and Luxemburg, along with Artois and the Franche Comté and the Duchy of Burgundy (modern Bourgogne). He also inherited the enmity of France, which overran Bourgogne and Picardy, but which was prevented from seizing the Franche Comté, Artois and Flanders (which she claimed) by Maximilian's victory over them at Guinegate, Artois, on 17 Aug 1479. Maximilian also inherited the Netherlands' extremely decentralized form of Gov, in which the Estates of the numerous provs and towns (dominated by the urbanized nobility and commercial aristocracy of this economically advanced area) had forced Mary to recognize their self-governing privileges (the *Grand Privilège*, 1477) in return for support. The external and internal problems intertwined as Maximilian tried to build up monarchical power in order to fight the French, while the States-Gen used French help to resist him, especially after the death of Mary (27 Mar 1482). The Estates now regarded, not Maximilian, but his son PHILIP as the head of State. It was the Estates, not Maximilian, which negotiated the Tr of Arras (Dec 1482) with France by which Maximilian's daughter Margaret was betrothed to the Dauphin (later K CHARLES VIII) with Artois, the Franche Comté, Charolais and Auxerre as her dowry. The cession of Bourgogne to France was also recognized. Later, Maximilian's struggles with the Estates grew more and more serious, until the rebellious city of Bruges imprisoned him from Feb to May 1488, when he was rescued by Imperial troops. When Maximilian left for Austria (Feb 1489) he left behind his Statthalter, Albert of Meissen, D of Saxony, who managed to discipline the towns in a 4-year struggle. Meanwhile (to hit France from behind) Maximilian m Anne, Dss of Brittany, by proxy (1490), but K Charles VIII m her instead (1491), repudiating Maximilian's betrothed daughter Margaret. This led to war, in which Maximilian beat off a French invasion at Salins (Franche Comté, Jan 1493), and to the Tr of Senlis (May 1493), whereby he got back Artois, the Franche Comté and Margaret. In Aug 1494, Maximilian handed the Netherlands over to his son PHILIP I (The Handsome); and after the latter's death (25 Sept 1506), Maximilian's daughter Margaret ruled as Regent (1509–30) for Philip's son, the future Emp CHARLES V. During this period Philip and Margaret wisely abandoned Maximilian's warlike policies in favour of retrenchment and the pursuit of the proper interests of the Netherlands.

The Italian Wars (*see* HABSBURG–VALOIS WARS). From 1493 (when he became Emp in effect) until 1516, Maximilian was involved in fruitless attempts to restore the authority of the Emp in Italy, and especially to counter the French claims to Milan, and to drive the Venetians out of Verona, off the mainland, and back to their islands. He never had sufficient troops, because the German Prs refused to finance what they regarded as madcap schemes for Habsburg family (ie non-German) interests, and they used his need of money as a means of weakening the power of the Emp inside Germany. He m (1494) Bianca Maria, niece of Ludovico SFORZA, ruler of Milan, in return for 440,000 ducats and the hope of pushing the Venetians into the sea. He then joined the League of Venice (Mar 1495) to expel K Charles VIII of France from Italy; and strengthened his alliance with Spain by a momentous double marriage: between his daughter Margaret and Don Juan, son and heir of FERDINAND and ISABELLA (1496 in Antwerp), and between his son Philip and Donna Joanna (later The Mad), 2nd daughter of Ferdinand and Isabella (1497, Burgos). In 1496 Maximilian fought as a *condottiere* in Venetian and Milanese pay (as he lacked German funds) to ward off a non-existent French invasion. He returned to Germany a laughing-stock, and eventually had to recognize the French annexation of Milan by the Tr of Blois (Sept 1504). Later, he formed the League of Cambrai with France (Dec 1508) for a further bout of useless campaigns against Venice; then, on Pp JULIUS II's illness, he toyed with the idea of becoming Pp (1511) (though this may only have been his idea of a joke); then he joined the Holy League (Apr 1513) for a campaign against France in the pay of K HENRY VIII of England (the German Prs refusing to provide the funds) and took part in the Battle of the Spurs (Guinegate, Artois, 16 Aug 1513). After K FRANCIS I's victory at Marignano, Milan (13/14 Sept 1515), he invaded Italy for the last time, even held Milan for 1 day (25 Mar 1516) and then retreated. So ended his Italian ventures, as he recognized in the Tr of Brussels (Dec 1516) with Francis I.

The Habsburg Provs (future Austrian Monarchy). Maximilian's policy here was, firstly, to gather the sovereignty of each of the provinces of Upper and Lower Austria into his own hands (instead of leaving them with branches of his family or under the occupation of Matthias Corvinus, K of Hungary); secondly, to add to them; thirdly, to unify them by central governing institutions. The Tyrol came into his hands (Mar 1490) when he persuaded D Siegmund to abdicate in his favour. Further E, Matthias Corvinus had conquered Styria and Carinthia, and occupied Vienna (1485) and Wiener Neustadt (1487). With his death, however (6 Apr 1490), his Kdom broke up into its constituent parts and Maximilian was able to reconquer all the Austrian lands. Moreover, in the Tr of Pressburg (Nov 1491) with WLADYSLAW JAGIELLO (who was K Vladislav II of Bohemia and also K Ulászló II of Hungary) he was recognized as the future K of Bohemia and Hungary should this K die without issue. Marriage treaties uniting the descendants of Maximilian and Wladyslaw were negotiated in 1502, 1506 and 1507, and found fruition in the treaties signed in Vienna (July–Aug 1515) whereby Maximilian adopted Wladyslaw's son Lewis as his son. Lewis was to marry Maximilian's granddaughter Mary, and Maximilian (aged 56) was betrothed to Wladyslaw's daughter Anna (aged 12). In 1516 Anna was m by proxy to FERDINAND (younger brother of the future Emp CHARLES V), who ultimately was elected K of both Hungary and Bohemia on the death of Lewis II in the battle of Mohács (26 Aug 1526) against Turkey. As an important contribution to the creation of the Austrian Monarchy, Maximilian set up a number of centralizing institutions. Councils were established at Innsbruck (1490) for Upper Austria and at Linz (1493) (later Vienna) for Lower Austria – not without opposition from the Estates of these provs. A separate central Treasury was also set up; and to cover the common problems of the Emp and Monarchy, Maximilian roughed out (1497–8) also the future *Hofrat* and *Hofkammer*.

Holy Roman Empire (Germany): Maximilian made no headway in the fundamental struggle between the Emp on the one hand, trying to turn Germany into a centralized absolutism, and the Estates on the other (ie, the nearly 400-strong Prs, cities and nobles) determined to keep their separate institutions of self-Gov. On his side, Maximilian wished to increase the powers of the Imperial Gov in order to raise men and money for his foreign schemes, which were more in the interests of the Habsburg family in Austria and Burgundy than in those of the German people. On their side, the Estates did not mind improving the central Gov's ability to suppress private warfare and keep law and order, so long as the real power was in the hands of their delegates. No lasting compromise was possible between his view of Germany as a monarchy under himself and theirs of it as a confederation ruled by an oligarchy, and his reign is filled by debates in the Diet (*Reichstag*) over Imperial reform which in practice came to nothing, though he made concessions from time to time (which he did not intend to carry out) in return for urgently required grants of taxation. The *Reichstag* of Worms (1495) proclaimed an Eternal Peace, and an end to feuds. Disputes henceforth were to be settled in the new Imperial Supreme Court (*Reichskammergericht*), which was to be independent of the Emp; and a new tax, the Common Penny, was to finance both this and Maximilian's schemes for driving K Charles VIII of France out of Italy. Maximilian refused to accept the *Reichstag*'s scheme for placing him under the supervision of an Executive Council (*Reichsregiment*) chosen by them, but agreed to an ineffective substitute whereby the *Reichstag* meeting for at least a month each year were to take all the main political decisions. In the absence of an Imperial bureaucracy, neither the political, nor the judicial, nor the financial reforms achieved much practical realization, except that they disturbed the Swiss into a rebellion which Maximilian could not put down. The Tr of Basle (Sept 1499) granted them practical independence. Further reforms were passed at the Diet of Augsburg (1500) where the Estates made Maximilian accept the setting-up of a 20-member *Reichsregiment* (with the Emp as President) as the supreme executive organ; secondly, they divided the Empire into 6 Circles for internal order and external defence. The Circles (increased to 10 in 1512) were effective and lasting; the *Reichskammergericht* and the *Reichsregiment* were out

Maximilian I

of action by 1502; while the death (21 Sept 1504) of the chief campaigner for reform, Berthold von Henneberg, Archbp of Mainz, took the steam out of the whole reform movement. At the Diet of Constance (1507) the *Reichskammergericht* was revived, and the basis of taxation went back to the traditional, but obsolete, assessment-lists, the *Matrikel* – both of which now lasted as long as the Empire. Further reforms were fruitlessly discussed at further Diets; and Maximilian spent his last Diet at Frankfurt (1518) trying to bribe a majority of the Electors to choose his grandson Charles as K of the Romans (and thus future Emp). He d, however, before this could be achieved. If as German K and universal knight-errant his success was small, as head of the Habsburgs he united the Austrian lands, sketched out the central institutions of the Austrian Monarchy, added Burgundy and also the worldwide possessions of the Crown of Spain, as well as a good chance of the succession to Bohemia and Hungary.

Maximilian I (17 Apr 1573–27 Sept 1651) D of Bavaria (1597), El of Bavaria (1623), the leading German Pr of his time. He established ABSOLUTISM in Bavaria by defeating the Estates and the Prots; and in Germany headed the Cath League, and during the THIRTY YEARS WAR played such a skilful diplomatic and military role – he opposed the Emp as a Pr but supported him as a Cath – that he gained the Upper Palatinate and the rank of El, both previously the possessions of Frederick V, the El Palatine.

Son of D William V and Renée of Lorraine; ed along with his cousin, the future Emp FERDINAND II, at the Jesuit college at Ingolstadt, Bavaria; m (1595) Prss Elizabeth of Lorraine (no children); succeeded when his sick father retired to a monastery (Oct 1597). Pale and thin, with adenoids and a piping voice, he dominated affairs at home and abroad with his very effective mixture of religious conviction, worldly wisdom and avarice tempered by an ability to wait his chance.

At home, his predecessors had eliminated the Prot problem, and he finished the job of making his rule absolute by suppressing the Estates; creating a well-trained army under Tilly; building a royal treasure through careful admin organized by an efficient central Gov and State-wide bureaucracy; and turning the Ch into an agent of the State, exercising a detailed supervision of the health, education, morals, manners and dress of the common people rarely found in Europe in that period.

Abroad, he was the leading Cath Pr in Germany under the Emp RUDOLF II, executing the Emp's ban in the Donauwörth Affair (1606–9); forming the Cath League in July 1609; using his army under Tilly during the Jülich-Cleves Succession Crisis (1609–14) to secure Jülich, Berg and Ravenstein for his brother-in-law, Wolfgang William, Count Palatine of Neuburg. During the Thirty Years War, Maximilian oscillated between backing the Emps Ferdinand II and FERDINAND III, when the Ch was in danger and territorial gains were on offer, and opposing them when they seemed militarily strong enough to threaten the liberties of the German Prs. At the same time, he opposed the interference in German affairs of foreign powers such as Denmark, Sweden, Spain and France; but was prepared to make use of them whenever it suited Bavaria. During the Bohemian War (1618–20), his army under Tilly suppressed the Prot Estates of Austria (which he then occupied and exploited, 1620–28), and defeated the Bohemian rebels at the White Mountain (8 Nov 1620). During the Palatinate

307

War (1621–3), Tilly conquered the Upper and Rhenish Palatinates; and for these services Maximilian was given the Palatinate and the rank of El belonging to its ruler, Frederick V – grants which were made secretly by the Emp in Sept 1621, and confirmed by the Electoral College in Feb 1623. During the Danish War (1624–9), the Emp tried to escape from his dependence upon Maximilian's armed forces by hiring his own army under WALLENSTEIN. Tilly defeated the main army of K CHRISTIAN IV of Denmark at Lutter (27 Aug 1626), and then co-operated with Wallenstein in driving the Danes out of N Germany. During the year of the Emperor's Pride and Fall (1629–30) it was Maximilian who led the opposition of the German Prs and who at the Regensburg Electors' Meeting (July–Aug 1630) forced the Emp to dismiss the too-successful Wallenstein and replaced him with his own Gen, Tilly. At the same meeting, Maximilian reached an understanding with France which, on and off, was to mark Franco-Bavarian relations into the C19. During the Swedish War (1630–35), Tilly captured and accidentally destroyed Magdeburg (20 May 1631); but was defeated by the combined Swedes and Saxons at Breitenfeld, Saxony, on 17 Nov 1631. He was now unable to prevent Sweden from thrusting across Germany to the upper Rhine, or Saxony from threatening Vienna through Bohemia. In fact, Maximilian now had the humiliation of seeing Tilly killed and Bavaria occupied. He had no alternative but to fall back on his alliance with the Emp, who jointly with Spain liberated Bavaria by defeating the Swedes at Nördlingen, Swabia, on 5/6 Sept 1634. Like most of the other German Prs, Maximilian now signed the Tr of Prague (May 1635). During the Franco-Habsburg War (1635–48), Maximilian began by playing a subordinate role to that of the Emp as his treasure and troops were so depleted; though his cavalry took part in the Spanish invasion of NE France which was halted at Corbie (1636). Resilient and hard-headed, however, he healed Bavaria's wounds, and by the mid-1640s once more had an army (under Franz von Mercy and Johan von Werth) which made both the Emp and RICHELIEU value his alliance again. Jointly with the Emp's forces, Mercy defeated the French at Tuttlingen, Württemberg (24 Nov 1643), and took Freiburg in July 1644, but had to retreat after a 3-day battle there (4–6 Aug 1644). Werth beat the French under Turenne at Mergentheim, Franconia, on 5 May 1645; but Turenne and Condé defeated Mercy at Allerheim (nr Nördlingen), Swabia, on 3 Aug 1645, a battle in which Mercy was killed. In June 1646 the Swedes and French invaded Bavaria again, forcing Maximilian to break with the Emp once more at the Tr of Ulm (Mar 1647). By Sept 1647, however, Maximilian had switched sides again, and the Franco-Swedes defeated the joint Bavarian and Imperial armies at Zusmarshausen, Bavaria, on 17 May 1648. Meanwhile, at the peace negotiations at Münster he co-operated with the French in getting as much advantage from the Emp for them both as possible; and by the ensuing Tr of Westphalia (Oct 1648) Maximilian kept the Upper Palatinate and the rank of El, but had to give up the Rhenish Palatinate.

Mazarin, Jules (Giulio Mazzarini) (14 July 1602–8/9 Mar 1661) Card (1641), chief minister of K LOUIS XIV of France during his minority, and favourite of the Q Mother, Anne of Austria. He continued the policies of RICHELIEU: at home, weathering the FRONDES and increasing the centralizing and absolutist powers of the Crown; abroad, consolidating Richelieu's THIRTY YEARS WAR efforts in the favourable Tr of Westphalia, withstanding Spanish counter-attacks in the NE and across the Pyrenees (though failing to make even a dent in Spain's predominance in Italy), and by the Tr of the Pyrenees (Nov 1659) establishing France's position as the greatest power in Europe.

b in Italy at Pescina, Abruzzi; eld son of Pietro Mazzarini, official in the household of Filippo Colonna; ed at Rome and Alcalá, Spain, in law; rose as a soldier and diplomat in the papal service, in which capacity he several times had dealings with Richelieu and impressed him so much that he was appointed unofficial representative of France at Rome (1631–9) and then joined the French service for good. Richelieu on his deathbed in Dec 1642 recommended him to K LOUIS XIII, who in turn appointed him to the Council of Regency which he provided in his will for the minority of Louis XIV. On Louis XIII's death, however, on 14 May 1643, the Q Mother got the Parlement of Paris to sidestep the will and declare her sole Regent. She then made Mazarin not only her chief minister, but probably also her lover and perhaps even her husband.

At home, as was to be expected under the Regency of a foreign Q Mother and the Gov of a foreign chief minister, there was immediate trouble from the Prs of the Blood. Mazarin had to break up the conspiracy against him of the D de Beaufort (grandson of K HENRY IV), the Dss de Chevreuse and others (the *Cabale des Importants*) by imprisoning Beaufort at Vincennes (Sept 1643). Mazarin had the same problems as Richelieu: to keep order at home by the increasing use of Intendants and whatever other means (peremptory or pliant) seemed appropriate, and to raise money by harsh taxation or crafty fiscal manipulations at the expense of the *rentiers* and the office-holders – all in aid of the main priorities, which were the successful completion of the THIRTY YEARS WAR (until 1648) and the protracted war against Spain (until 1659). In deciding to continue the Spanish war in 1648, Mazarin failed to appreciate the depth of suffering and the diversity of opposition his dictatorial methods and financial exactions were causing. As a result he was almost toppled by the Frondes (1648–53), a series of civil wars in which all the opponents of the Crown except the Hugs gave vent to their frustrations or ambitions: the Prs of the Blood, the Sword, the Robe, the office-holders, the peasants, the urban radicals and the provs, aided from time to time by the Spanish. Mazarin became the most hated man in France, for in a period of financial stringency and economic crisis he had not only accumulated a vast fortune in country estates, town houses, books, manuscripts and diamonds, but had also placed his brother as well as several nieces and nephews in lucrative posts or marriages, or both. Unlike Richelieu with his imperious bearing and forceful methods, Mazarin was gentle and subtle; and where Richelieu had struck hard blows, Mazarin was devious and yielding. He preferred to bide his time while his enemies destroyed one another, twice going into exile while the storms blew themselves out (Feb–Dec 1651 and Aug 1652–Feb 1653) each time carrying on the Gov of France in letters to the Q Mother. He was eventually triumphant, thanks to two powerful French emotions: loyalty to the legitimate K (Louis was declared of age on 7 Nov 1651 and he kept Mazarin in office), and fear of anarchy and foreign conquest. By using his fortune to raise troops and bribe his enemies, Mazarin re-established the authority of the Court, taking Bordeaux in Aug 1653, the last serious centre of resistance. Henceforth he ruled France as before, sending out Intendants (though not always under that name), manipulating the revenues and making a second fortune. One new feature must also be noticed: he taught Louis XIV how to rule without a chief minister, and trained his first brilliant generation of experts: Le Tellier, COLBERT and Lionne.

Abroad, he brought the Thirty Years War to a triumphant conclusion for France, operating mainly in the NE on the Belgian border where he beat the Spanish at Rocroi, Ardennes, on 19 May 1643, and stopped an Austro-Spanish invasion force at Lens, Artois, on 20 Aug 1648, and in the E, where he was thrusting through Bavaria towards Vienna in co-operation with Sweden. At Westphalia (Oct 1648) France gained full sovereignty over Metz, Toul and Verdun in Lorraine; took Breisach and Philippsburg on the E side of the Rhine, and Pinerolo in Piedmont; and effectively controlled Alsace. The war against Spain went through a dangerous phase at first because of the Frondes and because France no longer had the help of Holland, which had made peace in 1648; but France triumphed in the end, thanks to Turenne's generalship and Mazarin's imaginative diplomacy. Only in Italy did Mazarin have no success. His task was made difficult by the election of a pro-Spanish Pp, Innocent X (1644). The joint attack on Milan which Mazarin organized with his allies, Savoy and Modena, was a failure (1646–7). He captured some Tuscan towns in 1646, but lost them again in 1653. During the popular revolt which shook Naples in 1647–8 he was prevented by the Frondes from giving any effective anti-Spanish aid; and in 1652 the French were expelled from Casale in Piedmont. In Spain he aided the REVOLTS of CATALONIA and PORTUGAL, though the Spaniards recaptured Barcelona in Oct 1652, during the Frondes. In the NE, Spain made some gains during the Frondes, taking Gravelines (19 May 1652) and Dunkirk (16 Sept 1652); but Mazarin was able to counter-attack with the help of the English. In Oct/Nov 1655 he signed the commercial Tr of Westminster with CROMWELL, later enlarged into a military alliance, the fruit of which was the aid of the English fleet and the joint victory over Spain at the battle of the Dunes (14 June 1658) and the capture of Dunkirk (24 June 1658). Dunkirk was ceded to England; while Turenne was now able to strike at Brussels. In Germany, Mazarin conducted a vigorous diplomatic offensive to prevent the Emp giving any help to Spain. He made an alliance with Brandenburg (Feb 1656). On the death of the Emp FERDINAND III he tried to prevent the election of LEOPOLD I in favour of the El of Bavaria or even K Louis XIV. The Electors, however, voted unanimously for Leopold (July 1658), but, prompted by Mazarin, made him sign a Capitulation in which he guaranteed not to help Spain against France. In Aug 1658, Mazarin went further and organized the League of the Rhine (France, Sweden, Cologne, Trier, Mainz, Münster, Neuburg and others) aimed at hamstringing the Emp by guaranteeing German 'liberties'. Thus isolated, worn down and in decline, Spain agreed to make peace. By the Tr of the Pyrenees (Nov 1659), France gained Roussillon and Cerdagne in the Pyrenees, and Artois with some posts in Flanders, Hainault and Luxemburg in the NE. She also achieved a real grip on Lorraine, while Spain abandoned all claim to Alsace. France kept Pinerolo but renounced further claims in Italy, and gave up supporting the Catalans and Portuguese in Spain. France also withdrew from Franche Comté. Moreover, Louis pardoned Condé, the 1st Pr of the Blood, who had been fighting for Spain since the Frondes. Finally, according to the Tr, Louis m the Infanta Maria

Teresa, who renounced her rights to inherit Spain on condition that her dowry was paid. As it never was, this clause was the source of Louis' ambitious struggle for the Spanish Succession. In other words, when Mazarin d, France had passed beyond the stage of needing to break out of Habsburg encirclement, and could begin to contemplate aggression.

Melanchthon, Philipp (16 Feb 1497–19 Apr 1560) Theological lieutenant of LUTHER during the German REFORMATION.

Son of an armourer, and great-nephew of Reuchlin, the Humanist scholar, who supervised his career and gave him the Greek form of his original name, Schwarzerd, because of his knowledge of Greek; ed in HUMANISM at Heidelberg (1509) and Tübingen (1512), and, brilliant scholar as he was, became at 21 Prof of Greek at the Univ of Wittenberg, Saxony, in 1518; m Katherine Krapp. At Wittenberg he was converted by Luther and became his chief disciple. He accompanied him to the Leipzig Disputation with Eck from June–July 1519. He organized the religious outpourings of his master into the chief systematic theology of Lutheranism, his *Loci communes* (1st edn 1521). He was in charge at Wittenberg while Luther was taking refuge in the Wartburg (1521–2) but, since he was too tolerant with CARLSTADT and the other radical preachers from Zwickau, Luther had to pay a visit to Wittenberg to restore order in Mar 1522. A liberal and flexible theologian, Melanchthon belonged to the liberal wing of the Lutheran movement, taking almost the view of CALVIN on the Eucharist, believing, unlike the predestinarian Luther, that men's wills were free to co-operate or not with the divine grace, and drawing the important distinction between essentials and non-essentials in religion – the latter including Ch order and liturgy, and being negotiable with other denominations in the interests of peace. Thus the AUGSBURG CONFESSION of 1530, which he wrote, was thought by some Lutherans to make too many friendly gestures towards the papacy; the points of agreement he reached with the R C deputy, Contarini, at the discussions organized by the Emp CHARLES V at Regensburg (Apr–May 1541), were re-pudiated by both their headquarters, making reunion between R Cs and Prots impossible. Moreover, his readiness to accept the Emp's Augsburg Interim of May 1548 as a position from which to negotiate an agreement with the Pp lost him the support of the hard-line Lutherans (known as the 'Genuine Lutherans'), and heralded a deep division within Lutheranism. Melanchthon was also important as a leading educational reformer.

Michael (Mikhail Fedorovich) (12 July 1596–13 July 1645) Tsar of Russia (1613), the 1st of the Romanov dynasty, who restored peace, order and security after the TIME OF TROUBLES.

Son of Theodore Nikitich Romanov (who was nephew of IVAN IV's wife, Anastasia, and later called Patriarch Filaret) and his wife, Xenia Ivanovna Shestova. During the Time of Troubles Filaret was imprisoned in Poland, and Michael and his mother sheltered in a monastery at Kostroma until he very reluctantly agreed to become Tsar, having been elected to that office by a specially assembled *zemskii sobor* in Moscow; m 1st (1624) Maria Dolgorukaya, daughter of a *boyar* (d 4 months later); 2nd (1626) Eudoxia Streshneva, daughter of a small landowner (she left 1 son, the future Tsar ALEXIS). Michael had been chosen tsar because of his kinship with the old dynasty, but also because, being young, timid and in poor health, he was a non-entity around whom the warring groups in Russia could rally.

1613–19, with Filaret still in Poland, Michael was dominated by *boyars* of his mother's family, who, as well as lining their pockets, successfully dealt with the problems left by the Time of Troubles. At home, ordered Gov was restored as the anarchic *boyars*, COSSACKS, pretenders, Tatars and other marauders were suppressed. In the mood of national resurgence inspired by the popular levy (*opolchenie*), the *zemskii sobor* and the *boyars' duma* were kept in almost continous session (1613–22), helping to make more palatable the inevitable bitter medicine with which the Gov had to dose the nation: suppressing crime, re-assembling the plundered royal domain, taming the *boyars*, exacting services from the *dvoryane* and taxes from the people, intensifying serfdom. Abroad, peace of necessity had to be made with the invading foreigners: with Sweden by the Tr of Stolbovo (Feb 1617) by which GUSTAV II ADOLF returned Novgorod but gained Ingria and Karelia, thus blocking Russian access to the Baltic; with Poland (whose invasion of 1617–18 had reached, but failed to take, Moscow) by the 14-year Truce of Deulino (Dec 1618), which conceded Smolensk, Starodub, Novgorod Seversk and Chernigov to Poland.

1619–45: At home, the Tr of Deulino allowed Patriarch Filaret to return, and from his arrival in June 1619 until his death in Oct 1633 this dominating character ruled Russia, using the title Great Sovereign (*velikii gosudar*), and not paying much attention to the *zemskii sobor* or *boyars' duma*. No innovator, but an ideal-izer of the stability of the past, he drew strength from the *dvoryane* who manned the army and the bureaucracy, modernizing the former with foreign officers and a restored armaments industry, and streamlining the latter by strengthening the cumbersome 50 or so central departments (*prikazy*), by tightening control over the provs and cities with new officials, the *voevody*, who used their full military and civil power with increasing oppressiveness; and by consolidating the districts (*uezda*) into larger units (*razriady*). Abroad, (i) In the W Michael regarded Poland as the main enemy, and was in touch with the anti-Cath side in the THIRTY YEARS WAR (1618–48), subsidizing Gustav II Adolf against Poland by selling (1628–33) large consignments of cheap grain on which Sweden made a profit on the Amsterdam market. More directly, Russia embarked on the Smolensk War (1632–4) with the expiry of the Tr of Deulino and the death of SIGISMUND III; but unfortunately the military hero, *boyar* M. B. Shein, sur-rendered to the enemy under its new K, WLADYSLAW IV (Feb 1634), and Russia was forced to sign the Tr of Polianovka (Polanowo) (June 1634) confirming Poland in her gains of Deulino. On the other hand, Russia made some progress, for in return for 20,000 roubles Wladyslaw gave up his claim to the Russian throne. (ii) In the S where the marauding Crimean Tatars did so much damage – taking 200,000 Russians into slavery in the 1st half of C17 – Michael built a series of fortified towns (1630–46), the so-called Belgorod Line. But defence was all he could afford, and when the Don Cossacks captured the important Turkish fortress of Azov at the mouth of the Don on 21 June 1637 after a 9-week siege, and then fought off a vast Turkish army in an epic 4-month defence (June–Sept 1641), Michael could not contemplate a war with Turkey, and, after holding a *zemskii sobor* on the subject (Jan 1642), he ordered the Cossacks to give the fortress up. (iii) In the E, a Russian expedition reached the Pacific for the 1st time (1639); and the R Amur was explored as far as its mouth (1643) and contact made with China.

According to Soviet historians, with the death of Michael and the strengthening of the frontiers, the consolidation of the all-Russian central Gov based on the *dvoryane*, the creation of the all-Russian market and the development of capitalism in industry and commerce, and the entrenchment of serfdom, we are at the start of modern history.

Monasteries, Dissolution of the (1536–40) Thomas CROMWELL's method of ending K HENRY VIII of England's financial weakness, though it was supported by the wide and varied anti-clericalism which marked C16, especially among nobility and gentry with eyes on monastic property, or Prots who disapproved of monasticism on religious grounds, or Caths who believed in the monastic ideal but could see how far the monks fell short of it with their wealth and worldliness, lack of religious vocation, even non-performance of their social functions of charity and hospitality. Beginning with the assessment of the Ch's total wealth, which was recorded in the vast survey called the *Valor Ecclesiasticus* (1535), Cromwell (using his new power as Vicar-Gen) sent commissions on a visitation of the monasteries with a view to producing as black a picture as possible to present to Parl, which then passed the 1st Act of Dissolution (1536), dissolving all the smaller monasteries (with incomes under £200 a year). While this was being implemented, the Pilgrimage of Grace broke out and was suppressed (1536–7), enabling the Gov to confiscate the property of abbots who treasonably took part. After this, abbots of the larger monasteries one by one surrendered under pressure from Cromwell's agents, so that the 2nd Act of Dissolution (1539) simply legalized these surrenders and dissolutions, as well as any that should follow. The last to surrender was Waltham Abbey (Mar 1540).

As far as the human results are concerned, the abbots received large pensions, the monks small ones, and the friars nothing; but all had the possibility of Ch of England benefices – which the nuns, with very small pensions, did not; while the lay servants and labourers were probably taken over by the new owners. On the material side, there was great loss: plundered architecture, melted-down images, squandered libraries. The total income of the dissolved houses came to more than 3 times the income from the royal estate, and had it remained part of the royal domain, kings would have been better placed to resist the ambitions of Parl in C17. As it was, apart from founding 6 inadequately financed new bishoprics, 5 Regius Professorships and Trinity College at Cambridge, Henry VIII squandered most of this capital to finance his war against France (1543–6); and whether by gift or sale the monastic properties found their way into the hands of the nobility, gentry and yeomanry (two-thirds being gone by Henry's death). Thus the Dissolution marks a crucial shift in the social structure of England which added greatly to the numbers and wealth of the gentry and yeomanry at the expense of the ecclesiastical and baronial groups hitherto dominant, and helped to give England her peculiar economic and constitutional development; though it did not (as was once thought) hasten the advance of commercial agriculture, hard-faced landlordism, or urban pauperism (developments which were more tidal in their causes). The sale of the monastic lands also created a vested interest which prevented the re-creation of the monasteries under MARY I; while at the same time placing the clergy materially at the mercy of the Crown and laity, for with the land was transferred the right of presentation to about two-fifths of the parishes of England, as well as the ownership of much of the tithes.

Monck (Monk), George (6 Dec 1608–3 Jan 1670) 1st D of Albemarle (1660), professional soldier who fought on each side in turn in the English CIVIL WAR, becoming Gov of Scotland under CROMWELL. After the latter's death he used his army to overthrow the military rule of LAMBERT without bloodshed and restore the monarchy under K CHARLES II.

2nd son of Sir Thomas Monck; he fought in BUCKINGHAM's expeditions to Cádiz (Oct–Nov 1625) and the Isle of Rhé (July–Nov 1627), and spent the 1630s with an English regiment supporting the Dutch. Returning home, he fought for K CHARLES I against the Scots in the Bishops' Wars (1639–40) and against the Irish rebels (1642–3). Bringing over an Irish regiment to aid the K in the Civil War, he was defeated by FAIRFAX, the Parl leader, at Nantwich, Cheshire (24 Jan 1644), and imprisoned in the Tower for 2 years. Changing sides, he served under Cromwell in Ireland (1647–9) and in Scotland (1650–52), and as a Gen-at-Sea in the 1st Dutch War (1652–4); after which he consolidated the English grip on Scotland as Gov (1654–60). He m (1654) Mrs Anne Ratsford, laundress at the Tower, and his mistress since his imprisonment there. A bluff, handsome soldier of moderate views, sound political sense and excellent judgement of people, he sincerely believed in the subordination of the military power to the civil. During the year of anarchy which followed Cromwell's death on 3 Sept 1658, when a struggle for power ensued between, on the one hand the new Protector, Richard Cromwell – no soldier – and on the other Lambert and the Gens, with Republicans of the Rump and the City, and Royalists and other groups manoeuvring in between, he bided his time in Scotland, purged his army of unreliable political elements, and kept his plans to himself, though it is doubtful if he had worked out anything more precise than seeing – as he put it – 'my country freed from that intolerable slavery of a sword government': ie seeing that Lambert and his clique of officers did not set up a military dictatorship. He was in touch with Charles II from at least July 1659, but it is not known at what stage he decided to work for the restoration of the monarchy. He crossed into England in Jan 1660, his progress there greatly facilitated by Fairfax, who had come out of retirement and taken York on his behalf the day before. Lambert marched N to oppose him, but his army melted away. Monck's army trudged peacefully through an England under deep snow, reaching London on 3 Feb 1660. At first, Monck obeyed the civil power – the Rump – but gradually took control of the situation himself; fortified by the persuasion of his ambitious wife and the future 1st Earl of SHAFTESBURY – who spent most of the previous night arguing with him – he allowed the MPs who had been ejected by Pride's Purge to sit in Parl once more (Feb 1660). The restored Long Parl dissolved itself (Mar 1660) and ordered a general election. Meanwhile, by word of mouth, Monck advised Charles to move from Brussels (Spanish territory) to Breda in Holland, and there issue his conciliatory Declaration (Apr 1660), offering a general amnesty, liberty of conscience, a land settlement to be made by Parl and arrears of pay for the Army.

Similarly in London, Monck prevented the PRESBYTERIANS from imposing impossible conditions upon the returning monarch. The new Parl (the Convention Parl) met on 25 Apr 1660, and proclaimed Charles K on 8 May 1660. On 25 May 1660, when the K disembarked at Dover, Monck was there on the beach to receive him. It was a miracle which only an army could have worked, and only an army under a general of moderate ambitions and either great political skill or unusual luck. Monck desired, not power, but honours, to gratify his wife, and the new K lavished them on him, while keeping him in the political wings. He became Knight of the Garter, D of Albemarle, Capt-Gen, Master of the Horse, Ld Lieut of Ireland and Gen-at-Sea. In the last capacity he fought in the 2nd Dutch War (Feb 1665–July 1667), with his usual aggressive courage, if not with very great success.

Monmouth, James Scott, D of (9 Apr 1649–15 July 1685) Illegitimate son of K CHARLES II of England, who was executed after the failure of his rebellion against K JAMES II.

Son of Charles II (so the K believed) and his mistress, Lucy Walter; ed by courtiers as a Prot; made D of Monmouth (1663) by his father who spoiled him; m (1663) the very rich heiress, Anne Scott, Countess of Buccleuch in her own right. A handsome and athletic libertine without brains or judgement, he had the common touch and – unlike most Stuarts – knew how to ingratiate himself with the London mob and with peasants and craftsmen in the provs. He was rapidly promoted in the forces (Capt-Gen, 1670), fought in the 3rd Anglo-Dutch War (1672–4), and added to his martial reputation by suppressing the Scots Presbyterian rebellion at Bothwell Brig, Lanark, on the Clyde (1 June 1679). During the Exclusion crisis of 1679–81 (*see* SHAFTESBURY) the Whigs fixed on him as the alternative to the future K James II whom, as a Cath, they wished to keep off the throne. Monmouth did everything to encourage them, returning from Dutch exile without the K's permission (1679), making a rabble-rousing 'progress' through the provs as the 'Protestant Duke' (1680–82), and participating in the Rye House Plot (1683), after which he returned to exile in the Netherlands. On the accession of James (Feb 1685), he launched his badly timed rebellion: before the new K had taken any of his unpopular steps, and while he still enjoyed the backing of his Parl. Monmouth landed at Lyme Regis, Dorset, in June 1685 with 82 followers, and collected an army of about 7,000 Dissenting peasants, craftsmen and miners, who were possibly stimulated by the economic depression of that time. They were untrained and leaderless (the Gov having taken many radical gentry into preventive custody), and the cavalry were mounted on cart-horses. At Taunton, Somerset, Monmouth proclaimed himself K of England (18 June 1685) and, finding his advance on London blocked by John Churchill (the future MARLBOROUGH), he made a desperate nocturnal surprise attack on the royal army encamped on Sedgemoor, nr Bridgwater, Somerset, on 6 July 1685. He fled from the battlefield leaving his humble followers to be butchered, but was captured 2 days later. He was executed at the Tower of London, leaving WILLIAM and Mary as the only alternatives to James II, and providing William with lessons in the art of invading England from which he profited in the REVOLUTION OF 1688.

Montmorency, Anne Pierre Adrien, D de (15 Mar 1493–12 Nov 1567) Constable of France (1538), head of one of the 3 biggest family connections in C16 France, and leading soldier and statesman under K FRANCIS I and K HENRY II, who was eclipsed by the Guise family in the early stages of the FRENCH WARS OF RELIGION.

2nd son of Guillaume de Montmorency (minister of K CHARLES VIII and K LOUIS XII), and his wife, Anne Pot; ed at Court with the future K Francis I; m (1526) Madeleine of Savoy. He achieved fame in the HABSBURG–VALOIS WARS, eg at Ravenna (11 Apr 1512), Marignano (13/14 Sept 1515), in Provence when it was invaded by Charles III, D de Bourbon (1523–4), and at Pavia (24 Feb 1525), where he was captured by the Emp CHARLES V, along with Francis I. He helped to negotiate the Tr of Madrid (Jan 1526), and was Francis I's chief minister until enemies at Court forced his retirement (Mar 1541) for the rest of the reign. He regained power immediately on the accession of K Henry II (who hero-worshipped him) in Mar 1547; but in the 9th Habsburg–Valois War (1552–9) he was outshone by the rising military star, François, D de GUISE. Montmorency was defeated and captured by the Spanish at St-Quentin, Picardy, in Aug 1557, being later released to lead the French delegation to the talks which led to the Tr of Cateau-Cambrésis (Apr 1559). His prestige now sagged as he was blamed for losing both the war and the peace negotiations, and under K FRANCIS II he was ousted from power by the Guises. After the accession of K CHARLES IX, however, the Q Mother, CATHERINE DE MEDICI, invited him back to Court to break the monopoly of the Guise faction; though a bitter personal rival of the Guises, he was too inflexible in politics and religion to stomach the *Politique* programme advocated by L'HÔPITAL, and exemplified in the Q Mother's Colloquy of Poissy (Sept–Oct 1561) and January Edict (Jan 1562). Consequently he and his friend, the Maréchal de St-André, formed the so-called Triumvirate with Guise, and forced Catherine to accept them as the anti-Hug Gov. In the 1st War of Religion (Apr 1562–Mar 1563) he was taken prisoner – for the 3rd time – by the Hugs at the battle of Dreux (19 Dec 1562). In the 2nd War (Sept 1567–Mar 1568), he was wounded at the battle of St-Denis (10 Nov 1567) and d in Paris 2 days later.

More, Sir Thomas (1478–6 July 1535) Chancellor (1529–32), leading RC exponent of HUMANISM, who was martyred by K HENRY VIII of England for opposition to the REFORMATION.

Son of a judge, Sir John More; ed at St Anthony's Sch, London, and in the household of Archbp Morton, then at Oxford, then at the Inns of Court, London. His successful career as a lawyer, MP (1504) and Under-Sheriff in the City of London (1510), as well as his European prominence as a Humanist intellectual, friend of COLET and ERASMUS, and author of *Utopia* (1516), brought him to the notice of K Henry VIII, who sent him on a commercial embassy to the Netherlands (1515), made him a member of his Council (1518), knighted him (1521), brought him in to revise the K's book against LUTHER (1521), and had him elected Speaker of the H of C (1523). Meanwhile he had m 1st (1505) Jane Colte (d 1511); m 2nd Alice Middleton, a widow. Though critical of the state of the Ch, he believed that reform should come from within, and he feared the indiscipline which Protestantism promoted. In 1528 he wrote the *Dialogue concerning*

Heresies against Tyndale and the Lutherans; and in 1529 the *Supplication of Souls* against Simon Fish, the critic of the clergy. On the fall of Card WOLSEY, he was appointed Chancellor, the 1st layman to hold the office. In this capacity he notably developed the law of equity, but resigned in May 1532, the day after Convocation passed the Submission of the Clergy, agreeing not to legislate without the K's consent. More's move was made ostensibly on health grounds, but it probably resulted from his opposition to the Reformation. Like FISHER, he refused to take the oath required by the Succession Act of 1534. This repudiated the Pp, declared the marriage with CATHERINE OF ARAGON invalid, and acknowledged that the children of K Henry and Q Anne Boleyn were the legitimate heirs to the throne. More was committed to the Tower of London, 17 Apr 1534. Then, under the new Treasons Act of 1534, More's behaviour could be construed as treason. He was found guilty and beheaded at Tower Hill.

Newcastle, Thomas Pelham-Holles, 1st D of (21 July 1693–17 Nov 1768) Eld brother of Henry PELHAM, and wealthy political manager of the Old Corps of WHIGS under K GEORGE II in the ministries of WALPOLE and Pelham (1722–54). As Sec of State (1724–54) he built up Continental alliances against France, helping to provoke the DIPLOMATIC REVOLUTION. Then as 1st Ld of the Treasury (1754–6, 1757–62) he managed Parl and raised the revenue for the 2 Govs of PITT the Elder which won the SEVEN YEARS WAR (1756–63), until the accession of K GEORGE III ended his long political leadership, though he served as Ld Privy Seal in the ROCKINGHAM admin (1765–6).

Eld son of Thomas, 1st Bn Pelham, and his wife, Lady Grace Holles, sister of John Holles, D of Newcastle; ed Westminster Sch and Clare Hall, Cambridge (1709); m (1717) Lady Henrietta Godolphin (d 1776, no issue); added Holles to his name (1711) on succeeding to most of his uncle's estate; made Earl of Clare (1714), D of Newcastle-upon-Tyne (1715) and D of Newcastle-under-Lyme (1756).

Before 1754 he achieved prominence by maximizing the political value of his wealth and patronage, which he exploited with patient industry and meticulous attention to detail (though the extent of his so-called 'corruption' has been exaggerated, for he possessed only 9–12 pocket boroughs, even if he had influence in many more). Thanks to his following in the H of C, he became Ld Chamberlain (1717) in the STANHOPE–Sunderland admin; then Sec of State (S) under Walpole and Pelham (Apr 1724–Feb 1748), except for the joint resignation interval of 10–12 Feb 1746; then Sec of State (N) from Feb 1748–Mar 1754. In these posts he controlled Gov patronage, ecclesiastical and lay, and took a leading part in formulating British foreign policy. In the former role, he laboured fussily but successfully, during elections and in between them, to co-ordinate the influence exercised by the Crown and the political leaders so as to provide stable Parl majorities. In the latter, he followed a line midway between the isolationism of Walpole and Pelham and the deep Continental involvement of George II and CARTERET. He sought powerful European allies to counter the threat posed by France, though without disgorging huge subsidies simply to defend Hanover. He was deeply distressed by Walpole's refusal to support Britain's ally, Austria, in the WAR OF THE POLISH SUCCESSION (1733–5/8). He was prominent in running the WAR OF THE AUSTRIAN SUCCESSION (1740–48) and in negotiating the consequent Tr of Aix-la-Chapelle (Oct 1748), though he objected to Pelham's policy of forcing Austria to sacrifice Silesia to Prussia in order to facilitate peace-making. In the 1750s he continued to subsidize European allies, and thus came in for some rough handling by Pitt the Elder. A neurotic hypochondriac, he lacked the gifts for shaping high policy and accepting top responsibility. He was a good 2 i/c, a disinterested wheel-horse who laboured tirelessly for the public good. Untypical of the C18, he was incorruptible and ready to spend his own money on the K's business. He possessed above-average common sense and political judgement, though he was nervously incoherent in explaining himself, a twitterer known as 'hubble-bubble'.

After 1754, on the death of his brother, the PM, on 6 Mar 1754, Newcastle showed that he had not learned the lessons of C18 politics. He became 1st Ld of the Treasury (1754), planning to manage the H of C from the H of L, while keeping the leading speakers, Pitt and Henry FOX, in minor posts. In foreign affairs he was responsible for the Anglo-Russian Convention of St Petersburg of Sept 1755, though he misjudged Russia's motives By it Britain paid Russia to keep an army on the Prussian border ready to defend Hanover, but Russia looked on it as a method of attacking Prussia. This led to apprehensions in Prussia which prompted FREDERICK II to sign the Tr of Westminster with Britain (Jan 1756), a move which precipitated the Diplomatic Revolution. France and Russia were so angry with Prussia that they joined up with Austria (hitherto Britain's steadfast ally), forming a line-up which directly produced the Seven Years War. Britain's lack of preparedness and poor performance in the early stages of this war, along with the hostile speeches of Pitt and Fox from within his Gov, forced Newcastle 1st to offer Pitt a key post (but Pitt's conditions were too extreme for the K to stomach), then to make Fox Sec of State (S) (Nov 1755), then resign (Nov 1756). This proved that Parl management by itself was insufficient without backbench backing. The next ministry, the Devonshire–Pitt (1756–7), proved the converse, that backbench idols such as Pitt needed the support of the K and of political managers such as Newcastle: a truism recognized in the next admin, the Newcastle–Pitt (1757–61), which won the Seven Years War. With Newcastle as 1st Ld of the Treasury (July 1757), managing Parl and raising the finances, and Pitt as Sec of State (S) (June 1757) organizing the strategy and electrifying the nation, Britain reached a new peak of world power and founded the 1st British Emp. Unfortunately for Newcastle, when George II d (25 Oct 1760), he was succeeded by George III and his mentor BUTE, who were determined to eliminate George II's ministers and abandon their war policies. Pitt resigned in Oct 1761 because the K would not declare war on Spain. Newcastle resigned in May 1762 over Bute's abandonment of Britain's ally, Prussia. It was the end of an era, for not all the Old Corps resigned with them. Newcastle's magic had gone, for he was no longer the fount of patronage. Moreover, the new Gov under Bute (1762–3) furthered the fragmentation of the Old Whigs with the 'Massacre of the Pelhamite Innocents' – the dismissal from office, great and small, of all Newcastle's followers who would not back the peace Tr of Paris. During the next admin – GRENVILLE's (1763–5) – Newcastle and his remaining friends were in uneasy alliance with Pitt in opposition to the Gov's campaign against WILKES. In the next admin – that of Rockingham (1765–6), the leader of the new generation of the Old Corps – Newcastle was Ld Privy Seal (Aug 1765). It was a weak Gov that lacked the confidence of the K, a Gov of younger men who paid little attention to Newcastle; and it was dismissed to make way for Pitt on 9 July 1766.

Nikon (Nikita Minin) (24 May 1605–17 Aug 1681) Patriarch of Russia (1652–66), who for a time ruled Ch and State, and caused the great schism (*raskol*) by reforming the Ch; but was dismissed for trying to make the Ch superior to the State.

Son of a peasant family of Finnish origin; ed by monks; became a priest; m, but the death of his 3 children turned him into a monk and a hermit (1630s and 1640s). Pious, industrious and formidable, he belonged to the Ch reform movement, the Zealots of Piety, and rose in the Ch to become head of a monastery nr Novgorod (1643); then, by inspiring Tsar ALEXIS, Archimandrite (Abbot) of the Romanov family monastery of Novospasski, nr Moscow (1646); Metropolitan of Novgorod (1648); and Patriarch of Russia, being consecrated on 25 July 1652. While the Tsar was away at the 13 Years War (1654–67), Nikon was named Great Sovereign (*velikii gosudar*) and given as much power as if he were tsar. Fierce, impatient and overbearing, he enforced reforms in the Ch in a series of annual councils (1652–60) which brought about the schism. Unlike traditionalists who believed that Russia had been converted to Christianity by St Andrew independently of Greece, he saw the Russian Ch as a branch of Greek Orthodoxy, and found it full of incorrect usages and other deviations from the practice of the parent body, which he proceeded to put right. Sacred books, services and chants were all corrected with the help of Greek scholars from Kiev and elsewhere. Innovations not only shocked the mass of old-fashioned believers and clergy: they also alienated his old brethren in the Zealots of Piety. In fact, they split the Ch, and the Old Believers remained steadfast nonconformists down to the C20, their religious resistance mixed up with various forms of political and social protest, including hostility to westernization. In Nikon's day, the leader was Archpriest Avvakum, who after exile to Siberia then to the far N (where he wrote his famous *Life*, the 1st Russian autobiography), was burnt at the stake in Apr 1682. An important centre of resistance to the reforms was the Solovetskii Monastery on the White Sea, which held out against royal troops from 1667 to 1676. When it was finally taken, only 60 of the original 500 inhabitants were left. Between 1675 and 1695 about 20,000 Old Believers committed suicide by setting fire to their wooden churches. Meanwhile, Nikon himself had made many enemies with his arrogant methods of Gov, and his pretensions that the Ch should be above the State, exempt from secular courts, its property immune from taxation. Even the gentle Tsar Alexis screwed up enough courage to oppose him, and when Nikon sought to twist the royal arm by resigning (July 1658), Alexis called his bluff and refused to have him back. A Ch Council (1666–7) attended by the Patriarchs of Antioch and Alexandria stripped him of his priestly functions and exiled him to Beloozero in the far N (Dec 1666). The same Council confirmed Nikon's Ch reforms, but handed over to the State the job of punishing deviations. Nikon d on his way back to Moscow where he had been recalled by Theodore III. He had left the Ch in no position to resist subordination to the State over the next century.

Norfolk, Thomas Howard, 2nd D of (1443–21 May 1524) 1st Earl of Surrey (1483), 2nd D of Norfolk (1514), leading Yorkist who managed to restart his career under the Tudors and become a chief soldier and minister under Ks HENRY VII and HENRY VIII.

Son of John Howard, 1st D of Norfolk, and Catherine, daughter of Lord de Moleyns; ed at Ipswich Grammar School and at the court of K Edward IV; m (1472) wealthy Elizabeth Tilney; fought in the WARS OF THE ROSES under Edward IV and Richard III; at the battle of Bosworth his father was killed and he was taken prisoner by K Henry VII. He was one of those magnates whose attainder Henry VII achieved by dating his reign from the day before Bosworth. Norfolk was imprisoned until 1489, and his forfeited estates were returned to him only piecemeal as he demonstrated his loyalty to the new dynasty. He remained Earl of Surrey until 1514. In 1489 he became Lieutenant to Pr Arthur as Warden of the Marches at York (the embryonic Council of the North), a post in which his exceptional military gifts were put to good use in suppressing the rebellious northerners and keeping out the Scots. His loyalty once established, Norfolk moved into the inner circle of Henry VII's councillors, becoming Ld Treasurer (1501), and being used by the K on major diplomatic and military assignments, eg escorting Prss Margaret to Scotland for her marriage to K JAMES IV (Aug 1503). Under Henry VIII at first he remained chief minister (he was made Earl Marshal for life in July 1510), and was in command of the army which defeated the Scots at Flodden on 9 Sept 1513. Now over 70, he was created D of Norfolk, but found himself ousted from real power by WOLSEY, whom he regarded as an upstart. He found himself participating in the anti-aristocratic mood of this period when, as Ld High Steward, he had to pronounce the death sentence on his relative by marriage, Edward Stafford, 3rd D of Buckingham (May 1521), a duty which moved him to tears.

Norfolk, Thomas Howard, 3rd D of (1473–25 Aug 1554) Leading soldier and politician under K HENRY VIII of England who headed the conservative, aristocratic group at Court.

Son of the 2nd D of NORFOLK; m (1495) Anne, daughter of K Edward IV of England; became Earl of Surrey (1514), and D of Norfolk (1524); was appointed Ld Admiral (1513), Ld Deputy of Ireland (1520–21), Ld Treasurer (1522), Earl Marshal in tail male (1533). He fought in his father's army which was victorious over the Scots at Flodden (9 Sept 1513), and became one of Henry VIII's chief generals. He ravaged Normandy and Picardy in 1522, harassed Scotland (Apr–Sept 1523), suppressed the Pilgrimage of Grace (Oct–Dec 1536) and dealt out the subsequent harsh punishments, became Lieut when the Council of the North was created (1537), invaded Scotland and burnt Kelso (Oct 1542), landed at Calais and unsuccessfully besieged Montreuil (July 1546). As a politician, he led the aristocrats against the low-born career-men such as WOLSEY and CROMWELL, both of whom he helped to destroy, aided in each case by one of his nieces, 1st Anne Boleyn, then Catherine Howard. He backed the political aspects of Henry VIII's REFORMATION (ie the break with Rome, the Royal Supremacy over the Ch). With GARDINER in the 1530s and 1540s he led the conservative wing of Henry's Council and opposed Cromwell and CRANMER in their moves towards Protestantism. In this last capacity he toppled Cromwell and introduced the conservative Act of Six Articles in Parliament (1546); but he never achieved political dominance or a conservative reaction because Henry never lost trust in

Cranmer, while Norfolk became discredited by the fall of Catherine Howard in 1542. Moreover, he was simply a loyal soldier, and even in this capacity he was ousted in the 1540s by the rising generation headed by Edward SEYMOUR and John DUDLEY. Finally, he was attainted for treason, ie concealing the treason of his son, the Earl of SURREY, and condemned to be executed on 28 Jan 1547. He was reprieved, however, because K Henry himself d on that day; and he lived to spend 7 years in the Tower of London under K EDWARD VI, who deprived him of his Earl Marshalship. Under MARY I he was released and restored to his office, as well as to a certain political influence.

Norfolk, Thomas Howard, 4th D of (10 Mar 1536–2 June 1572) Leading peer of England under Q ELIZABETH I, who was executed for his involvement in the REVOLT OF THE NORTHERN EARLS and the Ridolfi Plot.

Eld son of the Earl of SURREY, the poet, who was executed under K HENRY VIII; ed by John Foxe, the martyrologist; m 1st (1556) Mary FitzAlan, daughter of the Earl of Arundel (d 1557); m 2nd (1558) Margaret, widow of Ld Henry Dudley (d 1563); m 3rd (1567) Elizabeth, widow of Thomas Ld Dacre, a keen Cath (d 1567). Restored in blood, he succeeded to the hereditary post of Earl Marshal on the death of his grandfather, the 3rd D of NORFOLK (1554). Under Q Elizabeth I he commanded the forces which invaded Scotland to expel the French in Mar 1560. As the cousin of the Q, the 1st peer of the realm and only D, and the wealthiest landowner, he joined the Privy Council in Oct 1562, but grew jealous of the power at Court of the Q's favourite, LEICESTER, and her Principal Sec, the future Ld BURGHLEY. In the late 1560s he began to dabble in treasonable schemes to marry MARY, Q OF SCOTS, who was at this time in custody in England – schemes which issued in the Revolt of the Northern Earls (Nov–Dec 1569). In Sept 1569, Norfolk left Court for Kenninghall, Norfolk, the centre of his territorial strength. He was dignified and popular, but lacked the political instincts and nerves of steel required by a revolutionary leader. He also suffered from migraines; when the Q summoned him to Court he obeyed and was imprisoned in the Tower (Oct 1569), a place he dreaded. After the Northern Earls had been defeated he was released in Aug 1570, but nevertheless became deeply enmeshed in the schemes of Roberto Ridolfi, a Florentine banker operating in London, through whose hands passed a good deal of financial aid and revolutionary advice from the Pp, France and Spain to Mary, Q of Scots, and English and Scottish Caths. Seemingly lacking any real basis apart from extreme plausibility, Ridolfi inveigled the gullible Norfolk into planning a rebellion supported by Spanish troops, supposedly to be dispatched by ALBA from the Netherlands – though both he and K PHILIP II were against such a policy at that time. Mary, Q of Scots, de Spes, the Spanish ambassador, and others were involved, and it was not long before Burghley was able to piece the plot together from correspondence captured while Ridolfi was travelling between Brussels, Rome and Madrid, unsuccessfully trying to get the authorities actively interested. Norfolk was arrested again (Sept 1571), tried by a court of 26 peers (Jan 1572), and executed at Tower Hill 5 months later, after strong Parl demands for his death.

North, Frederick, 7th Bn (13 Apr 1732–5 Aug 1792) KG (1772), 2nd Earl of

Guilford (1790), PM of Great Britain (1770–82) in the admin which fought and lost the WAR OF AMERICAN INDEPENDENCE (1776–83).

Son of Francis North, Whig MP (and descendant of C17 Tories) and his wife, Lady Lucy Montagu, daughter of George, Earl of Halifax; ed at Eton, Trinity, Oxford (1749–51), and on the Grand Tour (1751–4); m (1756) Anne, daughter of George Speke of Somerset. North became MP for the family pocket borough of Banbury, Oxfords (1754–90), and rose quickly in politics, thanks to family connections (his father was Gentleman of the Bedchamber to Frederick Louis, Pr of Wales, 1730–51; North was related to NEWCASTLE and other leading Whigs), also to his outstanding gifts as a Parl debater. Fat and clumsy, with thick lips, bulging, weak eyes, and a loud but indistinct voice, he attracted support by his unfailing amiability, his imperturbable resilience under attack, his steady good humour in the heat of debate, his flashes of wit, his sense of humour, and his easy-going informality. The backbenchers particularly liked his ability to master the mysteries of finance and explain it to them in simple terms, usually improvising.

His early career: He became a Ld of the Treasury (June 1759) in the Newcastle–PITT admin (1757–61) and stayed on under the BUTE admin (1761–3) and the GRENVILLE admin (1763–5), resigning when the Grenvilles were dismissed in July 1765. He made his Parl reputation leading for the Grenville admin in the great debates over WILKES and the *North Briton*. He opposed the ROCKINGHAM admin (1765–6); but under the Pitt admin (1766–8) he became Joint Paymaster-Gen (1766), member of the Privy Council (Dec 1766), then Chancellor of the Exchequer (Dec 1767) and leader of the H of C (Jan 1768). He continued in this post under the GRAFTON admin (1768–70), leading for the Gov in the debates over Wilkes and the Middlesex elections, and in the Cab meeting of May 1769 supporting the intransigent majority against the Pittite minority (5 to 4) in favour of repealing the Townshend duties in America, but retaining the tax on tea in order to assert the principle.

As Prime Minister (1770–82), North became 1st Ld of the Treasury (Feb 1770) on the resignation of Grafton, whose majority had been cut to shreds. (a) As Parl leader, within a month North had established his mastery over the H of C, achieving comfortable majorities; within a year he was in command in the Cab, having replaced recalcitrant Bedfordites with his own nominees, including some Grenvilles. Backed by the 2 chief sources of power – K and Parl – he brought a decade of stability, which the reign of George III had notably lacked thus far. As PM he was more of a chairman over departmental heads going their own way than an all-powerful dictator controlling all aspects of policy. He lacked the force of character and decisiveness to be a WALPOLE, but he acted as a steadying influence over the whole political scene. He was greatly helped by the confidence and friendliness of the K, a circumstance which did not turn him into a Favourite or puppet, as some have suggested for, though the K was the last person to keep his opinions to himself, he acted on policies laid down by the Cab, once he had appointed it. North was also helped by the crumbling of the opposition, the inability of the Pittites and the Rockinghams to co-operate, the death of the City Radical, Beckford, and the decline in popular militancy, as well as the general conservative reaction against the recent pro-Wilkes violence. He was also helped by the death of George Grenville (13 Nov 1770) and the union of his group with the Gov. Nevertheless, North was defeated from time to time: eg over the Grenville Committees Act of 1770 (*see* GRENVILLE) and over the printing of Parl debates in 1771 (*see* WILKES). (b) The Falkland Islands crisis (1770–71) saw North typically firm but conciliatory and concerned with saving money. Spain had long claimed these islands off S America, and she sent a force to occupy them in June 1770. Unlike his hard-line Bedfordite colleagues, North was anxious to avoid war, and he had his way. France was not prepared to back Spain to the point of fighting, and so Spain accepted a secret verbal promise that Britain would later surrender the islands (Jan 1771). The Spanish troops withdrew, North's face was saved, and his leadership of the Cab confirmed. (c) India – where vast areas, teeming millions and untold wealth were mismanaged by what was still only a commercial venture, the E India Co – was becoming more and more a political problem as its crying abuses demanded Gov intervention: eg the bankruptcy of the Co, despite the fortunes made by some of its members, and the corruption in the admin of its territories. North's 3 statutes mark the start of regular Gov intervention in the Co's affairs. The Regulating Act (1773) aimed at giving the Co more stability in London and firmer control in India by (i) raising the voting qualifications for the Court of Directors from £500 of stock to £1,000 held for one year, and holding elections every 4 years instead of annually; (ii) placing Bengal under a Gov-Gen (Warren Hastings) and a Council of 4; (iii) setting up a Supreme Court of Justice; and (iv) placing Bombay and Madras under the supervision of Bengal. By the Loan Act (1773), the Gov lent the E India Co £1,400,000; and by the Tea Act (1773) the Co was allowed customs concessions in the export of its surplus tea to America (a move which led directly to the Boston Tea Party). (d) Ireland became as restive as America, and with the same grievances. These evolved from a desire to free the Irish economy from the straitjacket of the navigation system (which kept Ireland poor to make England rich) to a demand for self-Gov. The American troubles exacerbated Irish troubles by causing a trade depression, by giving the Irish an example to copy, and by denuding Ireland of British troops. For his part, North wanted to make economic concessions in 1778, but was prevented by English business lobbies in Parl and Cab. In consequence, the Irish began to boycott English goods and to train a militia, the Volunteers; while the Rockinghams led the opposition in encouraging Irish seditiousness. These developments persuaded the English Parl to enact North's economic concessions: an Act allowing the Irish to export their wool and glass (1779), and an Act opening up trade to the Irish in America and the W Indies (1780). These concessions were too late, however, for the Irish, led by Henry Flood and Henry Grattan, had by this time moved on to the constitutional plane and were demanding legislative independence. As North's admin drew to its close, a convention of Volunteers met in a militant mood at Dungannon, County Tyrone, in Feb 1782, and Ireland was ready for rebellion. (e) Finance preoccupied North throughout his ministry, and his measures for improving the admin of the revenue, for keeping down taxes, and for reducing the National Debt would have given him the reputation of a great finance minister had not all his economies been ruined by the War of American Independence. Even so, in spite of a Civil Service which was inadequate for the task, he managed to find the revenue and raise supplies for the armed forces with more success than he used to be credited with. Moreover, it was he who introduced (1780) the

Commission on the Public Accounts whose work after North's day did so much to improve Civil Service efficiency and reduce corrupt influence. (f) America was North's downfall, making him notorious then and since as the PM who lost an Emp. Recently, however, the extent of his responsibility for provoking and then losing the war has been seen to be much less than was once thought. American independence now appears to be an inevitable development which no minister could have prevented. Moreover, the measures which North took – the Tea Act, the Coercion Acts, the Quebec Act etc – had the overwhelming support of the British political world; and even those who opposed them had nothing more practical to put in their place. Neither should North be held responsible for the military disasters. He had 3 tasks, each big enough in itself for one minister. He headed the Cab, which took the main policy decisions; he headed the Treasury, which raised the revenues; and he was the leader of the H of C, responsible for maintaining Gov majorities. Other ministers were responsible for running the war – foreign affairs, army and navy – and, according to the conventions of C18 Gov, North was not to blame for their failures. That there was a need for a co-ordinating PM of the modern type, responsible for all aspects of Gov, North more than once affirmed, but he denied that he himself had the abilities for the job. After the surrender at Saratoga (17 Oct 1777) he grew more depressed, indecisive and self-deprecatory, and he many times pleaded to resign – though without taking serious steps to do so. The K supplied the backbone that North lacked, even calling a Cab meeting (21 June 1779) – a royal initiative unprecedented since Q ANNE's reign. 'If others will not be active, I must drive,' said George as the Gov's difficulties accumulated. To the war with America was added war with France (1778), Spain (1779) and Holland (1780), as well as friction with the Armed Neutrality (1780 onwards), rebelliousness in Ireland (1779–82), the Radicals and the Association movement in England (1779–80), the Gordon Riots in London (1780) and in Parl a defeat on 6 Apr 1780 when the H of C passed John Dunning's opposition motion that 'the influence of the Crown has increased, is increasing, and ought to be diminished'. Meanwhile, nevertheless, the backbenchers supported North until the surrender at York-town (19 Oct 1781). After that, North – but not the K – accepted that independence must be conceded; when his majority dropped to single figures in Feb and Mar 1782, the K at last granted his request to resign (Mar 1782).

His later career: During the 2nd Rockingham admin (1782) and the Shelburne admin (1782–3), North and his 100 or so followers held the balance of power in Parl between Shelburne and the K's Friends on the one hand, and C. J. Fox and the Rockinghams on the other. By no means a royal Favourite, he was essentially the champion of Parl, defending it from attack, from no matter what quarter – the Crown, the Radicals or the Americans. 'It was here,' he told the H of C in May 1783, 'I was first known. You raised me up, you pulled me down.' He became increasingly alienated from the ungrateful K, who unfairly at first refused to reimburse him for the money he had spent on the Gen Election of 1780. Moreover, he could not co-operate with the Shelburne party because of Pitt the Younger's implacable opposition to him. Thus in the end he shocked the K and the country – and posterity – by making an agreement with his old enemy, C. J. Fox (Feb 1783) – an alliance which soon forced Shelburne to resign (Feb 1783) and obliged the K to appoint them, after a fruitless 5-week search for an alternative. The Portland admin – or Fox–North coalition (1783) – saw the D of Portland (Rockingham's political heir) as 1st Ld of the Treasury (Apr 1783). He made a constitutional innovation by insisting on appointing his junior ministers after the Gov had been formed instead of getting the K's prior agreement on all posts. North became Sec of State for home and colonial affairs. The K determined to get rid of them as soon as he could find an alternative. In Pitt the Younger George III found his man: a PM in the tradition of Walpole, Pelham and North himself. When Fox's India Bill was defeated in the H of L (partly on instructions from the K) the K dismissed the ministry on 18 Dec 1783 and appointed Pitt the next day. The 1st Pitt admin (1783–1801) was soon confirmed in office by its big victory in the Gen Election of Mar 1784 – a result which showed how unpopular the Fox–North coalition had been. North withdrew more and more from active politics through ill-health and growing blindness; and when he did appear in Parl he generally spoke out against innovations. He opposed the abolition of the slave trade (1783), Pitt's India Bill (1784), as well as his proposals for Parl Reform (1785) and trading concessions to Ireland (1785). He also opposed any further concessions to the Dissenters (1787 and 1789).

Nottingham, Daniel Finch, 2nd Earl of (2 July 1647–1 Jan 1730) Moderate High-Ch Tory leader under CHARLES II, JAMES II, WILLIAM III, ANNE and GEORGE I.

Son of Heneage Finch – moderate Royalist Anglican gentleman and lawyer-politician who became Attorney Gen (1670), Ld Keeper (1673), Ld Chancellor (1675) – and his wife, Elizabeth, daughter of Daniel Harvey, a prosperous London merchant; ed at Westminster Sch, the Inner Temple (1658), Christ Church, Oxford (1662) and on the Grand Tour (1665–8); m 1st (1674) Lady Essex Rich, co-heiress of the 3rd Earl of Warwick (d 1684); m 2nd (1685) 18-year-old Anne, daughter of Vt Hatton, by whom he had 22 children (d 1743).

Under Charles II in a by-election (Jan 1673) he was chosen MP for Great Bedwyn, Wilts, in the Cavalier Parl which was not dissolved until Jan 1679. He failed to win the seat in the 1st Exclusion Parl (Mar–July 1679). In the 2nd and 3rd Exclusion Parls (Oct 1679–Jan 1681 and Mar 1681) he was MP for Lichfield, Staffs. Sober, high-principled, holier-than-thou, tall and dark-complexioned, he was nicknamed Dismal, and he adhered to 'Things and Propositions, not men and Parties'. His stubborn devotion to points of principle made him impossible to ignore by contemporary politicians, while his lack of manipulative skill as a Parl leader meant that he never attracted sufficient followers to make him indispensable for long, especially as he was a prickly colleague. In the Exclusion crisis (see SHAFTESBURY), he opposed Exclusion and supported HALIFAX's policy of recognizing James as K while putting 'limitations' on his power. He was appointed a Commissioner for the Admiralty (1679), 1st Commissioner for the Admiralty (1680), and member of the Privy Council (Feb 1680).

Under James II he disapproved of the pro-Cath measures, but refused to sign the Invitation to William of Orange which initiated the REVOLUTION OF 1688 (though he was aware of its existence and concealed his knowledge). During the Revolution, when William was advancing on London from Devon, Nottingham was one of the 3 commissioners (along with Halifax and GODOLPHIN) whom James sent to negotiate with William at Hungerford, Berks, in Dec 1688. When they returned to London, James had fled. During the debates on the revolutionary settlement, Nottingham opposed the view that James had 'abdicated' and that therefore the throne was 'vacant'; and he favoured recognizing James as K with the royal powers exercised by a Regency. In the end, however, he accepted the inevitable, and agreed to support William as *de facto* K.

Under William III Nottingham was a member of the mixed ministry which opened the reign, as Sec of State (Mar 1689). He took the lead in the scheme for the 'comprehension' of PRESBYTERIANS in a broadened Anglican Ch and for the banning from public office of the extremists left out. When this was found to be politically impossible, he shepherded the Toleration Act (1689) through Parl, though it was not exactly to his liking (*see* REVOLUTION OF 1688). When the balance of power in Parl forced the K to give office to the Whig Junto, Nottingham was dismissed in Nov 1693; when, on the discovery of the 1696 plot to assassinate the K, Nottingham opposed the enforcement of an oath that William was 'rightful and lawful' K, the angry monarch struck him from the Privy Council (Mar 1696).

Under Anne, whom he had no qualms about recognizing, he became Sec of State (May 1702) under the triumvirate of MARLBOROUGH, Godolphin and HARLEY. In the War of the Spanish Succession (*see* LOUIS XIV) he opposed the 'blue-water' policy of some of the Tories, and also the concentration of the war effort in the Netherlands, which the Whigs favoured. He called for action in the Med, in Italy, in Spain and in the W Indies. On the domestic front he jeopardized the Gov's Parl position (they were only concerned to get the war measures voted) by leading the High-Ch Tories in 3 attempts to pass his Occasional Conformity Bill (1702, 1703, 1704), which would have prevented dissenters from taking Anglican communion once a year simply in order to qualify for public office. In the reconstruction of the ministry in 1704, when moderate Whigs and Tories were taken in, Nottingham lost his post (Apr 1704). He was a leading Hanover Tory and during 1705 ruined his reputation with Q Anne by proposing that the heiress to the throne – Sophia, Electress of Hanover – should reside in England, in order to head off any attempt at a Jacobite succession; it was partly the Q's opposition that kept him out of Harley's Tory Gov of 1710–14. In opposition, he supported the Whigs in their dislike of the Tory peace terms (1711), insisting that no peace should be signed which left Spain and the Indies in Bourbon hands. He also suspected that some of the ministers were Jacobites. In their turn, the Whigs voted for his Occasional Conformity Bill, which at last became law (Dec 1711).

Under George I, whose accession he had steadily supported, he was made Ld President of the Council (Sept 1714) in a mainly Whig Gov. He supported the impeachment proceedings against Harley, BOLINGBROKE and other Tories, but differed from the K and the Whigs over the question of punishing the Scots peers who had taken part in the Jacobite rebellion of 1715 – the 'FIFTEEN'. Nottingham voted against executing them, and was dismissed in Feb 1716. With the Hanoverian succession secure, he had outlived his usefulness to the Whigs.

Oldenbarnevelt, Johan van (14 Sept 1547–13 May 1619) *Lands-advocaat* (chief legal adviser) of the Prov of Holland, and pensionary (chairman) of the Estates of Holland, who used these offices to become one of the 2 leading statesmen of the United Provs after the assassination of WILLIAM I of Orange, and who led the Netherlands through the last years of the REVOLT against Spain up to the Truce of Apr 1609 and beyond. The other was his eventual rival, MAURICE of Orange, who succeeded in having Oldenbarnevelt executed after a political trial.

Ed in law at Louvain, Brabant and Bourges, France, and Heidelberg, Germany; followed by a grand tour of France and Italy; practised law at the Hague. Became a Calvinist and keen supporter of William of Orange, taking part in the sieges of Haarlem (1572–3) and Leiden (1574) in the Prov of Holland, but making his mark mainly in the Gov and diplomatic field, helping to organize the Union of Utrecht – future United Provs – in Jan 1579, and to drum up support for William and his son, Maurice. The United Provs was a loose collection of independent provs with an extremely decentralized form of Gov, and the only 2 men capable of imposing a semblance of unity on the diverse political, economic and religious interests were Oldenbarnevelt, from his position (1586 onwards) as leader of the Estates of Holland (the prov which supplied the bulk of the funds for the Revolt); and Maurice, whose power derived from the prestige of his father and from his office as Stadholder of several provs and thus head of their combined forces. Working together during the great Ten Years (1588–98) of the Dutch counter-attack, they drove the Spanish out of the N provs, making their new State impregnable behind its barrier of rivers, and signing an anti-Spanish tr of alliance with France and England (1596). Oldenbarnevelt and the Estates of Holland wished to carry the war into the S provs (Belgium) and liberate them all from Spain, to form a completely united Netherlands as William had wanted. Maurice, however, was against this policy, and only reluctantly obeyed orders to march across Flanders to defeat the Spanish at Nieuwpoort on 2 July 1600. But this victory was not followed up, partly because the S had no wish to rise against Spain. After a 3-year siege the Spanish retook Ostend on 20 Sept 1604, the N base in the S. From this point on, Oldenbarnevelt began to negotiate a truce with Spain which was eventually signed in Apr 1609. Here again, there was opposition from Maurice, as well as from the army and navy, the main body of merchants at Amsterdam (who profited richly from preying upon Spanish colonies in the W Indies), and the strict Calvinists (who opposed any accommodation with anti-Christ). Oldenbarnevelt's supporters were differently based, socially, politically and ideologically. He led the so-called Regents of Holland, the little group of urban aristocrats who had risen above commerce into finance and Gov. Their patronage system gave them political control in the decentralized system of Gov, which they wished to perpetuate and keep republican. They thus opposed any move towards unity or monarchy, which Maurice naturally favoured. Moreover, in religion they supported the more relaxed form of Calvinism advocated by Arminius, and favoured the subordination of the Ch to the State. And it was over the religious issue that the 2 parties became polarized until civil war threatened. The Arminians (known as Remonstrants, from their Remonstrance presented to the Estates of Holland and Zeeland in 1610) were opposed by the strict, predestinarian, semi-theocratic Counter-Remonstrants (or Gomarists). The social and political groups who supported the latter were broadly the same as those who supported Maurice; in July 1617 he became a Counter-Remonstrant for political reasons. Similarly, Oldenbarnevelt and his Regent supporters backed the Remonstrants; and in self-defence they persuaded the Estates of Holland to pass the so-called Sharp Resolution (Aug 1617). This authorized the towns to protect

Arminianism by recruiting locally paid troops – *waardgelders* – independent of Maurice's army, and ordered the soldiers in his army to swear obedience to the Estates. Here were 2 opposed visions of what kind of State the United Provs should become, which were to split them at least until the French Revolution: one patrician, republican and Arminian; the other democratic, monarchical and Gomarist. Maurice moved swiftly on the religious and political fronts to stop this threatened break-up of the United Provs. The packed Synod of Dort (Nov 1618–May 1619) settled the religious quarrel in favour of the Counter-Remonstrants. At the same time, Maurice outmanoeuvred Oldenbarnevelt politically by dismissing Remonstrant Regents and their *waardgelders* in the provs outside Holland; thus strengthened, he used the army to do the same in Holland. Given dictatorial powers by the States-Gen in Aug 1618, Maurice had Oldenbarnevelt arrested, condemned for treason by a special court, and executed at the Hague.

Olivares, Gaspar de Guzmán, Count-Duke of (6 Jan 1587–22 July 1645) Dynamic, swarthy and thick-set Favourite and chief minister of K PHILIP IV of Spain during the 1st 22 years of his reign (1621–43), who, when the DECLINE OF SPAIN was in full spate, committed her to foreign ventures far beyond her powers (notably the attempt to reconquer Holland and play a leading part in the THIRTY YEARS WAR, 1618–48); and at the same time, in trying to extend the centralizing power of Madrid over the non-Castilian provs, provoked the REVOLT OF CATALONIA and the REVOLT OF PORTUGAL.

Younger son of Enrique de Guzmán, 2nd Count of Olivares (Spanish ambassador to Rome, later Viceroy of Naples and Sicily) and his wife, Maria Pimentel de Fonseca; ed at Salamanca (1601–4) for the Ch, but gave that up when his eld brother's death made him heir to his father; m Inés de Zúñiga y Velasco, his cousin. Following a career at Court, he was appointed to the household of the future K Philip IV, over whom he established such an influence that on succeeding to the throne the young K made him chief minister, and as far as is known left the Gov to him, though without becoming a complete cipher. Olivares was created D of Sanlúcar la Mayor (Jan 1625), and was thenceforth known as the Count-Duke. Though belonging to an aspiring Andalusian landed family, Olivares was incorruptible, and more interested in power than in wealth. He wore himself out in body and mind in daily toil for the Spanish monarchy, being sometimes euphoric, sometimes dejected, but always mentally agile, and impatient with opponents, and with the facts. He steadily pushed aside all the other Grandees, and ended up surrounded by feeble flatterers. His main purpose was a foreign policy of aggression in defence of Spanish political, economic and religious interests in Europe and the world; supported by a home policy alternating between reform and dubious practices in vain attempts to raise sufficient revenue. In both fields he depended on the transatlantic silver shipments, which, after reaching a high level in 1624–6, declined, 1626–8, dropped decisively, 1629–31, and collapsed catastrophically, 1639–41, never to recover.

His foreign policy of aggression was mainly directed at Holland, that collection of once-Spanish provs which had mounted the REVOLT OF THE NETHERLANDS, and with which Spain had signed the humiliating 12-year Truce of 9 Apr 1609. On the expiry of the Truce, Olivares was determined that Spain should make a 2nd attempt at reconquering these provs, not only because they were

Spanish by rights, and posed a threat to the Spanish Netherlands (Belgium), and not merely because they were Prot, but mainly because of the aggressive way they had begun to penetrate the Portuguese and Spanish colonial Emps in the Indian Ocean and Far E, as well as in the Americas. For its part Holland – or at least the ascendant war party – was just as keen to revive the war in order to extend this aggression. In adopting his anti-Dutch programme, Olivares committed Spain to war, not only in Holland and the colonies, but also with England as well as Italy and Germany as a full participant in the Thirty Years War. Thus, though Olivares' aims were much more modest than the aggressive megalomania of K PHILIP II's day, they led him into a similar trap of over-extension.

In Holland the Truce was due to expire in Apr 1621, but Olivares' general, Spinola, was ready to pounce, having invaded the Rhine Palatinate (Aug 1620) on the outbreak of the Thirty Years War. He himself favoured a renewal of the Truce, but, over-ruled by Olivares, he took Jülich in Feb 1622 and besieged Bergen-op-Zoom on the border between N and S Netherlands. Mansfeld, on behalf of the Dutch, was able to relieve it in Oct 1622, but Spinola then laid siege to nearby Breda, Brabant, and took it in June 1625. (This victory was vividly depicted by Velázquez in *Las Lanzas*.) However, it was the furthest extent of Spanish success. The Dutch under FREDERICK HENRY now began to push the Spanish back, capturing Bois-le-Duc, Brabant (14 Sept 1629), Maastricht (23 Aug 1632), and Breda (10 Oct 1637), and conquering a strip of the S Netherlands eventually incorporated into the United Provs as the 'Generality'.

In the colonies the Dutch under Piet Heyn conquered the Portuguese possession of Bahia, Brazil (9 May 1624), but Olivares organized a joint Portuguese-Spanish expedition which soon recaptured it (1 May 1625). The Dutch pressed the attack, nevertheless. Piet Heyn captured practically the entire New Spain silver fleet off Matanzas, Cuba (8/9 Sept 1628); with the help of the proceeds, the Dutch began the conquest of the rich Prov of Pernambuco, Brazil (1630–35). They also took Curaçao (1634) and other Spanish Caribbean islands. Olivares was not in a position to counter-attack in Brazil until 1639, but his joint Portuguese-Spanish armada was beaten off by the Dutch in Jan 1640. On the outbreak of the Revolt of Portugal against Spain, Holland signed a 10-year truce with Portugal (June 1640); and it was not until 1654 that the Dutch were finally ejected from Brazil.

In England, whose friendship was needed to keep the Channel link with the Netherlands open, Olivares bemused JAMES I and CHARLES I for many years with the highly improbable Spanish marriage project, finally provoking them into war, the chief actions of which – Mansfeld's intervention in the Thirty Years War (1625), and BUCKINGHAM's attack on Cádiz (Oct–Nov 1625) – were incompetently executed.

In Italy, long the battleground of Spain's wars with France (*see* HABSBURG–VALOIS WARS), Olivares was also concerned with Holland, because the supply-route between Spain and the Netherlands – the 'Spanish Road' – passed through Genoa, Milan and the Valtelline to the Rhine valley, and Olivares could not afford to have it threatened by RICHELIEU, as it was in 1624–5 when the French occupied the Valtelline and threatened Genoa, and in 1627–31 during the War of Mantuan Succession. In the former case, Olivares was fortunate that Richelieu had Hug problems at home and had to withdraw (Tr of Monzón, Mar 1626). In the latter case Olivares failed to achieve his end, which was to prevent the

French D de Nevers from inheriting Mantua. By the Tr of Cherasco (Apr 1631), not only did Nevers keep his Duchy, but France kept the fortress of Pinerolo, Piedmont – a gateway into Italy.

In Germany, Olivares became deeply involved in the Thirty Years War because he considered that the Spanish reconquest of Holland depended upon a Cath and Imperial victory, thus keeping open the Spanish Road down the Rhine, and perhaps bringing help against the Dutch from the Emp. Throughout his period of office, Olivares committed huge funds to the war, occupying the Rhine Palatinate, and helping to organize joint action against the Danes, then the Swedes, then the French. It was a one-sided effort, however, for the Emp gave him no direct help against Holland, nor would WALLENSTEIN obey Spanish orders in Olivares' *almirantazgo* (1624–8) – a scheme for a Habsburg–Polish–Hanseatic seagoing union to ruin Holland by capturing her Baltic trade. Even his one victory became a long-term defeat, for when the joint Spanish-Imperial army under the K's brother Ferdinand, the Card-Infant, and the ArchD Ferdinand (the future FERDINAND III) smashed the Swedes at Nördlingen, Swabia on 26/27 Aug/5/6 Sept 1634, the only result was that Richelieu decided to commit France to open participation in the war. The Franco-Habsburg War, in which 1st Richelieu, then MAZARIN put the finishing touches to the decline of Spain, lasted beyond the Thirty Years War to 1659, and overstretched Spain to a fatal degree. In the course of it, Spain was attacked in N Italy again (Milan in 1635, the Valtelline in 1635–7 and Turin in 1640); and was pushed out of SW France at both ends of the Pyrenees, the French attacking Catalonia (1637) and Fuentarrabía, Guipúzcoa (1638), as well as aiding the revolutions in Catalonia and Portugal (1640 onwards), and conquering Perpignan (1642), and with it Roussillon. Moreover, on the Rhine the French took Breisach (17 Dec 1638) and other strongpoints, thus cutting the Spanish Road. In the Netherlands the fleet under Antonio de Oquendo, which was bringing reinforcements to the hard-pressed Spaniards, was destroyed in the battle of the Downs (21 Oct 1639) by Admiral Tromp – who thus closed the seagoing alternative to the Rhine. In NE France the French blocked a Spanish thrust to Paris at Corbie, nr Amiens (1636); conquered Artois (1639–40); and then, a few months after Olivares' fall from power, destroyed the Spanish army in the resounding victory at Rocroi, Ardennes, on 19 May 1643.

His home policy oscillated between attempts at reform and unfortunate expedients which made things worse, all with the purpose of scraping together the money and men with which to wage his disastrous foreign policy. He cut the expenses of the Court and household, and generally reduced the lavish extravagance which had marked Philip III's reign. He offended the nobility by his efforts to make them pay taxes, to reduce their spending by sumptuary laws, to stem the flow of favours granted by the K, and to eliminate corruption in the admin. At the same time, he sold titles of nobility, Crown lands, lordships, Gov posts and municipal offices. Moreover, beginning in June 1621 he debased the currency by issuing copper coins (*vellón*) which steadily declined in value, though occasionally he would suddenly reduce their value – by 50% in Aug 1628, by 25% in Sept 1642 – when holders of *vellón* received no compensation for their savage losses. On 31 Jan 1627 the Gov went bankrupt, paying off its creditors in Gov bonds (*juros*). Meanwhile, in the daily toil of Gov, Olivares was indefatigable, dedicated and domineering, insofar as the stone-walling Grandees allowed him to be. Unable to eliminate them from the Councils which governed Spain, he muffled their impact by extending the system of *juntas* – committees of experts, packed with his relatives and friends, to expedite the Councils' work and see that his wishes were carried out. From 1634 the *Junta de Ejecución* effectively replaced the Council of State as the chief policy-making organ in the State. He himself agreed with the proposals of the *Arbitristas* – the economic experts who were trying to halt Spain's decline – and he wrote many memoranda incorporating their ideas for reform: eg for pruning the bureaucracy; for replacing the *millones* and *alcabala* (purchase taxes which hit the masses) with rational taxes based on wealth; for reducing the sums spent on extravagant display; for ending the economically damaging preoccupation of Spaniards with honour and *limpieza* (purity of blood); and for removing the prejudice against business and hard work. Unfortunately, the deeply entrenched nobility blocked all reforms, which could only go through at their expense. Above all, in his secret memorandum of Dec 1624, Olivares argued strongly in favour of the unification and integration of the Spanish peninsula, proclaiming the duty of the non-Castilian provs to provide their share of men and money, and the duty of Castile to open up commercial privileges and Gov jobs to the provs of the periphery. This was a long-term programme, though; as a short-term contribution Olivares proposed the Union of Arms: an all-Spanish reserve of 140,000 men to be raised and supplied in fixed proportions by all the provs – in the Netherlands, Italy and the Americas, as well as in the Iberian peninsula. Aragon and Valencia voted small subsidies but no troops (1626), but the *cortes* of Catalonia (1626) turned down completely this invasion of their *fueros*. In the financial crisis of 1639–40 Olivares made a further attempt at what the other provs regarded as the Castilianization of the Spanish monarchy, in so doing provoking the Revolt of Catalonia (1640–52), the Revolt of Portugal (1640–68), and the conspiracy of his cousin, the Marqués de Ayamonte, to take Andalusia out of the monarchy (1641). These disasters, on top of the foreign failures, brought the inevitable revenge of the Grandees, who for some time had abandoned the Court and gone on strike on their estates. A faction led by the Count of Castrillo succeeded in having Olivares dismissed (Jan 1643). He d, broken in health and on the edge of madness.

Orléans, Jean Baptiste Gaston, D d' (25 Apr 1608–2 Feb 1660) Brother and, for much of his life, heir to K LOUIS XIII of France. He frequently conspired and rebelled against the K and his minister, RICHELIEU, and later participated in the FRONDES.

3rd son of K HENRY IV and Q MARIE DE MEDICI; m 1st (1626) Marie, daughter of the D de Montpensier (d 1627); m 2nd (1632, in secret) Marguerite de Vaudmont, sister of the D of Lorraine (d 1672). A spoilt and dissipated mother's favourite, treacherous and unstable, though not without attractive characteristics, he lacked brains and firmness of purpose. He replaced Henry, 3rd Pr de CONDÉ, as the leader of the Prs of the Blood and magnates in their opposition to the attempts of Louis XIII and Richelieu to increase the power of the central Gov. He vacillated between treasonable rebellions with aid of foreign powers, and profitable reconciliations with a Gov too nervous to treat him firmly. He played a leading role in the Chalais conspiracy of May 1626, after which he was made D d'Orléans (hitherto he had been D d'Anjou), but was forced against his will into his 1st marriage. He was in command of the army which besieged La Rochelle (1627–8), but left in a pique when the K took over from him on recovering from an illness. He joined forces with his mother in the Day of Dupes (10 Nov 1630), an abortive palace revolution to oust Richelieu, after which he fled to Brussels and Lorraine, where he secretly m the sister of the D, who was an enemy of France, in alliance with the Habsburgs. His next exploit was to invade France in support of Henri de Montmorency's rebellion in Languedoc which was defeated at the battle of Castelnaudary, 1 Oct 1632. Montmorency was executed (30 Oct 1632), but Orléans made his peace and escaped once more to the Netherlands till he returned again with an increase in income on reconciliation with the K in Oct 1634. He now took part in the campaign leading to the defeat of the Spanish invasion of Picardy in July 1636, though he had flounced off the battlefield in high dudgeon by the time that Richelieu received the Spanish surrender at Corbie in Nov 1636. In 1637 he was toying with a scheme to murder Richelieu; and in 1642 he was involved in the Cinq Mars conspiracy, aimed at murdering Richelieu and making Orléans the Lieut-Gen of France – all with Spanish help. When Richelieu discovered the plot, Orléans typically provided evidence of Cinq Mars' involvement. The latter was executed on 12 Sept 1642, but Orléans survived to become the Lieut-Gen of France in actual fact during the Regency of Q Anne of Austria and the rule of MAZARIN during the minority of LOUIS XIV. During the Frondes (1648–53), he manoeuvred between the competing Sword and Robe groups, achieving importance as leader of the PARLEMENT and population of Paris until, on Mazarin's return to power, he was exiled to his château at Blois (1652), where Mansart had built him the new Orléans wing.

Oxenstierna, Axel Gustafson, Count (16 June 1583–28 Aug 1654) Chancellor (1612) of K GUSTAV II ADOLF of Sweden, and after his death (16 Nov 1632) head of the Regency for Q CHRISTINA. Oxenstierna's personal collaboration with the K temporarily ended the rivalry between the Crown and the nobility, of which Oxenstierna was the leader. It enabled them both to reform all aspects of Swedish life, to defeat Denmark, Poland and Russia, to intervene decisively on the Prot side in the THIRTY YEARS WAR, and to raise Sweden from a position of insecurity to the rank of leading State in the Baltic and chief military power in Europe. He continued this policy during the minority of Q Christina (1632–44), but was at odds with her during her ten-year rule (1644–54).

Ed (1599–1603) in theology at the German univs of Rostock, Jena and Wittenberg; joined the Gov service and became (1609) a member of the Council (*riksråd*), the chief organ of the nobility in its struggle against K Charles IX. He forced the young K Gustav Adolf to accept the Accession Charter of Jan 1611 which limited royal power; but the K appointed him Chancellor, and together they were responsible for all the measures at home and abroad for which Gustav Adolf's reign became famous (*see* GUSTAV II ADOLF). After the K's death, Oxenstierna's career is noteworthy for his successful completion of Sweden's part in the Thirty Years War, and his conflict with the Q.

The Thirty Years War was in its *Swedish War* period (1630–35) when he joined Gustav Adolf in Germany in Nov 1631; and when the K was killed at Lützen he assumed supreme command. With his statesmanlike vision and unlimited endurance he was equal to the task. At this critical juncture he was faced with the complex problems of raising men and money for the Swedish army, holding the German Prot alliance together, fending off the attempts of his ally RICHELIEU to turn Sweden into a French puppet, and controlling a succession of headstrong generals: Bernard, D of Saxe-Weimar, Gustav Horn, Johan Baner, Lennart Torstensson, Karl Gustav Wrangel and Johan Christoph, Count von Königsmarck. (His diplomatic and military successes and failures in this war and the subsequent *Franco-Habsburg War* (1635–48), his vigorous thrusts at the Emp on the upper Rhine and in Bavaria in the W, and in N Germany and Bohemia in the E, his defeat of Denmark, and his refusal to make peace until the Emp conceded satisfactory territorial and financial compensation are detailed under the THIRTY YEARS WAR.) By the Tr of Westphalia (Oct 1648) Sweden gained: W Pomerania, including Stettin and the Oder estuary; Wismar in Mecklenburg; the Bprics of Bremen and Verden, giving her control over the Elbe and Weser estuaries; and 5 million talers for the troops.

Q Christina was not so congenial a monarch to him as her father had been. During her minority Oxenstierna ruled Sweden through a Regency of 5, headed by himself, and including a brother and a cousin. It was Oxenstierna who drew up the Form of Government (July 1634) embodying the thorough-going modernization of the Swedish admin which he and the K had worked out together – though the young Q regarded it with suspicion. She saw Oxenstierna as the leader of a revived aristocratic constitutionalism taking advantage of her age and sex; and from the time of his return from Germany in July 1636 until the crisis of 1650 their relations deteriorated, especially after she came of age (8 Dec 1644). She wanted a quick end to the war so as to get rid of him. She refused to marry and provide an heir, and she demanded that CHARLES GUSTAV, the nephew of Gustav Adolf whom Oxenstierna wanted her to marry, should be recognized as her successor. Oxenstierna and the nobles resisted this step in the direction of what they regarded as absolutism, for they were acustomed to extracting an Accession Charter from their would-be monarchs guaranteeing the nobility's role in the State. For her part, the Q allied with the mass of the people in the typical manner of her dynasty, and made use of the crisis of 1650 to get her way. This opportunity arose from the policy of Gustav Adolf and Oxenstierna of raising revenue for the wars by selling crown lands and other sources of income to nobles for ready cash. The long-term effects were to reduce the free peasants on these estates to a condition of vassalage to the nobles, and to give the nobles profits which by rights should have gone to the Crown, thus making higher taxation necessary. The non-noble Estates – the Burghers, Clergy and Peasants – had long demanded a resumption by the Crown of all these alienated properties, and in the Diet (*riksdag*) of 1650 they took the initiative and demanded not only a resumption but also other limitations on the powers and privileges of the nobles. The Q skilfully encouraged this campaign, and frightened Oxenstierna and the nobles into recognizing Charles Gustav as Hereditary Pr. Having achieved her main object, the Q now abandoned her radical allies and protected the nobles from the resumption. The only concession they had to make was the statute of 1652 which limited the extra labour-services of the free peasants on alienated lands; and, as a result, Oxenstierna's relations with the Q improved. When he d his family and his class were still firmly in control of Sweden.

333

Parker, Matthew (6 Aug 1504–17 May 1575) Archbp of Canterbury (1559) who presided over the creation and early enforcement of the Ch settlement of Q ELIZABETH I.

Ed at Corpus Christi, Cambridge (1520 onwards), where he was elected Fellow in 1527, the year of his ordination. He was influenced by the Prots who used to meet at the White Horse Inn; and also became a friend of the future Ld BURGH-LEY. He became Chaplain to Q Anne Boleyn (1535–6), Canon of Ely (1541), Master of Corpus Christi (1544), Vice-Chancellor of the Univ (1545) and Dean of Lincoln (1552). He m (1547) the gifted Margaret Harlestone of Norfolk, and thus under the Cath Q MARY I he had to retire into private life. He was gentle and retiring, with academic tastes; and he made an important contribution to medieval and Anglo-Saxon historical scholarship, leaving a valuable collection of documents. Under Q Elizabeth he was made Archbp of Canterbury, much against his wishes. Because of his moderate views he was specially selected by the Q and Cecil for the delicate task of setting up the Ch of England and defending it against Puritan and Cath criticism. He was no harsh persecutor of dissidents, but preferred to demonstrate the correctness of the Ch of England by historical research, and make its position clear in the series of publications he supervised: the Prayer Book (1559), *The Injunctions* (1559), the *39 Articles* (1563) and the *Advertisements* (1566). By the time he d he had succeeded in establishing a distinctive Ch of England; but Puritanism had already moved into its anti-episcopal, Presbyterian stage.

Parlements Regional supreme courts, of which there were 8 in C16 France: in Paris, Toulouse, Grenoble, Bordeaux, Dijon, Rouen, Aix and Rennes. A few others were added later. The Parlement of Paris was easily the most important, covering over one-third of the Kdom and acting as the highest court of appeal for the whole of France under the royal Council. Manned by Prs of the Blood and peers, as well as the ennobled career-lawyers (called the Nobility of the Robe) who did most of the technical work, the Parlement of Paris had two other important roles apart from hearing appeals: firstly, it possessed large admin powers (in Paris and other towns in its area) over police, markets, highways, fortifications, food prices, taverns, prostitutes, heretics etc; secondly, it possessed great political power, for royal edicts had to be registered in the Parlement before they had the force of law, and the Parlement could oppose royal policy by sending remonstrances to the K. In his turn, a strong K could get his way by presiding at a ceremony called a *lit de justice* in which the Parlement was browbeaten into registering the royal wishes. In the absence of the Estates-Gen, the Parlement of Paris was the only institution capable of standing up to absolute monarchy, and in C18 it led what it was pleased to think was a national resistance to the ministers of LOUIS XV and XVI. It borrowed the language of liberalism from its quite different counterpart in England; but, not being representative (except of the nobility), it played no creative role, but simply blocked progress by defending the rights of the privileged.

Parsons, Robert (24 June 1546–18 Apr 1610) English Cath exile under Q ELIZA-BETH I of England, who led the 1st underground Jesuit mission to England, and then intrigued with the Pp, Spain and France for the political overthrow of the Q.

Son of a blacksmith; ed at Taunton, then St Mary's Hall and Balliol, Oxford, becoming a Fellow of Balliol. Having quarrelled with his colleagues, he left Oxford (1575) for London, then Padua and Rome, where he joined the JESUITS (July 1575). He was placed at the head of the 9-man mission to England which included Edmund CAMPION. Parsons landed at Dover in June 1580, disguised as a soldier; changing lodgings frequently, he held services and organized a secret press, which printed his *A Brief Discourse containing certain Reasons why Catholics refuse to go to Church*. When Campion was captured Parsons decided to return to the Continent (Aug 1581) and spent the 1580s not only organizing the men and material for the English mission, but also moving about between Rome, Spain, France and the Netherlands, deeply involved in all the political activity which aimed at the forceful overthrow of the Q – a way of life more suited to this subtle and ambitious man of action than straightforward missionary work. He misunderstood the political leanings of English Caths, and misled K PHILIP II of Spain into believing that the Spanish ARMADA would be welcomed by a general Cath rising. At the same time, his intrigues with Spain did not endear him to English Caths; neither did his view that a community had the right to depose a heretic ruler. His pamphlet of 1594 called *The conference about the next succession* – in which he backed the Infanta Isabella Clara Eugenia in preference to the Stuarts for the succession – brought out into the open the deep rift in England between those Caths who supported the secular priests and were generally patriotic, and those who backed the Spanish-supported Jesuits.

Paul III (Alessandro Farnese) (prob Feb 1468–10 Nov 1549) Pp (1534), who supported the COUNTER-REFORMATION and raised the prestige of the Papacy in European politics.

Son of Pier Luigi Farnese and Giovanella Gaetano (high Roman aristocracy); ed at the Court of Lorenzo the Magnificent, Florence; thanks to the good looks of his sister, Giulia (who was the mistress of Pp ALEXANDER VI), he won quick promotion in the Ch, being created Card (1493) before being consecrated priest. Old and ailing by the time he became Pp, but also shrewd, tough and subtle, he took a more statesmanlike view of his duties than his predecessors during the Renaissance period. Although like them he had several illegitimate children (to whose material interests he sometimes sacrificed the higher destinies of the Ch and of Italy) and put much effort into outward beautification of Rome (beginning with the Farnese Palace, and employing Michelangelo in St Peter's and in the Sistine Chapel), he was anxious above all to bring an end to the HABSBURG–VALOIS WARS, to close the religious divisions of Europe, and to unite the Christian world against Turkey. Making a firm gesture towards the CATHOLIC REFORMATION, he included in his 1st promotions to the College of Cardinals some of the chief associates of the Oratory of Divine Love: Gasparo Contarini (1535), Jacopo Sadoleto (1536), Gian Pietro Caraffa (later Pp PAUL IV) and Giovanni Morone (1542); as well as the 2 opponents of K HENRY VIII of England, John FISHER (1535) and Reginald Pole (1536); but also 2 of his teen-aged grandsons. Similarly, he placed Contarini at the head of a 9-man reform commission (1536) which produced (1537) its secret report, the *Consilium de emendenda ecclesia* (*Advice on the Reform of the Church*) which was sharply critical of Ch abuses but superficial in its notion of what reform really entailed.

335

After a long period of doubt, Paul also put his weight behind the COUNTER-REFORMATION. He issued the Bull (Sept 1540) which recognized the new Society of Jesus (the JESUITS); persuaded by Caraffa he set up (July 1542) the reconstituted ROMAN INQUISITION; and he convened the COUNCIL OF TRENT, which first met in Dec 1545. To end the Habsburg–Valois War of 1536–8, he sailed to Nice and negotiated the 10-year truce with CHARLES V and FRANCIS I personally (June 1538); henceforth he switched from one to the other in accordance with his family ambitions and his conception of what the Counter-Reformation should concentrate on. He m his grandson Ottavio to Charles V's illegitimate daughter Margaret (1538). He angled for the marriage of his daughter Vittoria with the French D of Orléans. And, in the mid-1540s, he made a rapprochement with Charles V, who was now preparing to use force against the German Prots. Charles promised him Parma and Piacenza for his son Pier Luigi (1545). In return he agreed to call the Council of Trent, and guaranteed to help Charles fight the Prots with 12,000 infantry and 500 cavalry commanded by Ottavio, as well as a large sum of money from the resources of the Ch in Spain (June 1546). But this friendship soon ended: Charles's victory over the Prots at Mühlberg (24 Apr 1547) made him too powerful for Paul's comfort: capable, perhaps, of dealing with the GERMAN REFORMATION independently of the Pp, and free, perhaps, to interfere in Italy again. Also, they differed in their conception of the Council of Trent. For Charles, the prime task was the reform of abuses to facilitate the reconciliation of the Prots; for Paul, it was the definition of doctrine preparatory to all-out war on the heretics. In any case, the move of the delegates from Trent to Bologna (Mar 1547) effectively ended their usefulness to Charles. The assassination of Paul's son, Pier Luigi Farnese, at Piacenza by what seemed to be a Habsburg-inspired conspiracy (10 Sept 1547) widened the breach still further. Thus by the time of his death, Paul had resumed his favourite position of papal neutrality above the Habsburg–Valois contest. He was no nearer the solution of his major problems, but he had increased markedly the effectiveness of the papacy in European affairs.

Paul IV (Gian Pietro Caraffa) (28 June 1476–18 Aug 1559) Pp (1555), fanatical leader of the COUNTER-REFORMATION and hater of Spain.

Rose in the Ch with the help of his uncle who was a Cardinal. Created Archbp of Brindisi (1517), he played an important role in the CATHOLIC REFORMATION, until he abandoned the HUMANISM of this period, and turned into a violent and intolerant leader of the Counter-Reformation. It was he, eg, who persuaded Pp PAUL III to set up the ROMAN INQUISITION (July 1542); as its 1st Inquisitor-Gen he carried out a programme (covering all Italy) of vigorous and highly successful suppression, fitting up his own house in Rome with prison cells, burning men as well as books, and reducing both the Prot movement and his old allies of the Catholic Reformation movement to impotence. As a Neapolitan, he hated the Spanish who ruled in Naples and Milan (nothing but Jews and Arabs, he called them); as a consequence he opposed the JESUITS. He also set his face against Ch councils, and blocked any concessions to the German Prots. He believed the Pp was superior to the Emp; and when he became Pp, he gave rein to all these fierce prejudices to the point of insanity – though with more than a touch of the Renaissance still about him as he promoted his 3 highly disreputable (though real) nephews to high office in the Ch. In foreign affairs he revived the fatal policy of calling in the French to drive out the Habsburgs (alliance of Dec 1555); was a chief instigator of the last HABSBURG–VALOIS WAR (1552–9), in which French help to the German Prs led to the permanent failure to repress Protestantism in the Emp (PEACE OF AUGSBURG, 1555, denounced by Paul as a pact with heresy); and in which the defeat of the French at St Quentin (10 Aug 1557) placed Italy more completely under Habsburg control than ever. Forced to make peace with K PHILIP II of Spain (Sept 1557), he henceforth concentrated on Ch and Italian affairs. He attacked abuses in the papal Court, and in churches and monasteries up and down Italy. He turned against the allies of his youth (for the Catholic Reformation was now heretical), imprisoning Giovanni Morone, and excommunicating Reginald Pole, the Primate of England and ally of Spain. He issued the first INDEX (1559). He improved the efficiency of the INQUISITION. He tightened up the admin of the Papal States and improved the policing of the city of Rome. In a last fling in the wider world he refused to consecrate FERDINAND I as Emp; he instituted proceedings in the Roman Inquisition against CHARLES V and Philip II for heresy; in his last year, he was planning a Bull depriving the latter of his Kdom. On his death the Roman mob went berserk, burning the records of the Inquisition and breaking up his statue and throwing the pieces into the Tiber.

Peasants' War, The (June 1524–May 1525) A mass uprising of the German lower classes during the REFORMATION, fired by economic hardship and inspired by religious hopes.

During the early modern period in Europe the growth of a market economy, the PRICE REVOLUTION and the intermittent crises caused by bad harvests led landlords to squeeze more than the traditional income from their peasants. In E Europe the nobles succeeded in turning their tenants into serfs; in W Europe, where this was not possible, they ground them by raising entry fines, increasing labour dues, enclosing the commons, monopolizing hunting and fishing etc; in Central and SW Germany, where the Peasants' War began, these oppressive acts were the work not so much of the local nobility as of the numerous lay and ecclesiastical Prs with property on a provincial scale, and to them were added other provocations: the use of absolutist Roman Law in place of local custom, and the raising of taxes and tithes. Such oppressions had led to sporadic peasant rebellions in Switzerland and Germany during the C15, but the Peasants' War proved to be the biggest revolt of the German masses ever. It profited from the freedom of thought and speech brought about by LUTHER. In their economic and social despair the peasants were ready listeners to those preachers – such as Müntzer and other ANABAPTISTS – who carried Lutheranism far in the direction of religious anarchism, and who expected the Second Coming to bring about social justice. Beginning in SW Germany and spreading down the Danube into Austria (though not Bavaria) and down the Rhine into Central and N Germany, the outbreaks were widespread but unco-ordinated. Led by substantial peasants and urban craftsmen, the rebels sacked castles and monasteries, and issued demands in which clauses insisting on the return of the common waste mingled with plans for the election of pastors by their congregations. Luther violently attacked them in his brutal broadsheet *Against the thieving and murdering hordes of the peasants* of 1525. Once Prs such as Philip of Hesse organized repression, the peasants were slaughtered in their thousands, including the main body at Frankenhausen, Saxony, on 15 May 1525. The net effect was to strengthen the position of the Prs and their state Chs, at the expense of the lower classes, the local nobility and the Emp.

Pelham, Henry (*c* 1696–6 Mar 1754) Pupil and successor to WALPOLE who ruled as PM from at least 1746 until his death in a Gov which brought an end to the WAR OF THE AUSTRIAN SUCCESSION, and introduced many measures aimed at reducing Gov expenditure, stimulating economic growth, and dealing with social problems. One important aim behind these policies was to retain the support of both K and Parl, and thus continuance in office.

Younger son of Thomas, 1st Bn Pelham, and his 2nd wife, Lady Grace Holles, sister of John Holles, D of Newcastle; ed Westminster Sch, and Hart Hall, Oxford (1710); m (1726) Lady Catherine Manners (d 1780), eld daughter of the 2nd D of Rutland.

Early career (1717–42): MP for Seaford, Sussex (1717–22), then for Sussex (1722–54), he was appointed by Walpole a member of the Treasury board (Apr 1721); then Sec-at-War (Apr 1724); then Paymaster-Gen of the Forces (May 1730). Sane, temperate, industrious and reliable, he was a well-liked, honest bore who soon became a key figure in Walpole's political grouping – the Old Corps of WHIGS – with his admin efficiency and instinctive understanding of the workings of C18 political system, especially in the constituencies and the H of C.

The Old Corps and the New Whigs (1742–4): When Walpole lost the support of the backbenchers and was forced to resign (Feb 1742) because of Britain's poor performance in the War of the Austrian Succession (1740–48), there was no wholesale removal of the Gov. The Old Corps remained in office, but were reinforced by one of the opposition groups, the followers of CARTERET and Pulteney, known as the New Whigs. The other Out group – PITT and the Grenvilles – remained in opposition. For a time there was no clear leader. Pelham and his brother, the D of NEWCASTLE, and the Old Corps dominated the H of C, but in the Closet K GEORGE II was chiefly influenced by his favourites: John Carteret, who became Sec of State (N) (Feb 1742), and Spencer Compton, Earl of Wilmington, who became 1st Ld of the Treasury (Feb 1742). On the death of the latter on 2 July 1743, however, Pelham moved nearer the centre of power, possibly thanks to Walpole's continuing influence with the K behind the scenes. In Aug 1743 Pelham was made 1st Ld of the Treasury. The Cabinet was still split, between the Old Corps and the New Whigs, so long as Carteret and the K pursued their 'old system' of foreign policy, involving elaborate Continental alliances paid for by expensive subsidies, while Pelham had the job of keeping taxes down in order to maintain Parl support – not an easy task while Pitt and the Grenvilles were convincing the backbench Country elements that Great Britain's interests were being sacrificed to those of Hanover. Before long Carteret was forced out. Brilliant as he was in European diplomacy, his efforts were only leading to French victories, while, as a supercilious, easy-going *bon vivant*, he paid no attention to the mundane matter of securing a following, either in the Closet or in Parl. He resigned on 23 Nov 1744.

The Old Corps and the New Allies (1744–6): In the consequent reshuffle,

Pelham broadened the base of his support, to form the Broad-Bottom Admin. Unlike Walpole, who added to the opposition by his inability to stomach rivals of talent, Pelham was a conciliator who maximized his Parl support by tolerating all shades of opinion on the front bench. As well as to TORIES, he gave office to the leading Outs – the New Allies – including the Grenvilles, but not Pitt as yet, owing to the K's hatred of him. This Gov successfully rode the crisis of the Jacobite rebellion – the 'FORTYFIVE' (June 1745–Sept 1746) – but Pelham was still not really PM, for Carteret (Earl Granville) and Pulteney (Earl of Bath) were still advising the K 'behind the curtain'. It was to bring an end to this intolerable interference that the Gov staged its celebrated mass resignation on 10 and 11 Feb 1746. A day or two proved to George II that Granville and Bath were incapable of forming a Gov with a H of C majority, and on 14 Feb 1746 Pelham and his friends were back in office. Even Pitt received a post, becoming Joint-Vice-Treasurer of Ireland (Feb 1746), then Paymaster-Gen (May 1746). Pelham and Pitt agreed on foreign policy: they both opposed involvement in Continental wars, Pelham because of the expense, Pitt because of his 'blue-water' policy, ie colonial aggression.

Prime Minister (1746–54): Having achieved dominance in the Closet, Pelham used the election of 1747 – which he and his brother organized with their usual finesse – to confirm his mastery in the H of C. Thenceforth, till his death, he maintained political peace in the country such as had not been seen even under Walpole. All that rippled the surface were quarrels in the Cabinet: between Pelham and Newcastle (in which Henry FOX backed Pelham, and Pitt backed Newcastle), and between Newcastle and his fellow Sec of State, the D of Bedford, till the latter was forced out in June 1751. Abroad, Pelham brought an end to the war, with the Tr of Aix-la-Chapelle (Oct 1748), and then pursued a policy of peace at practically any price. Even if his habit of judging diplomacy mainly by its effect on the H of C led to the weak European position that Britain found herself in at the start of the SEVEN YEARS WAR (1756–63), nevertheless, Pelham was sufficiently flexible to favour abandoning the 'old system' of a pro-Austrian alliance to protect Hanover, in favour of an alliance with FREDERICK II of Prussia – a realignment which was brought about shortly after Pelham's death by the DIPLOMATIC REVOLUTION. At home, Pelham's ministry was noted for its encouragement of economic growth, and for its support of measures to solve social problems. With great financial and diplomatic skill he won the backing of both Parl and the City for his conversion of the National Debt, thus achieving a record low rate of interest of 3% on most of it by 1757. He reduced the army and navy; he lowered the land tax. He sponsored Chesterfield's Act (1751) to reform the calendar by adopting the New, or Gregorian, Style which Europe had been using since 1582. By this Act, the New Year began on 1 Jan 1752 (instead of 25 Mar 1752) and 11 days were omitted between 2 and 14 Sept 1752 – an excision which caused mob riots with the slogan: 'Give us back our eleven days'. He supported a bill for naturalizing foreign Prots, but shelved it because of the outcry. He supported the Jewish Naturalization Act (1753), which made it easier for Jews to become naturalized by private Act of Parl, but then repealed it because of popular hostility. His Gin Act (1751) brought the distillation and sale of spirits under closer Gov inspection. Moreover, with Gov encouragement the Bow Street magistrates became more effective in their suppression of crime and vice, while Hardwicke's Marriage Act (1753) introduced a more stringent State supervision of marriage ceremonies in order to protect girls. In general, Pelham's ministry brought peace, prosperity and social improvement. It became the very pattern of a stable Hanoverian admin; and, when Pelham d it was no wonder that George II remarked: 'Now I shall have no more peace.'

Pérez, Antonio (*c* 1540–3 Nov 1611) Sec to K PHILIP II of Spain (1566–79), whose corrupt and ruthless pursuit of supreme political power ended in disgrace and exile.

Illegitimate son of Gonzalo Pérez (a priest of plebeian, possibly Jewish, origin in Aragon, who rose by his talents to be Sec to the Emp CHARLES V and Philip II in turn); ed at Alcalá, Louvain, Salamanca, Padua and Venice; m (1568) Juana Coello. A brilliantly able and cultivated man, with an unsurpassed understanding of the European political scene, he profited fully from the advice and influence of his father (officially known as his uncle) and succeeded him in his office, at least in half of it, on his death. Philip, who disliked all-powerful servants, typically split the post in two, giving Pérez responsibility only for the N: France, England, the Netherlands and Germany. However, among other positions, he also became Sec to the Council of Castile, a look-out post from which he enjoyed an unrivalled view of all the internal affairs of the Spanish monarchy; and, out-doing all other officials in industry, ambition, acuity of perception and flexibility of morals, he rose to be the all-knowing adviser of the K, and the all-powerful intermediary for posts and favours. He grew rich on the gifts he received, and on the profits he made on the international markets, using his knowledge of State secrets. He irritated his fellow functionaries and the high nobility by living like a Grandee; he aroused the suspicions of the K by his evident desire to be a politician, not a civil servant, to be a Minister rather than a Sec. In the faction-divided Court, he was a member of the party led by the Pr of Eboli which favoured a conciliatory approach to the REVOLT OF THE NETHERLANDS; and at the Pr's death on 29 July 1573 he assumed the leadership of the group, and formed a liaison with the Pr's widow. To the one-eyed Prss of Eboli, Pérez was a young man who would go far; to the upstart Sec, she was a valuable link with the nobility who could turn the information he leaked her into hard cash. Theirs was probably not a physical affair, as was thought, but simply an alliance of opportunists to keep one another in the limelight. To call Pérez a 'double-dealer' would be to underestimate the complex nature of his chicanery. Like a dextrous puppeteer, he pulled strings all over Europe, and helped his rivals to plot one another's destruction; and his own destruction came when the K found out that Pérez had tricked him into actions his conscience revolted against. When Philip's half-brother, Don JOHN OF AUSTRIA, was appointed Gov-Gen of the Netherlands, his orders were to be conciliatory, but he kept demanding an army with which to conquer Holland, invade England, and m MARY, Q OF SCOTS. Pérez encouraged these romantic ambitions in Don John at the same time as he reported them to the K in order to discredit him. He placed one of his creatures, Juan de Escobedo, as Sec to Don John to spy on him; but Escobedo switched allegiances, and when Don John sent him to Madrid to plead for money and men, Pérez feared for his own safety, as Escobedo knew enough to hang him. To save his skin, Pérez persuaded Philip that Don John was plotting treason, and that Escobedo was his evil genius. He even induced the K to agree to the latter's elimination; Escobedo was murdered on 31 Mar 1578. After Don John himself d on 1 Oct 1578, his papers convinced the K both of his own innocence and of his Sec's trickery. Philip decided to break Pérez, especially as an important new policy was being adopted: the conquest of Portugal. Resolving to replace him with Card GRANVELLE, the K arrested Pérez on 28 July 1579, the day Granvelle arrived in Madrid from Italy, and confined the Prss of Eboli to her palace for the rest of her life. For 11 years Pérez was locked up and fully investigated. Philip was looking for evidence to convince his own conscience that Pérez, and not himself, was responsible for Escobedo's death. On 19 July 1590 Pérez escaped, and found refuge in Aragon, his arrival in Zaragoza coinciding with the Aragonese revolt of 1591–2. He was tried before the *Justicia*, but since this was the officer most responsible for preserving Aragon's constitutional liberties from infringement by Madrid, the hearings did not go the way Philip wanted, and Pérez used his public appearances to tell the world that the K had ordered Escobedo's murder. Twice the K succeeded in getting him handed over to the INQUISITION on charges fabricated for the occasion by the royal confessor, but each time (May and Sept 1591) he was rescued by anti-Castilian nobles at the head of an urban mob. In the end, Philip had to order the Castilian army to invade Aragon in Nov 1591. Resistance soon crumbled, and Pérez fled to Béarn, K HENRY IV of France's little Kdom. From there, and with French help, Pérez invaded Aragon in Feb 1592, but was quickly thrown out again. Thenceforth he lived in France and England, publishing his *Relaciones de su vida* in 1598, a biography which contributed much to the bad reputation of Philip II (part of the 'Black Legend').

Peter I (The Great) (30 May 1672–28 Jan 1725) Tsar of Russia (1682), who improved central and prov Gov, thus intensifying ABSOLUTISM and enabling the State to raise more taxes and recruit more men for the army, which he reformed, and the navy, which he created. At the same time, he brought the Ch and its property under State control, stimulated expansion in industry and commerce, consolidated the privileges of the *dvoryane* (serving nobility) and increased the subjection of the serfs. The purpose of these changes was an aggressive foreign policy on all fronts, but especially in the Baltic region, where his victories in the GREAT NORTHERN WAR (1700–21) gave him the coveted Baltic provs, made Russia instead of Sweden the chief power in N Europe, and gave Russia a permanent place thenceforth in European power politics and civilization.

14th child of Tsar ALEXIS and 1st of his 2nd wife, Natalia Naryshkina; ed in a desultory manner in practical crafts rather than academic disciplines, mainly away from Court at Preobrazhenskoe, a village near Moscow, where his family had to live during the ascendancy of the Miloslavky family, the relatives of Alexis's 1st wife (1676–89); m 1st (1689) Eudoxia Lopukhina, daughter of a palace functionary, whom he left after a few months and forced to take the veil in June 1699; m 2nd (1712) Catherine Skovorotski (future Empress CATHE-RINE I) a tough, illiterate peasant from Livonia, mistress of Alexander Menshikov before she became Peter's, c 1703. Peter's childhood was menaced by the deadly struggles between the factions surrounding the 2 widows of his father, when palace coups and Moscow riots brought quick changes of régime in which many of the losers were executed, tortured, exiled, or locked up in monasteries. On the death of his father (29 Jan 1676) Peter's eld brother succeeded as Theodore III. On his death (27 Apr 1682) the Naryshkins proclaimed Peter as Tsar, but they were soon overthrown by the Miloslavkys, backed by the Moscow *Streltsy* (musketeers), who proclaimed Peter and his half-blind and mentally deficient eld half-brother, Ivan, as joint Tsars (May 1682), with their rather masculine and hirsute sister, Sofia, as Regent. Sofia was in love with Pr V. V. Golitsin, whom she made chief minister; but his persecution of the Old Believers at home, and his alliance with Poland abroad (Tr of Moscow, the 'Eternal Peace', May 1686), followed by 2 disastrous campaigns against the Crimean Tatars (1687 and 1689) aroused enough opposition in Russia to enable Peter to carry out his coup of Aug 1689. He overthrew Sofia and made himself sole ruler in effect, though not in law until Ivan d in 1696. Unlike many Russian sovereigns who were enthroned by a *coup d'état*, Peter had the personality and industry to subdue not only his enemies but his supporters as well. Nearly 7 feet tall and broad in proportion, he was coarse-grained, loud-mouthed, violent, ruthless and impetuous. His massive intake of food and drink fuelled a demoniacal energy. He had walked when only 6 months old, and was incessantly active as an adult in every kind of practical task from carpentry and metal-work to training troops and torturing suspects. He heaved Russia forward and made her a great power.

The armed forces were enlarged and professionalized. They were the chief reason for the many other changes Peter made in Russian life. Previously, there had been 2 sorts of army unit: the militia and the 'new system' (*novyi stroi*). The militia were amateur drafts of villagers: landlords at the head of their bondsmen, or bailiffs of Crown or Ch land at the head of theirs. The 'new system' consisted of regulars such as the *Streltsy* and the COSSACKS and other units officered by foreign professionals. Peter united the two systems into one standing army (1699 onwards), all recruited, armed, dressed and trained alike. He disbanded the *Streltsy*, which had become too involved in politics, and made the two Guards' regiments – the Preobrazhenskii and the Semenovskii, with whom he had played soldiers as a boy – into the nucleus of a new, officer-training élite. Manpower was provided (1705 onwards) by the conscription of nobles and serfs for life-long service; and by the end of his reign Peter had about 130,000 men under arms, frugally provisioned and savagely disciplined, but equipped and trained up to European standards. As a proportion of the population, the Russian army was 3 times the size of other European forces. At the same time, Peter created a navy – a more revolutionary innovation – first at the mouth of the R Don, then on the Baltic. A combination of foreign expertise and native raw materials produced 48 ships of the line and nearly 800 galleys by the end of the reign. Crewed by native conscripts and foreign officers, they were capable of defeating CHARLES XII of Sweden and alarming GEORGE I of Britain.

The revenue was expanded 3-fold to pay for the armed forces and the wars they fought, all of which regularly took up about 85% of the royal income. The direct tax – the main source of income – was at first levied on households, but, since families evaded tax by joining together in larger and larger households, the revenue failed to keep pace with the population growth. As a remedy, Peter decreed (Nov 1718) that the tax should be levied on individual males (except nobles and clergy), and be called the 'soul' (*podushnyi*) tax – with the Old Believers paying double. If a male took flight, his tax had to be made up by his neighbours, a precaution which helped to pin down peasants in their villages and enserf them still further. Both the collection and the census on which it was based were carried out by the army. It took some years to complete the census, and the first year of the new tax was not until 1724. Indirect taxes – levied on such varied items as horse-collars, hot baths, bee-hives and beards – were 'farmed', usually by the favourites who invented them. Another source of income, royal monopolies, were also 'farmed', and at one time or another tobacco, salt, oil, dice and rhubarb came into this category.

The Church was deprived of its semi-autonomous position and subordinated to the State (peculiarly enough, without a murmur of resistance) mainly because Peter had an eye on its wealth, but partly because he despised and suspected an institution so rich in privileges, land and serfs, which contributed nothing to the State either in taxes or service people, and stubbornly resisted all Westernizing progress. When Patriarch Adrian d in 1700 he was not replaced, and in 1701 the control of the Ch's property was handed over to an old Gov dept now revived, the *Monastyrskii Prikaz*, which was to receive monastic revenues and pay monks a salary. The Patriarchate was formally abolished by the Ecclesiastical Regulation of 1721, and the Ch placed under the control of the Holy Synod and fully meshed into the State machine. The Regulation also laid down in minute detail what was to be the daily life of the clergy. They were to be disciplined on military lines with a view to inculcating complete submission to the State, both in them and in their congregations.

Education in non-religious matters was also introduced by Peter – essential to the armed forces if the gunners were to shoot straight and his sailors navigate. In Moscow the School of Navigation and Mathematics was founded in 1701, and run at first by English and Scottish schoolmasters. Later, special schools were established for Artillery (1701), Languages (1701), Medicine (1707) and Engineering (1712), while 30 or so Mathematical Schools were set up in prov towns, as well as numerous Garrison Schools and Diocesan Schools. At the top, the Academy of Sciences was created in 1724, and staffed at first by teachers and students imported from abroad; while for the educated public Peter started Russia's 1st newspaper in 1703: the *Vedomosti*, issued by the State. At the same time, many Russians were sent to the W to be educated in the latest technology, economics and political science. Having been captivated himself by W ideas – both through his youthful friendships in the Foreign Quarter of Moscow and his Great Embassy to the W (Mar 1697–July 1698) – Peter tried to westernize his subjects by decree: ordering them to shave off their beards, wear W clothes, hold W social gatherings, bring their women out of seclusion, develop capitalist enterprise and enjoy profit-making.

The economy preoccupied Peter greatly, especially after his Great Embassy, when he travelled through Germany, Holland and England, and then home via Austria and Poland, inspecting everything, but especially manufacturing methods. Back in Russia he applied W mercantilism in order to stimulate agriculture, industry and commerce so as to render Russia less dependent for armaments and uniforms on foreign exchange, and to raise the taxable capacity of its citizens. Though his achievements fell short of his aims, he set Russia on a course of economic growth which continued throughout C18. Unfortunately, a middle class stubbornly refused to flourish, a peculiarity of Russia which is not surprising in view of the overwhelming predominance of the State in all enterprises: as the source of capital, raw materials and labour, as well as the main market for the output, and the principal pocketer of the profits. Under Gov direction (from 1718, under 2 of the new central Colleges: of Commerce, and of Mines and Manufactures) iron foundries, armaments works, cloth factories etc, were set up, to be run by the State or 'farmed' out to privileged individuals. During Peter's reign the number of mining and manufacturing enterprises quadrupled. The State had the first call on all output, at prices fixed by itself. Private enterprise could make a profit only on the surplus that the State did not want; and any enterprise started by a private individual which became successful soon found itself taken over by the Crown. Agriculture remained overwhelmingly medieval in its methods and crops, though Peter made great efforts to introduce better ploughs and harrows, and to stimulate the production of silk, wool, flax, hemp and tobacco in order to encourage exports and save imports.

The Gov which Peter inherited was incapable of making the detailed impact on society which all these reforms required, and he experimented throughout his reign with admin improvements, which in fact merely continued the trends set up by his predecessors, MICHAEL and Alexis, and ultimately left Russian Gov in essence where he found it. In local Gov, by a decree of Jan 1699, towns were allowed to elect their own officials, called *Burgmestery*, to collect revenue, stimulate trade, and provide a check on the prov govs (*voevody*). A new Moscow office, the *Ratusha*, co-ordinated their work. The elected sheriff of the nobles in each locality – the *gubnoi starosta* – was replaced from 1702 by an elected board. Finally, in 1724, towns were ordered to govern themselves through elected gilds of the better-off. Apart from the *Ratusha*, hardly any of this machinery materialized, and local affairs continued under the arbitrary tyranny of the *voevody* and the landlords. In prov Gov, by a decree of Dec 1707, Peter divided Russia into 8 *guberniia*, each under a *Gubernator* with full powers, and divided into *uezda* (districts). By a decree of Nov 1718, a more carefully planned series of changes borrowed from Sweden began to take place. The number of *guberniia* was increased to 12, and these were subdivided into about 40 *provintsiia*, each under a *voevod* and consisting of a number of *uezda*. In central Gov, the autocratic Peter was advised at first by the Council (and no longer by the *Boyars' Duma*); and his orders were carried out by the chaotic 40 or so central depts, the *Prikazy*, some specializing in function (eg the Admiralty *Prikaz*), others having general responsibility over a certain area (eg the Ukraine *Prikaz*). In the rush of the early war years, Peter could do little more than tinker with these institutions and make *ad hoc* experiments. Then in 1711 he set up the 9-man Senate, which evolved into the chief executive organ and highest court of appeal. It was supervised on Peter's behalf by army officers: by an Inspector-Gen from 1715, and a Procurator-Gen from 1722 – the most powerful man under the Tsar. To fulfil the impossible task of ensuring the probity of the administrators, an *Oberfiscal* was appointed in 1711, aided by a staff of secret *Fiscals*, some of whom landed in gaol for corruption. In the meanwhile, the new organs of prov Gov had been absorbing some of the responsibilities of the central *Prikazy*, and from 1718 the latter were replaced by a more rational scheme, borrowed from Sweden, of 9 Colleges, each specializing in a certain function over the whole of Russia, and each run by a board of 10–12 men making collective decisions. The Table of Ranks was published in 1722 to regularize the compulsory State service of the hierarchies who manned the new armed forces and Gov depts. Supervised by a new officer, the *Herold-Meister*, the *dvoryane* were divided into 2 main sorts: military (army and navy) and civil (Court and admin), each arranged in a ladder of promotion made up of 14 ranks. Those who were commissioned in the forces (ie reached rank 14) and civil servants who reached rank 8 were granted hereditary nobility. It was a career open to the talents which really worked, though the inertia of the existing system weighed heavily on the side of the old nobility, especially in the topmost ranks. In general, this comment applies to most of Peter's internal reforms. Practice was very different from theory, and Russia changed very slowly. It remained an autocracy in which the Tsar had total power to issue orders, but few means of ensuring they were carried out, and no way of checking the arbitrary tyranny of his civil servants over the public. Peter's paper schemes for the creation of a systematic admin under the rule of law either never saw practice or were soon swept away; and Russian Gov remained what it always had been: a collection of irresponsible tyrannies, working through fear, and softened occasionally by bribery, crudely carrying out their primeval tasks – the extracting of money and the recruiting of men. For much of his reign Peter used soldiers rather than bureaucrats to enforce his will – an appropriate emergency measure when his overriding purpose is taken into account: foreign aggression.

Foreign policy followed tradition in pressing outward on all points of the compass: NW towards the Baltic, W into Poland, SW into the Ukraine, S towards the Black Sea, SE towards the Caspian and E into Siberia. The only break with the past was its sheer success.

The Azov campaigns opened Peter's reign: the 1st (1695), in which he fought as a bombardier, was a failure; the 2nd (1696), when he captained a ship, succeeded in taking Azov at the mouth of the R Don (19 July 1696), thanks to the fleet which had meanwhile been constructed upstream at Voronezh. Peter's Great Embassy was partly motivated by his wish to stimulate the formation of a coalition to continue the war against Turkey, but this proved to be the run-up period for 2 far more important European wars: the Great Northern War and the War of the Spanish Succession against LOUIS XIV. His erstwhile allies, the HREmp LEOPOLD I, Poland and Venice, therefore made the Tr of Carlowitz with Turkey behind his back (Jan 1699). He himself then had to make peace with Turkey in order to free himself for participation in the Great Northern War. By the Tr of Constantinople (July 1700) Turkey ceded the Azov district, and agreed that Russia was no longer obliged to pay tribute to the Tatar Khan of the Crimea. Peter built a naval base at nearby Taganrog on the Sea of Azov, and laid down a fleet.

The Great Northern War (1700–21) occupied most of the remainder of his reign, when he fought against K CHARLES XII alongside his allies, Christian V of Denmark, Augustus II of Saxony-Poland, joined later by Brandenburg and Hanover. After an initial disaster at Narva, Ingria, where Charles XII destroyed his army (19/30 Nov 1700), he steadily recovered, as all his domestic reforms made their contribution to his fighting forces. He conquered the Baltic provs from Sweden; founded St Petersburg (May 1703); gave support to Augustus and the pro-Russian party of nobles in Poland; and destroyed the army with which Charles struck at Moscow at the decisive battle of Poltava (27 June/8 July 1709), having previously captured Swedish reinforcements at Lesnaya (28 Sept/9 Oct 1708). The only set-back after this was the SW campaign against Turkey on the R Pruth (1711), in which he found himself surrounded by an unexpectedly large army and forced to yield Azov and the other gains of 1700 (Tr of Adrianople, June 1713). In the NW he advanced into Finland, his new Baltic fleet defeated Sweden off Hangö (Hangut) on 27 July 1714, and he was in a position to threaten the Swedish mainland, make client-States of some N German principalities, and alarm George I of Great Britain. By the Tr of Nystad (Aug/Sept 1721), which ended the war, Russia kept Livonia, Estonia and Ingria, and gave back Finland except for Kexholm and part of Karelia. Peter had made Russia into a great European power.

In the East he invaded Persia (1722–4) to keep it and the silk trade out of Turkish hands, conquering Derbent, Baku and Resht, and the whole W and S coasts of the Caspian Sea. He also sent expeditions into Siberia, founding Omsk (1717); and began the invasion of the Kamchatka peninsula.

Opposition to Peter's reforms and foreign wars was fierce throughout his reign. Old Believers and reformed Orthodox Christians alike were shocked by the impiety of westernization. Old *boyar* families who had been ousted by *dvoryane* in the reformed admin joined the opposition, as did those traditionalist rural nobles who could not see the point of the long war against Sweden. Moreover, protests from the peasant masses who bore the brunt of the taxation and conscription were endemic. The Cossacks too were a constant source of trouble, especially the Don Cossacks, who in 1707–8 broke out under Kondraty Bulavin in a revolt known to Soviet historians as the 3rd Peasant War, as it also set in flame the Russian serfs against their masters, and coincided with an anti-colonial revolt of the Bashkirs along the R Volga. Many of Peter's opponents pinned their faith in his pious and old-fashioned son by his 1st marriage, Tsarevich Alexis; but Peter – fearing he would destroy all his work on inheriting the throne – eliminated him and his circle in a blood-bath in 1718. His son Peter, by his 2nd marriage, d in 1719; lacking another son, and wishing to bar Alexis's son, the future PETER II, from the succession, he proclaimed (Feb 1722) his own right to appoint his successor. He d, however, before he could name anyone. The way was open for the palace revolutions of C18.

Peter II (2 Oct 1715–18 Jan 1730) Boy Emp of Russia (1727), whose short reign was dominated 1st by the Menshikov faction, then by the Dolgoruky.

Son of Tsarevich Alexis (the murdered son of PETER I) and the last male Romanov, he was the plaything of the magnates, under whose rule the autocracy of the Crown was further reduced in the interests of the *boyars*, while Russia played a passive role abroad. While Pr A. D. Menshikov was in power, Peter was affianced to his daughter, Maria (1727). On his fall (Sept 1727), Peter was betrothed to Pr Alexis Dolgoruky's daughter, Catherine (1729), but he d on the day fixed for the wedding.

Peter III (10 Feb 1728–6/17 July 1762) Emp of Russia (Dec 1761–June 1762), who admired K FREDERICK II of Prussia and saved him from destruction by ending Russia's participation in the SEVEN YEARS WAR (1756–63) against him. He also freed the nobility from compulsory State service and made other comparatively liberal changes until he was overthrown and killed in a guards coup which placed his wife on the throne as CATHERINE II.

b at Kiel, W Germany, son of Charles Frederick, D of Holstein-Gottorp, and his wife, Anna, daughter of Emp PETER I of Russia; was recognized as heir to the Russian throne by his aunt, Empss ELIZABETH; brought to Russia to be ed for this post, he was received into the Orthodox Ch (Nov 1742) and renamed Grand Duke Peter Feodorovich; m (1745) the future Empss Catherine II. Peter's reputation as a feeble-minded philanderer unfit for the throne is based on the hostile memoirs of Catherine and her friends. In fact, he enjoyed his books, spoke Russian, French and German, and played the violin; while his addiction to beer and practical jokes was nothing unusual at the Russian Court. He idolized Frederick the Great and all things Prussian, and neglected to cultivate the guards or the *dvoryane*, a mistake not made by his wife from whose bed he soon became an exile. On succeeding to the throne he wasted no time in making his presence felt at home and abroad. At home, in the famous Manifesto of the Emancipation of the Nobility (Feb 1762) he liberated the *dvoryane* from compulsory service to the State; but he also alienated powerful factions round the throne by bringing into office his new, untried entourage, and by starting to reorganize the guards on Prussian lines. He also horrified the pious by handing over Ch lands to the State to be run by the College of Economy, and turning monks and clergy into salaried officials of the Crown (decrees of Feb 1762 and Mar 1762). In addition, he decreed the abolition of many State monopolies (Mar 1762). Abroad, he withdrew from the Seven Years War. He signed a peace Tr with Prussia (Apr/May 1762), restoring all the Prussian lands that Russia had conquered, and then joined Prussia in an alliance against Austria (June 1762). He also planned a war against Denmark in order to recover Schleswig for his native Holstein. Meanwhile, his clever wife was organizing a palace coup with a faction of the guards and the connivance of leading politicians. She seized power on 28 June 1762, and Peter agreed to abdicate on the 29th. While under arrest at Ropshe, near St Petersburg, he was assassinated by a group of guardsmen in circumstances the details of which have never come to light.

Philip I (The Handsome) (22 July 1478–25 Sept 1506) ArchD of Burgundy (ie the Netherlands) (Mar 1482), K of Castile (Nov 1504).

Son of the future Emp MAXIMILIAN I and Mary, Dss of Burgundy, he became actual ruler of Burgundy when his father handed over to him in Aug 1494. He was less absolutist and more popular than his father. In accordance with the foreign policies of Maximilian and K FERDINAND II of Aragon, he m (1496) Joanna (The Mad), daughter of Ferdinand and ISABELLA, Q of Castile. He revived Anglo-Netherlands trade by the *Intercursus Magnus* Tr with K HENRY VII of England (Feb 1496). He visited Spain *via* Paris (1501–3); on Isabella's death (26 Nov 1504), he claimed to rule Castile on behalf of his mentally unstable wife (against the claim of his father-in-law, Ferdinand); he made a 2nd trip to Spain, this time by sea. Forced to take shelter in a storm at Weymouth (Jan 1506), he was entertained by Henry VII at Windsor (Jan 1506) and negotiated 2 Trs with him designed to win English support for his claims in Spain: the Tr of

Windsor (Feb 1506) and the *Malus Intercursus* Tr (Apr 1506), the latter, as its name implies, showing how far Philip was prepared to sacrifice the Netherlands trading interests to England in support of his personal ambitions in Spain. He was backed in Spain by the anti-absolutist, anti-Aragonese high nobility; Ferdinand was forced to sign the Tr of Villafavilla (June 1506), agreeing to leave Castile and allow Philip to take over. None of these Trs had much effect, however, for Philip d suddenly at Burgos, and Ferdinand resumed control.

Philip II (21 May 1527–13 Sept 1598) K of Spain (Jan 1556). During his reign Spain entered her Golden Age as the greatest power in Europe and a centre of high artistic and literary achievement. He inherited the Spanish peninsula (except for Portugal, which he conquered), the Netherlands, most of Italy, as well as Franche Comté, and a vast colonial emp. He failed in his attempts to invade England, dominate France, and stop the N Netherlands (Holland) from becoming independent; but he contained the Ottoman Emp, and made Spain, Italy and S Netherlands (Belgium) safe for the COUNTER-REFORMATION; he also gave his possessions an advanced system of Gov, combining centralized absolutism and regional self-Gov. But what he attempted was unrealistic and far beyond his resources. He drained Castile of money and manpower, and when he d the economic and psychological seeds of Spanish decline were already germinating.

Son of the Emp CHARLES V and Isabella of Portugal; ed in Spain by tutors who gave him a good grounding in history and politics, but left him weak at languages; from 1542 onwards he was Regent whenever his father left Spain; travelled, 1548–51, extensively in Italy, the Netherlands and Germany, though without learning much about the people or their languages; m 1st (1543) his 16-year-old cousin, Maria Manuela of Portugal (d 12 July 1545, 4 days after giving birth to Don CARLOS); m 2nd (1554) Q MARY I of England (d 17 Nov 1558); m 3rd (1560) Elizabeth of Valois, eld daughter of K HENRY II of France and CATHERINE DE MEDICI, a political marriage resulting from the Tr of Cateau-Cambrésis which turned into a love-match, producing 2 daughters of whom Philip was very fond: Isabella Clara Eugenia and Catherina Micaela. Elizabeth d on 3 Oct 1568, and Philip m 4th (1570) Anna of Austria, the daughter of the Emp Maximilian II, his cousin (d 1580, leaving one survivor out of 5 children: the future K PHILIP III). Philip inherited his share of Charles V's legacy (the Emp FERDINAND I taking the rest) in piece-meal fashion. He became K of Naples and D of Milan on the occasion of his marriage to Q Mary I of England; D of Burgundy (the Netherlands) when Charles V abdicated there on 25 Oct 1555; and K of Spain (ie K of Castile, Leon and Navarra, with the Indies, and K of Aragon and Catalonia with Sardinia), and K of Sicily on Charles V's abdication on 16 Jan 1556; then ruler of Franche Comté in Feb 1556. He remained in the Netherlands as ruler from Oct 1555 to Aug 1559, when he moved to Spain where he remained for the rest of his life. He chose Madrid as his capital in 1561, and d at nearby El Escorial, his favourite residence, which was a combination of a tomb for Charles V, a Hieronymite monastery and a royal palace, the building of which (1563–83) was his greatest pleasure.

His character: In lonely eminence he ruled his vast emp, a truly working monarch, spending long hours at his desk, red-eyed from reading and annotating a relentless deluge of documents. A small, aloof, austere, melancholy and scholarly person, in dark clothes, with a scarcely audible voice, a disconcerting stare and an icy smile, he submitted himself without reserve to the iron commands of duty and kept his feelings in a strait-jacket of composure, showing not a hint of glee at the victory of Lepanto, or of pain at the disaster of the ARMADA, and bearing a long and painful illness (possibly diabetic gangrene) to an exemplary death without a murmur of complaint. He was deeply religious, with a tender conscience which needed regular reassurance of rectitude, which his nimble-witted confessors were able to provide even in situations where he committed crimes to the glory of God. The arrest of his son, Don Carlos, the strangling of the Netherlands envoy, Montigny, the charge of heresy against his Secretary, PÉREZ, before the INQUISITION, were breaches of morality, which, by theologians as resourceful as any MACHIAVELLI, were justified as means to divine ends in the *raison d'état* of the Kdom of God. A barrier of sensitiveness and suspicion inside him cut him off from his fellow human beings, with the exception of his 3rd wife and their daughters. Long, loyal and distinguished service did not save Margaret of Austria, or ALBA, or Don JOHN, or Pérez, or FARNESE from being thrown away like squeezed oranges when their usefulness had passed.

His religion: The ends Philip pursued were the defence of the lands he had inherited and if possible their extension; though he fought the Turks and persecuted heretics, it would be an exaggeration to call him the secular champion of the Counter-Reformation. He attacked Islam and Protestantism only in so far as they were political threats to the Spanish monarchy. He refused the appeal of Pp Pius V for a crusade against the Ottoman Emp at the time of the Holy League; in order not to antagonize England or the German Prs he insisted that in trying to suppress the REVOLT OF THE NETHERLANDS he was fighting rebellion, not heresy; he spent the 1560s and 1570s trying to protect Prot England from papal hostility; he went to war against Pp PAUL IV, and quarrelled with most subsequent Pps about foreign policy and the extent of papal power in Spain. No K in Europe – not even the Prot Prs – had such power over his Ch as he had in Spain. For his relations with the papacy were criss-crossed with ambiguities. Abroad, politically-minded Pps worked against his domination of Italy and his ambitions in France, while religiously-minded Pps had no support from him for their unpragmatic crusades against Turkey or England. At home, he needed papal permission to collect the clerical taxation which outdid the revenues of the Indies; while, on the other hand, he fought a running battle with successive Pps over papal jurisdiction in Spain, as well as in Milan, Naples and Sicily. While his delegates ensured that the COUNCIL OF TRENT came out intransigently against compromise with Protestantism, he allowed the rulings of Trent to be put into effect in Spain only as and when he wanted, making sure that they brought about no diminution of the powers of the Crown, especially over the appointment of Bps. Though he pursued a policy of ruthless persecution of Jews, Moors and Prots, he also continued the deliberate policy of *regalismo* pursued by his predecessors since FERDINAND and ISABELLA. The Spanish Inquisition enjoyed his full support, partly because it was the only all-Spanish institution: the only court whose powers were not hampered by the *fueros*, or constitutional rights, of Aragon or the other non-Castilian provs. Under Fernando de Valdés, Archbp of Seville, and Inquisitor-Gen from 1547–68, the Inquisition made short work of Spain's puny Prot movement as well as intellectual deviationists in general. The Spanish *Index* was more severe than the papal one; and, to round off the intellectual *apartheid*, a decree of Nov 1559 forbade Spaniards to study in foreign universities. At the same time, papal power in Spain was severely restricted. The Council of Castile, eg, decreed in Oct 1572 that there was no appeal to courts outside Spain in ecclesiastical cases. The Carranza case illustrates the struggle between K and Pp. Bartolomé de Carranza, Archbp of Toledo and Primate of Spain, was arrested on 22 Aug 1559 on charges of heresy; despite papal bulls transferring the case to Rome, he was kept in a Spanish prison for 7 years. Even when the Pp succeeded in transferring the case to Rome (Dec 1566) Spanish ambassadors managed to delay a conclusion of the case until Apr 1576, when an ambiguous verdict was issued only a few weeks before Carranza's death.

His Government: With his emp, Philip inherited from Ferdinand and Isabella and Charles V the most advanced bureaucratic machinery in the world at that time. The 10 regions which constituted it – apart from Castile – were ruled by the viceroys of Aragon, Catalonia, Valencia, Navarra, Sardinia, Naples, Sicily, New Spain (Mexico) and Peru, and the Gov-Gen of the Netherlands. These were supervised by a series of councils sitting in Madrid. Philip himself added to these by creating the Council of Italy to supervise Milan, Naples and Sicily, hitherto under the Council of Aragon. Above these councils in the pyramid of gov were 1 or 2 specialized councils (eg the Council for Finance, the Council of the Inquisition) with, at the top, the Council of State which, however, never became a supreme policy-making cabinet, but remained a loose group of Grandees and ecclesiastics, favourites and ministers who gave Philip written opinions (*consultas*) on matters when he asked for them. All these councils had secs who corresponded with Philip through his private secretary. They had admin, legislative and judicial powers, but they were much concerned with the last, and ground slowly through their gov work, operating as courts of law. Philip alone knew everything and himself made policy, consulting a shifting *ad hoc* inner circle of servants he distrusted least. These last tended to divide themselves into factions, in rivalry for the ear of the K, and his remunerative posts and privileges, and advocating rival policies. Such were the Alba and Eboli factions in the early part of the reign – hawks and doves over the Netherlands, doves and hawks over England. Trusting no one, preferring letters to interviews, taking more notice of confessors than ministers, promoting bureaucrats who were jurists or clerics with univ degrees in preference to the amateur sons of the high nobility, Philip waded methodically through the tide of paper, taking his time over the petty as well as the momentous. In Castile, the core of his empire, he was absolute, the *Cortes* (or Parl) having already been deprived of any power to control taxation or legislation. In the other provs, Aragon, Catalonia, Navarra etc, the Crown had never succeeded in breaking the power of the *Cortes* mainly because it was hardly worth the trouble, so poor were they in wealth and manpower. It was Castile and her colonies which financed the rest of Philip's emp, and there, unfortunately for her future, he had the power and the machinery to milk her at will. On the whole, it was a system of Gov which was at its best under Philip, but which already revealed fatal defects: procrastination and caution, conservatism and corruption, the indiscipline caused by the sale of offices, the latent conflict between his centralizing tendencies and his respect for prov *fueros*, the revolts caused by the attempts at Castilianization and by the clamping on of the Counter-Reformation. To run it was well beyond the powers of such a glutton for Gov as Philip II: it overwhelmed his subnormal successors.

Foreign affairs. Philip's reign can be divided into 2 main periods. 1555-79 was a time of comparatively low revenues; when he was forced to make peace with France; maintain neutrality towards England; and concentrate his attention on the Med in order to contain the last thrusts of the Ottoman Turks and put down the Moriscos' revolt in Granada; and when his absolutist attempts to make the Netherlands pay their way sparked off the Revolt which outlasted his reign. 1580-98 saw a big increase in revenues, allowing him to indulge in more aggressive policies; a stalemate in the Turkish wars enabling him to concentrate on the Atlantic and N Europe, a switch which resulted in the conquest of Portugal, the suppression of the Aragonese revolt, and grandiose schemes for the final solution of his problems in England, France and the Netherlands by a fully orchestrated complex of diplomatic, military and naval aggression.

1555-79 (a) *Low revenues* limited his activities during these years. In spite of the fact that his income more than doubled, his expenses continually added to the debt of some 20 million ducats which he inherited from Charles V; at his death he left a debt of over 100 million ducats. Only 11-20 % of his income came from the silver and other resources of the Indies, while about 20 % came from the Ch, and the bulk was provided by savage taxation on the people of Castile. All the other provs, whether in the Spanish peninsula or in Italy or the Netherlands, were a drain on Castilian resources; and Philip only succeeded in financing his operations by borrowing from the bankers, 1st the Fuggers and then especially the Genoese, who also managed the international transfer of money among the widespread theatres of Philip's activity. Thus, while the Indies revenue was not a large proportion of his total income, the prospect of the next silver fleet enabled him to tide over present difficulties by borrowing from the future. Nevertheless, he went bankrupt twice in this period (1557 and 1575), not repudiating all his debts, but converting them into higher-interest, longer-term loans: again laying up trouble for his successors – for the deluge would ensue when the silver ceased to flow. In the meantime, the Indies revenue in the 1560s was only about a quarter of what it would become in the 1580s, and his early foreign ventures were modest in proportion. (b) *Peace with France* came at last in the Tr of Cateau-Cambrésis (Apr 1559) after Philip's moderately successful participation in the last of the HABSBURG–VALOIS WARS (1552–9). Though the French took Calais and kept Metz, Toul and Verdun, they abandoned their claims to Italy, leaving Spain supreme there. (c) *Neutrality towards England* was forced on Philip, first by the paucity of his resources in comparison with his responsibilities; second by the hope that a friendly England would not aid his enemies in the Netherlands and France; third by the danger that the elimination of Q ELIZABETH I might put MARY, Q OF SCOTS on the English throne and thus turn Britain into a satellite of France, which, under the rule of her family, the Guises, Philip regarded as a dangerous rival. Thus, in spite of Elizabeth's non-RC Ch settlement, Philip stopped Pp Pius IV from excommunicating her in 1561, and blocked an excommunication move at the Council of Trent in 1563. Similarly, in spite of Elizabeth's policy of giving comfort to the Hugs, shelter to the Dutch privateers, and support to HAWKINS's 3 piratical invasions of the Indies, Philip

turned down the Eboli faction's demand for war against England, did not invade
England during the Revolt of the Northern Earls of 1569 or the Ridolfi plot of
1571, did everything he could to prevent Pp Pius V from excommunicating
Elizabeth in 1570, and resisted papal exhortations for an anti-British crusade
until the political and economic situation required one. (d) *The war with Turkey*
was a defensive operation to protect Italy and Spain and the communications
between them from attacks from the Sultan's fleet and raids by his allies, the
N African corsairs. A realistic statesman first and a Christian second, Philip
refused to indulge in any grandiose schemes, advocated strongly by Pp Pius V,
for a crusade against the Infidel. As became clear in this period, the Med was far
too big for Spain to conquer Turkey, or vice versa. In any case, there was no
point in attacking Turkey without a large fleet, as Philip realized when he
prematurely conquered the island of Djerba, off Tripoli, on 13 Mar 1560 – only to
surrender it to the Turkish fleet on 29 July 1560, after great loss of men and
ships. Philip now organized the dockyards of Sicily, Naples and Catalonia into a
vast ship-building programme, which began to show results: eg when the Spanish
fought off the Algerian siege of Oran (Apr–May 1563), and the huge Turkish
enterprise against Malta (May–Nov 1565). The great Ottoman Emp SULAIMĀN
II d on 5/6 Sept 1566, but the next few years saw no Spanish aggression in the
Med, for Alba was involved in the Netherlands from 1567 onwards, and Don
John was putting down the revolt in Granada (1569–70). The Turks then conquered Cyprus from Venice (July 1570–July 1571), and the crusading zeal of Pp
Pius V managed to organize Venice and Spain into the Holy League (May 1571)
guaranteeing an annual campaign against Turkey for the next 3 years. Both
Venice and Spain were out for their own divergent ends – the former demanding a
campaign in the E Med, the latter cautiously limiting itself to a holding operation
in the centre and W – but the League held together long enough under Don John
to destroy the Turkish fleet off Lepanto, W Greece, on 7 Oct 1571, killing its
commander, Ali Pasha. It was a resounding victory, which greatly enhanced
Christian self-confidence, but also, unfortunately, inflated Philip's belief in himself and Spanish confidence in him. Otherwise it changed little. The following
year the Turks were able to put to sea with another great fleet. After the death
of Pius V on 1 May 1572 the League crumbled, Venice signing a separate peace
with Turkey (Mar 1573). The last engagement was the capture of Tunis (Oct
1573) – another pointless operation like the conquest of Djerba, for again Spain
could not hold it and soon surrendered to the Turks (13 Sept 1574), who had a
fleet bigger than either had had at Lepanto. After this both Spain and Turkey
withdrew from active operations against one another, both realizing that the
conquest of the whole Med was beyond their means. There was peace till the
1590s, maintained tacitly at first, and then by the truces of 1578, 1580, 1581 and
later. (e) *The Moriscos' revolt in Granada* was one result of the wars with Turkey
and Algiers, for Moors and Spaniards, once capable of living peacefully alongside each other, now became mortal enemies. Philip decided to turn the Moors
into Spanish RCs by force, and his decree of Jan 1567 rendered illegal their
language, customs and whole way of life. Aided by Algiers, the Moriscos revolted
on 24 Dec 1568, and it took Don John 2 years to repress them. By a decree of
Oct 1570, all the Moriscos were deported in chains from Granada and scattered
over the rest of Spain – a desperate measure which improved security along the

Granada coast, but which simply spread the Morisco problem over a wider area. (f) *The Revolt of the Netherlands* had its origins in Philip's financial difficulties and religious convictions. In order, first, to collect more revenue in the Netherlands so that these rich provs would cease to be a drain on Spanish resources; and, second, to stiffen the R C Ch there so that it would combat the spread of heresy more effectively; he began to install the machinery of centralized absolutism, locating the levers of power in Madrid, and hurting the pride of the native nobility, infringing on the privileges of the provs and cities, harming the prosperity of the business classes, starving the workers, scandalizing the R C supporters of HUMANISM, stirring the Calvinists into fanatical outbreaks of iconoclasm, and producing a deep and complex – and eventually successful – revolt, which was an exhausting drain on Castilian manpower and treasure for the rest of Philip's reign and beyond.

1580–98 (a) *The influx of silver* into Spain rose to 4 times what it had been in the 1st decades of the reign, as Castile basked in the prosperity of the Atlantic trade, which broke records from 1562 onwards, and as developing techniques allowed the full exploitation of the silver mines (eg at Potosí, Peru, discovered in 1545, and at Zacatecas, Mexico, discovered in 1548). This seemingly limitless flow of wealth, which was magnified by the elastic credit offered by the bankers, fatally inflated the ego of Philip and the Spanish, already deluded by visions of grandeur aroused by the decline of Turkey and the weakness of France. Philip's ambitions increased as he turned away from the Med to the Atlantic and N Europe as the main sphere of his activity. (b) *The Turkish stalemate* made this reorientation possible. Spain and Turkey ceased to attack each other, and there was peace from 1574 to the 1590s. (c) *The conquest of Portugal* was the 1st move in the new direction, and it was handled by a new and aggressive chief minister, for Card GRANVELLE now replaced Pérez, who went into exile and disgrace. The Kdom of Portugal – the only part of the Spanish peninsula not under Philip's rule – began to be available to him on the death of the young K Sebastian on 4 Aug 1578 at the battle of Alcázarquivir in Morocco, where the headstrong monarch had led a motley, ill-planned crusade. Since his heir, his epileptic great-uncle, Card Henry, did not have long to live, Philip began to prepare the diplomatic and military ground for a takeover. There were several claimants to the throne, but Philip, whose mother Isabella was the eldest daughter of K Manoel I (1495–1521), was the strongest. He was opposed by Dom Antonio, prior of Crato and illegitimate son of Card Henry's brother. On Card Henry's death on 31 Jan 1580, Portugal was divided and leaderless, the towns in the Cortes supporting Dom Antonio, while most of the nobility had either been killed at Alcázarquivir or been bribed by Philip. Alba was recalled from retirement, and he marched on Lisbon in June 1580, supported by Santa Cruz and his fleet, which sailed into the mouth of the Tagus. Lisbon surrendered on 25 Aug 1580; the Cortes of Thomar recognized Philip as K on 15 Apr 1581, while he in turn respected all their *fueros*. Dom Antonio was defeated by Santa Cruz as he and a French squadron attempted to make the Azores a base for a counter-attack (1582–3). With Portugal, Philip united the whole Spanish peninsula, and gained a million new subjects, a long Atlantic coastline, a strong fleet, and a commercial emp stretching from Brazil across to Goa and the E Indies. (d) *The revolt of Aragon* also enabled him to improve his position in the peninsula, though to a very small degree. Aragon was

353

a separate Kdom from Castile, consisting of the provs of Aragon, Catalonia, Valencia and others. The revolt occurred only in the prov of Aragon, and it typically received no support from the others. In Aragon the nobility resented the gentle attempts of Philip to reduce their *fueros* (their separate constitutional privileges) and to subordinate the prov to the centralized absolutism of Madrid. Like the Netherlands before them, they feared the loss of their identity in a policy of wholesale Castilianization. Moreover, they especially objected to the attempts of Madrid to reduce their still-medieval powers over their vassals. Thus, when Philip, breaking tradition, appointed a non-Aragonese Viceroy in 1590, they flung their *fueros* in his face. This protest happened to coincide with the disgrace and flight of Philip's Sec, Antonio Pérez, who crossed the border to seek the protection of Aragon's separate courts of justice. Philip's attempts to reclaim Pérez sparked off riots in Zaragoza, where urban mobs led by rebel nobles twice rescued him (May and Sept 1591). In Nov 1591, Philip ordered the Castilian army into Aragon, and soon put down the aristocratic constitutionalism of the obstreperous nobility, who lacked the 2 supports which successful rebellion required at that time: mass support based on religious fervour, and foreign help. Philip was now in a position to destroy the independence of Aragon, and incorporate it into the Castilian system of Gov; but, strange as it may seem in the light of later moves towards centralized absolutism, he faithfully and typically kept his promise to maintain the Aragonese *fueros*, making only minor changes in his hour of triumph. (e) *The Netherlands, England and France* moved up in this period into top place in Philip's programme, though he vacillated greatly over the relative importance he attached to them. In view of the complex interplay of all the factors in an ever-changing scene, it is not surprising that he made important errors in his appreciation of the situation and got his priorities wrong. In the 1st phase, the emphasis was on the Revolt of the Netherlands, where Farnese became Gov-Gen in Oct 1578 and gradually reconquered the S provs, Antwerp falling at last on 17 Aug 1585. Farnese was then in a position to fall on Holland and Zeeland in the N; but, in the 2nd phase, the whole situation was changed by the death of the D of Anjou on 10 June 1584, which made the Hug, Henry of Navarre, heir to the throne of France. Thenceforth Philip regarded the Guise family, not as dangerous rivals, but as weak allies who needed his support, both as the leaders of the Cath League in France, and in the person of Mary, Q of Scots in England. Philip signed the Tr of Joinville with the French League in Dec 1584, promising 50,000 *escudos* a month to keep the 8th of the FRENCH WARS OF RELIGION going (ie the war of the 3 Henries, 1585–9), Philip regarding the Card de Bourbon as heir to the French throne. At the same time, the friction with England turned into open hostility as Elizabeth I signed the Tr of Nonsuch in Aug 1585, and openly sent an expedition under LEICESTER to aid the Dutch. Philip now decided that by defeating England he could both safeguard his Atlantic emp and subdue the Dutch and the Hugs. He despatched the ARMADA against England in 1588, using the League to hold Paris and prevent K HENRY III from coming to Elizabeth's aid, and ordering the reluctant Farnese to turn his back on Holland and Zeeland and prepare to invade England. The 3rd, and last, phase stems from the defeat of the Armada (July 1588) and the assassination of K Henry III (2 Aug 1589) which made Navarre K HENRY IV of France. Philip now succumbed to the temptations of open imperialism, and concentrated on the task of securing the French throne for his daughter, Isabella Clara Eugenia, the granddaughter of K Henry II and Catherine de Medici. With an army pinned down in Spain by the revolt of Aragon (1591–2), he again ordered Farnese to withdraw his troops from the Dutch front-line, where MAURICE OF NASSAU with English and French help was reconquering the middle provs of the S Netherlands. Farnese invaded France and rescued Paris from Henry IV's siege in Sept 1590, and then Rouen, Normandy, in Apr 1592. Spanish troops landed in Brittany in Oct 1590; others invaded Languedoc in Mar 1591; but Philip's aggressions only aroused French patriotism, and he could not compete with the popular and legitimate heir, especially when Henry turned RC on 25 July 1593. Once more in Philip's mind, worldly ambition triumphed over religious faith as he tried to prevent Pp Clement VIII from giving Henry absolution, on the ground that his conversion was not genuine. The Pp absolved Henry, however, on 17 Sept 1595. The same year, Henry IV, the Dutch, and the English declared war on Spain. Inside France, the League began to crack as the leader, Mayenne, submitted to Henry in Oct 1595. England, having made a disastrous attempt to take Lisbon and start a Portuguese war of liberation (Apr–June 1589, *see* DRAKE), then sent 2 expeditions to help Henry IV in Brittany and Normandy in 1590 and 1591, carried on a series of attacks on Spain's Atlantic shipping, and made a damaging raid on Cádiz in 1596. For his part, Philip sent 2 more Armadas to aid the Irish in their rebellion against England, but both were driven back by storms (1596, 1597). He was now greatly overextended. On 29 Nov 1596 he went bankrupt for the 3rd time, and then conceded defeat in France by signing the Tr of Vervins (May 1598). The other 2 wars continued unsuccessfully into the new reign, the English until 1604, the Dutch until 1609. It is not so much that Philip had misjudged his priorities as that he had grossly over-estimated the resources of Castile, and set her targets which she was incapable of achieving. And the tragedy was that her heroic efforts to do so left her, already in 1598, embarked on her long, slow decline.

Philip III (14 Apr 1578–31 Mar 1621) K of Spain (1598) who presided over the beginnings of the DECLINE OF SPAIN, leaving Gov to Favourites who enriched themselves at Spain's expense.

Son of K PHILIP II and his 4th Q consort, Anna of Austria; m (1599) Archdss Margaret of Austria, sister of the future Emp FERDINAND II (d in childbirth, 1611). Short, fat, red-haired and Habsburg-jawed, he suffered from poor health and apathy and, concentrating on hunting, bull-fights, feasting and piety, he was too lazy to rule, taking up to 6 months to reply to a *consulta*. Reversing the whole trend of C16, he handed over central control to Favourites (*validos*), and allowed power to decentralize into the hands of the Grandees, setting precedents which were followed throughout C17. His 2 Favourites were the D de LERMA (in power 1598–1618) and his son, the D de Uceda, who ousted him (1618–21).

In foreign affairs he continued to act as if Spain were the leading power of Europe – an illusion created by the divisions of her enemies – and like a sleepwalker tried to follow the ambitious policies of Philip II, not so much expansionism as maintaining the existing situation by active diplomacy and periodic warfare in widely scattered parts of Europe. The Spanish financial crisis forced him to rely mainly on the former. With England, after an unsuccessful Armada invasion (1601) and landing in Kinsale, Ireland (1602), he allowed economic realities and ArchD Albert of the Netherlands to persuade him to make peace with K JAMES I by the Tr of London (Aug 1604). Similarly in the Netherlands (Belgium), after initial fighting (1600–4) when MAURICE and the Dutch invaded and were stopped at Nieuwpoort (2 July 1600), and when Spinola resumed the offensive for Spain by retaking Ostende (20 Sept 1604), and invading Frisia, the big fall in silver shipments (1604–5), leading to a royal bankruptcy (1607), made peace imperative, and Albert and OLDENBARNEVELT negotiated the 12-year Truce (Apr 1609). With France – temporarily and untypically pro-Spanish after the assassination of K HENRY IV (14 May 1610) had put power into the hands of the Q-Mother, MARIE DE MEDICI – Spain signed the Tr of Fontainebleau (Apr 1611) for the double marriage of K LOUIS XIII to the Spanish Infanta known as Anne of Austria, and her brother, the future K PHILIP IV, to Louis' sister, Elizabeth of Bourbon. The marriages were celebrated in 1615. In Italy (1613–17), Spain fought Charles Emmanuel I, D of Savoy, who had seized Monferrato from Mantua, eventually making him give it back (Tr of Pavia, Oct 1617). Spanish representatives such as the Gov of Milan, the Viceroy of Naples and the ambassador to Venice, seem to have run their own foreign policy without much oversight from Madrid. The Gov of Milan fortified the Valtelline, recognizing its importance as part of the 'Spanish Road'; but this offended Venice which backed Savoy and France. The 3 Spanish representatives are said to have hatched the 'Conspiracy of Venice' for the overthrow of the Republic (1618), but the truth about this mysterious episode has never been fully established. In Germany the Spanish ambassadors were similarly active, forming a powerful 'Spanish party' at the Court of the Emps RUDOLF II and MATTHIAS, urging these reluctant rulers to eliminate the Prots in their States, and generally heightening the tensions which led to the THIRTY YEARS WAR (1618–48). It was the Spanish ambassador, the Count of Oñate, who dominated the negotiations leading up to the Tr called after him (June and July 1617) which named the crusading absolutist, Ferdinand of Styria, as the next Emp (FERDINAND II). By 1618 the comparatively peaceful Lerma had been replaced by a more aggressive Gov, and on the outbreak of the Thirty Years War Spain occupied the Valtelline (July 1620) and the Rhine Palatinate (Sept 1620) – both to keep the 'Spanish Road' open – and also sent money and troops to aid the Emp at the battle of the White Mountain (8 Nov 1620). Thus when Philip III d his country's long death agonies had just begun.

Home affairs were dominated by the expulsion of the Moriscos and the economic crisis. The expulsion of the Moriscos, decided upon in Apr 1609, was a psychological compensation for the exactly contemporary Truce with the Dutch. These Moors, theoretically converted to Christianity, steadfastly refused full cultural integration with the Spanish; the *hidalgos* despised them for being non-Spanish and non-Christian, but most of all for being non-noble; while the masses envied them their enterprise and industry. They were especially a problem in Valencia and Aragon, where they were fast-growing minorities: 33% and 20% of the population, respectively. Between 1609 and 1614 about 275,000 from Spain as a whole were shepherded to the ports and shipped to Africa, a harsh solution, motivated mainly by religious fervour, but organized with a bureaucratic efficiency no other State could match at that time. The extent of the economic damage caused by the expulsion is still disputed by historians, but there is no doubt that with her population in decline this was a loss of manpower that Spain could ill afford. Moreover, it was a heavy blow to the urban middle classes, many of whom had lent money to the Moriscos, or to the noble land-lords of the Moriscos, who now defaulted, having lost their vassals. It was also a blow to the income of the INQUISITION in Valencia and Aragon, leaving them with few heretics to persecute and fine. In addition, the expulsion represented a significant interference by Castile in the internal affairs of these peripheral próvs. The K also intervened in Catalonia, aiming at curbing the private warfare of its brigand-like nobility and at raising more revenues from its prospering townsfolk; but this was only a tentative invasion of the rights of a very sensitive prov. It was left to PHILIP IV and OLIVARES to risk the full confrontation. The economic crisis was thus forcing Castile to take desperate measures. Its causes and cures were endlessly debated by perceptive economic experts (the *arbitristas*), but with no practical effect on a monarchy paralysed by personal and structural weak-nesses, and incapable of applying other than short-term remedies of desperation which only made the situation worse. The K and his Court were wantonly extravagant. His favourite, Lerma, cynically enriched himself and his relatives and friends out of public resources, partly as a means of building a faction and staying in power. Lacking the courage, and outside Castile the constitutional right, to increase taxation, the Gov could only supplement its declining income by recurring bankruptcies and periodic debasements, when the market was flooded with cheap copper coinage (*vellón*). Their occasional lurches back into monetary purity only increased business chaos. The replacement of Lerma by Uceda failed to appease the demons of economic recession, and when he d Philip left an empire in decay and a people without hope.

Philip IV (8 Apr 1605–17 Sept 1665) K of Spain (1621), who handed over power to Favourites, and hastened the decline of SPAIN by committing her abroad to tasks beyond her strength, and at home to coinage manipulation and other fatal financial devices to pay for them. He failed to reconquer Holland, which was continuing the REVOLT OF THE NETHERLANDS; showed no profit in the THIRTY YEARS WAR; lost a long war against the France of RICHELIEU and MAZARIN; had some success with the REVOLT OF CATALONIA, but none with the REVOLT OF PORTUGAL; and left his throne to his only legitimate son, the childless physical wreck, CHARLES II.

Eld son of K PHILIP III and his Q consort Margaret of Austria; m 1st (1615) Isabel of Bourbon, daughter of K HENRY IV of France (d 6 Oct 1644; and her son, Baltasar Carlos, d 9 Oct 1646); m 2nd (1649) Maria Anna (Mariana) of Austria, daughter of Emp FERDINAND III, her son becoming K Charles II. In addition he had numerous mistresses (mainly actresses selected for him by a network of agents) by whom he had at least 30 bastards, only one – Don John José of Austria, son of the sweet-voiced María Calderón – receiving official recognition. Thanks to the work of Velázquez, his features and those of his family and Court are well known. He swung between seasons of sexual de-bauchery and bouts of religious remorse, while in between he preferred the company of writers, artists and horses to the drudgery of Gov. Consequently, he left politics 1st to OLIVARES (1621–43), then to HARO (1643–61) and finally to the joint care of the Count of Castrillo and the D of Medina de las Torres (1661–5). The other important person in his life was Sor María, the mystical abbess of the Convent of the Immaculate Conception at Ágreda, Aragon, whom he met in July 1643, and who advised him by letter for the rest of his life. Thinking his lechery was the cause of Spain's collapse, he asked her to intercede with Heaven to make him chaste, but without success. He was thus chastised – to name only his chief afflictions – by the economic and moral decline of Spain, and the bankruptcy of its Gov; by the Tr of Münster (Jan 1648), granting independence to Holland; by the Trs of Westphalia (Oct 1648) and the Tr of the Pyrenees (Nov 1659), conceding victory to France; by the loss of Portugal, officially recognized (Tr of Lisbon, Feb 1668) soon after his death; and by the total inadequacy of his only heir.

Philip V (19 Dec 1683–9 July 1746) 1st Bourbon K of Spain (1700), who succeeded in winning his inheritance in spite of the challenge of the Habsburgs in the War of the Spanish Succession (*see* LOUIS XIV); and, spurred on by his Q, Isabella Farnese, started the revival of Spain after her C17 Decline (*see* SPAIN). At home he strengthened the monarchy and stimulated the economy; abroad he regained provs in Italy which had been lost to Austria, and challenged Great Britain in the colonies.

Son of Louis the Dauphin (son of K Louis XIV) and his wife, Marie Anne (daughter of Ferdinand, El of Bavaria); m 1st (1701) María Luisa of Savoy (d 1714, leaving 2 children who became K Luis I and K FERDINAND VI of Spain); m 2nd (1714, by proxy) Isabella Farnese (daughter of Odoardo, the eld son of Ranuccio II, D of Parma) by whom he had 2 sons: Don Carlos (later K CHARLES III) and Don Philip (she d 20 July 1766). In his youth – as the D of Anjou, and as the K of Spain fighting for his inheritance (1702–13/14) – he showed many signs of vigorous and courageous leadership; but after his 2nd marriage he declined into a depressed hypochondriac, totally enslaved to his iron-willed wife by sexual appetites out of the ordinary even in a Bourbon, and generally inclining to lassitude, religiosity, gloom, eccentricity and insanity. For a time, in a fit of conscientious ardour, he abdicated (Jan 1724) in favour of Luis I; but the latter soon d of smallpox, and Philip had to resume his responsibilities (Aug 1724).

In the War of the Spanish Succession he successfully defended the throne he had inherited by the will of K CHARLES II against the Habsburg claim in the person of the ArchD Charles (later the Emp CHARLES VI). His rival was backed by prov rebellions in Catalonia, Aragon and Valencia, well supplied by the British navy, but Philip had a powerful French army and the loyalty of the people of Castile. Eventually he prevailed in the peninsula, but at the cost of dependencies elsewhere. By the Trs of Utrecht (1713) and Rastatt (1714) Philip kept Spain and the colonies, but renounced the French throne and ceded the Netherlands (Belgium), Milan, Naples and Sardinia to Austria; Sicily to Savoy; and Minorca and Gibraltar to Britain, as well as the *asiento* (the monopoly of importing slaves into the Spanish colonies) and the *navio de permiso* (the right to send one ship a year to trade with Spanish America). This settlement gave Spain a great opportunity to climb out of her C17 decline by reducing her commitments abroad, and increasing her resources at home. First, it cut down Spain's responsibilities by trimming away those Continental possessions which had thus far given her such a false idea of her own strength, and seduced her into religious and political ambitions which were not in her interests. Second, it increased the monarchy's resources by enabling it to eliminate the constitutional liberties (*fueros*) of the rebel provs. Aragon and Valencia were given new forms of Gov in 1707, Majorca in 1715, and Catalonia in 1716 (by the new constitution, the *Nueva Planta*). These changes left only Navarra and the Basque provs still in possession of their *fueros*, and enabled the Crown to incorporate the rest into the Castilian admin system, increase its revenue by more rational taxation methods, stimulate the economy by reducing internal customs barriers, and loosen the archaic grip of the COUNTER-REFORMATION on intellectual life by founding such institutions as the Academy of Language, the National Library and the Royal Academy of History. Philip and his ministers grasped this opportunity at home, but frittered it away abroad.

At home, 1700–14, Spain was effectively ruled from a distance by Louis XIV through ministers sent from France, eg Jean Jacques Amelot, the French ambassador, and Jean Henri Louis Orry, a financial specialist. Backed by Philip's sensible 1st Q, and opposed by the usual forces of resistance – the nobles, the Ch and the provs – these ministers submitted Spain to healthy doses of what COLBERT had done for France: the reform of the admin system, the stimulation of the economy, and increase in the revenues. After 1714, when Isabella Farnese took control, the ministers she brought in continued this trend towards centralized ABSOLUTISM. From 1716 to 1719 Giulio Alberoni governed Spain as the Q's confidant, though he lacked a state office. The son of a gardener in Piacenza who rose to be a Card (1717), he extended the power of the Crown by reducing the role of the slow and routine-bound Councils; he used this power to reform the Treasury, rationalize taxation, reduce waste and peculation, build an army, a war fleet and a merchant fleet, attract foreign artisans, and in other mercantilist ways stimulate trade and industry, both in Spain and the colonies. From 1719 to 1726 Bn Juan Guillermo Ripperdá occupied a similar position and followed similar policies. A Prot colonel from Holland who became a Cath and a Grandee, he was full of new plans for economic growth, but lost his post before much could be done. From 1726 to 1736 Don José Patiño took charge after a long and valuable career as *intendente* in several provs, where he was mainly concerned with naval admin. Appointed Sec of the Navy and the Indies, then also of the Treasury, he was chiefly responsible for producing the revenue, the ships and the troops required by the Q's adventurous foreign policy. From 1738 to 1743 Don José del Campillo and (1743–54) Zenón de Somodevilla, Marqués de la Ensenada, continued these efforts at admin reform, economic revival and rearmament.

Abroad Spain's main fields of activity were Italy and the American colonies. Italy became an obsession of the Spanish Crown. Even after the Utrecht settlement Spain and Austria remained technically at war until 1720, because Philip refused to acknowledge his Italian losses to Charles VI, and the latter still hankered after the Spanish throne. In addition, Philip also asserted his claim to the throne of France, where the child-K LOUIS XV was not expected to survive. The main drive towards war in Italy, though, was the determination of the Q to win the 2 Duchies of Parma-Piacenza and Tuscany for her sons, Don Carlos and Don Philip. The war of 1717–20 formed part of Alberoni's aggressive designs and began with the Spanish invasion of Sardinia (Aug 1717) and Sicily (July 1718). France, Britain and Holland in their Triple Alliance of Jan 1717, however, were determined to preserve peace and the Utrecht settlement. Without declaring war, the British fleet destroyed the new Spanish squadron off Cape Passaro, Sicily (31 July/11 Aug 1718); while Austria joined the alliance, making it Quadruple (July/Aug 1718); and French armies invaded Spain at both ends of the Pyrenees (1719–20). This was too much for Spain. Alberoni fell in Dec 1719, and Philip made peace, accepting the terms of the Quadruple Alliance (Jan 1720). He gave Sardinia back to Savoy, and renounced his claim to Sicily; but Don Carlos and Don Philip were promised the succession to Parma-Piacenza and Tuscany, respectively, where the ruling families (Farnese and Medici) were nearing extinction. Under Ripperdá, 1719–26, Spain despaired of Franco-British aid for the Q's ambitions in Italy, and temporarily adopted the opposite policy of an alliance with Austria. The 1st Tr of Vienna (Apr 1725) was a minor diplomatic revolution which threw Britain, France and their many satellites into a counter-alliance – the Tr of Hanover (Aug/Sept 1725). War seemed imminent, but Austria proved not prepared to fight for Spanish interests, and Spain soon reverted to her old allies. Under Patiño (1721–36), Spain signed the Tr of Seville (Oct/Nov 1729) with France and Britain, settling commercial and other grievances, and agreeing that Don Carlos should become the D of Parma on the death of the last Farnese, D Antonio. When this occurred in Jan 1731, Britain and France negotiated the 2nd Tr of Vienna with Austria, then Holland and Spain (Mar–July 1731) whereby, among other agreements, Austria allowed Spanish troops into Parma, Piacenza and Tuscany. Don Carlos formally took up his duties as D of Parma in Oct 1732, and the 1st of Isabella Farnese's ambitions was realized. She achieved the 2nd in the WAR OF THE POLISH SUCCESSION (1733–5/8) by an act of opportunist aggression. Joining France in the Tr of the Escorial (1st Family Compact, Nov 1733), Spain conquered Naples, where Don Carlos entered in triumph on 10 May 1734. By the Tr of Vienna which ended the war (Nov 1738) Don Carlos gave up his claims to Parma, Piacenza and Tuscany, and received Naples and Sicily in return, becoming K Charles III of the Two Sicilies.

America became more and more of a problem as aggressive British merchants did all in their power to turn the trading concessions of the Tr of Utrecht (the *asiento* and the *navio de permiso*) into a wholesale economic invasion of the Spanish emp. Under Campillo (1736–43) and Ensenada (1743–54) – though the Italian ambitions of the Q still dominated foreign policy – America gradually gained more attention as British merchants bent the law as far as sheer piracy, and Spanish officials retaliated in ways which reminded the British public of the INQUISITION. The Anglo-Spanish War of Jenkins' Ear (which public opinion forced the British PM, WALPOLE, to declare on 19/30 Oct 1739) quickly evolved into the European WAR OF THE AUSTRIAN SUCCESSION (1740–48), which began on the death of the Emp Charles VI. Urged on by the Q, for whom peace-time was an unnatural waste of life, Philip entered a claim to the Austrian monarchy, since Charles VI had left no male heir. Before long Spain and France renewed their alliance by the Tr of Fontainebleau (2nd Family Compact, Oct 1743) and Franco-Spanish troops with naval support made a double thrust at Austrian positions in central and N Italy, striking N from Naples and S from Piedmont; though co-operating badly together. By the Tr of Aix-la-Chapelle

(Oct 1748) Don Philip at last received a principality to rule, gaining Parma and Piacenza as well as Guastalla from Austria. His mother had succeeded in her aims, but she was no longer in command of the Spanish foreign office. After Philip d, Spain's rulers wisely abandoned Italian ambitions, and concentrated instead on the struggle for the colonial empire.

Pitt, William, the Elder (15 Nov 1708–11 May 1778) Great statesman under GEORGE II and GEORGE III of Great Britain, who, beginning in the opposition to WALPOLE and PELHAM, forced his way into supreme office in the teeth of George II's hostility (1756–61). Ahead of his time, he could visualize Britain as the centre of a world network of colonies and trading relations; and with his global war effort he brought Britain victoriously through the SEVEN YEARS WAR (1756–63) and the consequent founding of the 1st British Emp. During the 1st decade of George III's reign, Pitt made a big contribution to the chronic instability of Gov: his incapacitating bouts of illness preventing him from being an effective PM over his own disastrous admin (1766–8), and his megalomania preventing anyone else from doing so until NORTH established himself as PM (1770–82). By temperament and belief a typical Country politician, he lacked the pragmatism necessary for Gov in C18 conditions. He was against corruption and party Gov; he opposed the attack on WILKES by a Parl influenced by the Court; he proposed Parl reform; and over the WAR OF AMERICAN INDEPENDENCE he favoured conciliation, but not withdrawal.

Younger son of Robert Pitt, Tory MP for Old Sarum, Wilts (and son of the Whig Thomas 'Diamond' Pitt, a rich, self-made India merchant) and his wife, Lady Harriet Villiers, daughter of Vt Grandison; ed at Eton (1718–26), Trinity, Oxford (1727), and the Univ of Utrecht, Holland (1728); m (1754) Hester Grenville, youngest sister of Earl Temple and George GRENVILLE: a very successful marriage. As an impecunious younger son, Pitt began his career in the army, obtaining a cornetcy in Cobham's Horse (1731), a dragoon regiment commanded by Vt Cobham, the very rich uncle of Pitt's school friend, George Lyttelton. He was chosen MP for Old Sarum, Wilts (a family borough) in 1735 and 1741; for Seaford, Sussex, 1747 and Aldborough, Yorks, 1754 (both NEW-CASTLE's boroughs); for Okehampton, Devon, 1756 (in the Lyttelton interest); and for Bath, Somerset, 1757 (backed by the corporation).

Under George II he first made his mark in the opposition to the Walpole admin (1721–42) in company with the followers of Vt Cobham: George Lyttelton and his cousins, the Grenville brothers: Richard (later 1st Earl Temple), George and James. Known as Cobham's Cubs or the Boy Patriots, these young men reinforced the older generation of Walpole's enemies led by CARTERET and Pulteney, and they appealed to the prejudices and principles of the Country and Tory backbenchers with policies based on the ideas of BOLINGBROKE. They also linked up with the Leicester House faction, led by Frederick, Pr of Wales, whose Groom of the Bedchamber at £400 a year Pitt became (1737–45). Pitt was a tall and commanding figure with a Roman nose, an 'eye that would cut a diamond' (as Shelburne put it), stagey behaviour, and an organ-like voice which filled the H of C and overflowed outside. Though he was maladroit in personal relationships and difficult to make friends with, his platform performances were unequalled in their day for their ability to raise mundane matters to the level of first principles and high drama. His rhetoric enraptured Parl and galvanized the nation. He stung Walpole and the K with his support of the Pr of Wales and his attacks on Walpole's foreign policy. Britain's colonial interests, he said, were being neglected in favour of Hanover: 'when trade is at stake . . . you must defend it or perish'. He was deprived of his commission in 1736, but nevertheless continued to play a major part in the opposition campaigns which eventually forced Walpole to resign (Feb 1742).

During the Pelham–Carteret admin (1742–4) he continued his attacks, posing as the voice of the people against a corrupt Court which was fighting the WAR OF THE AUSTRIAN SUCCESSION (1740–48) as a Continental, instead of a colonial and maritime, war, and which, even on the Continent, was attacking the enemy with insufficient vigour for fear of provoking attacks on the K's Electorate of Hanover, which was neutral. Britain, he said, was being treated like 'a province of a despicable Electorate'. In May 1744 Pitt fell seriously ill for the 1st time, with a cluster of symptoms which cut him off from public life many times later, and which defy satisfactory diagnosis: 'gout in the stomach', bowel disorders, high fever, insomnia, loss of appetite, nervous prostration and 'gout in the head', or insanity (probably manic depression), to name the chief ones. On the other hand, a fervent admirer, Sarah, the widow of MARLBOROUGH, d in Oct 1744 and eased his financial position considerably by leaving him £10,000 and the reversion of some very valuable estates.

The Pelham admin (1744–54) included the Grenvilles, but not at first Pitt, owing to the K's hostility, and possibly Pitt's bad health. George II's resistance was not overcome till 1746 when the K put himself in a weak position. He tried – and failed – to bring Carteret back into office, and then had to recall the Pelhams who had resigned in a body (Feb 1746). Among other concessions, the K had to give Pitt a post: Joint-Vice-Treasurer of Ireland (Feb 1746), then Paymaster-Gen of the Forces (May 1746), in which post Pitt ostentatiously refused to touch the usual perquisites, out of which holders of this office usually made a fortune. On the other hand, while projecting this image of Country purity, Pitt sat for 2 corrupt little pocket-boroughs in succession. At the same time, Pitt faithfully served the Gov in the H of C until his 2nd bout of serious illness threw him out of public life from Aug 1751 to Sept 1753.

The Newcastle admin (1754–6) kept on both Pitt and Henry FOX in their minor posts. Both were after high office, and both were H of C giants, capable of making political life impossible for the PM as he strove to run the Gov from the H of L. Pitt grew restive and renewed his contacts with the Leicester House faction, which since Frederick's death (23 Mar 1751) was led by his widow and BUTE, the tutor of the new Pr of Wales, the future K George III. He also attacked his own Gov in the H of C. This was the period of the DIPLOMATIC REVOLUTION and the run-up to the Seven Years War (1756–63). True to his 'blue-water' policy, Pitt opposed Newcastle for neglecting Britain's colonial and mercantile interests, seriously menaced by France, and buying expensive Continental allies in order to defend Hanover. He was dismissed in Nov 1755, while Fox was silenced with the post of Sec of State (S) (Nov 1755); but the disasters of the Seven Years War's 1st year and Pitt's savage denunciations and awesome appearance struck terror into the front bench and forced the Gov's resignation (Nov 1756). Approaches had been made to Pitt, but he haughtily refused to serve with Newcastle, and imperiously insisted on being in charge, with direct access to the K.

The Devonshire–Pitt admin (1756–7) contained Pitt as Sec of State (S) (Dec 1756). He had 'stormed the Closet'; and he immediately began to issue the orders which would galvanize Britain's war preparations. 'I am sure I can save this country, and nobody else can,' he told Devonshire, but no Gov could survive based only on backbench idealism, and lacking the co-operation of the K and the pragmatism of the chief political group, the Old Corps of WHIGS. The K dismissed Pitt on 6 Apr 1757, but it took nearly 3 months of negotiation before he eventually accepted the only workable solution.

The Newcastle–Pitt admin (1757–61) provided the broad-based stability needed to win the war. Pitt ran the war, while Newcastle managed Parl. Newcastle saw the revenue bills through both Houses, Pitt put the money to the most effective use. As Sec of State (S) from June 1757 he reached the peak of his greatness. Though he did much of his work in the sick-room, his warlike spirit animated the whole nation. Seeing the war as a world-wide system of interconnected battle fronts, he abandoned his former hostility to Continental warfare. He at last appreciated that the subsidies paid to Prussia and the reinforcements sent to the Army of Observation were not simply measures to protect Hanover; by pinning down French armies, they also reduced the pressure on Britain and the colonies. And in addition to these arrangements 'to win Canada on the banks of the Elbe', as he put it, he issued clear, detailed, aggressive plans for global strategy. He reorganized the navy and set in train a huge building programme. He defeated the French fleets, or blockaded them in harbour; and he made seaborne attacks on French coastal stations to prevent them from invading Britain or reinforcing their colonies. He put into force his scheme for raising a militia in the English counties; and he raised 2 regiments of infantry from the Highland clans who had not long before taken part in the 'FORTYFIVE' rebellion. At the same time his strategy embraced Canada, the W Indies, W Africa, India and the Philippines; and for it he was ready to look beyond seniority of service and promote young commanders of ability. His schemes rose to a crescendo of success in 1759 and 1760, but they were cut short by the death of George II (25 Oct 1760) and the accession of a new K and the appointment of a new Gov.

George III was determined to abandon the policies and politicians of his much-hated grandfather, and so he gave his favourite, Bute, in effect, supreme office. Under the Bute admin (1761–3), Pitt wished to anticipate Spain's expected entry into the war on the side of France by declaring war on her, but the K refused and Pitt resigned (5 Oct 1761) and went into opposition. When the peace preliminaries were debated in Dec 1762, Pitt attacked them without mercy. He had been thought too ill to take part, but he theatrically appeared at the last moment, dressed in black velvet and wrapped in flannel, with big boots and thick gloves; leaning on a crutch, he was helped to his place by friends. He spoke for 3 hours 25 minutes, blaming the Gov for being too generous to the enemy, for giving back too many sugar islands and too many concessions in the Canadian fisheries; in fact, for failing to cripple France so thoroughly that she would never again recover and endanger Britain. After Bute was driven from office, Pitt's aloof and prickly behaviour, as well as his physical and mental incapacity, forced the K to accept 2 Govs in succession under leaders – Grenville and ROCKINGHAM – he strongly objected to.

Under the Grenville admin (1763–5) the chief political issue was the Wilkes affair; and Pitt spent his time either criticizing the PM – his brother-in-law and life-long ally – or waiting in the wings in the country for a summons from the K. Typically, Pitt castigated Wilkes and his methods, but spoke strongly in support of his freedom from arrest as an MP, and in favour of the liberty of the press from Gov interference. Moreover, it was Pitt's ally and relative, Earl Temple, who was Wilkes's chief patron; and Chief Justice Pratt, the chief lawyer in Pitt's circle, who upheld Wilkes's Parl immunity from arrest in the Court of Common Pleas, and who condemned general warrants. In the long H of C debates on general warrants (Feb 1764) Pitt spoke many times in the opposition until, already a sick man again, he fell out of action till Jan 1766. The K was at his wits' end to free himself from Grenville's clutches, and made 3 attempts to bring Pitt back into office: in Aug 1763 through Bute, in May 1765 through Cumberland, and in June 1765 in direct conversations. Pitt was impossibly difficult, making egocentric demands in ambiguous but subservient language, and in the end the attempts failed.

Under the Rockingham admin (1765–6), when the chief issue was the quarrel which led to the War of American Independence, Pitt was able to appear in Parl again, Jan–May 1766. Taking his own peculiar line, he supported the repeal of the Stamp Act, but opposed the passing of the Declaratory Act, becoming the hero of the RADICALS in the City as well as the colonists in America. He argued that Britain was sovereign over the colonies, and could levy external duties on their commerce for the purpose of regulating the economy in Britain's interests, but that internal taxes for revenue purposes were illegal, since taxation was not part of the powers of governing, but a voluntary gift, which the colonists could not make as they were not represented in Parl. In July 1766 the K made a further attempt to persuade Pitt to take office, this time through Northington, and this time successful.

The Pitt admin (1766–8) was a catastrophe in spite of being the sort of mixed, non-party Gov that both Pitt and the K favoured. It included King's Friends and some Rockinghams, apart from followers of Pitt, while in the opposition were the other Rockinghams, as well as the Grenvilles and the Bedford gang. Pitt – till then famous as the Great Commoner – became the Earl of Chatham and Ld Privy Seal (July 1766), thus cutting himself off from the H of C, which already saw too little of him through his illness. In any case, he soon became seriously ill again for the 3rd time, and by Mar 1767 was no longer in charge of the Gov. He spent his time in a darkened room, communicating with the outside world only through his wife, and leaving GRAFTON, the 1st Ld of the Treasury, in command, though in practice each minister went his own way. Abroad, Pitt's scheme for an alliance with Prussia and Russia failed because at that time these States were only interested in E European affairs. Over India, the Gov was divided on how far the State should take over the responsibilities and income of the E India Co, until Grafton worked out a temporary compromise (June 1767). In America, the colonists were defying the Mutiny Act (1766), and Townshend, the brilliant but unrealistic Chancellor of the Exchequer, thought he had cleverly solved the revenue problem with his external duties (May 1767), but these simply turned the

Americans into enemies of all taxation imposed by Britain, whether internal or external. At home, the opposition in Parl forced the Gov to reduce the land tax from 4 shillings in the pound to 3. Most of the Rockinghams left the ministry in Nov 1766. A further reshuffle in the winter of 1767–8 brought in the Bedfords, who very soon dominated it with their harder line on the American problem. Ultimately, Pitt and his supporter Shelburne both resigned in Oct 1768, leaving Grafton as P M.

During the Grafton Admin (1768–70) Pitt became reconciled with the Grenvilles, and co-operated with the Rockinghams in trying to bring the Gov down. These were years of economic crisis and political unrest, with mounting American resistance, continuing emotion over Wilkes, the burgeoning Radical movement, and the savage satire of the letters of *Junius*. Pitt came out of his 3-year retirement in Jan 1770 and made strong Country-type attacks on the purity of the H of C, defiled as it was by royal 'influence'. He called the boroughs 'the rotten part of the constitution', and demanded Parl reform and the repeal of the Septennial Act. Grafton resigned (Jan 1770), and a further reshuffle placed Ld NORTH at the helm.

The North admin (1770–82) soon restored public stability, but Pitt became ever more hostile whenever he was fit, acting in concert with the City Radicals, and becoming too extreme for the aristocratic Rockinghams. (He was out of action May 1771–May 1774 and again Feb 1775–May 1777.) He even attacked the K, referring to his old enemy, George II, as 'the late good old king'. He attacked the Gov's conciliatory settlement of the Falkland Islands quarrel with Spain (1770–71). He supported attempts to reverse the H of C persecution of Wilkes (Apr 1770). He backed a bill to make it easier for Dissenters to hold public office (May 1772). He continued to regard the American rebels as law-abiding subjects who had been provoked into resistance by unwise measures; and after the Boston Tea Party (16 Dec 1773) he opposed the coercive measures, as well as the Quebec Act (1774). Nevertheless, he did not approve of the new Rockingham policy of granting independence to the colonists. He continued to assert the theory of 'the supreme legislative authority and superintending power' of Britain over the colonies, but called for moderation in practice. His last speech in the H of L on 7 Apr 1778 was an attack on the Rockingham independence proposals. He collapsed in the middle of it, and d a month later.

Pizarro, Francisco (*c* 1475–26 June 1541) Spanish conqueror of Peru.

Illegitimate son of Capt Gonzalo Pizarro and Francisca González; he was active in transatlantic exploration from 1502 onwards. He was appointed Mayor of Panamá (1519–23), and led 2 voyages (1524–5, 1526–7) to explore the N W coast of S America. This area – which he named Peru – was the territory of the despotic Inca Emp, the last and most advanced of the Indian civilizations that had ruled there for 1,000 years. The Gov of Panamá opposed his projects, and ordered him to return in the middle of his 2nd voyage. Pizarro, however, along with 13 volunteers, pushed on S, and discovered the coastal town of Túmbez. Side-stepping the Gov, Pizarro returned to Spain (1528) and convinced the Emp CHARLES V of the value of his scheme in an interview. On 26 July 1529 the Q Empss Isabella presented him with his mandate, making him Gov and Capt-Gen of the new prov. Returning to Panamá (Jan 1530), Pizarro took 4 of his half-brothers with him, and they, together with Diego de Almagro, a soldier, and Hernando de Luque, a priest, formed the leadership of the *conquista*. With 180 men and 37 horses in one ship (later reinforced by 2 more), the fearless and ruthless Pizarro set off to conquer the 12-million-strong Inca Emp. From the heat of the coast at Túmbez they turned to penetrate the icy mountains of the interior. Pizarro used surprise, terror and treachery to exploit the divisions among the Incas, who, at that time, were split over a disputed succession between Atahuallpa and his half-brother, Huescar. Arriving at Cajamarca on 15 Nov 1531, Pizarro sent a deputation to Atahuallpa, who received them with magnificence and ceremony, but refused to become Christian or accept Charles V as his overlord. On Pizarro's orders, the Spaniards suddenly fell on the Incas. Atahuallpa was imprisoned (Nov 1532); released so that he could kill Huescar, then imprisoned again, in spite of offering Pizarro a large room full of gold. On 29 Aug 1533, after becoming a Christian, Atahuallpa was strangled and burned. Without its head, the Inca despotism collapsed before the Spaniards, and in Nov 1533 Pizarro entered the capital, Cuzco. After that, it was a matter of consolidating the Spanish dominion, and exploiting the Incas' riches. Pizarro founded Lima in 1535 as part of this process. His partner, Almagro, who grew dissatisfied with his share of the spoils, rebelled against Pizarro, but was defeated and killed in 1538. Some of his followers, however, attacked the palace at Lima, and Pizarro was killed in the fighting.

Polish Succession, War of the (1733–5/8) In which Russia and Austria on one side and France on the other fought for the control of Poland, while France, aided by Spain and Savoy-Sardinia, attacked Austrian possessions in Lorraine and Italy.

In Poland hostilities began when, on the death of K Augustus II of Poland (who was also the El Frederick Augustus I of Saxony) on 1 Feb 1733, a faction of Polish nobles backed by France elected as the new K Stanislas Leszczyński (Sept 1733) the father-in-law of LOUIS XV of France. (He had already been K of Poland once before, 1704–9, during the GREAT NORTHERN WAR.) Russia immediately invaded Poland in Oct 1733 and induced a pro-Russian and Austrian faction of nobles to elect their candidate, Frederick Augustus II of Saxony, as K Augustus III (Sept/Oct 1733). Stanislas fled from Warsaw to Danzig, where he was besieged by the Russian army until the city capitulated (June 1734), the French having sent only a small squadron to his aid. Stanislas escaped disguised as a peasant.

In W Europe France allied with Savoy-Sardinia (Sept 1733) and Spain (the Family Compact, Nov 1733) and declared war on the Emp CHARLES VI (Oct 1733), seeking the aid of Bavaria, Sweden and Turkey. Great Britain under WALPOLE refused to go to the Emp's aid, even though she had promised this in the Tr of Vienna (1731). Franco-Spanish invasions of W Germany and N and S Italy prevented Austria from going to war in Poland. France occupied Lorraine (May–June 1734) whose D – Francis Stephen – shortly m the heiress of the Austrian monarchy, MARIA THERESA (Feb 1736). Austrian possessions in Italy were also attacked. Aided by Savoy-Sardinia, France invaded Lombardy, while further S Don Carlos (the future K CHARLES III of Spain, and D of Parma since 1731) conquered Naples. The peace preliminaries were agreed in Oct 1735, but the definitive Tr of Vienna was not signed by all the powers until Nov 1738. By it, Augustus III, the Russo-Austrian candidate, remained K of Poland. Stanislas renounced the crown of Poland (Jan 1736), but not the title, and in compensation received Lorraine and Bar from Francis Stephen. On the death of Stanislas, Lorraine and Bar were to revert to France. Francis Stephen in compensation received Tuscany, where the Medici line ran out in 1737. Don Carlos received Naples and Sicily from Austria, with the title of K Charles III. He gave Parma and Piacenza to Austria. Austria kept Lombardy, but gave Tortona and Novara to Savoy-Sardinia. France guaranteed the Pragmatic Sanction (the arrangement whereby the Emp Charles VI bequeathed Austria to his daughter, Maria Theresa).

Popish Plot, The (1678) A tissue of lies, half-truths, and truths woven by Titus Oates, to the effect that Caths were about to murder K CHARLES II, replace him with his Cath brother, the D of York (future K JAMES II), massacre the Prots, and make England Cath. Oates was a homosexual renegade Anglican parson with a capacious memory and a fertile imagination, who joined the Cath Ch and gained an intimate knowledge of the activities of English JESUITS and their colleagues in Spain and France. He also nursed a personal grievance against them. He revealed the Plot to the K through an intermediary in Aug 1678, and subsequently invented further complications, but what convinced the public were two valuable coincidences: the discovery that one of the conspirators he named – Edward Coleman, fanatical Cath and ex-Sec of both the D and Dss of York – had actually been in treasonable correspondence with France; and the murder of Sir Edmund Berry Godfrey – the magistrate before whom Oates swore his testimony – whose body was found at the foot of Primrose Hill on 17 Oct 1678. The suspicions of the public, fed earlier by the GUNPOWDER PLOT (1605) and the story that the Fire of London (1666) had been started by Papists, and nourished by the pro-French and pro-Cath behaviour of the K and his brother and their Cath wives, now seemed justified. A wave of irrational credulity warped the nation's judgement, and any crank or criminal with a Cath horror story found an appreciative audience. Sub-plots and by-plots abounded, the atmosphere heightened by the slump of 1678-9 and the consequent unemployment in London. At the same time, the politicians added fuel to the flames. The K and his ministers, though healthily sceptical, had to investigate every charge. As HALIFAX said, 'the Plot must be handled as if it were true, whether it were so or not'. The opposition, for their part, pursued their own inquiries, led by SHAFTESBURY. In the end, the Plot led to the passing of the Parliamentary Test Act, the fall of DANBY, the exile of the D of York, the dissolution of the Cavalier Parl, the campaign, led by Shaftesbury, to exclude James from the succession, and the election of the 3 Exclusion Parls. Surprisingly, in all the popular excitement, not one person was killed on the streets, though 35 Caths were executed. Before long, the Plot faded away. Oates lost his allowance from the K in Sept 1681. Under James II he was found guilty of perjury, fined and imprisoned for life, with regular whippings and appearances in the pillory. Under WILLIAM III he was given a free pardon and £10 a week out of the secret-service money. He m a rich widow (1693), joined the Baptists, and d in comparative obscurity on 12 July 1705.

Poynings, Sir Edward (1459–Oct 1521) Soldier, administrator and Ld Deputy of Ireland under K HENRY VII of England.

Son of Robert Poynings, a Kentish gentleman, and Elizabeth Paston, he was with the future Henry VII in exile, and after the battle of Bosworth had a prominent place on his Council. He was Admiral of the small fleet which, in aid of the Emp MAXIMILIAN I, captured the castle of Sluys, Netherlands, on 13 Oct 1492; along with WARHAM he negotiated with Mary, Dss of Burgundy, in the summer of 1493, in an attempt to persuade her not to support Perkin WARBECK. He is best known for the laws for the subjugation of Ireland which were named after him. Hitherto the Yorkists and Henry VII had ruled the wild chieftains through the Earl of Kildare, the biggest chieftain of them all, as Ld Deputy. For direct rule by England was limited to the Pale: an area stretching about 50 miles inland from Dublin. Owing to the Irish support of Lambert SIMNEL, Henry dismissed Kildare in 1492, and tried to bring the Irish directly within the English admin machinery. Young Pr Henry (the future K HENRY VIII) became Ld Lieutenant, and Poynings went to Ireland in 1494 as his Ld Deputy. The Irish Parl met at Drogheda in Dec 1494 and passed the so-called Poynings' Laws, the chief 2 of which laid down that future Irish Parls needed to get prior approval from K and Council for their meetings and agendas, and that henceforth English statutes applied also to Ireland. Other laws passed included measures for putting down over-mighty subjects, and for generally applying to Ireland the law-and-order machinery used in England. Judging by the lack of support that Perkin Warbeck found in Ireland, Poynings' Laws were a great success in the short run. He was recalled, however, in Dec 1495, and Kildare was once more sworn in as Ld Deputy (Aug 1496) – though Poynings' Laws were not repealed until 1782. Kildare kept peace with England, which was as much as Henry VII could afford to achieve. He postponed the real problem of governing Ireland for his successors.

Presbyterians PURITANS who supported the hierarchical form of Ch Gov worked out by CALVIN, in which discipline was exercised through a pyramid of authorities topped by the national synod working through provincial synods, district presbyteries and single congregations. They could be theocratic, as in Scotland, or Erastian, as in England, where strong anti-clerical feeling always insisted on the rule of lay elders, and on the ultimate authority of Parl. English Presbyterianism as it was worked out by the Westminster Assembly under the rule of Oliver CROMWELL, where JPs and MPs had the whip hand, tended to be an upper-, and upper-middle-class Ch; while its opponents – the INDEPENDENTS – belonged generally to the lower-middle classes. Presbyterians should not be confused with 'Presbyterians', a political grouping in the Long Parl (*see* CHARLES I).

Price Revolution, The A period of inflation during C16 whose timing varied from country to country. In Germany and Poland it seems to have begun in late C15, in Spain *c* 1500, in Italy *c* 1550, while in England it ran from 1510 to 1620. The total amount of inflation also varied. Prices rose 5-fold during the century in England, 4-fold in Spain, 2½-fold in Poland, but less than this in Italy and Sweden. The rise also affected different commodities differently, agricultural products rising earlier and faster than manufactured goods. Moreover, though contemporaries then and historians since have been quite sure that the inflation existed, they have not been able to chart its progress with reliable figures, and probably never will. At the same time, historians are far from agreed on the causes and results of the price rise.

As far as causes are concerned, monetary explanations held the field till the 1960s; the main sources of the increased money supply that historians have pointed to have been one or more of the following: debasement of the coinage, heavy Gov spending, expanding credit facilities, higher output from the German and Bohemian silver mines in the 1st half of C16 and from the S American mines in the 2nd half. None of these explanations can be statistically proved, and each has been criticized in various ways. Since the 1960s, historians have tended to favour the pressure of rising population on inelastic resources – especially food – as the chief cause, though accurate population figures are as hard to come by as price indices, while statistics of food production probably never will be arrived at. The results have been similarly debated by historians. The Price Revolution used to be thought of as the main drive behind the development of capitalism in C16. According to this view, entrepreneurs enjoyed increased profit margins as the price of goods rose ahead of wages and rents, which were held back by institutional rigidities. This thesis, however, has been subjected to so much criticism as to be no longer tenable. Inflation has also been cited as the explanation of the swifter economic growth experienced by N Europe in comparison with S Europe. It has also been quoted as the cause of the rise of the bourgeoisie, the rise of the gentry, and so on; but such changes in the social structure are difficult to chart and impossible to prove at present. All that can be said with confidence about the social classes is that landless labourers, urban and rural, felt the pinch very badly, suffering periods of intense destitution and undergoing a general decline in income over the century. Tenants did well or badly according to how secure their tenures were, how fixed their rents, and how big their output: whether it was so big that they had a surplus for sale, or so small that they had to buy food themselves. The fortunes of landowners – the nobility, the gentry and the yeomen – varied according to how enterprising they were in producing for the market, and how successful they were in raising the rents of their tenants.

Puritans Stricter than average Prots in C16 and C17 in England, though the content of the word expanded and contracted according to circumstances. Broadly speaking, Puritans were motivated by piety, not only in Ch on Sundays, but in all aspects of daily life: in the family, at work, in society. They tended to be morally upright and censorious, self-reliant and independent-minded, given to ordered living, diary keeping, Bible reading, sermons and family prayers. It is not sufficient to call them Calvinists, because the Ch of England under Q ELIZABETH I and K JAMES I was Calvinist in theology. The essential difference came with Ch organization. Puritans under Elizabeth believed that the REFORMATION had not gone far enough, and that non-Biblical, 'Popish' remnants, such as clerical vestments and Ch ceremonies, still needed to be eliminated. When WHITGIFT and the bps ordered them to conform, they began to doubt the divine origins of episcopacy, and many moved over into support of the Presbyterian form of Ch organization, eg Thomas CARTWRIGHT. Sometimes the word

'Puritan' refers to Christians to the left again of these: separatists who did not want a Ch composed of the mass of humanity, but only a community of the elect, God's chosen people. Under the 1st 2 Stuarts the word further modified its meaning as Archbp LAUD and the ARMINIANS captured control of the Anglican Ch. If we call Puritans at this time the opponents of the Arminians, then they were the majority of the Ch of England. But they were also the majority of those outside it: PRESBYTERIANS and INDEPENDENTS, and the extremist groups beyond those. During the fragmentation of churches which marked the CIVIL WAR period, the word 'Puritan' lost what usefulness it still possessed. Those who disagreed with the proposals of the Westminster Assembly of Divines began to be called 'dissenters', and the extremists – who heard voices, or saw the inner light, or were filled with the Holy Spirit, eg Baptists, Quakers, FIFTH MONARCHY MEN, Ranters and Antinomians – are conveniently referred to as 'sectaries'.

Pym, John (?1584–8 Dec 1643) Statesmanlike leading opponent of K CHARLES I of England in the Long Parl, who launched the impeachment of STRAFFORD, the Grand Remonstrance, and other revolutionary legislation of 1641, and, on the outbreak of the CIVIL WAR, organized the war-effort of the Parl side, especially the financial provision and the alliance with the Scots.

Son of Alexander Pym, landowner; ed in the Puritan household of his mother's 2nd husband, and at Pembroke, Oxford (1599) and the Middle Temple (1602); m (between 1614 and 1620) Anne Hooke (or Hooker) (d 1620). He entered politics as a client of the neighbouring Russell family, Earls of Bedford, and sat in the 3rd Parl of James I (Jan 1621–Jan 1622), where he joined in opposition to BUCKINGHAM's pro-Spanish and pro-Cath policies, attacked monopolies, and supported the Protestation of Dec 1621, which the K tore from the H of C Journals. On the dissolution he was placed under house arrest for 3 months. In the 1st 4 Parls of K Charles I he rose in prominence as an opponent of the Court, helping to impeach Buckingham (1626) and pass the Petition of Right (1628). During the 11 Years' Personal Rule (1629–40), he was a keen supporter of transatlantic colonization as a refuge for victims of the Court and as a base for attacks on Spanish shipping. He became Treasurer of the Providence Island Co, and since the other directors were leading Puritan Parliamentarians, the meetings of its board provided opportunities for concerting action against the K – eg the refusal of John HAMPDEN to pay Ship Money. In the Short Parl (Apr–May 1640) and the Long Parl (beginning Nov 1640) he emerged as the leading opponent of the K and his ministers. In the former, he limited himself to a policy of refusing to vote taxes before grievances had been settled; in the latter he became convinced that the K, Strafford and LAUD were negotiating with a European-wide Cath conspiracy to destroy English liberties, and he moved forward to a determination to remove Strafford and Laud, and henceforth place ministers under Parl control. A persuasive debater who carried his audience by sound argument rather than emotional rhetoric, he was a subtle, realistic and conciliatory moderate, the inspiration behind opposition policy, the architect of the strategy and tactics which united the diverse enemies of the Court and passed the revolutionary legislation of 1641, destroying the K's ministers, suppressing the prerogative courts, forbidding non-Parl taxation, and forcing the K to call Parl at least every 3 years. This unity, of course, cracked in the autumn of 1641, when deep rifts appeared, especially over the future shape of the Ch, and over who should command the troops used to suppress the Irish rebellion which had just broken out. Pym was convinced that the K was not to be trusted and that the statutes of 1641 would be repealed if Parl did not secure command of his armed forces and control of his choice of ministers. With Parl splitting into the future Parl and Royalist parties, Pym began to appeal to public opinion outside, in the City of London, and in the country at large. Parl passed the Grand Remonstrance with a majority of only 11 (Nov 1641), but Pym had it printed and published; it is not surprising that he was one of the 5 members whom the K tried to arrest on 4 Jan 1642. They escaped down river to the City, where the radicals had just captured control of the Common Council in the elections of Dec 1641. Soon the 5 members were back, and Pym took the lead of the middle group of MPs which held the balance between the war party, who favoured all-out war on the K, and the peace party, who looked for a settlement with him as soon as possible. The middle group favoured negotiation backed by effective war preparations, and Pym became the leader of the Parl side in the Civil War, organizing the system of committees which raised taxes and troops, and negotiating the Solemn League and Covenant with the Scots, which Parl confirmed in Sept 1643.

Radicals The name given to the agitators (eg WILKES) of the reign of K GEORGE III, whose main demand was Parl Reform, whose main power-base was the extra-Parl masses in county and borough, and whose campaigns exploited new political techniques, especially the use of the press, by then a network covering the whole nation. There had been a continuous underground stream of republican and radical thought since the English CIVIL WAR of C17 (eg the 'Commonwealth Men'); this surfaced again in late C18 at a time of economic depression, unstable admins, conflict between the K and the politicians, the development of disciplined parties, and rebelliousness in America and Ireland. There were 3 main periods of Radical agitation: 1768–9, over the Middlesex elections and the expulsion of Wilkes; 1779–80, the Association Movement, in which representatives of the county freeholders and borough freemen tried to create a national organization which could supersede Parl; and 1793–4, the working-class unrest under the stimulus of the French Revolution. The Radicals moved beyond the traditional Tory and Country opposition programme, which aimed at making the existing constitution work better by increasing the independence of Parl with Place Acts and other forms of Economical Reform – thus reducing the influence of the Crown – and with the transference of seats from rotten boroughs to the counties and populous boroughs, and with the reduction of the life of each Parl from 7 years to 3. Strongly affected by the American slogan of 'no taxation without representation', the Radicals wished to alter the constitution itself by making Parl dependent upon the wishes of the people, by redistributing seats and extending the franchise so that MPs represented people not property, and by holding annual elections. Moreover, in appealing to the masses of the population, the Radicals exploited the new methods of agitation so well developed by Wilkes: the press, county meetings, street demonstrations, instructions to MPs, petitions to Parl, remonstrances to the K, local and national associations and political clubs. Finally, unlike the popular agitators of late C17 and early C18, who were fostered by the aristocratic leaders as a stick with which to beat the Court, the Radicals were a self-reliant popular movement, helped by opposition factions, of course (eg the Rockinghams and the Pittites), but not dependent upon them – rather the converse.

Ralegh (Raleigh), Sir Walter (c 1554–29 Oct 1618) Histrionic Renaissance scholar and man of action, favourite of Q ELIZABETH I of England, poet and historian, and important as an early advocate of American colonization, who was executed by K JAMES I to appease Spain.

Younger son of Sir Walter Ralegh by his 3rd wife, Katherine Gilbert (who was also the mother of Sir Humphrey GILBERT); ed at Oriel, Oxford, and the Middle Temple.

Under Elizabeth, after fighting for the Hugs (1569) and against Spanish shipping (1578), he came to the Q's notice for his military service against the Munster rebels in Ireland (1580–81). At Court (1581 onwards) his good looks, extravagant clothes, his charm and wit soon made him the favourite of the Q, who enriched him with monopolies, estates and offices, knighting him (1585) and appointing him Capt of the Q's Guard (1587). He became an early and imaginative proponent of transatlantic colonization, privateering and trade – schemes later taken up by PYM's Providence Island Co, and given State support in Oliver CROMWELL's Western Design. He sent a series of unsuccessful expeditions (1584–9) to found a colony near Roanoke Island on what is now the coast of N Carolina, but then called Virginia by him after the Q. In 1591, he secretly m Elizabeth Throckmorton, a Maid of Honour to Elizabeth, an affront which led to his imprisonment and disgrace (1592–7) when the Q discovered it. He sailed (1595) in search of El Dorado, the fabulous city of untold wealth, and, though he failed to find it, he explored 3–400 miles of the valley of the R Orinoco, Venezuela. He sailed with ESSEX in the attack on Cádiz (June–Aug 1596), and was in joint command with him on the Islands Voyage (July–Oct 1597), an unsuccessful attempt to destroy the new Spanish Armada and capture the silver fleet.

Under James I – and possibly 'framed' by his rival, SALISBURY – he was arrested (17 July 1603) for plotting with Spain to place Arabella Stuart on the throne, and sentenced to death at his trial at Winchester, Hants (Sept 1603), where COKE led the prosecution with very weak evidence, and Ralegh used the trial as a platform for self-advertisement. Reprieved, he remained in the Tower, where he carried out experiments and wrote his *History of the World* (1614), until BUCKINGHAM secured his release in Mar 1616 to lead an expedition to Guiana in search of gold. A condition of his release was that he would not interfere with Spanish possessions, but unfortunately his men attacked San Thomé, and on his empty-handed return James I – pro-Spanish in his foreign policy at this stage – had him beheaded at Westminster for his crime of 1603. He faced his death with enormous courage, saying, of the axe, 'This is sharp medicine; but it is a sure cure for all diseases'; and calling to the hesitant executioner: 'What dost thou fear? Strike, man, strike.'

Reformation, The The break-away of certain states and peoples from the RC Ch and the formation of a variety of Prot Chs. The intense convictions of Martin

LUTHER, leading to his resolute defiance of the Ch hierarchy (1517 onwards) and their widespread broadcast by means of the printing press, set in train this vast complex of events, but would not have done so had not the time been ripe in certain important respects.

The rotten condition of the Ch from top to bottom made it crumble under this impact. The C14 crisis of the Avignon captivity of the Pp, and the Great Schism when there were 2 (or 3) rival Pps; followed by the Council of Constance (1414–18) where the Bps struggled with the Pp to turn the Ch into a limited, instead of an absolute, monarchy; all seriously damaged the effectiveness of papal government, harmed the reputation of the Ch in the eyes of the laity, led Pps (such as ALEXANDER VI, JULIUS II, LEO X and CLEMENT VII) to resist the reform of crying abuses through fear of a council, and to strengthen their position by using their spiritual power (along with war and diplomacy) to acquire material wealth and political strength as territorial Prs in Italy. Similarly, the Ch hierarchy was riddled throughout with pluralism, simony, absenteeism and lack of vocation, as a result of the exploitation of clerical patronage by the laity in all the states of Europe, in such a way that posts in the Ch were convenient sources of income for the political servants of the princes and the poor relations of the nobility. Moreover, the religious orders in their monasteries and convents were without a true vocation, and the priests of the parishes were uneducated and poorly paid. Even where the clergy were conscientious, religious life for the mass of the people rose little above the superstitious observance of external ceremonies mechanically repeated to ward off fears of hell-fire. However, there was nothing new in all this in 1517: these were faults of long standing. It was anti-clericalism that was new: a tide of criticism which now overwhelmed the Ch, fed partly by streams from within the Ch, but swelled mainly by the complex flood of hostility in the laity. In the first place, economic growth and social evolution were producing wealth, urbanization, education and reading matter, and creating a laity confident enough to challenge the intellectual monopoly of the traditional Ch; to require a higher standard of performance of its religious duties; to insist on an end to its taxes; to claim a share in its material wealth; and to demand freedom from the myriad ways in which the Ch courts could hamstring social and economic change. In most W European countries this trend was encouraged, if not headed, by an analogous anti-clericalism among the Erastian Ks and Prs who were building up centralized and absolutist States, stimulating patriotic emotions, and treating the Ch at home or the papacy abroad as they did any other internal rival or external power. On the other hand, these economic, social and political changes were worsening the standard of life of masses of peasants and labourers in the villages, and craftsmen and workmen in the towns, where day-to-day hardships were periodically turned into catastrophe by slump, famine and disease. All these changes, in the second place, were bringing about cultural shifts, were preparing the minds of the people (according to their various situations) perhaps to respond to Renaissance HUMANISM by using the latest scholarly techniques to strip Christianity of its unbiblical accretions and reveal what Jesus and the apostles really said; or perhaps to listen more closely to the underground followers of early reform movements (eg the Lollards in England, the Hussites in Bohemia, the Vaudois in N Italy and S France) which anticipated Luther by replacing the clerical trappings of external observances with the inwardness and independent-mindedness of personal salvation; or to pay attention to the mysticism, asceticism and piety of the *devotio moderna*, a lay religious movement with great influence in the Netherlands and N Germany; or even hearken to the rantings of the revivalists who could periodically set villages aflame with religious ecstasy, with preparations for the Second Coming, and with blueprints for the equalization of material wealth. Of course, the state of the Ch and the material and mental foundations of anti-clericalism varied from country to country; but so did the idiosyncrasies of the reform leaders – the psychological disturbances of Luther for example, or the political and marital imperatives of K HENRY VIII of England; or the intellectual struggles of ZWINGLI or CALVIN with their city councils. The outcome was a rich variety of Prot churches on the one hand, facing a revived and reformed Catholicism on the other. *See* REFORMATION, The English; REFORMATION, The German; CALVIN; GUSTAV I VASA; KNOX; LUTHER; ZWINGLI.

Reformation, The English The series of changes whereby the Ch in England separated from the RC Ch and was placed under the supreme headship of the monarch. Also included in the changes were the DISSOLUTION OF THE MONASTERIES, and certain moves in the direction of Protestantism. The Reformation was initiated by K HENRY VIII, carried further by K EDWARD VI, reversed by Q MARY I, and re-established by Q ELIZABETH I. It was precipitated by Thomas CROMWELL's revolutionary solutions to the problem of Henry VIII's divorce from Q CATHERINE OF ARAGON; but these could not have succeeded, had not certain long-term trends disposed the minds of the nation to support them.

The Ch in England had not deteriorated: its faults had been only too apparent for a century and more. The upper clergy, trained in the law and not in theology, were civil servants, not servants of God; the lower clergy were hardly trained at all; the monks were in the main a scandal; and even among conscientious Christians, clergy and laity innocent of pluralism, absenteeism, simony and worldly behaviour, religious observances were too limited to the mechanical acquisition of the rights to reduced purgatory or eternal salvation by going on pilgrimages, invoking saints, saying masses, kissing relics etc. What was new was the emergence of an educated laity who, for one reason or another, were no longer prepared to tolerate this state of affairs, and who formed an anti-clerical public opinion which was made up of a number of different strands, the chief of which were as follows. (a) The supporters of Christian HUMANISM (eg COLET, MORE, ERASMUS) who abandoned scholastic theology and went back to the Bible itself and studied it as a text according to the philological, historical and literary methods of the Renaissance. (b) The followers of the *devotio moderna*, who aimed at contact with the Divine through austere and contemplative pietism, rather than ceremonies and other ostentatious 'works'. (c) The descendants of the Lollards, who had been C14 anticipators of all the doctrines of LUTHER except that of justification by faith alone, and who now formed a persecuted underground movement among townsmen, merchants, gentry and some lower clergy which was attractive, like Lutheranism, to all those who sought individual responsibility for their own souls. (d) Those who wished to reduce the wealth, power and privileges of the Ch, either because of greed or because they objected to paying tithes and other Ch dues, or because they were frustrated by wrongdoers sheltering from justice behind the rights of sanctuary and benefit of clergy, or because they resented the jurisdiction of the Ch over wills, perjury, sexual offences and trading misdemeanours. (e) Those – a sophisticated minority, cluding Thomas Cromwell – who believed that the future of human civilization depended upon the build-up of the absolute, sovereign, Erastian state, independent of all external authorities such as the Papacy, and omnicompetent within. (f) Those – a large number – who disliked the Papacy out of sheer xenophobia. (g) Those who fell under the influence of the Continental reformers (first Luther, then ZWINGLI), and met together at Cambridge in the 1520s and came very much under the influence of Tyndale.

Under Henry VIII, the monarch placed himself at the head of these movements in so far as they coincided with his own wishes for a divorce from Cathemrine of Aragon, for independence from Rome, and for Erastian control of the Ch; and he resisted it in so far as it involved demands for doctrinal and other changes in the direction of Protestantism. In the years 1529–31 Henry was putting pressure on the Pp for his divorce by rallying the anti-clericalism of Parl and by disciplining the clergy. In the first session of the so-called Reformation Parl (Nov–Dec 1529), Henry gave the hitherto spontaneous anti-clericalism of Parl its head with the passage of statutes lopping mortuary and probate fees, restricting sanctuary, limiting pluralism and non-residence and forbidding clerical trading. The whole clergy were charged with offences against the statute of Praemunire for unlawfully exercising their spiritual jurisdiction (Dec 1530); then they were granted the royal pardon on payment of £118,000 (Jan and Feb 1531). During the years 1532–6, when Thomas Cromwell was chief minister, a new policy was displayed: the breach with Rome, the assertion of the absolute sovereignty of England (and thus the purely English divorce), and of the Royal Supremacy over the Ch of England – a revolutionary development brought about in the following chief measures: (a) The Commons' Supplication against the Ordinaries (Mar 1532) – a petition against the legislative and judicial powers of the clergy leading to the Submission of the Clergy (May 1532) by which, after strong resistance, Convocation agreed not to legislate without royal consent, a concession put into legislative form in the Act for the Submission of the Clergy (1534). (b) The Act in Restraint of Appeals (1533) with its famous preamble stating that 'this realm of England is an empire', asserted the judicial independence of England, and thus allowed the royal divorce (now urgent on Anne Boleyn's pregnancy, Dec 1532). (c) The Act in Conditional Restraint of Annates (1532) which was brought into force by Letters Patent in July 1533 and then replaced by the Act in Absolute Restraint of Annates (1534). (d) The 1st Act of Succession (1534) making the children of Henry and Anne Boleyn heirs to the throne. (e) The Act of Supremacy (1534) which declared that Henry was the Supreme Head of the Ch of England. These same years (1532–6) also saw Henry ruthlessly stamp out the sparks of the exiguous opposition, bright though some of them were. Elizabeth Barton, the deluded 'Nun of Kent', prophesied against the K's marriage to Anne Boleyn; she was hanged with 5 male accomplices at Tyburn on 20 Apr 1534. Bp John FISHER and Sir Thomas More opposed the royal supremacy and the divorce, and were beheaded on 22 June and 6 July 1535, respectively, for refusing to take the oath required by the Succession Act. The years 1536–47 saw the Dissolution of the Monasteries (1536–40); and

Henry's doctrinal vacillations between Catholicism and Protestantism. His position depended on how successfully he was manipulated by the conservatives on the royal Council, led by the 3rd D of NORFOLK, and Bp GARDINER, or by the pro-Lutherans, led by Cromwell and CRANMER; and also on how far he was swayed by his appreciation of the diplomatic situation abroad or influenced by public opinion at home. In general, his religious posture remained flexible, ambiguous, and comprehensive enough to deserve the name 'Anglican' already, as it was put before the public in the *Ten Articles* (1536), the *Bishops' Book* (1537), the *Injunctions* (1538), the Act of Six Articles (1539), the *King's Book* (1543). These years also included the still debated final moves of the reign which indicate steps in the direction of Protestantism: eg the education of the future K EDWARD VI by Prots; the rise in the royal Council of the young Prots, Edward SEYMOUR and John DUDLEY; the destruction of the conservative Norfolk faction; and the naming of the Council of Regency for young Edward VI, a body which had a strong Prot bias and which deliberately omitted Stephen Gardiner.

Under K Edward VI the Reformation moved in a more Prot direction in 2 stages, at 1st moderate, then more extreme. Under the rule of Edward Seymour, D of Somerset (1547–9), Parliament allowed communion in both kinds (1547), and passed an Act repealing the Act of Six Articles and virtually all the anti-heresy laws: a liberal step which flooded the country with Calvinist and Zwinglian preachers from all over Europe and stirred up a rich but dangerous broth of religious sectarianism. At the same time, further secularization of Ch land was enacted in a statute of 1547 dissolving the chantries and other religious foundations, for educational and charitable purposes. New *Injunctions* (1547) were issued again shrines, paintings, stained glass etc; and Cranmer's 1st English Prayer Book was published in 1549: a moderately Prot work written with deliberate ambiguity so as to embrace the widest possible range of Caths and Prots, and enforced by the 1st Act of Uniformity (1549). A further Act of 1549 allowed priests to marry. During the rule of John Dudley, D of Northumberland, secularization went on apace as the political leaders enriched themselves by depriving conservative Bps and replacing them with Prots who were forced to hand over large tracts of Ch land. Moreover, Cranmer's 2nd, more Prot, Prayer Book was issued in 1552, enforced by the more savage 2nd Act of Uniformity (1552); the establishment of Protestantism was completed by Cranmer's *42 Articles* of 1553, an explanation of Christian faith which formed the basis of the later *39 Articles* of Q ELIZABETH's reign.

Under Q MARY I the Protestant legislation of the previous reign was repealed and the situation restored as it was in 1547 by the statute of 1554. Leading Protestants such as LATIMER, RIDLEY and Cranmer were at once arrested and deprived; during the reign about 1,500–2,000 married clergy were ejected. Card Pole, the COUNTER-REFORMATION leader, returned to England; in Nov 1554 he gave England absolution and received her back into the RC Ch. Also in 1554 Parl passed an Act repealing all the anti-papal legislation passed since 1529, the year when the English Reformation began, except, of course, the Dissolution of the Monasteries. It also revived the old laws against heresy and passed a new Treasons Act. Thus armed, the authorities were now able to begin the enforcement of orthodoxy by burning Latimer, Ridley and Cranmer at the stake, as well as about 300 artisans and yeomen, while some 800 members of the gentry and middle classes fled abroad. The result of this persecution was a deep and lasting hatred of the R C Ch in England.

Under Q Elizabeth I the Ch settlement was embodied in the Act of Supremacy (Apr 1559) reversing Mary's reconciliation with Rome, and declaring the Q in Parl to be the Supreme Governor of the Ch; and the Act of Uniformity (May 1559) enforcing the 1552 (more Prot) Prayer Book of Edward VI, modified in a Cath direction as far as the Communion Service and clerical vestments were concerned. Q Elizabeth was a *politique* head of the Ch, and she aimed at a broad settlement which would attract the loyalty of the majority of the nation, and avoid provoking foreign powers. Nevertheless, she had to spend her reign defending the Ch from Cath and Prot extremists, both at home and abroad.

Reformation, The German In Germany, the pressures which brought about the REFORMATION in general were felt with a special intensity. The Ch was more wealthy and powerful, and its abuses correspondingly more oppressive, and the anti-clericalism of the public more explosive. In the political field, the Prs were able to stop Emps such as MAXIMILIAN I from turning Germany into a unified and absolutist State; but not yet strong enough to create the numerous small-State absolutisms typical of Germany a century later. In the consequent power-vacuum (in contrast to the conditions in England, France and Spain) clerical, as well as other, abuses flourished luxuriantly. Germany was plundered to gorge an alien papacy, and the vulnerable sections of society suffered misfortunes against which the political authorities were as yet unable to defend them. In the resultant material misery, spiritual despair, and patriotic indignation the call of LUTHER (Oct 1517), broadcast by the press, found a profound response which turned an academic dispute into a national upheaval. When Luther attacked Tetzel's sale of INDULGENCES, defied Pp, Emp and General Council, and broke with Catholicism, over not only abuses but also major points of doctrine (1517–20), his cause was espoused by a varied array of supporters: the masses of sincere Germans hoping to slake their religious thirst; the imperial Knights waging a hopeless war (1522–3) in defence of their social class; the Peasants fighting (1524–5) for the far more radical religious and social demands which the ANABAPTISTS and other sects put forward; scholars moved by religious zeal, such as Philipp MELANCHTHON, who joined Luther at Wittenberg, and Martin BUCER, who led the slightly more radical Reformation in Strassburg; Prs and city councils from a mixture of motives. To these last (aside from religious considerations) Protestantism had at least two other important functions: externally, as a stick with which to beat the steadfastly R C Emp CHARLES V, and internally, as a pretext for confiscating R C property and for setting up Prot churches subordinate to the temporal ruler. Thus, Charles V was prevented from nipping Lutheranism in the bud by the activities, for example, of the El FREDERICK the Wise, who supported Luther in Saxony when the Ban of Emp was pronounced against him at the Diet of Worms (May 1521); of the Prs and cities who signed the Protestation (the first 'Protestants') against the decision of the Diet of Speier banning religious change (Apr 1529); of the scholars and politicians who backed the AUGSBURG CONFESSION (June 1530), the statement of Lutheran faith drawn up in the face of R C intransigence at the Diet of Augsburg (June–Sept 1530); of the leaders who formed the League of Schmalkalden (Feb 1531) for the military defence of Protestantism, and fought against the Emp in the war of 1546–7. But support inside Germany was not the only factor which prevented Charles V from suppressing Lutheranism: he was hamstrung also by external considerations. First, he had to absent himself frequently from Germany in order to cope with the Gov of his other territories, such as Spain and the Netherlands; and second, he had to defend himself in the HABSBURG– VALOIS WARS from the attacks of France, the Pp, Turkey and other powers, sometimes in alliance with the German Prots. It is not surprising that Lutheranism evolved from a religious revolt into an ordered establishment which had to be officially recognized in the TR OF AUGSBURG (Sept 1555), whereby each territory was to follow the religion of its Pr or city council, RC or Lutheran, but no other – an arrangement which was later summarized as *cuius regio eius religio*.

Revolt of Catalonia, The (1640–52) Against the attempt by OLIVARES to make the non-Castilian provs of Spain provide their share of men and money towards all-Spanish needs, hitherto met solely by Castile. The Catalan *cortes* refused (1626–32) on the grounds that this was a breach of their *fueros* (their constitutional liberties). Olivares needed their aid to finance Spain's part in the THIRTY YEARS WAR (1618–48), especially the long struggle with the France of RICHELIEU; and he tried to involve the prov in these responsibilities by attacking France through Catalonia, hoping that this would break down local prejudice in favour of an all-Spanish patriotism. Unfortunately, the bad behaviour of the royal army which Olivares billeted in Catalonia during the winter of 1639/40 caused such resentment that rebellion broke out in May 1640. In Barcelona there were 5 days of rioting, and on 7 June 1640 the Viceroy was assassinated on the beach as he was trying to escape by sea. This rebellion, initiated by the nobility and bourgeoisie, then turned into a 2-tier revolution when the peasants, workers and bandits revolted against them; and in this crisis the backward-looking Catalan upper classes handed the prov over to France in return for military protection (Jan 1641). But French ABSOLUTISM turned out to be less desirable than Castilian – it was more efficient – and soon a pro-Castilian party formed, while the pro-French group split over personal rivalries. Thus weakened by vertical and horizontal divisions, and lacking effective leaders, the Catalans were gradually rolled back by K PHILIP IV's troops until 1648 saw the withdrawal of French aid because of the FRONDES, and 1650–54 saw the prov laid low by the plague. Barcelona – besieged (1651–2) by Don John José of Austria – surrendered in May 1652. The K issued a general pardon, and Catalonia returned to its normal ungovernability with all its *fueros* intact.

Revolt of the Netherlands, The (1567–1648) The 17 provs of the Duchy of Burgundy rebelled against the centralizing ABSOLUTISM and religious persecution of their D, who was also K PHILIP II of Spain. Eventually, the N (the future Netherlands) split away from the S (the future Belgium) and succeeded in gaining their independence in the Truce of 1609, confirmed in the Tr of Münster (1648); while the S remained under Spanish rule. The Revolt began as a defensive response of traditionalist nobles, provs and cities to Philip's acceleration of the progress towards centralizing the Gov in Brussels (in continuation of the policies of MAXIMILIAN I, PHILIP I and CHARLES V), and subordinating it to Madrid (his innovation); but it later broadened out into a patriotic war and religious crusade.

In the political field Philip II was intent on eliminating the federal form of Gov of the Netherlands (provs which he regarded as a distant and not very important appendage to the Spanish monarchy), and turning it into a centralized and obedient unit, above all producing its fair share of revenue. Although these provs at the mouth of the Rhine were the most advanced in Europe from the point of view of commerce, industry, banking, agriculture, fishing, mining, social differentiation, cultural level and wealth, nevertheless, the powers of the central Gov were so restricted by the liberties which each province and city had inherited from the Middle Ages that the Duchy had ceased to be a source of strength to the Habsburg monarchy, and had begun to be a drain on resources which Philip wished to use for what he regarded as more important purposes, such as the wars against SULAIMĀN II, the Turkish Emp, or against the traditional enemy, France, or against heretic England. Moreover, a land in which the Estates not only had the right to vote taxation but also ran the machinery which collected it, was highly antipathetic to him. Shortly after becoming D of Burgundy on his father's abdication (Oct 1555), Philip left for Spain (Aug 1559), and progressively grew more out of touch with a people he never saw again and whose language he could not understand. He appointed his half-sister, Margaret of Austria, Dss of Parma, as his Regent, but on the Council of State he entrusted all his business to Card GRANVELLE, a native of Franche Comté who had reached a high position in the Spanish Gov. Unfortunately, this clumsily handled Hispanicization policy so angered one group of the aristocracy who had traditionally made high policy in their native land, that, led by WILLIAM I (the 'Silent'), Pr of Orange, and Lamoral, Count of Egmont, they resigned from the Council in protest in July 1563. A rival group of aristocrats under the D of Aerschot – a leading noble of the Walloon district in the deep S – supported Granvelle, but Spain's measures caused such deep resentment against him that Philip at last allowed him to resign (Jan 1564). Magnates such as Orange, with vast estates all over the Netherlands, were not averse to centralization, but took exception to receiving Spain's orders from an alien bureaucracy – especially when these orders included religious measures which soon antagonized, not only the nobility at large led by William's brother, Pr LOUIS OF NASSAU, but the mass of the urban populace as well. Philip's policy over religion was the single-minded enforcement of the Catholicism of the COUNTER-REFORMATION by all possible means including terror. Now Spanish religious rigour confronted in the Netherlands a cultural climate as different from it as it was possible to be in C16 Christendom. The majority of the people were R Cs either of the worldly sort typical of early modern Europe, or of the tolerant sort affected by the HUMANISM of ERASMUS and others. Small groups of the middle class had become affected by the doctrines of LUTHER in the 1520s; some workers became ANABAPTISTS in the 1530s; from the 1540s, and especially after 1559, the ideas of CALVIN spread from France, affecting elements of all classes. Philip's policies alienated all these groups, R C and Prot alike. The JESUITS, the shock-troops of the Counter-Reformation, began operations in the Netherlands in 1556. The

INQUISITION of the Netherlands also began a fierce enforcement of the Placards – laws against heresy – burning Prots at the stake. A new Univ at Douai in Walloon Flanders was founded by Papal Bull in 1559. Most disturbing of all, Papal Bulls of 1559 and 1561 put into force the long-planned reform of the Ch in the Netherlands, broadly speaking, making its organization more rational and streamlined, more effective against heresy, and more responsive to orders from Madrid. The Ch was broken up into 18 – instead of 4 – sees, paid for partly out of the revenues of the richer monasteries, and manned by 3 Archbps and 15 Bps appointed by the Crown and working according to the rulings of the COUNCIL OF TRENT which were promulgated by Philip in the Netherlands in 1564. It was a grievous blow at the easy-going life of the upper clergy and at the income and patronage of their fathers and elder brothers, ie the nobles who had hitherto had these appointments in their gift. Fearing religious war such as was then breaking out in France, Orange and the magnates appealed to Philip for toleration. His reply, given in 2 famous letters to Margaret sent from Segovia, Old Castile, in Oct 1565, was to command the strictest punishment of heresy. And now members of the lesser nobility, both RC and Prot, led by Louis of Nassau and the hot-headed Henry of Brederode, formed a defensive league called the Compromise; when 200 of them rode into Brussels to demand an end to religious persecution on 5 Apr 1566, one of Margaret's councillors called them *Gueux* – beggars. They proudly called themselves *Gueux* from then on. It was at this stage that real beggars come into the story, when a slump turned a noble protest into a popular revolt. The economic crisis of 1563–6 – the result of the Northern Seven Years War of 1563–70, a crash in the English cloth trade, and bad weather, among other factors – brought unemployment and hunger to the workers of the Flemish industrial towns, eg Antwerp and Ghent in the severe winter of 1565/6, which exploded into the so-called Altar Riots. Anti-clerical in normal times, the workers now became especially receptive to the hell-fire sermons of Calvinists, and they enjoyed the support of the armed bands provided by the wilder nobles of the Compromise. Iconoclastic riots began at Steenvoorde in W Flanders in Aug 1566 and spread to Antwerp, Amsterdam and Ghent. As urban mobs ran amok wrecking churches and monasteries, Margaret called off the persecution until she felt able to fight back – and this was not until Feb 1567, when funds arrived from Spain, and enough nobles had been scared by the social unrest to swing over to the side of order. Orange himself played a conciliatory role and was mistrusted by the extremists of both sides. At this stage, he was his own man and was not yet leader of the Revolt. In fact, at this stage there was no Revolt, only a variety of rebellions. It needed the provocation of Madrid to forge a Revolt out of the disparate discontents of the magnates, the nobles, the provs, the towns, the congregations, and the workers; Philip provided this when the hawks gained the ascendancy on his councils and he decided to send the D of ALBA with an army from Italy to teach the Netherlanders their place. As Alba set out from Spain in Apr 1567, Orange retired to his estates at Dillenburg, Nassau, in Germany, to organize resistance. Egmont and his ally Hoorn stayed in the Netherlands, loyal to Philip and anxious to negotiate a friendly settlement; but William had no intention of being reduced to the level of a cog in the Spanish imperial machine.

The Revolt (1567–1609) passed through various vicissitudes marked by Philip's oscillations between terror and conciliation – swings which were perhaps basically determined by the extent of Turkish aggressiveness in the Med, a problem which he rated as more serious than the Revolt. The second chief characteristic was William's evolution into a statesmanlike figure, into the *Politique* focus of revolutionary loyalties, the peacemaker between clashing political, religious and social groups, and the organizer of foreign military and diplomatic aid. Third was the emergence of Holland and Zeeland as the bastions of the Revolt, their desperate attempts to fuse all 17 provs into one revolutionary movement, their reluctant acceptance of the eventual split between N and S, their astounding endurance in the face of overwhelming dangers, their unprecedented economic aggressiveness as they penetrated deep into Spain's world-wide colonial emp and amassed the wealth that guaranteed Dutch survival.

The rule of Alba (Aug 1567–Dec 1573) brought the resignation of Margaret and the start of the Revolt. In carrying out his secret instructions to 'make all the states into one kingdom, with Brussels as its capital', Alba used his army to terrorize the population. His agents interfered in prov and urban Gov, thrusting aside centuries-old liberties. He formed a tribunal, nicknamed the Council of Blood, which during his rule tried 12,302 victims, and executed or banished 1,105. He suddenly executed Egmont and Hoorn (5 June 1568), both unshakeable R Cs and loyal subjects. He introduced new taxes in an effort to relieve the central Gov from control by the Estates and to make the Netherlanders pay for the Spanish army. One of these, the 100th Penny, a once-only 1% tax on property, was passed by the States-Gen in Mar 1569. The other two taxes – the 20th Penny (5% on land sales) and the 10th Penny (a 10% sales tax reminiscent of the Spanish *alcabala*) – were resisted all over the Netherlands as a menace to trade, their life-blood; and a great deal of the money was never collected. The Netherlands continued to the end to be a drain on Spanish revenues. Meanwhile, Orange was planning an armed attack, one branch of which was the Sea Beggars (*Gueux de Mer*), a pirate force of noble and commoner exiles who flew the Orange flag and raised supplies by preying on shipping. As havens, they used Emden in Germany, the French Hug port of La Rochelle and certain English ports. These aristocratic pirates now brought the Revolt to a new stage – though initially to William's alarm. Expelled from English ports by Q ELIZABETH I's proclamation of Mar 1572, a squadron of 25 Sea-Beggar ships under William de la Marck captured the town of Brill in Zeeland on 1 Apr 1572, finding it temporarily unoccupied by Spanish troops. A week later Flushing fell likewise, and one by one the towns of Holland and Zeeland were either taken from the outside by the Sea Beggars or went through an internal *coup d'état* with Sea-Beggar help. All this was possible partly because in the economic crisis of 1571–2 the urban élites were more afraid of their own masses than they were of the Spanish; and partly because Alba had denuded the N of troops in order to meet an external threat from the S. COLIGNY was temporarily in power in France, and was organizing a Hug thrust into the S Netherlands in conjunction with an invasion there also by Louis of Nassau, who captured Mons in Hainault on 23 May 1572. It was a temporary conjuncture, soon to be ended by the Massacre of St Bartholomew on 23/24 Aug 1572 and the surrender of Mons by Louis on 19 Oct 1572, but it was sufficient for many of the towns and cities of Holland and Zeeland to be taken over by a minority of Calvinist fanatics. As a result, the Revolt now had a land, as well as a sea, base. It also had a leader. William of

Orange, who in July 1572 was chosen as Stadholder by the States of Holland, arrived there near the end of Oct 1572. Relieved of French pressure, Alba now reasserted his control over the S, and began the reconquest of the N, capturing Haarlem, Holland, after a long siege (Dec 1572–July 1573), but meeting only failure in Zeeland. Lacking money and ships – Spanish resources having that season been concentrated on the Med campaign which culminated in Lepanto – he could make no headway against the Sea Beggars, who at this stage were being transformed from a pirate squadron into the Dutch navy, fully in control of the Netherlands coast and the sea-lanes to Spain.

Replacing Alba with Requesens (Nov 1573–Mar 1576): Philip now swung from terror to conciliation, except on the religious question, where he was immovable. The Dutch captured the important port of Middleburgh on 18 Feb 1574 after a 2-year siege; the Spaniards wiped out Louis of Nassau's army at Mook near Nijmegen, killing Louis and his brother Henry (14 Apr 1574). In the N, a turning-point was reached when Leiden was relieved after a long Spanish siege from May–Oct 1574. The Dutch opened their dikes and flooded the area, allowing the Sea Beggars to float in relief, and forcing the Spanish to evacuate (Oct 1574), just as the burghers were about to surrender through starvation and disease. In a peace conference at Breda (Feb–July 1575) between his delegates and deputies from Holland and Zeeland, Requesens agreed to remove Spanish soldiers and bureaucrats, but discussion ended when he refused to countenance any religion other than the R C. This was the chief point in the eyes of the Dutch also. Their local and prov Gov was now in the hands of Calvinists, and the Revolt had become a religious war.

Unity, then Division (1576–9): The years after Requesens d of fever on 5 Mar 1576 were a confused time in which Orange in the N, the D of Aerschot in the S, Don JOHN OF AUSTRIA as the new Spanish Gov, the ArchD MATTHIAS from Vienna, John Casimir from the Palatinate, François D of Alençon from France, the Estates of Holland and Zeeland, and the States-Gen of the Netherlands all jockeyed for position, each using military and diplomatic coups to try to gain control of a very fluid situation. It was a period in which Orange almost succeeded in uniting all the provs into one anti-Spanish union; but in which eventually the shifting political and military scene allowed the extremists on both sides to gain control and split the Netherlands into two. What gave the *politiques* of N and S their chance to promote a union based on toleration was the collapse of discipline in the Spanish army after Requesens' death. Lacking pay since Philip had gone bankrupt on 1 Sept 1575, the soldiers ran wild in a plundering expedition which culminated in the sack of Antwerp – 11 days of anarchy beginning on 4 Nov 1576, in which 7,000 were killed and one-third of the city destroyed. The revulsion in the S caused by the 'Spanish Fury' enabled Aerschot to grasp control and help to organize the Pacification of Ghent (8 Nov 1576), an agreement signed by N and S, leaving the religious question undecided, but calling for the withdrawal of foreign troops. The new Gov, Don John, had to accept this on his arrival by signing the Eternal Edict (Feb 1577) – a promise to evacuate the Spanish army. Since the Edict also promised a return to the R C religion everywhere, however, Holland and Zeeland refused to sign it, or accept Don John as Gov. Meanwhile Orange lost control of his own extremists. In the middle (Flemish) S, the Calvinist movement was proletarian not bourgeois, and in Aug

1577 the workers of Brussels, Antwerp, Bruges, Ghent and other industrial towns overthrew their R C magistrates and began to sack the churches. This social and religious revolution in its turn caused Aerschot to move in the direction of *his* extremists, as he and the S retreated from the policy of the Pacification of Ghent back to closer co-operation with Spain. Meanwhile Don John, out for his own ends, suddenly seized Namur on 24 July 1577; and so the States-Gen abandoned him in Dec 1577 and appointed the ArchD Matthias as Gov, with Orange as Lieut-Gov in Jan 1578. Don John replied by attacking and beating the N army at Gembloux, Brabant, on 30 Jan 1578, with the help of his newly-arrived nephew, Alessandro FARNESE. In the deep (Walloon) S, however, the Malcontents, a group of S nobles worried by the social threat posed by Calvinism, made François, D of Alençon, the 'Defender of the Liberties of the Low Countries against the tyranny of the Spanish and their adherents' (Aug 1578); while John Casimir arrived from Germany to head the Calvinist crusade in the cities (Oct 1578). Don John d of typhus on 1 Oct 1578, leaving Farnese as commander of his army – a man who shortly transformed the whole scene. Head and shoulders above all these individuals and groups in statesmanship, William of Orange juggled desperately with them all in the hopes of finding a combination which would hold the fragile union together. However, the religious tensions and the social prejudices – even the personal rivalry between himself and Aerschot – were all against him; and N and S drifted apart, the S forming the Union of Arras on 7 Jan 1579 and the N the Union of Utrecht on 23 Jan 1579.

Alessandro Farnese, who was in command Oct 1578–Dec 1592, was a skilful enough diplomatist to overcome the anti-Spanish prejudice of the Walloon nobility in the deep S; using the deep S as a base, he was then a skilful enough general to recover most of the middle S. He would have done more – perhaps reconquered the N – had he not been repeatedly deflected from these tasks by orders from Madrid, first to co-operate with the Spanish ARMADA in its attack on England, then to make 3 incursions into the FRENCH WARS OF RELIGION. (a) The United Provs are born. In a desperate bid for French and possibly English help against Spain, Orange offered the sovereignty of the Netherlands to the French K's brother, François, D of Alençon – now become D of Anjou. Philip's reply to this treasonable move was to declare Orange an outlaw with a price of 25,000 *écus* on his head (June 1580). Orange replied with his *Apologie* of Dec 1580, a combination of exaggerated slanders on Philip and a philosophical justification of his life's work. The breach with Spain was made complete, and the new State of the United Provs founded when the States-Gen of the Union of Utrecht formally deposed Philip in the Act of Abjuration (July 1581). Their new theoretical sovereign, Anjou, arrived in Feb 1582 without proving himself of any practical use against Farnese. Seeking to create a Kdom for himself, he made an attack on Antwerp on 17 Jan 1583, failed, and went home to France to die of fever on 10 June 1584. A month later, on 10 July 1584 Orange was assassinated. (b) Farnese's advance. During these moves in the N, Farnese was patiently conducting his diplomatic conquest of the Walloon S and his military reconquest of the Flemish S. With the former he signed the Tr of Arras (May 1579), whereby the Union of Arras confirmed Philip II as their sovereign, and Farnese confirmed them in the privileges contained in the Pacification of Ghent and the Eternal Edict. As these included the departure of the Spanish army, Farnese was somewhat restricted in his campaign, but his conciliatory attitude to the Malcontents and his capture of Maastricht (29 June 1579) and Tournai (Dec 1581) won the confidence of the Arras provs until in 1582 they agreed to the return of the Spanish army. Farnese now proceeded to capture Flemish towns in the S one by one: Oudenarde in July 1582, Dunkirk in July 1583, Bruges in 1584, Ghent in Sept 1584, Brussels in Mar 1585 and Antwerp on 17 Aug 1585 after a sensational 14-month siege. (c) English intervention resulted from the deaths of Orange and Anjou, and came by the Tr of Nonsuch (Aug 1585) by which Q Elizabeth I provided 6,000 men for the duration of the war. The expedition under the Earl of LEICESTER landed at Flushing on 9/19 Dec 1585 but, for two main reasons, achieved only modest results. First, the United Provs aimed at an all-out war against Spain, while Elizabeth intended only a small intervention simply to bring pressure to bear on Spain in Europe in general. Second, Leicester accepted the post of Gov-Gen (Jan 1586) against Elizabeth's orders and, like his predecessors in the post, he interfered for his own ends in a ham-fisted way in the delicate web of political, economic and religious rivalries which were threatening to break up the new republic. As a result, Farnese continued his reconquest of the Netherlands, taking Grave and Venloo in June 1586; then Zutphen (Oct 1586), Deventer (Jan 1587) and Gertruidenberg (Apr 1589) from the English. With these bridgeheads N of the Rhine and Meuse he was poised for an onslaught on Holland and Zeeland, when policy decisions in Madrid changed the whole situation. Putting the Netherlands low in his list of priorities as usual, Philip ordered Farnese first to concentrate his forces at Dunkirk and Nieuwpoort in July 1588 in order to go aboard the Armada and invade England; second, to invade France in order to help the Cath League against HENRY IV in Aug 1590, Apr 1592 and Dec 1592. It was a repetition of 1572, when Alva's preoccupation with France had enabled the Sea Beggars to gain their first foothold in the N.

The counter-attack, the Truce and the ultimate survival of the new State were thus due partly to English help and Spanish mistakes, but mainly to the people's own internal strength. This was the result, in the first place, of the moral fibre deriving from Calvinism and from their devotion to prov liberties. Second, their financial strength accrued from Holland's incredible economic expansion, when Amsterdam replaced Antwerp as the financial hub of Europe, when Calvinist refugees from the S contributed many new industrial skills, and when Dutch ships began not only to dominate the Baltic, the North Sea and the Med, but also to penetrate across the Atlantic and into the Indian Ocean, making useful profits from trading even with Spain herself. A third source of strength was the political skill of Johan van OLDENBARNEVELT, the leader of the Estates of Holland, who achieved the miracle of a united war effort by successfully fending off the Earl of Leicester (who left at the end of 1587), getting Orange's son, MAURICE of Nassau, appointed Capt-Gen and Stadholder of most of the provs, and henceforth doing without the dubious advantage of calling in a foreign Pr as sovereign. A fourth advantage was the military genius of Maurice who, basing himself on the classical authors, turned the Dutch army into one of the finest in Europe, regularly paid, supplied and drilled, and incorporating artillery, engineering and pioneer sections, and using a new unit, smaller than the *tercio*: the battalion of 550 officers and men. Fifth, the geographical position of the N provs made them practically impregnable as they sheltered behind the Rhine and the Meuse, and the sea, dominated by the Dutch navy. Backed by these advantages, Maurice retook Breda, Zutphen and Deventer in 1590 and 1591, and in the next 10 years steadily removed the Spanish from their other bridgeheads in the N. Moreover, on 16/26 May 1596 Holland as a sovereign State jointly went to war against Spain with England and France. Her Revolt had thus become an international war. By 1600 Maurice was able to invade Flanders, but not very deeply. This time, the Flemish masses did not rise in support. Spain in decline had made peace with France (May 1598) and England (Aug 1604), and now conceded Dutch demands in the 12-year Truce of Apr 1609. Maurice opposed the Truce, but Oldenbarnevelt won the day. It gave the United Provs international recognition, and by it Spain agreed to close the R Scheldt (thus confirming the ruination of Antwerp) and give the Dutch free trading access to the West Indies. When the 12 years were over, neither Spain nor the Dutch would renew the Truce, so warfare began again (1621–48), this time as part of the general European conflicts of the THIRTY YEARS WAR (1618–48). In the Tr of Münster (Jan 1648) the Spanish concessions of 1609 were confirmed; in addition the United Provs kept cities which had been conquered by Maurice's brother, FREDERICK HENRY, during the fighting, including 's Hertogenbosch, Breda and Maastricht. As well as separation from Spain, the Dutch achieved independence from the HR Emp, to which they had been theoretically attached hitherto.

Revolt of the Northern Earls, The (Nov–Dec 1569) The last, and unsuccessful, attempt by the great clientage networks of the N of England to reassert regional independence against Tudor centralization, Catholicism against Protestantism and the old nobility against new bureaucrats such as William Cecil, the future Ld BURGHLEY.

The Revolt was one of 3 centres of opposition to Q ELIZABETH I and her Sec, Cecil, the others being the alliance at Court between the 4th D of NORFOLK and the Earl of LEICESTER to overthrow Cecil and ensure the succession to the throne by the marriage of Norfolk to MARY, Q OF SCOTS, now in custody in England; and the activities of Roberto Ridolfi, a Florentine banker in London, who offered rebels aid from Spain, France and the Pp. When the Q got wind of the plots, Leicester made a clean breast and received forgiveness; but Norfolk left Court for E Anglia (Apr 1569) to organize resistance where his landed strength lay. When the Q ordered him back to London, however, his nerve cracked and he obeyed. He was placed in the Tower on 8 Oct 1569 after he had told the N Earls not to rise. In the N, nevertheless, on the lands and among the followers of the 3 great families – the Percies, the Nevilles and the Dacres – feelings ran very deep. In this remote region, economically backward and poor in communications, the Ch of England had hardly penetrated, and the power of the Crown was felt only indirectly through the local magnates. When Thomas Percy, Earl of Northumberland, and Charles Neville, Earl of Westmorland, were summoned to Court, they refused to obey, and on 13 Nov 1569 they were pronounced rebels. The rebels took Durham and celebrated Mass in the cathedral on 14 Nov 1569; but it was a revolt confined to these 3 families – the other gentry holding back – and not the wide regional movement that the Pilgrimage of Grace had been. Gov troops soon scattered the rebels, and in Dec 1569 the leaders took refuge in Scotland. Northumberland was later handed over and executed at

York on 22 Aug 1572, and Westmorland fled to Flanders to spend the rest of his life in exile. Severe punishment, with about 500–800 executions, brought an end to what proved a crucial episode in English history: confirming Cecil in office, and the Q on the throne, and ensuring the survival of the Ch of England and the centralization of the administration.

Revolt of Portugal against Spain, The (1640–68) Beginning on 1 Dec 1640 with the proclamation of the 7th D of Bragança as K John IV, it resulted from the convergence of a number of causes. The Portuguese masses had resented the Spanish connection ever since 1580, when PHILIP II conquered them. The nobility and bourgeoisie, however, had so far favoured Spanish rule, for it protected the Portuguese colonies from Dutch aggression, and allowed Portuguese merchants the unofficial possibility of tapping the trade of the Spanish colonies of Mexico and Peru from their own colony of Brazil. By 1640, however, these advantages no longer existed as the decline of SPAIN became manifest. Spain under OLIVARES: was unable to prevent the Dutch from conquering Pernambuco, Brazil; was pushing the Portuguese merchants out of Mexico and Peru; was trying to centralize the independent Portuguese admin under Castile; and was taxing the Portuguese to provide revenues for all-Spanish purposes. Moreover, Spain in 1640 was in desperate straits, with military defeats on all fronts; with naval strength gone – one fleet having been destroyed by the Dutch in the battle of the Downs (21 Oct 1639) and another defeated by them off Pernambuco in Jan 1640; and with the REVOLT OF CATALONIA in full swing (May 1640). Like the Catalans, the Portuguese had the benefit of help from RICHELIEU and MAZARIN; but they enjoyed further advantages which eventually conferred success on their struggle for independence. They had help from the England of both CROMWELL and CHARLES II. Geography aided them. They were a united clergy and people, fired by patriotism. They had a K, and they were led by a dynamic and creative upper class fully experienced in world-wide commerce, and untrammelled by attempts at social revolution. They had an Emp in Africa and Brazil, and after ejecting the Dutch from Angola in 1648 and Brazil in 1654, they enjoyed the profits of trade in slaves and sugar. Most of the fighting took place on or near the road from Lisbon to Badajoz, Estremadura. The Portuguese invaded Spain as far as Badajoz in 1657. They stopped a Spanish invasion of Portugal at Elvas, Alentejo (14 Jan 1659). They defeated the Spanish at Ameixial, nr Estremos (8 June 1663); and when the Spanish made a thrust at Vila Viçosa, the home of the Braganças, the Portuguese beat them at nearby Montes Claros (17 June 1665). With the death of the intransigent K PHILIP IV, peace negotiations became feasible, and at last his widow, the Regent Mariana, recognized the independence of Portugal in the Tr of Lisbon (Feb 1668).

Revolution of 1688 The overthrow of K JAMES II of Great Britain and Ireland and his replacement by K WILLIAM III and Q Mary II, followed by important constitutional enactments. James was dethroned after an invasion by William of Orange from Holland, supported in England by defections and risings of leading WHIGS and TORIES. These had been radicalized by the dangerous attempts of James to turn Britain into a Cath ABSOLUTISM, using a standing army illegally officered by Caths, and preparing for the election of a subservient Parl by using middle-class Dissenters and Caths to oust the normal rulers of England, the nobility and gentry. William landed at Torbay, Devon, on 5/15 Nov 1688; James fled to France on 23 Dec 1688; and William called a Convention Parl (Jan 1689–Feb 1690) which passed the chief legislation of the Revolution settlement, though further statutes followed later. The men who made the settlement thought of themselves as restoring the traditional constitution after it had been upset by the revolutionary moves of James II. Their settlement, though temporarily making the Crown almost elective, left it in full command as head of the executive – making appointments and deciding on policy. On the other hand, the settlement in effect made annual meetings of Parl essential, and forced the K to choose men and measures which could achieve a majority there. In addition, the independence of the judiciary was strengthened, and the rights of the individual against the State fortified.

The Bill of Rights (Dec 1689) declared James to have abdicated, and settled the vacant throne on William and Mary and their heirs, then on ANNE and hers. This arrangement was a compromise between the views of different groups: the strict legitimists who wanted William to be Regent for a theoretically still reigning James; William himself who refused to stay in England unless he had full regal powers; Tories who regarded Mary as the legitimate heir to James (most people believing, or pretending to believe, that Pr James Edward was not a genuine son of James); and Whigs who believed that the people should choose their ruler. In addition, the Bill of Rights forbade the monarch to be, or to marry, a Cath; it also declared the following illegal: the suspending power, and the dispensing power as James had used it; prerogative courts such as the Ecclesiastical Commission; non-Parl taxation; a standing army without Parl consent; and prosecutions for petitioning the Crown. It went on to call for frequent Parls, free elections, and free Parl debates, and to extend the judicial rights of the individual against the State.

The Mutiny Act (Mar 1689) gave the Crown the legal means to maintain army discipline; but Parl prevented military dictatorship and made Parl co-operation necessary by enacting this for only 6 months at a time (later one year).

The Toleration Act (May 1689) did not enact religious toleration, but exempted Dissenters (except Caths and Unitarians) from certain laws. In practice they achieved freedom of worship, but not full citizenship, as the Test and Corporation Acts were still in force.

The Triennial Act (Dec 1694) ordered that no Parl and no dissolution should exceed 3 years.

The Civil List (Dec 1698): the financial provision for the K's ordinary expenditure was henceforth provided in the Civil List, under the K's control; while each item of extraordinary expenditure was voted, appropriated and audited by Parl. As the extraordinary expenditure increased, especially with the long and frequent wars of the next century, so did the dependence of the Crown on Parl.

The Act of Settlement (June 1701) conferred the Crown (should Anne die without issue) upon the Electress Sophia of Hanover and her heirs, being Prot; among other measures, it ordered that the monarch must be in communion with the Ch of England, that judges should be appointed during good behaviour and not during the K's pleasure, and that the royal pardon could not be pleaded in impeachment trials.

Richelieu, Armand Jean du Plessis de (9 Sept 1585–4 Dec 1642) Card (1622), *Duc et paire* (1631), chief minister of K LOUIS XIII of France, who strengthened the power of the Crown without making any fundamental reforms in the social and admin structure (though he defeated the magnates, eliminated the 'state within a state' of the Hugs, and built a navy), and who led France to victory in the THIRTY YEARS WAR (through diplomacy until 1635, thereafter through war), thwarting the Habsburg attempts to unite Germany and encircle France, and gaining valuable additions to the frontiers on the Rhine and in the Pyrenees; though at the cost of much suffering to the French masses.

3rd son of François du Plessis, Ld of Richelieu in Poitou, and his wife Susanne de La Porte, daughter of a Poitiers lawyer; ed in Paris at the Collège de Navarre, then at a military academy, then at the Collège de Calvi, where he studied theology in preparation for taking over the family Bpric at Luçon in Poitou. Being under age, he had to go to Rome and persuade Pp Paul V to grant the necessary dispensation, and there in Apr 1607 he was ordained priest and consecrated Bp. Thereafter the main elements in his career were: his rise to power from the comparative obscurity of a minor noble family in the provs; his efforts to stay in power – ie to retain the confidence, against continuous attempts at sabotage, of Louis XIII, a K who could be just as suggestible and ruthless as any democratic electorate; his build-up of centralized ABSOLUTISM, not by any systematic and rational plan, but by a pragmatic mixture of dictatorial strokes against, and realistic compromises with, the chief opponents of the Crown (the Hugs, and the Prs of the Blood, the magnates and the office-holders); and his foreign policy of frustrating the joint efforts of the Spanish and Austrian Habsburgs to encircle France and dominate Europe by taking diplomatic and military action in Italy, Germany and Spain.

His rise to power was fuelled by his intense ambition and outstanding abilities. Tall and thin, pale and delicate, he possessed an imperious bearing and hypnotic gaze, persuasive eloquence and unbending will, which either enslaved or repelled all who came into personal contact with him. Between Dec 1608 and Oct 1614 he administered his improverished little diocese; but as a representative of the Poitevin clergy at the Estates-Gen of Oct 1614–Feb 1615 he distinguished himself as a speaker on the side of the pro-*dévot*, pro-Spanish policies of the then Regent, MARIE DE MEDICI, and her favourite, Concini. His reward was to be appointed Chaplain to the new Spanish Q of France, Anne of Austria (Nov 1615), and then Sec of State for War and Foreign Affairs in Concini's reconstructed Gov until the latter's murder on 24 Apr 1617. Under the new Gov of LUYNES, Richelieu went to Blois with the exiled Marie de Medici, then to Luçon, and then to exile in Avignon in Apr 1618. During Marie's various rebellions, defeats and reconciliations (1619–21), Richelieu acted as her adviser and go-between, and on the death of Luynes he negotiated her return to the K's Council (1622) where she put forward his ideas, and gradually persuaded the sceptical K of Richelieu's ability and honesty. Neither the Gov of the Brûlart brothers, nor that of La Vieuville, who replaced them in Feb 1624, was clever enough to handle the critical diplomatic situation in which France found herself during the early years of the Thirty Years War (1618–48), when Habsburg aggressions in N Italy and on the Rhine threatened her with encirclement. Richelieu hired pamphleteers, and Marie de Medici exploited her maternal situation, and between them they persuaded the K that Richelieu had the right policy, as well as the subtlety to put it into practice. In Apr 1624 he was given a seat on the Council, and on 13 Aug 1624 supreme power.

His efforts to stay in power ended only with his death, for his career lay at the mercy of a K with mediocre abilities, but with a high sense of his position and duties, who was constantly assailed by opposition groups – self-seeking and conscientious, in the Court and in the country – and who was conscious that he needed the intellectual and moral stiffening of a minister such as Richelieu, but who nevertheless always had the last word. (a) The Chalais conspiracy (May 1626) was the first serious challenge that Richelieu unearthed at Court. It was an attempt by the Prs of the Blood (Gaston, the K's brother, the Vendômes, his 2 bastard half-brothers, CONDÉ and Soissons, his cousins, Anne of Austria, his Q) and some associated Court magnates (notably the libidinous Dss de Chevreuse, ie the widow of Luynes who had promptly remarried, and her lover, Chalais) to kill Richelieu, depose Louis, and share out the power and perquisites among themselves. With typical selectivity, Richelieu arrested the Vendôme brothers, exiled Chevreuse and others, executed Chalais (Aug 1626), but promoted Gaston to be D d'ORLÉANS and brought him on to the Council. (b) The Day of Dupes (10 Nov 1630) was a more principled attack on his position, led by his old sponsor, Marie de Medici, in alliance with a group of his colleagues under the Keeper of the Seals, Michel de Marillac. It got its name from the hysterical, fruitless, but at first seemingly successful, attempt to browbeat the K into dismissing Richelieu and change his policies. Hitherto a faithful *dévot*, Richelieu had now embarked upon his life-long struggle with the Habsburgs, a campaign so expensive that it became impossible to spend time and money trying to convert or persecute the Hugs, as Marie wanted, or to undertake fundamental reforms in the *Ancien Régime*, which the Marillacs advocated. Rightly or wrongly, the K accepted Richelieu's appreciation of the situation, and confirmed him in supreme power. (c) The Languedoc rebellion (1632) was mounted by a combination of the Prs of the Blood (represented by Gaston d'Orléans and Marie de Medici operating from exile in enemy territory – Lorraine and the Spanish Netherlands) in support of a great magnate, Henri II, D de Montmorency, Gov of Languedoc, who was leading the forces of separatism in the prov against the attempts of the Gov to turn it into a *pays d'élections*. The rebels were defeated in battle at Castelnaudary on 1 Sept 1632, and Montmorency was beheaded in Toulouse. Orléans, on the contrary, was temporarily reconciled. (d) The Comte de Soissons' invasion (1641) was mounted with help of Spanish troops. Soissons defeated the French at La Marfée on the Meuse near Sedan (6 July 1641); but his plot came to nothing as he was immediately killed on the battlefield as he raised his visor. (e) The Cinq Mars conspiracy (1642) occupied the very last days of Richelieu's life, when this young favourite of the K plotted to kill Richelieu, put Gaston d'Orléans in power, and make peace with Spain. It was the last aspect which forced Louis to execute Cinq Mars on 12 Sept 1642, 2 months before Richelieu's own death.

In his build-up of centralized absolutism Richelieu continued the policies of his predecessors, as and when he could, not following a sophisticated master-plan of State-building, but acting as dictatorially as he dared in the varying circumstances, with a view to smashing opposition, maintaining order, stimulating the economy and shaping mens' minds, all in order to raise the resources for his 1st priority: the anti-Habsburg struggle.

The Hugs – running what he called 'a state within a state' – occupied his attention from the very start, for like Luynes before him, he realized that the Prs of the Blood and the high nobility would never be tamed so long as they had this republic within a monarchy as a power-base and a refuge. The situation of the Prots had changed since the Edict of Nantes (Apr 1598) had brought an end to the FRENCH WARS OF RELIGION. They had become concentrated in the fortified towns and mountain fastnesses of Poitou, Guyenne and Languedoc. They were organized into 8 circles, with a C-in-C and an army; they met in prov assemblies and a gen assembly; declining in numbers, no longer aided by the Germans or the Dutch (now allied to the French Crown), and fearful of extermination at the hands of the *dévots* and other agencies of the French COUNTER-REFORMATION, they took to arms under the D de ROHAN whenever a noble rebellion or foreign crisis offered them the opportunity to consolidate their position, extend their boundaries, or even achieve the status of an independent republic as the Dutch had done. To Frenchmen, the Hug enclave was a political monstrosity unique in Europe, and Richelieu regarded its elimination as more urgent, even, than the war against Spain. When he took action to keep the Rhine and the Valtelline out of Spanish hands (1624–5), the Hugs of La Rochelle seized the islands of Oléron and Rhé, which covered their city from the sea (1625), forcing Richelieu to make peace with them (Tr of La Rochelle, Feb 1626), then with Spain (Tr of Monzon, Mar 1626). He prepared for final showdown – a move pleasing to his *dévot* colleagues and backers, but also urgent in view of the Hugs' alliance with England. He and the K took personal control of the operations against La Rochelle. The English expedition under BUCKINGHAM, which landed on the Isle of Rhé on 12/22 July 1627, was forced off again on 8/18 Nov 1627, with only half its complement. A mole was built across La Rochelle harbour to keep off further English relief attempts, and on 28 Oct 1628 the starving city surrendered. Rohan continued the struggle in Languedoc until the English made peace (Tr of Suze, Apr 1629). Though he then made an alliance with Spain in May 1629 Rohan could not withstand the royal armies, and the rebellion ended with the Grace of Alais (Alès) on 28 June 1629. The Hugs kept their religious privileges, but their military strongholds and political organization were destroyed.

The Prs of the Blood, the magnates and the office-holders were considerably weakened by Richelieu's success against the Hugs, and against the various plots and rebellions to overthrow him. He had no plan to oust the nobility – Sword or Robe – from political activity: he wished to stop them from using their clientage connections and the organs of prov separatism *against* the Crown, and get them to work *for* the Crown *within* the admin structure of the French state. To this end he held an Assembly of Notables (Dec 1626–Feb 1627) – the last before 1788 – but since each group (Clergy, Sword and Robe) thought of nothing beyond the defence of their own corporate privileges, little came of the elaborate plans of Richelieu and Marillac for quartering the army in the provs, demolishing castles, abolishing the *paulette*, repurchasing the royal domain and reducing taxation. Only Richelieu's mercantilist plans for building a fleet and forming trading companies were approved; and Richelieu was obliged for the rest of his rule to fall back on the old financial expedients which were to prove so disastrous in the long term: the sale of offices, forced loans and increased *taille*. Unlike Marillac, Richelieu was against postponing foreign action in order to have a confrontation with the privileged and a basic reform of the *Ancien Régime*. The so-called *Code Michaux*, which Marillac issued in 1629 and which contained his schemes, was not enforced by Richelieu after his colleague's fall. He did not favour Marillac's head-on campaign (1629-31) for turning the remaining *pays d'états* into *pays d'élections* by bringing them into the normal tax-collecting system and making them pay their fair share of the national revenue. Of course, he acted drastically against Montmorency and his Languedoc rebellion which these reforms provoked (see above); but he compromised with the *pays d'états*. They kept their privileges, but promised a higher *don gratuit*. Nor did he have uniform proposals for dealing with prov Govs, except for breaking recalcitrant ones when a good chance offered, and replacing these with reliable men, or taking over the job himself as he did in Brittany after getting rid of the D de Vendôme. In some provs he made more and more use of Intendants to keep an eye on the Gov; to supervise the office-holders, who were capable not only of failing to collect the taxes but also of encouraging the populace not to pay them; to bring the Estates in the *pays d'états* into line by persuasion or brute force. Similarly in the case of the PARLEMENT of Paris and the prov Parlements – the chief institutions of the Robe – Richelieu preferred undermining their authority to meeting them head-on. He used other courts to try eminent rebels when they would not co-operate. The Council was given power from 1632 onwards to overrule decrees of the Parlement which it considered not in the public interest. When Parlements refused to register new taxes, they could be brought to heel by the arrest of individual members, the exile of others, the use of *lits de justice* and *lettres de cachet*, or severe lectures from the K, or by diluting their strength by selling new offices in them. Finally, the decree of Feb 1641 allowed them only 2 remonstrances before registering financial edicts, and permitted the discussion of affairs of State only *after* registration. Getting them to register *this* edict was a distinct victory for Richelieu. At the same time he deployed every device of the modern State to keep the population in general patriotic: spies and *agents-provocateurs*, pamphleteers and journalists, literature, architecture and painting. A Gov-inspired weekly, the *Gazette*, came out from 1631 onwards: and in Jan 1635 the K officially recognized the *Académie Française* which Richelieu had founded earlier. He built the imposing Palais Cardinal (after his death called the Palais Royal) as his residence. And, fundamental to the whole structure, the army was reformed by François Sublet de Noyers into an instrument capable not only of challenging over-mighty subjects but also of defeating Spain. It was an oppressive régime, powerful enough to plunder the nation, but too weak to assess taxation according to income. The rich and powerful were able to unload the main weight of the fiscal exactions onto the urban and rural masses – and this in a period marked by recurrent harvest failures and economic crises. The consequence was that not a year of Richelieu's rule passed without riots against the tax-collectors by peasants and workers, often encouraged by the local nobility and bourgeoisie. In the famine of 1629-30 the peasants attacked Dijon, Caen, Lyons and Angers; in the most serious episode – the *Va-nu-pieds* (Barefoot) risings in Normandy against the introduction of the salt-tax in 1639–40 – the Chancellor Séguier himself had to take over the prov with an army (Jan 1640), suspend the normal prov and local organs of Gov, and suppress the rebellion by terror.

His foreign policy consisted of the defence of France's interests by whatever measures the situation required, religious considerations playing no part. Ahead of his time, he was prepared to fight alongside R Cs or Calvinists, Moslems or members of the Ch of England. Pp Urban VIII and Père Joseph went to some lengths to ease tender consciences with cleverly-worked-out theological arguments in support of war against members of the true Ch; but Richelieu's policies were simply based on that separation of politics from religion which has since become quite normal. They were designed to prevent the Austrian and Spanish Habsburgs from achieving victory in the Thirty Years War, and to frustrate Spanish attempts to encircle and penetrate France. They consisted of diplomacy and war in Italy, Germany and the N, and Spain.

In Italy he considered it vital to gain footholds so as to prevent Spain sending troops into N Europe, either via the Valtelline (the upper valley of the R Adda which led through the Alps into Tyrol and the Rhine), or via Savoy and Franche Comté into the Rhine valley. Thus in 1624–5 he sent help to the Grisons canton (owners of the Valtelline) who were rebelling against Austria, and laid siege to Genoa, the port where Spanish supplies and men were landed on their way to Milan and the Valtelline. The Hug revolt of 1625 at La Rochelle, however, forced him to withdraw and make the Tr of Monzon in Mar 1626. When, with the Grace of Alais, he had dealt with the Hugs, he intervened in Italy again, this time in the War of the Mantuan Succession (1627–31). The last of the Gonzaga rulers of Mantua and Monferrato d on 26 Dec 1627 and was succeeded by a French magnate, the D de Nevers. The Emp and Spain disputed this, and, though Nevers established himself in Mantua, Spanish troops in alliance with Savoy occupied Monferrato. Regarding this as a vital French interest, Richelieu conquered Savoy and reinforced the anti-Spanish fortress of Casale in Monferrato (18 Mar 1629). The following year he took Pinerolo in Piedmont (23 Mar 1630), but the Spanish took Mantua (18 July 1630). Nevertheless, French diplomatic pressure at Regensburg, Germany, where the Emp and the Electors were meeting, enabled Richelieu to achieve the favourable Tr of Cherasco (Apr 1631), whereby Nevers got Mantua and Monferrato, while France kept Pinerolo, giving Savoy part of Monferrato in compensation. This crucial decision to hold on to Pinerolo and commit France to a long war with the Habsburgs was taken by the K with his eyes open to the consequences, which, as Richelieu had explained to him in his memorandum of Apr 1630, involved 'giving up all thought of rest, or economizing, and of putting right the internal affairs of the kingdom'. This was the issue on which Richelieu split with Marie de Medici and Marillac, and which led to the Day of Dupes. Henceforth, he continued to harass the Spanish in Italy. On 11 July 1635 he organized a joint attack on Spanish-held Milan by Savoy, Mantua and Parma – an enterprise which had scant success. That same year Rohan achieved control of the Valtelline, but the Spanish regained it in 1637. And in Sept 1640, the French army took Turin; but by this time Italy was not so vital. The main war areas were in Germany and in Spain itself.

In Germany and the N, Richelieu attacked the Habsburgs indirectly until 1635 by the diplomatic and financial incitement of their enemies, and directly thereafter by open warfare. (a) His indirect warfare on Spain and Austria consisted, first, of close co-operation with Holland, from the Tr of Compiègne of June 1624 onwards, in her attack on the Spanish Netherlands (Belgium). Second, his diplomatists were prominent in the organization of the Hague agreement of Dec 1625, whereby CHRISTIAN IV of Denmark, Holland, JAMES I of England and FREDERICK V of the Palatinate allied to inaugurate the Danish War period of the Thirty Years War (1625–9) with the approval of such widely scattered friends as BETHLEN GÁBOR, Pr of Transylvania, Murad IV, Sultan of Turkey, and Pp Urban VIII. Third, Richelieu facilitated the entry of GUSTAV II ADOLF of Sweden into the Swedish War period (1630–35) by negotiating the Tr of Altmark (Sept 1629), ending the war between Sweden and Poland, and the Tr of Bärwalde (Jan 1631), whereby Sweden promised to keep an army in Germany, and France promised to subsidize it to the tune of 400,000 *taler* a year for 5 years. Fourth, Richelieu's agents were prominent at the meeting of the Emp and the German Els at Regensburg (June–Aug 1630), and succeeded in reaching an understanding with MAXIMILIAN I, El of Bavaria, who vacillated between supporting the Emp on religious grounds and opposing him on political. Fifth, and more directly, he took the Els of Trier and Cologne under French protection, and occupied Ehrenbreitstein and Philippsburg on the Rhine, as well as Nancy, the capital of Lorraine (1631). This vast network of allies, all pursuing their own interests, was immensely difficult to manage, especially the independent-minded Gustav Adolf who stormed down to SW Germany against Richelieu's wishes and frightened Maximilian of Bavaria back on to the side of the Emp. After Gustav Adolf's death (16 Nov 1632), his chief minister, OXENSTIERNA, organized the League of Heilbronn with the German Prot Prs (Apr 1633); but Richelieu succeeded in making France rather than Sweden the dominating influence in it, and paid his subsidies to the League, not to Sweden. The days of this limited involvement were over, however, for, when Sweden was crushingly defeated by the Austro-Spanish army at Nördlingen (5–6 Sept 1634), Richelieu had no alternative but to emerge from the background into open warfare. (b) Direct action now being imperative, Richelieu occupied strong points in Alsace and Lorraine, and made 1635 a year of intense activity in diplomacy – for France was not yet ready to field an army of her own. He renewed the alliance with Holland in Feb 1635 for a joint attack on the Spanish Netherlands. He renewed the alliance with Sweden for another 3 years (Tr of Compiègne, Apr 1635). He ceremonially declared war on Spain (May 1635) by sending a herald to Brussels. He organized Savoy, Parma and Mantua into a league against Milan (July 1635). He helped to negotiate the Tr of Stuhmsdorf (Sept 1635) releasing Sweden from the Polish War for further action in Germany. He took Bernard, D of Saxe-Weimar, the successful commander of the Swedish army, into French pay (Oct 1635). Nevertheless, the next year – the 'year of Corbie' – was one of intense danger to France. An Austrian army invaded Franche Comté and Burgundy. A Spanish army from the Netherlands penetrated Picardy and took Corbie, nr Amiens (14 Aug 1636), while the cavalry managed to reach Compiègne. In Paris, 80 kilometres away, there was panic; but the firmness of the K and the Card saved the day, and soon the overextended enemy had to retreat. Henceforth, with his highly trained, if small, new army, commanded by 2 rising military stars, Turenne and d'Enghien (the future Great Condé), Richelieu took the offensive in 2 main areas. First, in the Netherlands, while the Dutch struck at the Spanish from the N – taking Breda on 10 Oct 1637 – the French hammered at them from the S, completing the conquest of Artois by taking Hesdin (1639) and Arras (1640); and, 5 months after Richelieu's death, destroying the Spanish army and military reputation at the famous battle of Rocroi (19 May 1643). Second, astride the Rhine in Alsace and the Breisgau, Bernard took Rheinfelden (3 Mar 1638), and with Turenne's help, after a 6-month siege, took Breisach on 17 Dec 1638. It was at once a gateway into Germany and a blockhouse on the Rhine which cut the Spanish Road between Milan and the Netherlands and made the Valtelline irrelevant. Fortunately for Richelieu, just as Bernard was proving self-interested and hard to manage – he aimed at creating a German duchy of Alsace for himself – he d, suddenly on 18 July 1639, and Richelieu was able to purchase his army and the ground it stood on. He was thus in a position to bite deep into Germany in co-operation with Sweden, with whom he renewed his alliance, involving annual payments of a million *livres* (Tr of Hamburg, Mar 1638) – a necessary refresher, as Oxenstierna was meditating a separate peace with the Emp. Thus Richelieu left France in a powerful position, which MAZARIN after him was able to consolidate in the Trs of Westphalia (Oct 1648).

In Spain, where the war continued until the Tr of the Pyrenees (Nov 1659), Richelieu first had to push back invasions of Languedoc and Guyenne from each end of the Pyrenees; then, from 1637 onwards, carry the war into Spain by land and sea. French troops invaded Catalonia at one end of the Pyrenees in 1637, and then laid siege to Fuentarrabía, Guipúzcoa, at the other in 1638. The siege failed, but the new navy defeated a Spanish force coming to relieve it. On 19 July 1639 France took Salses, nr Perpignan, Roussillon, but had to abandon it on 6 Jan 1640. Nevertheless, Richelieu encouraged the 1640 revolutions in Catalonia and Portugal; and, on 19 Sept 1642, just before his death, Perpignan fell, completing the French grip on Roussillon – hitherto Rosellón, a Spanish prov N of the Pyrenees.

In sum, Richelieu had gone far towards achieving all his objects. He had thrown out Spanish invasions; and he had made them less likely in the future by pushing back the frontiers to include Artois in the NE, much of Alsace on the Rhine and Roussillon in the Pyrenees. With Pinerolo in Piedmont and Breisach on the Rhine he had openings into Italy and Germany, while Breisach cut the Spanish Road and breached Spanish encirclement.

Ridley, Nicholas (*c* 1503–16 Oct 1555) Bp of Rochester (1547–50), Bp of London (1550–53), English Prot theologian who was burned at the stake under Q MARY I.

Son of Christopher Ridley of the Northumberland gentry; ed at Newcastle and Pembroke Hall, Cambridge, then at the Sorbonne, Paris, and Louvain, then again at Cambridge from 1530–37, during which time, probably, he became a Prot. He became private chaplain and intellectual aide to Archbp CRANMER in 1537, and then Master of Pembroke (1540), Bp of Rochester (1547), then, after the deprivation of BONNER, Bp of London (1550). An important contributor to the foundation of Anglican doctrine and practice, he took a leading part in the scholarly disputations over transubstantiation and other controversies raised by the English REFORMATION under K EDWARD VI, as well as in the more practical tasks of removing images and ceremonies from the churches under his command. On K Edward's death on 6 July 1553 he supported the ill-fated coup of Lady Jane Grey; and on the accession of Q Mary I he was arrested and deprived of his Bpric. Along with LATIMER and Cranmer he was found guilty of heresy by a delegation of Convocation at Oxford (Apr 1554); condemned to death on 30 Sept 1555 and burnt at the stake at Oxford with Latimer, suffering unbearable agonies because of the inefficiency of the executioners.

Rockingham, Charles Watson-Wentworth, 2nd Marquis of (13 May 1730–1 July 1782) Leader of the Old Corps of WHIGS after NEWCASTLE, and twice PM under K GEORGE III (1765–6 and 1782), who repealed the Stamp Act, favoured independence for the American colonies, brought in Economical Reform (but remained suspicious of Parl Reform), and granted legislative independence to Ireland. Under his leadership the Old Corps changed from being the party of the Court, kept in power by Parl management and the help of the Crown – as it was in the days of WALPOLE, PELHAM and Newcastle – to become a party of opposition, with a belief in party Gov with a party programme, suspicious of the influence of the Crown, looking for support among the merchants and freeholders of the boroughs and counties, and sticking to its principles, rather than making the pragmatic compromises necessary to achieve and keep office.

5th and only surviving son of Thomas Watson-Wentworth, 1st Marquis of Rockingham (a rich landowner with vast estates in Yorks and Ireland) and his wife, Mary, daughter of Daniel Finch, 2nd Earl of NOTTINGHAM; ed at Westminster Sch and St John's, Cambridge; succeeded on 14 Dec 1750; m (1752) Mary, daughter of Thomas Bright of Badsworth, Yorks (d 19 Dec 1804, no issue). Like his father, Rockingham became one of the leading aristocrats in the Old Corps of Whigs in the days of the Pelham brothers, being (1751 onwards) Ld of the Bedchamber and Ld Lieut of the N and W Ridings of Yorks, losing both posts when the Old Corps monopoly of power was ended by the BUTE admin (1761–3). He resigned the Bedchamber (Nov 1762) in sympathy with Old Corps colleagues whom George III was ousting, and was then dismissed from his Ld Lieutenancies (Dec 1762). Wealthy, genial, hospitable, and conscientious, he headed the younger generation of Whigs and succeeded Newcastle as leader of the Old Corps.

In his 1st admin (1765–6) he was 1st Ld of the Treasury (July 1765) in a Gov of which the D of Cumberland (the young K's uncle) was the real leader until his death on 31 Oct 1765, after which Rockingham became PM, by accident as it were. A keen supporter of party Gov, he decimated Bute's office-holders, high and low, and replaced them with his own followers; but he suspected that the K's Friends who remained (for Northington and Egmont had stayed on from the Bute admin) were secretly used by the K to sabotage his own work. His deep, but unwarranted, suspicion of George III (which soon formed part of Whig mythology and then of C19 historiography) prevented him from co-operating with Bute and the K's Friends, the very elements which could have assured him a stable and long-lived admin, though they would have cost him his prized popularity with the people. Rockingham thus departed significantly from the practices of the earlier Old Corps leaders; and he found himself in charge of a divided admin which lacked Court backing and was opposed by the Grenvilles and the

Bedfords. The Rockingham Whigs prided themselves on a new article of faith – their consistency, ie practising in office what they preached in opposition. They repealed Bute's Cider Tax, carried a H of C resolution condemning general warrants, and tried to revive the Prussian alliance in a forward policy against France and Spain. They also, in a Country-like manner, looked to public opinion in the boroughs and countries for support, and brought in several measures to help trade. Moreover, it was under pressure from the merchant lobby that they belatedly adopted the policy of repealing the Stamp Act, though, since his followers were split on the issue (Newcastle and the elders opposed repeal), Rockingham accompanied this measure with the Declaratory Act (*see* the WAR OF AMERICAN INDEPENDENCE) to rally support. Rockingham, however, was not endowed by nature to be a PM. He was lazy, procrastinating, inefficient and valetudinarian; he much preferred the horse races at Doncaster and York to the rat-race of Whitehall and Westminster. He spoke in Parl only twice during this admin, and once forgot to attend one of his own Cab meetings. He was convinced that the K had instructed the K's Friends to vote against the repeal of the Stamp Act, and he angered George with his aristocratic rudeness and his patent contempt for the K's views on men and measures. Moreover, he made the admin look foolish by wooing the support of PITT the Elder, who only despised him. His ministry was further weakened by the resignation in May 1766 of GRAFTON, his Sec of State (N) because of the failure to acquire his hero, Pitt. Finally, the K managed to persuade Pitt to form a Gov, and Rockingham was dismissed on 9 July 1766. A number of Rockinghams stayed on in the Pitt admin (1766–8) until one of them, Ld Edgcumbe, was demoted with inadequate compensation, when Rockingham persuaded them all to resign (Nov 1766), except Gen Conway, and the Rockinghams spent the next 16 years in opposition.

In opposition (1766–82) Rockingham and his group naturally espoused Country causes, though they were far from effective, partly because they could not co-operate with Pitt, who was also in opposition, 1768 onwards. Rockingham opposed the Grafton admin (1768–70) and the NORTH admin (1770–82) over the persecution of WILKES, the Falkland Islands affair (1770–71), the need for reforming the law of libel (1770) and the printing of Parl debates (1771); but by 1772 the steam had gone out of these issues, and North was firmly in command of Parl. The Rockinghams were still just another aristocratic faction jockeying for office; but the years 1772–82 saw big changes in their theory and practice as they took advantage of the shattering political upsets which that decade produced: the Association Movement in England (1779–80), Grattan's rebellious campaign in Ireland (1779–82) and, above all, the economic and constitutional shake-up caused by the War of American Independence (1776–83). Aided by his very clever sec, Edmund Burke, and his brilliant new recruit, Charles James Fox, Rockingham forged the new Whig theory. According to this, George III had revived Stuart power through his influence in Parl (thanks to the K's Friends) and through his Favourite, Bute, and similar 'behind-the-curtain' ministers, who formed a second, secret, Cab, which sabotaged the work of the ostensible Cab. The remedy for this absolutism was for the politicians to form a party with which to bring trade-union pressure to bear on the self-willed monarch – a party based on principles, enunciated in opposition and adhered to in office, a party drawing strength from its contact with the extra-Parl agitators among the RADICALS, and making use of the new political techniques developed during the campaigns of John Wilkes. Exploiting the perennial Country desire to reduce Gov expenditure, Burke produced the Economical Reform programme to reduce the number of placemen, and thus royal influence and Gov expenditure at one and the same time. Rockingham did not go so far as Fox in support of Parl Reform, though he favoured a small measure. His main concern was to limit the K's power in the interests of the politicians, not of the people. Similarly, Ireland and especially America were useful sticks with which to beat the Crown. Rockingham had adopted a pro-colonial stance almost accidentally in repealing the Stamp Act and, being consistent, he continued to back the Americans, unrealistically thinking that conciliation could bring them back to their former allegiance and revive the old commercial relations. More wisely, he also said that it was impossible to suppress the Americans, and therefore unwise to try. Fox introduced a deeper ideological note into this pragmatism, supporting the Americans as allies against a common enemy – George III – and taking the view that a K who was victorious over the colonists would be a menace to liberty in the mother country. Then, with the British surrender at Saratoga (17 Oct 1777) and the entry of France on the American side (6 Feb 1778), the policy of the Rockinghams evolved a stage further. They favoured recognizing American independence and reviving Anglo-American business ties by giving the colonists favourable terms, so that Britain could concentrate on the war against France. And, remembering their love of consistency, they also conveyed the impression that they had always been liberal towards American demands.

His 2nd admin (1782) was forced on the unwilling K by the lack of an alternative after the fall of North. Moreover, Rockingham made a substantial constitutional innovation: he made the K agree in advance to accept 2 policy measures which the Rockinghams had advocated in opposition, namely, Economical Reform and independence for America. Rockingham was 1st Ld of the Treasury (Mar 1782) presiding over a divided Gov. Half the members were followers of Shelburne (through whom the K had communicated with the Rockinghams), and 1 – Thurlow, the Ld Chancellor – was a K's Friend in their midst. Bitter disagreement arose between the 2 Secs of State, Shelburne and Fox, whose responsibilities were for the 1st time allocated in the modern way, with Fox dealing with foreign affairs, and Shelburne dealing with home and colonial affairs. (a) Economical Reform – which in the event caused only a small reduction in Crown influence compared with Pitt the Younger's later admin reforms – consisted of 3 statutes. These were Crewe's Act for the disfranchisement of the revenue officers (1782); Clerke's Act disqualifying Gov contractors from being MPs (June 1782); and Burke's Civil Establishment Act (1782) pruning the number of sinecures at the K's disposal. (b) The H of C voted (May 1782) to expunge from the Journal the resolutions expelling Wilkes over the Middlesex elections; but rejected 2 motions (proposed by Pitt) to inquire into the redistribution of Parl seats and to shorten the life of Parl. (c) The Irish Parl was granted legislative independence (May 1782). (d) Progress towards American independence was hampered by the quarrels between the 2 Secs of State, each of whom was involved in the peace negotiations: Shelburne with the Americans and Fox with the Europeans. A settlement had not been reached when the ministry was suddenly brought to an end when Rockingham d of influenza.

Rohan, Henry, D de (21 Aug 1579–13 Apr 1638) Pr de Léon, leading French magnate and soldier who unsuccessfully led the Hugs against K LOUIS XIII of France and RICHELIEU.

Son of René II, Count of Rohan; ed at the Court of K HENRY IV, for whom he fought in the last of the FRENCH WARS OF RELIGION (1589–98); m (1605) Marguerite de Béthune, daughter of SULLY; made *Duc et paire* (1603). A proud aristocrat who was prepared to rough it with his men, he was also a sincere Prot who happened to believe that the maintenance and extension of the Hug 'state within a state' which had been endorsed by the Edict of Nantes (Apr 1598) was the only effective guarantee of the liberties of the great nobles in their provs against the centralizing policies of the monarchy. In the 1st 10 years of Louis XIII's reign (1610–20), when the magnates were in frequent rebellion against the Crown, he built himself a strong position among the Hugs in the S and SW, especially in the mountainous area of Upper Guyenne and Languedoc. Co-operating with his brother, the Seigneur de Soubise, who was dominant in Poitou, especially La Rochelle, Rohan saw himself as a WILLIAM of Orange in a breakaway Hug republic. When Louis defeated his mother, MARIE DE MEDICI, and the magnates at Ponts-de-Cé, Poitou, on 7 Aug 1620, and decided to eliminate the Hugs, his chief minister, LUYNES, began a series of successful campaigns in the SW and S, which were later completed by Richelieu (1625–9). Throughout the period, Rohan was the tireless organizer, not only of resistance among the somewhat incompatible city councillors and rural nobles of the gradually con-tracting Hug zone, but also of foreign help from Prot England (under BUCKING-HAM) and even RC Spain. He saved Montauban from capture during the siege of Aug–Nov 1621, but could not do the same for Montpellier (Aug–Oct 1622). By the Tr of Montpellier (Oct 1622), the Hugs were reduced to 5 cities and the Cevennes area, having lost the majority of their territory. Nevertheless, while Richelieu was occupied with the Habsburg threats in the THIRTY YEARS WAR, Rohan and Soubise broke out again in open revolt at La Rochelle in 1625, forcing Richelieu to make peace with them in the Tr of La Rochelle of Feb 1626 and with Spain in the Tr of Monzon of May 1626. Richelieu now determined to liquidate the Hug problem once and for all, and besieged La Rochelle until it surrendered on 28 Oct 1628. Rohan continued to hold out in the S, even signing an alliance with Spain on 3 May 1629; but his movement collapsed as England made peace in the Tr of Suze (Apr 1629), and as the Hugs accepted the Grace of Alais (June 1629). Rohan now spent the rest of his life in exile, partly as a Gen employed by Venice; partly fighting for France in the Valtelline (1635–7), where his Protestantism helped him for a time to win over the Swiss to the French side; and ultimately joining the army of Bernard of Saxe-Weimar on the upper Rhine.

Roses, Wars of the (1455–87) So-called, unhistorically, in C19 – the Red Rose and the White Rose supposedly having been the emblems of the Lancastrians and the Yorkists. The former claimed the throne of England through their direct male descent from John of Gaunt, 3rd son of K Edward III; the latter through their descent from the D of Clarence, 2nd son of K Edward III, but through Clarence's daughter. This legal quarrel would not have led to civil war if K Henry VI (1422–61 and 1470–71) had not been incapable of strong rule, first during his minority (1422–36) and then through some form of mental breakdown. One faction of magnates took possession of the K's Council and all the chief offices, thereby causing the gradual formation of a discontented opposition party out of which Richard, D of York, emerged as leader, demanding in 1450 a place on a new Council, and then in 1460 the throne itself. The fighting concerned only a small number of magnates and their retinues, without bothering the mass of the people; and the amount of campaigning totalled only 12–13 weeks in 32 years; yet there were at least 17 engagements, and the crown changed hands 5 times: Henry VI, 1422–61; Edward IV, 1461–70; Henry VI, 1470–71; Edward IV, 1471–83; Richard III, 1483–5; and finally the accession of HENRY VII, 1485. One of the chief claims to fame of the last is that, after defeating the Yorkists with the false claimant, Lambert SIMNEL, at the battle of Stoke in 1487, he ensured that that was the last battle of these wars.

Rudolf II (18 July 1552–20 Jan 1612) ArchD of Austria (Oct 1576–June 1608), K of Hungary (Sept 1572–June 1608), K of Bohemia (Sept 1575–June 1608), HREmp (Oct 1576), whose Court at Prague sheltered seers from all over Europe – experts in the occult arts, trying to penetrate the secrets of the universe, which for them was animated by hidden powers and criss-crossed by magical correspondences. Rudolf sought to reconcile RCs and Prots in some higher religious synthesis, and thus preserve Christianity and the Emp; but his eccentric, even insane, behaviour led to such a paralysis of Habsburg power, both in the Austrian Monarchy and in the HREmp (Germany), during the build-up of the tensions in the years preceding the THIRTY YEARS WAR, that his family forced him to abdicate in favour of his brother, MATTHIAS.

Eldest son of the Emp Maximilian II and Maria, daughter of the Emp CHARLES V; ed at Court and at the Court of K PHILIP II of Spain, safe from the Prot influences which then plagued Vienna; though he did not turn out to be the crusader for the COUNTER-REFORMATION that Philip hoped for. He was shy and melancholy, unstable and procrastinating, neurotic, deranged; and much happier consorting with the artists and scientists he collected round him than with the daily drudgery of Gov. He was as likely to take political advice from his valet as from his ministers. Leaving Austria to be ruled in practice by his brother, Ernest, until his death in 1595, and then by Matthias, he made Prague his capital (1583 onwards), and scholars and charlatans of all types enjoyed his patronage in the Hradčin, high above the city. Both the astronomers, Tycho Brahe and Johann Kepler, were briefly employed by him, and so was Giordano Bruno. Rudolf was deeply interested in alchemy and astrology, precious stones and exotic birds, botany, mathematics and Mannerist art. Eschewing the fanaticism of both Calvinistic Protestantism and Counter-Reformation Catholicism which was shortly to swamp his Kdom, he and his Court maintained the tolerant and cosmopolitan traditions of Renaissance HUMANISM.

In the Austrian Monarchy, the main features of his reign – the Turkish War, the resistance of the Estates, the spread of Protestantism, and his quarrel with his brother, Matthias – all worked together to weaken the Crown. In return for taxes voted for the war, Rudolf had to confirm, even extend, the privileges of the Estates. In their turn, the Estates represented the separatist interests of the various provs – Upper Austria, Lower Austria, Hungary, Bohemia, Moravia, Silesia etc – and also the class interests of the nobles and urban patricians. One of these interests was freedom of worship for Protestantism, now deeply entrenched in these classes. Moreover, the Estates gained and the monarchy lost as Rudolf and his brother bid against each other in offering advantages to the various Estates in order to win their support. Overall, the reign of Rudolf saw the monarchy slide dangerously towards decentralization and republicanism. The Turkish War (1593–1606) resulted partly from the ambitious plans of Rudolf to unite the Emp and Europe, R Cs and Prots, in a crusade against the enemy of Christianity, partly from the renewed aggressiveness of Turks in Hungary now that the stars were favourable and they were free (1590) of their long war with Persia. Successful during the 1st few years, Rudolf began to persecute the Hungarian Prots, who had hitherto been tolerated by Turkey. The Prot Estates of Hungary rebelled in alliance with the Calvinist István Bocskay, the new Turkish-backed Pr of Transylvania, whom they elected K of Hungary in place of Rudolf. Bocskay tried to widen the Prot front by invading Moravia and Bohemia in May 1605, but here both Prots and R Cs joined in opposing him – Czech national feeling against Hungary and Turkey outdoing religious zeal. Meanwhile, Rudolf's eccentric behaviour deteriorated into mental derangement from 1600 onwards. He quarrelled violently with his brother, who with his Habsburg cousins now began to plan his removal. Meeting in Vienna on 25 Apr 1606, they recognized Matthias as head of the family with full powers to regulate the succession and make war and peace. Matthias ended the Turkish War by making the Tr of Vienna with Bocskay (June 1606), recognizing him as Pr of Transylvania; and the Tr of Zsitva-Torok with Sultan Ahmed I of Turkey (Nov 1606) – neither of which Trs was accepted by Rudolf. The Estates of the various provs gained political and religious liberties at the expense of the monarchy in this period. Though aiming at greater centralization and absolutism, Rudolf was forced to guarantee prov liberties in order to get the Estates to vote taxes for the Turkish War. His quarrel with Matthias now had the same effect, for the latter bribed the Estates of Hungary, Austria and Moravia with religious and political concessions in order to get them to recognize him as sovereign instead of Rudolf (Tr of Libeň, or Lieben, June 1608). He invaded Bohemia to force Rudolf to recognize the peace Trs, but Bohemia and Silesia remained loyal to Rudolf, who likewise was forced to grant concessions to the Estates. In Prague, the so-called Spanish Party, favouring the aggressive Catholicism of Philip II, had been in power since the appointment of Zdeněk Lobkovic as Chancellor (1599); supported by the papal nuncio and the Spanish ambassador, they stiffened Rudolf into an attack on the nobles' privileges. For their part, the Bohemian Estates, led by Heinrich Matthias, Count von Thurn and Václav Budovec, prepared for armed resistance, and so Rudolf capitulated, issuing the famous Letter of Majesty (*Majestätsbrief*) on 9 July 1609, which was extended to Silesia on 20 July 1609. By it the Prots were granted full freedom of worship, the right to build churches and schools, full access to the universities etc – all guaranteed by certain powers that were given to the Estates. Henceforth, the Estates could elect 30 *defensors* to guard Prot rights. The Estates were also placed in charge of the admin of the Ch and Univ of Prague; and the Prot members could assemble whenever they wanted without the K's consent. The Letter placed Bohemia in the vanguard of European progress as far as self-gov and religious toleration were concerned. In economic evolution she was similarly placed. Moreover, the Estates made further gains when Rudolf tried to suppress them with undisciplined soldiery hired from his nephew and neighbour, ArchD Leopold, the Bp of Passau, in Jan 1611. The Estates' reply to this plundering expedition was to transfer their allegiance to Matthias, who invaded Bohemia and pressurized Rudolf into resigning (11 Aug 1611), having been elected K of Bohemia in his place by the Estates on 23 May 1611.

As HREmp, Rudolf was even less effective, as he presided over the early stages of those tensions which eventually produced the Thirty Years War: the spread of the REFORMATION and the Counter-Reformation, the mutinous behaviour of the German Prs, and the interference of foreign powers. Three developments brought war nearer. (a) The Donauwörth affair (1606–9). In this imperial, but Prot, city in Swabia, a riot between the RC minority and the Prot authorities in 1606 led the Emp to revoke its privileges, appointing MAXI- MILIAN I of Bavaria to execute the ban (1608). He annexed the city (1609) and re-catholicized it, because the Emp could not afford to pay his expenses. In the face of this violation of the Tr of Augsburg (Sept 1555), (b) The Prot Union was formed in May 1608 at Ahausen, nr Constance, under the leadership of Frederick V of the Palatinate; in reply to which Maximilian I of Bavaria formed the Cath League in July 1609 at Munich. (c) The Jülich-Cleves succession crisis (1609–14) was caused when D John William, ruler of Jülich, Cleves, Mark, Berg and Ravensberg, a group of provs on the lower Rhine between Cologne and the Netherlands frontier, d without issue on 25 Mar 1609. Using Leopold of Passau again, the Emp seized the provs in order to keep out the Prot claimants; but K HENRY IV of France made an alliance with the Prot Prs (Feb 1610) with a view to using the dispute in order to strike a blow at the Habsburgs. MAURICE of Orange of Holland occupied Jülich and general war was averted only by the assassination of Henry IV (14 May 1610). By the Tr of Xanten of Nov 1614, the disputed provs were divided between the legitimate heirs of the D: Brandenburg (Prot) and Neuburg (RC) – an arrangement negotiated by England and France. All these crises found the institutions of the Emp in a state of paralysis; though before the deluge came Rudolf d, refusing the last rites of the Ch.

Salisbury, Robert Cecil, 1st Earl of (1 June 1563–24 May 1612) Knight (1591), Baron Cecil of Essendine, Rutland (1603), Vt Cranborne (1604), Earl of Salisbury (May 1605); Sec (July 1596), Chancellor of the Duchy of Lancaster (1597), Ld Privy Seal (1597), Master of the Wards (1598), Ld High Treasurer (1608); chief minister of Q ELIZABETH I of England (1598–1603) and K JAMES VI AND I (1603–12), who brought England safely through the transition from one reign to the other.

2nd son of Ld BURGHLEY and his 2nd wife, Mildred; ed at home and at St John's, Cambridge, and Grey's Inn; m (1589) Elizabeth, daughter of William Brooke, 7th Ld Cobham (d 1591); trained for statesmanship by his father. A 5-foot hunchback – 'my pygmy', the Q called him, 'my little beagle', the K – he seemed too frail to bear the immense load of work he loyally carried day after day, and he eventually broke under the strain; yet with his sharp intellect, cautious attitude, patience, self-control and realism, he was head and shoulders above his contemporaries as a politician and statesman in both reigns, though similar to them in the intensity of his ambition and his ability to wax rich on Gov office.

Under Elizabeth in the 1590s he unofficially did the work of Sec after WAL-SINGHAM's death, as an apprentice to his father, until he was officially appointed to the office. During the last 10 years of the Q he was the chief Gov spokesman and manager in the H of C, and after his father's death, chief minister, though he achieved the latter position only after a prolonged struggle with the favourite, ESSEX, and his followers. He was chiefly responsible for guiding England safely through the problems that beset the last years of the Q: the struggle with Spain, the war in Ireland, the crisis in the economy, the demands of the Puritan and Cath minorities, the testiness of the H of C, the factious fights at Court, and the succession question.

Under James he toiled with scant recognition for a workshy K till the latter's mind became poisoned against him by the favourite, Robert CARR. In foreign affairs he made peace with Spain (Aug 1604), contributed to the negotiation of the 12-year truce between Spain and the Netherlands (Apr 1609), and supervised the *rapprochement* with the German Prots, symbolized later in the marriage of Prss Elizabeth and Frederick V, Count Palatine of the Rhine (14/24 Feb 1613). In religion he drove a wedge between the JESUITS and the secular clergy, and their followers, with a view to retaining the political loyalty of the latter, though his accommodating approach was made difficult by the GUNPOWDER PLOT. He lost the opportunity of reconciling the moderate PURITANS by satisfying their demands for reform, though he had little chance of creating a 'good and learned' ministry so long as the Ch was impoverished by lay patronage in over 40% of the benefices, to remove which would have amounted to a social revolution. In gov he improved the K's financial position. Prevented from reducing Gov expenditure by the crass extravagance of the K and the Court, he was forced to increase Gov income in ways which incurred the hostility of the people. The Crown leased the bulk of the customs collection to 3 financiers for a fixed rent: the Great Farm of 1604. Gov agents sought out Crown lands in private hands, called in old debts, and extracted more profit from the royal domain. Above all, Salisbury took advantage of the judges' decision in Bate's Case (July 1606), allowing the Crown to impose extra customs duties without Parl consent if the aim was to regulate trade. In July 1608 he extended impositions – as they came to be called – to practically every import, except foodstuffs, munitions and ships' stores. Finally in 1610 he negotiated the Great Contract, an attempt to put royal income on a rational basis. James would receive £200,000 annually in exchange for abandoning purveyance, wardship and other feudal rights. Unfortunately, there was insufficient trust between K and Parl for concessions of this kind to be agreed, and Parl was dissolved before the scheme was accepted. By this time Salisbury felt the hostility of both the K's enemies in Parl and his friends at Court. In Parl, the H of C got out of hand, mainly for reasons outside Salisbury's control, but partly because he found it increasingly difficult to manage the Commons from his seat in the Lords. At Court, the K was in the thrall of Robert Carr and his minions, who detested Salisbury, for the latter had no way of doing good for the country except at their expense. James treated his overworked statesman with callous indifference, blaming him for the trouble with Parl, and quietly excluding him from real power until Salisbury's health collapsed.

Savonarola, Gerolamo (21 Sept 1452–23 May 1498) Florentine religious reformer, democrat and martyr.

Son of Niccolò Savonarola, physician to the Court of Este; he left home secretly to join a Dominican priory at Bologna (Apr 1475). Becoming Prior of San Marco in Florence, he carried out a reform of the Order in Tuscany, and, somewhat in the manner of the ANABAPTISTS and SPIRITUALISTS of the REFORMATION, he began to mesmerize large congregations with his attacks on tyranny in the State and corruption in the Ch, and with his warnings of the imminence of divine wrath. When K CHARLES VIII of France invaded Italy in 1494 he seemed like the fulfilment of the prophecy, and when the ruler of Florence, Piero de' Medici, first opposed Charles and then made a humiliating submission, the popular party overthrew the Medici family on 9 Nov 1494, and under the guidance of Savonarola created a fairly democratic republic. While Savonarola preached against RENAISSANCE ideas and art, turned Florence into a stronghold of puritanism with his public burnings of 'vanities' such as gaming tables and jewellery, pictures and books, introduced pawnshops for the poor, attacked the authority of Pp ALEXANDER VI as 'a simoniac, heretic and infidel', and maintained Florence as a satellite of France, Florence itself became politically isolated in Italy, as the Holy League of Venice (31 Mar 1495) drove out the French. The defeat of Charles VIII, the papal excommunication (13 May 1497), and Savonarola's failure to answer the Franciscan challenge that he should demonstrate his boasted power to walk through fire (Apr 1498) all weakened his credibility in the eyes of Florentines who had also had enough of popular Gov and State prying into private lives. The various opposition factions in the city managed to gain the ascendancy, and Savonarola and 2 of his Dominican supporters were found guilty by a papal commission and then handed over to the magistrates of Florence, who had them crucified before the crowd on the Piazza della Signoria, and then burned.

Seven Years War, The (1756–63) A European and a colonial and naval war between Great Britain and Prussia on one side, and France, Austria, Russia, Sweden and Saxony on the other; in which Prussia was confirmed as a great power, and in which Britain defeated France and acquired the 1st British Emp. The European war arose out of the DIPLOMATIC REVOLUTION in which a coalition of France, Austria, Russia and Sweden aimed at taming the upstart Prussia of FREDERICK II, which had just conquered Silesia from Austria in the WAR OF THE AUSTRIAN SUCCESSION (1740–48). The colonial and naval war was a continuation of the long Anglo-French struggle for the control of the seas and of N America, the W Indies, W Africa and India. The 2 wars were interdependent, as Britain was in alliance with Prussia, and provided her with an annual subsidy, while Prussian military activity pinned down French troops and reduced the French effort in the colonies. At the same time, Britain not only maintained the so-called Army of Observation (of Hanoverians, Hessians and others) in W Germany to protect Prussia and Hanover from French attack, but also made attacks on the French fleet and on the French coastline, both of which reduced France's pressure on Prussia.

1756–8: The European war opened when Prussia invaded Saxony (29 Aug 1756), took Dresden (May 1757), then invaded Bohemia to be defeated by

Austria at Kolin, Bohemia (18 June 1757), after which Prussia had to withdraw. Thenceforth the war followed the same pattern each year, with Frederick II and his armies constantly on the move, fighting off repeated attacks from Russia, Sweden, Austria and France, winning tactical victories, but failing to change the overall strategical stalemate. In the W, France invaded Hanover and there defeated the Army of Observation under the D of Cumberland at Hastenbeck (26 July 1757), after which Cumberland concluded the disastrous Convention of Kloster-Zeven (Sept 1757) neutralizing his army and thus exposing Prussia and Hanover to French attack. In the E, Russia invaded E Prussia (Aug 1757), defeated Prussia at Gross Jägerndorf (19/30 Aug 1757), but then retreated back into Russia. Sweden invaded Pomerania (Oct 1757). Austria struck through Silesia, and briefly occupied Berlin (16 Oct 1757); but Prussia won 2 important victories: one against the Franco-Saxon army at Rossbach, Saxony (5 Nov 1757), and the other against Austria at Leuthen, Silesia (5 Dec 1757). Britain, where PITT the Elder had assumed control of the war, then repudiated the cease-fire of Kloster-Zeven (28 Nov 1757), assumed financial responsibility for the Army of Observation, reinforced it, and replaced Cumberland with Pr Ferdinand of Brunswick, who proceeded to drive the French out of Hanover and then back over the Rhine at Emmerich (27 Mar 1758). At the same time, by the 2nd Tr of Westminster (Apr 1758), Britain began to pay Prussia an annual subsidy. In the E, once more, Russia invaded E Prussia, taking Königsberg (11/22 Jan 1758) and occupying the prov for the rest of the war. In conjunction with Sweden, Russia then invaded Brandenburg; but Prussia defeated them at Zorndorf (14/25 Aug 1758), at great loss, in what proved to be the bloodiest battle of the war. Subsequently at Hochkirk, Saxony, Austria defeated Prussia on 14 Oct 1758, but failed to follow up the victory.

The colonial and naval war: Though Britain was officially at peace with France until 15 May 1756, unofficial warfare between the 2 peoples had continued since the War of the Austrian Succession. (a) In India the E India Companies of Britain and France were fighting for commercial dominance in an increasingly unstable continent where the decaying Mogul Emp was breaking up to the advantage of numerous warlike Prs. Though Pitt sent out reinforcements – as did the French – the war in India depended on the leaders on the spot much more than on the European Govs. In Bengal, the new Nawab, Siraj-ud-Daulah, captured the British station at Calcutta and, according to tradition, one of his subordinates locked up 146 British in the so-called Black Hole for the night (20 June 1756), and 123 of them d. Sailing from Madras, Robert Clive recaptured Calcutta in Jan 1757, defeated the Nawab at Plassey (23 June 1757), replaced him with a puppet – Mir Jafar – drove the French out of their station at nearby Chandernagore, and established the British E India Co's control over all Bengal, Bihar and Orissa. (b) In Africa Britain was trying to drive the French out of Senegal and thus increase its stake in the valuable slave trade with America and its control of the sea-lanes. A small expedition took Fort Louis from France in Apr 1758; a second squadron captured Goree (Dakar) further S on 31 Dec 1758. (c) In America the French were attempting to link up their settlements in Louisiana in the S with those in Canada in the N by a chain of forts along the Ohio and Mississippi valleys; the British colonists on the E seaboard were determined to break through this barrier and expand into the Middle W. At the same time, Britain wanted to take over the fur trade and fishing industry of Canada. Already a force of Virginians under young George Washington had surrendered to the French and their Indian allies in a struggle over one of the new strongpoints, Fort Duquesne (3 July 1754); while Gen James Braddock, with reinforcements from England, was killed and his men captured 9 miles from the same place on 9 July 1755. Moreover, on 14 Aug 1756, the French under their warlike new commander, the Marquis de Montcalm, captured Fort Oswego on Lake Ontario, along with 1,400 men. When Pitt came to power, Britain concentrated on driving the French from Canada with a new intensity. The 1st blow failed, when the expedition against Louisbourg at the mouth of the St Lawrence withdrew without making an attack (May–June 1757). Pitt now put into action a 3-fold attack: 1st up the St Lawrence via Louisbourg and Quebec; 2nd from the Hudson valley via Ticonderoga and Crown Point and the Great Lakes; 3rd into the Ohio valley against Fort Duquesne. The 1st and 3rd began successfully, with the capture of Louisbourg (26 July 1758) by Gen Amherst and Admiral Boscawen, and of Fort Duquesne (25 Nov 1758) by Brigadier Forbes – a fortress soon renamed Pittsburgh. Unfortunately, the 2nd expedition under Gen Abercromby failed to take Ticonderoga (8 July 1758). (d) In the W Indies France and Britain were fighting for as many rich sugar islands as they could capture, but Pitt was unable to mount a big effort there as yet. (e) In Europe the French began the sea war well by conquering Minorca (28 June 1756), a British disaster for which Admiral Byng was later executed as a scapegoat (14 Mar 1757). Pitt tried to relieve pressure on the colonies and on Prussia by raids on the French coasts, the value of which was disputed then, and still is by historians. The attack on Rochefort (10 miles up the R Charente) was a failure (Sept–Oct 1757). In June 1758 an expedition landed at St Malo, Brittany, and set fire to it. On 8 Aug 1758 Cherbourg, Normandy, was taken, the fortifications demolished, and the town pillaged. A 2nd attempt to take St Malo in Sept 1758 failed. At the same time, the British fleet blockaded the 2 French naval bases: Brest in Brittany and Toulon in Provence.

1759–60: The European war continued its slow torture of Frederick II, though the pressure on him was reduced slightly by the decision of the new French chief minister, Choiseul, to reduce French aid to Austria (3rd Tr of Versailles, Mar 1759) so as to concentrate on Britain. In W Germany, Ferdinand of Brunswick saved the situation by heavily defeating the French at Minden, Westphalia, on 1 Aug 1759, a victory which confirmed Pitt in his new policy of strengthening the Army of Observation. In E Germany, Russia and Austria invaded Brandenburg, and gave Frederick II his worst defeat of the war at Kunersdorf (1/12 Aug 1759), though through mutual distrust they failed to follow up this success. Austria invaded Saxony, took Dresden (14 Sept 1759), and forced the Prussian army to capitulate at Maxen (21 Nov 1759). In Silesia, Austria beat Prussia at Landshut (23 June 1760), but combined Russo-Austrian forces failed to co-operate and were defeated by Prussia at Leignitz (4/15 Aug 1760). In Brandenburg, a joint Russo-Austrian force made a ceremonial entry into Berlin on 28 Sept/9 Oct 1760, but left 4 days later; in Saxony, Prussia beat Austria at Torgau (3 Nov 1760), though without loosening Austria's hold on most of Saxony and Silesia.

In the colonial and naval war these were years of Britain's crucial victories over France. (a) In India the main Anglo-French struggle was in the Carnatic, where the new French general, Lally-Tollendal, besieged Madras (Dec 1758–Mar 1759) until reinforcements from Britain relieved the city and then defeated the French at Wandewash (22 Jan 1760). Further N the French were driven out of Masulipatam (8 Apr 1759), leaving them only Pondicherry, which itself fell in Jan 1761. (b) In America the remaining 2 tasks of Pitt's triple assault on the French under new commanders were completed with total success. One expedition under Gen Wolfe and Admiral Saunders advanced up the St Lawrence and took Quebec from Montcalm on 18 Sept 1759; the other force under Gen Amherst, approaching by the Hudson and the Lakes, took Fort Niagara, between Lakes Ontario and Erie, in June 1759, and Ticonderoga and Crown Point on Lake Champlain in July and Aug 1759; after this they captured Montreal (8 Sept 1760), and with it all Canada. (c) In the W Indies the British took Guadelupe on 1 May 1759, and Marie Galante in the following month. (d) In Europe France mounted an ambitious scheme to invade England in order to take British pressure off France in Europe and the colonies, but this was rendered impossible by Admiral Boscawen's destruction of the Toulon fleet off Lagos Bay, S Portugal (19 Aug 1759), and Admiral Hawke's victory over the Brest fleet off Quiberon Bay, Brittany (20–22 Nov 1759), two victories which not only ended French plans to invade England but also made it impossible to reinforce their defences in America and the West Indies.

1761–2: Political changes began to ease the way towards peace. In Britain the new K, GEORGE III, ascended the throne on 25 Oct 1760, and he and most of his ministers except Pitt were war-weary and chary of humiliating France further. Anglo-French peace-talks began in Mar 1761, but Choiseul's position hardened as France began to receive support from Spain. In Spain the new K, CHARLES III, who succeeded on 10 Aug 1759, was hostile to Britain and revived old Spanish grievances: that British privateers were not respecting Spanish neutrality, that British merchants were illegally taking logwood (for dyes) from Honduras, and that Spain ought to have a share in Canadian fishing. As a result, France and Spain renewed their old alliance, the Family Compact (Aug 1761), whereby Spain promised to join in the war on France's side if no satisfactory peace had been signed by 1 Apr 1762. In Britain, Pitt wished to strike first by declaring war on Spain, but his colleagues disagreed and he resigned (5 Oct 1761). The reconstructed Gov under BUTE reduced aid to Prussia, but nevertheless eventually declared war on Spain on 2 Jan 1762.

The European war continued to stretch Prussia's resources to breaking point, with, in the E, Russia and Sweden overrunning Pomerania, and Austria and Russia expelling Prussia from Silesia and Saxony; and, in the W, Pr Ferdinand's army fighting indecisive engagements with the French. Prussia's position grew desperate with the cut-back in British aid, but good fortune saved Frederick from destruction. On 5 Jan 1762 the Empress ELIZABETH of Russia d, and her successor, PETER III, long an ardent admirer of Frederick II, ordered an end to Russian attacks. Russia made peace with Prussia on 24 Apr/5 May 1762; Sweden made peace with Prussia on 22 May 1762; and all conquests were returned. In view of this, and of France's concentration on Britain, Austria had to cede that the reconquest of Silesia was impossible. The way to peace was open.

The colonial and naval war continued to follow Pitt's plans, whether he was in office or not. (a) In Europe Britain took Belle Ile, Brittany (8 June 1761). (b) In the W Indies Britain took Martinique from France (Jan 1762), followed by St Lucia, St Vincent, Grenada and Tobago; as well as Havana, Cuba, from Spain (Aug 1762). (c) In the Philippines Britain also took Manila from Spain in Oct 1762.

The Peace Treaties: The Tr of Paris (10 Feb 1763) between Britain and France (and Spain in Aug 1763). (a) In America France ceded to Britain Canada, Cape Breton Island and the Middle W as far as the Mississippi; but shared the fishing rights off Newfoundland and in the St Lawrence and received the islands of St Pierre and Miquelon as fishing bases. Spain ceded Florida to Britain, allowed logwood cutters in Honduras, and renounced her Canadian fishing claims. France ceded Louisiana to Spain. (b) In the W Indies France ceded to Britain Grenada, Dominica, St Vincent and Tobago; but recovered Martinique, St Lucia, Guadelupe and Marie Galante; while Spain recovered Havana. (c) In the Philippines Spain recovered Manila. (d) In Africa France ceded Senegal to Britain, but recovered Goree. (e) In India France and Britain restored their mutual conquests, returning to the territorial position of 1749; but French power was at an end in India as she was not allowed to rebuild her fortifications; while Britain was firmly in control of Bengal which had been conquered from the Indians. (f) In Europe Britain recovered Minorca; France recovered Belle Ile; and France had to evacuate and restore territories conquered in Hanover, Hesse and Brunswick; and also evacuate Prussia's Rhenish territories, as well as Ostend and Nieuwpoort in the Austrian Netherlands.

The Tr of Hubertusburg (15 Feb 1763) between Prussia, Austria and Saxony restored the pre-war situation (Prussia kept Silesia); and Prussia promised to vote for MARIA THERESA's son, Joseph, as K of Rome, and thus future H R Emp JOSEPH II.

Seymour, Edward (c 1505–22 Jan 1552) Vt Beauchamp (1536), Earl of Hertford (1537), D of Somerset (1547), Ld Protector of England (1547), Tudor soldier and statesman who became leading minister of K EDWARD VI until he was ousted by his erstwhile ally, John DUDLEY, D of Northumberland, and executed.

Eldest son of Sir John Seymour of Savernake, Wilts, and Margaret Wentworth (and thus brother of Q Jane Seymour); m Anne Stanhope; became courtier to K HENRY VIII and rose in his councils as a soldier, diplomat and politician. He was Ld Admiral (1542–3), saw military service in Scotland (May 1544 and Sept 1545), and in France (1545 and 1546), and was made Lieut of the Kdom during Henry VIII's last visit to France in 1544. By 1546 he and John Dudley were Protestants and leaders of the new generation who were opposed to the 3rd D of NORFOLK and his conservative faction, and who, as leading councillors, contributed to the overthrow of their rivals in the last hours of the old K's reign. Keeping the K's death secret from 28 to 31 Jan 1547 – while he made his dispositions and also made free with the K's will – he announced himself Governor of the young K Edward VI and Protector of the realm. Shortly after he promoted himself D of Somerset, and placed the Gov in the hands of CRANMER and Dudley, pushing aside the conservative Norfolks, including GARDINER and BONNER. Ambitious and arrogant, but also refined and idealistic, he embarked at once upon an ambitious programme of: settling the Franco-Scottish problem with inadequate resources; moving moderately towards Protestantism in the

Ch while so disarming the State that it was powerless to block the rush into religious anarchy and theological radicalism; and attempting to solve the social and economic problems on the basis of a false diagnosis of their causes.

In Scotland he formed a visionary scheme of forcing an Anglo-Scottish union on the basis of the marriage of K Edward VI and MARY, Q OF SCOTS (betrothed July 1543); but the only union he achieved by his invasion of Scotland and his victory at Pinkie, near Musselburgh, on 10 Sept 1547 – and his hand-out of free Bibles there – was the union of all the Scots against England. They sent Mary to France, and he had to abandon the hopeless task of dominating them. In France K HENRY II was making inroads on the defences of Boulogne, which Henry VIII had captured on 18 Sept 1544. Seymour was forced to sign the Tr of Boulogne (Mar 1550), by which he had to hand back Boulogne immediately in exchange for only 400,000 crowns, instead of the previous arrangement laid down in the Tr of Ardres (June 1546) whereby the K of England was to get 2 million crowns for handing it back in 1554.

In the Church Seymour ceased to enforce the anti-Prot laws of Henry VIII, as well as the Treason laws and other means of enforcing them, a policy of dangerous liberalism which filled the country with Continental preachers of every hue and spawned a mixed brood of radical sects. At the same time *Injunctions* (1547) were issued against shrines, stained glass etc; Cranmer's rather Zwinglian *Homilies* were ordered to be read in churches by the clergy; every Ch was to possess a copy of ERASMUS's *Paraphrases*; services were to be in English. Seymour also continued the policy initiated by Henry VIII of the DISSOLUTION OF THE MONASTERIES: he secularized the property of the Chantries and other charitable institutions founded by the Ch (1547). Another Act allowed communion in both kinds (1547), while the Act of Uniformity (1549) enforced Cranmer's moderately Prot 1st Prayer Book in English, and clerical marriage was legalized by statute the same year. The unrest which these swift changes stimulated (eg the rebellion in Devon and Cornwall of June–Aug 1549, where English was not spoken and the new Prayer Book seemed 'like a Christmas game') was also partly due to social distress.

The social problem was the result of the PRICE REVOLUTION (at its peak 1547–51 due to Gov manipulation of the currency) and the speeding up of the growth of capitalism, especially the enclosure of the common fields and pastures (rampant 1540–55), which led to pauperism, unemployment and the disappearance of villages, and caused much discontent and rioting. Seymour's policy was that of the 'Commonwealth Men', who believed that the problem was the result of the greed of hard-faced landlords; and he backed John Hales who tried to get legislation passed forbidding enclosures and profiteering, and giving security of tenure to the peasants. Composed as it was of landlords, Parl not merely rejected these bills, but also enacted savage measures against the able-bodied poor (1547). Baulked here, Seymour issued proclamations against enclosures and set up Royal Commissions to investigate the problem (1548). In this atmosphere, Kett's Rebellion broke out (July 1549) in Norfolk, where a force of 12,000 farmers, thinking the 'good Duke' was on their side in their opposition to the enclosure of the commons, rising rents etc, dominated Norwich practically as a separate political unit from 12 July to 27 Aug, the day on which they were cut to pieces at Dussindale nearby by troops under John Dudley, Earl of Warwick. This failure to maintain law and order – even this encouragement of disorder – was a serious blow to Seymour's prestige, while the victory over the rebels was a feather in Dudley's cap as far as the upper classes were concerned. A further blow was the judicial murder of his own brother, Thomas, Ld Seymour of Sudely. This ambitious but corrupt Ld Admiral and husband of ex-Q Catherine Parr was condemned by Act of Attainder for conspiring against the Protector and beheaded on 20 Mar 1549. Moreover, Seymour was just as haughty and tactless in his dealings with his fellow councillors as he was impolitic in alienating the powerful in the country at large; his extravagant building of Somerset House in the Strand, London, from 1547 onwards – involving as it did the destruction of the town houses of 2 Bps and the confiscation of much ecclesiastical property – shocked everyone. Dudley pretended to be friendly towards Catholicism, and soon outmanoeuvred Seymour on the Council and in the mind of the young K. Seymour was arrested on 10 Oct 1549, but released again on 2 Feb 1550 while Dudley made ready for the kill. On a false charge of conspiracy he was arrested again on 16 Oct 1551 and executed for felony on Tower Hill. His liberal policy had alienated Caths and moderate Prots without satisfying the radicals. His 'Commonwealth' attitude to society had scared all property owners without giving the poor much practical help. His foreign disasters shamed everyone. And to suppress the riots which his policies provoked he relied on his most dangerous rival. In the circumstances, efficient pragmatism would have been better than his high-minded incompetence.

Sforza, Ludovico ('il Moro') (27 July 1452–27 May 1508) D of Milan (1494) who invited K CHARLES VIII of France to invade Italy, but who was taken prisoner by K LOUIS XII to France, where he d.

Younger son of Francesco Sforza, a leading *condottiere* who was chosen D of Milan by the people in 1450 after he conquered it. Ludovico's elder, illegitimate brother, Galeazzo Maria Sforza, succeeded their father as D in Mar 1466, but was assassinated on 26 Dec 1476 and succeeded by his son, Gian Galeazzo. It was during the rule of this boy that his uncle Ludovico, a skilful and ruthless politician, managed to become the *de facto* ruler from 1479 onwards. He m (1491) Beatrice d'Este, a wise, gifted, and cultivated collaborator, who helped him make Milan a centre of Renaissance art and literature, employing Donato Bramante and Leonardo da Vinci, among others. Sforza was deeply involved in the 1st 2 HABSBURG–VALOIS WARS of 1494–5 and 1499–1505, during which 2 successive French Ks invaded Italy. Here the 40-year-long peace since the Tr of Lodi (1454), based on the triple alliance of Milan, Florence and Naples, began to be threatened by the death of Lorenzo the Magnificent of Florence on 8 Apr 1492, and by strife which broke out between Milan and Naples, partly due to family quarrels. Feeling isolated, Sforza encouraged Charles VIII of France, who claimed Naples, to invade Italy and take attention away from Milan; but with the easy French conquest of Naples on 22 Feb 1495 he switched sides to join the Holy League of Venice (Mar 1495) which expelled the French from Italy after the battle of Fornovo on 6 July 1495. At the same time he m his niece Bianca Maria to the Emp MAXIMILIAN I (Mar 1494), provided him with 440,000 ducats, and rendered other services too, all of which stood him in good stead when his nephew, D Gian Galeazzo, d on 22 Oct 1494. Sforza was able to get himself recognized as D (although Gian Galeazzo had a son) both by the Milanese (1494), and by the Emp, who officially invested him with the Duchy in return for further financial aid in 1495. The 2nd French invasion of Italy, however, was directed at Milan itself, for Louis XII's claim derived from his wife's descent from the Visconti family – predecessors of the Sforzas as Ds of Milan. On the French approach Sforza fled to the Tyrol (Sept 1499) to seek the Emp's help, and the French K solemnly took possession of the city on 6 Oct 1499. Hiring Swiss mercenaries and taking advantage of the anti-French unrest among the Milanese, Sforza retook his capital on 5 Feb 1500. However, he was defeated at nearby Novara on 8 Apr 1500, when his Swiss refused to fight Louis' Swiss, and was captured as he was trying to pass through the French lines disguised as a common soldier (10 Apr 1500). He spent the rest of his life in a dungeon in the Château of Loches, on the Indre in France.

Shaftesbury, Anthony Ashley Cooper, 1st Earl of (22 July 1621–21 Jan 1683) Great landowner with City and colonial interests, who fought for the K and then Parl in the CIVIL WAR, becoming a minister to the restored CHARLES II – the only Commonwealth backer to do so – but later gaining notoriety as the opposition leader who without scruple exploited the odious perpetrators of the POPISH PLOT in a campaign to exclude the future K JAMES II from the throne, and in so doing provided the driving force behind the opposition groupings who came to be known as the WHIGS. In the history of the Country v Court struggle he was the link between the Civil War generation and that of the REVOLUTION OF 1688.

Eld surviving son of John Cooper and Anne Ashley, representatives of 2 families which had prospered under the Tudors, and whose combined estates made Shaftesbury exceedingly wealthy; ed privately as a Puritan, then at Exeter, Oxford (1637) and Lincoln's Inn (1638); m 1st (1639) Lady Margaret Coventry, daughter of Thomas, 1st Ld Coventry, Ld Keeper of the Privy Seal (d 11 July 1649); m 2nd (1650) Lady Frances Cecil, of the family of BURGHLEY and SALISBURY (d 31 Dec 1652); m 3rd (1655) Lady Margaret Spencer, sister of the 1st Earl of Sunderland.

1640–60, during the Civil War and Interregnum, he became MP for Tewkesbury, Glos, in the Short Parl (Apr–May 1640) – one of the youngest members – and then was elected for Downton, Pembrokeshire, in the Long Parl (3 Nov 1640 onwards), but his election was disputed and the issue not decided for 17 years, with the result that he took no part in the revolutionary debates of 1641–2, though his later career shows that he must have learned a great deal from PYM's activities in the art of managing Parl and exploiting public feeling outside. On the outbreak of the Civil War he raised troops for the K (1643), but then joined Parl (Feb 1644), probably disliking the absolutist pro-Cath elements among the Royalists. He was chosen for Barebone's Parl (July–Dec 1653) as well as the Council of State (July 1653), belonging to the conservative group which voted to dissolve the Parl early one morning before the radicals and visionaries had arrived. A typical Whig, he opposed absolute monarchy, but also feared democracy, and he later remarked to Evelyn on 'the misery of being under a mechanic tyranny'. Moreover, though he was a Puritan he was no sectary. He opposed the clerical pretensions of churchmen such as LAUD, but nevertheless favoured an established Ch with tithes and patronage, but also with toleration for dissenters.

His many changes of side earned him an evil reputation until recently for cynical careerism, but it can be argued that he remained faithful to his ideals throughout, and that his slipperiness – he was known as the 'Dorsetshire eel' – resulted from his exploitation of the changing situation in order best to realize them. He backed the *Instrument of Gov* (Dec 1653) which made CROMWELL Ld Protector, being MP in the 1st Protectorate Parl (Sept 1654–Jan 1655) and a member of the Council of State, until he broke with Cromwell for dissolving Parl. He was MP in the 2nd Protectorate Parl (Sept 1656–Feb 1658), but was one of the awkward members whom the Protector excluded from sitting. In the anarchy after Cromwell's death (3 Sept 1658) he sat in Richard Cromwell's Parl (Jan–Apr 1659); but could not sit in the recalled Rump (May–Oct 1659) because his Downton dispute was still unsettled, though he was in the Council of State it chose (May 1659). When LAMBERT and the Gen dispersed the Rump and aimed at the perpetuation of their own power, Shaftesbury conspired with Scot and Haslerig and other Rump Republicans, and also made contact with MONCK, the Gov of Scotland. The Rump was recalled (Dec 1659) and decided the Downton dispute in his favour so that he could at last take his seat (Jan 1660). Shaftesbury, however, discovered that the Rump was also out to perpetuate its own power; he put his weight behind Monck who reached London with his army on 3 Feb 1660, took charge, and organized the restoration of the monarchy. Though no Cavalier, Shaftesbury supported the return of the K as the only way to eliminate the army, the Republicans and the fanatics, and secure a return to genuine Parl Gov. He was MP in the Convention Parl (Apr–Dec 1660) and was one of the commissioners sent to the Hague to invite Charles to return.

1660–73, when he was in the Gov, he served in the 1st 2 ministries of Charles II, that of CLARENDON (1660–67), and that of the Cabal (1667–73), becoming Ld Ashley (1661) and Chancellor of the Exchequer (1661), a regular member of the Cab Council or Committee of Foreign Affairs (autumn 1670 onwards), President of the Council of Trade and Plantations (1672), Earl of Shaftesbury (1672), and Ld Chancellor (1672). During these years he proved himself a skilled frontbench spokesman in the H of L, and a diligent and innovating administrator, who helped to organize the Restoration settlement, backed the change-over from farming the customs to Gov collection (1671), opposed the Stop of the Exchequer (1672) – though he had no alternative solution – supported the 2nd Dutch War (1672–4) – witness his resounding *Delenda est Carthago* speech of 5 Feb 1673 – and appreciated the importance of trade and colonization more than any other politician of his time. By now tending towards deism, he took a latitudinarian, anti-clerical line in religious policy, and supported any moves to aid the Dissenters, eg the Declarations of Indulgence of Dec 1662 and Mar 1672. On the other hand, he supported the Test Act (Mar 1673), which drove all Caths out of public office, for by this time a significant change had occurred in the situation. The Q had proved to be barren, and James, D of York – the future K James II and now heir to the throne – was a Cath. Moreover, Shaftesbury now began to realize how the K had deceived him with his pro-Cath, pro-French, and pro-absolutist secret Tr of Dover (May 1670) with France. Thus the Test Act may have been inconsistent with the tolerance shown in the Declarations of Indulgence, but the problem was no longer the freedom of worship of peaceable Cath citizens, but the danger of the State being captured by a ruler bent on turning it into a Cath

411

ABSOLUTISM by force and with French help. It was to avoid this catastrophe that Shaftesbury began to take an independent line and concentrate on keeping James off the throne – the policy of Exclusion. The K dismissed him on 9 Nov 1673, partly at James's request. By this time, Shaftesbury's small frail body was already tortured and bent by the disability which plagued him for the rest of his life, and which brought him prematurely aged to an early grave. Severe pains on the left side which he had known since youth so intensified in May 1668 that he agreed to an operation – a courageous decision in those days without anaesthetics or antiseptics. Thanks to the notes taken by John Locke – a friend and member of Shaftesbury's household, 1667 onwards – modern medicine can identify his trouble as a hydatid cyst of the liver. After its removal, the surgeon inserted a tube to drain it, which Shaftesbury had to endure for the rest of his life, and which gave Tory writers the chance to call him 'Tapski' and make jokes about his surname, Cooper.

1673–83, in opposition, Shaftesbury henceforth concentrated his political skills on the Exclusion campaign. By this time the Cavalier Parl (May 1661–Jan 1679) no longer deserved its name, having ceased to be the co-operative Ch-and-K assembly it was initially. Diverse new opposition groups appeared, each with its own grievances or ideals, belonging to a variety of social groups, and consisting of either original Cavaliers now disillusioned, or younger men brought in at by-elections. These added themselves to the original 60 or so ex-Roundheads who had always opposed the Court: former 'Presbyterians' who disliked the Restoration religious settlement. Among the opposition members were stiff-necked Country MPs – the permanent Outs – who despised the Court for its extravagance, its corruption, its weak foreign policy, or its absolutist and Cath tendencies. There were also the Outs who were longing to be in, some of whom backed the K's bastard son, MONMOUTH, for K. In addition, there were the urban radicals patronized by the 2nd D of Buckingham, heirs of the LEVELLERS and Republicans, who did not become MPs, but agitated in the constituencies under Parl leadership. It was Shaftesbury's pioneering achievement to compound these gritty elements, not into a party in the modern sense – though they came to be called the Whig party from 1681 – but into a grouping sufficiently united to overthrow the new chief minister, DANBY, and his Court – or Tory – party, force the dissolution of the Cavalier Parl, and win the elections to the 3 Exclusion Parls (Mar–July 1679, Oct 1679–Jan 1681 and 21–28 Mar 1681) only to be blocked in the end by 2 obstacles he could not circumvent. One was the split in the Exclusionists between those who favoured WILLIAM and Mary as the replacements for James, and Shaftesbury's followers who backed Monmouth, though Shaftesbury himself never disclosed his own view. The other obstacle was the cheerful obduracy of Charles II, and his ability (1681–5) to do without Parl, thanks to financial assistance from LOUIS XIV. Shaftesbury fused the opposition together by giving them a cause – Exclusion – around which they could unite; by exploiting to the full the Popish Plot and Montagu's revelations about Danby's correspondence with France; and by using all the methods of managing Parl and swaying public opinion that had been invented in Pym's day and developed since. He used rational arguments, and appealed to the most unlovely prejudices. He made threats and promises, exploited influence, had Parl votes printed and published and, with the help of Locke, he produced pamphlets such as his 'Letter from a Person of Quality to his Friend in the Country' (Nov 1675). In 1676 he moved his residence to Thanet House, Aldersgate Street, in the City, an address from which he could sway City elections, whip up the enthusiasm of the Green Ribbon Club in Chancery Lane – green had been the Levellers' colour – organize petitions to the Gov and instructions to M Ps, and bring the mob out on to the streets in massive Pope-burning processions. Even his arrest and imprisonment in the Tower (16 Feb 1677–27 Feb 1678), and the brilliant satire of Dryden's *Absolom and Achitophel* (1681), merely highlighted him as the Whig leader. Moreover, his short period of office as Ld President of the Council (Apr–Oct 1679) – when the K reluctantly added opposition members to the Privy Council in the hope of buying them off – did not clip his wings, for Charles did not consult his new ministers, and Shaftesbury certainly did not behave like a member of the Court. His second arrest (2 July 1681) on a charge of high treason only added to his glory. Thanks to the Whig machine, the City elections of June 1681 produced a Whig victory, so that Whig sheriffs could nominate a Whig Grand Jury which at the Old Bailey on 24 Oct 1681 dismissed the charge, causing the City to stay up all night carousing round bonfires. Shaftesbury was released on bail by the Court of K's Bench (Nov 1681), but in Feb 1682 the charge against him was dropped. The K was aiming at him from another angle: the attack on the borough charters. On 28 Sept 1682, by blatant trickery, Charles succeeded in having Tory sheriffs sworn in. The next day, Shaftesbury went into hiding, mainly in Wapping, then in Amsterdam, where he arrived to take refuge with Brownist exiles on 2 Dec 1682. But by now he was already a very sick man. By 26 Dec 1682 the discharge through his tube had ceased and he was unable to retain food, but in the end his death was sudden and peaceful.

Sickingen, Franz von (2 Mar 1481–7 May 1523) German knight prominent in private warfare who became the self-styled protector of the Prots during the REFORMATION.

He enriched himself by private warfare, trying to build up a landed position which would raise him above the knightly class, which was going down before the rising power of the Prs and the cities. He attacked Worms in 1513 and Mainz in 1518, and then in 1519 led the army of the Swabian League against the D of Württemberg, who had murdered Hans von Hutten during a hunting party. This brought von Sickingen in contact with the latter's kinsman, Ulrich von HUTTEN, under whose influence he now set himself up as the protector of the Prot cause. BUCER became his chaplain in 1522, while he himself became the focus of German national discontent with Rome, and the champion of the knightly class against all its enemies. Attacking Trier in 1522, he began the KNIGHTS' WAR (1522–3), in which he was fatally wounded in his stronghold at Landstuhl, Palatinate.

Sigismund (Zygmunt) III Vasa (20 June 1566–30 Apr 1632) K of Poland (1587), K of Sweden (1592–99), who was deposed by the Swedes; and whose pursuit of narrow family and Ch aims as K of Poland, as well as his over-involvement in foreign wars, ensured that his attempts to end the chronic lack of central authority in the Polish constitution were successfully opposed by the nobility and gentry. In his wars with Russia, Turkey and Sweden, he had only limited success,

413

despite the favourable circumstances provided by the Russian TIME OF TROUBLES (1598–1613) and the THIRTY YEARS WAR (1618–48).

Eld son of K John III of Sweden and his Q consort, Catherine Jagiello; ed as a Cath by his mother; m 1st (1592) Anna of Styria (d 10 Feb 1598); m 2nd (1605) Constance of Styria (d 10 July 1631), both sisters of the Emp FERDINAND II. Cultured and pious, he was too haughty to secure the co-operation of his subjects and too naive to cope successfully with harsh political realities. In Sweden he left in charge an aristocratic Regency led by his uncle, Charles of Södermanland, the youngest son of GUSTAV I VASA. Charles made a typical Vasa alliance with the masses and overthrew Sigismund (1598) and deposed him, soon after becoming K himself as Charles IX (1604). This led to many wars over Polish claims to the Swedish throne, exacerbated by the religious conflict between Prot Sweden and Cath Poland.

In Poland he had been elected K partly because his mother was a Jagiello, and partly because both Poland and Sweden were considering action against the Wward advance of Russia. (a) The political power of the Crown was already inferior to that of the Diet (*Seym*), which consisted of the Senate (magnates) and the Chamber of Deputies (mainly *szlachta*, or gentry), and whose consent was required for important matters such as taxation and foreign policy. The Diet was ineffective, however, since action required a unanimous vote; thus power was decentralized into the hands of the magnates with their vast estates, private armies and sway over prov assemblies. In the Diet of 1606, Sigismund's measures to introduce majority voting, a permanent revenue and a standing army provoked a revolt of the anarchic gentry led by Mikolaj Zebrzydowski (1606–9) which was put down, but which ensured the continuation of central-Gov paralysis. (b) In the Ch, where the COUNTER-REFORMATION, spearheaded by the JESUITS from the 1560s, was having great success, Sigismund gave such wholehearted support to the reconversion of Prots that Poland became the bastion of militant Catholicism in E Europe and Sigismund earned the title of the 'Polish PHILIP II'. He supported the Union of Brześć (Brest) (1596) which created the Uniate Ch: a joint Cath-Orthodox organization recognizing the Pp but also allowing E rites. By no means all the Orthodox joined, however, especially in E Poland among the White Russians and Ukrainians, where the Orthodox cause was sustained with help from Russians and COSSACKS. (c) Foreign policy was complicated by this. In the Russian War (1609–19), Sigismund took advantage of the Time of Troubles (1598–1613) to aim at the Russian throne and to establish the Cath Ch there. His forces beat the Russo-Swedish army at Klushino (24 June/4 July 1610) and took Moscow in Oct 1610 and Smolensk in June 1611. A faction of *boyars* even elected his son, WLADYSLAW, tsar in 1610. However, the revival of Russian patriotism and Orthodox fervour, as well as the election of MICHAEL Romanov (Feb 1613), put a stop to these fantasies. Moreover, a 2nd campaign by Wladyslaw of 1617–18 failed to conquer Russia, though by the Tr of Deulino (Dec 1618) Poland gained Smolensk, Starodub, Novgorod-Seversk and Chernigov. In the Turkish War (1617–21), the Turks attacked Poland in retaliation for Cossack raids on Tatars and Turks, but Sigismund's army beat the Turks at Chocim (Khotin) on the Dniester (28 Sept 1621), and by the Tr signed there (Oct 1621) peace was agreed, strengthened by setting up a Christianized Moldavia as a buffer between them. The Swedish War continued intermittently and unsuccessfully for Sigismund,

1600–11, 1617–22, 1626–9; and by the 6-year Tr of Altmark (Sept 1629) he had to concede to GUSTAV II ADOLF Livonia and the Prussian ports of Memel, Pillau, Elbing etc, along with their immense customs revenue.

Simnel, Lambert (?1475–?1535) Yorkist imposter and pretender to the throne of England.

A good-looking son of an Oxford joiner, he resembled the sons of K Edward IV – the 'princes in the Tower' – so well that his tutor, the priest Richard Symonds, groomed him to impersonate, 1st, one of them (Richard, D of York) and then Edward, Earl of Warwick, who was rumoured to have disappeared from the Tower where K HENRY VII had imprisoned him since the battle of Bosworth. Henry's Yorkist enemies, led by Ld Lovell and John de la Pole, Earl of Lincoln, fell in with the scheme, which also received the backing of 2,000 German mercenaries provided by Margaret, Dss of Burgundy. Ireland, where Kildare and the other chieftains were Yorkists, was chosen as the invasion base, and Simnel was solemnly crowned K Edward VI of England in Dublin Cathedral on 24 May 1487, in spite of the fact that Henry had had the real Warwick exhibited to the public in London the previous February. Lincoln and Lovell invaded England at Furness, Lancs, on 4 June 1487, crossed into Yorkshire, turned S and were beaten by Henry's army at Stoke on 16 June 1487: the last battle of the WARS OF THE ROSES. The Yorkist leaders were killed (or not seen again), Symonds imprisoned, and the harmless Simnel made turnspit and then falconer in the royal household.

'South Sea Bubble', The (Feb–Sept 1720) A financial boom and slump which shook Hanoverian England to its foundations, and enabled WALPOLE to achieve supreme office. The South Sea Co, founded in 1711 by HARLEY as a Tory rival to the Bank of England, had a monopoly of the S American trade, but by 1720 was a financial rather than a trading corporation. The Gov of K GEORGE I under STANHOPE and Sunderland wished to reduce the tax burden necessitated by paying interest on the National Debt, and they promoted a scheme – passed by Parl in Feb 1720 – whereby ⅗ths of the Debt was converted into South Sea stock: ie all the Debt not held by the 2 other big financial corporations, the Bank of England and the East India Co. In an optimistic atmosphere promoted by John Law's similar Mississippi scheme in Paris, and encouraged by the possibility of great trading profits in S America, a feverish wave of buying ensued, pushing up the price of South Sea stock till £100 of it sold for £1,050 on 24 June 1720. In this speculative boom, the directors of the Co used sharp practice to make vast profits, while in the City of London many other companies were floated – some with improbable purposes, such as buying up bogs in Ireland or saving Englishmen from being sold into slavery – whose shares were all snapped up by frenzied speculators. At the top of the boom the Gov was reconstructed, and Walpole, who had been in opposition since Apr 1717, became Paymster-Gen of the Forces on 11 June 1720. He had opposed the South Sea scheme, and supported an alternative one proposed by his friends in the Bank of England. Moreover, he had criticized details of the South Sea scheme, though he had not been prepared for the panic which followed its adoption. In fact, he bought and sold shares at the wrong moments, and was only saved from great losses by his banker. Nevertheless, such was his reputation as a financier that, when the inevitable crash came in Sept 1720, he was the only leader capable of restoring business confidence. Moreover, only he had the political skill to perform another essential function: to screen the royal family and the ministry from the scandal of a Parl inquiry – for they had all indulged in very shady – if very profitable – deals. In the teeth of a hostile Parl whose members were enraged by fortunes gained and lost, he managed, by sacrificing a few, to save the rest. John Aislabie, the Chancellor of the Exchequer, and a few directors were convicted and stripped of their gains; but Walpole saved Stanhope and Sunderland and the Court. The economic condition of England was fundamentally sound, and public credit was quickly restored, while the 'Skreen-Master General' – as Walpole was dubbed – became PM for the next 2 decades.

Spain, The Decline of Characterized the reigns of PHILIP III, PHILIP IV and CHARLES II in C17, and can be seen with hindsight to have had roots in the reign of PHILIP II, who overstretched Spain's resources in an ambitious foreign policy, and anticipated the revenues of the Indies years in advance, leaving imperial responsibilities and vast debts – a weight round the necks of his heirs which sank them. If decline was not already visible in the defeat of the Spanish ARMADA (July–Aug 1588), it certainly was in Spain's recognition of Holland's independence, temporarily in 1609, permanently in 1648; in the defeat by France at Rocroi (19 May 1643); in the losses of land to France in the Tr of the Pyrenees (Nov 1659); in the brutal invasions of Spanish interests by LOUIS XIV; and in the humiliating War of the Spanish Succession (1702–13/14), when France, Holland, Great Britain and Austria scuffled like vultures for joints of Spain's decaying corpse.

Among the complex causes of Spain's decline was her feeble economy, the poor performance of which owed much to the fall in population. In its turn, this was due to disastrous attacks of famine and plague, losses in warfare and emigration, the expulsion of the MORISCOS (1609–14), the decrepit agriculture, and the drift of peasants into urban beggary. The weakness in agriculture derived from unusually adverse geographical conditions, and a land-holding system which produced the contradiction of (a) vast uncultivated estates (inalienable because of mortmain in the Ch, entail among the aristocracy, in addition to the privileges of the Mesta, the sheep-raising combine which had vast pastures reserved for it by royal command), and (b) hordes of land-hungry small-holders and landless labourers unable to find work. At the same time, the once-profitable transatlantic trade withered as the colonies began to produce their own cloth, oil, wine and flour; as silver shipments halved; and as industry and commerce at home were starved of capital because savings were invested in Gov bonds or jobs.

The social structure also discouraged enterprise, with its minority of Grandees owning lands so extensive that estate-management was superfluous; the decaying middle and lower nobles – the *hidalgos* – losing wealth and worrying about their honour and the purity of their blood from Jewish or Arab taints; the crowds of unproductive clergy, civil servants, soldiers and students; the vagabonds whom the Spanish value-system encouraged with indiscriminate alms-giving.

The cultural and psychological condition of Spain owed much to the immense power of the Ch, with its monopoly of education, the pulpit and the press, all backed by the INQUISITION; its vast apparatus of cathedrals and parish churches, monasteries and convents, holy days, pilgrimages and carnivals; its economic power; and its great prestige since the Reconquest, the CATHOLIC REFORMATION, and the COUNTER-REFORMATION, the persecution of the Jews, the Moors, the Prots and the innovating intellectuals. The Spaniards despised manual labour, thought that the spirit of capitalism was fit only for Jews, Arabs and other aliens, regarded usury as sinful, allowed their business world to be captured by foreigners and, through their educational system, remained ignorant of science and the empirical outlook. They saw their country's catastrophes as God's judgement on their personal wickedness; in pessimistic mood, instead of clearing up the mess, they resigned themselves to the divine will. The Gov also played its part in Spain's decline. Remedial measures were hampered by structural weaknesses such as the sale of offices; the sprawling bureaucracy, too powerful and too corrupt to be controlled from Madrid; the inability of the Crown – while absolute enough to suck Castile dry – to make the other provs – Aragon, Catalonia, Valencia, the Balearic Islands, Navarra and the Basque provs – pay their fair share in taxes and troops of Spain's requirements, because of the incompleteness of her centralization and the consequent ability of the peripheral provs to shelter behind their constitutional privileges – their *fueros*. Personal weaknesses of diverse sorts also played their parts, placing these 3 Ks under the control of the Grandees and preventing them from doing anything to relieve the sufferings of their patient subjects; while policy errors only made them worse: their over-extended foreign adventures and their desperate financial expedients to pay for them, such as price-fixing, tampering with the coinage, and excessively taxing the poor, all causing economic chaos.

In 1700 when Spain's Habsburg dynasty petered out with the death of Charles II, Louis XIV succeeded in placing his grandson on the Spanish throne as PHILIP V; and this Bourbon capture of the Spanish crown is a fitting end to a century of decline, for the causes outlined above tell only half the story. The other half consists of the rise of France under HENRY IV, LOUIS XIII, RICHELIEU, MAZARIN and LOUIS XIV.

Spiritualists Part of the radical wing of the REFORMATION (the other part being the ANABAPTISTS). They were mystics giving chief place to the 'continuous revelation' which comes, not through reading the Bible or listening to sermons, but through the inward experience of Christ, the reading of the 'inner word' written in the heart by God. They were thus indifferent to outward aids such as ecclesiastical organization or religious ceremonies, and they believed that the true Ch was the invisible communion of the faithful. As these were a minority, the Spiritualists did not, like the Anabaptists, stir up the masses into social revolution. They did not accept predestination, but believed that men by the effort of free will could ensure salvation by active co-operation with the divine.

Stanhope, James Stanhope, 1st Earl (1673–5 Feb 1721) General and diplomat in the War of the Spanish Succession against LOUIS XIV, who became the leader of the 1st ministries (1714–21) of K GEORGE I of Great Britain, and whose masterly Europe-wide diplomacy was the chief factor in securing European peace in his time and under WALPOLE after him.

Eld son of Alexander Stanhope and his wife, Catherine Burghill; ed at Eton and Trinity, Oxford (1688), and at his father's embassies in Holland and Spain, where he became fluent in French and Spanish, as well as gaining an intimate knowledge of Continental politics; m (1713) Lucy, daughter of Thomas Pitt, merchant grandfather of PITT the Elder (d 24 Feb 1723); MP (1701–17); performed top military and diplomatic tasks in the War of the Spanish Succession (1702–13/14), mainly in Spain, where at Brihuega (28 Nov/8 Dec 1710) he was taken prisoner along with 4,000 men. A bookish man of complete integrity, statesmanlike vision, with charm, good looks and intellectual powers, he aimed at a military career; but, as one who under Q ANNE suffered the attacks of the TORIES (1710–14) and then took a leading part in organizing the Prot succession, he became a minister, eventually chief minister, of George I. He became Sec of State (S) (Sept 1714–Dec 1716); Sec of State (N) (Dec 1716–Apr 1717); 1st Ld of the Treasury (Apr 1717–Mar 1718); Sec of State (N) (Mar 1718 until his death). He was raised to the peerage as Bn (1717), then Earl (1718).

At home (*see* GEORGE I) his Gov suppressed the Jacobite rebellion, the 'FIFTEEN' (1715–16); passed the Septennial Act (1716); and repealed the Occasional Conformity and Schism Acts (1718), for Stanhope strongly favoured toleration and would have repealed the Test and Corporation Acts, as well as liberalized the anti-Cath legislation, but for the opposition of the Ch of England. He also put into force Walpole's scheme for a Sinking Fund (1717); but was defeated over the Peerage Bill (1719). His Gov was also responsible for the 'SOUTH SEA BUBBLE' (1720), though he was not directly involved, nor touched by any of the scandal. His ministry split (1717–20) when Townshend and Walpole resigned because of Stanhope's over-active and expensive foreign policy.

Abroad, where Stanhope found his main field of activity, he aimed to end the isolation in which the Tories had left Britain at the end of the War of the Spanish Succession, and to consolidate European peace by settling the international disputes that remained after the peace-making of 1713/14. The chief areas of discord were the Med, where Austria and Spain were still disputing the control of Italy, and the Baltic, where the GREAT NORTHERN WAR was still raging. Ready to travel frequently to the main European capitals, gifted with unusual powers of persuasion, willing to take responsibility, and armed with a grasp of the diplomatic scene unrivalled in Britain except by that of George I, he became the chief guide of European affairs. He pacified those 2 areas, and secured free passage in the Baltic for British ships; though he failed to achieve one major object: to prevent Russia becoming the dominant power in that sea. He also established that working relationship with the old enemy, France, which became the basic precondition of the peace and prosperity of Britain under Walpole.

Strafford, Thomas Wentworth, Earl of (13 Apr 1593–12 May 1641) Authoritarian and efficient minister of K CHARLES I of England during the 11 years' personal rule, who was executed in the early stages of the Long Parl.

Eld surviving son of Sir William Wentworth, of Wentworth Woodhouse, Yorks; ed at St John's, Cambridge, and the Inner Temple, followed by a tour of France (1611–13); m 1st (1611) Lady Margaret Clifford, daughter of the Earl of Cumberland (d Aug 1622); m 2nd (1625) Arabella Holles, daughter of the Earl of Clare (d 5 Oct 1631); m 3rd (1632) Elizabeth Rhodes, daughter of his neighbour,

Sir Godfrey Rhodes. In the 1st phase of his public career he was an opposition MP, sitting in the last 3 Parls of JAMES I and the 1st 3 of Charles I, except that he did not sit in the 1626 Parl, since he was one of those opponents whom Charles had picked as sheriffs to keep them out of the H of C. He joined in the attacks on the favourite, BUCKINGHAM, and his pro-Spanish foreign policy; he was imprisoned in the Marshalsea for a while (1627–8) for being one of the 76 who refused to contribute to the forced loan; and he supported the campaign which produced the Petition of Right (June 1628). He was no Puritan, of course, and he did not support the more radical methods and measures of ELIOT. The 2nd phase of his career began during the summer recess, when Buckingham was assassinated (23 Aug 1628), and Strafford changed sides, becoming Ld President of the Council of the North (Dec 1628). Though he agreed with the opposition on the necessity of preserving the balance of the constitution, when it came to a choice between increasing the K's power or the people's, he was firmly on the side of the K. Arrogant, ruthless and awe-inspiring, he promoted the K's Gov, and his own fortune, with the same managerial skills; along with LAUD in London, he followed a policy in the N – and later in Ireland – known as 'Thorough', or 'Through', ie putting through the K's policies with the utmost efficiency. In the N, he spent the 11 years' Personal Rule (1629–40) reducing the prov separatism of the magnates, keeping a close watch on the J Ps, enforcing law and order in the remotest corners, and generally using the powers of the centralizing State to protect the weak from the strong: ie to enforce the Poor Law, regulate enclosures, and relieve hunger. Then, still retaining this post, he became also the Ld Deputy of Ireland (July 1633), and moved to Dublin to perform similar functions. For 7 years he knocked the wild frontier colony into shape, imperiously issuing decrees, manipulating Parl, sweeping aside opponents, and generally antagonizing the Irish, the English and the Ulstermen. He succeeded in creating a small army, extending the area of English settlement, resuming Ch and Crown lands, putting down pirates, maintaining law and order, stimulating agriculture, industry and trade, tripling the customs revenue, in sum, making Ireland a source of profit to the K (and to himself) instead of a drain on English resources – all on a temporary basis, however, for his work collapsed on his return home. On 12 Sept 1639 he sailed from Dublin having been recalled by the K to deal with the crisis of the Bishops' Wars with Scotland. He became the Earl of Strafford (Jan 1640) and for the 1st time was at the centre of affairs. He allowed the management of the Short Parl (Apr–May 1640) to fall into the hands of PYM and the opposition, and when appointed Capt-Gen he failed to keep the Scots out of Northumberland and Durham, though on a return trip to Dublin he secured the support of the Irish Parl. Back in London he negotiated with Spain for support, and called the Long Parl (3 Nov 1640), hoping to outbid Pym for a majority in it, and then impeach him for treason in negotiating with the Scots. Unfortunately, with his money-making and his centralizing reforms he had accumulated a host of enemies; in any case, the K was hesitant, while Pym anticipated him at every stage, and was determined to destroy him. The opposition really believed that Strafford was about to clamp a Cath dictatorship on England with foreign help. Strafford would have been wise to seek refuge abroad, but the K guaranteed his protection, saying that Strafford 'should not suffer in his person, honour, or fortune'. Pym impeached him and locked him in the Tower on 11 Nov 1640, accusing him of a series of non-treasonable acts which together, he claimed, constituted treason, including subverting the laws and planning to bring the K's Irish army over to England. Strafford defended himself with moving eloquence and powerful reasoning, and Pym realized that the H of L, before whom the impeachment was tried, would not find him guilty. He therefore attacked him with another weapon – an Act of Attainder – which the H of L passed on 3 May 1640, terrorized by a howling London mob. Meanwhile, Strafford had nobly released Charles from his promise to protect him, and so the K signed the Bill, fearful for the safety of his wife and children in the popular anger – perhaps his greatest error. Strafford was beheaded at Tower Hill before a crowd of about 200,000 people.

Sulaimān II ('The Magnificent' or 'The Lawgiver') (Dec 1494 or Apr 1495–5/6 Sept 1566) Sultan of the Ottoman Emp (Turkey) from 1520, who spent his life in Asia becoming the chief Moslem power, in Europe attacking the Christian States in the Balkans and the Med, and at home supporting the arts and sciences.

Only son of Selim I ('The Grim', 1512–20), he became Sanjak Beg (prov Gov) of Kaffa (Crimea) and then Manisa (Anatolia) before succeeding. Then, proud, aggressive, though literate and artistic, he determined to further his father's policy of conquest. (Under Selim I the Ottoman Emp had been extended from its kernel in the Balkans and Anatolia by the conquest of E Anatolia and Kurdistan from Persia (1515), Syria and Egypt from the Mameluke Sultans (1516, 1517), including the Holy Cities of Mecca and Medina – important conquests in view of the fact that the wars with Persia were partly religious conflicts between the orthodox Sunnites of Turkey and the heretical Shiites of Persia.) Though tolerant to Christians and Jews within their Emp, the Ottomans conceived it to be their religious mission to conquer the world – an ambitious plan adopted by Sulaimān.

In Asia, he invaded Persia and took Tabriz, overran Mesopotamia, took Baghdad, and kept it all except Tabriz (1534–5). He then sent an expedition down the Red Sea, annexing Yemen and Aden (Aug 1538); and, in alliance with Gujerat (NW India), he attacked the Portuguese fort of Diu, but had to abandon the attempt (Nov 1538). He attacked Persia again, took Tabriz again, but had to retreat (1548–9). Persia counterattacked and reconquered the prov of Erzerum on his E frontier in Anatolia (1552); and when peace was signed (1553), Turkey again handed back Tabriz.

Two years of indecisive war were followed by a peace Tr based on the status quo (1554–5). Sulaimān's failure to keep Tabriz demonstrates the fact that Turkey's military and admin effectiveness reached its limits about 800–1,000 miles (or $2\frac{1}{2}$–3 months' journey) away from Constantinople. In Europe, Vienna was similarly beyond his grasp.

In Europe, Sulaimān attacked in 2 areas: through the Balkans, and through the Med, in both cases co-ordinating his efforts with the fortunes of the HABS-BURG–VALOIS WARS, and sometimes acting in alliance with K FRANCIS I of France (while the Emp CHARLES V kept in touch with Persia). In the Balkans (while the Habsburg–Valois Wars of 1521–9 were in progress) he took Belgrade (28/9 Aug 1521), invaded Hungary, defeated and killed K Lewis II at Mohács (29 Aug 1526), took Buda but could not hold it. 2 Ks of Hungary were elected to succeed Lewis: John Zápolyai, Pr of Transylvania, and FERDINAND I, ArchD of Austria (and future Emp). Sulaimān recognized Zápolyai, who became his vassal (1528); retook Buda (1529) and invaded Austria, unsuccessfully besieging Vienna (Sept–Oct 1529). He later mounted another campaign, but, being held up for 3 months by the heroic defence of Güns, he simply made another foray through Croatia, Carinthia and Styria, and once more threatened Vienna (Sept 1532) – but no more. Peace was signed (1533) recognizing Zápolyai in Transylvania, and leaving Sulaimān free for his 1st attack on Persia. On the death of Zápolyai (21 July 1540), Sulaimān annexed Hungary and, in spite of many years of claims and invasions by Ferdinand I, held on to all of it, except a narrow strip in the E, for which Ferdinand had to pay an annual tribute of 30,000 Hungarian ducats (truces of 1545 and 1547, and the Tr of Constantinople of 1562). (Some of this warfare coincided with the Habsburg–Valois wars of 1536–8, and 1542–4, when Sulaimān was in alliance with K Francis I of France.) Austrian attacks after the death of Ferdinand (25 July 1564) provoked further war in 1566, and it was in the unsuccessful siege of Szigetvár (W Hungary) that Sulaimān d. Hungary remained in Turkish hands for another century and more.

In the Med, Sulaimān was a serious menace to Venice in the E, and to the Spain of Charles V and PHILIP II in the W, especially when in alliance with K Francis I, and in control of the Med islands and of the coast of N Africa. He took Rhodes after a long siege (June–Dec 1522) from the Knights of St John, who thereafter established themselves in Tripoli and Malta (1530). In order to have the benefit of the most modern naval equipment and techniques of sea-warfare, Sulaimān took into his pay the highly successful corsair captain, Kair ad-Dín (known as Barbarossa), who had established himself as ruler of the State of Algiers under the Sultan's protection. Summoned to Constantinople (1534) and promoted to the high command of the Turkish fleet, Barbarossa took and held Tunis (Aug 1534) till Charles V reconquered it (June–Aug 1535). In 1537, he attacked the Venetians in Otranto in Apulia (S Italy) and besieged Corfu (Adriatic), giving up in Sept 1537. In self-defence Venice joined the Holy League with the Emp and Pp (Feb 1538), but the Turks defeated the combined Spanish and Venetian fleets off Prevesa (Greece, 28 Sept 1538), gaining the naval initiative in the Med till the battle of Lepanto (1571). Getting no further help from her allies, Venice made peace (2 Oct 1540), giving up her last posts in the Morea (Greece) and her last islands in the Aegean Sea. Charles V, however, continued the struggle and made an unsuccessful attack on Algiers (Oct 1541). Sulaimān now made an alliance with Francis I (Habsburg–Valois War of 1542–4), and Barbarossa burned Reggio in Calabria (S Italy) and, in alliance with a French naval squadron, sacked Nice (6 Sept 1543), and used Toulon as winter quarters (Sept 1543–Mar 1544). In 1551 Dragut, one of Barbarossa's captains, conquered Tripoli from the Knights of St John; a loss which the new K of Spain, Philip II, tried to make good by his attack on Djerba, a neighbouring island (May 1560), the defeat of which established Sulaimān along the whole N African coast, constituting, it seemed, a most dangerous menace to Spain and Christianity. The Ottoman Emp had reached its limits, however, and the failure of the Turks to conquer Malta from the Knights of St John (1565), though a very close thing, marks a turning point in Ottoman Med history. Sulaimān d the following year, and the long decline of Turkey had begun; the causes of which, though, were mainly internal.

At home, Sulaimān had autocratic powers over a magnificent Emp, which he

421

used not only to conquer new provs, but also to construct Mosques, roads and bridges, to codify the laws, and to patronize scholarship, literature and the arts. The Ottoman Sultan ruled in a most unusual way, through an army and a civil service consisting of foreign slaves. These were boys who volunteered, were captured in battle, or were bought in the markets of the Middle E; but mostly they were recruited through the *devshirme* system: a regular 5-yearly levy of boys in Christian families, mostly in the Balkans. Converted to Islam, and thoroughly trained in the monastic conditions of the palace schools, these boys formed the Sipāhis (cavalry) and Janissaries (infantry) of the army, and the bureacrats of the royal household and public admin. It was a career wide open to the talents, for they could rise to the very top and, still slaves, exercise supreme power and marry into the sultan's family. They provided only part of the cavalry, for the bulk of this consisted of holders of special military, but non-hereditary, fiefs. Turkey was beginning to decline because this system in its ideal state was rigid, and, reinforced by the conservative Moslem religion, became too resistant to the advances in technology, warfare and bureaucracy, which the W European States were then making. It did not remain ideal, however. It depended on the presence of an ever-expanding frontier to provide a steady supply of slaves, plunder and land for military fiefs. Under Sulaimān, however magnificent a conqueror and beautifier of cities he was, the limits of 800–1,000 miles from the capital had been reached. The frontier stopped advancing; the military and admin structures became eaten away by patronage, bribery and the sale of offices; the Janissaries began to marry and acquire family interests; the military fiefs began to pass from father to son. Worst of all, Sulaimān was followed by totally inadequate successors. Turkey was unfortunate in not yet possessing a fixed law of succession; and whoever became Sultan used to have all his brothers strangled so as to avoid later attempts at usurpation. Sulaimān's eldest son, Mustafa, had serious rivals in Selim and Bayazid, the 2 sons of his favourite and much beloved wife, Roxelana. In alliance with Rustem Pasha, the Grand Vizier (or head of the admin), who had married her daughter, she so poisoned the sultan's mind against Mustafa that the latter began to form a party among the discontented fief-holders of Anatolia. Sulaimān had him strangled, however (1553); and the two favoured sons, Selim and Bayazid, in their turn attracted a following, especially after the death of their mother (1558). Bayazid eventually lost the struggle and fled to Persia; but, in return for a large sum of money, the Shah handed him back, to be executed along with his sons (1561). When Sulaimān d, therefore, the way to the throne was clear for Selim II ('The Sot'), the 1st of a long line of cretins.

Sully, Maximilien de Béthune, Baron de Rosny, D de (12 or 13 Dec 1560–22 Dec 1641) Leading Hug during the FRENCH WARS OF RELIGION, whose work as K HENRY IV's chief minister during the post-war reconstruction, especially in the fields of financial admin, communications, fortifications and town planning, helped to lay the foundations of ABSOLUTISM upon which such rulers as RICHELIEU and LOUIS XIV later built.

Son of a minor Sword noble, François de Béthune, and Charlotte Dauvet, daughter of a *président* in the Paris *chambre des comptes*, both Hugs; ed at home and then in Paris, where he went in 1572. His 2 Prot tutors were not seen again after the Massacre of St Bartholomew (23/24 Aug 1572), but Sully was given shelter by the Principal of the *Collège de Bourgogne*. A few years later he returned home to complete his military ed in mathematics, geography etc, and in 1576 joined the army of K Henry of Navarre, while 2 of his brothers fought for the RCs. He m 1st (1583) Anne de Courtenay (d 1589); m 2nd (1592) Rachel de Cochefilet, who survived him. In the Wars of Religion he fought at Arques (21 Sept 1589) and Ivry (14 Mar 1590), being prominent as a skilled gunner and engineer: but he was also very useful at raising supplies, and also valued by the K after his conversion to Catholicism as a link with the Hugs. He was a member of the *conseil d'état* (1594 onwards), and by June 1598 he was head of the revenue system on the *conseil des finances*, and a member of the small inner *conseil des affaires*, being given the official title of *surintendant des finances* in 1600. He accumulated a number of other posts and titles, being *grand maître de l'artillerie* (1599), *grand voyer* (head of communications, 1599), *surintendant des bâtiments* (1600), Gov of the Bastille (1602), Gov of Poitou (1603), Duc de Sully (1606) and *Maréchal de France* (1634).

As *surintendant des finances* he turned a deficit into a surplus by increasing the efficiency of the financial system without making any fundamental reform. The structure, and often the very personnel, had managed to survive the various changes of régime brought about by the Wars of Religion, and Sully concentrated on building up a strong central secretariat and a prov infrastructure so as to bring the whole under a closer central supervision than it had ever known. He attacked corruption, reduced expenses, raised the tax load, spread it more equitably, and increased the proportion that eventually reached the treasury. He also reduced the interest on the *rentes*, and made a start on the repurchase of alienated sections of the royal domain. To a certain extent, he replaced chaos with order, custom with rationality: eg it had been assumed that there were 1,700,000 parishes in France, but he reduced the estimate to 40,000, when in fact there were only 22,600. Another achievement was to succeed in producing the expensive presents which the K regularly demanded to purchase the favours of his numerous mistresses. On the other hand, his functionaries still used Roman numerals and were ignorant of double-entry book-keeping. Moreover, like all his successors until 1789, he was powerless to make any inroads on the fundamental financial problem of the *Ancien Régime*: the tax-privileges of the nobility, the clergy, the *pays d'états*, the office-holders and other sub-groups, all protected by the PARLEMENTS. In one respect he made things worse. In 1604 he introduced the Paulette, an annual tax of one-sixtieth of the value of offices, the payers of which could make their offices hereditary. It aided the Crown in the short run by creating a new source of revenue, and by attaching civil servants to the State instead of to some over-mighty subject; but in the long run it made the *Ancien Régime* the prisoner of its own bureaucracy, unable to reform itself. As *grand voyer* he greatly improved communications, especially bridges and waterways, and especially in the *pays d'états*. The Briare Canal linking the Loire with the Seine was one of his great works, though it was not completed in his lifetime, and not opened till 1642. He also reduced the plague of municipal and private tolls which battened on French commerce; and, on the whole, invested money in transport at a rate which was probably not equalled again until mid C18. As *surintendant des fortifications* he improved the defensive works all round the French border, and as *surintendant des bâtiments* he made his contribution to the slowly accumulating Louvre, finished the Pont Neuf (1606), began the Place Dauphine (1608), and built the Place Royale (now Place des Vosges, 1605–12): all still admired by lovers of Paris. As *grand maître de l'artillerie* he made the Arsénal in Paris his home, and was responsible for the organization, manufacture, purchase and transport of cannon, powder and shot for Henry IV's wars. But he was by no means office-bound, and commanded the artillery himself at the sieges of Charbonnières (Sept 1600) and Montmélian (Oct–Nov 1600) during the war against Savoy. In addition, he revived France's fleet of galleys in the Med. And important diplomatic tasks came his way, such as arranging the K's marriage with MARIE DE MEDICI (Oct 1600), negotiating the Tr of Lyons with Savoy (Jan 1601), and heading a special embassy to K JAMES I of England on his accession (June–July 1603). In all these posts, Sully was fully backed by the K, who was his senior by 6 years: and he co-operated fully with other ministers – eg Laffemas – in the political and economic revival of France. He believed in a policy of centralized absolutism and, like Richelieu, tried, first, to destroy the prov power of the nobility by demolishing their castles and dismantling their clientage networks; second, to incorporate them in the admin framework as servants, not rivals, of the monarch. Similarly in economic matters, he was not an out-and-out free-trader as used to be thought, but played a central role along with Laffemas in the State protection and regulation of trade and industry. In foreign affairs he backed the K's resolute defence of French interests, and the legend that he and Henry had a 'grand design' for universal peace based on the balance of power is due to C18 misreadings of his writings. As the ruthless agent of a demanding monarch, Sully was bound to make many enemies, and soon after Henry's assassination on 14 May 1610 he was forced out of office by the Q Mother and her supporters among the great nobles. In Jan 1611, he went into private life. Within 3 years the 10 million *livres* cash-in-hand and the 5 million surplus in the Bastille which he had accumulated by 1610 were all spent. Likewise, his central secretariat was dispersed, and the old abuses reappeared throughout the admin. His work had to be tackled afresh, and on much the same lines, by LUYNES and Richelieu after him.

Sunderland, Robert Spencer, 2nd Earl of (1641–28 Sept 1702) A non-party political 'manager' under the later Stuarts, who supported the Exclusion from the throne of JAMES II, became his chief minister, but survived the REVOLUTION OF 1688 to become the leading confidential adviser of WILLIAM III.

Son of the moderate Royalist Henry, 3rd Bn Spencer, later 1st Earl of Sunderland and his wife, Dorothy, daughter of Robert Sidney, 2nd Earl of Leicester; ed privately and at Christ Ch, Oxford, and on the Grand Tour; m (1665) Anne, daughter of George Digby, 2nd Earl of Bristol.

Under CHARLES II after a series of ambassadorial appointments he became Sec of State (Feb 1679). During the Exclusion crisis (1679–81) he supported the Exclusion of the future James II from the throne (though he favoured William and Mary, rather than MONMOUTH, as the alternative), and was dismissed in Jan 1681. Thanks to his brilliant intellect, his urbane charm, his unruffled self-confidence, his unrivalled grasp of the European situation, and perhaps above all his influence with the K's mistress, the Dss of Portsmouth, he was soon reconciled to the Court. Appointed Sec of State (Jan 1683), he was one of the chief ministers (the 'Chits') who managed the period of absolute rule which ended the reign (1681–5).

Under James II, as Sec of State, and then Ld President of the Council in addition (Dec 1685), he backed the K in his pro-French foreign policy and his attempt to establish a Cath ABSOLUTISM at home, becoming chief minister after the dismissal in Jan 1687 of his chief rivals, the pro-Anglican Hyde brothers, the Earl of Clarendon and the Earl of Rochester. He was the master-mind behind the illegal appointment of Caths to public office, and behind the elaborate campaign to secure a subservient Parl, based on Dissenting support, by wholesale tampering with the constituencies and the organs of local Gov (see JAMES II). He even became Cath himself (June 1688), but with the imminence of the Revolution of 1688 he advised the K to cancel the whole campaign, and James dismissed him on 27 Oct 1688. He had been in touch with William of Orange, of course, and when the success of the Revolution appeared certain it was to Holland he fled, not France, thus feeding rumours that he had encouraged James in his folly simply to ruin him and secure William's accession. Whatever the truth, he had so impoverished himself by reckless gambling that he needed public office to stave off bankruptcy, no matter who was K. He was back in England in May 1690, reconverted to Protestantism, and from 1693 was the K's chief behind-the-scenes intermediary between the Crown and the party leaders. Though a non-party man himself, he taught William the lesson that it was impossible to rule England as if parties did not exist, advising him to take in the Whig Junto in 1694, and probably counselling him to turn to the TORIES in the reshuffle of 1700. He also taught William to govern with a small inner circle of 6 or so ministers instead of a Council twice that size: 'the true architect of Cabinet government', as J. H. Plumb has said. He was made Ld Chamberlain in Apr 1697, but public hostility forced him to resign in Dec 1697.

Surrey, Henry Howard, Earl of (1517–19 Jan 1547) Courtier, soldier and poet, who was executed for treason against K HENRY VIII of England.

Eldest son of Thomas Howard, 3rd D of NORFOLK; ed in HUMANISM at Windsor and in France along with the D of Richmond, bastard son of K Henry VIII, who m Surrey's sister Mary in 1533; m (?1532) Lady Frances de Vere, daughter of the Earl of Oxford; and matured as a brilliant but wayward swashbuckler, writer of Italianate sonnets, expounder of Prot views, perpetrator of youthful pranks, and unsuccessful soldier, who was defeated by the French near Boulogne in 1545 and replaced there as C-in-C by Edward SEYMOUR, his deadly rival (Mar 1546). As K Henry VIII's death approached, Surrey began to publicize his royal descent, quartered his arms with those of K Edward the Confessor, and suggested that his father should rule as Regent for young K EDWARD VI on Henry's death. Seymour, who was now in supreme power, brought about Surrey's ruin. He was found guility of treason at Guildhall on 13 Jan 1547, and beheaded at Tower Hill on 19 Jan 1547.

Theodore I (Fedor Ivanovich) (31 May 1557–7 Jan 1598) Tsar of Russia (Mar 1584) for whom BORIS GODUNOV ruled the country.

3rd son of IVAN IV and his 1st wife, Anastasia Romanovna Zakharina-Yurieva; m (1580) Irina Fedorovna, sister of Boris Godunov (d 5 Nov 1603).

Known as the 'sanctified tsar', he was benevolent and pious, but weak at the knees, with a fixed smile on his face, and a bowed attitude of submission. He enjoyed bell-ringing, and left politics to his brother-in-law. His death ended the dynasty of Rurik which had ruled Muscovy since C9, and started the TIME OF TROUBLES.

Thirty Years War, The (23 May 1618–24 Oct 1648) A series of wars beginning in the Austrian Monarchy, then spreading to the HREmp (Germany), and then involving practically the whole of Europe.

The origins: (a) In the Austrian Monarchy a politico-religious rebellion of the Estates and the Prots of Bohemia broke out against the centralizing ABSOLUTISM and COUNTER-REFORMATION fanaticism of the new Austrian monarch, FERDINAND II. The result was disaster for Bohemia, which was turned into an Austrian colony. (b) In the HREmp, where Ferdinand II was also Emp, the war spread because the tensions created by the 2 basic problems of the Emp CHARLES V's time had been only temporarily settled by the TR OF AUGSBURG (Sept 1555), and were now ready to break out into violence again. These were: on the one hand the political struggle between the Emp, trying to unite Germany under his absolute rule, and the Prs, trying to preserve their independence; on the other, the religious struggle between the Emp, bent on re-catholicizing Germany, and the Prots, defending their Lutheranism and Calvinism. Here the outcome was that the Emp lost both struggles. (c) Europe as a whole became involved because the ambitions of Ferdinand II in alliance with Spain revived the apprehensions of France, and inaugurated another stage in the long Franco-Habsburg power-struggle (earlier fought out in the HABSBURG–VALOIS WARS), with each side allied to a network of lesser States, each with its own interests and fears to fight for. The War in Europe left Spain in decline and France on the threshold of European predominance.

The fighting consisted of (a) the Bohemian War (1618–20), when Frederick V and the rebels were defeated by the Emp and Bavaria at the White Mountain; (b) the Palatinate War (1621–3), when the Upper Palatinate was conquered by Bavaria, when the Rhenish Palatinate was jointly conquered by Bavaria and Spain, and when Spain and Holland renewed the REVOLT OF THE NETHERLANDS; (c) the Danish War (1624–9), when a Europe-wide anti-Habsburg coalition organized by Holland was defeated and its leader, Denmark, knocked out of the War at the battle of Lutter and the Tr of Lübeck by the armies of Bavaria and WALLENSTEIN; (d) the Emp's pride and fall, the former expressed in (i) Wallenstein's pretensions to military dominance and (ii) the Edict of Restitution's Cath aggressiveness; the latter in (iii) the Regensburg Electors' Meeting which forced the Emp to dismiss Wallenstein; (e) the Swedish War (1630–35), when GUSTAV II ADOLF invaded N Germany under French pay, forced the Prot Prs into alliance, defeated the Caths at Breitenfeld, conquered SW Germany, and turned E into Bavaria, forcing Bavaria to renew its alliance with the Emp, and the Emp to recall Wallenstein. The latter drew Sweden N away from Vienna, and at Lützen Wallenstein was defeated, but Gustav Adolf was killed. Sweden now organized the German Prots into the Heilbronn League, but this broke up when defeated by the Austro-Spanish army at Nördlingen.

German Prs now signed the Tr of Prague with the Emp, and the War became international. (f) The Franco-Habsburg War (1635–48) consisted of (i) the French war on Spain in N Italy, Spain itself, along the Rhine (helped by Sweden), in NE France (conquest of Artois); (ii) the Dutch war on Spain in the S Netherlands, where the Generality was conquered; (iii) the Swedish-French conquests in SW Germany, including Breisach on the Rhine, the Swedish reconquest of N Germany, repeated Swedish invasions of Bohemia and Moravia aiming at Prague and Vienna, interrupted by the Swedish-Danish War; (iv) the Franco-Swedish 2-pronged thrust at Vienna through Bohemia and through Bavaria; simultaneously with (v) the peace negotiations at Münster and Osnabrück, Westphalia. The Tr of Westphalia registered (a) the independence of Holland and Switzerland; (b) the territorial gains in Germany of France, Sweden, Saxony, Brandenburg and Bavaria – at the expense of the HREmp rather than the Austrian Monarchy; (c) the recognition of Lutherans and Calvinists; and (d) the practical sovereignty of the many Prs and cities of the HREmp.

The Results include the political and religious fragmentation of Germany and the damage to its economic and social framework.

The origins

(a) In the Austrian Monarchy the feeble rule of the Emps RUDOLF II and MAT-THIAS had enabled the Estates and the Prots in all three regions (Austria, Bohemia and Hungary) to win such power that the Monarchy was really a confederation of constitutional monarchies, the most privileged of which was Bohemia. It is not surprising that it was here that the trouble arose, for it was the most advanced section of the Austrian Monarchy, in fact, in the forefront of European progress as a whole from the point of view of economic development, social diversification, urban and prov self-Gov, freedom of thought and religious toleration. Beneath the basic struggle between Bohemia and the Austrian Monarchy there were also damped down a number of internal disputes: between the separate provs of Bohemia, Moravia, Silesia and Lusatia; between the religious denominations of RCs, Hussites, New Utraquists, Lutherans, Calvinists and Czech Brethren; between urban business men, faced with C17 depression, and rural nobility, who were adopting capitalist methods to refeudalize society, ie who were entering industry and commerce themselves, and crushing the towns and enserfing the peasants. The new Emp was thus igniting combustible material when he began to repeat in the whole Monarchy what he had achieved as ArchD in Inner Austria: ie wipe out the Prots and tame the Estates. In Bohemia, where the Estates voted to 'accept' him as K on 17 June 1617, Ferdinand's attempt to limit the application of the Letter of Majesty – the famous guarantee of Czech religious freedom won from Rudolf II on 9 July 1609 – led to the first act of violence. Under the leadership of Heinrich Matthias, Count von Thurn, an assembly in Prague of Prot nobles – the *defensors* under the Letter of Majesty – invaded the royal palace, the Hradčin, on 23 May 1618, and threw out of the window 2 RC Govs – Vilém Slavata and Jaroslav Martinic – and a sec. Their lives were saved since they fell on a heap of rubbish, though the pious were convinced that angels were involved. The Bohemian Prot leaders now expelled the JESUITS (9 June 1618), raised a militia, and made contact with the other Estates in the Monarchy, with other provs in Germany, and other states in Europe. They deposed Ferdinand, unfortunately electing as K in his place the frivolous Frederick V, Count Palatine of the Rhine (26 Aug 1619). He arrived in Prague on 31 Oct 1619, and involved Germany as a whole with the Bohemian Rebellion.

(b) In Germany, Ferdinand was elected HR Emp on 28 Aug 1619, 2 days after his deposition in Bohemia. With single-minded determination he was already organizing the isolation and destruction of the Bohemian rebels. Their Prot neighbour, JOHN GEORGE I, El of Saxony, was no help to them. He was a Lutheran, while Frederick was a Calvinist, and in any case the Emp had seduced him with the promise of Lusatia. Moreover, in Germany as a whole, the Prs of the Prot Union signed the Tr of Ulm (July 1620) with the Cath League to maintain German neutrality in the Bohemian affair. On the other hand, Germany could not be forever insulated from the Bohemian Rebellion, for Ferdinand was determined to unify and Catholicize the Emp as well; and Prs and Prots now had to look to the defence of their own liberties, especially in the mounting tension that had marked the reigns of the last 2 Emps, Rudolf II and Matthias, when such disturbances as the Donauwörth Affair (1606–9), the formation of the Prot Union (1608) and the Cath League (1609), and the Jülich-Cleves Succession Crisis (1609–14) had almost sparked off general war 8 years earlier. In any case, the K of Bohemia was an El in the HR Emp, and the question as to who held this position was important to all Germans – crucial, in fact, since a Prot K of Bohemia would give a 4–3 majority to the Prot Els, who could then elect a Prot Emp.

(c) Europe as a whole became involved because the Emp brought in his Spanish cousins, especially K PHILIP IV and OLIVARES who firstly were keen to strike at heretics wherever they raised their head; and secondly were about to renew their attempt to put down the REVOLT OF THE NETHERLANDS, where the 12-year Truce of 1609 was about to expire. This co-operation between the 2 houses of Habsburg brought in France, especially under K LOUIS XIII and RICHELIEU, who regarded French security as placed in jeopardy by Austrian predominance in Germany and by Spanish encirclement of their frontiers. Each side brought in its allies. The Habsburgs had SIGISMUND III and WLADISLAW IV of Poland, 'the Spain of the N'. The French had Holland, CHRISTIAN IV of Denmark, Gustav II Adolf of Sweden, JAMES I of England and MICHAEL, Tsar of Russia, in N Europe; Pp Urban VIII, Charles Emmanuel I and II of Savoy, and the Republic of Venice ('honorary Prots') in Italy; and BETHLEN GÁBOR, Pr of Transylvania. Beneath these political and religious rivalries, historians have discerned a more general polarization, seeing the War as a struggle between 2 opposed ways of life, the one characterized by Protestantism, free institutions, intellectual inquiry, religious toleration and middle-class private enterprise; the other by the Counter-Reformation, centralized absolutism, the INQUISITION, the closing of minds and the persecution of heretics, and the enserfment of the peasants by the nobles.

The Fighting

(a) The Bohemian War (1618–20) was soon over. The Bohemians were weak through ineffectual leadership, through political, religious and social rivalries, and through the absence of effective outside help. The Cath side enjoyed the advantages of Ferdinand's pious determination, and the ample and prompt support of his allies. The Bohemian rebels were a group of self-seeking nobles whose plans for turning the country into an aristocratic republic alienated their new K, Frederick V, as well as other would-be friendly monarchs. Moreover, their haughty refusal to accept help from their compatriots in the middle and lower classes sapped the vitals of Czech resistance. Of their allies, Holland sent money and a few troops, Charles Emmanuel I, D of Savoy, sent his soldier of fortune, Mansfeld, with an army, James I of England sent advice, and Bethlen Gábor of Transylvania struck at Austria several times from the E; but this did not prevent the Emp's army under Bucquoy and MAXIMILIAN I of Bavaria's army under Tilly invading Bohemia from Austria and decisively defeating the rebels outside Prague on the chalk of the White Mountain on 8 Nov 1620. Frederick fled, and Bohemia lay at Ferdinand's mercy. In the next few years he subdued it, executing 27 leaders, confiscating about half the total landed property and transferring it to new, reliable owners of various nationalities, forcing about 130,000 Czechs into exile, and eliminating most of its self-Gov institutions by the Renewed Constitution of 10 May 1627 for Bohemia and 1 July 1628 for Moravia. This made the throne hereditary in the Habsburg family, transferred the Chancery from Prague to Vienna, and generally placed the Kdom under the sway of royal bureaucrats. In the next few decades (except in Silesia) he forcibly re-Catholicized its Prot parishes, and refeudalized its developed economy.

(b) The Palatinate War (1621–3) was fought at the same time. Spanish troops from the S Netherlands under Spinola conquered the Rhenish Palatinate W of the Rhine, taking Mainz on 19 Aug 1620, while Bavarian troops under Tilly conquered the Upper Palatinate (1620–21) and then the E side of the Rhenish Palatinate, defeating the armies raised by Dutch diplomacy and money, and taking Heidelberg, the capital, on 16 Sept 1622. At this stage, in Apr 1621, Spain and Holland renewed the Eighty Years War, which had begun as the Revolt of the Netherlands, but had been halted by the 12-year truce of 1609. Spinola took Jülich in Feb 1622, and then attacked Holland, beginning hostilities which lasted until 1648, and which are difficult to disentangle from the Thirty Years War. In this period, Holland was led by MAURICE, and then by FREDERICK HENRY.

(c) The Danish War (1624–9) resulted from the alliance organized and partly financed by Holland, which included England and France, and had the blessing of the Pp and the Sultan, among others (Tr of the Hague, Dec 1625). Christian of Brunswick and K Christian IV of Denmark operated in NW Germany while Mansfeld invaded Bohemia from the W, aided by Bethlen Gábor of Transylvania thrusting at the Emp from the E. On the Cath side, Ferdinand appointed Wallenstein, the Bohemian military entrepreneur, as C-in-C of his forces on 7 Apr 1625. This rescued him from his irksome dependence upon Maximilian I of Bavaria and the troops of the Cath League under Tilly. Wallenstein advanced N and defeated Mansfeld at Dessau on the Elbe on 25 Apr 1626. Tilly defeated Christian IV of Denmark at Lutter in NW Germany on 27 Aug 1626. Wallenstein then turned to prevent Mansfeld and Bethlen Gábor co-operating in an attack on Vienna (1626); after which he joined Tilly in driving the Danes out of N Germany (July 1627). In pursuit of the Spanish *almirantazgo* – a plan for the Habsburg takeover of the Baltic trade – Wallenstein now occupied Pomerania and Mecklenburg, took the HANSEATIC LEAGUE ports of Wismar (1627) and Rostock (1628), and laid siege to Stralsund, soon having to abandon the attempt (July–Aug 1628). Denmark now withdrew from the war by the Tr of Lübeck (May 1629).

(d) The Emp's Pride and Fall (1629–30) occupied the year which marked the turning-point in the War, when Sweden took over from Denmark as the spearhead of Protestantism, and when France replaced Holland as the paymaster. In this interval, the Emp seemed near to achieving absolute power until the Prs and the Prots united again to bring him within bounds. (i) Wallenstein's pretensions in Germany roused the centuries-old apprehensions for German liberty among the Prs. On 11 Mar 1628 he was made D of Mecklenburg in place of that duchy's defeated and deprived rightful owners. On 21 Apr 1628 he was made 'Gen of the Whole Imperial Fleet and Ld of the Ocean and of the Baltic'. He was poised to extend the Emp's power across the whole N German coast and on to the seas. (ii) The Edict of Restitution, issued by the Emp on 6 Mar 1629, stirred those fears and resentments further. Capitalizing on his military success – and without consulting the Prs – Ferdinand ordered the return of all lands taken over by the Prots since the Tr of Passau (Aug 1552). He also allowed Cath rulers to expel Prots, and gave no recognition to Calvinists. This high-handed juggling with private property touched Prots and Caths alike where it hurt most, especially Maximilian I, who was a rival of the Emp's for some of the richest spoils. (iii) The Regensburg Electors' Meeting (June–Aug 1630) pooled the Prs' resentments. Ferdinand was present, hoping for 2 concessions: supplies to aid Spain in Holland and N Italy, and the election of his son as K of the Romans (ie future Emp). A French delegation was also there to settle the War of the Mantuan Succession (1627–31), and Richelieu's agent, Father Joseph, skilfully guided the anti-imperial Prs led by Maximilian I into forcing Ferdinand to dismiss Wallenstein (13 Aug 1630) – replacing him with Tilly – and to allow the workings of the Edict of Restitution to be supervised by the Diet. In return, however, the Emp failed to get his *quid pro quo*: neither of his requests was granted.

(e) The Swedish War (1630–35) began when K Gustav II Adolf, with Richelieu's help, had extricated himself from his war against K Sigismund III of Poland by the Tr of Altmark (Sept 1629). His invasion of Germany began when he landed at Peenemünde, Usedom, on 26 June/6 July 1630, and overran Pomerania, Mecklenburg and other small N German provs, including the Neumark area of Brandenburg, where he signed the 5-year Tr of Bärwalde with France in Jan 1631. By this, Sweden was to provide the troops and France was to find the money. The 2 chief Prot Prs, GEORGE WILLIAM of Brandenburg and JOHN GEORGE I of Saxony, called a Prot conference at Leipzig (Feb–Apr 1631) in an endeavour to form a 3rd party: one committed to defending the Prs against the Emp, but independent of non-German powers such as Sweden. When, however, Tilly and the League army took and destroyed Magdeburg on the Elbe (20 May 1631), Gustav Adolf overran Brandenburg and forced George William into an alliance (May 1631). Tilly now invaded Saxony, a mistake which shocked John George also into an alliance with Sweden (Tr of Coswig, Sept 1631). Thus fortified by Saxon troops, Gustav Adolf heavily defeated Tilly at Breitenfeld, Saxony, on 7/17 Sept 1631. The way was now open to S Germany, though what now ensued was far in excess of what Richelieu had in mind. Sending the Saxon army under Hans Georg von Arnim into Silesia and Bohemia (where he took Prague on 10 Nov 1631), Gustav Adolf swiftly struck into SW Germany through Swabia and Franconia to the Upper Rhine, an area thick with rich bprics which fell to him like ripe plums. He took Würzburg on 4/14 Oct 1631 and Frankfurt on Main on 12/22 Dec 1631 – but he could not take the middle and lower Rhine, since Richelieu, in self-defence against his insubordinate ally, had occupied strongpoints in Cologne, Trier and Lorraine. Gustav Adolf spent that winter organizing his area under OXENSTIERNA as Gov-Gen, and distributing some of the plums to his generals. His ambitions had expanded with his achievements, and he now proposed to use this area as a base from which to conquer the rest of the H R Emp: ie Bavaria and the Austrian Monarchy, helped by Saxony descending from Prague. He crossed the R Lech into Bavaria on 5/15 Apr 1632 (Tilly was fatally wounded in the battle) and conquered the whole prov except Ingolstadt. Maximilian I was forced back into alliance with the Emp, and the Emp was forced back into dependence on Wallenstein. Reappointed on 16 Apr 1632, Wallenstein drove the Saxons out of Bohemia, and then managed by skilful strategic withdrawals to attract Gustav Adolf away from Vienna and N into Saxony. Here, at the battle of Lützen on 6/16 Nov 1632, the Swedes defeated Wallenstein, but suffered the loss of their beloved leader. The Swedish Chancellor, Oxenstierna, now organized the Prot Prs (except Saxony) into the Heilbronn League (Apr 1633), which was financed by France, since Richelieu was not yet ready for direct intervention. On the Cath side, the Emp dismissed Wallenstein again (24 Jan 1634) and organized his murder (25 Feb 1634). The imperial army now came under the command of the Emp's son, the future FERDINAND III, advised by Count Matthias Gallas. This army linked up with the Bavarian army, and with a Spanish army newly arrived from N Italy and commanded by the 'Cardinal-Infant', also called Ferdinand, who was on his way down the Rhine to become Gov of the Netherlands. The joint forces heavily defeated the armies of the League of Heilbronn under Bernard, D of Saxe-Weimar, and the Swedish marshal Gustav Horn, at Nördlingen, Swabia, on 26–27 Aug/5–6 Sept 1634. As a result, the League of Heilbronn broke up, helped on its way by John George of Saxony who made peace with the Emp in the Tr of Prague (May 1635). According to this, John George was confirmed in his possession of Lusatia (part of Bohemia which he had conquered during the Bohemian War), and his son in the possession of Magdeburg. On the other side, the Emp postponed the operation of the Edict of Restitution for 40 years (for ever, in effect), allowing the possession of Ch lands to remain as it was on 12 Nov 1627 (instead of 2 Aug 1552). By these concessions Ferdinand won over the rest of the German Prs who one by one signed the Tr of Prague; and the War was over insofar as it was a German civil war. Unfortunately, it was continued for another 13 years as an international war by the other European powers – France, Sweden and Holland on the one side, and Spain and the Emp on the other – who had not yet achieved their war aims.

(f) The Franco-Habsburg War (1635–48) was essentially the successful attempt by 1st Richelieu and then MAZARIN to break the Spanish encirclement of France and strengthen the French frontiers, in conjunction with Holland's successful conclusion under Frederick Henry of the Revolt against Spain, and Sweden's attempt under Oxenstierna to gain territory in Germany and guarantee the safety of the Prots there. In Germany itself, exhaustion was overtaking both sides, and the War consisted of short, unco-ordinated campaigns by States protecting their own interests. (i) France declared war on Spain on 19 May 1635. In N Italy, Richelieu organized an unsuccessful joint attack on the Spanish in

Milan by Savoy, Mantua and Parma (1635); ROHAN took the Valtelline in 1635 but lost it in 1637; and France took Turin in 1640. In Spain itself, Richelieu pushed the Spanish out of SW France at both ends of the Pyrenees, unsuccessfully invaded Catalonia (1637) and Guipúzcoa (at Fuentarrabía, 1638), aided the revolutions in Catalonia and Portugal (1640), and took Perpignan (1642), and with it Roussillon. On the Rhine, he took the Swedish army of Bernard of Saxe-Weimar into French pay and conquered a number of strongpoints, including Breisach on the Rhine (17 Dec 1638), which gave him entry into Germany and enabled him to cut the 'Spanish road' between N Italy and the Netherlands. In the NE, he renewed his alliance with Holland on 8 Feb 1635; saved France from the Spanish-Bavarian invasion from the S Netherlands, which advanced as far as Corbie, nr Amiens (1636); conquered Artois (Hesdin, 1639; Arras, 1640); then Mazarin destroyed the Spanish army at Rocroi, Ardennes, on 19 May 1643; and finally smashed a last desperate Austro-Spanish attempt to throw him back at Lens, Artois, on 20 Aug 1648. (ii) Holland continued her Eighty Years War with Spain by renewing her alliance with France on 8 Feb 1635 for the joint conquest of the S Netherlands. Frederick Henry had already taken Bois-le-Duc ('s Hertogenbosch) (Sept 1629) and Maastricht (Aug 1632); he now proceeded to capture Breda on 10 Oct 1637, while Admiral Tromp destroyed a Spanish armada bringing reinforcements at the battle of the Downs in the Channel on 10 Oct 1639. Thus, while France conquered Artois in the S of the S Netherlands, Holland conquered the strip of N Flanders and N Brabant which eventually joined the United Provs as the 'Lands of the Generality'. (iii) Sweden renewed her French alliance by the Tr of Compiègne (Apr 1635); and signed the Tr of Stuhmsdorf with Poland (Sept 1635), whereby Sweden gave up the Prussian ports with their invaluable customs revenue – thus freeing her for further action in Germany (the reason why France negotiated the Tr). In SW Germany, Bernard of Saxe-Weimar and his Swedish army co-operated with the French in conquering Alsace (1637) and taking a number of Rhine citadels, including Breisach on 17 Dec 1638. In N and E Germany, the Swedes under Baner and Torstensson regained control of Pomerania and Mecklenburg, and defeated the armies of Saxony and the Emp at Wittstock, Brandenburg, on 4 Oct 1636. After this, Torstensson made several thrusts into Bohemia in 1639, 1641 and 1642, taking Olomouc (Olmütz), the capital of Moravia, on 14 June 1642, and then defeating the Emp's forces at the 2nd battle of Breitenfeld, Saxony, on 2 Nov 1642. Torstensson at this point had to postpone his march on Vienna in order to turn N, where he hammered K Christian IV of Denmark in the Swedish-Danish War of 1643–5. (This had been provoked by the envious Christian, and is described under his name.) The profitable Tr of Brömsebro (Aug 1645) freed Torstensson once more to menace Vienna. (iv) A 2-pronged attack on Vienna was now mounted by France and Sweden working in co-operation, from the N through Bohemia, and from the W through the Black Forest and Bavaria. Torstensson annihilated a large army fielded by Bavaria and the Emp in Bohemia at Jankov (Jankau) on 24 Feb/6 Mar 1645, and thrust S into Austria. At this stage he was in alliance with György Rákóczi, Pr of Transylvania, who invaded Hungary from the E, but soon made peace (Tr of Linz, Sept 1645). Meanwhile, the Bavarian army under Mercy and Werth revived, and for 2 years held off attempts by Turenne and Condé to invade the Black Forest. The French were beaten at Tuttlingen, Württemberg (24 Nov 1643). Mercy then captured Freiburg in July 1644, but had to retreat before the French after a 3-day battle there (4–6 Aug 1644). He defeated the French again at Mergentheim, Franconia, on 5 May 1645; but was himself beaten and killed by Turenne and Condé at Allerheim (nr Nördlingen), Swabia, on 3 Aug 1645. The following year in June the Swedes under Wrangel invaded Bavaria in conjunction with the French under Turenne, forcing Maximilian I to make peace (Tr of Ulm, Mar 1647); but, when the Emp forced Maximilian back into action on his side again, the joint Swedish–French army beat them both at Zusmarshausen, Bavaria, on 7/17 May 1648. The way to Vienna from the W was open. It was almost open from the N also. A Swedish army under Johan Christoph von Königsmarck besieged Prague (July–Oct 1648), taking the W districts on 26 Aug 1648. The Tr of Westphalia (Oct 1648) saved the city from capture, however, though this – the last fighting of the War – went on till 2 Nov 1648, when the news of the peace arrived. (v) Peace negotiations had begun at least as early as 1638 at Hamburg, and the Tr of Dec 1641 fixed meeting places at Cath Münster and Prot Osnabrück, little towns in Westphalia, 55 km apart, the former for negotiations between the Emp and France, the latter for the Emp and Sweden. The conference at Münster officially opened on 4 Dec 1644, but full discussions were not under way until mid 1645, and then they were spun out for a further 3½ years as the participants tried to extract the maximum benefits from the course of the fighting. All European States were there except Britain, Poland, Russia and Turkey; though there was no question of peace between France and Spain, who continued fighting until the Tr of the Pyrenees (Nov 1659). Spain and Holland signed the Tr of Münster (Jan 1648) bringing about the independence of the new republic, and also its separation from the H R Emp.

The Tr of Westphalia (24 Oct 1648)

(a) France gained (i) sovereignty over Metz, Toul and Verdun, the Bprics over which she had had a protectorate since 1552; (ii) Philippsburgh and Breisach on the E side of the Rhine, and Pinerolo in Piedmont, Italy; (iii) undefined rights (because of the inscrutably worded and mutually contradictory clauses in the Tr) in Alsace, a conglomeration of free cities, feudal holdings, ecclesiastical jurisdictions and monastic properties, which provided opportunities for much legal hair-splitting in subsequent years. (b) Sweden gained (i) W Pomerania, including Stettin and the Oder estuary; (ii) Wismar, Mecklenburg; (iii) the Bprics of Bremen and Verden, giving control of the Elbe and Weser estuaries; (iv) 5 million *taler* 'for the contentment of the soldiery'. (c) Saxony kept Lusatia. (d) Bavaria kept (i) the Upper Palatinate; (ii) the title of Elector. (e) The Rhenish Palatinate was restored to Karl Ludwig, son of Frederick V, and an 8th Electorate created for him. (f) Brandenburg gained (i) E Pomerania; (ii) the Bprics of Kammin, Halberstadt and Minden; (iii) the succession to the Archbpric of Magdeburg. (g) The Swiss Confederation was separated from the H R Emp. (h) The H R Emp (i) made all the above concessions from the Emp, not from the Habsburg Monarchy, which lost only Breisach and its vague claims in Alsace; (ii) repealed the Edict of Restitution and the Tr of Prague, and fixed 1 Jan 1624 as the base date for settling religious questions: ie the situation on that day was to be the criterion for judging disputes over Ch property, the use of churches, and freedom of worship; (iii) granted the same rights to Calvinists as Lutherans enjoyed by the Tr of Augsburg; in effect, allowing full sovereignty to all the Prs and cities.

Results

(a) Politically, this Tr marks the failure of the Emp to turn Germany into an absolute monarchy. Instead, the Prs turned it into a collection of absolute monarchies, the most powerful of which was the Austrian Monarchy (ie Austria, Bohemia and Hungary) which the Emp ruled as the head of the House of Habsburg. (b) Religiously, it marks the failure of the Emp to apply the Counter-Reformation to the whole of Germany, though in the Austrian Monarchy the powerful Prot movements in Austria, Bohemia and Hungary were either eliminated or driven underground; and in all the Cath states of S Germany the Ch entered upon its baroque and rococo glory. The Pp tried without success to prevent the official toleration of heresy, and in the open letter *Zelo Domus Dei*, dated 20 Nov 1648 and published 3 Jan 1651, he condemned the Tr of Westphalia. The European States, however, paid little attention, acknowledging the separation of politics and religion which now became customary. Henceforth, the religious boundaries of Europe changed little. (c) Socially and economically, the effects of the War do not now seem to have been so catastrophic as used to be thought. There was, of course, much human suffering, pillaging of property, decay of towns, stagnation of trade, enserfment of peasants, fall in population, internal migration – the worst-hit areas being in a band stretching from the S W to the N E. As causes of these calamities, however, it is not easy to disentangle the War from the general economic recession which plagued Europe before the fighting began; nor is it easy to give them firm statistical foundations.

Time of Troubles, The (1598–1613) A period of anarchy in Russia marked by economic crisis, violent changes of régime, civil wars, peasant revolts, brigandage, tribal rebellions and foreign invasions.

The death of THEODORE I without heirs (7 Jan 1598) preceded by the mysterious death of his brother Dmitri (15 May 1591), and followed by the election of a *boyar*, BORIS GODUNOV, to the throne, encouraged other *boyar* families to aim at power, aided at times by Poland or Sweden. At the same time, in the aftermath of the savage reign of IVAN IV ('The Terrible'), and in the stress of the famine and depopulation of 1601–3, there were many discontented groups in Russia ready for violence: colonial tribesmen and prov Russians objecting to Russian centralization; peasants forced into serfdom by the economic crisis and Gov legislation in favour of the *dvoryane* (service nobility); as well as invading Tatars and wandering COSSACKS. On top of this, the incomplete admin revolution in which the *dvoryane* were ousting the *boyars* had left the Gov machine with weakened effectiveness, and at the mercy of a series of pretenders. In the end, a surge of nationalist and Orthodox feeling against the Poles as foreigners and Caths led to the defeat of the invaders, the election of MICHAEL Romanov as Tsar (Feb 1613) and the restoration of order.

1598–1605: Boris Godunov reigned as tsar, and was overthrown by the clever and courageous ginger-haired ex-monk, False Dmitri I, who invaded from Poland, purporting to be Ivan IV's youngest son, and claiming to have escaped death at Uglich.

1605–6: False Dmitri I reigned, recalling the Romanovs, the Shuiskys and other *boyar* families who had been exiled by Boris Godunov, though failing to endear himself to the Russian people, in spite of being recognized as genuine by the real Dmitri's mother (May 1605) – who had taken the veil and the name of Martha. His tactless disregard of Russia's religious and other customs, his marriage to the Polish Cath, Maryna Mniszech (1606), and the behaviour of her large retinue, so upset the Muscovites that a faction of *boyars* led by Pr Basil Shuisky and Pr Basil Golitsin was able to overthrow and kill Dmitri (16/17 May 1606) and choose Basil Shuisky as Tsar (19 May 1606).

1606–10: Basil Shuisky, sometimes called the '*boyar* Tsar', reigned over a Russia splitting up along its social seams and prov boundaries. (a) 1606–8: Ivan Bolotnikov's complex revolt pitted Cossacks, serfs, slaves and vagabonds against landlords and bureaucrats (it is known to Soviet historians as the '1st Peasant War'). They ravaged the S, then besieged Moscow for 5 weeks (Oct–Dec 1606), then were besieged themselves in Tula (June–Oct 1607) until they surrendered to Shuisky's army. (b) 1607–8: False Dmitri II meanwhile emerged with Cossack and Polish backing, the support of the *dvoryane*, and the assurance of Maryna and Martha – the wife and the mother – that he was authentic. He threatened Moscow in June 1608, then set up a parallel Court and Gov at nearby Tushino, hence his other name, the Felon of Tushino. (c) 1609–10: Sweden and Poland then intervened, Sweden helping Shuisky eject False Dmitri II from Tushino, while SIGISMUND III of Poland besieged Smolensk (Feb 1609) and made an agreement with the Tushino *dvoryane* that his son, the future K WLADYSLAW IV, should be Tsar (Feb 1610). Shuisky's huge army sent to relieve Smolensk was wiped out by the Polish Hetman, Stanislaw Zólkiewski, at Klushino, halfway from Moscow, on 24 June/4 July 1610. Zólkiewski advanced on Moscow where on 17 July 1610 a *boyar*-organized popular revolt overthrew Basil Shuisky and forced him to take the tonsure. False Dmitri II and his Cossacks also threatened the capital.

1610–13: The interregnum. (a) Wladyslaw was now elected tsar by a *zemskii sobor* of Moscow *boyars* and their supporters (17 Aug 1610), according to conditions agreed upon with Zólkiewski. Sigismund III at Smolensk, however, wanting the throne for himself – and without conditions – rejected the deal. Meanwhile Zólkiewski took Moscow (Oct 1610), and False Dmitri II was murdered by one of his own men at Kaluga on 11 Dec 1610. (b) 1611: The 1st popular levy (*opolchenie*) resulted from the efforts of Patriarch Hermogen who through the Ch – the steadiest institution during the Time of Troubles – played an epic role in inspiring a nationalistic and Orthodox revival. The *opolchenie*, formed in Ryazan under Procopy Liapunov from *dvoryane*, townsmen, Cossacks and others, besieged the Poles in the Moscow Kremlin, but shortly broke up into its constituent parts and collapsed (Aug 1611). At the same time the Poles under Sigismund captured Smolensk (3/13 June 1611); Novgorod accepted Swedish rule (July 1611); and several other pretenders appeared, including False Dmitri III. (c) The 2nd popular levy was formed at Nizhnii Novgorod in Oct 1612 by Kuzma Minin, a leading butcher, and commanded by Pr Dmitri Pozharskii, a local noble; it was soon joined by forces from other areas. Working in unhappy and intermittent alliance with the Cossacks under Pr Dmitri Trubetskoi, and administering its part of Russia like a mobile *zemskii sobor*, the levy took Moscow (22–26 Oct 1612).

1613: Election of Michael Romanov. As the new tsar, a specially assembled *sobor* elected Michael, great-nephew of Ivan IV's 1st wife, Anastasia. He was chosen because, being only 16 and a weak character in poor health, as well as a relative of the old dynasty, he divided the Russians least. His reign marks the end of the Time of Troubles, and the start of a new period in Russian history.

The results mainly consisted of an intensification of trends already visible in Russian history: (a) the growth of centralized ABSOLUTISM as a safeguard against further social anarchy, prov separatism, and foreign intervention; (b) the consequent rise of the *dvoryane* and decline of the *boyars*; and (c) the intensification of serfdom; and (d) the rise in power and prestige of the Ch.

Tordesillas, Tr of (7 June 1494) Between Spain and Portugal, demarcating their respective halves of the world for exploration.

To settle the rivalry between Spain and Portugal in the New World, Pp ALEXANDER VI issued a series of Bulls, the most important of which, *Inter Caetera* (May 1493), drew the dividing line from pole to pole 100 leagues W of the Cape Verde and Azores islands, with Portugal taking lands to the E, and Spain to the W. By the Tr of Tordesillas, Portuguese pressure managed to get the line shifted 270 leagues further W – thus allowing CABRAL to claim Brazil (22 Apr 1500). This Tr needed modification later when Portugal and Spain, sailing E and W respectively, began to clash in the Pacific, especially over the Moluccas, or Spice Islands, which a Spanish expedition under MAGELLAN first reached by sailing W in Nov 1521. The dispute was settled by the Tr of Zaragoza (Apr 1529), which confirmed the Moluccas as Portuguese, by drawing the Pacific dividing-line 297.5 leagues E of the islands, and which compensated Spain with 350,000 ducats. France, England, Holland, and other powers, of course, did not regard themselves as bound by any of these arrangements.

Tories The name given by the WHIGS to the Court party formed by DANBY under K CHARLES II during the last months of the Cavalier Parl (May 1661–Jan 1679) and the Exclusion crisis (1679–81). In origin, it was the name of some Irish Cath bandits, but it was adopted by the followers of Danby; and he pioneered the use of influence, patronage and other methods of Parl management which became normal in C18. Tories believed in divine right, hereditary succession, and non-resistance to the K's prerogative. At the same time they defended the Anglican Ch against Caths and Dissenters. Under the Cath JAMES II, they were forced to choose between their 2 loyalties, to their K and to their Ch, and those who chose the latter helped the Whigs carry out the REVOLUTION OF 1688. The Revolution settlement also found them divided. In practice, they reluctantly had to accept WILLIAM and Mary as joint sovereigns, but, trying to be consistent, they wanted to regard them as regents for the theoretically still-reigning James II. Some were prepared to regard Mary, since she was James's eld daughter, as the rightful sovereign, but William blocked this compromise by insisting on full regal powers for himself as well as for Mary. Tories certainly could not accept the Whig theory that Parl could choose a monarch to fill a vacant throne. The Revolution split them into Court Tories and Country Tories; the latter, with their opposition to William III's Continental wars, their dislike of toleration for

Dissenters, their fears that the Ch was in danger from science and reason, and with it the traditional social order and moral norms, their dislike of the 'financial revolution' and their opposition to the growth of the 'money'd interest' in the City and to the expansion of the central Gov depts, were skilfully joined up to the Country Whigs by HARLEY, a non-party 'manager', for his own purposes. He formed them into the new Country Party under William III, which became the Tory Party of Q ANNE's reign (1702–14). Under a legitimate Q (now that James was dead, and assuming, as they thankfully did, that the Old Pretender was not his genuine son) and also a Q with strong Tory and Anglican feelings, Court and Country Tories could now once more act together. In this reign they usually enjoyed majorities in the H of C, but split into factions over the chief issues of the day: for and against the persecution of Dissenters, for and against the signing of peace with France behind the allies' back and without first conquering Spain, for a Jacobite or a Hanoverian succession to the throne. Complicating these divisions was the bitter personal rivalry between Harley and BOLINGBROKE; when the crisis came with the death of Anne on 1 Aug 1714 only the Whigs were of one mind and ready for action. They organized the succession of K GEORGE I, and, thanks to Bolingbroke's flight abroad to join the Old Pretender, and to the Jacobite rebellion of 1715 (the 'FIFTEEN'), were able to accuse the Tories of Jacobitism, and keep them out of office for the rest of C18. The Tory party became identified with the Country views of the backbench squires and lower clergy, the groups who failed to prosper in the 1st half of the century – the permanent opposition. Any would-be Court Tory joined the Whigs, or resigned himself to the wilderness. During this period, Bolingbroke made repeated efforts to unite the Tories with the Jacobites, the Country Whigs, and the Whig Outs, with an up-to-date programme capable of ousting the Whigs. No longer mentioning the religious issue, he reiterated the point that since 1688 'Whig' and 'Tory' were meaningless terms, since the Tories accepted the Revolution and no longer believed in divine right, non-resistance and prerogative Gov. It was WALPOLE and the Whigs, said Bolingbroke, who were upsetting the balance of the constitution. The 'financial revolution' which followed 1688 had created a newly-rich 'money'd interest' at the expense of the land-tax-paying gentry whose seats in Parl the upstarts were buying up. At the same time, the Septennial Act (1716) and the expansion of the central Gov depts enabled Walpole to flout the wishes of the people by using corruption in order to stay in power. Appealing to the squires and the small prov merchants, Bolingbroke opposed the great privileged trading Cos, a large standing army, and an expensive foreign policy (especially one in the interests of Hanover). He supported the 'blue-water' policy, using the navy to protect British colonies and trading posts. He also backed the usual Country complaints about big Gov, Septennial Parls, placemen in Parl and other forms of corruption. Later, when Frederick Louis, Pr of Wales, quarrelled with K GEORGE II and found himself courted by the opposition, Bolingbroke added another weapon to the Tory armoury: the idea of a Patriot K, a virtuous monarch who would choose a ministry of the best people, irrespective of party. Unfortunately for Bolingbroke, his reputation had long been too unsavoury, and Walpole's political skill was far too great, for the Tories to achieve anything but occasional negative successes. Moreover, the opposition factions were incapable of agreeing with one another for long at a time; while social and economic change was bringing such prosperity as to render archaic the notion that land was suffering from the development of capitalism. Tories were thus destined to remain the Country opposition for the rest of the reign. Under K GEORGE III they disappeared as an organized group, some appearing at Court and accepting office, others joining one or other of the Whig factions, the remainder continuing as independent backbenchers. At the same time, their Country attitudes were espoused by Country Whigs and RADICALS.

Trent, Council of (13 Dec 1545–4 Dec 1563) To define doctrine and reform abuses in the RC Ch.

Producing a body of legislation bulkier than that of all the previous 18 General Councils put together, the Council of Trent marks a crucial stage in Ch history. As a result of what was to be the last Gen Council till 1869–70, the Ch emerged as the typical instrument of the COUNTER-REFORMATION: rigid and uncompromising over doctrine, liturgy etc; absolutist and centralized in its power-structure; ready to wage war on heresy and to impose a uniform religious and moral life on RCs the whole world over, right down to parish level. Pps had long resisted the demands of the Emp CHARLES V for a Council, fearing that it would reduce the Pp's power, and turn the Ch into a limited monarchy, and that it would facilitate a reconciliation between Charles and the German Prots, and leave the Emp with far too much power in Italian and European politics for the comfort of the papacy. And when Pp PAUL III finally summoned the Council (22 May 1542) he had a different conception of its role from that entertained by Charles V. The Emp wanted the reform of abuses to take priority – so as to win back the Lutherans. The Pp desired a clear definition of doctrine – so that heretics could easily be identified and persecuted. In all three of the stages of the Council the papacy had its way: partly because Trent was in Italy (though also in the Tyrol, ie in the Emp) and about ⅔rds of the delegates were Italians, and partly because the papal delegates who took the chair adopted procedural rules which favoured the papacy.

The first stage (13 Dec 1545–11 Mar 1547) was the decisive one, when vague measures to correct abuses such as pluralism and absenteeism were promulgated; but also when several points of doctrine were defined in such a way as to make reconciliation with Lutheranism impossible and to mark the victory of the old-fashioned scholastics over Christian HUMANISM: eg, Justification by Faith alone was condemned; the traditions of the Ch were placed on a par with the Scriptures as a source of theological authority; the Vulgate, as interpreted by the Pp, was the authentic text of the Bible; original sin did not leave man totally depraved, as LUTHER said; and man was free to co-operate or not with divine grace; the seven sacraments were fully efficacious, conferring grace irrespective of the merits of the persons administering or receiving them. This stage effectively ended with the victory of Charles V over the German Prots at Mühlberg (24 Apr 1547), after the delegates had moved to Bologna, ostensibly to avoid the plague.

The second stage (1 May 1551–28 Apr 1552) was called by Pp Julius III (1550–55), and though it included Prots it continued the trend towards the rigid definition of doctrine and the growth of papal ABSOLUTISM. It affirmed transubstantiation eg, and condemned communion in both kinds and other aspects of the Prot view of the Eucharist. This stage ended with the successful rebellion of MAURICE of Saxony in 1552. When the Emp was forced to flee from Innsbruck into the Alps, the delegates of Trent went home.

The third stage (18 Jan 1562–4 Dec 1563) was called by Pp Pius IV (1559–66), who managed, by playing off the warring factions against one another, to further increase the power of the Pp and the rigidity of Ch orthodoxy. While the non-Italian delegates agreed together in demanding a reform of the papacy and a reduction in its power, they disagreed over doctrine. The German delegates of the Emp FERDINAND I favoured doctrinal concessions (eg clerical marriage, communion in both kinds) in order to reconcile the Prots; the Spanish delegates of K PHILIP II opposed all changes in ceremonies and beliefs; while the French delegates wavered in accordance with the situation at home where the FRENCH WARS OF RELIGION were just beginning. The papal delegates – especially Card Morone – used eloquence, diplomacy, horse-trading and bribery, and succeeded in getting through the measures they favoured and bringing the Council to an end. Decrees were voted tightening up discipline among the bps, parish clergy and religious orders; while on the chief doctrinal questions decisions were taken which confirmed tradition and made no concessions to Prots or liberal Caths: eg on the Mass, purgatory, indulgences, invocation of saints, the nature of holy orders and clerical celibacy. The decrees of the whole Council were confirmed by Pius IV on 26 Jan 1564. They armed the Ch with the two chief weapons – doctrinal clarity and ecclesiastical discipline – with which it waged the war of the Counter-Reformation over the next 2 centuries.

Union with Scotland, Act of (6 Mar 1707) Ended the separate Scottish Parl and gave Scotland 16 peers in the H of L and 45 MPs in the H of C; was brought about by the English, mainly to eliminate the risk that always existed so long as there was a separate Scottish Parl: ie that Scotland would choose a different K from England, and pursue policies (especially foreign policies) inimical to English interests, especially during the War of the Spanish Succession (1702–13/14). It was agreed to by the Scots mainly because it gave them full participation in the English economy. The initiative was taken on the English side by GODOL-PHIN and HARLEY, aided by the Whig Junto; and common sense and realism eventually prevailed on both sides over centuries-long enmities produced by national pride, religious odium and economic rivalry. The supporters of the Union also enjoyed the advantage that their multifarious opponents could never agree amongst themselves. The Union brought political, economic, cultural and other advantages to both nations, and henceforth Anglo-Scottish co-operation contrasted strongly with the misunderstandings which poisoned England's relations with the American colonies and Ireland.

Vasily III (26 Mar 1479–3 Dec 1533) Grand Pr of Moscow (1505), who continued the policies of internal consolidation and external expansion of IVAN III.

Son of Ivan III by his 2nd wife, Sofia Palaeologa, he was ruthless and despotic like his father, but lacked his greatness. He was also pious and haughty. He m 1st (1505) Solomonia, who proved barren and had to be divorced (1526), causing scandal among the *boyars*, and a rift in the Ch; m 2nd (1527) Elena, niece of the Lithuanian Pr Mikhail Glinsky, who gave birth to the future IVAN IV ('The Terrible') near the end of the reign.

In Great Russia he completed the absorption by Moscow of the remaining provs by annexing the republic of Pskov (1510), the rest of the principality of Ryazan (1517), and the principalities of Starodub and Novgorod-Seversk (1523). The Tatars in the E and S gave him more trouble than his father, partly because of his poor diplomacy, but mainly because the Crimean Khan changed his policy from friendship to hostility. With the Golden Horde eliminated as a rival (1502), the Crimean Khan no longer needed Moscow's help, but began to fear her as a rival. Moreover, he nursed bigger ambitions than the regular raiding parties of his fathers: he planned the conquest of Moscow itself by forming a grandiose coalition with Kazan, Turkey and Poland. Vasily just managed to ward off an attack on Moscow (1521), thanks to a timely attack on the Crimea by the Mongols of Astrakhan. He also managed to set up a pro-Muscovite Khan in Kazan for much of the time, though the constant need to be on the alert all along this front was a big drain on his resources. Against Lithuania he fought 2 big campaigns (1507–8, 1512–14) in alliance with Mikhail Glinsky, the biggest landowner there, and leader of the pro-Muscovite faction. He captured Smolensk, the gateway to the W, in July 1514, and hung on to it in spite of Lithuanian counterattacks. It was confirmed as his by Tr (1522).

At home he continued the build-up of absolute power and internal unity by using the serving nobility (*dvoryane*) increasingly as army officers and bureaucrats, and by reducing the role of the Prs and *boyars*, whose appanages had been swallowed by the state of Moscow. When he d in Moscow, he had made a significant contribution to the rise of Moscow as a European power, having been in diplomatic contact with the H R Emp, the Pp, SULAIMĀN II of Turkey and Barbar, the founder of the Mogul Emp in India. On the other hand, his son Ivan IV ('The Terrible') was only a child, and so Vasily bequeathed to Moscow a period of *boyar* reaction and anarchy.

Wallenstein (Waldstein, Valdštejn), Albrecht Eusebius von (24 Sept 1583–25 Feb 1634) D of Friedland (1625), D of Mecklenburg (1628), Czech magnate and military entrepreneur who twice became C-in-C of the army of the Emp in the THIRTY YEARS WAR, and was murdered on the orders of FERDINAND II for excessive ambition.

Son of Prot minor nobility; orphaned at 13; ed by an uncle in the beliefs of the Bohemian Brethren at school in Goldberg, Silesia, and then in the faculty of theology in the Lutheran Univ of Altdorf (1599–1600). After a grand tour (1600–2), he became a soldier, then a Cath convert (1606), rising to prominence in military circles in Moravia; m 1st (1609) Lucrezia Neksch of Landeck, the wealthy widow of Arkleb of Víckov, and also a Cath convert (d 1614); m 2nd (1623) Isabella Katherina von Harrach, daughter of one of Emp Ferdinand's chief ministers. It was on the basis of his 1st wife's estates in Moravia that he began his career as the most successful military entrepreneur of the Thirty Years War. With capital borrowed from speculators – his chief financial agent being the Dutch Calvinist, Jan de Witte, a Prague banker – he raised troops which he supplied from his estates and from levies on the population (friendly or not) that lay in the path of his advance, the profit being lands conquered in war, and estates, offices and other favours granted by his employer, the Emp, to whom he also lent money at a high rate of interest. He took part in the 1615–17 war between

Ferdinand (when he was ArchD in Styria) and Venice, at the head of his own cavalry; and came to the future Emp's notice for his spirited defence of Gradisca against a Venetian siege (1617). In the gathering storm of the Thirty Years War, he supported the Emp, and not his fellow Czech rebels; and during the Bohemian War his troops played an important part in the war against Mansfeld, in the White Mountain campaign, and in the subsequent suppression, expropriation and Catholicization of his fellow countrymen. In Dec 1621 he became Gov of Bohemia, and with a consortium of highly placed Cath profiteers made a fortune out of debasing the coinage of Bohemia, Moravia and Austria, and using the profits to buy up nearly 60 estates of executed or exiled Czech nobles. With his associated subordinates, he became the apex of the largest feudal network in Bohemia, centred on Friedland in the N, and occupying about half the country. Living like a Pr in the Palais Waldstein in Prague and other baroque castles which he built, he ruled his properties almost as though they formed an independent State. Haughty and ambitious, he was indifferent to religion, but somewhat neurotically under the spell of astrology. His horoscope was cast by no less an astronomer than Johann Kepler. He amassed kingly riches by taking unscrupulous advantage of his neighbour's misfortune; but he administered his properties on enlightened and business-like lines, making a profit, of course, but also treating his tenants with patrimonial humanity, instead of enserfing them as was becoming customary in E Europe. At the same time, he maintained unusual discipline in his armies with the result that the peasants and burghers on his estates were safe from plunder, and prospered. During the Danish War he was made C-in-C of the imperial forces on 7 Apr 1625, and raised an army of 24,000 men for Ferdinand II, who was anxious to end his irksome reliance on the troops of MAXIMILIAN I of Bavaria and the Cath League. Marching N down the R Elbe, he defeated the invading army of Mansfeld at the bridge at Dessau (25 Apr 1626), and then, back in Bohemia, he prevented Mansfeld and BETHLEN GÁBOR, Pr of Transylvania, from co-operating in an attack on Vienna. In 1627 he fought alongside the Cath League general, Tilly, in throwing the Danes out of N Germany and invading Denmark itself; then, elbowing Tilly aside, he took control of Mecklenburg and Pomerania on the Baltic coast. Here he began to build a fleet and to put into practical form the plans of the Spanish chief minister, OLIVARES, for the *almirantazgo*, a scheme whereby the Habsburg rulers in Madrid, Brussels and Vienna would take over the Baltic trade, eliminating Holland, co-operating with SIGISMUND III of Poland, and using the cities of the HANSEATIC LEAGUE as bases. There was an important variation, though: it was going to be Wallenstein's sea-going Emp, not Spain's or the Emp's. He occupied the Mecklenburg cities of Wismar (1627) and Rostock (1628), becoming D of Mecklenburg, and then 'General of the Whole Imperial Fleet and Lord of the Ocean and Baltic Sea' (Apr 1628). His scheme, however, required Stralsund, Pomerania, as its naval base, but now Denmark and Sweden untypically co-operated to stop him, and his siege of July–Aug 1628 had to be abandoned. This was the summit of his success, however, for the jealous German Prs, Cath and Prot alike, forced the Emp at the Regensburg Meeting of Electors to dimiss his too successful Gen (13 Aug 1630), and rely once more on Tilly and the Cath League. A month after this blow, de Witte's financial empire collapsed, and its owner committed suicide in Prague (11 Sept 1630). Wallenstein himself returned to Bohemia, but the success of

GUSTAV II ADOLF in the Swedish War compelled his recall. On 16 Apr 1632 Wallenstein was given full military command once more and, on his own insistence, enough political initiative to make him practically a sovereign Pr. He drove the invading Saxons out of Bohemia, and then by skilful defensive strategy drew Gustav Adolf northwards, away from Bavaria and Austria. On 3 Sept 1632, he fought off a Swedish attack near Nürnberg, and then moved further N into Saxony, drawing Gustav Adolf after him. In the ensuing battle at Lützen, nr Leipzig (16 Nov 1632), Wallenstein was defeated, but Gustav Adolf was killed, two events which drastically reduced Wallenstein's importance in the Emp's scheme of things. In the ensuing months the two drew apart as Wallenstein opposed the influence of Spain at Vienna, refused to aid Maximilian of Bavaria against Sweden, and negotiated with Sweden and France, the Prot Prs and the Bohemian *émigrés*. He behaved less like a general than an autonomous power (the aim of every military entrepreneur), and toyed with proposals (still far from clear, but inconsistent with one another) of putting himself at the head of the Bohemian nation, or of uniting the German folk. In the end, his shiftiness and indecision lost him the trust of all, including some of his own officers; but it is still not certain whether the explanation lies in his bad health, his dependence on the stars, or whether he simply over-reached himself with megalomaniac diplomacy. On 12 Jan 1634 at Pilsen, Bohemia, he made 50 of his generals sign a pledge of support, but others kept Vienna informed. On 24 Jan 1634 Ferdinand II dismissed him in a secret decree, and on 18 Feb 1634 published a call for his capture, dead or alive. Wallenstein's end came at Eger, Bohemia, where he had moved with a small force of trusted men to be nearer the Swedes. On 25 Feb 1634 his hosts, the Irish general, Walter Butler, and 2 Scottish colonels, Walter Leslie and John Gordon, murdered Wallenstein's chief aides; then an Irish captain, Walter Devereux, stabbed Wallenstein to death. His vast properties were broken up and distributed among these and many other parvenu and foreign henchmen of the Emp. He was the last of his kind, for, with the military revolution of C17, armies became too elaborate and important to be left outside the machinery of the absolute State.

Walpole, Sir Robert (26 Aug 1676–18 Mar 1745) 1st Ld of the Treasury (Apr 1721–Feb 1742), and generally regarded as Great Britain's 1st PM. As well as making a fortune for himself and his family (eg rebuilding Houghton Hall in the Palladian style and filling it with works of art) he consolidated the settlement brought by the REVOLUTION OF 1688 and the Hanoverian succession, gave the WHIGS the monopoly of office, and achieved political stability for Britain and longevity for himself in office by wise policies, convincingly publicized and efficiently administered, of peace, low taxes, business expansion and lack of innovation on the one hand; on the other, the skilful management of Parl, the constituencies, the Cabinet and the Closet, by methods which became the standard practice of C18.

3rd son of Col Robert Walpole, country gentleman and Whig MP, and his wife, Mary, daughter of Sir Jeffery Burwell of Rougham, Suffolk; ed at Great Dunham, Norfolk (1682), Eton (1690) and King's, Cambridge (1696–8), his univ career being cut short by the death of his elder brothers, which obliged him to return home to manage the estate – which he inherited on his father's death

(18 Nov 1700); m 1st (1700) Catherine, daughter of John Shorter of Bybrook, Kent, a Baltic timber merchant (d 1737); m 2nd (1738) Maria Skerritt, his mistress from 1724 onwards (d in childbirth, 1738).

He became MP for Castle Rising, Norfolk, the family borough (Jan 1701); then for King's Lynn, Norfolk (July 1702), a seat which he held for most of the next 40 years. A convinced Whig, a vigorous orator and an industrious organizer, he became a leading junior member of the Whig Junto, being aided in his advancement by his cousin and brother-in-law, the 2nd Vt Townshend. He was appointed member of Pr George's Admiralty Council (June 1705), made Sec-at-War (Feb 1708), and Treasurer of the Navy (Jan 1710) – all posts which involved him in the running of the War of the Spanish Succession (1702–13/14) in all its aspects. On the appointment of Q ANNE's Tory Gov under HARLEY he was dismissed (Jan 1711); but Harley also wanted him removed from the political scene during the peace-Tr debates, and so he was impeached for corruption. Parl found him guilty, expelled him, and imprisoned him in the Tower (Jan–July 1712), though no evidence to justify this has come to light.

Rise to power 1714–21: In the Gov (Sept 1714–Apr 1717) he was Paymaster-Gen of the Forces (Sept 1714), then 1st Ld of the Treasury and Chancellor of the Exchequer (Oct 1715). This ministry safely suppressed the Jacobite rising known as the 'FIFTEEN' (Oct 1715–Apr 1716), of which Walpole made the fullest use to brand the TORIES as Jacobites, and therefore as incapable of holding office. Moreover, the Gov made certain of the Whig victory by passing the Septennial Act (1716) which extended the life of the existing and subsequent Parls from 3 to 7 years. In the Treasury Walpole introduced a sound conversion scheme for reducing the interest on the National Debt, and a Sinking Fund with which to redeem part of it each year. Unfortunately, he and Townshend quarrelled with the other 2 chief ministers – STANHOPE and Sunderland – partly through personal rivalry in getting the ear of the new K, GEORGE I, and partly through Walpole's and Townshend's disapproval of the Gov's active foreign policy. The other ministers' deep involvement in diplomacy and war preparations in the Med and the Baltic jeopardized Walpole's economy measures and endangered their majority in the H of C. In consequence Walpole and his friends resigned.

In the opposition (Apr 1717–June 1720), Walpole attacked the Gov, giving no quarter. He rallied the motley factions with typical Jacobite, Tory and Country Whig policies; and paid court to the Pr of Wales (the future K GEORGE II) who quarrelled with his father in Sept 1717 and set up a rival household at Leicester House. Here Walpole got on very well with the Prss of Wales – Caroline of Ansbach – and turned her into a life-long political ally. By 1720 his factious behaviour had succeeded in its aims, and he and Townshend were reinstated in office in return for persuading the Pr of Wales to become reconciled with the K.

In the Gov (June 1720–Apr 1722), he was made Paymaster-Gen (June 1720) at the peak of the 'SOUTH SEA BUBBLE' fever, and then promoted 1st Ld of the Treasury and Chancellor of the Exchequer (Apr 1721) to clear up the mess when it burst. He had opposed the South Sea Co's scheme (favouring an alternative Bank of England arrangement), and became thought of as a financial wizard who was untainted by South Sea corruption. In fact, he had speculated incompetently and lost, and had been saved from ruin only by his banker and a delay in the post. His first 2 tasks – in which he was highly successful – were to restore public credit and to shield the Court and as many ministers as possible from the scandal of a Parl inquiry. 'Skreen-Master General' was the title he earned for himself; after the opportune deaths of Stanhope on 5 Feb 1721 and Sunderland on 19 Apr 1722, he became in effect PM for the next 20 years, though it was a title he repudiated.

In power 1722–42, Walpole displayed gifts of survival unequalled in English politics; he brought a stability to the political scene which had been missing for almost a century. 20 stone in weight, short and ruddy-cheeked, he had the common touch; but his Norfolk accent and rustic manner belied the steel of his ambition and the capacity of his intellect, as well as his appetite for work and his instinctive understanding of men and women. He stayed in power so long by raising the arts of political management to higher levels of sophistication and thoroughness, and by pursuing policies which attracted the loyalty of key groups in the community.

Political management involved (a) winning the support of the K in the Closet; (b) dominating the Court and the Cab; and (c) mustering majorities in Parl and the constituencies. (a) In the Closet Walpole won the confidence of George I with his ability to do the K's business in Parl: eg settle the South Sea Bubble crisis, vote the K a generous Civil List, root out the Jacobite plot of 1722 and punish suspects without mercy – notably Francis Atterbury, Bp of Rochester and Dean of Westminster, who was condemned to perpetual exile by Act of Parl (May 1723). From time to time a donation to the K's mistress, the Dss of Kendal, also helped the K to see Walpole's point of view. After George I's death (11 June 1727) the new K – who hated his father – tried at first to do without his father's ministers. Instead, he planned to make his friend, Spencer Compton, chief minister, but within 24 hours he recalled Walpole when it was clear that only he had sufficient mastery of the H of C to raise the increased Civil List he wanted and also to achieve a generous separate income for Q Caroline. Walpole had long before achieved a working partnership with Caroline: she planted Walpole's ideas in George's mind until he thought they were his own. Moreover, the K's support survived the Q's death (20 Nov 1737); he was in tears when he eventually accepted Walpole's resignation when it was forced on him by the H of C in Feb 1742. (b) In the Court and Cab Walpole insisted on complete subservience to his leadership; to this end, instead of the large formal Cab where public divisions could arise, he consulted an inner Cab of close associates, 4- or 5-strong. Independent-minded ministers had no place there. John CARTERET, Sec of State (S), was such a case. He encouraged George I in his expensively active foreign policy, until Walpole secured his dismissal (Apr 1724) and transfer to Ireland as Ld Lieut, out of harm's way (Oct 1724). Moreover, in this reshuffle of 1724 he refused to give a post to his ambitious old ally, William Pulteney, thus turning him into a life-long enemy. Instead, he promoted the more amenable Pelham faction: the D of NEWCASTLE, who became Sec of State (S) on 6 Apr 1724; his brother, Henry PELHAM, who became Sec-at-War (1 Apr 1724); and their friend, Philip Yorke (later Earl of Hardwicke), who became Attorney-Gen (31 Jan 1724). Even his brother-in-law and cousin, Townshend, was ousted from his post as Sec of State (N) on 15 May 1730 for pursuing too active a foreign policy. Similarly, after the Excise crisis of 1733 (see below), Walpole got George II to dismiss a whole phalanx of disobedient aristocrats from their posts in the

Household, Gov and army, each of whom helped to swell the growing opposition in the H of L. (c) Parl and the constituencies needed careful manipulation, because in his ability to keep majorities lay his usefulness to the K, and thus his continuance in office. On the other hand, his hold over the K gave him control over all appointments in the Gov's gift, a stock-pile of patronage which was continually growing in C18 with the expansion of Gov activity, not least in warfare and empire-building. As far as possible, Walpole centralized this patronage under his own control: jobs great and small in the Household, the Ch, the Law, the Civil Service and the armed forces, as well as Gov contracts. He used it with an unprecedented degree of sophistication so as to derive from it the maximum political benefit. With it he built up a disciplined body of faithful M Ps – the 'Court and Treasury Party'. This was the core of all his Parl majorities, but not of course a majority in itself. Unlike a modern PM, Walpole could not rely on a disciplined party to give him automatic control of the H of C. About half the M Ps were independent country gentry whose support could be attracted only by sound policies convincingly put over. Here was the secret of Walpole's power. Unlike previous chief ministers, Walpole stayed in the H of C. At every opportunity he crippled the Tories by branding them as Jacobites. As for the Whigs, he studied the national interest and the interests of the conflicting groups, and tried to steer a middle course between Ch and Dissent, land and business, Court and Country, producer and consumer, peace and security, the desirable and the possible. He excelled in admin despatch, knowledge of the subject, the ability to explain matters simply to country gentry, and the gift of winning their confidence. Moreover, he was prepared to abandon measures which proved unpopular. In Aug 1725 he withdrew William Wood's patent for making half-pennies for Ireland because it caused such political resentment, especially when attacked by Swift's *Drapier's Letters*. In Apr 1733 he withdrew his sound scheme for replacing customs duties with an excise on tobacco and wines, a reform which the opposition branded as persecution of the poor, an invasion of liberty and an increase in corruption because of the extra civil servants it would require. In May 1737 he watered down a bill for fining and punishing the City of Edinburgh for allowing the mob to assassinate Captain Porteous, the commander of the army there. And against his better judgement he declared war on Spain (19 Oct 1739), thus starting the War of Jenkins' Ear which led to his downfall.

His policies helped to produce peace, prosperity, and ideological quiet. In the Church, he resisted Whiggish plans to please Dissenters by repealing the Test and Corporations Acts – a measure which would have once more aroused Anglican fears for the 'Church in danger' – and instead he passed annual Indemnity Acts (1727 onwards), excusing Dissenters who illegally held public office. In finance, he aimed at low taxation, evenly spread. Under his rule – until the war years of 1740 onwards – he kept the land tax at 2 shillings or 1 shilling in the pound every year except 1727–9. His Sinking Fund (which Stanhope introduced in 1717) had the purpose of redeeming parts of the National Debt and lowering the interest on it. In fact, not much redemption took place, and he occasionally raided the Fund for revenue to avoid adding to the tax burden. Nevertheless, public confidence in the National Debt grew high, and soon recovered from the shock of the South Sea Bubble to become an essential prerequisite of the revolutionary commercial and industrial expansion of C18, as well as of Britain's military victories. Anxious to keep the land tax low and to lose as little revenue as possible through smuggling, Walpole placed excise instead of customs duties on tea, coffee, cocoa and chocolate (1723); but he was forced to beat a retreat when he tried to extend the excise to tobacco and wines (1733). Commerce and industry also received much of his attention, and he fostered them by the mercantilist measures which were in vogue at that time. He encouraged the export of manufactured goods by abolishing export duties, and by paying export bounties in some cases. He encouraged the import of essential raw materials by lowering or abolishing import duties on them. High duties were levied on foreign manufactured goods and luxuries, and the export of English raw materials needed in English industry – eg wool – was forbidden. Ireland and the American colonies were forbidden to manufacture wares which rivalled England's, and certain of their raw materials could be exported only to England. At the same time, the Gov helped employers keep wages low, and workers in due submission. Trade unions were forbidden, and the law treated attacks on property with the utmost ferocity. It was under Walpole's administration that the notorious Waltham Black Act was passed (May 1723), creating some 50 new capital offences. Moreover, in the City of London, Walpole steadily supported the interests of the big financial and commercial corporations against those of the smaller and prov merchants. How far his policies were responsible for the economic growth of that period it is impossible to compute. Probably the effects were small – and certainly little was done to help the chief industry, agriculture. The burgeoning prosperity was plain for all to see, however; and it sweetened Walpole's task of entrenching the Revolution of 1688, and consolidating the Hanoverian Succession. Foreign affairs were not Walpole's province at first, but the issues of war and peace profoundly affected the level of taxation and with it the mood of the backbench country squires. He therefore had to master the problems of European diplomacy in order to control decisions in the Closet and the Cab, and to explain policy effectively in the H of C. His policy was one of peace, based on an alliance with France and the settlement of international disputes by negotiation. He failed to appreciate that, for France, the alliance with Britain was a temporary convenience, and that the disputes between the great powers – France, Spain, Austria and Britain – would in the long run have to be settled by war. He clashed with a series of Secs of State who believed that Britain's security depended on diplomatic strength deriving from alliances and military preparedness: Stanhope, in his early days, then Carteret, Townshend and Newcastle. It was because of Carteret's wide-ranging diplomatic activity in N and E Europe that Walpole procured his dismissal in 1724. Townshend followed the same course. When Spain and Austria –rivals until then – revolutionized the European situation by the signing of the 1st Tr of Vienna (2 parts, 30 Apr and 1 May 1725) settling their differences and threatening an Austro-Spanish revival, Townshend increased the peacetime army, hired Hessian troops, put the navy on a war footing and formed a very expensive N European alliance by the Tr of Hanover (Aug/Sept 1725). Walpole disagreed. He thought that Spain was the real danger, not Austria, and so he negotiated the Tr of Seville (Oct/Nov 1729) between Britain and Spain: a shallow attempt to settle the commercial disputes between them which had long been rumbling across the Atlantic Ocean. Townshend resigned and chose private life (May 1730), while Walpole went on to negotiate a settlement with the Emp CHARLES VI. By the 2nd Tr of Vienna, to which Holland and Spain also adhered (1731), Charles VI allowed Spanish troops into Parma and Piacenza, and abolished the Ostend Co, while Britain recognized the Pragmatic Sanction whereby Charles's daughter, MARIA THERESA, was to succeed him in all his possessions. But Walpole's ambitious scheme of pacification was nothing but paper over the cracks. France had no wish to help the Emp, and began to abandon her alliance with Britain. In the WAR OF POLISH SUCCESSION (1733–5/8) Austria fought France and Spain (all 3 Walpole's allies), while Britain stayed neutral and broke her obligations to the Emp. At the same time, France and Spain formed the Family Compact (Nov 1733), and by the late 1730s Britain was without a friend in Europe.

His decline had already set in by this time. His 1st wife d in 1737, his 2nd in 1738. In the Closet, he lost the help of Q Caroline who d 20 Nov 1737. Moreover, Frederick, Pr of Wales, had fled from the Court on 31 July 1737 and led the opposition from his separate household, 1st at Carlton House, then at Norfolk House. In the Cab, his pacific foreign policy made his 2 Secs of State – Newcastle and Harrington – and the whole Pelham group restive. In Parl, a steadily increasing opposition alliance was consolidating, consisting of Jacobites under William Shippen, Tories under Sir William Wyndham, and sundry Whig backbenchers and Outs, led by his old enemies, BOLINGBROKE, Pulteney and Carteret, stimulated by the *Craftsman* (1726–36) and other sheets, reinforced by the disgruntled Whigs whom Walpole had deprived of their places, and refreshed by the talents of the 'Boy Patriots', led by William PITT the Elder, who entered the H of C in 1735. In the country at large, the indignation of urban RADICALS and county freeholders fuelled the explosion of opposition in which Walpole was trounced for his stranglehold on power through corruption, his neglect of Britain in favour of Hanover, and especially his weak-kneed attitude to the aggressions of Spain, whose coastguards across the Atlantic were persecuting English merchants in ways reminiscent of the INQUISITION – witness Captain Robert Jenkins, who claimed to have had his ear torn off by them (1731). Abroad, Walpole's supine policies encouraged both Spanish intransigence and British nationalism; in spite of his desperate attempts to cool things with the conciliatory Convention of El Pardo (Jan 1739) he was forced to declare war on 19 Oct 1739. Not surprisingly, he ran the War of Jenkins' Ear so badly that backbench support drained away. He was defeated on a minor issue (2 Feb 1742) and resigned, becoming the Earl of Orford (9 Feb 1742), and remaining an active adviser behind the scenes to George II and his successors, the Pelhams, till he d. One testimonial to his greatness was the failure of the Jacobite rebellion: the 'FORTY-FIVE'.

Walsingham, Sir Francis (*c* 1532–6 Apr 1590) Principal Sec (1577) and Chancellor of the Duchy of Lancaster (1587) to Q ELIZABETH I of England, who advocated pro-Prot policies at home and abroad, and whose intelligence network ensnared MARY, Q OF SCOTS.

Son of William Walsingham, lawyer, and his wife, Joyce Denny; ed at the Prot King's College, Cambridge (1548–50), France and Italy (1550–52), Gray's Inn, London (1552–3), abroad again (1553–60) under Q MARY I, including a spell at the Univ of Padua, Italy (1555–6); m 1st (1562) Anne Barnes; m 2nd (1564)

Ursula St Barbe, both widows; MP for Lyme Regis (1562). A gifted linguist, he was employed by BURGHLEY (1568 onwards) to report on spies and other foreigners in London, and he gradually built up out of his own resources an intelligence network with agents in all the major cities of Europe. In Aug 1570 he went on a mission to the French Court, where COLIGNY and the Hugs were in the ascendancy, becoming ambassador, Nov 1570–Apr 1573. Being a sincere Puritan he fully supported the project that Coligny was planning with LOUIS OF NASSAU for a French attack on the Spanish in the Netherlands, where the REVOLT had begun; but he had also to obey orders from England and discuss the possible marriage between the Q and the D of Anjou, the French K's brother, who was planning a leading role for himself in the Netherlands. Walsingham's function – and the marriage's function – was to control French intervention in the Netherlands, for a French success there would have been just as dangerous for England as the Spanish military presence. Walsingham negotiated the Tr of Blois (Apr 1572) between England and France, but his efforts were nullified when the Massacre of St Bartholomew (23–4 Aug 1572) revolutionized the political situation. Back in England, Walsingham became Sec (Dec 1573); MP for Surrey (1576); and a knight (1577). In the Privy Council he was the leading advocate, along with LEICESTER, of open war in favour of the Dutch and French Prots, but until 1585 he was overruled by the more moderate Burghley, and the much more cautious Q. He spent June–Sept 1578 in the Netherlands unsuccessfully trying to limit Dutch dependence on the youngest French Pr, the D of Alençon (now himself called Anjou). With the same object in mind he spent July–Sept 1581 in France discussing the possible marriage between Anjou and the Q; and during Sept–Oct 1583 he was in Scotland trying to wean K JAMES VI away from French influence. At the same time, his agents uncovered the Throckmorton Plot (Oct 1583) and the Babington Plot (Aug 1586) to assassinate the Q. In the latter he deliberately trapped Mary, Q of Scots, so that she provided the evidence for her own trial and execution. Walsingham was also an enthusiastic supporter of exploration and colonization in the New World, where he had a Cape named after him.

Warbeck, Perkin (*c* 1474–23 Nov 1499) Yorkist imposter and pretender who was executed by K HENRY VII of England.

Son of a boatman and customsman of Tournai, Flanders (according to his own confession), he arrived in Cork, Ireland in 1491, the handsome member of the crew of a ship belonging to a Breton silk-merchant. Some Irish Yorkists, apparently impressed by the stylish way he wore his master's silks – perhaps as an advertisement – persuaded him, with some difficulty, to impersonate Richard, D of York, the younger of the sons of K Edward IV, the 'Prs in the Tower'. The story is full of obscurities, and perhaps did not begin at this point. Warbeck may already have been drawn into Yorkist plotting by Margaret, Dss of Burgundy, or K CHARLES VIII of France. Whatever the true details, he became a serious nuisance to Henry VII until his execution, being recognized at various times by the Yorkists, by JAMES IV of Scotland, Charles VIII of France, the Emp MAXIMILIAN I, the ArchD PHILIP I, Margaret of Burgundy, and other rulers looking for a stick with which to beat Henry in international diplomacy. From Ireland, Warbeck went to France, until the Tr of Etaples (Nov 1492) between

England and France forced his removal to the Netherlands, where Margaret's support so incensed Henry that he broke off commercial relations with the Netherlands from Sept 1493 until the Tr of *Magnus Intercursus* of Feb 1496. Meanwhile Henry's agents were unearthing Yorkist supporters (or putative supporters) of Warbeck, and during 1494 he executed a number of leaders and struck such terror into the rest that Warbeck found little active English support for his various invasion attempts. His blow at Deal, Kent, on 3 Aug 1495 was easily defeated; his siege of Waterford, Ireland, in Aug 1495 failed, thanks to the reforms of POYNINGS; but in Scotland, his next call, he was welcomed by K JAMES IV on 27 Nov 1495, and given Lady Catherine Gordon, of royal blood, as a bride. James made 2 unsuccessful assaults on England (Sept 1496 and July–Aug 1497), while the Cornish Rising of June 1497 encouraged Warbeck to try another point of entry. He went to Cork once more on 26 July 1497, but still received no backing, and then invaded Cornwall at Whitesand Bay, near Land's End, on 7 Sept 1497, proclaiming himself K Richard IV. What little support appeared was soon suppressed by Henry's troops; and Henry's good luck and skilful diplomacy had by now knocked away all Warbeck's international support. Losing heart – he was no leader – he sought sanctuary in Beaulieu Abbey, Hampshire, and then gave himself up and confessed his guilt to Henry at Taunton, Somerset, on 5 Oct 1497. At first he was treated leniently; but after 2 attempts to escape in 1498 and 1499, he was found guilty of treason and hanged at Tyburn, London.

Warham, William (*c* 1450–22 Aug 1532) Bp of London (1502–3), Archbp of Canterbury (1503–32), Chancellor (1504–15), ecclesiastical lawyer, diplomat and minister of K HENRY VIII of England.

Ed at Winchester and New College, Oxford, he became a leading English lawyer, and thenceforth pursued a career typical of a medieval prelate in the royal admin. He was employed on various diplomatic missions by HENRY VII and Henry VIII – till the rise of WOLSEY – negotiating, eg, the marriage of Pr Arthur with CATHERINE OF ARAGON. He was promoted to Canterbury over the head of the more suitable Richard Fox, but Henry VII was particularly keen on pliable prelates. In his turn, Warham was completely overshadowed by Wolsey, who became Card and Legate; and, though he opposed Henry VIII's divorce from Catherine of Aragon as well as the English REFORMATION, he was too old and malleable to be an effective defender of the Ch against Henry VIII and CROMWELL, and he d before men really had to stand up and be counted.

Warwick, Robert Rich, 2nd Earl of (*c* June 1587–19 Apr 1658) Puritan opponent of K CHARLES I of England, though wealthy and very cheerful, who helped to win the CIVIL WAR by taking the navy over to the side of Parl.

Eld son of Robert Rich, 1st Earl of Warwick, and his wife, Penelope Devereux, sister of the 2nd Earl of ESSEX; ed at Emmanuel, Cambridge (1603), then the Inner Temple (1604); MP in JAMES I's 1st and 2nd Parls (1610–11 and 1614); succeeded his father in Mar 1619; m 1st (1605) Frances, daughter of Sir William Hatton (d 1634); 2nd Susan, widow of William Halliday, Alderman of London (d 1646); 3rd (1646) Eleanor, daughter of Sir Edward Wortley. Though it is uncertain whether he was a Presbyterian or Episcopalian, he was a friend of

Sir John ELIOT, and one of the leading opponents of Archbp LAUD and K Charles I. He played a prominent part in anti-Spanish privateering expeditions and transatlantic colonizing ventures, joining many trading companies, including the Providence Island Co, on the board of which he and PYM, HAMPDEN and others concerted their opposition to the Court, including their refusal to pay Ship Money. When K and Parl were on the point of civil war, Parl appointed Warwick to the post of Admiral of the Fleet (Mar 1642) in spite of the K's objections; and in June 1642 he induced the navy to fight on the Parl side. As Ld High Admiral (Dec 1643–Apr 1645) he made a vital contribution to the Parl war effort in clearing the seas of Royalists and supplying the Parl armies, particularly the garrisons at Plymouth and Hull. In accordance with the Self-Denying Ordinance (Apr 1645) he resigned his commission; but became Ld High Admiral again (May 1648–Feb 1649) during the 2nd Civil War, when the Parl navy was in danger of going over to the K. The execution of Charles and the establishment of the republic were steps which were too radical for Warwick, and he retired to private life.

Wentworth, Peter (*c* 1524–1597) Puritan M P under Q ELIZABETH I of England, whose outspoken defence of the privileges of Parl against the Crown anticipated the work of ELIOT and PYM, and landed him in the Tower several times.

Eld son of Sir Nicholas Wentworth; ed at Lincoln's Inn; m 1st Letitia Lane, second cousin to Q Catherine Parr; m 2nd Elizabeth, sister of WALSINGHAM; he sat in all the Parls from 1571 onwards, except that of 1584–5. Prickly and awkward, deaf to the other side of the question and incapable of apologizing, waspish in language but recklessly courageous, and devoted to the Q, he was ahead of his time in the skill with which he transformed Parl disputes with the Crown over policy into struggles over the H of C's privilege of free speech. The Q forbade the House to debate what she called 'matters of State': the Ch, foreign policy, her marriage and the succession; Wentworth claimed that Parl could freely debate, and initiate legislation on, any matter of importance to the community. Both views were too extreme, in an area of constitutional practice which had not yet crystallized into law; though, of course, Wentworth's was the view of the future. He strongly objected to the way the work of the House was inhibited by 'rumours' from the Court that the Q disliked a certain policy, or 'messages' forbidding the discussion of certain subjects; on 8 Feb 1576 he made a strong speech condemning them. 'I would to God,' he said, '. . . that these two were buried in hell: I mean rumours and messages. None is without fault: no, not our noble queen. Since, then, her majesty has committed great faults . . .' – at which point the aghast Commons stopped him and, on 12 Mar 1576, lodged him in the Tower for a month. In the Parl of 1586–7, when the Q blocked a bill to reshape the Ch on Presbyterian lines – Anthony Cope's 'bill and book' – Wentworth urged the House to adopt 10 articles of his as rules of the House for the preservation of freedom of speech. The Q lodged him and 4 others in the Tower (1 Mar 1587). After this Wentworth concentrated on trying to browbeat the Q into adopting the erroneous policy of announcing her successor. The contents of his ms pamphlet, 'A Pithy Exhortation to Her Majesty for Establishing the Succession', leaked, and the Council again imprisoned him (Aug–Nov 1591). In the Parl of 1593 he worked hard to build up a party of new M Ps to campaign for a decision on the succession. He had a speech and a bill already drafted, as well as a list of objections and answers, a vote of thanks to the Q in case of victory, and a rebuke if not; but his attempts to form a faction could not be kept quiet, and once more the Council locked him in the Tower (Feb 1593). This time it was until he d, for he steadfastly refused to give the promise of silence on the succession question which would have released him.

Whigs The name given by the TORIES to the Country opposition led by SHAFTES-BURY against K CHARLES II of Great Britain and his chief minister, DANBY. Originally a term of abuse – meaning Scottish Presbyterian rebels – it was proudly adopted as a label to cover the disparate groups who co-operated during the Exclusion crisis (1679–81) in a campaign to exclude the future JAMES II from the throne because he was a Cath. The chief ingredients of the movement when it formed during the last months of the Cavalier Parl (May 1661–Jan 1679) were ex-Roundheads who had always opposed the Court; ex-Cavaliers who had become disillusioned with Charles II; Prebyterians who disliked the Restoration religious settlement; backbench gentry who generally opposed the Court for its extravagance and corruption; career politicians who wanted office – Outs who wanted to be in; and urban radicals stirred into action by the wilder aristocrats. They argued that the consent of the people was the source of political authority, and that Ks were put into office by contract with the community, who retained the right to resist monarchs who broke it. The other main plank in their platform was toleration of Dissenters. Outwitted by Charles II in the Exclusion campaign, they resisted the Cath and absolutist policies of James II, and put their theories into practice by carrying out the REVOLUTION OF 1688 in alliance with some Tories. Under WILLIAM III they split into Court Whigs and Country Whigs. The latter – mainly the radical elements – coalesced with the Country Tories under HARLEY to form the New Country Party, or the Tory Party of Q ANNE's reign. The Court Whigs, led by the Junto, took office under William III – their K – and in this period (1694–8) took on the persona which identified them for most of the next C. They became the party of the Gov, the Court, the nobility and the richer gentry, and the 'money'd' men of the City produced by the financial revolution. They fully supported the forward foreign policy and Continental wars of William III and MARLBOROUGH, and exploited to the full the patronage and other forms of influence which the expanding machinery of Gov afforded in order to gain firm political control at the centre and in the localities. Firmly pro-Hanoverian, they confidently organized the accession of K GEORGE I in 1714, tainted the Tories with Jacobitism (keeping them in the wilderness for the rest of the C), strengthened themselves with the Septennial Act (1716), and in K GEORGE II's reign (under WALPOLE, PELHAM and NEWCASTLE) consolidated their main body as the Old Corps of Whigs, the party of the established order of things. Under K GEORGE III who resumed control of Gov patronage (the Court and Treasury Party becoming known as the K's Friends) the Whig aristocrats were limited to their own private sources of patronage. They were hammered by Henry FOX in the 'Massacre of the Pelhamite Innocents', and broke up into factions: the Old Corps under Newcastle, the Bedfords, the Grenvilles, the Pittites etc. Under ROCKINGHAM, who succeeded Newcastle as leader, the trimmed-down Old Corps evolved into a Country party once more, accusing the K of tyranny, and espousing the causes which opposed him: WILKES, the

Americans, the Irish, Economical Reform, and Parl Reform. They also employed the new political techniques of the late C18: the creation of a disciplined party (instead of a mere personal connection) with a consistent programme and making full use of the press, county meetings, petitions, remonstrances and associations. At the same time the rest of the Whigs co-operated with the K and the K's Friends to form the 2 stable admins of NORTH (1770–82) and Pitt the Younger (1783–1801), both very reminiscent of the days of Walpole and Pelham. Under Rockingham's successor, the D of Portland, the Rockinghams split (1793–4), when Portland and most of the aristocrats joined Pitt's Gov (in the crisis of the French Revolutionary War and the RADICAL unrest) to form what became the Tory Party of C19, while the minority under Charles James Fox preserved their radical tenets and took Whiggism into the next C.

Whitgift, John (*c* 1530–29 Feb 1604) Archbp of Canterbury (Aug 1583) who co-operated with Q ELIZABETH I of England in a vigorous anti-Puritan campaign.

Son of a prosperous merchant, and nephew of the Abbot of Wellow, who supervised his upbringing; ed at St Anthony's Sch., London, Queens' and Pembroke, Cambridge. Under Q MARY I he was elected Fellow of Peterhouse (1555) and continued his studies while many of his contemporaries fled abroad. He was ordained in 1560, chosen Lady Margaret Prof of Divinity in 1563, and Master of Pembroke in 1567. The pay at Pembroke was so poor, however, that he became Master of Trinity the same year, as well as Chaplain to Q Elizabeth I, Regius Prof of Divinity and Vice-Chancellor of the University. He led the campaign in Cambridge which deprived the Presbyterian theorist, Thomas CARTWRIGHT, of his Lady Margaret Professorship of Divinity (1570) and Fellowship of Trinity (1572). He also collected a few more sources of income by becoming a Prebendary of Ely (1568), Dean of Lincoln (1571) and Bp of Worcester (1577). As Archbp of Canterbury, and, from Feb 1586 onwards, member of the Privy Council, he worked closely with BURGHLEY and the Q at the task of suppressing the Presbyterian movement inside the Ch of England, as well as the Congregationalists outside it. He issued orders to his Bps to enforce the laws on Ch attendance, vestments and ceremonial; and refused to allow clergy to officiate who would not subscribe to the Royal Supremacy, the Book of Common Prayer and the *39 Articles*. He controlled the press through the Star Chamber; he enforced discipline through the new Commission for Ecclesiastical Causes, with himself at its head. The Congregationalists, John Greenwood and Henry Barrow, were hanged at Tyburn on 6 Apr 1593 for sedition, and a third, John Penry, was executed for treason on 29 May 1593. By this stage Whitgift had broken the back of the Puritan movement in the Ch of England but, as he had concentrated on achieving sheer uniformity rather than trying to reform abuses, there was sufficient wrong with the Ch to nourish a renewed Puritan attack in the next reign. Whitgift was present at the death of Elizabeth, and he crowned K JAMES I.

Wilkes, John (17 Oct 1725–26 Dec 1797) Upstart rogue under K GEORGE III, whose brilliant anti-Gov journalism and pro-radical demagogy enlarged the liberties of the subject against the State, especially liberty of expression, and publicized and extended the extra-Parl techniques of agitation which became the mainstay of the RADICALS.

2nd son of Israel Wilkes, successful London malt distiller, and his wife, Sarah; ed privately in Hertford and Aylesbury, then at Lincolns Inn (1742) and Leiden Univ, Holland (1744–6); m (1747) Mary (d 4 Apr 1784), daughter of John Mead, a rich London merchant settled in Aylesbury, through whom he joined the gentry of Bucks who looked up to the opposition politician, Earl Temple (brother of GRENVILLE) as their patron and leader. As well as becoming a prominent debauchee in the Hell-Fire Club and the sacrilegious Medmenham Monks, he became High Sheriff of Bucks (1754–5) and colonel in the Bucks militia (1762–3). Ugly and squinting, but charming and witty, he was an impudent careerist who exploited public causes for his own ends with brilliance and panache. Though an indifferent debater and public speaker, he was mesmeric in conversation; but his greatest gifts were his pungent journalism and his genius for all forms of publicity. He was an C18 master of the media, and in the 1st 20 years of George III's reign he rode the crest of the Radical agitation which marked this period of unstable Govs, economic depression, rebellion in America and Ireland, and rioting in Britain.

He achieved notoriety in 2 big causes: that of the *North Briton*, and that of the Middlesex elections. The *North Briton* was a scintillating weekly (June 1762 onwards), sponsored by Earl Temple, and edited by Wilkes and Charles Churchill, which contributed significantly to the nervous collapse of George III's Favourite and 1st PM, BUTE (1761–3), partly by hinting at improper relations between Bute and the Q Mother. Under the Grenville admin (1763–5) it continued the attack, in edition No 45 (23 Apr 1763) sharply criticizing the K's speech. On 26 Apr 1763 the Sec of State issued a general warrant (ie one against the authors, printers and publishers, without mentioning names) and Wilkes was locked up in the Tower (30 Apr 1763). Judicial proceedings now took place in the courts and in Parl. In the courts, Chief Justice Pratt (a member of PITT's entourage) in the Court of Common Pleas ordered Wilkes's release on the grounds of his Parl privilege (May 1763). At the same time, a campaign of mass demonstrations with the slogan 'Wilkes and Liberty' was orchestrated by the Parl opposition and the City Radicals. The Gov strengthened its hand by seizing a copy of the *Essay on Woman* – a 100-line mock-scholarly parody of Pope's *Essay on Man*, written by Wilkes and Thomas Potter (son of the Archbp) in praise of sex. In Parl the *Essay* was read out in the H of L by the new Sec of State, the Earl of Sandwich (who had been one of Wilkes's former cronies at Medmenham), and the Lords condemned it as 'a most scandalous, obscene, and impious libel' (Nov 1763). At the same time, the H of C voted that No 45 was 'a false, scandalous, and seditious libel' (15 Nov 1763); that Parl privilege did not extend to libel (24 Nov 1763), and that Wilkes was expelled from the House (Jan 1764). Meanwhile, Wilkes was wounded in a duel (16 Nov 1763) and fled abroad (Dec 1763) for 4 years; in the courts he was found guilty of publishing 'a seditious libel' and 'an obscene and impious libel', and pronounced an outlaw. As a result of Wilkes and others suing the Sec of State and his servants, important judgements were pronounced: by Ld Mansfield in the case of *Leach v Money* (18 June 1765) condemning general warrants, and by Pratt (Ld Camden) in *Entick v Carrington* (1765) denying that the Sec of State could imprison people (except for treason) and denying the validity of a warrant to search, seize and carry away papers. The Middlesex elections (1768–9) saw Wilkes back at the head of the Radical movement again

453

after he had surrendered to the courts (27 Apr 1768), got his outlawry reversed (8 June 1768), and been condemned to 22 months' imprisonment and £1,000 in fines. He was elected MP for Middlesex (Mar 1768), expelled by H of C resolution (3 Feb 1769); elected for the 2nd time (16 Feb 1769) and re-expelled and pronounced 'incapable of being elected' (17 Feb 1769); elected for the 3rd time (16 Mar 1769) and expelled (17 Mar 1769); elected for the 4th time (13 Apr 1769), when his opponent, Henry Lawes Luttrell, was declared MP (15 Apr 1769). These events high-lighted an important constitutional conflict between (a) those who believed that Parl privileges (including H of C control over its own membership) should be safeguarded, both from the Crown (which had been the struggle in C16 and 17) and from the mob (the new struggle); and (b) those who believed that the H of C had no right to incapacitate a member, or otherwise flout the wishes of the electorate, and who feared that Parl was corruptly managed by the Court and therefore should be reformed. Wilkes's imprisonment ended on 18 Apr 1770; backed by the Society of Supporters of the Bill of Rights – which had been founded (20 Feb 1769) to pay his debts and get him into Parl – he harassed the NORTH admin for the next decade from his 2 power-bases: the City of London, where he was Alderman (Jan 1769 onwards), and the county of Middlesex, where he was elected unopposed for the 5th, 6th and 7th times (Oct 1774, Sept 1780 and Apr 1784). He supported any popular cause with which he could hammer the Gov; the resistance brewing in America and Ireland, and the depressed state of the economy in Britain supplied him with plenty of material to work on. He played a leading part in winning the freedom of the press to print Parl debates, which the H of C until 1771 had regarded as a breach of Parl privilege. Under the North admin (1770–82) some City printers were summoned to appear at the bar of the H of C in Feb 1771; encouraged by Alderman Wilkes, they refused to do so. In the ensuing struggle, Wilkes fully exploited the propaganda value of the incident. He outmanoeuvred the Gov by turning the affair into a conflict between Parl and the City, in which the H of C appeared to be interfering with the City's privileges. Anxious to avoid trouble with the volatile London crowd, Parl brought no further cases of this sort against journalists. In these years also – years which brought the WAR OF AMERICAN INDEPENDENCE (1776–83) – Wilkes encouraged colonial resistance. Moreover, on 21 Mar 1776 he spoke in the H of C in favour of Parl reform. Later he was involved in the massive Association Movement which the Radicals mounted in 1779 and 1780; but threw his weight behind law and order during the anti-Cath Gordon Riots (2–12 June 1780). After middle age he mellowed. He called himself an extinct volcano, and said to the K: 'I was never a Wilkite.' Under the ROCKINGHAM admin (1782–3) the H of C at last expunged from the Journal the resolutions expelling him in the Middlesex elections affair (May 1782). Moreover, the Radical movement cooled down temporarily in the 1780s, though by that time Wilkes was recognized for what he was: an opportunist scoundrel, and not a friend of the people.

William I (The Silent) (24 Apr 1533–10 July 1584) Pr of Orange, S France, and Count of Nassau, Germany, richest member of the high nobility of the Netherlands who became the leader of the Dutch people in the REVOLT OF THE NETHERLANDS, and, until his assassination, one of the chief factors in its success.

Eldest son of the Lutheran William, Count of Nassau-Dillenburg, and Juliana von Stolberg; in 1544 he inherited extensive estates in the Netherlands, Franche Comté, Charolais and Orange; ed by the Emp CHARLES V at Breda and Brussels as an RC; m 1st (1551) Anne van Buren, a rich heiress of the Egmont family (d 24 Mar 1558); m 2nd (1561) Anna of Saxony, daughter of the Lutheran El MAURICE, whose deranged behaviour and adultery with, among others, a lawyer, John Rubens (later father of the painter) led to their divorce in 1571; m 3rd (1575) Charlotte de Bourbon-Montpensier (d 6 May 1582); m 4th (1583) Louise, daughter of the Admiral COLIGNY. He had 10 daughters and 3 sons: Philip William, who was kidnapped and Catholicized in Spain, MAURICE and FREDERICK HENRY, who continued William's work after his death. He survived the 1st attack on his life at Antwerp (18 Mar 1582) by Juan Jauréguy, clerk to a Portuguese merchant; but not the 2nd, when he was killed in the Prinsenhof at Delft, Holland, by Balthasar Gérard, a fanatical, pro-Spanish, cabinet-maker's apprentice from Franche Comté. William's life went through 3 main phases: as a courtier in the entourage of the Emp Charles V; as a politician leading the aristocratic resistance to Philip II's attempt to reduce their privileges; and as a statesman heroically guiding the Dutch people in their Revolt against Spain.

As a courtier, he began as a typical member of the high nobility of the Netherlands, trained for diplomatic, military and admin co-operation with the then D of Burgundy (who was also the Emp Charles V) in the uphill task of easing the 17 provs into a closer union so as to give them more weight in international affairs. As a young man it was upon his shoulders that Charles V leaned when he enacted his solemn abdication ceremony in Brussels on 25 Oct 1555; later he was a member of the Habsburg delegation to the peace conference at Cateau-Cambrésis (Feb–Apr 1559). It was natural that under K PHILIP II he should be Stadholder (Gov) of Holland, Zeeland and Utrecht and a member of the Council of State of the Netherlands.

As a politician he became prominent when Philip left the Netherlands for good (20 Aug 1559), thrusting aside the native nobility, and trusting high policy to his faithful servant from Franche Comté, GRANVELLE. It was when this policy emerged as a combination of, firstly, religious persecution in a land noted for the tolerant HUMANISM of its RCs and for the existence of numerous different groups of Prots, and, secondly, centralized ABSOLUTISM, infringing the entrenched privileges of the nobility, the provs and the cities in that very loosely federated area, that William emerged as the leader of the party of aristocratic resistance. He and Egmont resigned from the Council of State (July 1563), and their hostile attitude eventually forced the K to dismiss Granvelle in Mar 1564.

As a statesman William began to take shape at the point when Philip provoked the Revolt itself by sending the D of ALBA and an army to terrorize all ranks into becoming disciplined supporters of the COUNTER-REFORMATION and obedient subjects of the Spanish monarchy. Under the rule of Alba (Aug 1567–Dec 1573), William's sympathies broadened and deepened, and his aspirations rose. From being the leader of a narrow noble faction defending its traditional liberties, he evolved into the father of the Dutch people fighting for the broad principles of religious toleration and political freedom. He operated, on the one hand, as a Pr of international renown who could negotiate on their own level with the monarchies of Europe and marry into their families; on the other, as a hero with the

455

common touch who could inspire devotion in his humblest subjects. During 1565–6, when the wilder elements among the lower nobility were indulging in anti-Spanish brigandage, and the urban proletariat exploded in the iconoclastic Altar Riots, he played a mediating role, saving Antwerp from being sacked by the extremists (Feb and Mar 1567), and earning the curses of the fanatics on both sides. He was aware of the moral fervour of the Calvinists, and of the physical force provided by hungry proletarians. He later provided leadership for them both. But he was also well aware that the Netherlands was overwhelmingly R C, and that it contained social groups that were terrified at the democratic notions of the urban mobs. Moreover, he had in mind seeking help from Lutheran Prs in Germany and from the R C rulers of France. He therefore aimed to avoid identification with any one minority group. Alone among the multifarious opponents of the Spanish in the Netherlands he had a vision of the 17 separate provs merging into one united people and, at the same time, allowing more than one religion in the same State: a revolutionary concept. When he learned of the approach of Alba he left the Netherlands for his home in Dillenburg, Germany (Apr 1567), determined to resist by all means in his power; and to that task he devoted the rest of his life. He saw military action at the head of his troops, and the example of his endurance brought the Revolt through the darkest hours of defeat; but his most important contributions were, firstly, in organizing diplomatic, military and financial aid from Germany, from France, from England, from all the enemies of Spain, even Turkey; secondly, in rising above all the internal disputes that splintered the Netherlands – whether caused by personal jealousies, class animosities, religious prejudices, or prov rivalries – to provide a flexible and *politique* leadership, to open an umbrella under which the broadest possible range of Netherlands society could take shelter. He was a deep and complex character, and very difficult to fathom. He was subtle, devious and passionate, yet tolerant, his head inspired by high ideals, his heart moved by deep devotion, his feet planted securely in reality. He led an army across the Maas on 6 Oct 1568, striking towards Brussels in the S but, finding no popular support, he had to retreat, defeated. He fought with the Hugs in 1569 to get French help. This almost materialized in 1572, when COLIGNY planned to attack Spain in the Netherlands. As part of this scheme, William made a 2nd invasion of the S on 27 July 1572, this time to relieve his brother LOUIS OF NASSAU, besieged in Mons. The Massacre of St Bartholomew in Paris on the night of 23/24 Aug 1572 brusquely ended these hopes of French help; but meanwhile the Calvinist minorities, helped by the Sea Beggars, were seizing power in the towns and cities of Holland and Zeeland, provs which henceforth became the hard core of the Revolt. William was recognized as Stadholder by the Estates of Holland on 19 July 1572. He joined the N rebels in Oct 1572; he joined the Calvinist Ch in Apr 1573. These were his geographical and ideological bases, which he first had to defend from Spanish attack, and from which he then spread out into the remainder of the N and into the middle, Flemish regions of the S, plagued constantly by the narrow-minded localism of Holland and Zeeland, which alienated the other provs, and by the missionary zeal of the Calvinists, which scared off the rest of the population because of its tendency to stimulate social revolution. He was in the thick of the negotiations which led to the hopeful Pacification of Ghent of Nov 1576 – a brief union of the N and S which left the religious problem undetermined, but which called for the evacuation of Spanish troops. The honeymoon was soon over, however. On the one side, Philip II's new Gov-Gen, DON JOHN, while agreeing to the evacuation of Spanish troops, refused to tolerate Protestantism. On the other, Calvinist mobs seized power and sacked churches in Brussels, Antwerp and all the main cities of the Flemish S (Aug 1577). Hard as he worked, negotiating with all parties, and seeking foreign support, William could not prevent the Netherlands from splitting in two, into the Union of Arras in the S, formed on 7 Jan 1579 (the future Belgium), and the Union of Utrecht in the N of 23 Jan 1579 (the future United Provs). Philip II now outlawed William, putting a price of 20,000 *écus* on his head (June 1580). William published a retort, his *Apologie* (Dec 1580), which justified his life's work. When the assassin's bullet found its mark, the N provs were in retreat before the armies of Alessandro FARNESE, the new Gov-Gen; but, thanks partly to the foundations William had laid, they came through the struggle and rightly called him *un père de la patrie*. But the survival of the separate states of Belgium and Holland would have appeared to William as the failure of all his efforts.

William II, Pr of Orange (27 May 1626–6 Nov 1650) Stadholder of Holland and other provs in the United Provs (1647), whose attempted coup and sudden death ushered in the rule of Johan de WITT.

Son of Pr FREDERICK HENRY and his wife, Amalia von Solms; m (1641) Mary Stuart, eld daughter of K CHARLES I of Britain; became Stadholder of 5 of the provs on the death of his father (Mar 1647), and leader of the Orange interest in the United Provs, the chief supports of which were the common people, the extreme Calvinist clergy and the wealth and patronage of the Orange family; and the main policies of which were the centralization of the Gov, the increase in the monarchical power of the Stadholder, and military adventures abroad. Opposed to him were the middle-class Regents and the moderate Calvinists, led by the Estates of Holland, upholders of the decentralized form of Gov, and opponents of war, which increased taxation, interfered with business and increased the power of the Stadholder. The Tr of Münster (the United Provs' separate peace with Spain at the end of the THIRTY YEARS WAR) was their work (1648), and after it they voted in the States Gen for the disbandment of the army (1648, 1649, 1650) for whose upkeep they provided most of the taxes. William II opposed the peace and the disbandment. He wished to use the army to help MAZARIN against Spain, and K CHARLES I of Britain against CROMWELL. It was fortunate for his opponents that he was fat, lazy and dissolute. He arrested 6 leading members of the Estates of Holland (30 July 1650) and locked them in the fortress of Loevestein. He sent an army to take Amsterdam, but bungled the coup, the city having been warned. Then he suddenly d of smallpox a week before the birth of his son, WILLIAM III. The scene was set in the United Provs for the rule of Johan de Witt and the 1st 'Stadholderless period'.

William III, Pr of Orange (4/14 Nov 1650–8/19 Mar 1702) K of Great Britain (13 Feb 1689), who rescued the United Provs from conquest by K LOUIS XIV of France in the Franco-Dutch War (1672–9) and governed it successfully in co-operation with the Regents. He devoted his life to countering French aggression by diplomacy and war, a programme which included the capture of the English throne in the REVOLUTION OF 1688, and the consolidation of the post-revolutionary form of Gov.

Posthumous and only child of Pr WILLIAM II and his wife, Mary Stuart, daughter of K CHARLES I of Britain; ed by Heer van Zuylestein, bastard son of Pr FREDERICK HENRY, as a sincere Calvinist, and connoisseur of the arts who could speak Dutch, French, English, German, Latin and Spanish. Frail, thin, pale and asthmatic, with a hump on his back and brilliant blue eyes, he suffered the insecurities of an upbringing as the head of the Orange party during the rule of the anti-Orange party under Johan de WITT. He m (1677) Mary, tall and beautiful eld daughter of K JAMES II of Britain: a political union which later became a love match. (She d 28 Dec 1694.) He achieved power in the United Provs in the so-called 'revolution of 1672', when the Dutch, with the French at their throats, overthrew de Witt and his party, and made William Capt-Gen and Admiral-Gen of the United Provs, as well as Stadholder of the various provs, in spite of the laws passed against this under de Witt's régime. 1672–88: William governed the United Provs and fought Louis XIV from the Hague; 1688–1702: he concentrated on Britain, leaving the United Provs to what was an unofficial 'stadholderless period' under the Grand Pensionary, Anthonie Heinsius.

1672–88 at first saw William leading his country – occupied by the French and flooded on his orders – out of the mortal danger of the Franco-Dutch War, 1672–9. A visionary who could see what was needed, a leader who inspired devotion, a commander who got things done, he cleared the French out of his country by 1674, made peace with Britain, and joined up in a Grand Alliance with the Emp LEOPOLD I, Spain, Brandenburg and Lorraine: a European coalition which he knew was the only protection for the United Provs from French aggression. The war moved away from Dutch territory, and William's problem then was to convince the inward-looking Regents that, even if Dutch trade and Protestantism were their only interests, their safety lay only in European-wide diplomacy and war. He succeeded, and by the Trs of Nijmegen (1678/9) France returned all her Dutch conquests and repealed the anti-Dutch tariff of 1667. As ruler of the United Provs, William was unusually successful. He turned a number of de Witt's followers out of their offices, but replaced them with moderates: Regents of the same social class who were prepared to collaborate. Somehow he managed to make the federated system of Gov – where real power often lay with prov Estates, even city Councils – work effectively. He used a mixture of cunning and ruthlessness, bribery, influence and patronage, persuasion and inspiration, and gradually knocked some unity of direction into a society notoriously at cross-purposes. He was an Orange leader who managed to carry the Regents with him – or at least drag them a little way behind him. During the *Réunions* and the following years (1679–88), when Louis XIV was grabbing Rhineland territories in peacetime by a mixture of bullying and so-called legal process, William at first found it impossible to awaken the Regents to their long-term danger. Their main concern was trade, and they regarded war as an aristocratic hobby and the first step to ABSOLUTISM and centralization. When France went to extremes, however, William's warnings began to be heard. Louis XIV revoked the Edict of Nantes and filled the United Provs with Prot refugees. He laid claim to the whole Spanish inheritance, and thus threatened Dutch participation in the Spanish economy. Henceforth the Regents backed William's diplomatic efforts to unite the enemies of France. Much more, they voted him the ships and the men to invade England and carry out the Revolution of 1688; and they backed him to the hilt in the subsequent 2 long anti-French wars.

1688–1702 in England: At home, William's main purposes in accepting the invitation of the Whig and Tory group to invade England were to assert the hereditary rights of his wife and himself, and to recruit a valuable ally in his world-wide crusade against France. He never understood the prejudices of the English, for whom the Revolution had quite a different purpose, and to most of whom foreign alliances, standing armies and Continental warfare were totally alien. Nor was the English political system easy to understand, for the Revolution had brought about a reconstruction of the parties. The pre-Revolution Whig party split into Court WHIGS and Country Whigs, the former – with leaders soon to be called the Junto – supporting the K as the embodiment of the Revolution, the latter continuing to be backbenchers and still nursing suspicions of the K and Court. At the same time, the TORIES, who opposed the Court because on religious and political grounds they did not regard William and Mary as the legitimate sovereigns of Britain, coalesced with the Country Whigs in opposition and adopted some of their principles. William relied on non-party, pro-Court 'managers' such as the 2nd Earl of SUNDERLAND and the D of Shrewsbury to form and reform ministries for him and to manage his business in Parl, though, of course, there was never anything approaching a PM. Working late into the night, William kept control of overall policy and in effect ran several departments himself: the Treasury, foreign affairs and the armed forces, besides being generalissimo and the main diplomatic drive behind the European Grand Alliance. His ideal was to govern with mixed ministries and so escape the clutches of party. His 1st ministry was of this kind (it included HALIFAX, Shrewsbury, NOTTINGHAM and DANBY), but by 1693 it became necessary to make concessions to the Whigs, who were enthusiastically behind the War of the League of Augsburg, and to shed Tories, who opposed it. The increasingly Whig ministry's job was to finance the war; and in creating the National Debt (1693 onwards), founding the Bank of England (1694), and carrying through the recoinage (1696) they achieved a 'financial revolution' which not merely defeated Louis XIV but also, by underpinning the modern financial world with Gov and Parl support, provided the financial preconditions of the Commercial Revolution and the INDUSTRIAL REVOLUTION of C17 and 18. In the meantime, Robert HARLEY, building upon backbench prejudice against standing armies, the Whig Bank of England, placemen and other forms of Gov 'influence', managed to build the New Country Party out of opposition Whigs and Tories; and with the war over (1697) William was obliged to abandon his Whig ministers (1698) and see them impeached for having supported his policy over the Partitions Trs. He also had to accept Tory ministers (1700); but when the War of the Spanish Succession became imminent (1701–2) the Whigs closed ranks again and a pro-war Whig ministry was formed (1701): a clear-cut party Gov on a clear-cut party issue.

As well as establishing himself as K of England and consolidating the Revolution settlement, William had to defeat the attempts at counter-revolution by JAMES II which merged into the European-wide War of the League of Augsburg against Louis XIV (under whom it is described). William had to defeat James in Ireland

and his supporters in Scotland, and wage a gruelling war against France at sea and in the Netherlands, eventually forcing France to sign the Tr of Rijswijk (1697) in which she abandoned all her war aims and returned all her post-1678 conquests except Strasbourg. But the crucial war had yet to be fought, for Louis was aiming at inheriting the Spanish empire, and neither William nor the Emp Leopold I were prepared to accept that without war. William signed the 1st and 2nd Partition Trs with France (Oct 1698, June 1699). The aim was to avoid war by breaking up the Spanish inheritance between France and the Emp; but this policy failed when K CHARLES II of Spain left the whole inheritance in his will to the French Pr Philip of Anjou, and Louis XIV accepted it. William thus headed a European coalition preparing to fight the War of the Spanish Succession when an accident robbed him of the chance of seeing his life's work completed. He caught a chill after breaking his collar-bone while trying out a new horse in Richmond Park. He d at Kensington Palace.

Witt, Johan de (24 Sept 1625–20 Aug 1672) Grand Pensionary of Holland (1653–72), and in effect ruler of the United Provs during most of the 1st 'Stadholderless period' (1650–72), ie between the death of Pr WILLIAM II and the coming of age of Pr WILLIAM III – a period of high prosperity, diplomatic leadership, artistic genius, and intellectual advance.

Son of Jacob de Witt, one of the 6 leading members of the Estates of Holland who were arrested by Pr William II in 1650; ed at Leiden Univ and on tour in France and England; practised as a lawyer at the Hague (1647 onwards); chosen Pensionary of Dordrecht (Dec 1650) and Grand Pensionary of Holland (July 1653); m (1655) Wendela Bicker, daughter of a leading Regent of Amsterdam, who added to his political strength in Holland. Cultured, arrogant, ruthless and realistic, he ruled the United Provs from his post in Holland, showing short-term political skill of a high order, though not long-term statesmanship.

At home, he carried out financial reforms and encouraged world-wide trade. Moreover, he opposed all attempts to unify the United Provs. His main preoccupation was to manipulate the decentralized form of Gov in the United Provs so as to maintain himself, his family and his Regent allies in power in the Estates of Holland, and keep Holland as the leading force in the States General of the United Provs. He used patronage, persuasion, influence and corruption, and all the other management techniques common in Parl régimes at that time. His chief enemy was the Orange party, which was backed by the lower classes, the strict Calvinist clergy, and the landowners of the less commercialized provs, but which lacked leadership during the minority of Pr William III. His other enemies were the middle group of Regents led by Gillis Valkenier, Coenraad van Beuninghen and Gaspar Fagel. These were 'outs' who wished to replace the de Witt group, and they backed moderate pro-Orange policies in order to do so. On 1 May 1654 de Witt had his hand forced by Oliver CROMWELL in the negotiations to end the 1st Anglo-Dutch War (1652–4). De Witt had to get the Estates of Holland to pass a secret Act of Seclusion which excluded the House of Orange from all its former offices: Capt-Gen, Stadholder etc. This Act was repealed on 25 Sept 1660 with the Restoration in England of William's ally and uncle, K CHARLES II. To maintain his predominance, de Witt then took control of William III's upbringing by having him declared a Child of State (Apr 1666).

On 5 Aug 1666, however, the Estates of Holland, led by the middle group, passed the Eternal Edict declaring that William could not become Capt-Gen until he was 22, and that when he did he could not also be Stadholder of any prov. This was an apparent victory for de Witt, but in reality a defeat, for as the other provs accepted it (in the Harmony of 1670) it was clear that William was bound to take power one day.

Foreign affairs saw the United Provs in an apparently dominating position, an illusion due to the temporary weakness of rival powers. De Witt tried to avoid war, which upset trade, put up taxes and inflated the power of the Orange party. Nevertheless, he was forced by English aggressiveness into the 1st Anglo-Dutch War (1652–4). He also had to intervene (1658–60) in the War of the North (1655–60) to protect Denmark from Sweden, and thus ensure in the Tr of Copenhagen between them (1660) – which his mediation brought about – that no one power dominated the Baltic, that the Sound was kept open, and that the United Provs' richest trading area was safeguarded. After the Stuart Restoration in England, which strengthened the Orange party, de Witt made an alliance with France (1662); and then successfully fought the 2nd Anglo-Dutch War (1665–7) with French military, if not naval, aid. By this time, however, the situation was being transformed by the aggressive policies of K LOUIS XIV of France, in particular his invasion of the Spanish Netherlands in the War of Devolution (1667–8). Having France as an ally was one thing: having her as a neighbour was quite another; and so de Witt signed the Tr of the Hague with England (1668), which became the Triple Alliance when Sweden joined a month later. Louis responded by making peace, but he never forgave de Witt's independent attitude; when the next onslaught was launched it was against the United Provs itself (Franco-Dutch War, 1672–9). De Witt fought alone, having allowed Louis to isolate him diplomatically. Too rigid in his thinking, de Witt had failed to appreciate the new diplomatic situation in which the United Provs' period of luck was over. Moreover, he clung greedily and brutally to power, making it impossible for a transition to a different régime to take place without violence. The swift French invasion of Holland and Zeeland led directly to his downfall. The masses and the middle group rallied to the Orange party. William III was declared Capt-Gen and Admiral-Gen (Feb 1672). De Witt resigned as Grand Pensionary (Aug 1672). His brother, Cornelis, had been imprisoned in the Gevangenpoort at the Hague on a charge of conspiring against William, but when Johan paid him a visit the mob broke in, tore them both limb from limb, and sold the pieces. It was an end hardly suitable to a statesman who had led the United Provs through the years of its greatest glory.

Wladyslaw Jagiello (1 Mar 1456–13 Mar 1516) K Vladislav II of Bohemia (1471) and K Ulászló II of Hungary (1490), whose reign in both States was characterized by an increase in the power of the nobility at the expense of the serfs, the towns and the Crown; while abroad he was a satellite of the Habsburgs.

Eld son of Casimir IV Jagiello, Grd D of Lithuania and K of Poland (1447–92), and Elizabeth of Habsburg; m 1st (1475) Barbara, daughter of Albert Achilles of Brandenburg (by proxy only); m 2nd (1490) comely Beatrix of Aragon, widow of K Matthias Corvinus of Hungary (in secret); m 3rd (1502) Anne de Candalle (niece of Anne of Brittany) after the Pp had declared his 1st 2 marriages invalid (she d 1506). He was elected K of Bohemia, and then K of Hungary.

As K of Bohemia he was easy-going and indecisive – vices which had encouraged the Estates to elect him K in the first place – and he became known as King Dobre (King All Right). From before his election (when he had had to accept a reduction in the rights of the Crown) to the end of his reign, the nobles and knights steadily reduced his powers over revenue, the armed forces, and policy-making in general, until the Constitution of 1500 showed Bohemia to be nothing more than an aristocratic republic marked by struggles for office between factions of the nobility, and between the nobility and the knights. Another firm trend was the enserfment of the peasantry, legalized in 1497 and in the Constitution of 1500. Moreover, the nobles extended their grip on the towns, reducing their commercial and other rights, and excluding them from the Diet (1500–8). The towns fought back, forming a union (1513); and in the compromise of 1517 they regained some of their independence, though they had to give up their monopoly over brewing and selling beer.

In Hungary, also, the magnates elected him precisely because his weakness made him a welcome change from his predecessor, Matthias Corvinus. As in Bohemia, they reduced him to a cipher by demanding a more stringent coronation oath, keeping him short of money, plundering the royal domain, and establishing the principle (1507) that no royal decree could have effect until it had been confirmed by the Council of State. Also as in Bohemia, there were struggles within the aristocratic order (lay and ecclesiastical), and between them and the lesser nobles, who managed to get their position on the central and county diets affirmed in the *Tripartitum*, a theoretical work on constitutional law (1514) which henceforth became regarded as *the* authority on the Hungarian constitution. As well as subduing the K, the nobles attacked urban liberties and enserfed the peasantry (a change also legally enshrined in the *Tripartitum*), and put down savagely the terrible peasants' revolt led by George Dósza (1514).

In foreign affairs, Wladyslaw became a Habsburg satellite, handing back the conquests of Matthias Corvinus and recognizing MAXIMILIAN I as future K of Hungary, should Wladyslaw die without issue (Tr of Pressburg, 1491); and later, when he did have children, agreeing to marry his son, Lewis, to Maximilian's granddaughter Mary, and his daughter, Anne, to Maximilian's grandson, the future Emp FERDINAND I. Although the Tr of 1491 had been accepted by the Diet at Buda, the opposition party among the nobility, led by the Zápolyai family, got the Diet to pass a declaration (Oct 1505) that no foreigner could succeed, should the K die without an heir. When Wladyslaw d, however, there was no opposition by the magnates to the election of his son, LEWIS.

Wladyslaw IV Vasa (19 June 1595–20 May 1648) K of Poland (1632), who was forced to preside over the continuing decline of Poland because of the powerlessness of the Crown in the face of the decentralizing nobility, the diversity of religions and races, and the rise of aggressive neighbours.

Son of SIGISMUND III by his 1st wife, Anna of Styria; m 1st (1637) Archdss Cecilia Renata of Austria, daughter of Emp FERDINAND II (d 24 Mar 1644); m 2nd (1645) Marie Louise de Gonzague-Nevers of France (d 9 May 1667). As a young man during the Russian TIME OF TROUBLES (1598–1613), he was elected tsar by a group of *boyars* (Aug 1610), but his father rejected the conditions, and in any case he wanted the throne for himself. In 1617–18 Wladyslaw fought an unsuccessful campaign as far as Moscow to enforce his rights, but had to be satisfied with the considerable territorial gains conceded in the 14-year Tr of Deulino (1618). After this he saw action in the Turkish War (1617–21). As K, Wladyslaw was hamstrung in his foreign policy by his weak position at home.

His foreign policy was defensive through lack of resources. (a) In the Russian War (Smolensk War) (1632–4), launched by MICHAEL on the expiry of Deulino which coincided with the death of Sigismund III), Wladyslaw forced the Russian commander, Shein, to surrender his army at Smolensk on 19/29 Feb 1634. By the Tr of Polanowo (Polianovka) (June 1634) Poland kept the gains of Deulino, but Wladyslaw abandoned his claim to be tsar of Russia. (b) In the Turkish War (1633–4) a Turkish invasion of S Poland – taking the opportunity of the Smolensk War – brought swift counteraction from Wladyslaw which forced Turkey to make peace (Oct 1634), based on a division of interests in Moldavia and Wallachia (Romania), and a Polish guarantee to restrain the COSSACKS matched by a Turkish promise to check the Tatars. (c) With Sweden, which wanted peace in order to concentrate on the THIRTY YEARS WAR, Wladyslaw made the 26-year Tr of Stuhmsdorf (Sept 1635) with RICHELIEU's help, whereby Sweden made the huge sacrifice of the Prussian ports with their valuable revenues. (d) With the Emp, Wladyslaw made an alliance (1633), and then his 1st marriage (1637), but nevertheless could take no part in the Thirty Years War in spite of pressing invitations. (e) In the Baltic, where he expanded the navy and its base at Wladyslawowo, his plans for defending Polish trading interests in an active way were scotched by the Seym (Diet) and he was forced (1638 onwards) to sell his ships and let the harbour rot.

At home it was Wladyslaw's position as perhaps the most limited monarch in Europe which explains Poland's weak international performance. He was an elected K whose ministers, exclusively magnates, were rather agents of the Seym than of the Crown, and could not be dismissed once appointed. Legislation, finance and the armed forces were controlled by the Seym which often went home without deciding anything because of the unanimity requirement, but which was in any case itself limited by the fact that the delegates were under orders from the prov diets. Effective power – financial and military – was exercised by the magnates scattered about the country on their vast estates worked by serf labour. They commanded private armies, headed clientage networks of gentry and, in order to preserve their 'Golden Freedom' as they called it, were determined to stop any move to strengthen the Polish monarchy. Thus, though Poland was a great power, extensive, populous and rich, profiting handsomely from its exports of grain down the Vistula through Danzig, the busiest Baltic port, neither Wladyslaw nor anyone else had the strength to mobilize its resources and save it from decay. Wladyslaw, an energetic ruler, a popular politician – he wore Polish moustaches rather than the Swedish pointed beard – and an imaginative statesman, was full of ideas and tried many initiatives – utopian in various degrees – and all of them failures. The nobility not only scuttled his navy, they banned his scheme for raising a royal army of mercenaries. When he tried to split the magnates by binding some of them more closely to himself in a Spanish-type Cavalry of the Order of the Immaculate Conception of the Virgin Mary (1637), they frustrated that. In a country of many religious denominations which was falling prey to the regimentation of the COUNTER-REFORMATION, he threw his weight on the side of toleration: for Prots in W Poland, where he sponsored a Prot–Cath colloquy at Toruń (Thorn) (1645), and for the Orthodox in Lithuania and the Ukraine, to whom he granted religious liberty and recognition of their underground hierarchy (1633), in the form of the Metropolitan of Kiev and 4 bps. Nevertheless, the JESUITS with their baroque churches and grip on education were succeeding in cutting Poland off from the intellectual progress of the W. Moreover, since the Crown was too weak to subordinate the Ch to the State, the hierarchy and the Pp were increasingly influential in Poland's policy-making, especially in foreign affairs. And finally Wladyslaw found the Ukrainian problem too difficult to solve. The Cossacks were growing desperate as the Polish magnates colonized the Dnieper area, turned them into serfs instead of 'registered Cossacks', brought them under the machinery of the Polish State, and persecuted their Orthodox forms of worship. An explosive mixture of racial, social and religious hatred brought the Cossacks out in armed rebellions in 1625, 1630, 1637 and 1638. Between 1638 and 1648 Wladyslaw enforced a period of 'golden peace', from a new fortress at Kudak on the lower Dnieper. At the same time he hatched a grandiose scheme for neutralizing the Cossacks once and for all by eliminating the Tatar danger further S. The Crimean Tatars agitated the Cossacks, sometimes by raiding their lands, sometimes by joining them in anti-Polish alliances; but the only satisfactory way of curbing them was to defeat their over-lord, the Ottoman Emp. In the late 1640s, Wladyslaw began negotiating a visionary anti-Turkish crusade in conjunction with Venice, the Pp, France and others. He encouraged the Cossacks to prepare for battle with hints of further privileges, but kept the scheme secret from the Seym until 1646, when they for-bade it. Disappointment proved the last straw for the Cossacks and, led by a skilful soldier and diplomat, Bohdan Chmielnicki, who had private grievances against Poland, they broke into violence on the eve of Wladyslaw's death, and began a momentous rebellion which rocked Poland in the reign of JOHN II CASIMIR, his successor.

Wolsey, Thomas (c 1473–29 Nov 1530) Archbp of York (1514–30), Chancellor (1515–29), Card (1515), Legate *a latere* (1518), chief minister of K HENRY VIII of England (1514–29).

Son of a butcher and cattle-dealer; ed at Magdalen, Oxford, he held successive private chaplaincies till his unusual managerial abilities, grasp of detail, swift judgement and appetite for work recommended him to K HENRY VII, whose chaplain he became in 1507. Under K Henry VIII, as royal Almoner (1511), he rose in influence as unofficial royal sec and intermediary between the K and absent ministers, until by 1514 he had outstripped his willing sponsors, Richard Fox and William WARHAM. He had also begun to acquire that vast collection of ecclesiastical and political offices which made him, after the K, the most powerful man in Ch and State. He became Bp of Tournai (1513–18), Bp of Lincoln (1514), Archbp of York (1514–30), Bp of Bath and Wells (1518–24), Abbot of St Albans (1521), Bp of Durham (1524–9) and Bp of Winchester (1529), benefices which provided his basic, but by no means his total, income, and which enabled him to afford such residences as York Place, London (where Whitehall now is), and Hampton Court in the country, as well as to adopt that ostentatious style of life which so fed the ire of his enemies. In addition he became Card (1515) and Legate *a latere* (1518), the latter office making him a special, but permanent, representative of the Pp, wielding supreme power over both provs of the Ch of England, and turning Warham, the Archbp of Canterbury, into a mere cipher. His power in the State derived from his office of Chancellor (1515) through which he lorded it over the royal Council, quickly elbowing aside Warham and Fox, and sharply taming the aristocrats who had threatened a comeback on the death of Henry VII. Broadly speaking, he monopolized the power hitherto shared by the inner ring of the Council; and from then until 1529 he relieved the pleasure-loving K of the tedium of day-to-day decision-making, though Henry was ultimately responsible for the broad outlines of policy – and he could suddenly intervene over details as well – and, of course, for the making and breaking of Wolsey himself.

In home affairs, Wolsey's greatest achievements were in: (a) the judiciary. He established Chancery as the regular court of equity in civil cases, which gradually accumulated a body of case-law from the decisions of Wolsey and his successors, thus filling in gaps in the common law, and bringing it up to date. He revived and extended the competence of the Court of Requests for Poor Men's Causes. He increased the activity and authority of the Star Chamber, ie the Council sitting as a court in a room of that name at Westminster, and reinforcing – and sometimes ousting – the common-law courts in criminal cases of rioting, private warfare and rebellion, as well as in cases of perjury, libel and forgery, hitherto the province of the Ch courts. (b) In admin he left the Gov machine ticking over much as he inherited it from Henry VII. His financial policy left the K short of money, since Wolsey both over-spent and failed to increase revenue, partly because his misunderstanding of economics led to a neglect of trade, and partly because his dictatorial approach to Parl only resulted in inadequate financial votes. His attempt to secure a forced loan in 1524, eg – known as the Amicable Grant – led to violent resistance, and had to be abandoned. Moreover, he misunderstood the nature of the long-term social and economic trends of C16, which were, broadly, the PRICE REVOLUTION, the rise in population, the steady replacement of medieval peasant husbandry by modern commercial agriculture, and the transformation of society to produce the basic structure of landlord, tenant-farmer and landless labourer. Wolsey tried ineffectually to assuage the unpleasant results of these changes – vagrancy and pauperism – by concentrating on one symptom: by trying to stop enclosure with his Commissions of 1517, 1518 and 1526). (c) In the Ch, as legate *a latere*, he tyrannized over the bench of Bps, encroached on their jurisdiction, soaked up their wealth and, far from effecting any of the reforms he promised so loudly, flamboyantly exemplified in himself all the worst vices of the clergy of that time: pluralism, absenteeism, simony, worldliness and sexual immorality. He eased the passage of the REFORMATION in England, firstly by intensifying the anti-clerical and anti-papal prejudices which gave Henry VIII the backing of the laity and, secondly, by lowering the spiritual vigour, and thus the powers of resistance, of the clergy.

In foreign affairs (his main interest) he strove to reconcile several tasks: (a) to indulge Henry VIII's chivalric descents upon France, anachronistically reviving the 100 Years War; (b) to ensure the security of England by peaceful or warlike action (preferably the former) in the ever-shifting international rivalries of the Emp CHARLES V and K FRANCIS I of France; (c) to safeguard his Legatine power by being friendly with whoever dominated the papacy – even by trying to become Pp himself in 1521, 1523 and 1529, though this was the K's idea; (d) to take the lead in negotiating a stable peace in Europe. He failed because, characteristically, this flamboyant great-power role was quite beyond the resources of a near-bankrupt monarchy. Finally (e) he caused his own downfall by his failure to negotiate a divorce for Henry from Q CATHERINE OF ARAGON.

His fall was inevitable as, abroad, Charles V and Francis I signed the Tr of Cambrai behind his back in Aug 1529, thus reconciling Pp and Emp and changing the whole set of premises from which Wolsey had deduced his foreign policy; and as at home his enemies gathered for the kill: common lawyers resentful of the encroachments of Chancery and Star Chamber, M Ps angered by his financial demands, clergy resisting his tyranny over the Ch and his milking of its wealth, gentry disliking his support of the poor, nobility thirsting for the political power he denied them, and the nation at large hating him as the arrogant and ostentatious representative of a foreign power. By late 1529 the 3rd D of NORFOLK was dominant at Court, along with his niece, Anne Boleyn, and her relatives. On 22 Sept 1529 Wolsey was dismissed as Chancellor. A month later he was no longer Bp of Winchester or Abbot of St Albans. He had not given up hope, however, and was negotiating secretly with the Pp, Charles V and Francis I. In view of this, Norfolk and the Boleyns persuaded Henry to send him out of the way to his see of York; and at last, at the end of Apr 1530, he set foot for the first time there. However, Henry's policy suddenly hardened again, and Wolsey was arrested on 4 Nov 1530, and d at Leicester Abbey on his way S to the Tower of London.

Ximénez de Cisneros, Fray Francisco (1436–8 Nov 1517) Spanish Card; R C reformer and statesman.

Son of poor noble stock; ed Alcalá de Henares, Salamanca, and Rome. The Pp gave him a written guarantee of a benefice in Toledo, but the Archbp there imprisoned him (1473–9). Appointed Vicar-Gen of the diocese of Sigüenza (1482), he abandoned it (1484) for the full rigour of Franciscan asceticism in the monastery of San Juan de los Reyes at Toledo. He became confessor to Q ISABELLA (1492), Provincial of the Franciscan Order in Castile (1494), Archbp of Toledo and Primate of Spain (1495), President of the Council of Regency of Castile between the death of K PHILIP I and the return of K FERDINAND II (1506), Card and Inquisitor-Gen (1507), Regent of Castile between the death of K Ferdinand II and the arrival of K Charles I (Emp CHARLES V) (1516–17).

One of the greatest statesmen in Spanish history (though a reluctant one) he was the chief agent of stability and continuity through 3 reigns; the reformer of the finances; the re-organizer of the army; the inspiration behind the forceful conversion of the Moriscos; the financial backer of K Ferdinand II's conquests in N Africa (where the Moslems were allies of the Moriscos); but, chief of all, the agent of the pre-Lutheran CATHOLIC REFORMATION in Spain. He instituted the reform of the Franciscans, the Dominicans etc, attacking their worldly habits and making them observe the strict rules of their orders. He also banned INDULGENCES in Spain before LUTHER attacked them in Germany. Moreover, he was one of the chief architects of the INQUISITION. He founded the Univ of Alcalá de Henares (1498) for the study of nominalist, as well as Thomist, theology – a

centre of scholarship which became one of the chief diffusers of Christian
HUMANISM in Spain.

Zwingli, Huldreich (1 Jan 1484–11 Oct 1531) Swiss REFORMATION leader.

Son of a free peasant; ed at the univs of Vienna (1498–1502) and Basle (1502–6);
m (1524) Anna Reihard, a widow. Appointed parish priest of Glarus (1506–16),
he served in Italy as chaplain to the Glarus soldiers who were fighting as mercenaries in the HABSBURG–VALOIS WARS (at Novara on 6 June 1513, and
Marignano on 13/14 Sept 1515). At Glarus and at Einsiedeln, his next living
(1516–18), he began to reach Lutheran conclusions by way of his studies in
HUMANISM: possibly independently of Luther, whose work he did not know
until he moved to Zürich as Common Preacher (*Leutpriester*) at the Great
Minster (1518). Here his sermons expounding the Bible played an important
part in producing the Zürich Reformation, by their influence on the townsmen,
but more especially by their conversion of the majority of the city Council.
Under his leadership during the early 1520s, the clergy and magistrates together
turned the city into a stronghold of Protestantism, a revolution which was followed by similar changes in Berne (1528) and Basle (1529). Zwingli's *67 Articles*,
which he published in connection with his disputation with the representatives of
the local Bp of Constance (Jan 1523), were adopted as official doctrine: over the
next two years rapid steps were taken in the direction of reform: the liturgy of
the Great Minster was simplified, preaching and bible-readings ('prophesyings')
were stepped up, images and relics were frowned upon, sausages were eaten
during Lent, clerical marriage was allowed, monks and nuns came out into the
world, monasteries were dissolved and their resources devoted to education and
poor-relief. In 1525 Zürich broke with the Bp of Constance and with Rome, and
replaced the Mass with a simple ceremony of commemoration in which the laity
partook of both the bread and the wine – these being regarded by Zwinglians
only as symbols of the body and blood of Christ. Moreover, the Ch began to
exercise that strict supervision of moral behaviour which, 15 years later, became
a crucial aspect of CALVIN's work at Geneva.

Like other religious reformers Zwingli had to defend his chosen theological
position from radical as well as conservative attacks. ANABAPTISTS were
numerous in Zürich. Led by Conrad Grebel, they were followers of Zwingli who
continued his deductions further than he was prepared to go in the direction of
adult baptism, or the creation of 'gathered' churches of the saved, independent of
the magistrates. Zwingli engaged in inconclusive disputations with them in
1525 – they were mainly peasants and craftsmen from the surrounding villages
rather than citizens of Zürich – and finally fell in with the magistrates' decision
(1526) to chastise, exile or drown them. As for the Lutherans, Philip of Hesse,
in an effort to unite the Prot movement in the face of the military threat of the
Emp CHARLES V, organized a meeting between LUTHER and Zwingli at Marburg (1–3 Oct 1529), but to no avail. Though they agreed on much, they broke
over the interpretation of the Lord's Supper, Luther sticking to his literal interpretation of Christ's words: 'This is my body', and Zwingli insisting that 'is'
meant 'signifies'. The Catholic Ch remained strong in the 5 forest cantons, where
the rural inhabitants feared the unification of the Swiss Confederation by a too
powerful Zürich. Moreover, they were economically dependent on the export of

mercenaries, a trade which Zwingli attacked. When they formed a Christian Union with the Austrian Monarchy (Apr 1529), the old army chaplain Zwingli preached religious war against them. Two campaigns were fought (1529 and 1531), in the latter of which Zwingli was killed at the battle of Kappel (11 Oct 1531). His work in Zürich was carried on by Heinrich Bullinger (1504–75).

Subjects listed in small capital letters and page numbers shown in heavy type in the Index indicate a main entry in the Dictionary. Battles are indicated by crossed swords (✕). For abbreviations used in the Index, see pages 9–10.

Index

MORE ABOUT PENGUINS, PELICANS AND PUFFINS

For further information about books available from Penguins please write to Dept EP, Penguin Books Ltd, Harmondsworth, Middlesex UB7 0DA.

In the U.S.A.: For a complete list of books available from Penguins in the United States write to Dept DG, Penguin Books, 299 Murray Hill Parkway, East Rutherford, New Jersey 07073.

In Canada: For a complete list of books available from Penguins in Canada write to Penguin Books Canada Ltd, 2801 John Street, Markham, Ontario L3R 1B4.

In Australia: For a complete list of books available from Penguins in Australia write to the Marketing Department, Penguin Books Australia Ltd, P.O. Box 257, Ringwood, Victoria 3134.

In New Zealand: For a complete list of books available from Penguins in New Zealand write to the Marketing Department, Penguin Books (N.Z.) Ltd, P.O. Box 4019, Auckland 10.

In India: For a complete list of books available from Penguins in India write to Penguin Overseas Ltd, 706 Eros Apartments, 56 Nehru Place, New Delhi 110019.